CENSUS OF INDIA 1911

CENSUS OF INDIA, 1911

VOLUME - III

ASSAM

PART II - TABLES

J. McsWINEY

GYAN

Published by

GYAN

Gyan Publishing House
5, Ansari Road
Daryaganj, New Delhi-110002
Phone: 011-47034999, 9811692060
E-mail: books@gyanbooks.com

Distribution Network
gyanbooks.com
India, USA, Canada, UK, Australia

ISBN: 978-81-212-7127-1 (Set) 23 Vols. In 41 Bindings

ISBN: 978-81-212-7499-9 (PB) Vol. III, Pt. II

First Published, 1912

2nd Impression 2024

Printed at: Gyan Press, Delhi.

CENSUS OF INDIA 1911

CENSUS OF INDIA, 1911.
VOLUME III.

ASSAM.

PART II.
TABLES.

BY

J. McSWINEY, M.A.

OF THE INDIAN CIVIL SERVICE.

SUPERINTENDENT OF CENSUS OPERATIONS IN ASSAM.

SHILLONG:

PRINTED AT THE ASSAM SECRETARIAT PRINTING OFFICE.

1912.

CENSUS OF INDIA, 1911.

VOL. III.

ASSAM.

PART II.—TABLES.

Agents for the sale of Books published by the Assam Administration.

Agents in India.

(1) Messrs. Thacker, Spink & Co., Calcutta.

(2) Messrs. W. Newman & Co., Calcutta.

(3) Messrs. S. K. Lahiri & Co., Calcutta.

(4) Messrs. A. M. and J. Ferguson, Ceylon.

(5) Messrs. R. Cambray & Co., 6 and 8/2, Hastings Street Calcutta.

(6) Messrs. Thompson & Co., Madras.

(7) Babu Hari Ram Dhar, B.A., Popular Library, Dacca.

(8) Messrs. D. B. Taraporevala Sons & Co., 103 Meadows Street Fort, Post Box No. 187. Bombay.

Agents in England.

(1) Messrs. Constable & Co., 10, Orange Street, Leicester Square, W. C.

(2) Messrs. Kegan Paul, Trench, Trübner & Co., 43, Gerrard Street, Soho, W., London.

(3) Mr. B. Quaritch, 11, Grafton Street, New Bond Street, W.

(4) Messrs. P. S. King & Son, 9, Bridge Street, Westminster, S. W., London.

(5) Mr. B. H. Blackwell, 50 and 51, Broad Street, Oxford.

(6) Messrs. Deighton Bell & Co., Cambridge.

(7) Messrs. Henry S. King & Co., 65, Cornhill, E. C., London,

(8) Messrs. Grindlay & Co., 54, Parliament Street, S. W., London,

(9) Mr. T. Fisher Unwin, 1, Adelphi Terrace, London, W.C.

(10) Messrs. W. Thacker & Co., 2, Creed Lane, London, E. C.

(11) Messrs. Luzac & Co., 46, Great Russell Street, London, W. C.

Agents on the Continent of Europe.

(1) MM. Friedländer & Sohn, 11, Carlstrasse, Berlin.

(2) M. Otto Harrassowitz, Leipzig.

(3) M. Karl Hiersemann, Leipzig.

(4) M. Ernest Leroux, 28, Rue Bonaparte, Paris.

(5) Martinus Nijhoff, The Hague.

SHILLONG:

PRINTED BY H. H. KING, PRESS SUPERINTENDENT ASSAM.

PART II.

TABLES.

CONTENTS.

PAGE

IMPERIAL TABLES.

PROVINCIAL TABLES.

TABLE I.

AREA, HOUSES AND POPULATION.

THIS table shows for each district and the State of Manipur the area, the number of towns and villages, the number of occupied houses, and the total urban and rural population, male and female. The districts are arranged in this and other tables in the order prescribed by Government.

The areas given have been obtained from the District Gazetteers under the orders of Government: where they differ from those given in 1901, the change is due to revised survey: the area shown for Naga Hills, which is the same as in 1901, is for the surveyed area only and excludes the previously unadministered territory added since 1901, the area of which is unknown.

For the purpose of column 3 (number of towns) cantonments have been treated as forming part of the municipalities which they adjoin.

NOTE.—Similar statistics for areas smaller than districts are contained in Provincial Table I, which is printed at the end of the Imperial Tables.

TABLE I.—AREA, HOUSES AND POPULATION.

DISTRICT OR STATE.	Area in square miles.	Towns.	Villages.	OCCUPIED HOUSES. Total.	OCCUPIED HOUSES. In towns.	OCCUPIED HOUSES. In villages.	POPULATION. PERSONS. Total.	PERSONS. Urban.	PERSONS. Rural.	MALES. Total.	MALES. Urban.	MALES. Rural.	FEMALES. Total.	FEMALES. Urban.	FEMALES. Rural.
1	2	3	4	5	6	7	8	9	10	11	12	13	14	15	16
ASSAM	*61,471*	*21*	*29,352*	*1,521,510*	*45,745*	*1,475,765*	*7,059,857*	*211,318*	*6,848,539*	*3,638,287*	*119,893*	*3,518,394*	*3,421,570*	*91,425*	*3,330,145*
(1) ***British Territory***	*53,015*	*20*	*27,875*	*1,452,019*	*30,423*	*1,421,596*	*6,713,635*	*136,668*	*6,576,967*	*3,467,621*	*83,500*	*3,384,121*	*3,246,014*	*53,168*	*3,192,846*
SURMA VALLEY AND HILL DISTRICTS	*25,277*	*9*	*15,112*	*760,478*	*13,370*	*747,108*	*3,446,030*	*60,511*	*3,385,519*	*1,761,134*	*37,275*	*1,723,859*	*1,684,896*	*23,236*	*1,661,660*
Cachar	3,565	2	1,413	**115,442**	2,301	113,141	**497,463**	10,247	487,216	**260,444**	6,888	253,556	**237,019**	3,359	233,660
Sylhet	5,388	5	10,776	**547,655**	7,515	540,140	**2,472 671**	34,202	2,438,469	**1,268,469**	20,934	1,247,535	**1,204,202**	13,268	1,190,934
Khasi and Jaintia Hills	6,027	1	2,140	**37,816**	2,962	34,854	**235,069**	13,639	221,430	**114,442**	7,762	106,680	**120,627**	5,877	114,750
Naga Hills...	3,070	1	407	**41,232**	592	40,640	**149,623**	2,423	147,200	**74,751**	1,691	73,060	**74,872**	732	74,140
Lushai Hills	7,227	...	376	**18,333**	...	18,333	**91,204**	...	91,204	**43,028**	...	43,028	**48,176**	...	48,176
ASSAM VALLEY DISTRICTS	*27,738*	*11*	*12,763*	*691,541*	*17,053*	*674,488*	*3,267,605*	*76,157*	*3,191,448*	*1,706,487*	*46,225*	*1,660,262*	*1,561,118*	*29,932*	*1,531,186*
Goalpara	3,954	2	2,135	**112,298**	2,653	109,645	**600,643**	11,772	588,871	**318,475**	7,712	310,763	**282,168**	4,060	278,108
Kamrup	3,858	2	1,952	**131,493**	5,024	126,469	**667,828**	23,220	644,608	**339,398**	13,399	325,999	**328,430**	9,821	318,609
Darrang	3,418	1	1,405	**87,517**	1,264	86,253	**377,314**	5,355	371,959	**198,581**	3,759	194,822	**178,733**	1,596	177,137
Nowgong	3,843	1	1,494	**62,159**	1,223	60,936	**303,596**	5,433	298,163	**154,938**	3,145	151,793	**148,658**	2,288	146,370
Sibsagar	4,996	4	2,139	**150,803**	3,599	147,204	**690,299**	15,814	674,485	**364,810**	9,314	355,496	**325,489**	6,500	318,989
Lakhimpur	4,529	1	1,701	**114,498**	3,290	111,208	**468,989**	14,563	454,426	**249,021**	8,896	240,125	**219,968**	5,667	214,301
Garo Hills	3,140	...	1,937	**32,773**	...	32,773	**158,936**	...	158,936	**81,264**	...	81,264	**77,672**	...	77,672
(2) ***Manipur State***	*8,456*	*1*	*1,477*	*69,491*	*15,322*	*54,169*	*346,222*	*74,650*	*271,572*	*170,666*	*36,393*	*134,273*	*175,556*	*38,257*	*137,299*

TABLE II.

VARIATION IN POPULATION SINCE 1872.

THIS table compares the population as now ascertained with that of the four previous censuses. The figures for the latter in some districts differ slightly from those shown in the old Census Reports. This is due to subsequent changes of jurisdiction, *i.e.*, transfers of area from one district to another. The effect of these changes on the population of the districts concerned has been calculated, and the figures have been adjusted accordingly.

The following are the districts which have undergone changes of jurisdiction :—

Between 1872 *and* 1881—

Goalpara.

Between 1891 *and* 1901—

Naga Hills, Goalpara, Darrang, Nowgong and Sibsagar.

In columns 19, 20 and 21 the variations shown against the Province, British Territory, Surma Valley and Hill Districts and Manipur are the variations of the total population shown against them and not the sum of the variations of their districts. Both Lushai Hills and Manipur were excluded from the census of 1872, and in 1881 Manipur alone was enumerated ; in 1891 the census papers of Manipur were destroyed in the insurrection, while the Lushai Hills was not censused but an estimate was formed of the population of the northern portion, which was the only part then in Assam.

The variation shown against Naga Hills between 1901 and 1911 is mainly due to the addition of territory unadministered in 1901, *viz.*, the Sema and Eastern Angami villages, with a population of 39,586 persons.

NOTE.—Similar statistics for areas smaller than districts are contained in Provincial Table I, which is printed at the end of the Imperial Tables.

TABLE II.—Variation in Population since 1872.

District or State.	Persons. 1911.	1901.	1891.	1881.	1872.	Males. 1911.	1901.	1891.	1881.	1872.
1	2	3	4	5	6	7	8	9	10	11
ASSAM	***7,059,857***	***6,126,343***	***5,477,302***	***5,128,862***	***4,150,769***	***3,638,287***	***3,143,692***	***2,819,936***	***2,626,449***	***2,133,774***
(1) British Territory	***6,713,635***	***5,841,878***	***5,477,302***	***4,907,792***	***4,150,769***	***3,467,621***	***3,004,060***	***2,819,936***	***2,516,885***	***2,133,774***
SURMA VALLEY AND HILL DISTRICTS	***3,446,030***	***3,084,537***	***2,879,251***	***2,546,241***	***2,165,943***	***1,761,134***	***1,573,103***	***1,471,146***	***1,294,932***	***1,109,065***
Cachar	497,463	455,593	386,483	313,858	235,027	260,444	244,161	203,679	166,936	125,373
Sylhet	2,472,671	2,241,818	2,154,593	1,969,009	1,719,539	1,208,469	1,141,060	1,100,938	999,785	880,330
Khasi and Jaintia Hills	235,069	202,250	197,904	167,804	140,356	114,442	97,221	94,606	79,765	67,852
Naga Hills	149,623	102,402	96,637	94,570	71,021	74,751	51,656	49,084	48,446	35,510
Lushai Hills	91,204	82,434	43,634	...	...	43,028	39,004	22,839	...	...
ASSAM VALLEY DISTRICTS	***3,267,605***	***2,757,351***	***2,598,051***	***2,361,551***	***1,984,826***	***1,706,487***	***1,430,958***	***1,348,796***	***1,221,953***	***1,024,709***
Goalpara	600,643	462,052	452,773	446,700	387,341	318,475	242,685	236,863	229,383	193,670
Kamrup	667,898	589,187	634,249	644,960	561,681	339,398	292,869	321,029	329,061	292,688
Darrang	377,314	337,313	307,440	273,012	235,720	198,581	176,030	161,220	142,257	122,693
Nowgong	303,596	261,160	347,307	314,893	260,238	154,938	132,995	179,374	162,637	136,031
Sibsagar	690,299	597,969	480,659	393,545	317,799	364,810	316,985	252,687	206,329	165,545
Lakhimpur	465,989	371,396	254,053	179,893	121,267	249,021	190,359	135,404	96,335	64,692
Garo Hills	158,936	138,274	121,570	109,548	100,780	81,264	70,035	61,213	55,951	50,390
(2) Manipur State	***346,222***	***284,465***	...	***221,070***	...	***170,666***	***139,632***	...	***109,557***	...

District or State.	Females. 1911.	1901.	1891.	1881.	1872.	Variation. Increase (+), Decrease (−). 1901—1911.	1891—1901.	1881—1891.	1872—1881.	Net variation in period 1872—1911. Increase (+). Decrease (−).
	12	13	14	15	16	17	18	19	20	21
ASSAM	***3,421,570***	***2,982,651***	***2,657,366***	***2,502,420***	***2,016,995***	+ ***933,514***	+ ***649,041***	+ ***348,440***	+ ***978,093***	+ ***2,909,088***
(1) British Territory	***3,246,014***	***2,837,818***	***2,657,366***	***2,390,907***	***2,016,995***	+ ***871,757***	+ ***364,576***	+ ***569,510***	+ ***757,023***	+ ***2,562,866***
SURMA VALLEY AND HILL DISTRICTS	***1,684,896***	***1,511,435***	***1,408,105***	***1,251,809***	***1,056,878***	+ ***361,503***	+ ***205,276***	+ ***333,010***	+ ***380,298***	+ ***1,280,087***
Cachar	237,019	211,432	182,804	146,922	109,654	+ 41,870	+ 69,110	+ 72,625	+ 78,831	+ 262,436
Sylhet	1,204,202	1,100,788	1,053,655	969,224	839,209	+ 230,823	+ 87,255	+ 185,584	+ 249,470	+ 753,132
Khasi and Jaintia Hills	120,627	105,029	103,298	88,039	72,504	+ 32,819	+ 4,346	+ 30,100	+ 27,448	+ 94,713
Naga Hills	74,872	50,746	47,553	47,124	35,511	+ 47,221	+ 5,765	+ 1,067	+ 24,549	+ 78,602
Lushai Hills	48,176	43,430	20,795	...	...	+ 8,770	+ 38,800	...	...	...
ASSAM VALLEY DISTRICTS	***1,561,118***	***1,396,393***	***1,249,261***	***1,139,598***	***960,117***	+ ***510,254***	+ ***159,300***	+ ***236,500***	+ ***376,725***	+ ***1,282,779***
Goalpara	282,168	219,367	215,910	217,317	193,671	+ 138,591	+ 9,279	+ 6,073	+ 59,359	+ 213,302
Kamrup	328,430	296,318	313,220	315,899	268,993	+ 78,641	− 45,062	− 10,711	+ 83,279	+ 106,147
Darrang	178,733	161,283	146,220	130,755	113,027	+ 40,001	+ 29,873	+ 34,428	+ 37,292	+ 141,594
Nowgong	148,658	128,165	167,933	152,256	125,207	+ 42,436	− 86,147	+ 32,414	+ 54,655	+ 43,358
Sibsagar	325,489	280,984	227,972	186,216	152,254	+ 92,330	+ 117,310	+ 88,114	+ 74,746	+ 372,500
Lakhimpur	219,968	172,037	117,649	83,558	56,575	+ 97,593	+ 117,343	+ 74,160	+ 58,626	+ 347,722
Garo Hills	77,672	68,239	60,357	53,597	50,390	+ 20,662	+ 16,704	+ 12,022	+ 8,768	+ 58,156
(2) Manipur State	***175,556***	***144,833***	...	***111,513***	...	+ ***61,757***	...	...	...	...

TABLE III.

TOWNS AND VILLAGES CLASSIFIED BY POPULATION.

IN this table, as in Tables I and IV, cantonments have been treated as forming part of the municipalities which they adjoin.

In Cachar, Kamrup, Darrang, Nowgong, Sibsagar and Lakhimpur and in the valley of the State of Manipur the cadastral village has been taken as the village. Elsewhere it is the residential village or group of houses bearing a separate name; small outlying hamlets have been treated as part of the main residential village to which they appertain.

TABLE III.—Towns and Villages classified by Population.

District or State.	Total number of inhabited towns and villages.	Population.	Under 500.		500—1,000.		1,000—2,000.		2,000—5,000.		5,000—10,000.		10,000—20,000.		50,000—100,000.		Encampments, Boat and Railway population unclassed.
			Number.	Population.	Number.	Population.	Number.	Population.	Number.	Population.	Number.	Population.	Number.	Population.	Number.	Population.	
1	2	3	4	5	6	7	8	9	10	11	12	13	14	15	16	17	18
ASSAM	*29,373*	*7,059,857*	*26,011*	*3,836,109*	*2,526*	*1,716,040*	*673*	*907,385*	*146*	*384,265*	*11*	*65,680*	*5*	*65,117*	*1*	*74,650*	*10,611*
(1) ***British Territory***	*27,895*	*6,713,635*	*24,658*	*3,667,903*	*2,424*	*1,647,368*	*654*	*882,006*	*143*	*374,950*	*11*	*65,680*	*5*	*65,117*	...	...	*10,611*
SURMA VALLEY AND HILL DISTRICTS	*15,121*	*3,446,030*	*13,474*	*1,979,968*	*1,963*	*864,161*	*303*	*406,780*	*55*	*136,819*	*4*	*26,599*	*2*	*28,096*	...	...	*4,314*
Cachar	1,415	497,463	1,054	194,332	298	197,491	68	85,626	4	9,231	1	8,785	...	...	...	...	1,998
Sylhet	10,781	2,472,671	9,608	1,473,100	855	569,072	207	281,487	47	116,440	3	17,814	1	14,457	...	...	1,301
Khasi and Jaintia Hills	2,141	235,069	2,095	184,061	40	25,844	3	5,077	2	5,620	...	...	1	13,639	...	...	828
Naga Hills	406	149,623	317	65,899	68	50,040	21	28,163	3	5,582	...	...	...	...	...	...	...
Lushai Hills	376	91,204	340	61,876	32	22,714	4	6,427	...	...	...	...	...	...	...	...	187
ASSAM VALLEY DISTRICTS	*12,774*	*3,267,605*	*11,184*	*1,688,635*	*1,141*	*783,207*	*351*	*475,226*	*88*	*238,138*	*7*	*39,081*	*3*	*37,021*	...	...	*6,297*
Goalpara	2,137	600,643	1,851	302,167	195	133,342	67	90,546	22	62,728	2	11,772	...	...	...	...	90
Kamrup	1,954	667,828	1,550	272,996	289	196,727	96	135,765	17	46,096	...	...	2	22,458	...	...	3,786
Darrang	1,406	377,314	1,248	229,058	115	79,935	38	54,117	4	8,528	1	5,355	...	...	...	...	421
Nowgong	1,495	303,596	1,334	169,488	135	92,787	22	8,272	3	6,815	1	5,360	...	...	...	...	874
Sibsagar	2,143	690,299	1,737	321,164	316	217,617	73	99,488	14	34,988	3	16,594	...	...	...	...	448
Lakhimpur	1,702	463,989	1,535	242,661	86	59,200	52	72,902	28	78,985	...	...	1	14,563	...	...	678
Garo Hills	1,937	156,936	1,929	151,201	5	3,599	3	4,136	...	...	...	...	...	...	...	...	...
(2) ***Manipur State***	*1,478*	*346,222*	*1,353*	*168,206*	*109*	*68,672*	*19*	*25,379*	*3*	*9,815*	...	...	...	...	*1*	*74,650*	...

TABLE IV.

POPULATION OF TOWNS WITH VARIATION SINCE 1872.

The table shows the population of all municipalities, unions and cantonments and also of certain other places (chiefly subdivisional headquarters) which are of an urban character, though not under municipal government.

The population of the cantonments, which has been added to that of the towns which they adjoin, is shown below:—

Cantonment.	Town with which included.	Persons.	Males.	Females.
Shillong	Shillong	2,511	1,661	850
Kohima	Kohima	322	288	34
Dibrugarh	Dibrugarh ...	730	586	144
Imphal	Imphal	1,063	827	236

The population of the towns of Shillong, Tezpur and Imphal as returned at previous enumerations has been adjusted on account of subsequent changes in boundaries. The figures now given represent the population of the area now included in each municipality or town.

It has been found impossible to ascertain the former population of places now treated as towns for the first time; Hailakandi and Nazira Unions are treated as towns now for the first time.

TABLE IV.—Towns classified by Population with variation since 1872.

Town.	District or State.	Municipality, Suburbs, Cantonment, etc.	Population. 1911.	Population. 1901.	Population. 1891.	Population. 1881.	Population. 1872.	Variation. Increase (+), Decrease (−). 1901 to 1911.	1891 to 1901.	1881 to 1891.	1872 to 1881.	Variation in period 1872—1911. Increase (+) Decrease (−).	Males. 1911.	Males. 1901.	Males. 1891.	Females. 1911.	Females. 1901.	Females. 1891.
1	2	3	4	5	6	7	8	9	10	11	12	13	14	15	16	17	18	19
TOTAL URBAN POPULATION ...		*21 Towns* ...	*211,318*	*187,162*	*100,736*	*92,047*	*60,084*	*+24,156*	*+86,426*	*+8,689*	*+31,963*	*+151,234*	*119,893*	*107,712*	*62,519*	*91,425*	*79,450*	*37,924*
CLASS II—50,000—100,000 ...	...	*1 Town* ...	*74,650*	*72,234*	...	...	...	*+ 2,416*	...	...	...	...	*36,393*	*35,487*	...	*38,257*	*36,747*	...
Imphal	Manipur ...	*	74,650	72,234	...	...	...	+ 2,416	...	...	...	...	36,393	35,487	†	38,257	36,747	†
CLASS IV—10,000—20,000 ...	...	*5 Towns* ...	*65,879*	*55,149*	*49,428*	*48,875*	*41,718*	*+ 10,730*	*+5,721*	*+553*	*+7,157*	*+24,161*	*38,371*	*32,873*	*28,538*	*27,508*	*22,276*	*20,890*
Dibrugarh	Lakhimpur ...	Municipality	14,563	11,227	9,876	7,153	2,774	+ 3,336	+ 1,351	+ 2,723	+ 4,379	+11,789	8,896	7,001	6,100	5,667	4,136	3,776
Sylhet	Sylhet ...	Ditto ...	14,457	13,893	14,027	14,407	16,846	+ 564	− 134	− 380	− 2,439	− 2,389	8,314	8,212	7,976	6,143	5,681	6,051
Shillong	Khasi and Jaintia Hills	Ditto ...	13,639	9,621	7,900	4,288	...	+ 4,018	+ 1,721	+ 3,612	...	...	7,762	5,577	4,638	5,877	4,044	3,262
Gauhati	Kamrup ...	Ditto ...	12,481	11,661	8,283	11,695	11,492	+ 820	+ 3,378	− 3,412	+ 203	+ 989	8,138	7,772	5,280	4,343	3,889	3,003
Barpeta	Ditto ...	Ditto ...	10,739	8,747	9,342	11,332	10,606	+ 1,992	− 595	− 1,990	+ 726	+ 133	5,261	4,221	4,544	5,478	4,526	4,798
CLASS V—5,000—10,000 ...	...	*9 Towns* ...	*55,096*	*48,316*	*41,548*	*36,774*	*18,366*	*+6,780*	*+ 6,768*	*+ 4,774*	*+ 18,408*	*+ 36,730*	*34,908*	*31,784*	*27,860*	*20,188*	*16,532*	*13,688*
Silchar	Cachar ...	Municipality	8,785	9,256	7,523	6,567	4,925	− 471	+ 1,733	+ 966	+ 1,642	+ 3,860	5,900	6,575	5,728	2,885	2,681	1,795
Karimganj	Sylhet ...	*	6,512	5,692	3,340	2,810	...	+ 820	+ 2,343	+ 530	...	...	4,027	3,470	2,144	2,485	2,222	1,205
Habiganj	Ditto ...	Union ...	6,244	5,236	4,161	4,061	...	+ 1,008	+ 1,075	+ 100	...	...	3,912	3,361	2,709	2,332	1,875	1,452
Goalpara	Goalpara ...	Municipality	5,964	6,287	5,440	6,697	4,323	− 323	+ 847	− 1,257	+ 2,374	+ 1,641	3,802	4,198	3,605	2,162	2,089	1,835
Dhubri	Ditto ...	Ditto ...	5,808	3,737	4,825	2,893	...	+ 2,071	− 1,088	+ 1,932	...	...	3,910	2,670	3,688	1,898	1,067	1,137
Sibsagar	Sibsagar ...	Station ...	5,764	5,712	5,249	4,583	3,993	+ 52	+ 463	+ 666	+ 590	+ 1,771	3,228	3,420	3,078	2,536	2,292	2,171
Nowgong	Nowgong ...	Municipality ...	5,433	4,430	4,815	4,248	3,241	+ 1,003	− 385	+ 567	+ 1,007	+ 2,192	3,145	2,659	2,838	2,288	1,771	1,977
Tezpur	Darrang ...	Ditto ...	5,355	5,067	4,027	2,922	1,884	+ 288	+ 1,040	+ 1,105	+ 1,038	+ 3,471	3,759	3,582	2,683	1,596	1,485	1,344
Jorhat	Sibsagar ...	Ditto ...	5,231	2,899	2,159	1,984	...	+ 2,332	+ 740	+ 175	...	...	3,225	1,849	1,387	2,006	1,050	772
CLASS VI—UNDER 5,000 ...	...	*6 Towns* ...	*15,693*	*11,463*	*9,760*	*6,398*	...	*+4,230*	*+1,705*	*+ 3,362*	...	...	*10,291*	*7,568*	*6,414*	*5,479*	*3,895*	*3,346*
Sunamganj	Sylhet ...	*	4,620	3,530	3,139	1,020	...	+ 1,090	+ 391	+ 2,119	...	...	3,084	2,282	2,124	1,536	1,248	1,015
Nazira	Sibsagar ...	Union ...	2,583	...	...	...	...	...	...	...	...	...	1,501	...	...	1,082	...	...
Kohima	Naga Hills ...	*	2,423	3,093	1,781	1,380	...	− 670	+ 1,312	+ 401	...	...	1,691	2,174	1,247	732	919	534
Maulvi Bazar	Sylhet ...	*	2,369	2,481	2,629	1,857	...	− 112	− 148	+ 772	...	...	1,597	1,721	1,725	772	760	904
Golaghat	Sibsagar ...	Union ...	2,236	2,359	2,211	2,141	...	− 123	+ 148	+ 70	...	...	1,360	1,391	1,318	876	968	893
Hailakandi	Cachar ...	Ditto ...	1,462	...	...	...	...	...	...	...	...	...	988	...	...	474	...	...

* Treated as town for census purposes although neither a Municipality nor a Cantonment.
† Not censused.

TABLE V.

TOWNS ARRANGED TERRITORIALLY WITH POPULATION BY RELIGION.

The column "Others" includes the following :—

Town.	Religion.	Persons.	Males.	Females.
1	2	3	4	5
Tezpur	Jew	1	1	...
Kohima Cantonment	Confucian ...	1	1	...
Total ...	......	2	2	...

TABLE V.—Towns arranged Terri

Serial No.	District or State.	Town, Municipality, Suburbs, Cantonments, etc.	POPULATION.			HINDU.			BRAHMO.			SIKH.		
			Persons.	Males.	Females.	Persons.	Males.	Females.	Persons.	Males.	Females.	Persons.	Males.	Females.
	1	2	3	4	5	6	7	8	9	10	11	12	13	14
	ASSAM	...	*211,318*	*119,893*	*91,425*	*157,966*	*89,044*	*68,922*	*170*	*94*	*76*	*110*	*90*	*20*
	(1) British Territory	...	*136,66 8*	*83,500*	*53,168*	*86,898*	*54,782*	*32,116*	*170*	*94*	*76*	*103*	*85*	*18*
	SURMA VALLEY AND HILL DISTRICTS.		*60,511*	*37,275*	*23,236*	*31,022*	*20,780*	*10,242*	*72*	*43*	*29*	*53*	*41*	*12*
1	Cachar ...	Silchar ...	**8,785**	5,900	2,885	**6,260**	4,203	2,057	**10**	8	2	...	...	...
2	Ditto ...	Hailakandi ...	**1,462**	988	474	**1,102**	726	376	...	...	...	...	...	...
3	Sylhet ...	Sylhet ...	**14,457**	8,314	6,143	**6,529**	4,088	2,441	**9**	6	3	...	...	...
4	Ditto ...	Habiganj ...	**6,244**	3,912	2,332	**4,022**	2,614	1,408	...	...	...	...	...	...
5	Ditto ...	Sunamganj ...	**4,620**	3,084	1,536	**2,041**	1,563	478	...	...	...	...	...	...
6	Ditto ...	Karimganj ...	**6,512**	4,027	2,485	**2,975**	1,940	1,035	...	...	...	...	...	...
7	Ditto ...	Maulvi Bazar ...	**2,369**	1,597	772	**1,368**	968	400	**6**	4	2	...	...	...
8	Khasi and Jaintia Hills.	Shillong ...	**13,639**	7,762	5,877	**5,446**	3,780	1,666	**47**	25	22	**53**	41	12
9	Naga Hills ...	Kohima ...	**2,423**	1,691	732	**1,279**	898	381	...	...	...	...	...	...
	ASSAM VALLEY DISTRICTS...		*76,157*	*46,225*	*29,932*	*55,876*	*34,002*	*21,874*	*98*	*51*	*47*	*50*	*44*	*6*
10	Goalpara ...	Dhubri ...	**5,808**	3,910	1,898	**3,732**	2,547	1,185	**43**	22	21	**7**	6	1
11	Ditto ...	Goalpara ...	**5,964**	3,802	2,162	**3,846**	2,484	1,362	**4**	3	1	...	...	...
12	Kamrup ...	Gauhati ...	**12,481**	8,138	4,343	**8,790**	5,843	2,947	**10**	5	5	**10**	8	2
13	Ditto ...	Barpeta ...	**10,739**	5,261	5,478	**10,481**	5,062	5,419	...	...	...	...	...	...
14	Darrang ...	Tezpur ...	**5,355**	3,759	1,596	**3,871**	2,726	1,145	**12**	6	6	**1**	1	...
15	Nowgong ...	Nowgong ...	**5,433**	3,145	2,288	**3,605**	2,168	1,437	...	...	...	**14**	11	3
16	Sibsagar ...	Sibsagar ...	**5,764**	3,228	2,536	**4,021**	2,289	1,732	...	...	...	**2**	2	...
17	Ditto ...	Nazira ...	**2,583**	1,501	1,082	**1,834**	1,046	788	...	...	...	...	...	...
18	Ditto ...	Jorhat... ...	**5,231**	3,225	2,006	**3,791**	2,404	1,387	...	...	...	...	...	...
19	Ditto ...	Golaghat ...	**2,236**	1,360	876	**1,421**	920	501	...	...	...	...	...	...
20	Lakhimpur ...	Dibrugarh ...	**14,563**	8,896	5,667	**10,484**	6,513	3,971	**29**	15	14	**16**	16	...
	(2) Manipur State	...	*74,650*	*36,393*	*38,257*	*71,068*	*34,262*	*36,806*	...	...	...	*7*	*5*	*2*
21	Manipur ...	Imphal ...	**74,650**	36,393	38,257	**71,068**	34,262	36,806	...	...	...	**7**	5	2

TORIALLY WITH POPULATION BY RELIGIONS.

JAIN.			BUDDHIST.			MUSALMAN.			CHRISTIAN.			ANIMIST.			OTHERS.			Serial No.
Persons.	Males.	Females.	Persons.	Males.	Females.	Persons.	Males.	Females.	Persons.	Males.	Females.	Persons.	Males.	Females.	Persons.	Males.	Females.	
15	16	17	18	19	20	21	22	23	24	25	26	27	28	29	30	31	32	
665	*572*	*93*	*203*	*128*	*75*	*40,513*	*24,086*	*16,427*	*3,465*	*1,748*	*1,717*	*8, 24*	*4,129*	*4,095*	*2*	*2*	...	
558	*471*	*87*	*202*	*127*	*75*	*38,551*	*22,809*	*15,742*	*3,401*	*1,709*	*1,692*	*6,783*	*3,421*	*3,362*	*2*	*2*	...	
141	*132*	*9*	*56*	*44*	*12*	*20,793*	*12,241*	*8,552*	*2,498*	*1,214*	*1,284*	*5,875*	*2,779*	*3,096*	*1*	*1*	...	
...	...	...	3	3	...	2,359	1,616	743	104	47	57	49	23	26	...	...	...	1
...	...	...	...	...	...	357	260	97	3	2	1	...	...	...	...	...	...	2
33	24	9	...	...	...	7,746	4,120	3,626	120	56	64	20	20	...	...	...	...	3
...	...	...	...	...	...	2,204	1,288	916	18	10	8	...	...	...	...	...	...	4
5	5	...	...	...	...	2,569	1,511	1,058	5	5	...	...	...	...	...	...	...	5
44	44	...	...	...	...	3,466	2,031	1,435	27	12	15	...	...	...	...	...	...	6
18	18	...	...	...	...	973	605	368	4	2	2	...	...	...	...	...	...	7
4	4	...	51	39	12	847	570	277	2,162	1,043	1,119	5,029	2,260	2,769	...	...	...	8
37	37	...	2	2	...	272	240	32	55	37	18	777	476	301	1	1	...	9
417	*339*	*78*	*146*	*83*	*63*	*17,758*	*10,568*	*7,190*	*905*	*495*	*408*	*908*	*642*	*266*	*1*	*1*	...	
51	40	11	...	...	...	1,927	1,266	661	21	10	11	27	19	8	...	...	...	10
85	81	4	...	...	...	1,983	1,195	788	42	35	7	4	4	...	...	...	...	11
28	24	4	13	10	3	3,075	1,870	1,205	217	130	87	338	248	90	...	...	...	12
5	4	1	1	1	...	248	190	58	...	...	...	4	4	...	...	...	...	13
70	53	17	2	2	...	1,088	759	329	69	44	25	241	167	74	1	1	...	14
53	41	12	1	1	...	1,443	765	678	179	70	109	138	89	49	...	...	...	15
...	...	...	...	...	...	1,614	871	743	124	63	61	3	3	...	...	...	...	16
14	8	6	...	...	...	727	440	287	3	2	1	5	5	...	...	...	...	17
38	30	8	10	2	8	1,317	743	574	37	18	19	38	28	10	...	...	...	18
4	4	...	1	1	...	780	419	361	23	11	12	7	5	2	...	...	...	19
69	54	15	118	66	52	3,556	2,050	1,506	188	112	76	103	70	33	...	...	...	20
107	*101*	*6*	*1*	*1*	...	*1,962*	*1,277*	*685*	*64*	*39*	*25*	*1,441*	*708*	*733*	...	...	...	
107	101	6	1	1	...	1,962	1,277	685	64	39	25	1,441	708	733	...	...	...	21

TABLE VI.

RELIGIONS.

The head "Minor Religions" includes the following :—

District.	Religion.	Persons.	Males.	Females.
1	2	3	4	5
Naga Hills	Confucian ...	1	1	...
Kamrup	Parsi	1	1	...
Darrang	Jew	1	1	...
Lakhimpur	Parsi	4	4	...
	Atheist	1	1	...
Total ...	......	8	8	...

TABLE VI.—RELIGIONS.

District or State.	Population.			I.—Indo-Aryan. Hindu.			Brahmo.			Sikh.			Jain.			Buddhist.		
	Persons.	Males.	Females.	Persons.	Males.	Females.	Persons.	Males.	Females.	Persons.	Males.	Females.	Persons.	Males.	Females.	Persons.	Males.	Females.
1	2	3	4	5	6	7	8	9	10	11	12	13	14	15	16	17	18	19
ASSAM	*7,059,857*	*3,638,287*	*3,421,570*	*3,838,769*	*1,997,724*	*1,841,045*	*428*	*241*	*187*	*757*	*475*	*282*	*2,508*	*2,136*	*372*	*10,513*	*6,204*	*4,309*
(1) ***British Territory***	*6,713,635*	*3,467,621*	*3,246,014*	*3,637,400*	*1,898,460*	*1,738,940*	*428*	*241*	*187*	*750*	*470*	*280*	*2,398*	*2,032*	*366*	*10,506*	*6,199*	*4,307*
SURMA VALLEY AND HILL DISTRICTS ...	*3,446,030*	*1,761,134*	*1,684,896*	*1,436,284*	*743,597*	*692,637*	*285*	*156*	*129*	*118*	*97*	*21*	*206*	*190*	*16*	*430*	*294*	*136*
Cachar	497 463	260,444	237,019	320.104	167,424	152,680	13	11	2	21	16	5	19	13	6	33	28	5
Sylhet	2,472,671	1,268,469	1,204.202	1,098 950	564,268	534,684	20	11	9	9	8	1	146	136	10	20	14	6
Khasi and Jaintia Hills	235 069	114,442	120,627	9 454	6,738	2,716	252	134	118	59	45	14	4	4	...	62	47	15
Naga Hills	149.623	74,751	74,872	4,218	2,737	1,476	...	...	...	3	2	1	37	37	...	3	3	...
Lushai Hills	91,204	43,028	48,176	3,513	2,432	1,081	...	...	...	26	26	...	...	...	...	312	202	110
ASSAM VALLEY DISTRICTS	*3,267,605*	*1,706,487*	*1,561,118*	*2,201,166*	*1,154,863*	*1,046,303*	*143*	*85*	*58*	*632*	*373*	*259*	*2,192*	*1,842*	*350*	*10,076*	*5,905*	*4,171*
Goalpara	600.643	318,475	282,168	334,720	178,673	156,047	71	40	31	32	21	11	712	617	95	955	606	349
Kamrup	667 828	339,398	328,430	459.227	235,014	224,213	12	7	5	12	10	2	264	180	84	574	441	133
Darrang	377 314	198,581	178,733	245 341	129,631	115,710	22	16	6	16	15	1	376	339	37	609	435	174
Nowgong	303 596	154,938	148,658	177,795	91,213	86,582	...	...	...	399	215	184	232	207	25	41	30	11
Sibsagar	690.299	364,810	325,489	595.266	313,748	281,518	2	2	...	56	34	23	303	259	44	1,964	1,099	865
Lakhimpur	468 989	249,021	219,968	367.990	195,291	172,699	36	20	16	117	78	39	284	225	59	5,648	3,147	2,501
Garo Hills	158,936	81,264	77,672	20.827	11,293	9,534	...	...	...	...	...	...	21	15	6	285	147	138
(2) ***Manipur State***	*346,222*	*170,666*	*175.556*	*201,369*	*99,264*	*102,105*	...	...	...	*7*	*5*	*2*	*110*	*104*	*6*	*7*	*5*	*2*

District or State.	II.—Semetic. Musalman.			Christian.			III.—Primitive. Animist.			IV.—Miscellaneous. Minor religions.		
	Persons.	Males.	Females.	Persons.	Males.	Females.	Persons.	Males.	Females.	Persons.	Males.	Females.
	20	21	22	23	24	25	26	27	28	29	30	31
ASSAM	*1,901,032*	*984,968*	*916,064*	*66,562*	*33,632*	*32,930*	*1,239,280*	*612,899*	*626,381*	*8*	*8*	...
(1) ***British Territory***	*1,886,528*	*977,463*	*909,065*	*66,430*	*33,548*	*32,882*	*1,109,187*	*549,200*	*559,987*	*8*	*8*	...
SURMA VALLEY AND HILL DISTRICTS ...	*1,522,988*	*783,772*	*739,216*	*39,719*	*19,184*	*20,535*	*446,049*	*213,843*	*232,206*	*1*	*1*	...
Cachar	156,096	82,560	73,536	1,181	649	532	19,996	9,743	10,253	...	...	...
Sylhet	1,364.739	699,470	665,269	1 512	863	649	7.275	3,701	3,574	...	...	...
Khasi and Jaintia Hills	1,528	1,172	356	31,257	14,855	16,402	192,453	91,447	101,006	...	...	...
Naga Hills	318	281	37	3,308	1,554	1,754	141.740	70,136	71,604	1	1	...
Lushai Hills	307	289	18	2,461	1,263	1,198	84,585	38,816	45,769	...	...	...
ASSAM VALLEY DISTRICTS	*363,540*	*193,691*	*169,849*	*26,711*	*14,364*	*12,347*	*663,138*	*335,357*	*327,781*	*7*	*7*	...
Goalpara	211 562	111,917	99,645	5.252	2,731	2,521	47,339	23,870	23,469	...	...	...
Kamrup	64 627	33,723	30,904	2 535	1,373	1,162	140.576	68,649	71,927	1	1	...
Darrang	20.305	11,073	9,232	1,913	1,028	885	108.731	56.043	52,688	1	1	...
Nowgong	15.689	8,163	7,526	1,373	707	666	108.067	54,403	53,664	...	...	...
Sibsagar	29.718	16,373	13,345	5,410	2,933	2,477	57 580	30,362	27,218	...	...	...
Lakhimpur	13,419	7,986	5,433	4.789	2,647	2,142	76,701	39,622	37,079	5	5	...
Garo Hills	8,220	4,456	3,764	5,439	2,945	2,494	124,144	62,408	61,736	...	...	...
(2) ***Manipur State***	*14,504*	*7,505*	*6,999*	*132*	*84*	*48*	*130,093*	*63,699*	*66,394*	...	...	...

TABLE VII.

AGE, SEX AND CIVIL CONDITION.

THIS table is divided into two parts : *Part A* shows the distribution, for the Province as a whole, of the total population and of each religion by age, sex and civil condition. *Part B* shows the distribution for districts and Manipur State of the total population and of the main religions by age, sex and civil condition; but in this part, in order to economise space, the age statistics have been given in less detail than in the provincial summary.

TABLE VII.

Age, Sex and Civil Condition. Part A.—Provencial Summary.

Religion.	Age.	POPULATION.			UNMARRIED.			MARRIED.			WIDOWED.		
		Persons.	Males.	Females.	Persons.	Males.	Females.	Persons.	Males.	Females.	Persons.	Males.	Females.
	1	2	3	4	5	6	7	8	9	10	11	12	13
ALL RELIGIONS.	0—1	245,124	122,290	122,825	245,124	122,299	122,825	...	...	...	...	...	...
	1—2	131.502	64,413	67,089	131.502	64,413	67,080	...	...	...	...	...	...
	2—3	236,737	114,884	121,853	236,733	114,881	121,852	4	3	1	...	...	...
	3—4	251.331	121,620	129,711	251 309	121,613	129,696	21	7	14	1	...	1
	4—5	242,259	119,758	122,501	242,182	119,747	122,435	68	11	57	9	...	9
	TOTAL 0—5	*1,106,953*	*542,974*	*563,979*	*1,106,850*	*542,953*	*563,897*	*93*	*21*	*72*	*10*	...	*10*
	5—10	1,120.929	565,185	555,744	1,106 868	563,333	543,475	13 380	1,796	11,584	741	56	685
	10—15	705,117	388,026	317,091	605.848	378,936	226,912	95,735	8,729	87,006	3,534	361	3,173
	15—20	565 922	273,169	292,753	303 005	231,277	68,728	248.275	36,985	211,290	14.642	1,907	12,735
	20—25	586 207	269,692	316,515	164.662	145,787	18,876	389 872	116,637	273,235	31.673	7,268	24,405
	25—30	669.766	335,834	333,932	92 042	85,677	6,365	520.759	233,099	287,660	56.965	17,058	39,907
	30—35	589,918	310,332	279,586	36 509	33,298	3,211	476.677	255,581	2[illegible]1,096	76,732	21,443	5[illegible],289
	35—40	443 861	258,702	185,159	15 546	13 989	1,557	352.415	223,905	128,450	75,900	20,748	55,152
	40—45	400.764	222,663	178,101	9.264	8,047	1,217	291.113	192,640	98,473	100,387	21,976	78,411
	45—50	226.042	131,700	94,312	4,044	3,578	466	155 011	113,147	41,864	66.967	14,975	52,013
	50—55	256.053	138,191	117,862	3.737	3,198	539	150.952	114,653	36,209	101 364	20,340	81,024
	55—60	100,471	55,982	44,489	1.330	1,133	197	57,940	44,954	12,086	42,101	9,895	32,206
	60—65	151.984	76,341	75,643	1,811	1,406	345	70,386	58,559	11,827	79,787	16,316	63,471
	65—70	36,798	19,396	17,402	570	488	82	17.400	14,332	3,068	18 823	4,576	14,252
	70 and over	99,072	50,110	48,962	1,425	1,095	330	40,251	34,285	5,966	57,396	14,730	42,666
	TOTAL	*7,059,857*	*3,638,287*	*3,421,570*	*3,453,451*	*2,017,255*	*1,436,196*	*2,879,359*	*1,449,383*	*1,429,976*	*797,047*	*171,649*	*555,398*
HINDU.	0—1	128.657	64,181	64,476	128.657	64,181	64,476	...	...	...	...	...	...
	1—2	65.963	32,665	33,298	65 963	32,665	33,208	...	...	...	...	...	...
	2—3	115,564	56,298	59,[illegible]66	115,862	56,296	59,566	2	2	...	...	...	...
	3—4	126,459	60,850	65.609	126.450	60,848	65,602	8	2	6	1	...	1
	4—5	122,156	60,675	61,481	122,107	60,671	61,436	45	4	41	4	...	4
	TOTAL 0—5	*559,099*	*274,669*	*284,430*	*559,039*	*274.661*	*284,378*	*55*	*8*	*47*	*5*	...	*5*
	5—10	560.798	293,110	287,688	571,340	292,002	279,338	8,984	1,065	7,919	474	48	431
	10—15	372 236	204,267	167,969	314,171	198,776	115,395	55.839	5,218	50,621	2.226	273	1,953
	15—20	300.471	149,514	150,957	162.745	129,006	33,739	128.952	19,378	109,574	8.774	1,130	7,644
	20—25	325 871	154,796	171,075	95 520	87,854	7,666	210.483	62,672	147,[illegible]11	19.868	4,270	15,59[illegible]
	25—30	380.556	193,719	186,837	56.450	54,000	2,450	286.799	129,033	157,766	37 307	10,696	26,621
	30—35	337.646	178,667	158,079	24,764	[illegible]	1,244	262.371	140,907	121,464	50 511	14,240	36,271
	35—40	259.964	152,595	107,369	10,462	9,774	689	198 642	128,543	70,099	50 860	14,278	36,582
	40—45	227.022	127,842	99,1[illegible]0	6.276	5,769	507	157,241	107,091	50,1[illegible]0	63 595	14,982	48,52[illegible]
	45—50	132.067	77,730	54,337	2 844	2,649	195	85 930	64,561	21,3[illegible]9	43 293	10,520	32,773
	50—55	147,305	79,606	67,699	2,588	2,358	230	80,917	62,951	17,966	63 800	14,297	49,5[illegible]3
	55—60	61.965	34,392	27,573	972	890	82	32,423	26,311	6,112	28 570	7,191	21,379
	60—65	83 849	41,615	42,234	1,197	1,070	127	34 360	29,461	4,899	48.292	11,084	37,2[illegible]8
	65—70	20.676	10,742	9,934	361	322	39	8,547	7,355	1,192	11.768	3,065	8,703
	70 and over	49,244	24,460	24,784	709	615	94	16,784	14,885	1,899	31,751	8,960	22,791
	TOTAL	*3,838,769*	*1,997,724*	*1,841,045*	*1,809,438*	*1,083,266*	*726,172*	*1,568,327*	*799,439*	*768,888*	*461,004*	*115,019*	*345,985*

TABLE VII.

Age, Sex and Civil Condition. Part A.—Provincial Summary—*contd.*

Religion.	Age.	POPULATION.			UNMARRIED.			MARRIED.			WIDOWED.		
		Persons.	Males.	Females.	Persons.	Males.	Females.	Persons.	Males.	Females.	Persons.	Males.	Females.
	1	2	3	4	5	6	7	8	9	10	11	12	13
BRAHMO.	0—1	15	5	10	15	5	10	...	...	...	...	...	...
	1—2	5	2	3	5	2	3	...	...	...	...	...	...
	2—3	14	7	7	14	7	7	...	...	...	...	...	...
	3—4	13	6	7	13	6	7	...	...	...	...	...	...
	4—5	13	5	8	13	5	8	...	...	...	...	...	...
	TOTAL 0—5	*60*	*25*	*35*	*60*	*25*	*35*	...	...	...	...	...	...
	5—10	56	32	24	53	31	22	3	1	2	...	...	...
	10—15	36	22	14	36	22	14	...	...	...	...	...	...
	15—20	31	13	18	24	13	11	5	...	5	2	...	2
	20—25	46	29	17	29	26	3	15	3	12	2	...	2
	25—30	53	26	27	18	10	8	31	14	17	4	2	2
	30—35	34	18	16	3	2	1	28	15	13	3	1	2
	35—40	39	27	12	1	1	...	32	22	10	6	4	2
	40—45	28	15	13	1	1	...	21	12	9	6	2	4
	45—50	11	9	2	...	...	...	8	7	1	3	2	1
	50—55	23	16	7	1	1	...	17	15	2	5	...	5
	55—60	5	3	2	...	...	...	4	3	1	1	...	1
	60—65	1	1	...	...	...	...	1	1	...	...	...	...
	65—70	4	4	...	...	...	...	2	2	...	2	2	...
	70 and over	1	1	...	...	...	...	1	1	...	...	...	...
	TOTAL	*428*	*241*	*187*	*226*	*139*	*94*	*168*	*96*	*72*	*34*	*13*	*21*
SIKH.	0—1	19	10	9	19	10	9	...	...	...	...	...	...
	1—2	21	13	8	21	13	8	...	...	...	...	...	...
	2—3	20	14	6	20	14	6	...	...	...	...	...	...
	3—4	4	...	4	4	...	4	...	...	...	...	...	...
	4—5	22	11	11	22	11	11	...	...	...	...	...	...
	TOTAL 0—5	*86*	*48*	*38*	*86*	*48*	*38*	...	...	...	...	...	...
	5—10	72	34	38	71	34	37	1	...	1	...	...	...
	10—15	66	37	29	60	34	26	6	3	3	...	...	...
	15—20	59	37	22	25	25	...	28	9	19	6	3	3
	20—25	86	52	34	21	18	3	62	33	29	3	1	2
	25—30	110	72	38	18	17	1	86	52	34	6	3	3
	30—35	92	63	29	7	7	...	74	50	24	11	6	5
	35—40	60	39	21	...	...	...	52	36	16	8	3	5
	40—45	50	40	10	3	3	...	39	34	5	8	3	5
	45—50	28	21	7	...	...	...	18	17	1	10	4	6
	50—55	15	13	2	...	...	...	12	12	...	3	1	2
	55—60	11	6	5	1	1	...	7	5	2	3	...	3
	60—65	16	8	8	1	1	...	9	6	3	6	1	5
	65—70	1	...	1	...	...	...	...	...	...	1	...	1
	70 and over	5	5	...	...	...	...	4	4	...	1	1	...
	TOTAL	*757*	*475*	*289*	*293*	*188*	*105*	*398*	*261*	*137*	*66*	*26*	*40*

TABLE VII.

Age, Sex and Civil Condition. Part A.—Provincial Summary—*contd.*

Religion.	Age.	Population. Persons.	Population. Males.	Population. Females.	Unmarried. Persons.	Unmarried. Males.	Unmarried. Females.	Married. Persons.	Married. Males.	Married. Females.	Widowed. Persons.	Widowed. Males.	Widowed. Females.
	1	2	3	4	5	6	7	8	9	10	11	12	13
JAIN.	0—1	22	15	7	22	15	7	...	...	...	...	...	...
	1—2	24	11	13	24	11	13	...	...	...	...	...	...
	2—3	34	19	15	34	19	15	...	...	...	...	...	...
	3—4	31	21	10	31	21	10	...	...	...	...	...	...
	4—5	21	13	8	21	18	8	...	...	...	...	...	...
	TOTAL 0—5	*132*	*79*	*53*	*132*	*79*	*53*	...	...	...	...	...	...
	5—10	126	74	52	124	72	52	2	2	...	...	...	...
	10—15	224	196	28	191	176	15	30	17	13	3	3	...
	15—20	339	290	49	212	211	1	123	77	46	4	2	2
	20—25	432	382	50	207	205	2	218	170	48	7	7	...
	25—30	391	341	50	131	129	2	243	200	43	17	12	5
	30—35	273	250	23	50	50	...	205	184	21	18	16	2
	35—40	192	167	25	26	28	...	152	139	23	14	12	2
	40—45	159	141	18	15	15	...	127	114	13	17	12	5
	45—50	91	80	11	4	4	...	72	65	7	15	11	4
	50—55	83	77	6	3	3	...	63	60	3	17	14	3
	55—60	31	31	...	1	1	...	23	23	...	7	7	...
	60—65	26	22	4	1	1	...	17	17	...	8	4	4
	65—70	4	3	1	...	...	...	2	2	...	2	1	1
	70 and over	5	3	2	...	...	...	2	2	...	3	1	2
	TOTAL	*2,508*	*2,136*	*372*	*1,097*	*972*	*125*	*1,279*	*1,062*	*217*	*132*	*102*	*30*
BUDDHIST.	0—1	313	168	145	313	168	145	...	...	...	...	...	...
	1—2	161	90	71	161	90	71	...	...	...	...	...	...
	2—3	280	139	141	280	139	141	...	...	...	...	...	...
	3—4	309	154	155	309	154	155	...	...	...	...	...	...
	4—5	282	150	132	282	150	132	...	...	...	...	...	...
	TOTAL 0—5	*1,345*	*701*	*644*	*1,345*	*701*	*644*	...	...	...	...	...	...
	5—10	1,331	677	654	1,323	672	651	7	5	2	1	...	1
	10—15	880	483	397	832	466	366	44	17	27	4	...	4
	15—20	851	475	376	584	419	165	252	51	201	15	5	10
	20—25	1,240	756	484	446	404	42	733	321	412	61	31	30
	25—30	1,256	782	474	248	222	26	932	510	422	76	50	26
	30—35	1,066	609	367	124	108	16	827	516	311	115	75	40
	35—40	645	436	209	56	49	7	505	338	167	84	49	35
	40—45	669	436	233	45	42	3	501	344	157	123	50	73
	45—50	361	221	140	17	17	...	260	177	83	84	27	57
	50—55	376	256	120	20	19	1	252	191	61	104	46	58
	55—60	145	91	54	3	2	1	106	82	24	36	7	29
	60—65	183	105	78	6	6	...	81	67	14	96	32	64
	65—70	54	26	28	...	...	...	23	19	4	31	7	24
	70 and over	111	60	51	1	1	...	61	44	17	49	15	34
	TOTAL	*10,513*	*6,204*	*4,309*	*5,050*	*3,128*	*1,922*	*4,584*	*2,682*	*1,902*	*879*	*394*	*485*

TABLE VII.

Age, Sex and Civil Condition. Part A.—Provincial Summary—*contd.*

Religion.	Age.	Population.			Unmarried.			Married.			Widowed.		
		Persons.	Males.	Females.	Persons.	Males.	Females.	Persons.	Males.	Females.	Persons.	Males.	Females.
	1	2	3	4	5	6	7	8	9	10	11	12	13
MUSALMAN.	0—1	71,242	35,818	35,429	71,242	35,818	35,429	...	...	...	...	...	...
	1—2	33,471	16,252	17,219	33,471	16,252	17,219	...	...	...	...	...	...
	2—3	69,916	33,770	36,146	69,914	33,769	36,145	2	1	1	...	...	...
	3—4	73,208	35,409	37,799	73,200	35,404	37,796	8	5	3	...	...	...
	4—5	72,423	35,760	36,663	72,413	35,737	36,656	9	3	6	1	...	1
	TOTAL 0—5	*320,260*	*157,004*	*163,256*	*320,240*	*156,995*	*163,245*	*19*	*9*	*10*	*1*	...	*1*
	5—10	342,490	172,269	170,221	338,766	171,802	166,964	3,515	458	3,057	209	9	200
	10—15	200,771	115,399	85,372	166,807	113,262	53,545	32,932	2,095	30,837	1,032	42	990
	15—20	160,627	75,862	84,765	71,658	65,473	6,185	85,421	10,049	75,372	3,548	340	3,208
	20—25	156,722	69,692	87,030	37,704	36,241	1,463	112,841	32,078	80,763	6,177	1,373	4,804
	25—30	173,474	88,338	87,136	20,379	19,679	700	144,158	65,453	78,705	10,937	3,206	7,731
	30—35	145,502	78,482	67,020	5,210	4,746	464	124,615	70,184	54,431	15,677	3,552	12,125
	35—40	103,550	62,945	40,605	1,854	1,620	234	86,367	58,237	28,130	15,329	3,088	12,241
	40—45	93,476	52,365	41,111	1,184	960	224	69,324	48,264	21,060	22,968	3,141	19,827
	45—50	50,424	30,508	19,916	484	401	83	35,702	28,136	7,566	14,238	1,971	12,267
	50—55	60,185	32,348	27,837	425	343	82	36,252	29,234	7,018	23,508	2,771	20,737
	55—60	19,079	11,401	7,678	129	98	31	11,631	10,175	1,456	7,319	1,128	6,191
	60—65	39,259	20,028	19,231	251	175	76	19,443	17,230	2,213	19,565	2,623	16,942
	65—70	7,653	4,380	3,273	118	111	7	3,967	3,633	334	3,568	636	2,932
	70 and over	25,560	13,947	11,613	199	144	55	11,553	10,842	711	13,868	2,961	10,847
	TOTAL	*1,301,032*	*984,968*	*916,064*	*965,408*	*572,050*	*393,358*	*777,740*	*386,077*	*391,663*	*157,884*	*26,841*	*131,043*
CHRISTIAN.	0—1	2,245	1,085	1,160	2,245	1,085	1,160	...	...	...	...	...	...
	1—2	1,522	775	747	1,522	775	747	...	...	...	...	...	...
	2—3	2,211	1,098	1,113	2,211	1,098	1,113	...	...	...	...	...	...
	3—4	2,274	1,124	1,150	2,274	1,124	1,150	...	...	...	...	...	...
	4—5	2,205	1,066	1,139	2,205	1,066	1,139	...	...	...	...	...	...
	TOTAL 0—5	*10,457*	*5,148*	*5,309*	*10,457*	*5,148*	*5,309*	...	...	...	...	...	...
	5—10	9,649	4,897	4,752	9,610	4,876	4,734	37	21	16	2	...	2
	10—15	7,598	3,975	3,553	7,361	3,944	3,417	159	31	128	8	...	8
	15—20	6,233	2,942	3,291	4,414	2,661	1,753	1,701	263	1,438	118	18	100
	20—25	5,822	2,657	3,165	1,912	1,410	502	3,649	1,169	2,480	261	78	183
	25—30	6,643	3,266	3,377	1,045	846	199	5,134	2,263	2,871	464	157	307
	30—35	5,136	2,663	2,474	481	385	96	4,202	2,139	2,063	453	138	315
	35—40	4,413	2,510	1,903	267	220	47	3,597	2,134	1,463	549	156	393
	40—45	3,386	1,797	1,589	143	102	41	2,643	1,564	1,079	600	131	469
	45—50	2,102	1,152	950	69	56	13	1,557	1,006	551	476	90	386
	50—55	1,914	1,011	903	47	39	8	1,263	853	410	604	119	485
	55—60	934	499	435	19	13	6	586	411	175	329	75	254
	60—65	1,084	547	537	11	7	4	606	458	148	467	82	385
	65—70	378	179	199	11	5	6	205	152	53	162	22	140
	70 and over	883	390	493	9	4	5	371	284	87	503	102	401
	TOTAL	*66,562*	*33,632*	*32,930*	*35,856*	*19,716*	*16,140*	*25,710*	*12,748*	*12,962*	*4,996*	*1,168*	*3,828*

TABLE VII.

Age, Sex and Civil Condition. Part A.—Provincial Summary—*contd.*

Religion.	Age.	POPULATION.			UNMARRIED.			MARRIED.			WIDOWED.		
		Persons.	Males.	Females.	Persons.	Males.	Females.	Persons.	Males.	Females.	Persons.	Males.	Females.
	1	2	3	4	5	6	7	8	9	10	11	12	13
ANIMIST.	0–1	42,611	21,022	21,589	42,611	21,022	21,589	...	...	...	...	...	...
	1–2	30,335	14,605	15,730	30,335	14,605	15,730	...	...	...	...	...	...
	2–3	48,398	23,539	24,859	48,398	23,539	24,859	...	...	...	...	...	...
	3–4	49,033	24,056	24,977	49,028	24,056	24,972	5	...	5	...	...	...
	4–5	45,137	22,078	23,059	45,119	22,074	23,045	14	4	10	4	...	4
	TOTAL 0–5	*215,514*	*105,300*	*110,214*	*215,491*	*105,296*	*110,195*	*19*	*4*	*15*	*4*	...	*4*
	5–10	186,407	94,092	92,315	185,521	93,844	91,677	831	244	587	55	4	51
	10–15	123,376	63,647	59,729	116,390	62,256	54,134	6,725	1,348	5,377	261	43	218
	15–20	97,309	44,034	53,275	63,341	36,467	26,874	31,793	7,158	24,635	2,175	409	1,766
	20–25	95,988	41,328	54,660	28,823	19,629	9,194	61,871	20,191	41,680	5,294	1,508	3,786
	25–30	105,283	49,290	55,993	13,753	10,774	2,979	83,376	35,574	47,802	8,154	2,942	5,212
	30–35	100,167	49,479	50,688	5,870	4,480	1,390	84,353	41,584	42,769	9,944	3,415	6,529
	35–40	74,997	39,982	35,015	2,880	2,299	581	63,067	34,525	28,542	9,050	3,158	5,892
	40–45	75,971	40,024	35,947	1,596	1,154	442	61,215	35,215	26,000	13,160	3,655	9,505
	45–50	40,958	21,979	18,979	626	451	175	31,464	19,178	12,286	8,868	2,350	6,518
	50–55	46,152	24,864	21,288	653	435	218	32,176	21,837	10,339	13,323	3,092	10,231
	55–60	18,301	9,559	8,742	205	128	77	12,260	7,944	4,316	5,836	1,487	4,349
	60–65	27,566	14,015	13,551	344	206	138	15,869	11,319	4,550	11,353	2,480	8,863
	65–70	8,028	4,062	3,966	80	50	30	4,654	3,169	1,485	3,294	843	2,451
	70 and over	23,263	11,244	12,019	507	331	176	11,475	8,223	3,252	11,281	2,690	8,591
	TOTAL	*1,239,280*	*612,899*	*626,381*	*636,080*	*337,800*	*298,280*	*501,148*	*247,013*	*254,135*	*102,052*	*28,086*	*73,966*
PARSI.	0–1	...	...	...	...	...	...	...	...	...	...	...	...
	1–2	...	...	...	...	...	...	...	...	...	...	...	...
	2–3	...	...	...	...	...	...	...	...	...	...	...	...
	3–4	...	...	...	...	...	...	...	...	...	...	...	...
	4–5	...	...	...	...	...	...	...	...	...	...	...	...
	TOTAL 0–5	...	...	...	...	...	...	...	...	...	...	...	...
	5–10	...	...	...	...	...	...	...	...	...	...	...	...
	10–15	...	...	...	...	...	...	...	...	...	...	...	...
	15–20	2	2	...	2	2	...	...	...	...	...	...	...
	20–25	...	...	...	...	...	...	...	...	...	...	...	...
	25–30	...	...	...	...	...	...	...	...	...	...	...	...
	30–35	1	1	...	...	...	...	1	1	...	...	...	...
	35–40	...	...	...	...	...	...	...	...	...	...	...	...
	40–45	2	2	...	...	...	...	2	2	...	...	...	...
	45–50	...	...	...	...	...	...	...	...	...	...	...	...
	50–55	...	...	...	...	...	...	...	...	...	...	...	...
	55–60	...	...	...	...	...	...	...	...	...	...	...	...
	60–65	...	...	...	...	...	...	...	...	...	...	...	...
	65–70	...	...	...	...	...	...	...	...	...	...	...	...
	70 and over	...	...	...	...	...	...	...	...	...	...	...	...
	TOTAL	*5*	*5*	...	*2*	*2*	...	*3*	*3*	...	...	...	...

TABLE VII.

Age, Sex and Civil Condition. Part A.—Provincial Summary—*contd.*

Religion.	Age.	Population. Persons.	Population. Males.	Population. Females.	Unmarried. Persons.	Unmarried. Males.	Unmarried. Females.	Married. Persons.	Married. Males.	Married. Females.	Widowed. Persons.	Widowed. Males.	Widowed. Females.
	1	2	3	4	5	6	7	8	9	10	11	12	13
JEW.	0—1	...	...	...	...	...	...	...	...	...	...	...	...
	1—2	...	...	...	...	...	...	...	...	...	...	...	...
	2—3	...	...	...	...	...	...	...	...	...	...	...	...
	3—4	...	...	...	...	...	...	...	...	...	...	...	...
	4—5	...	...	...	...	...	...	...	...	...	...	...	...
	TOTAL 0—5	...	...	...	...	...	...	...	...	...	...	...	...
	5—10	...	...	...	...	...	...	...	...	...	...	...	...
	10—15	...	...	...	...	...	...	...	...	...	...	...	...
	15—20	...	...	...	...	...	...	...	...	...	...	...	...
	20—25	...	...	...	...	...	...	...	...	...	...	...	...
	25—30	...	...	...	...	...	...	...	...	...	...	...	...
	30—35	...	...	...	...	...	...	...	...	...	...	...	...
	35—40	...	...	...	...	...	...	...	...	...	...	...	...
	40—45	1	1	...	1	1	...	...	...	...	...	...	...
	45—50	...	...	...	...	...	...	...	...	...	...	...	...
	50—55	...	...	...	...	...	...	...	...	...	...	...	...
	55—60	...	...	...	...	...	...	...	...	...	...	...	...
	60—65	...	...	...	...	...	...	...	...	...	...	...	...
	65—70	...	...	...	...	...	...	...	...	...	...	...	...
	70 and over	...	...	...	...	...	...	...	...	...	...	...	...
	TOTAL	*1*	*1*	...	*1*	*1*	...	...	...	...	...	...	...
ATHEIST.	0—1	...	...	...	...	...	...	...	...	...	...	...	...
	1—2	...	...	...	...	...	...	...	...	...	...	...	...
	2—3	...	...	...	...	...	...	...	...	...	...	...	...
	3—4	...	...	...	...	...	...	...	...	...	...	...	...
	4—5	...	...	...	...	...	...	...	...	...	...	...	...
	TOTAL 0—5	...	...	...	...	...	...	...	...	...	...	...	...
	5—10	...	...	...	...	...	...	...	...	...	...	...	...
	10—15	...	...	...	...	...	...	...	...	...	...	...	...
	15—20	...	...	...	...	...	...	...	...	...	...	...	...
	20—25	...	...	...	...	...	...	...	...	...	...	...	...
	25—30	...	...	...	...	...	...	...	...	...	...	...	...
	30—35	1	1	...	...	...	...	1	1	...	...	...	...
	35—40	...	...	...	...	...	...	...	...	...	...	...	...
	40—45	...	...	...	...	...	...	...	...	...	...	...	...
	45—50	...	...	...	...	...	...	...	...	...	...	...	...
	50—55	...	...	...	...	...	...	...	...	...	...	...	...
	55—60	...	...	...	...	...	...	...	...	...	...	...	...
	60—65	...	...	...	...	...	...	...	...	...	...	...	...
	65—70	...	...	...	...	...	...	...	...	...	...	...	...
	70 and over	...	...	...	...	...	...	...	...	...	...	...	...
	TOTAL	*1*	*1*	...	...	...	...	*1*	*1*	...	...	...	...

TABLE VII.

Age, Sex and Civil Condition. Part A.—Provincial Summary—*concld.*

Religion.	Age.	Population.			Unmarried.			Married.			Widowed.		
		Persons.	Males.	Females.	Persons.	Males.	Females.	Persons.	Males.	Females.	Persons.	Males.	Females.
	1	2	3	4	5	6	7	8	9	10	11	12	13
Confucian.	0—1	...	...	...	...	...	...	...	...	...	...	...	...
	1—2	...	...	...	...	...	...	...	...	...	...	...	...
	2—3	...	...	...	...	...	...	...	...	...	...	...	...
	3—4	...	...	...	...	...	...	...	...	...	...	...	...
	4—5	...	...	...	...	...	...	...	...	...	...	...	...
	TOTAL 0—5	...	...	...	...	...	...	...	...	...	...	...	...
	5—10	...	...	...	...	...	...	...	...	...	...	...	...
	10—15	...	...	...	...	...	...	...	...	...	...	...	...
	15—20	...	...	...	...	...	...	...	...	...	...	...	...
	20—25	...	...	...	...	...	...	...	...	...	...	...	...
	25—30	...	...	...	...	...	...	...	...	...	...	...	...
	30—35	1	1	...	...	...	...	1	1	...	...	...	...
	35—40	...	...	...	...	...	...	...	...	...	...	...	...
	40—45	...	...	...	...	...	...	...	...	...	...	...	...
	45—50	...	...	...	...	...	...	...	...	...	...	...	...
	50—55	...	...	...	...	...	...	...	...	...	...	...	...
	55—60	...	...	...	...	...	...	...	...	...	...	...	...
	60—65	...	...	...	...	...	...	...	...	...	...	...	...
	65—70	...	...	...	...	...	...	...	...	...	...	...	...
	70 and over	...	...	...	...	...	...	...	...	...	...	...	...
	TOTAL	*1*	*1*	...	...	...	...	*1*	*1*	...	...	...	...

TABLE VII.

AGE, SEX AND CIVIL CONDITION. PART B.—DETAILS FOR DISTRICTS.

District.		Population.			Unmarried.			Married.			Widowed.		
		Persons.	Males.	Females.	Persons.	Males.	Females.	Persons.	Males.	Females.	Persons.	Males.	Females.
	1	2	3	4	5	6	7	8	9	10	11	12	13
CACHAR.	ALL RELIGIONS ...	*497,463*	*260,444*	*237,019*	*233,934*	*138,502*	*95,432*	*213,687*	*109,362*	*104,335*	*49,842*	*12,580*	*37,262*
	0—5 ...	77,212	37,968	39,244	77,188	37,968	39,220	22	...	22	2	...	2
	5—10 ...	77,650	39,313	38,337	76,337	30,077	37,260	1,249	230	1,019	64	6	58
	10—15 ...	48,247	26,801	21,446	46,113	25,957	14,156	7,833	805	7,028	301	39	262
	15—20 ...	39,433	19,008	20,425	18,885	15,855	3,030	19,532	3,031	16,501	1,016	122	894
	20—40 ...	167,644	88,032	79,612	20,035	18,542	1,493	131,107	64,519	66,588	16,502	4,971	11,531
	40—60 ...	67,512	38,810	28,702	1,151	936	215	45,127	33,123	12,004	21,234	4,751	16,483
	60 and over ...	19,765	10,512	9,253	225	167	58	8,817	7,654	1,163	10,723	2,691	8,032
	HINDU ...	*320,104*	*167,424*	*152,680*	*143,058*	*85,670*	*57,388*	*141,254*	*72,051*	*69,203*	*35,792*	*9,703*	*26,089*
	0—5 ...	45,784	22,427	23,357	45,763	22,427	23,336	20	...	20	1	...	1
	5—10 ...	47,398	24,076	23,232	46,170	23,893	22,277	1,093	180	913	45	3	42
	10—15 ...	30,643	16,620	14,023	24,644	15,898	8,746	5,761	686	5,075	238	36	202
	15—20 ...	25,081	12,104	12,977	11,840	9,871	1,969	12,535	2,147	10,388	706	86	620
	20—40 ...	112,632	58,950	53,682	13,612	12,735	877	86,730	42,454	44,276	12,290	3,761	8,529
	40—60 ...	46,121	26,563	19,558	879	730	149	29,854	22,005	7,849	15,388	3,828	11,560
	60 and over ...	12,535	6,684	5,851	150	116	34	5,261	4,579	682	7,124	1,989	5,135
	MUSALMAN ...	*156,096*	*82,560*	*73,536*	*80,080*	*47,149*	*32,931*	*64,017*	*33,069*	*30,948*	*11,999*	*2,342*	*9,657*
	0—5 ...	27,982	13,918	14,064	27,981	13,918	14,063	1	...	1	...	...	...
	5—10 ...	27,395	13,737	13,658	27,237	13,689	13,548	140	45	95	18	3	15
	10—15 ...	15,628	9,102	6,431	13,563	9,075	4,488	2,002	114	1,888	58	3	55
	15—20 ...	12,685	6,167	6,518	5,861	5,323	538	6,547	814	5,733	277	30	247
	20—40 ...	47,772	25,614	22,158	5,183	4,953	230	39,060	19,634	19,426	3,529	1,027	2,502
	40—60 ...	18,386	10,585	7,801	195	149	46	13,158	9,724	3,434	5,033	712	4,321
	60 and over ...	6,253	3,347	2,906	60	42	18	3,109	2,738	371	3,084	567	2,517
	ANIMIST ...	*19,996*	*9,743*	*10,253*	*10,111*	*5,276*	*4,835*	*7,899*	*3,963*	*3,936*	*1,986*	*504*	*1,482*
	0—5 ...	3,281	1,546	1,735	3,279	1,546	1,733	1	...	1	1	...	1
	5—10 ...	2,734	1,417	1,367	2,769	1,414	1,355	14	3	11	1	...	1
	10—15 ...	1,868	930	938	1,798	925	873	65	5	60	5	...	5
	15—20 ...	1,578	697	881	1,125	625	500	420	66	354	33	6	27
	20—40 ...	6,728	3,171	3,557	1,074	724	350	4,996	2,277	2,719	658	170	488
	40—60 ...	2,811	1,523	1,288	52	34	18	1,974	1,291	683	785	198	587
	60 and over ...	946	459	487	14	8	6	429	321	108	503	130	373
SYLHET.	ALL RELIGIONS ...	*2,472,671*	*1,268,469*	*1,204,202*	*1,180,616*	*724,185*	*456,431*	*1,005,323*	*495,708*	*509,615*	*286,732*	*48,576*	*238,156*
	0—5 ...	366,396	179,173	187,224	366,361	179,162	187,199	33	10	23	2	...	2
	5—10 ...	411,763	205,657	206,106	405,302	205,181	200,121	6,073	460	5,613	388	16	372
	10—15 ...	251,638	143,297	108,341	198,934	140,616	58,318	50,877	2,613	48,264	1,827	68	1,759
	15—20 ...	209,380	99,001	110,379	93,072	86,921	6,151	109,836	11,699	98,137	6,472	381	6,091
	20—40 ...	801,605	408,036	393,569	109,218	105,398	3,820	595,522	286,170	309,352	96,865	16,468	80,397
	40—60 ...	328,[illegible]	180,379	147,907	6,289	5,652	637	200,028	155,287	44,741	122,029	19,440	102,589
	60 and over ...	103,543	52,927	50,616	1,440	1,255	185	42,954	39,460	3,485	59,149	12,203	46,946

TABLE VII.

Age, Sex and Civil Condit.on. Part B.—Details for Districts—*continued.*

District.	Age.	POPULATION.			UNMARRIED.			MARRIED.			WIDOWED.		
		Persons.	Males.	Females.	Persons.	Males.	Females.	Persons.	Males.	Females.	Persons.	Males.	Females.
	1	2	3	4	5	6	7	8	9	10	11	12	13
SYLHET—*concld.*	HINDU	*1,098,950*	*564,266*	*534,684*	*476,981*	*307,969*	*169,012*	*451,199*	*296,057*	*235,142*	*170,770*	*30,240*	*140,530*
	0—5	138,035	67,380	70,646	138,013	67,383	70,630	21	6	15	1	...	1
	5—10	160,066	79,400	80,606	155,513	79,174	76,339	4 237	212	4,025	256	14	242
	10—15	103,971	58,644	45,327	75,150	57,238	17,912	27,783	1,367	26,416	1,038	39	999
	15—20	92,822	44,916	47,906	41,395	39,279	2,116	47.678	5,481	42,197	3,749	156	3,593
	20—40	381'121	195,828	185,303	61.037	59,390	1,647	259,375	127,679	131,696	60,709	8,759	51,950
	40—60	171'172	92,654	78,518	4,798	4,506	292	94,174	74,733	19,441	72,200	13,415	58,785
	60 and over	51'823	25,435	26,388	1,075	990	76	17,931	16,570	1,352	32,817	7,857	24,960
	MUSALMAN	*1,364,739*	*699,470*	*665,269*	*699,230*	*413,637*	*285,593*	*550,376*	*267,732*	*282,644*	*115,133*	*18,101*	*97,032*
	0—5	227,114	111,167	115,947	227.101	111,163	115,938	12	4	8	1	...	1
	5—10	250,399	125,567	124,833	248.444	125,319	123,125	1,824	246	1,578	131	2	129
	10—15	146,806	84,189	62,617	122.980	82,924	40,056	23,042	1,241	21,801	784	24	760
	15—20	115,906	53,775	62,131	51.307	47,376	3,931	61 891	6,177	55,714	2,708	222	2,486
	20—40	417,193	210,481	206,712	47,605	45,506	2,099	333,724	157,349	176,375	35,864	7,626	28,238
	40—60	155,889	86,960	68,929	1,429	1,094	335	105.006	79,919	25,057	49,454	5.917	43,537
	60 and over	51,432	27,331	24,101	364	255	109	24,877	22,766	2,111	26,191	4,310	21,881
KHASI AND JAINTIA HILLS.	ALL RELIGIONS	*235,069*	*114,442*	*120,627*	*119,324*	*62,980*	*56,244*	*90,854*	*45,666*	*45,188*	*24,991*	*5,796*	*19,195*
	0—5	40,279	19,581	20,608	40,279	19,581	20,698	...	...	...	...	...	...
	5—10	32,272	16,050	16,222	32.208	16,030	16,178	56	20	36	8	...	8
	10—15	23,148	11,930	11,218	22,599	11,841	10,758	490	80	410	59	9	50
	15—20	20,970	9,598	11,372	13,936	8,133	5,803	6,143	1,317	4,826	891	148	743
	20—40	74'393	36,184	38,209	9,601	6,975	2,626	56,035	26,768	29,267	8,757	2,441	6,316
	40—60	32'080	15,970	16,110	456	322	134	22.664	13,732	8,932	8.960	1,916	7,044
	60 and over	11'927	5,129	6,798	145	98	47	5,466	3,740	1,717	6.316	1,282	5,034
	ANIMIST	*192,453*	*91,447*	*101,006*	*97,577*	*50,862*	*46,715*	*73,355*	*35,733*	*37,622*	*21,521*	*4,852*	*16,669*
	0—5	33,964	16,523	17,441	33,964	16,523	17,441	...	...	...	...	...	...
	5—10	26,804	13,260	13,544	26,757	13,245	13,512	41	15	26	6	...	6
	10—15	18,939	9,748	9,161	18,443	9,670	8,773	414	69	345	52	9	43
	15—20	16,922	7,591	9,331	11,046	6,361	4,685	5,074	1,097	3,977	802	133	669
	20—40	58,810	27,055	31,755	6,921	4,755	2,166	44,337	20,299	24,038	7,552	2,001	5,551
	40—60	26,620	12,823	13,707	325	224	101	18,702	11,012	7,090	7,593	1,587	6,006
	60 and over	10'424	4,447	5,977	121	84	37	4,787	3,241	1,546	5 516	1,122	4,394
	CHRISTIAN	*31,257*	*14,855*	*16,402*	*17,009*	*8,817*	*8,192*	*11,421*	*5,482*	*5,939*	*2,827*	*556*	*2,271*
	0—5	5,138	2,498	2,640	5.138	2,498	2,640	...	...	...	...	...	...
	5—10	4.565	2,309	2,256	4,558	2,309	2,249	5	...	5	2	...	2
	10—15	3,608	1,799	1,809	3,585	1,797	1,788	18	2	16	5	...	5
	15—20	3,091	1,393	1,698	2,350	1,288	1,062	667	94	573	74	11	63
	20—40	9.706	4,497	5,209	1,310	895	415	7,470	3,359	4,111	926	243	683
	40—60	3,879	1,846	2,033	54	24	30	2,714	1,641	1,073	1,111	181	930
	60 and over	1,270	513	757	14	6	8	547	386	161	709	121	588

TABLE VII.

Age, Sex and Civil Condition. Part B.—Details for Districts—*continued.*

District.	Age.	Population.			Unmarried.			Married.			Widowed.		
		Persons.	Males.	Females.	Persons.	Males.	Females.	Persons.	Males.	Females.	Persons.	Males.	Females.
	1	2	3	4	5	6	7	8	9	10	11	12	13
NAGA HILLS.	ALL RELIGIONS	*149,623*	*74,751*	*74,872*	*74,077*	*39,469*	*34,608*	*60,758*	*30,590*	*30,168*	*14,788*	*4,692*	*10,096*
	0—5	21,106	10,383	10,723	21,106	10,383	10,723	...	...	...	...	...	...
	5—10	21,569	10,562	11,017	21.561	10,551	11,010	7	1	6	1	...	1
	10—15	15,020	7,850	7,170	14.848	7,835	7,013	166	15	151	6	...	6
	15—20	10.483	5,202	5,281	8 442	4,761	3,691	1,748	434	1,314	293	17	276
	20—40	44,797	21,086	28,811	7,438	5,434	2,004	32,769	14,770	17,990	4 599	1,782	2,817
	40—60	27,174	13,963	13,212	488	347	141	20,787	11,837	8,950	5 899	1,778	4,121
	60 and over	9,474	4,816	4,658	194	168	26	5,290	3,533	1,757	3,990	1,115	2,875
	ANIMIST	*141,740*	*70,136*	*71,604*	*70,136*	*37,117*	*33,019*	*57,359*	*28,480*	*28,879*	*14,245*	*4,539*	*9,706*
	0—5	19.990	9,828	10,163	19.990	9,828	10,162	...	...	...	...	...	...
	5—10	20 529	10,031	10,498	20,521	10,030	10,491	7	1	6	1	...	1
	10—15	14 366	7,508	6,858	14 216	7,494	6,722	144	14	130	6	...	6
	15—20	9 848	4,883	4,965	8.022	4,480	3,542	1,547	388	1,159	279	15	264
	20—40	41,654	19,917	21,737	6,745	4,797	1,948	30,533	13,425	17,108	4.376	1,695	2,681
	40—60	26.123	13,283	12,841	453	322	131	19,973	11,233	8,740	5,697	1,727	3,970
	60 and over	9,230	4,687	4,543	189	166	23	5,155	3,419	1,736	3,886	1,102	2,784
LUSHAI HILLS.	ALL RELIGIONS	*91,204*	*43,028*	*48,176*	*48,925*	*24,929*	*23,996*	*32,165*	*16,381*	*15,784*	*10,114*	*1,718*	*8,396*
	0—5	12,336	5,904	6,432	12.329	5,900	6,420	13	4	9	3	...	3
	5—10	11.895	5,783	6,112	11.825	5,763	6,062	44	19	25	26	1	25
	10—15	10.322	5,124	5,198	10.216	5,084	5,132	95	30	56	11	1	10
	15—20	8.907	4,027	4,880	7.364	3,674	3,690	1,290	308	982	253	45	208
	20—40	28,593	13,358	15,235	6.810	4,320	2,490	18 346	8,134	10,212	3 437	904	2,633
	40—60	14.270	6,771	7,499	319	160	150	10,132	6,141	3,991	3,819	470	3,340
	60 and over	4,881	2,061	2,820	71	28	43	2,245	1,736	509	2,565	297	2,268
	ANIMIST	*84,585*	*38,816*	*45,769*	*45,476*	*22,698*	*22,778*	*29,367*	*14,507*	*14,860*	*9,742*	*1,611*	*8,131*
	0—	11.461	5,469	5,990	11.445	5,458	5,987	13	4	9	3	...	3
	5—10	11,192	5,434	5,758	11.122	5,414	5,708	44	19	25	26	1	25
	10—15	9.744	4,798	4,946	9.664	4,763	4,901	69	34	35	11	1	10
	15—20	8.319	3,672	4,647	6 935	3,370	3,565	1,139	257	883	245	45	200
	20—40	25.002	11,[illegible]31	14,431	5.971	3,550	2,421	16 399	6,837	9,553	3.301	844	2,457
	40—60	13.500	6,[illegible]7	7,263	275	118	157	9,550	5,687	3,863	3 675	432	3,243
	60 and over	4,707	1,983	2,725	64	25	39	2,162	1,669	493	2,481	288	2,193
GOALPARA.	ALL RELIGIONS	*600,643*	*318,475*	*282,168*	*286,028*	*172,040*	*113,988*	*258,229*	*135,477*	*122,752*	*56,386*	*10,958*	*45,428*
	0—5	102.392	49,735	53,657	102.383	49,735	53,648	7	...	7	2	...	2
	5—10	98 346	50,683	47,663	95.662	50,480	45,173	2,569	100	2,379	115	4	111
	10—15	57,608	32,262	25,346	43.512	31,016	12,496	13.647	1,221	12,426	449	25	424
	15—20	51,051	24,841	26,210	21.966	19,504	2,462	27.786	5,222	22,564	1,299	115	1,184
	20—40	183.379	99,501	83,788	21.126	20,035	1,091	145 599	75,883	69,716	16,654	3,673	12,981
	40—60	79 897	47,069	32,828	1,153	1,064	89	55,509	41,707	13,803	23,235	4,298	18,937
	60 and over	27,970	14,294	13,676	226	197	29	13,112	11,254	1,858	14,632	2,843	11,789

TABLE VII.

AGE, SEX AND CIVIL CONDITION. PART B.—DETAILS FOR DISTRICTS—*continued.*

District.	Age.	POPULATION.			UNMARRIED.			MARRIED.			WIDOWED.		
		Persons.	Males.	Females.	Persons.	Males.	Females.	Persons.	Males.	Females.	Persons.	Males.	Females.
	1	2	3	4	5	6	7	8	9	10	11	12	13
GOALPARA—*concld.*	HINDU	*334,720*	*178,673*	*156,047*	*157,076*	*94,820*	*62,256*	*141,154*	*76,205*	*64,949*	*36,490*	*7,648*	*28,842*
	0—5	54,628	26,502	28,126	54,619	26,502	28,117	7	...	7	2	...	2
	5—10	52,404	26,975	25,429	50,965	26,885	24,080	1,381	89	1,292	58	1	57
	10—15	30,691	16,772	13,919	23,642	16,105	7,537	6,770	650	6,120	279	17	262
	15—20	27,770	13,795	13,975	12,655	10,937	1,718	14,247	2,789	11,458	868	69	799
	20—40	105,518	58,417	47,101	14,201	13,473	728	79,927	42,527	37,400	11,390	2,417	8,973
	40—60	46,992	27,789	19,203	875	817	58	31,475	23,870	7,605	14,642	3,102	11,540
	60 and over	16,717	8,423	8,294	119	101	18	7,347	6,280	1,067	9,251	2,042	7,209
	MUSALMAN	*211,562*	*111,917*	*99,645*	*101,014*	*61,784*	*39,230*	*93,721*	*47,601*	*46,120*	*16,827*	*2,532*	*14,295*
	0—5	37,432	18,159	19,273	37,432	18,159	19,273	...	...	...	...	...	...
	5—10	36,923	19,020	17,903	35,714	18,921	16,793	1,152	96	1,056	57	3	54
	10—15	21,223	12,500	8,723	14,832	12,031	2,701	6,242	462	5,780	159	7	152
	15—20	19,045	9,117	9,928	7,326	7,116	210	11,346	1,960	9,386	373	41	332
	20—40	62,586	33,453	29,133	5,436	5,298	138	52,619	27,165	25,454	4,531	990	3,541
	40—60	25,780	15,258	10,522	191	173	18	18,236	14,177	4,059	7,353	908	6,445
	60 and over	8,573	4,410	4,163	93	86	7	4,126	3,741	385	4,354	583	3,771
	ANIMIST	*47,339*	*23,870*	*23,469*	*24,394*	*13,285*	*11,109*	*20,251*	*9,920*	*10,331*	*2,694*	*665*	*2,029*
	0—5	9,404	4,598	4,806	9,404	4,598	4,806	...	...	...	...	...	...
	5—10	8,042	4,178	3,864	8,010	4,175	3,835	32	3	29	...	...	...
	10—15	4,802	2,477	2,325	4,197	2,379	1,818	594	97	497	11	1	10
	15—20	3,475	1,520	1,955	1,556	1,124	432	1,869	394	1,475	50	2	48
	20—40	12,844	6,230	6,614	1,140	930	201	11,094	5,077	6,017	610	214	396
	40—60	6,305	3,528	2,777	74	61	13	5,150	3,215	1,935	1,081	252	829
	60 and over	2,467	1,339	1,128	13	9	4	1,512	1,134	378	942	196	746
KAMRUP.	ALL RELIGIONS	*667,828*	*339,398*	*328,430*	*337,911*	*194,395*	*143,516*	*261,616*	*130,948*	*130,668*	*68,301*	*14,055*	*54,246*
	0—5	117,109	57,036	60,073	117,102	57,030	60,072	7	6	1	...	...	...
	5—10	107,611	54,539	53,072	106,558	54,382	52,176	1,018	154	864	35	3	32
	10—15	65,624	36,290	29,334	58,339	35,553	22,786	7,091	702	6,389	194	35	159
	15—20	48,463	24,933	23,530	27,215	21,618	5,597	20,521	3,201	17,320	727	114	613
	20—40	201,662	99,630	102,032	27,169	24,519	2,650	156,849	71,038	85,811	17,644	4,073	13,571
	40—60	99,248	53,512	45,736	1,321	1,121	200	65,259	46,360	18,899	32,668	6,031	26,637
	60 and over	28,111	13,458	14,653	207	172	35	10,871	9,487	1,384	17,033	3,799	13,234
	HINDU	*459,227*	*235,014*	*224,213*	*229,767*	*135,651*	*94,116*	*177,705*	*89,360*	*88,345*	*51,755*	*10,003*	*41,752*
	0—5	76,207	37,193	39,014	76,206	37,192	39,014	1	1	...	...	...	...
	5—10	72,685	36,815	35,870	71,924	36,710	35,214	727	102	625	34	3	31
	10—15	45,474	25,569	19,905	39,997	25,163	14,834	5,326	386	4,940	151	20	131
	15—20	34,209	18,301	15,908	19,689	16,357	3,332	13,983	1,873	12,110	537	71	466
	20—40	140,841	70,269	70,572	20,813	19,237	1,576	106,426	48,226	58,200	13,602	2,806	10,796
	40—60	69,738	37,342	32,396	973	855	118	43,903	32,184	11,719	24,862	4,303	20,559
	60 and over	20,073	9,525	10,548	165	137	28	7,339	6,588	751	12,569	2,800	9,769

TABLE VII.

Age, Sex and Civil Condition. Part B.—Details for Districts—*continued.*

District.	Age.	Population. Persons.	Population. Males.	Population. Females.	Unmarried. Persons.	Unmarried. Males.	Unmarried. Females.	Married. Persons.	Married. Males.	Married. Females.	Widowed. Persons.	Widowed. Males.	Widowed. Females.
	1	2	3	4	5	6	7	8	9	10	11	12	13
KAMRUP—concld.	MUSALMAN	*64,627*	*33,723*	*30,904*	*32,376*	*18,764*	*13,612*	*26,915*	*13,873*	*13,042*	*5,336*	*1,086*	*4,250*
	0—5	11,416	5,645	5,771	11,411	5,640	5,771	5	5	...	...	...	...
	5—10	11,083	5,658	5,425	10,878	5,637	5,241	205	21	184	...	...	...
	10—15	6,325	3,586	2,739	5,557	3,467	2,090	758	115	643	10	4	6
	15—20	4,582	2,397	2,185	2,312	1,971	341	2,227	417	1,810	43	9	34
	20—40	19,299	9,844	9,455	2,104	1,948	156	15,897	7,535	8,362	1,298	361	937
	40—60	9,158	5,230	3,919	105	92	13	6,601	4,718	1,883	2,452	429	2,023
	60 and over	2,764	1,354	1,410	9	9	...	1,222	1,062	160	1,533	283	1,250
	ANIMIST	*140,576*	*68,649*	*71,927*	*74,055*	*38,923*	*35,132*	*55,482*	*26,824*	*28,658*	*11,039*	*2,902*	*8,137*
	0—5	29,053	13,978	15,075	29,052	13,978	15,074	1	...	1	...	...	...
	5—10	23,400	11,838	11,562	23,315	11,807	11,508	84	31	53	1	...	1
	10—15	13,461	6,912	6,549	12,432	6,700	5,732	996	201	795	33	11	22
	15—20	9,372	4,081	5,291	5,014	3,154	1,860	4,213	893	3,320	145	34	111
	20—40	40,239	18,725	21,514	3,986	3,100	886	33,556	14,734	18,822	2,697	891	1,806
	40—60	19,892	10,616	9,276	225	160	65	14,389	9,184	5,205	5,278	1,272	4,006
	60 and over	5,159	2,499	2,660	31	24	7	2,243	1,781	462	2,885	694	2,191
DARRANG.	ALL RELIGIONS	*377,314*	*198,581*	*178,733*	*177,934*	*102,487*	*75,447*	*157,813*	*81,572*	*76,241*	*41,567*	*14,522*	*27,045*
	0—5	56,618	28,024	28,594	56,616	28,024	28,592	2	...	2	...	...	...
	5—10	54,367	27,410	26,957	53,942	27,265	26,677	409	139	270	16	6	10
	10—15	36,001	19,871	16,130	32,812	19,218	13,594	3,063	613	2,450	126	40	86
	15—20	25,812	13,049	12,763	15,216	10,899	4,317	9,891	1,962	8,029	605	188	417
	20—40	137,643	72,130	65,513	18,103	15,893	2,210	103,645	49,464	54,191	15,895	6,783	9,112
	40—60	55,646	32,361	23,285	1,148	1,092	56	38,289	25,703	10,586	18,209	5,566	12,643
	60 and over	11,227	5,736	5,491	97	96	1	4,414	3,701	713	6,716	1,930	4,777
	HINDU	*245,341*	*129,631*	*115,710*	*112,795*	*66,204*	*46,591*	*102,337*	*53,111*	*49,226*	*30,209*	*10,316*	*19,893*
	0—5	33,395	16,619	16,776	33,395	16,619	16,776	...	...	...	...	...	...
	5—10	34,342	17,336	17,006	34,059	17,244	16,815	272	87	185	11	5	6
	10—15	23,206	12,831	10,375	21,132	12,449	8,683	1,971	347	1,624	103	35	68
	15—20	17,112	8,787	8,325	10,448	7,581	2,867	6,206	1,064	5,142	458	142	316
	20—40	92,629	48,834	43,795	12,915	11,502	1,413	67,904	32,425	35,479	11,810	4,907	6,903
	40—60	37,034	21,413	15,621	789	753	36	23,190	16,789	6,401	13,055	3,871	9,184
	60 and over	7,623	3,811	3,812	57	56	1	2,794	2,399	395	4,772	1,356	3,416
	MUSALMAN	*20,305*	*11,073*	*9,232*	*9,872*	*5,853*	*4,019*	*8,558*	*4,735*	*3,823*	*1,875*	*485*	*1,390*
	0—5	3,249	1,634	1,615	3,248	1,634	1,614	1	...	1	...	...	...
	5—10	3,219	1,575	1,644	3,151	1,564	1,587	66	11	55	2	...	2
	10—15	1,953	1,173	780	1,755	1,131	624	196	42	154	2	...	2
	15—20	1,435	779	656	801	649	152	612	126	486	22	4	18
	20—40	6,748	3,825	2,923	868	826	42	5,333	2,778	2,555	547	221	326
	40—60	2,936	1,707	1,229	43	43	...	2,030	1,491	539	863	173	690
	60 and over	765	380	385	6	6	...	320	287	33	439	87	352

TABLE VII.

Age, Sex and Civil Condition. Part B.—Details for Districts—*continued.*

District.	Age.	Population.			Unmarried.			Married.			Widowed.		
		Persons.	Males.	Females.	Persons.	Males.	Females.	Persons.	Males.	Females.	Persons.	Males.	Females.
	1	2	3	4	5	6	7	8	9	10	11	12	13
DARRANG—concld.	ANIMIST	*108,731*	*56,043*	*52,688*	*53,814*	*29,493*	*24,321*	*45,609*	*22,923*	*22,686*	*9,308*	*3,627*	*5,681*
	0—5	19,596	9,587	10,009	19 595	9,587	10,008	1	...	1	...	...	...
	5—10	16 455	8,319	8,136	16 382	8,278	8,104	70	40	30	3	1	2
	10—15	10 589	5,714	4,875	9 690	5,493	4,197	879	216	663	20	5	15
	15—20	7.058	3,353	3,705	3 836	2,563	1,274	3.100	749	2,351	122	42	80
	20—40	36 989	18,633	18,356	4,005	3,285	720	29 527	13,740	15,787	3,457	1,608	1,849
	40—60	15 268	8,041	6,337	276	258	18	10.772	7,197	3,575	4 220	1,486	2,734
	60 and over	2,776	1,496	1,280	30	30	...	1,260	981	279	1,486	485	1,001

NOWGONG.

District.	Age.	Population.			Unmarried.			Married.			Widowed.		
		Persons.	Males.	Females.	Persons.	Males.	Females.	Persons.	Males.	Females.	Persons.	Males.	Females.
	ALL RELIGIONS	*303,596*	*154,938*	*148,658*	*157,603*	*87,991*	*69,612*	*115,184*	*58,949*	*56,235*	*30,809*	*7,998*	*22,811*
	0—5	53,423	26,132	27,291	53.423	26,132	27,291	...	...	...	...	...	...
	5—10	50,020	25,140	24,880	49.950	25,116	24,834	66	22	44	4	2	2
	10—15	26,906	14,672	12,234	25 816	14,493	11,324	1.021	171	850	69	9	60
	15—20	21.358	10,288	11,070	14.183	9,238	4,948	6 804	979	5,825	368	71	297
	20—40	95 794	48,648	47,146	13,446	12,302	1,144	72.579	33,255	30,334	9,769	3,001	6,678
	40—60	43.938	24,080	19,848	710	653	57	29.426	20,245	9,181	13,792	3,182	10,610
	60 and over	12,167	5,978	6,189	72	58	14	5.288	4,277	1,011	6,807	1,643	5,164
	HINDU	*177,795*	*91,213*	*86,582*	*91,285*	*52,179*	*39,106*	*65,793*	*33,787*	*32,006*	*20,717*	*5,247*	*15,470*
	0—5	[illegible]25	14,435	14,990	29,425	14,435	14,990	...	...	...	...	...	...
	5—10	29,649	14,830	14,819	29.612	14,817	14,795	36	13	23	1	...	1
	10—15	15 668	8,783	6,885	15,021	8,684	6,337	632	93	539	15	6	9
	15—20	12,072	6,138	5,934	8,088	5,649	2,439	3,756	453	3,303	228	36	192
	20—40	57 369	29,228	28,141	8,647	8,120	527	42,172	19,127	23,045	6,550	1,981	4,569
	40—60	26,673	14,472	12,201	449	436	13	16,655	11,907	4,748	9,569	2,129	7,440
	60 and over	6,939	3,327	3,612	43	38	5	2,542	2,194	348	4,354	1,095	3,259
	ANIMIST	*108,067*	*54,403*	*53,664*	*57,054*	*30,621*	*26,433*	*42,412*	*21,447*	*20,965*	*8,601*	*2,335*	*6,266*
	0—5	20.977	10,257	10,720	20.977	10,257	10,720	...	...	...	...	...	...
	5—10	17.399	8,847	8,543	17.364	8,839	8,525	23	6	17	3	2	1
	10—15	9 580	4,978	4,602	9.210	4,909	4,301	317	66	251	53	3	50
	15—20	7.960	3,480	4,480	5.260	2,995	2,265	2,578	454	2,124	122	31	91
	20—40	32 774	16,344	16,430	4,005	3,433	572	26,033	11,974	14,059	2.736	937	1,799
	40—60	14 815	8,190	6,625	214	173	41	11,025	7,120	3,905	3.576	897	2,679
	60 and over	4,571	2,307	2,264	24	15	9	2,436	1,827	609	2,111	465	1,646

SIBSAGAR.

District.	Age.	Population.			Unmarried.			Married.			Widowed.		
		Persons.	Males.	Females.	Persons.	Males.	Females.	Persons.	Males.	Females.	Persons.	Males.	Females.
	ALL RELIGIONS	*690,299*	*364,810*	*325,489*	*350,813*	*200,314*	*150,499*	*274,412*	*139,226*	*135,186*	*65,074*	*25,270*	*39,804*
	0—5	104 949	52,048	52,892	104 933	52,047	52,886	6	1	5	1	...	1
	5—10	107.940	54,867	53,073	107 023	54,526	52,497	877	331	546	40	10	30
	10—15	70 703	38,185	32,518	66,198	37,131	29,067	4,298	989	3,309	207	65	142
	15—20	51,378	26,237	25,141	34 694	23,211	11,483	15.727	2,728	12,999	957	298	659
	20—40	236 106	123,431	112,680	34,986	30,798	4,188	177 743	81,838	95,905	23.371	10,795	12,576
	40—60	98 741	58,718	40,023	2,561	2,253	308	66 868	46,074	20,794	29,312	10,391	18,921
	60 and over	20,497	11,324	9,173	418	348	70	8,893	7,265	1,628	11,136	3,711	7,425

TABLE VII.

Age, Sex and Civil Condition. Part B.—Details for Districts—*continued.*

District.	Age.	POPULATION.			UNMARRIED.			MARRIED.			WIDOWED.		
		Persons.	Males.	Females.	Persons.	Males.	Females.	Persons.	Males.	Females.	Persons.	Males.	Females.
	1	2.	3	4	5	6	7	8	9	10	11	12	13
SIBSAGAR—*concld.*	HINDU	*505,266*	*313,748*	*281,518*	*300,724*	*172,005*	*128,719*	*236,428*	*119,242*	*117,186*	*58,114*	*22,501*	*35,613*
	0—5	89,976	44,606	45,370	89,969	44,605	45,364	6	1	5	1	...	1
	5—10	93,003	47,222	45,781	92,268	46,959	45,309	697	253	444	38	10	28
	10—15	60,393	32,633	27,760	56,582	31,772	24,810	3,630	803	2,828	181	59	122
	15—20	43,884	23,352	21,532	29,576	19,840	9,736	13,498	2,266	11,232	810	246	564
	20—40	205,159	106,778	98,381	29,885	26,663	3,222	154,452	70,526	83,926	20,822	9,589	11,233
	40—60	85,618	50,710	34,908	2,096	1,869	227	57,142	39,526	17,616	26,380	9,315	17,065
	60 and over	17,233	9,447	7,786	348	297	51	7,003	5,868	1,135	9,882	3,282	6,600
	MUSALMAN	*29,718*	*16,373*	*13,345*	*15,774*	*9,191*	*6,583*	*11,363*	*6,177*	*5,186*	*2,581*	*1,005*	*1,576*
	0—5	4,383	2,213	2,170	4,383	2,213	2,170	...	...	...	...	...	...
	5—10	4,974	2,509	2,465	4,912	2,489	2,423	62	20	42	...	...	...
	10—15	3,494	1,868	1,626	3,270	1,820	1,450	215	45	170	9	3	6
	15—20	2,461	1,274	1,187	1,561	1,143	418	859	124	735	41	7	34
	20—40	9,504	5,420	4,084	1,506	1,390	116	7,092	3,627	3,465	906	403	503
	40—60	3,983	2,522	1,461	126	122	4	2,704	1,983	721	1,153	417	736
	60 and over	919	567	352	16	14	2	431	378	53	472	175	297
	ANIMIST	*57,580*	*30,362*	*27,218*	*30,377*	*16,761*	*13,616*	*23,409*	*12,086*	*11,316*	*3,801*	*1,515*	*2,286*
	0—5	9,417	4,637	4,780	9,417	4,637	4,780	...	...	...	...	...	...
	5—10	8,861	4,567	4,294	8,743	4,511	4,232	116	56	60	2	...	2
	10—15	6,088	3,281	2,807	5,656	3,141	2,515	417	137	280	15	3	12
	15—20	4,467	2,295	2,172	3,203	1,955	1,248	1,175	303	872	89	37	52
	20—40	18,573	9,615	8,958	3,035	2,274	761	14,119	6,656	7,463	1,419	685	734
	40—60	8,015	4,771	3,244	270	207	63	6,214	4,000	2,214	1,531	564	967
	60 and over	2,159	1,196	963	53	36	17	1,361	934	427	745	226	519
LAKHIMPUR.	ALL RELIGIONS	*468,989*	*249,021*	*219,968*	*226,508*	*128,542*	*97,966*	*200,117*	*102,810*	*97,307*	*42,304*	*17,669*	*24,695*
	0—5	71,021	35,022	35,999	71,018	35,022	35,996	3	...	3	...	...	...
	5—10	69 509	35,697	33.812	68,949	35,534	33,415	537	155	382	23	8	15
	10—15	44 318	23,540	20,778	40.963	22,679	18,284	3,178	801	2,377	177	60	117
	15—20	32·486	15,618	16,868	20,865	12,884	7,981	10,860	2,449	8,411	761	285	476
	20—40	176,399	93,923	82,476	23,008	20,783	2,225	135,015	64,042	70,973	18,376	9,098	9,278
	40—60	63.411	38,955	24,456	1,535	1,477	58	44 858	31,069	13,789	17.018	6,409	10,609
	60 and over	11,845	6,266	5,579	170	163	7	5,666	4,294	1,372	6,009	1,809	4,200
	HINDU	*367,990*	*195,291*	*172,699*	*174,542*	*99,448*	*75,094*	*158,947*	*81,372*	*77,575*	*34,501*	*14,471*	*20,030*
	0—5	54,591	27,050	27,541	54,591	27,050	27,541	...	...	...	...	...	...
	5—10	53,795	27,506	26,289	53,356	27,397	25,959	419	102	317	20	7	13
	10—15	34 705	18,438	16,267	31 857	17,693	14,164	2,686	688	1,098	162	57	105
	15—20	25 095	12,064	13.031	15,938	9,873	6,065	8,526	1,938	6,588	631	253	378
	20—40	141,114	75,101	66,013	17,478	16,143	1,335	108,444	51,408	57,036	15,192	7,550	7,642
	40—60	49 716	30,400	19.316	1,184	1,157	27	34 651	24,037	10,614	13,881	5,206	8,675
	60 and over	8,974	4,732	4,242	138	135	3	4,221	3,199	1,022	4,615	1,398	3,217

TABLE VII.

Age, Sex and Civil Condition. Part B.—Details for Districts—*continued.*

District.	Age.	Population, Persons.	Population, Males.	Population, Females.	Unmarried, Persons.	Unmarried, Males.	Unmarried, Females.	Married, Persons.	Married, Males.	Married, Females.	Widowed, Persons.	Widowed, Males.	Widowed, Females.
	1	2	3	4	5	6	7	8	9	10	11	12	13
LAKHIMPUR—*concld.*	ANIMIST	*76,701*	*39,622*	*37,079*	*40,353*	*22,002*	*18,351*	*30,433*	*15,253*	*15,180*	*5,915*	*2,367*	*3,548*
	0–5	13,304	6,404	6,900	13,301	6,404	6,897	3	...	3	...	...	...
	5–10	12,411	6,553	5,888	12 368	6,530	5,838	72	23	49	1	...	1
	10–15	7,370	3,855	3,515	7,024	3,791	3,233	336	62	274	10	2	8
	15–20	5,509	2530	2,979	3,754	2,148	1,606	1,656	361	1,295	99	21	78
	20–40	25,702	12,916	12,786	3,686	2,939	747	19,626	8,858	10,768	2,390	1,119	1,271
	40–60	10,230	6,257	3,973	205	177	28	7.680	5,170	2,510	2,345	910	1,435
	60 and over	2,145	1,107	1,038	15	13	2	1,060	779	281	1,070	315	755
GARO HILLS.	ALL RELIGIONS	*158,936*	*81,264*	*77,672*	*77,654*	*43,635*	*34,019*	*74,617*	*36,015*	*38,602*	*6,665*	*1,614*	*5,051*
	0–5	27,685	14,050	13,635	27,685	14,050	13,635	...	...	...	...	...	...
	5–10	23 928	12,441	11,487	23,632	12,410	11,222	296	31	265	...	...	...
	10–15	17,237	8,933	8,304	14,495	8,527	5,968	2,697	401	2,296	45	5	40
	15–20	15,858	6,854	9,004	7,125	4,872	2,253	8,545	1,947	6,598	188	35	153
	20–40	46,894	23,[illegible]22	23,582	4,429	3,496	933	40 382	19,199	21,183	1,993	527	1,466
	40–60	19,332	10,950	8,382	226	219	7	16,618	10,165	6,453	2,488	506	1,922
	60 and over	8,092	4,814	3,278	62	61	1	6,979	4,272	1,807	1,951	481	1,470
	HINDU	*20,827*	*11,293*	*9,534*	*10,498*	*6,134*	*4,364*	*8,409*	*4,599*	*3,810*	*1,920*	*560*	*1,360*
	0–5	3,390	1,573	1,817	3 390	1,573	1,817	...	...	...	...	...	...
	5–10	3 067	1,573	1,494	3,044	1,573	1,471	23	...	23	...	...	...
	10–15	2,195	1,182	1,013	1 910	1,154	756	277	28	249	8	...	8
	15–20	1.748	864	884	947	729	218	752	123	629	49	12	37
	20–40	6.851	4,031	2,820	1.126	1,024	102	5,137	2,794	2,343	588	213	375
	40–60	2,574	1,558	1,016	71	71	...	1.757	1,275	482	746	212	534
	60 and over	1.002	512	400	10	10	...	463	379	84	529	123	406
	ANIMIST	*124,144*	*69,408*	*61,736*	*60.167*	*33,214*	*26,953*	*60,147*	*28,301*	*31,846*	*3,830*	*893*	*2,937*
	0–5	22,090	11,373	10,717	22,090	11,373	10,717	...	...	...	...	...	...
	5–10	18,845	9,839	9,006	18 601	9,812	8,789	244	27	217	...	...	...
	10–15	13,436	6,810	6,626	11,241	6,457	4,784	2,166	348	1,818	29	5	24
	15–20	12,574	5,185	7,389	5 343	3,463	1,880	7,105	1,701	5,404	126	21	105
	20–40	35,433	16,714	18.719	2,714	1,931	783	31,601	14,527	17,074	1,118	256	862
	40–60	15,119	8,440	6,679	129	129	...	13,674	8,026	5,648	1,316	285	1,031
	60 and over	6,647	4,047	2,600	49	49	...	5,357	3,672	1,685	1,241	326	915
MANIPUR.	ALL RELIGIONS	*346,222*	*170,666*	*175,556*	*182,224*	*97,786*	*84,438*	*134,584*	*66,679*	*67,905*	*29,414*	*6,201*	*23,213*
	0–5	56,436	27,919	28,517	56,436	27,919	28,517	...	...	...	...	...	...
	5–10	54,059	27,053	27,006	53,859	27,009	26,850	179	44	135	21	...	21
	10–15	38,345	19,271	19 074	37.033	18.987	18,016	1,279	279	1,000	63	5	58
	15–20	30,343	14,513	15,830	20,039	12,717	7,322	9,492	1,708	7,784	812	88	724
	20–40	94,939	46,379	48,560	13.390	10,256	3,134	74,141	34,212	39,929	7,408	1,911	5,497
	40–60	53,745	26,999	26,746	1,018	660	358	40,551	23,951	16,600	12,176	2,388	9,788
	60 and over	18,355	8,532	9,823	479	238	241	8,942	6,485	2,457	8,934	1,809	7.125

TABLE VII.

Age, Sex and Civil Condition. Part B.—Details for Districts—*concluded.*

District.	Age.	Population.			Unmarried.			Married.			Widowed.		
		Persons.	Males.	Females.	Persons.	Males.	Females.	Persons.	Males.	Females.	Persons.	Males.	Females.
	1	2	3	4	5	6	7	8	9	10	11	12	13
MANIPUR—concld.	HINDU	*201,369*	*99,264*	*102,105*	*104,843*	*57,728*	*47,115*	*76,564*	*37,615*	*38,949*	*19,962*	*3,921*	*16,041*
	0—5	31,592	15,859	15,733	31,592	15,859	15,733	...	...	...	...	...	...
	5—10	32,884	16,504	16,380	32,782	16,481	16,301	91	23	68	11	...	11
	10—15	24,159	12,150	12,009	23,203	11,985	11,218	907	161	746	49	4	45
	15—20	19,292	9,330	9,962	11,387	8,223	3,164	7,188	1,053	6,135	717	54	663
	20—40	52,409	25,814	26,595	5,290	4,720	570	41,834	19,804	22,030	5,285	1,290	3,906
	40—60	30,521	14,914	15,607	440	352	88	21,950	13,111	8,839	8,131	1,451	6,680
	60 and over	10,512	4,693	5,819	149	108	41	4,594	3,403	1,131	5.769	1,122	4,647
	ANIMIST	*130,093*	*63,699*	*66,394*	*69,007*	*35,555*	*33,482*	*52,405*	*26,065*	*26,340*	*8,651*	*2,079*	*6,572*
	0-5	21,946	10,597	11,349	21,946	10,597	11,349	...	...	...	...	...	...
	5—10	18,491	9,221	9,270	18,405	9,203	9,202	76	18	58	10	...	10
	10—15	12,454	6,256	6,198	12,154	6,161	5,993	286	94	192	14	1	13
	15—20	9,694	4,498	5,196	7,945	4,015	3,930	1,695	462	1,233	54	21	33
	20—40	38,475	18,276	20,199	7.704	5,165	2,539	28,894	12,574	16,320	1,877	537	1,340
	40—60	21,649	11,227	10,422	555	286	269	17,335	10,062	7,273	3.759	879	2,850
	60 and over	7,384	3,624	3,700	328	128	200	4,119	2,855	1,364	2,937	641	2,296

TABLE VIII.

EDUCATION BY RELIGION AND AGE.

THIS table, like Table VII, is divided into two parts. *Part A* shows the extent of literacy in the Province as a whole amongst the total population and for each religion returned; *Part B* gives details, for Districts and Manipur State, of the total population and of each main religion.

The table shows the number of persons literate in any language as well as those literate in English, the figures in columns 12 to 14 being included in those in columns 6 to 8.

The following statement shows the literates among Indian Christians and other Christians separately :—

Race.	Population.									Literate in English.		
	Total.			Literate.			Illiterate.					
	Persons.	Males.	Females.	Persons.	Males.	Females.	Persons.	Males.	Females.	Persons.	Males.	Females.
(1) Indian Christians, including Feringis.	63,837	31,762	32,07	10,142	6,762	3,380	53,695	25,000	28,695	1,785	1,370	415
(2) Other Christians ...	2,725	1,870	855	2,427	1,731	696	298	139	159	2,395	1,715	680
Total	66.562	33,633	32,930	12,569	8,493	4,076	53,993	25,139	28,854	4,180	3,085	1,095

TABLE VIII.—EDUCATION BY RELIGION AND AGE. PART A.—PROVINCIAL SUMMARY.

RELIGION AND AGE.	POPULATION.									LITERATE IN ENGLISH.		
	TOTAL.			LITERATE.			ILLITERATE.					
	Persons.	Males.	Females.	Persons.	Males.	Females.	Persons.	Males.	Females.	Persons.	Males.	Females.
1	2	3	4	5	6	7	8	9	10	11	12	13
ALL RELIGIONS	*7,059,857*	*3,638,287*	*3,421,570*	*333,672*	*312,919*	*20,753*	*6,726,185*	*3,325,368*	*3,400,817*	*35,855*	*34,333*	*1,522*
0—10	2,227,882	1,108,159	1,119,723	18,912	16,530	2,382	2,208,970	1,091,629	1,117,341	501	433	68
10—15	705,117	388,026	317,091	39 823	36,434	3,389	665,294	351,592	313,702	3,570	3,410	160
15—20	565 922	273,169	292,753	37,906	34,371	3,535	528,016	238,798	289,218	5,593	5,364	220
20 and over	3,560,936	1,868,933	1,692,003	237,031	225,584	11,447	3,323,905	1,643,349	1,680,556	26,191	25,126	1,06
HINDU...	*3,838,769*	*1,997,724*	*1,841,045*	*251,182*	*237,123*	*14,059*	*3,587,587*	*1,760,601*	*1,826,986*	*26,236*	*25,927*	*309*
0—10	1,139,897	567,779	572,118	14,755	12,931	1,824	1,125,142	554,848	570,294	351	335	16
10—15	372,236	204,267	167,969	29,588	27,275	2,313	342,648	176,992	165,656	2,649	2,599	50
15—20	300,471	149,514	150,957	28 103	25,771	2,332	272 368	123,743	148,625	4.207	4,137	70
20 and over	2,026,165	1,076,164	950,001	178,736	171,146	7,590	1,847,429	905,018	942,411	19,029	18,856	173
BRAHMO	*428*	*241*	*187*	*203*	*134*	*69*	*225*	*107*	*118*	*104*	*84*	*20*
0—10	116	57	59	28	17	11	88	40	48	4	4	...
10—15	36	22	14	23	15	8	13	7	6	10	9	1
15—20	31	13	18	18	8	10	13	5	8	12	6	6
20 and over	245	149	96	134	94	40	111	55	56	78	65	13
SIKH ...	*757*	*475*	*282*	*212*	*194*	*18*	*545*	*281*	*264*	*33*	*30*	*3*
0—10	158	82	76	4	3	1	154	79	75	2	1	1
10—15	66	37	29	11	10	1	55	27	28	4	4	...
15—20	59	37	22	24	23	1	35	14	21	6	6	...
20 and over	474	319	155	173	158		301	161	140	21	19	2
JAIN ...	*2,508*	*2,136*	*372*	*1,576*	*1,557*	*19*	*932*	*579*	*353*	*20*	*19*	*1*
0—10	258	163	105	17	17	...	241	136	105	...	...	...
10—15	224	196	28	137	135	2	87	61	26	1	1	...
15—20	339	290	49	240	234	6	99	56	43	1	1	...
20 and over	1,687	1,497	190	1,182	1,171	11	505	326	179	18	17	1
BUDDHIST	*10,513*	*6,204*	*4,309*	*720*	*700*	*20*	*9,793*	*5,504*	*4,289*	*38*	*36*	*2*
0—10	2,676	1,378	1,298	11	10	1	2,665	1,368	1,297	...	...	...
10—15	880	483	397	41	39	2	839	444	395	1	1	...
15—20	851	475	376	72	71	1	779	404	375	1	1	...
20 and over	6,106	3,868	2,238	596	580	16	5,510	3,288	2,222	36	34	2

TABLE VIII.—EDUCATION BY RELIGION AND AGE. PART A.—PROVINCIAL SUMMARY—*concluded*.

RELIGION AND AGE.	POPULATION.									LITERATE IN ENGLISH.		
	TOTAL.			LITERATE.			ILLITERATE.					
	Persons.	Males.	Females.	Persons.	Males.	Females.	Persons.	Males.	Females.	Persons.	Males.	Females.
1	2	3	4	5	6	7	8	9	10	11	12	13
PARSI ...	*5*	*5*	...	*4*	*4*	...	*1*	*1*	...	*4*	*4*	...
0—10	...	...	...	...	...	...	...	...	...	...	...	...
10—15	...	...	...	...	...	...	...	...	...	...	...	...
15—20	2	2	...	2	2	...	...	...	...	2	2	...
20 and over	3	3	...	2	2	...	1	1	...	2	2	...
MUSALMAN	*1,901,032*	*984,968*	*916,064*	*58,440*	*56,625*	*1,815*	*1,842,592*	*928,343*	*914,249*	*4,611*	*4,551*	*60*
0—10	662 750	329,273	333,477	3,280	3,022	258	659,470	326,251	333,219	51	50	1
10—15	200,771	115,399	85,372	7,548	7,215	333	193,223	108,184	85,039	590	582	8
15—20	160,627	75,862	84,765	6,416	6,110	306	154,211	69,752	84,459	872	852	20
20 and over	876,884	461,434	412,450	41,196	40,278	918	835,688	424,156	411,532	3,098	3,067	31
CHRISTIAN	*66,562*	*33,632*	*32,930*	*12,569*	*8,493*	*4,076*	*53,993*	*25,139*	*28,854*	*4,180*	*3,085*	*1,095*
0—10	20,106	10,045	10,061	531	293	238	19,575	9,752	9,823	90	40	50
10—15	7,528	3,975	3,553	1,559	924	635	5,969	3,051	2,918	238	143	95
15—20	6,233	2,942	3,291	1,902	1,138	764	4,331	1,804	2,527	390	261	129
20 and over	32,695	16,670	16,025	8,577	6,138	2,439	24,118	10,532	13,586	3,462	2,641	821
JEW ...	*1*	*1*	...	*1*	*1*	...	...	...	...	*1*	*1*	...
0—10	...	...	...	...	...	...	...	...	...	...	...	...
10—15	...	...	...	...	...	...	...	...	...	...	...	...
15—20	...	...	...	...	...	...	...	...	...	...	...	...
20 and over	1	1	...	1	1	...	...	...	...	1	1	...
ANIMIST	*1,239,280*	*612,899*	*626,381*	*8,764*	*8,087*	*677*	*1,230,516*	*604,812*	*625,704*	*698*	*596*	*32*
0—10	401 921	199,392	202,529	286	237	49	401,635	199,155	202,480	3	3	...
10—15	123 376	63,647	59,729	916	821	95	122,460	62,826	59,634	77	71	6
15—20	97 309	44,034	53,275	1,129	1,014	115	96,180	43,020	53,160	102	98	4
20 and over	616,674	305,826	310,848	6,433	6,015	418	610,241	299,811	310,430	446	424	22
ATHEIST	*1*	*1*	...	*1*	*1*	...	...	...	...	...	...	...
0—10	...	...	...	...	...	...	...	...	...	...	...	...
10—15	...	...	...	...	...	...	...	...	...	...	...	...
15—20	...	...	...	...	...	...	...	...	...	...	...	...
20 and over	1	1	...	1	1	...	...	...	...	...	...	...
CONFUCIAN	*1*	*1*	...	...	...	...	*1*	*1*	...	...	...	...
0—10	...	...	...	...	...	...	...	...	...	...	...	...
10—15	...	...	...	...	...	...	...	...	...	...	...	...
15—20	...	...	...	...	...	...	...	...	...	...	...	...
20 and over	1	1	...	...	...	...	1	1	...	...	...	...

TABLE VIII.—Education by Religion and Age. Part B.—Details for Districts.

District.	Age.	Population. Total. Persons.	Total. Males.	Total. Females.	Literate. Persons.	Literate. Males.	Literate. Females.	Illiterate. Persons.	Illiterate. Males.	Illiterate. Females.	Literate in English.		
	1	2	3	4	5	6	7	8	9	10	11	12	13
CACHAR.	ALL RELIGIONS	*497,463*	*260,444*	*237,019*	*29,489*	*27,738*	*1,751*	*467,974*	*232,706*	*235,268*	*2,844*	*2,726*	*118*
	0—10	154.862	77,281	77.581	1.977	1,682	295	152,885	75,599	77,286	21	20	1
	10—15	48,247	26,801	21,446	3,307	3.072	235	44.940	23,729	21,211	297	283	14
	15—20	39.433	19,008	20.425	3,121	2,854	267	36.312	16,154	20,158	404	385	19
	20 and over	254,921	13[illegible],354	117,507	21,084	20,130	954	233,837	117,224	116,613	2,122	2,038	84
	HINDU	*320,104*	*167,424*	*152,680*	*22,182*	*20,679*	*1,503*	*297,922*	*146,745*	*151,177*	*2,125*	*2,096*	*29*
	0—10	93,092	46,503	46,589	1,435	1,168	267	91,657	45.335	46,322	16	16	...
	10—15	30,643	16,620	14,023	2,326	2,117	209	28,317	14,503	13,814	227	215	12
	15—20	25,081	12,104	12,977	2.333	2,100	233	22,748	10,004	12,744	288	282	6
	20 and over	171,288	82,197	79,091	16.088	15,294	704	155,200	76,903	78,297	1,594	1,583	11
	MUSALMAN	*156,096*	*82,560*	*73,536*	*6,775*	*6,674*	*101*	*149,321*	*75,886*	*73,435*	*422*	*416*	*6*
	0—10	55,377	27.655	27,722	523	504	19	54,854	27,151	27,703	4	4	...
	10—15	15,623	9,102	6,431	958	943	15	14,665	8,249	6,416	65	65	...
	15—20	12.685	6,167	6,518	747	729	18	11,938	5,438	6,500	98	96	2
	20 and over	72.411	39,546	32,865	4,547	4,498	49	67,864	35,048	32,816	255	251	4
	ANIMIST	*19,996*	*9,743*	*10,253*	*103*	*88*	*15*	*19,893*	*9,655*	*10,238*	*3*	*3*	...
	0—10	6,065	2,963	3,102	4	1	3	6,061	2,962	3,099	...	...	...
	10—15	1.868	930	938	7	6	1	1,861	924	937	...	...	...
	15—20	1,578	697	881	9	8	1	1,569	689	880	1	1	...
	20 and over	10,485	5,153	5,332	83	73	10	10,402	5,080	5,322	2	2	...
SYLHET.	ALL RELIGIONS	*2,472,671*	*1,268,469*	*1 204,202*	*132,495*	*124,785*	*7,710*	*2,340,176*	*1,143,684*	*1,196,492*	*10,980*	*10,739*	*241*
	0—10	778 159	384,829	393,330	8.653	7,724	929	769,506	377,105	392,401	109	100	9
	10—15	251,638	143,297	108,341	17.044	15.811	1,233	234.594	127,486	107.108	1,250	1,233	17
	15—20	209.380	99,001	110,379	14.965	13,735	1,2[illegible]0	194,415	85,266	109,149	1974	1,933	41
	20 and over	1,233,494	641,342	592,152	91,833	87.515	4,318	1,141,661	553,827	587,834	7,647	7,473	174
	HINDU	*1,098,950*	*564,266*	*534,684*	*95,826*	*89,197*	*6,629*	*1,003,124*	*475,069*	*528,055*	*8,496*	*8,400*	*96*
	0—10	298,041	146,789	151,252	6,626	5,818	808	291,415	140,971	150,444	77	75	2
	10—15	103,971	58,644	45,327	12,205	11,115	1,090	91,766	47,529	44,237	945	933	12
	15—20	92,822	44,916	47,906	10,839	9,782	1,057	81,983	35,134	46,849	1,506	1,484	22
	20 and over	604,116	313,917	290,199	66,156	62,482	3 674	537,960	261,435	286,525	5,968	5,908	60

TABLE VIII.—EDUCATION BY RELIGION AND AGE. PART B.—DETAILS FOR DISTRICTS—*continued.*

District.	Age.	Population. Total. Persons.	Population. Total. Males.	Population. Total. Females.	Population. Literate. Persons.	Population. Literate. Males.	Population. Literate. Females.	Population. Illiterate. Persons.	Population. Illiterate. Males.	Population. Illiterate. Females.	Literate in English. Persons.	Literate in English. Males.	Literate in English. Females.
	1	2	3	4	5	6	7	8	9	10	11	12	13
SYLHET—*concld.*	**MUSALMAN**	*1,364,739*	*699,470*	*665,269*	*35,885*	*34,983*	*902*	*1,328 854*	*664,487*	*664,367*	*1,969*	*1,959*	*10*
	0—10	477,513	236,734	240,779	1,993	1,888	105	475,520	234,846	240,674	22	22	...
	10—15	146 806	84,189	62,617	4 789	4,658	131	142,017	79,531	62,486	293	290	3
	15—20	115,906	53,775	62,131	4 060	3,909	151	111,846	49 866	61,980	442	439	3
	20 and over	624,514	324,772	299,742	25,043	24,528	515	599,471	300,244	299,227	1,212	1,208	4
KHASI AND JAINTIA HILLS.	**ALL RELIGIONS**	*235,069*	*114,442*	*120,627*	*12,940*	*9,242*	*3,698*	*222,129*	*105,200*	*116,929*	*2,717*	*2,216*	*501*
	0—10	72 551	35,631	36,920	610	360	250	71,941	35,271	36,670	76	49	27
	10—15	23 148	11,930	11,218	1 586	959	627	21,562	10,971	10 591	278	198	80
	15—20	20,970	9,598	11,372	1,864	1,126	738	19,106	8,472	10,634	363	271	92
	20 and over	118,400	57,283	61,117	8,880	6,797	2,083	109,520	50,486	59,034	2,000	1,098	02
	ANIMIST	*192,453*	*91,447*	*101,006*	*2,993*	*2,420*	*573*	*189,460*	*89,027*	*100,433*	*401*	*373*	*28*
	0—10	60,768	29,783	30,985	105	70	35	60,663	29,713	30,950	2	2	...
	10—15	18,909	9 748	9,161	365	283	82	18 544	9,465	9 079	49	43	6
	15—20	16,922	7,591	9,331	406	305	101	16,516	7,280	9,230	48	44	4
	20 and over	95,854	44,325	51,529	2,117	1,762	355	93 737	42,563	51,174	302	284	18
	CHRISTIAN	*31,257*	*14,855*	*16,402*	*6,736*	*4,021*	*2,715*	*24,521*	*10,834*	*13,687*	*1,378*	*952*	*426*
	0—10	9 703	4,807	4,896	340	185	155	9,363	4,622	4,741	41	18	23
	10—15	3 608	1,799	1 809	1 035	545	490	2 573	1,254	1,319	158	89	69
	15—20	3 091	1,393	1,698	1 181	614	567	1,910	779	1,131	214	141	73
	20 and over	14 855	6,856	7,999	4,180	2,677	1,503	10,675	4,179	6,496	965	704	261
NAGA HILLS.	**ALL RELIGIONS**	*149,623*	*74,751*	*74,872*	*1,287*	*1,233*	*54*	*148,336*	*73,518*	*74,818*	*184*	*169*	*15*
	0—10	42,675	20,935	21,740	27	26	1	42 648	20,909	21,759	1	1	...
	10—15	15,020	7,850	7,170	89	84	5	14,931	7,766	7,165	4	3	1
	15—20	10,483	5,202	5,281	133	125	8	10 350	6,077	5,273	25	23	2
	20 and over	81,445	40,764	40,681	1,038	998	40	80,407	39,766	40,641	154	142	12
	ANIMIST	*141,740*	*70,136*	*71,604*	*129*	*128*	*1*	*141,611*	*70,008*	*71,603*	*24*	*24*	...
	0—10	40,519	19,859	20,660	3	3	...	40,516	19,856	20,660	...	...	...
	10—15	14,366	7,508	6,858	24	24	...	14,342	7,484	6,858	1	...	...
	15—20	9 848	4,883	4,965	33	33	...	9 815	4,850	4,965	10	10	...
	20 and over	77,007	37,886	39,121	69	68	1	76,938	37,818	39,120	13	13	...

TABLE VIII.—Education by Religion and Age. Part B.—Details for Districts—*continued*.

District.	Age.	Population. Total. Persons.	Total. Males.	Total. Females.	Literate. Persons.	Literate. Males.	Literate. Females.	Illiterate. Persons.	Illiterate. Males.	Illiterate. Females.	Literate in English. Persons.	Literate in English. Males.	Literate in English. Females.
	1	2	3	4	5	6	7	8	9	10	11	12	13
LUSHAI HILLS.	ALL RELIGIONS	*91,204*	*43,098*	*48,176*	*3,635*	*3,498*	*137*	*87,569*	*39,530*	*48,039*	*199*	*185*	*14*
	0—10	24,231	11,687	12,544	32	29	3	24,199	11,658	12,541	3	3	1
	10—15	10,322	5,124	5,198	269	247	22	10,053	4,877	5,176	...	...	...
	15—20	8,907	4,027	4,880	511	479	32	8,396	3,548	4,848	37	36	1
	20 and over	47,744	22,190	25,554	2,823	2,743	80	44,921	19,447	25,474	159	147	12
	ANIMIST	*84,585*	*38,816*	*45,769*	*1,892*	*1,865*	*27*	*82,693*	*36,951*	*45,742*	*17*	*17*	...
	0—10	22,653	10,896	11,757	6	5	1	22,047	10,891	11,756	5	...	...
	10—15	9,744	4,798	4,946	141	140	1	9,603	4,658	4,945	...	...	...
	15—20	8,319	3,672	4,647	318	314	4	8,001	3,358	4,643	...	5	...
	20 and over	43,869	19,450	24,419	1,427	1,406	21	42,442	18,044	24,398	12	12	...
GOALPARA.	ALL RELIGIONS	*600,643*	*318,475*	*282,168*	*24,653*	*23,523*	*1,130*	*575,990*	*294,952*	*281,038*	*2,151*	*2,097*	*54*
	0—10	200,738	100,418	100,320	1,164	1,018	146	199,574	99,400	100,174	44	39	5
	10—15	57,606	32,262	25,340	2,482	2,304	178	55,128	29,958	25,168	230	224	6
	15—20	51,051	24,841	26,210	2,548	2,345	203	48,503	22,496	26,007	390	385	5
	20 and over	291,246	160,954	130,292	18,459	17,856	603	272,787	143,098	129,689	1,487	1,449	38
	HINDU	*334,720*	*178,673*	*156,047*	*18,399*	*17,548*	*851*	*316,391*	*161,195*	*155,196*	*1,692*	*1,681*	*11*
	0—10	107,032	53,477	53,555	946	833	113	106,086	52,644	53,442	35	33	2
	10—15	30,691	16,772	13,919	1,878	1,755	123	28,813	15,017	13,796	190	188	2
	15—20	27,770	13,795	13,975	1,871	1,714	157	25,899	12,081	13,818	303	303	...
	20 and over	169,227	94,629	74,598	13,704	13,246	458	155,523	81,383	74,140	1,164	1,157	7
	MUSALMAN	*211,562*	*111,917*	*99,645*	*4,869*	*4,743*	*126*	*206,693*	*107,174*	*99,519*	*255*	*255*	...
	0—10	74,355	37,179	37,176	184	160	24	74,171	37,019	37,152	...	...	...
	10—15	21,223	12,500	8,723	464	433	31	20,759	12,067	8,692	22	22	...
	15—20	19,045	9,117	9,928	500	482	18	18,545	8,635	9,910	63	63	...
	20 and over	96,939	53,121	43,818	3,721	3,668	53	93,218	49,453	43,765	170	170	...
	ANIMIST	*47,339*	*23,870*	*23,469*	*216*	*215*	*1*	*47,123*	*23,655*	*23,468*	*8*	*8*	...
	0—10	17,446	8,776	8,670	6	6	...	17,440	8,770	8,670	...	...	...
	10—15	4,802	2,477	2,325	16	16	...	4,786	2,461	2,325	1	1	...
	15—20	3,475	1,520	1,955	17	17	...	3,458	1,503	1,955	1	1	...
	20 and over	21,616	11,097	10,519	177	176	1	21,439	10,921	10,518	6	6	...

TABLE VIII.—EDUCATION BY RELIGION AND AGE. PART B.—DETAILS FOR DISTRICTS—*continued.*

District.	Age.	Population. Total. Persons.	Total. Males.	Total. Females.	Literate. Persons.	Literate. Males.	Literate. Females.	Illiterate. Persons.	Illiterate. Males.	Illiterate. Females.	Literate in English. Persons.	Literate in English. Males.	Literate in English. Females.
	1	2	3	4	5	6	7	8	9	10	11	12	13
KAMRUP.	ALL RELIGIONS	*667,328*	*339,398*	*328,430*	*36,194*	*34,580*	*1,614*	*631,634*	*304,818*	*326,816*	*3,094*	*2,993*	*101*
	0—10	224,720	111,575	113,145	1,811	1,608	203	222,909	109,967	112,942	44	40	4
	10—15	65,624	36,290	29,334	4,929	4,651	278	60,695	31,639	29,056	380	373	7
	15—20	48,463	24,933	23,530	4,564	4,279	285	43,899	20,654	23,245	639	623	16
	20 and over	329,021	166,600	162,421	24,890	24,042	848	304,131	142,548	161,573	2,031	1,957	74
	HINDU	*459,227*	*235,014*	*224,213*	*31,559*	*30,290*	*1,269*	*427,668*	*204,724*	*222,944*	*2,530*	*2,500*	*30*
	0—10	148,892	74,008	74,884	1,580	1,410	170	147,312	72,598	74,714	35	34	1
	10—15	45,474	25,569	19,905	4,275	4,058	217	41,199	21,511	19,688	314	310	4
	15—20	34,207	18,301	15,906	4,026	3,800	226	30,183	14,501	15,082	560	552	8
	20 and over	230,652	117,136	113,516	21,678	21,023	656	208,974	96,114	112,860	1,621	1,604	17
	MUSALMAN	*64,627*	*33,723*	*30,904*	*2,963*	*2,800*	*163*	*61,664*	*30,923*	*30,741*	*351*	*339*	*12*
	0—10	22,499	11,303	11,196	173	153	20	22,326	11,150	11,176	4	4	...
	10—15	6,325	3,586	2,739	469	430	39	5,856	3,156	2,700	62	60	2
	15—20	4,582	2,397	2,185	335	308	27	4,247	2,089	2,158	61	57	4
	20 and over	31,221	16,437	14,784	1,986	1,909	77	29,235	14,528	14,707	224	218	6
	ANIMIST	*140,576*	*68,640*	*71,927*	*941*	*929*	*12*	*139,635*	*67,720*	*71,915*	*23*	*23*	...
	0—10	52,453	25,816	26,637	40	36	4	52,413	25,780	26,633	...	...	...
	10—15	13,461	6,912	6,549	107	104	3	13,354	6,808	6,546	1	1	...
	15—20	9,372	4,081	5,291	98	97	1	9,274	3,984	5,290	11	11	...
	20 and over	65,290	31,840	33,450	696	692	4	64,594	31,148	33,446	11	11	...
DARRANG.	ALL RELIGIONS	*377,314*	*198,581*	*178,733*	*12,755*	*12,240*	*515*	*364,559*	*186,341*	*178,218*	*1,631*	*1,569*	*62*
	0—10	110,985	55,434	55,551	492	432	60	110,493	55,002	55,491	17	16	1
	10—15	36,001	19,871	16,130	1,126	1,062	64	34,875	18,809	16,066	82	81	1
	15—20	25,812	13,049	12,763	1,208	1,120	88	24,604	11,929	12,675	164	162	2
	20 and over	204,516	110,227	94,289	9,929	9,626	303	194,587	100,601	93,986	1,368	1,310	58
	HINDU	*245,341*	*129,631*	*115,710*	*10,682*	*10,271*	*411*	*234,659*	*119,360*	*115,299*	*1,270*	*1,259*	*11*
	0—10	67,737	33,955	33,782	447	393	54	67,290	33,562	33,728	15	14	1
	10—15	23,206	12,831	10,375	899	840	59	22,307	11,891	10,316	79	78	1
	15—20	17,112	8,787	8,325	1,067	989	78	16,045	7,798	8,247	148	147	1
	20 and over	137,286	74,058	63,228	8,160	7,940	220	129,117	66,109	63,008	1,028	1,020	8

TABLE VIII.—Education by Religion and Age. Part B.—Details for Districts—*continued.*

District.	Age.	Population: Total: Persons.	Total: Males.	Total: Females.	Literate: Persons.	Literate: Males.	Literate: Females.	Illiterate: Persons.	Illiterate: Males.	Illiterate: Females.	Literate in English: Persons.	Literate in English: Males.	Literate in English: Females.
	1	2	3	4	5	6	7	8	9	10	11	12	13
DARRANG—*concld.*	MUSALMAN	*20,305*	*11,073*	*9,232*	*934*	*910*	24	*19,371*	*10,163*	*9,208*	*103*	*103*	...
	0—10	6,468	3,209	3,259	22	18	4	6 446	3,191	3,255	...	...	...
	10—15	1 953	1,173	780	64	60	4	1 889	1,113	776	1	1	...
	15—20	1 435	779	656	72	68	4	1 363	711	652	9	9	...
	20 and over	10,449	5,912	4,537	776	764	12	9.673	5,148	4,525	93	93	...
	ANIMIST	*108,731*	*56,043*	*52,688*	*533*	*530*	*3*	*108,198*	*55,513*	*52,685*	*17*	*17*	...
	0—10	36 051	17,906	18,145	19	18	1	36 032	17,888	18,144	...	...	...
	10—15	10 589	5,714	4,875	37	37	...	10 552	5,677	4,875	1	1	...
	15—20	7,058	3,353	3,705	31	30	1	7.027	3,323	3,704	...	...	...
	20 and over	55,033	29,070	25,963	446	445	1	54 587	28,625	25,962	16	16	...
NOWGONG.	ALL RELIGIONS	*303,596*	*154,938*	*148,658*	*15,401*	*14,654*	*747*	*288,195*	*140,284*	*147,911*	*1,475*	*1,427*	*48*
	0—10	103·443	51,272	52,171	1 058	943	115	102 385	50,329	52.056	22	20	2
	10—15	26 906	14,672	12,234	1 775	1,636	139	25 131	13,036	12.095	136	133	3
	15—20	21 358	10,288	11,070	1 572	1,452	120	19 786	8.836	10,950	194	183	11
	20 and over	151.889	78,706	73,183	10.996	10,623	373	140 893	68,083	72,810	1.123	1,091	32
	HINDU	*177,795*	*91,213*	*86,582*	*12,908*	*12,424*	*484*	*164.887*	*78.789*	*86,098*	*1,068*	*1,064*	*4*
	0—10	59 074	29,265	29,809	897	829	68	58.177	28,436	29,741	14	14	...
	10—15	15 668	8.783	6,885	1 498	1,412	86	14 170	7,371	6,799	107	106	1
	15—20	12 072	6,138	5,934	1 308	1.232	76	10.764	4.906	5,858	135	135	...
	20 and over	90 981	47,027	43,954	9 205	8,951	254	81.776	38,076	43,700	812	809	3
	ANIMIST	*108,067*	*54,403*	*53,664*	*737*	*728*	*9*	*107.330*	*53,675*	*53,655*	*17*	*17*	...
	0—10	38 367	19,104	19,263	43	41	2	38 324	19,063	19,261	...	...	...
	10—15	9 580	4.978	4,602	67	64	3	9 513	4,914	4,599	...	...	...
	15—20	7 960	3.480	4,480	70	68	2	7 890	3,412	4,478	1	1	...
	20 and over	52.160	26,841	25,319	557	555	2	51.603	26,286	25,317	16	16	...
SIBSAGAR.	ALL RELIGIONS	*690.299*	*364,810*	*325,489*	*34,799*	*32,978*	*1,821*	*655,500*	*331,839*	*323.668*	*5,691*	*5,529*	*162*
	0—10	212 880	106,915	105.965	1 818	1,617	201	211 062	105,298	105,764	106	99	7
	10—15	70 703	38,185	32,518	4 054	3.729	325	66 649	34,456	32,193	573	558	15
	15—20	51 378	26 237	25,141	4 042	3,743	299	47 336	22 494	24 842	832	815	17
	20 and over	355.338	193,473	161,865	24 885	23,889	996	330,453	169,584	160.869	4.180	4,057	123

TABLE VIII.—Education by Religion and Age. Part B.—Details for Districts—*continued.*

District	Age	Population: Total: Persons	Total: Males	Total: Females	Literate: Persons	Literate: Males	Literate: Females	Illiterate: Persons	Illiterate: Males	Illiterate: Females	Literate in English: Persons	Literate in English: Males	Literate in English: Females
1		2	3	4	5	6	7	8	9	10	11	12	13
SIBSAGAR—*concld.*	HINDU ...	*595,266*	*313,748*	*281,518*	*30,553*	*29,119*	*1,434*	*564,713*	*284,629*	*280,084*	*4,509*	*4,458*	*51*
	0—10 ...	182,979	91,828	91,151	1,572	1,424	148	181,407	90,404	91,003	87	83	4
	10—15 ...	60,393	32,633	27,760	3,559	3,305	254	56,834	29,328	27,506	467	462	5
	15—20 ...	43,884	22,352	21,532	3,559	3,302	257	40,325	19,050	21,275	692	678	14
	20 and over ...	308,010	166,935	141,075	21,863	21,088	775	286,147	145,847	140,300	3,263	3,235	28
	MUSALMAN ...	*29,718*	*16,373*	*13,345*	*3,018*	*2,800*	*218*	*26,700*	*13,573*	*13,127*	*697*	*688*	*9*
	0—10 ...	9,357	4,722	4,635	213	170	43	9,144	4,552	4,592	12	11	1
	10—15 ...	3,494	1,908	1,626	427	367	60	3,067	1,501	1,566	92	90	2
	15—20 ...	2,461	1,274	1,187	369	339	30	2,092	935	1,157	119	118	1
	20 and over ...	14,406	8,509	5,897	2,009	1,924	85	12,397	6,585	5,812	474	469	5
	ANIMIST ...	*57,580*	*30,362*	*27,218*	*238*	*228*	*10*	*57,342*	*30,134*	*27,208*	*9*	*9*	...
	0—10 ...	18,278	9,204	9,074	4	3	1	18,274	9,201	9,073	...	...	...
	10—15 ...	6,088	3,281	2,807	13	13	...	6,075	3,268	2,807	...	...	...
	15—20 ...	4,467	2,295	2,172	22	19	3	4,445	2,276	2,169	3	3	...
	20 and over ...	28,747	15,582	13,165	199	193	6	28,548	15,389	13,159	6	6	...
LAKHIMPUR.	ALL RELIGIONS ...	*468,989*	*249,021*	*219,968*	*21,082*	*19,892*	*1,190*	*447,907*	*229,129*	*218,778*	*4,172*	*3,995*	*177*
	0—10 ...	140,530	70,719	69,811	1,007	860	147	139,523	69,859	69,664	52	41	11
	10—15 ...	44,318	23,540	20,778	2,155	1,930	225	42,163	21,610	20,553	273	261	12
	15—20 ...	32,486	15,618	16,868	2,076	1,884	192	30,410	13,734	16,676	438	418	20
	20 and over ...	251,655	139,144	112,511	15,844	15,218	626	235,811	123,926	111,885	3,409	3,275	134
	HINDU ...	*367,990*	*195,291*	*172,699*	*17,282*	*16,386*	*896*	*350,708*	*178,905*	*171,803*	*3,169*	*3,126*	*43*
	0—10 ...	108,386	54,556	53,830	850	726	124	107,536	53,830	53,706	40	37	3
	10—15 ...	34,705	18,438	16,267	1,801	1,616	185	32,904	16,822	16,082	223	215	8
	15—20 ...	25,095	12,064	13,031	1,788	1,636	152	23,307	10,428	12,879	392	384	8
	20 and over ...	199,804	110,233	89,571	12,843	12,408	435	186,961	97,825	89,136	2,514	2,490	24
	ANIMIST ...	*76,701*	*39,622*	*37,079*	*655*	*651*	*'4*	*76,046*	*38,971*	*37,075*	*19*	*19*	...
	0—10 ...	25,745	12,957	12,788	43	43	...	25,702	12,914	12,788	...	...	...
	10—15 ...	7,370	3,855	3,515	77	76	1	7,293	3,779	3,514	5	5	...
	15—20 ...	5,506	2,530	2,979	76	76	...	5,433	2,454	2,979	2	2	...
	20 and over ...	38,077	20,280	17,797	459	456	3	37,618	19,824	17,794	12	12	...

TABLE VIII.—EDUCATION BY RELIGION AND AGE. PART B.—DETAILS FOR DISTRICTS—*concluded.*

District.	Age.	POPULATION.									LITERATE IN ENGLISH.		
		TOTAL.			LITERATE.			ILLITERATE.					
		Persons.	Males.	Females.	Persons.	Males.	Females.	Persons.	Males.	Females.	Persons.	Males.	Females.
	1	2	3	4	5	6	7	8	9	10	11	12	13
GARO HILLS.	ALL RELIGIONS	*158,936*	*81,264*	*77,672*	*1,836*	*1,667*	*169*	*157,100*	*79,597*	*77,503*	*158*	*147*	*11*
	0–10	51,613	26,491	25,122	37	27	10	51,576	26,464	25,112	...	...	...
	10–15	17,237	8,933	8,304	175	152	23	17,062	8,781	8,281	4	4	...
	15–20	15,855	6,851	9,004	314	273	41	15,544	6,581	8,963	24	22	2
	20 and over	74,228	38,086	35,242	1,310	1,215	95	72,918	37,771	35,147	130	121	9
	HINDU	*20,827*	*11,293*	*9,534*	*788*	*757*	*31*	*20,039*	*10,536*	*9,503*	*51*	*50*	*1*
	0–10	6,457	3,146	3,311	18	15	3	6,439	3,131	3,308	...	...	...
	10–15	2,195	1,182	1,013	49	45	4	2,146	1,137	1,009	1	1	...
	15–20	1,748	864	884	78	73	5	1,670	701	879	...	...	...
	20 and over	10,427	6,101	4,326	643	624	19	9,784	5,477	4,307	50	49	1
	ANIMIST	*124,144*	*62,408*	*61,736*	*113*	*110*	*3*	*124,031*	*62,298*	*61,733*	*1*	*1*	...
	0–10	40,935	21,212	19,723	2	2	...	40,933	21,210	19,723	...	...	...
	10–15	13,436	6,810	6,626	5	5	...	13,431	6,805	6,626	...	...	...
	15–20	12,574	5,185	7,389	13	13	...	12,561	5,172	7,389	...	...	...
	20 and over	57,199	29,201	27,998	93	90	3	57,106	29,111	27,995	1	1	...
MANIPUR.	ALL RELIGIONS	*346,222*	*170,666*	*175,556*	*7,106*	*6,889*	*217*	*339,116*	*163,777*	*175,339*	*559*	*541*	*18*
	0–10	110,495	54,972	55,523	226	204	22	110,269	54,768	55,501	6	6	...
	10–15	38,345	19,271	19,074	832	797	35	37,513	18,474	19,039	63	59	4
	15–20	30,343	14,513	15,830	988	956	32	29,355	13,557	15,798	109	108	1
	20 and over	167,039	81,910	85,129	5,060	4,932	128	161,979	76,978	85,001	381	368	13
	HINDU	*201,369*	*99,264*	*102,105*	*6,463*	*6,298*	*165*	*194,906*	*92,966*	*101,940*	*384*	*384*	...
	0–10	64,476	32,363	32,113	205	188	17	64,271	32,175	32,096	2	2	...
	10–15	24,159	12,150	12,009	740	714	26	23,419	11,436	11,983	29	29	...
	15–20	19,292	9,330	9,962	893	866	27	18,399	8,464	9,935	80	80	...
	20 and over	93,442	45,421	48,021	4,625	4,530	95	88,817	40,891	47,926	273	273	...
	ANIMIST	*130,093*	*63,699*	*66,394*	*164*	*148*	*16*	*129,929*	*63,551*	*66,378*	*81*	*79*	*2*
	0–10	40,437	19,818	20,619	11	9	2	40,426	19,809	20,617	1	1	...
	10–15	12,454	6,256	6,198	49	46	3	12,405	6,210	6,195	19	19	...
	15–20	9,694	4,498	5,196	33	31	2	9,661	4,467	5,194	20	20	...
	20 and over	67,508	33,127	34,381	71	62	9	67,437	33,065	34,372	41	39	2

TABLE IX.

EDUCATION.

BY SELECTED CASTES, TRIBES OR RACES.

THIS table repeats the information given in Table VIII in respect of education with this difference that, whereas in that table the population is distributed by age and religion, it is here arranged according to caste or tribe. Moreover in Table VIII the whole population is dealt with, but this table refers only to selected castes and tribes ; the minor castes and tribes have been left out of account altogether, and even those selected for inclusion have been taken only for the districts where they were specially numerous. To save space, figures have been given, not for each district separately, but for groups of districts, the local conditions of which may be presumed to be fairly uniform.

It may be explained that the total district strength of a caste in this table does not necessarily tally with that in Table XIII and Table XII-A, as the latter include and exclude figures added and subtracted in the course of classification, which the present table does not.

TABLE IX.—EDUCATION BY SELECTED CASTES, TRIBES OR RACES.

Caste, Tribe or Race.	Locality.	POPULATION. Total. Persons.	Total. Males.	Total. Females.	Literate. Persons.	Literate. Males.	Literate. Females.	Illiterate. Persons.	Illiterate. Males.	Illiterate. Females.	LITERATE IN ENGLISH. Persons.	Literate in English. Males.	Literate in English. Females.
1	2	3	4	5	6	7	8	9	10	11	12	13	14
AHOM (Hindu)	Brahmaputra Valley	192,560	99,418	93,142	11,652	11,361	291	180,908	88,057	92,851	1,686	1,670	16
BAIDYA (Hindu)	Province	5,609	3,049	2,560	3,139	2,213	926	2,470	836	1,634	1,331	1,285	46
BARUI (Hindu)	Surma Valley	24,542	12,504	12,038	2,363	2,297	66	22,179	10,207	11,972	100	100	...
BHUINMALI (Hindu)	Sylhet	32,067	16,694	15,373	656	637	19	31,411	16,057	15,354	10	10	...
BHUIYA (Hindu)	Total	54,677	28,399	26,278	415	398	17	54,262	28,001	26,261	11	11	...
	Surma Valley	15,604	8,145	7,459	276	274	2	15,328	7,871	7,457	6	6	...
	Brahmaputra Valley	39,073	20,254	18,819	139	124	15	38,934	20,130	18,804	5	5	...
BHUIYA (Animist)	Ditto	1,868	989	879	4	4	...	1,864	985	879	...	...	...
BRAHMAN (Hindu)	Province	124,506	68,361	56,145	40,359	37,318	3,041	84,147	31,043	53,104	6,092	6,032	60
CHAMAR (Hindu)	Surma Valley	38,969	19,541	19,428	382	375	7	38,587	19,166	19,421	3	3	...
CHUTIYA (Hindu)	Upper Brahmaputra Valley	82,164	42,359	39,805	4,149	4,078	71	78,015	38,281	39,734	340	339	1
CHUTIYA (Animist)	Ditto	228	119	109	3	3	...	225	116	109	...	...	...
DHOBA (Hindu)	Sylhet	23,093	11,870	11,223	521	504	17	22,572	11,366	11,206	8	8	...
GARO (Hindu)	Garo Hills and Contiguous Districts	232	118	114	8	8	...	224	110	114	...	...	...
GARO (Animist)	Ditto	137,338	69,048	68,290	183	180	3	137,155	68,868	68,287	5	5	...
GOALA (Hindu)	Province	40,858	22,800	18,058	1,277	1,237	40	39,581	21,563	18,018	50	49	1
INDIAN CHRISTIAN	Ditto	63,837	31,762	32,075	10,145	6,758	3,387	53,692	25,004	28,688	1,787	1,368	419
JOGI or JUGI (Hindu)	Ditto	167,521	85,287	82,234	9,865	9,470	395	157,656	75,817	81,839	299	298	1

TABLE IX.—Education by Selected Castes, Tribes or Races—*continued.*

Caste, Tribe or Race.	Locality.	Population. Total. Persons.	Total. Males.	Total. Females.	Literate. Persons.	Literate. Males.	Literate. Females.	Illiterate. Persons.	Illiterate. Males.	Illiterate. Females.	Literate in English. Persons.	Literate in English. Males.	Literate in English. Females.
1	2	3	4	5	6	7	8	9	10	11	12	13	14
KACHARI (Hindu)	Total	*52,379*	*28,487*	*23,892*	*2,413*	*2,368*	*45*	*49,966*	*26,110*	*23,847*	*382*	*381*	*1*
	Cachar	12,969	6,431	6,538	227	219	8	12,742	6,212	6,530	36	36	...
	Brahmaputra Valley	39,410	22,056	17,354	2,186	2,149	37	37,224	19,907	17,317	346	345	1
KACHARI (Animist)	Ditto	*168,429*	*84,277*	*84,152*	*1,213*	*1,201*	*12*	*167,216*	*83,076*	*84,140*	*27*	*25*	*2*
KAIBARTTA CHASI (Hindu) ... ... (Mahishya).	Province	*63,552*	*33,295*	*30,257*	*5,218*	*4,969*	*249*	*58,334*	*28,326*	*30,008*	*373*	*371*	*2*
KALITA (Hindu)	Brahmaputra Valley	*220,640*	*114,886*	*105,754*	*17,460*	*16,904*	*556*	*203,180*	*97,982*	*105,198*	*1,793*	*1,791*	*2*
KAMAR (Hindu)	Province	*35,633*	*17,977*	*17,656*	*1,586*	*1,552*	*34*	*34,047*	*16,425*	*17,622*	*63*	*63*	...
KAYASTHA (Hindu)	Ditto	*81,177*	*43,600*	*37,577*	*29,232*	*24,795*	*4,437*	*51,945*	*18,805*	*33,140*	*6,811*	*6,719*	*92*
KEWAT (Hindu)	Brahmaputra Valley	*88,047*	*44,891*	*43,156*	*5,206*	*5,055*	*151*	*82,841*	*39,836*	*43,005*	*532*	*528*	*4*
KHASI (Animist)	Khasi and Jaintia Hills	*115,664*	*54,627*	*61,037*	*2,665*	*2,129*	*536*	*112,999*	*52,498*	*60,501*	*374*	*349*	*25*
KSHATTRIYA (Hindu)*	Total	*248,279*	*123,656*	*124,623*	*11,912*	*11,655*	*257*	*236,367*	*112,001*	*124,366*	*487*	*485*	*2*
	Cachar and Sylhet	76,733	39,564	37,169	7,373	7,222	151	69,360	32,342	37,018	210	208	2
	Manipur	171,546	84,092	87,454	4,539	4,433	106	167,007	79,659	87,348	277	277	...
KOCH (Hindu)	Brahmaputra Valley	*203,775*	*103,960*	*99,815*	*9,201*	*8,970*	*231*	*194,574*	*94,990*	*99,584*	*667*	*665*	*2*
KUKI (Animist)	Province	*20,619*	*10,185*	*10,434*	*44*	*44*	...	*20,575*	*10,141*	*10,434*	*3*	*3*	...
KUMHAR (Hindu)	Total	*19,638*	*9,927*	*9,711*	*856*	*843*	*13*	*18,782*	*9,084*	*9,698*	*81*	*81*	...
	Sylhet	12,197	6,167	6,030	598	589	9	11,599	5,578	6,021	70	70	...
	Kamrup	7,441	3,760	3,681	258	254	4	7,183	3,506	3,677	11	11	...
LAKHER (Animist)	Lushai Hills	*3,639*	*1,751*	*1,888*	*36*	*36*	...	*3,603*	*1,715*	*1,888*	...	...	...

* Kshattriya includes 19,410 persons who returned themselves as Manipuris.

TABLE IX.—Education by Selected Castes, Tribes or Races—*continued.*

Caste, Tribe or Race.	Locality.	Population. Total. Persons.	Total. Males.	Total. Females.	Literate. Persons.	Literate. Males.	Literate. Females.	Illiterate. Persons.	Illiterate. Males.	Illiterate. Females.	Literate in English. Persons.	Literate in English. Males.	Literate in English. Females.
1	2	3	4	5	6	7	8	9	10	11	12	13	14
LALUNG (Animist)	Nowgong	32,790	16,027	16,763	231	229	2	32,559	15,798	16,761	2	2	...
LUSHAI (Animist)	Lushai Hills	32,808	14,826	17,982	831	815	16	31,977	14,011	17,966	10	10	...
„ MHAR (Animist)	Ditto	12,050	5,523	6,527	261	259	2	11,789	5,264	6,525	2	2	...
„ PAITE (Animist)	Ditto	3,686	1,822	1,864	61	59	2	3,625	1,763	1,862	...	...	...
„ RALTE (Animist)	Ditto	15,931	7,136	8,795	384	381	3	15,547	6,755	8,792	2	2	...
„ POI (Animist)	Ditto	10,938	5,098	5,840	103	103	...	10,835	4,995	5,840	1	1	...
„ FANAI (Animist)	Ditto	3,631	1,681	1,950	55	53	2	3,576	1,628	1,948	1	1	...
„ SAILO " (Animist)	Ditto	1,261	586	675	102	101	1	1,159	485	674	1	1	...
MALO (Hindu)	Sylhet	13,460	7,002	6,458	255	247	8	13,205	6,755	6,450	5	5	...
MECH (Hindu)	Goalpara	68,591	34,170	34,421	1,389	1,383	6	67,202	32,787	34,415	16	16	...
MECH (Animist)	Ditto	24,437	12,006	12,431	91	91	...	24,346	11,915	12,431	3	3	...
MIKIR (Animist)	Province	102,212	52,180	50,032	354	348	6	101,858	51,832	50,026	12	12	...
MIRI (Hindu)	Sibsagar and Lakhimpur	13,256	6,753	6,503	76	76	...	13,180	6,677	6,503	...	...	...
MIRI (Animist)	Ditto	37,471	19,357	18,114	418	414	4	37,053	18,943	18,110	10	10	...
MUCHI (Hindu)	Sylhet	4,542	2,405	2,137	39	37	2	4,503	2,368	2,135	...	...	...
MUNDA (Hindu)	Total	56,647	29,988	26,659	307	301	6	56,340	29,687	26,653	11	11	...
	Surma Valley	12,624	6,438	6,186	145	143	2	12,479	6,295	6,184	4	4	...
	Darrang, Sibsagar and Lakhimpur	44,023	23,550	20,473	162	158	4	43,861	23,392	20,469	7	7	...

TABLE IX.—EDUCATION BY SELECTED CASTES, TRIBES OR RACES—*continued*.

Caste, Tribe or Race.	Locality.	POPULATION.									LITERATE IN ENGLISH.		
		TOTAL.			LITERATE.			ILLITERATE.					
		Persons.	Males.	Females.	Persons.	Males.	Females.	Persons.	Males.	Females.	Persons.	Males.	Females.
1	2	3	4	5	6	7	8	9	10	11	12	13	14
MUNDA (Animist)	Total	*26,689*	*13,701*	*12,988*	*111*	*68*	*43*	*26,578*	*13,633*	*12,945*	*2*	*2*	...
	Surma Valley	344	174	170	4	4	...	340	170	170	...	...	...
	Darrang, Sibsagar and Lakhimpur	26,345	13,527	12,818	107	64	43	26,238	13,463	12,775	2	2	...
NADIYAL (Hindu)	Brahmaputra Valley...	*63,281*	*32,026*	*31,255*	*2,347*	*2,251*	*96*	*60,934*	*29,775*	*31,159*	*176*	*174*	*2*
NAGA KACHHA (Animist)	Total	*9,307*	*4,581*	*4,726*	*1*	*1*	...	*9,306*	*4,580*	*4,726*	*1*	*1*	...
	Naga Hills	9,011	4,424	4,587	1	1	...	9,010	4,423	4,587	1	1	...
	Manipur	296	157	139	...	...	...	296	157	139	...	...	...
„ ANGAMI (Animist)	Naga Hills	*39,672*	*19,875*	*19,797*	*77*	*77*	...	*39,595*	*19,798*	*19,797*	*18*	*18*	...
„ KABUI (Animist)	Manipur	*12,435*	*5,920*	*6,515*	...	...	...	*12,435*	*5,920*	*6,515*	...	...	...
„ LHOTA (Animist)	Naga Hills	*19,498*	*9,437*	*10,061*	*8*	*8*	...	*19,490*	*9,429*	*10,061*	*2*	*2*	...
„ SEMA (Animist)	Ditto	*32,726*	*16,304*	*16,422*	*5*	*5*	...	*32,721*	*16,299*	*16,422*	*1*	*1*	...
„ TANGKHUL (Animist)	Manipur	*26,577*	*12,506*	*14,071*	*78*	*74*	*4*	*26,499*	*12,432*	*14,067*	*41*	*39*	*2*
„ AO (Animist)	Naga Hills	*26,505*	*12,533*	*13,972*	*6*	*6*	...	*26,499*	*12,527*	*13,972*	*1*	*1*	...
„ KEZHAMA (Animist)	Ditto	*4,685*	*2,600*	*2,085*	*1*	*1*	...	*4,684*	*2,599*	*2,085*	...	...	...
„ RENGMA (Animist)	Ditto	*4,370*	*2,016*	*2,354*	*11*	*11*	...	*4,359*	*2,005*	*2,354*	*1*	*1*	...
„ UNSPECIFIED (Animist)	Ditto	*1,709*	*1,267*	*442*	*1*	*1*	...	*1,708*	*1,266*	*442*	...	...	...
NAMASUDRA (Hindu)	Total	*171,214*	*88,650*	*82,564*	*3,871*	*3,785*	*86*	*167,343*	*84,865*	*82,478*	*40*	*39*	*1*
	Surma Valley	152,702	78,635	74,067	3,134	3,055	79	140,568	75,580	73,988	32	31	1
	Goalpara, Kamrup and Nowgong	18,512	10,015	8,497	737	730	7	17,775	9,285	8,490	8	8	...
NAPIT (Hindu)	Total	*29,396*	*14,981*	*14,415*	*1,871*	*1,827*	*44*	*27,525*	*13,154*	*14,371*	*60*	*60*	...
	Sylhet	23,682	12,229	11,453	1,641	1,603	38	22,041	10,626	11,415	52	52	...
	Kamrup	5,714	2,752	2,962	230	224	6	5,484	2,528	2,956	8	8	...

TABLE IX.—Education by Selected Castes, Tribes or Races—*concluded.*

Caste, Tribe or Race.	Locality.	POPULATION.									LITERATE IN ENGLISH.		
		Total.			Literate.			Illiterate.					
		Persons.	Males.	Females.	Persons.	Males.	Females.	Persons.	Males.	Females.	Persons.	Males.	Females.
1	2	3	4	5	6	7	8	9	10	11	12	13	14
ORAON (Hindu)	Total	*12,905*	*6,665*	*6,240*	*56*	*56*	...	*12,849*	*6,609*	*6,240*	*1*	*1*	...
	Cachar	2,378	1,224	1,154	26	26	...	2,352	1,198	1,154	...	...	...
	Brahmaputra Valley	10,527	5,441	5,086	30	30	...	10,497	5,411	5,086	1	1	...
ORAON (Animist)	Total	*11,006*	*5,321*	*5,685*	*17*	*17*	...	*10,989*	*5,304*	*5,685*	...	...	...
	Cachar	300	147	153	...	...	...	300	147	153	...	...	...
	Brahmaputra Valley	10,706	5,174	5,532	17	17	...	10,689	5,157	5,532	...	...	...
PATNI (Hindu)	Surma Valley	*110,858*	*56,721*	*54,137*	*4,023*	*3,792*	*231*	*106,835*	*52,929*	*53,906*	*91*	*90*	*1*
RAJBANSI (Hindu)	Goalpara	*127,946*	*65,747*	*62,199*	*7,192*	*7,037*	*155*	*120,754*	*58,710*	*62,044*	*218*	*218*	...
SANTAL (Hindu)	Total	*26,939*	*13,659*	*13,280*	*147*	*144*	*3*	*26,792*	*13,515*	*13,277*	*6*	*6*	...
	Surma Valley	5,534	2,911	2,623	74	73	1	5,460	2,838	2,622	1	1	...
	Brahmaputra Valley	21,405	10,748	10,657	73	71	2	21,332	10,677	10,655	5	5	...
SANTHAL (Animist)	Total	*22,206*	*11,486*	*10,720*	*89*	*84*	*5*	*22,117*	*11,402*	*10,715*	...	...	...
	Surma Valley	4,630	2,360	2,270	40	36	4	4,590	2,324	2,266	...	...	...
	Brahmaputra Valley	17,576	9,126	8,450	49	48	1	17,527	9,078	8,449	...	...	...
SUDRA (Hindu)	Sylhet	*115,141*	*59,400*	*55,741*	*10,392*	*9,967*	*425*	*104,749*	*49,433*	*55,316*	*625*	*623*	*2*
SUTRADHAR (Hindu)...	Total	*15,424*	*8,103*	*7,321*	*750*	*735*	*15*	*14,674*	*7,368*	*7,306*	*15*	*15*	...
	Sylhet	13,187	6,803	6,384	630	616	14	12,557	6,187	6,370	12	12	...
	Goalpara	2,237	1,300	937	120	119	1	2,117	1,181	936	3	3	...
SYNTENG (Animist)	Khasi and Jaintia Hills	*42,124*	*19,629*	*22,495*	*276*	*242*	*34*	*41,848*	*19,387*	*22,461*	*22*	*21*	*1*
TANTI (Hindu)	Sibsagar and Lakhimpur	*23,375*	*11,602*	*11,773*	*207*	*193*	*14*	*23,168*	*11,409*	*11,759*	*34*	*33*	*1*
TELI OR TILI (Hindu)	Sylhet	*28,011*	*14,368*	*13,643*	*3,054*	*2,898*	*156*	*24,957*	*11,470*	*13,487*	*142*	*142*	...

TABLE X.

LANGUAGE.

In this table the languages returned at the census are arranged under the following headings :—

A. Vernaculars of India ...
- (1) Aryan.
- (2) Tibeto-Burman.
- (3) Siameso-Chinese.
- (4) Mon-Khmer.
- (5) Munda.
- (6) Dravidian.

B. Vernaculars of Asiatic countries beyond India.
C. European languages.

Languages which are either numerically insignificant or too localized for separate entry are grouped together under the head "Others." Details of these minor languages are given in Appendix I printed at the end of the table. A classification of languages by linguistic families will be found in Chapter IX of the Report. Appendix II gives the details of the dialects shown together as Naga unclassed.

TABLE X.—LANGUAGE.

District or State.	POPULATION. Persons.	Males.	Females.	A.—VERNACULARS OF INDIA. I.—ARYAN. Assamese. Persons.	Males.	Females.	Bengali. Persons.	Males.	Females.	Hindi. Persons.	Males.	Females.	Marathi. Persons.	Males.	Females.
1	2	3	4	5	6	7	8	9	10	11	12	13	14	15	16
ASSAM	*7,059,857*	*3,638,287*	*3,421,570*	*1,532,393*	*784,932*	*747,461*	*3,224,604*	*1,665,600*	*1,559,004*	*430,778*	*244,452*	*186,326*	*1,397*	*66*	*531*
(1) ***British Territory***	*6,713,635*	*3,467,621*	*3,246,014*	*1,532,332*	*784,889*	*747,443*	*3,224,130*	*1,665,230*	*1,558,900*	*428,822*	*242,904*	*185,918*	*1,396*	*865*	*531*
SURMA VALLEY AND HILL DISTRICTS	*3,446,030*	*1,761,134*	*1,684,896*	*4,188*	*2,597*	*1,591*	*2,573,988*	*1,323,327*	*1,250,661*	*223,961*	*119,596*	*104,365*	*52*	*31*	*21*
Cachar	497,463	260,444	237,019	1,461	859	602	287,759	151,761	135,998	101,209	53,445	47,764	43	22	21
Sylhet	2,472,671	1,268,469	1,204,202	1,052	569	483	2,282,738	1,169,016	1,113,722	119 218	63,371	55,847	3	3	...
Khasi and Jaintia Hills	235,069	114,442	120,627	884	555	329	2,627	1,874	753	2.820	2,186	634	5	5	...
Naga Hills	149,623	74,751	74,872	685	550	135	91	69	22	535	452	83	1	1	...
Lushai Hills	91,204	43,028	48,176	106	64	42	773	607	166	179	142	37	...	...	...
ASSAM VALLEY DISTRICTS	*3,267,605*	*1,706,487*	*1,561,118*	*1,528,144*	*782,292*	*745,852*	*650,142*	*341,903*	*308,239*	*204,861*	*123,308*	*81,553*	*1,344*	*834*	*510*
Goalpara	600,643	318,475	282,168	85,329	43,565	41,764	347,772	183,073	164,699	22,041	17,385	4,656	3	3	...
Kamrup	667,828	339,398	328,430	529,387	266,198	263,189	8 378	5,654	2,724	12 435	9,330	3,105	12	5	7
Darrang	377,314	198,581	178,733	167,405	86,128	81,277	58,131	30,382	27,749	21,532	12,842	8,690	19	8	11
Nowgong	303,596	154,938	148,658	195 649	97,310	98,339	12 715	7,233	5,482	17 378	9,934	7,444	...	...	...
Sibsagar	690,299	364,810	325,489	391 584	205,767	185,817	127 816	86,615	61,201	43 276	24,412	18,864	858	431	427
Lakhimpur	468,989	249,021	219,968	158,481	83,137	75,344	76 417	38,872	37,545	87 572	48,852	38,720	452	387	65
Garo Hills	158,936	81,264	77,672	309	187	122	18,913	10,074	8,839	627	553	74	...	...	...
(2) ***Manipur State***	*346,222*	*170,666*	*175,556*	*61*	*43*	*18*	*474*	*370*	*104*	*1,956*	*1,548*	*408*	1	1	...

District or State.	A.—VERNACULARS OF INDIA—continued. 1.—ARYAN—*concluded.* Naipali. Persons.	Males.	Females.	Oriya. Persons.	Males.	Females.	Panjabi. Persons.	Males.	Females.	Pashto. Persons.	Males.	Females.	Rajasthani. Persons.	Males.	Females.	2.—TIBETO-BURMAN. Abor. Persons.	Males.	Females.
1	17	18	19	20	21	22	23	24	25	26	27	28	29	30	31	32	33	34
ASSAM	*47,110*	*29,681*	*17,429*	*61,187*	*30,541*	*30,646*	*851*	*705*	*146*	*702*	*664*	*38*	*11,679*	*8,852*	*2,827*	*1,147*	*669*	*478*
(1) ***British Territory***	*45,214*	*28,513*	*16,701*	*61,182*	*30,537*	*30,645*	*823*	*683*	*140*	*702*	*664*	*38*	*11,611*	*8,790*	*2,821*	*1,147*	*669*	*478*
SURMA VALLEY AND HILL DISTRICTS	*6,781*	*4,702*	*2,079*	*15,256*	*7,456*	*7,800*	*302*	*251*	*51*	*269*	*254*	*15*	*762*	*492*	*270*	...	...	...
Cachar	1 041	693	348	3 135	1,531	1.604	136	107	29	113	100	13	51	32	19	...	...	...
Sylhet	273	242	31	12,039	5,840	6,190	4	4	...	115	115	...	518	315	203	...	...	...
Khasi and Jaintia Hills	2,701	1,935	766	58	53	5	100	82	18	41	39	2	115	82	33	...	...	...
Naga Hills	1,020	602	418	13	13	...	32	31	1	...	...	...	71	60	11	...	...	...
Lushai Hills	1,746	1,230	516	11	10	1	30	27	3	...	...	...	7	3	4	...	...	...
ASSAM VALLEY DISTRICTS	*38,433*	*23,811*	*14,622*	*45,926*	*23,081*	*22,845*	*521*	*432*	*89*	*433*	*410*	*23*	*10,849*	*8,298*	*2,551*	*1,147*	*669*	*478*
Goalpara	3 804	2,528	1,276	215	160	55	38	31	7	30	30	...	1,071	871	200	...	...	...
Kamrup	4 020	2,540	1,480	359	262	97	70	56	14	30	30	...	1 569	984	585	...	...	...
Darrang	13,953	8,165	5,788	9 608	4,853	14,755	22	19	3	53	53	...	879	794	85	...	...	...
Nowgong	2.412	1.616	796	2 333	1,229	1,104	144	116	28	49	44	5	973	864	109	...	...	...
Sibsagar	3.672	2,330	1,342	14 213	7,157	7,056	75	59	16	67	56	11	3 502	2,672	830	2	2	...
Lakhimpur	9,070	5,648	3,422	19,196	9,418	9,778	172	151	21	204	197	7	2 820	2,084	736	1,145	667	478
Garo Hills	1,502	984	518	2	2	...	...	...	...	...	...	...	35	29	6	...	...	...
(2) ***Manipur State***	*1,896*	*1,168*	*728*	*5*	*4*	*1*	*28*	*22*	*6*	...	...	...	*68*	*62*	*6*	...	...	...

TABLE X.—LANGUAGE—*continued.*

A.—VERNACULARS OF INDIA—continued.

2.—TIBETO-BURMAN—*continued.*

District or State.	Anal.			Angami.			Ao.			Bhotia of Bhutan.			Bhotia of Tibet.		
	Persons.	Males.	Females.	Persons.	Males.	Females.	Persons.	Males.	Females.	Persons.	Males.	Females.	Persons.	Males.	Females.
1	35	36	37	38	39	40	41	42	43	44	45	46	47	48	49
ASSAM	*2,659*	*1,370*	*1,289*	*38,714*	*20,059*	*18,655*	*29,064*	*13,742*	*15,322*	*536*	*413*	*123*	*759*	*486*	*273*
(1) British Territory	...	...	...	*38,699*	*20,048*	*18,651*	*29,064*	*13,742*	*15,322*	*536*	*413*	*123*	*759*	*486*	*273*
SURMA VALLEY AND HILL DISTRICTS	...	...	...	*38,657*	*19,919*	*18,638*	*28,877*	*13,617*	*15,260*	*17*	*10*	*7*	...	...	...
Cachar	...	...	...	...	...	...	...	...	...	2	1	1	...	...	...
Sylhet	...	...	...	...	...	...	...	...	...	...	...	...	...	...	...
Khasi and Jaintia Hills	...	...	...	...	...	...	...	...	...	15	9	6	...	...	...
Naga Hills	...	...	...	38,557	19,919	18,638	28,877	13,617	15,260	...	...	...	...	...	...
Lushai Hills	...	...	...	...	...	...	...	...	...	...	...	...	...	...	...
ASSAM VALLEY DISTRICTS	...	...	...	*142*	*129*	*13*	*187*	*125*	*62*	*519*	*403*	*116*	*759*	*486*	*273*
Goalpara	...	...	...	...	...	...	...	...	...	38	26	12	47	46	1
Kamrup	...	...	...	...	...	...	...	...	...	470	370	100	3	3	...
Darrang	...	...	...	...	...	...	...	...	...	...	...	...	147	121	26
Nowgong	...	...	...	...	...	...	...	...	...	...	...	...	...	...	...
Sibsagar	...	...	...	141	128	13	104	68	36	...	...	...	...	...	...
Lakhimpur	...	...	...	...	...	...	83	57	26	...	...	...	1	1	...
Garo Hills	...	...	...	1	1	...	...	...	...	11	7	4	561	315	246
(2) Manipur State	*2,659*	*1,370*	*1,289*	*15*	*11*	*4*	...	...	...	...	...	...	...	...	...

A.—VERNACULARS OF INDIA—continued.

2.—TIBETO-BURMAN—*continued.*

District or State.	Bodo, Mech or Plains Kachari.			Chiru.			Chutia.			Dafla.			Dimasa.			Empeo or Kachcha Naga.		
	Persons.	Males.	Females.	Persons.	Males.	Females.	Persons.	Males.	Females.	Persons.	Males.	Females.	Persons.	Males.	Females.	Persons.	Males.	Females.
1	50	51	52	53	54	55	56	57	58	59	60	61	62	63	64	65	66	67
ASSAM	*261,255*	*130,605*	*130,650*	*1,298*	*593*	*705*	*3,107*	*1,431*	*1,676*	*951*	*527*	*424*	*16,483*	*8,230*	*8,253*	*8,169*	*4,160*	*4,009*
(1) British Territory	*261,112*	*130,528*	*130,584*	...	...	...	*3,107*	*1,431*	*1,676*	*951*	*527*	*424*	*16,483*	*8,230*	*8,253*	*6,885*	*3,455*	*3,430*
SURMA VALLEY AND HILL DISTRICTS	*8,647*	*4,326*	*4,321*	...	...	...	*8*	*8*	...	*5*	*5*	...	*16,430*	*8,202*	*8,228*	*6,868*	*3,438*	*3,430*
Cachar	8,235	4,063	4,172	...	...	...	8	8	...	5	5	...	15,305	7,648	7,657	...	...	...
Sylhet	228	153	75	...	...	...	...	...	...	...	...	...	...	...	...	...	...	...
Khasi and Jaintia Hills	114	66	48	...	...	...	...	...	...	...	...	...	...	...	...	...	...	...
Naga Hills	70	44	26	...	...	...	...	...	...	...	...	...	1,125	554	571	6,868	3,438	3,430
Lushai Hills	...	...	...	...	...	...	...	...	...	...	...	...	...	...	...	...	...	...
ASSAM VALLEY DISTRICTS	*252,465*	*126,202*	*126,263*	...	...	...	*3,099*	*1,423*	*1,676*	*946*	*522*	*424*	*53*	*28*	*25*	*17*	*17*	...
Goalpara	92,636	45,893	46,743	...	...	...	...	...	...	...	...	...	...	...	...	...	...	...
Kamrup	91,114	43,602	47,512	...	...	...	...	...	...	...	...	...	...	...	...	...	...	...
Darrang	55,007	28,592	26,415	...	...	...	...	...	...	518	313	205	...	...	...	...	...	...
Nowgong	9,145	4,698	4,447	...	...	...	...	...	...	...	...	...	...	...	...	...	...	...
Sibsagar	2,710	2,114	596	...	...	...	700	280	420	8	8	...	53	28	25	...	...	...
Lakhimpur	729	673	56	...	...	...	2,399	1,143	1,256	420	201	219	...	...	...	17	17	...
Garo Hills	1,124	630	494	...	...	...	...	...	...	...	...	...	...	...	...	...	...	...
(2) Manipur State	*143*	*77*	*66*	*1,298*	*593*	*705*	...	...	...	...	...	...	...	...	...	*1,284*	*705*	*579*

TABLE X.—Language—*continued.*

A.—*VERNACULARS OF INDIA*—continued.

2.—TIBETO-BURMAN—*continued.*

District or State	Garo. Persons.	Garo. Males.	Garo. Females.	Gurung. Persons.	Gurung. Males.	Gurung. Females.	Kabui. Persons.	Kabui. Males.	Kabui. Females.	Kachin or Singpho. Persons.	Kachin or Singpho. Males.	Kachin or Singpho. Females.	Kezhama. Persons.	Kezhama. Males.	Kezhama. Females.	Khairao. Persons.	Khairao. Males.	Khairao. Females.
1	68	69	70	71	72	73	74	75	76	77	78	79	80	81	82	83	84	85
ASSAM	*153,766*	*77,607*	*76,159*	*1,001*	*723*	*278*	*17,230*	*8,178*	*9,052*	*1,880*	*992*	*888*	*5,035*	*2,600*	*2,435*	*1,026*	*495*	*531*
(1) British Territory	*153,766*	*77,607*	*76,159*	*1,001*	*723*	*278*	*18*	*12*	*6*	*1,880*	*992*	*888*	*5,035*	*2,600*	*2,435*	...	...	...
SURMA VALLEY AND HILL DISTRICTS	*6,694*	*3,481*	*3,213*	*677*	*505*	*172*	*18*	*12*	*6*	...	...	...	*5,035*	*2,600*	*2,435*	...	...	...
Cachar	...	...	...	38	27	11	...	...	...	...	...	...	...	...	...	...	...	...
Sylhet	388	189	199	...	...	...	...	...	...	...	...	...	...	...	...	...	...	...
Khasi and Jaintia Hills	6,282	3,274	3,008	480	370	110	...	...	...	...	...	...	...	...	...	...	...	...
Naga Hills	24	18	6	67	46	21	18	12	6	...	...	...	5,035	2,600	2,435	...	...	...
Lushai Hills	...	...	...	92	62	30	...	...	...	...	...	...	...	...	...	...	...	...
ASSAM VALLEY DISTRICTS	*147,072*	*74,126*	*72,946*	*324*	*218*	*106*	...	...	...	*1,880*	*992*	*888*	...	...	...	...	...	...
Goalpara	15,323	7,701	7,622	72	55	17	...	...	...	...	...	...	...	...	...	...	...	...
Kamrup	5,702	2,934	2,768	21	13	8	...	...	...	...	...	...	...	...	...	...	...	...
Darrang	477	251	226	19	13	6	...	...	...	...	...	...	...	...	...	...	...	...
Nowgong	509	275	234	28	22	6	...	...	...	...	...	...	...	...	...	...	...	...
Sibsagar	667	279	388	113	74	39	...	...	...	127	78	49	...	...	...	...	...	...
Lakhimpur	38	9	29	...	...	...	...	...	...	1,753	914	839	...	...	...	...	...	...
Garo Hills	124,356	62,677	61,679	71	41	30	...	...	...	...	...	...	...	...	...	...	...	...
(2) Manipur State	...	...	...	...	...	...	*17,212*	*8,166*	*9,046*	...	...	...	...	...	...	*1,026*	*495*	*531*

A.—*VERNACULARS OF INDIA*—continued.

2.—TIBETO-BURMAN—*continued.*

District or State.	Khambu. Persons.	Khambu. Males.	Khambu. Females.	Koch. Persons.	Koch. Males.	Koch. Females.	Koireng. Persons.	Koireng. Males.	Koireng. Females.	Kom. Persons.	Kom. Males.	Kom. Females.	Kuki (Unspecified). Persons.	Kuki (Unspecified). Males.	Kuki (Unspecified). Females.	Lakher (Lai). Persons.	Lakher (Lai). Males.	Lakher (Lai). Females.
1	86	87	88	89	90	91	92	93	94	95	96	97	98	99	100	101	102	103
ASSAM	*1,320*	*1,058*	*262*	*3,658*	*1,831*	*1,827*	*1,026*	*493*	*533*	*2,087*	*960*	*1,127*	*19,607*	*9,740*	*9,867*	*3,523*	*1,701*	*1,822*
(1) British Territory	*1,320*	*1,058*	*262*	*3,658*	*1,831*	*1,827*	*392*	*195*	*197*	...	...	...	*12,920*	*6,258*	*6,662*	*3,523*	*1,701*	*1,822*
SURMA VALLEY AND HILL DISTRICTS	*181*	*125*	*56*	...	...	...	*392*	*195*	*197*	...	...	...	*12,838*	*6,215*	*6,623*	*3,523*	*1,701*	*1,822*
Cachar	80	46	34	...	...	...	...	...	...	...	...	...	7,784	3,791	3,993	...	...	...
Sylhet	...	...	...	...	...	...	...	...	...	...	...	...	838	363	475	...	...	...
Khasi and Jaintia Hills	4	3	1	...	...	...	392	195	197	...	...	...	1,025	571	454	...	...	...
Naga Hills	97	76	21	...	...	...	...	...	...	...	...	...	3,189	1,490	1,699	...	...	...
Lushai Hills	...	...	...	...	...	...	...	...	...	...	...	...	2	...	2	3,523	1,701	1,822
ASSAM VALLEY DISTRICTS	*1,139*	*933*	*206*	*3,658*	*1,831*	*1,827*	...	...	...	...	...	...	*82*	*43*	*39*	...	...	...
Goalpara	845	725	120	...	...	...	...	...	...	...	...	...	...	...	...	...	...	...
Kamrup	9	7	2	...	...	...	...	...	...	...	...	...	...	...	...	...	...	...
Darrang	104	76	28	...	...	...	...	...	...	...	...	...	...	...	1	...	...	...
Nowgong	8	5	3	...	...	...	...	...	...	...	...	...	7	39	38	...	...	...
Sibsagar	...	...	...	1	1	...	...	...	...	...	...	...	...	4	...	...	...	...
Lakhimpur	166	120	46	...	...	...	...	...	...	...	...	...	...	...	...	...	...	...
Garo Hills	7	...	7	3,657	1,830	1,827	...	...	...	...	...	...	...	...	...	...	...	...
(2) Manipur State	...	...	...	...	...	...	*634*	*298*	*336*	*2,087*	*960*	*1,127*	*6,687*	*3,482*	*3,205*	...	...	...

TABLE X.—LANGUAGE—*continued.*

A.—*VERNACULARS OF INDIA*—continued.

2.—TIBETO-BURMAN—*continued.*

District or State.	Lalung. Persons.	Lalung. Males.	Lalung. Females.	Lhota or Tsontsu. Persons.	Lhota or Tsontsu. Males.	Lhota or Tsontsu. Females.	Limbu. Persons.	Limbu. Males.	Limbu. Females.	Lushai or Dulien. Persons.	Lushai or Dulien. Males.	Lushai or Dulien. Females.	Mangar. Persons.	Mangar. Males.	Mangar. Females.	Manipuri, Meithei, Kathe or Ponnu. Persons.	Manipuri, Meithei, Kathe or Ponnu. Males.	Manipuri, Meithei, Kathe or Ponnu. Females.
1	104	105	106	107	108	109	110	111	112	113	114	115	116	117	118	119	120	121
ASSAM	*12,187*	*5,940*	*6,247*	*19,627*	*9,512*	*10,115*	*1,874*	*1,298*	*576*	*68,826*	*32,042*	*36,784*	*2,745*	*1,817*	*928*	*295,425*	*146,595*	*148,830*
(1) British Territory	*12,187*	*5,940*	*6,247*	*19,627*	*9,512*	*10,115*	*1,874*	*1,298*	*576*	*68,713*	*31,979*	*36,734*	*2,745*	*1,817*	*928*	*83,734*	*42,900*	*40,834*
SURMA VALLEY AND HILL DISTRICTS	*3,389*	*1,659*	*1,730*	*19,600*	*9,493*	*10,107*	*351*	*240*	*111*	*68,713*	*31,979*	*36,734*	*1,301*	*912*	*389*	*82,894*	*42,277*	*40,617*
Cachar	6	4	2	...	...	...	20	13	7	2	...	2	123	88	35	52,367	26,705	25,662
Sylhet	...	...	...	...	...	...	...	...	...	4	4	...	...	...	...	30,082	15,191	14,891
Khasi and Jaintia Hills...	3,382	1,654	1,728	...	...	...	14	9	5	14	14	...	800	569	231	75	41	34
Naga Hills	1	1	...	19,600	9,493	10,107	115	68	47	...	...	...	253	158	95	322	297	25
Lushai Hills	...	...	...	...	...	...	202	150	52	68,693	31,961	36,732	125	97	28	48	43	5
ASSAM VALLEY DISTRICTS	*8,798*	*4,281*	*4,517*	*27*	*19*	*8*	*1,523*	*1,058*	*465*	...	...	...	*1,444*	*905*	*539*	*840*	*623*	*217*
Goalpara	...	...	...	...	...	...	873	668	205	...	...	...	347	221	126	1	1	...
Kamrup	1,015	491	524	...	...	...	72	34	38	...	...	...	240	158	82	83	51	32
Darrang	...	...	...	...	...	...	260	158	102	...	...	...	447	278	169	7	6	1
Nowgong	7,776	3,790	3,986	...	...	...	36	29	7	...	...	...	50	34	16	11	5	6
Sibsagar	3	...	3	27	19	...	40	24	16	...	...	...	93	61	32	507	396	111
Lakhimpur	4	...	4	...	...	...	9	4	5	...	...	...	99	44	55	231	164	67
Garo Hills	...	...	...	...	...	...	233	141	92	...	...	...	168	109	59	...	...	...
(2) Manipur State	...	...	...	...	...	...	...	...	...	*113*	*63*	*50*	...	...	...	*211,691*	*103,695*	*107,906*

A.—*VERNACULARS OF INDIA*—continued.

2.—TIBETO-BURMAN—*continued.*

District or State.	Maram. Persons.	Maram. Males.	Maram. Females.	Maring. Persons.	Maring. Males.	Maring. Females.	Mhar. Persons.	Mhar. Males.	Mhar. Females.	Mikir. Persons.	Mikir. Males.	Mikir. Females.	Miri. Persons.	Miri. Males.	Miri. Females.	Mojung. Persons.	Mojung. Males.	Mojung. Females.
1	122	123	124	125	126	127	128	129	130	131	132	133	134	135	136	137	138	139
ASSAM	*3,259*	*1,593*	*1,666*	*2,674*	*1,294*	*1,380*	*5,430*	*2,476*	*2,954*	*103,063*	*52,766*	*50,297*	*55,647*	*28,262*	*27,385*	*643*	*321*	*322*
(1) British Territory	...	...	...	...	...	...	*3,196*	*1,416*	*1,780*	*103,063*	*52,766*	*50,297*	*55,647*	*28,262*	*27,385*	*643*	*321*	*322*
SURMA VALLEY AND HILL DISTRICTS	...	...	...	...	...	...	*3,196*	*1,416*	*1,780*	*19,211*	*9,941*	*9,270*	*291*	*142*	*149*	*596*	*281*	*315*
Cachar	...	...	...	...	...	...	...	...	...	2,581	1,298	1,283	...	...	...	...	...	...
Sylhet	...	...	...	...	...	...	...	...	...	115	61	54	...	...	...	...	...	...
Khasi and Jaintia Hills	...	...	...	...	...	...	...	...	...	16,511	8,578	7,933	...	...	...	...	...	...
Naga Hills	...	...	...	...	...	...	...	...	...	3	3	...	...	...	...	...	...	...
Lushai Hills	...	...	...	...	...	...	3,196	1,416	1,780	1	1	...	291	142	149	596	281	315
ASSAM VALLEY DISTRICTS	...	...	...	...	...	...	...	...	...	*83,852*	*42,825*	*41,027*	*55,356*	*28,120*	*27,236*	*47*	*40*	*7*
Goalpara	...	...	...	...	...	...	...	...	...	...	...	...	...	...	...	...	...	...
Kamrup	...	...	...	...	...	...	...	...	...	10,508	5,330	5,178	...	...	...	...	...	...
Darrang	...	...	...	...	...	...	...	...	...	3,190	1,676	1,514	4,416	2,233	2,183	...	...	...
Nowgong	...	...	...	...	...	...	...	...	...	45,120	22,936	22,184	...	...	...	...	...	...
Sibsagar	...	...	...	...	...	...	...	...	...	25,030	12,879	12,151	21,949	11,180	10,769	...	...	...
Lakhimpur	...	...	...	...	...	...	...	...	...	4	4	...	28,991	14,707	14,284	47	40	7
Garo Hills	...	...	...	...	...	...	...	...	...	...	...	...	...	...	...	...	...	...
(2) Manipur State	*3,259*	*1,593*	*1,666*	*2,674*	*1,294*	*1,380*	*2,234*	*1,060*	*1,174*	...	...	...	...	...	...	...	...	...

TABLE X.—LANGUAGE—*continued.*

A.—VERNACULARS OF INDIA—*continued.*

2.—TIBETO-BURMAN—*continued.*

District or State.	Murmi. Persons.	Murmi. Males.	Murmi. Females.	Naga unclassed.* Persons.	Naga unclassed.* Males.	Naga unclassed.* Females.	Naga unspecified. Persons.	Naga unspecified. Males.	Naga unspecified. Females.	Newari. Persons.	Newari. Males.	Newari. Females.	Pahri. Persons.	Pahri. Males.	Pahri. Females.	Paite. Persons.	Paite. Males.	Paite. Females.
1	140	141	142	143	144	145	146	147	148	149	150	151	152	153	154	155	156	157
ASSAM	*1,615*	*1,030*	*585*	*2,133*	*1,078*	*1,055*	*14,629*	*7,676*	*6,953*	*831*	*509*	*322*	*1,051*	*571*	*480*	*15,567*	*7,336*	*8,231*
(1) British Territory	*1,615*	*1,030*	*585*	*2,133*	*1,078*	*1,055*	*10,391*	*5,624*	*4,767*	*831*	*509*	*322*	*1,051*	*571*	*480*	*7,239*	*3,016*	*4,223*
SURMA VALLEY AND HILL DISTRICTS	*169*	*91*	*78*	*2,133*	*1,078*	*1,055*	*2,341*	*1,082*	*1,259*	*93*	*64*	*29*	*2*	...	*2*	*7,239*	*3,016*	*4,223*
Cachar	59	33	26	...	...	...	2,226	1,013	1,213	58	38	20	2	...	2	...	...	...
Sylhet	...	...	...	...	...	...	40	28	12	...	...	...	...	...	...	...	...	...
Khasi and Jaintia Hills	2	1	1	...	...	...	15	12	3	6	6	...	...	...	...	...	...	...
Naga Hills	105	55	50	2,133	1,078	1,055	...	...	...	22	15	7	...	...	...	...	...	...
Lushai Hills	3	2	1	...	...	...	60	29	31	7	5	2	...	...	...	7,239	3,016	4,223
ASSAM VALLEY DISTRICTS	*1,446*	*939*	*507*	...	...	...	*8,050*	*4,542*	*3,508*	*738*	*445*	*293*	*1,049*	*571*	*478*	...	...	...
Goalpara	525	304	221	...	...	...	1	1	...	208	136	72	21	11	10	...	...	...
Kamrup	39	23	16	...	...	...	14	12	2	83	48	35	65	31	31	...	...	...
Darrang	243	155	88	...	...	...	25	25	...	221	125	96	3	3	...	...	...	...
Nowgong	11	6	5	...	...	...	9	7	2	63	41	22	...	...	...	...	...	...
Sibsagar	175	130	45	...	...	...	2,806	1,686	1,120	42	19	23	309	179	180	...	...	...
Lakhimpur	419	299	120	...	...	...	5,195	2,811	2,381	48	36	12	651	344	307	...	...	...
Garo Hills	34	22	12	...	...	...	...	...	...	73	40	33	...	...	...	...	...	...
(2) Manipur State	...	...	...	...	...	...	*4,238*	*2,052*	*2,186*	...	...	...	...	...	...	*8,328*	*4,320*	*4,008*

* For details see Appendix II to Table X.

A.—VERNACULARS OF INDIA—*continued.*

2.—TIBETO-BURMAN—*continued.*

District or State.	Purum. Persons.	Purum. Males.	Purum. Females.	Rabha. Persons.	Rabha. Males.	Rabha. Females.	Balte. Persons.	Balte. Males.	Balte. Females.	Rengma. Persons.	Rengma. Males.	Rengma. Females.	Sema. Persons.	Sema. Males.	Sema. Females.	Sokte. Persons.	Sokte. Males.	Sokte. Females.
1	158	159	160	161	162	163	164	165	166	167	168	169	170	171	172	173	174	175
ASSAM	*1,036*	*510*	*526*	*27,995*	*13,925*	*14,070*	*7,493*	*3,405*	*4,088*	*4,389*	*2,025*	*2,364*	*32,922*	*16,366*	*16,556*	*4,221*	*2,163*	*2,058*
(1) British Territory	...	...	...	*27,995*	*13,925*	*14,070*	*4,015*	*1,709*	*2,306*	*4,389*	*2,025*	*2,364*	*32,921*	*16,365*	*16,556*	...	...	...
SURMA VALLEY AND HILL DISTRICTS	...	...	...	*42*	*25*	*17*	*4,015*	*1,709*	*2,306*	*4,367*	*2,015*	*2,352*	*32,851*	*16,319*	*16,532*	...	...	...
Cachar	...	...	...	10	7	3	...	...	...	...	...	...	...	...	...	...	...	...
Sylhet	...	...	...	...	...	...	...	...	...	...	...	...	...	...	...	...	...	...
Khasi and Jaintia Hills	...	...	...	24	11	13	...	...	...	...	...	...	...	...	...	...	...	...
Naga Hills	...	...	...	4	3	1	...	...	...	4,367	2,015	2,352	32,851	16,319	16,632	...	...	...
Lushai Hills	...	...	...	4	4	...	4,015	1,709	2,306	...	...	...	...	...	...	...	...	...
ASSAM VALLEY DISTRICTS	...	...	...	*27,953*	*13,900*	*14,053*	...	...	...	*22*	*10*	*12*	*70*	*46*	*24*	...	...	...
Goalpara	...	...	...	20,169	9,979	10,190	...	...	...	...	...	...	...	...	...	...	...	...
Kamrup	...	...	...	85	48	37	...	...	...	...	...	...	...	...	...	...	...	...
Darrang	...	...	...	43	35	8	...	...	...	...	...	...	...	...	...	...	...	...
Nowgong	...	...	...	2	2	...	...	...	...	...	...	...	...	...	...	...	...	...
Sibsagar	...	...	...	5	4	1	...	...	...	22	10	12	70	46	24	...	...	...
Lakhimpur	...	...	...	...	...	...	...	...	...	...	...	...	...	...	...	...	...	...
Garo Hills	...	...	...	7,649	3,832	3,817	...	...	...	...	...	...	...	...	...	...	...	...
(2) Manipur State	*1,06*	*510*	*526*	...	...	...	*3,478*	*1,696*	*1,782*	...	...	...	*1*	*1*	..	*4,221*	*2,163*	*2,058*

TABLE X.—LANGUAGE—*continued.*

District or State.	A.—VERNACULARS OF INDIA—*continued.* 2.—TIBETO-BURMAN—*continued.* Sopvoma. Persons.	Sopvoma. Males.	Sopvoma. Females.	Tamlu. Persons.	Tamlu. Males.	Tamlu. Females.	Tangkhul. Persons.	Tangkhul. Males.	Tangkhul. Females.	Thado or Jangshen. Persons.	Thado or Jangshen. Males.	Thado or Jangshen. Females.	Tipura or Mrung. Persons.	Tipura or Mrung. Males.	Tipura or Mrung. Females.
1	176	177	178	179	180	181	182	183	184	185	186	187	188	189	190
ASSAM	***10,100***	***5,287***	***4,813***	***1,998***	***940***	***1,058***	***27,285***	***12,868***	***14,417***	***26,571***	***13,030***	***13,541***	***9,676***	***4,917***	***4,759***
(1) British Territory	...	...	...	***1,998***	***940***	***1,058***	***13***	***13***	...	***116***	***51***	***65***	***9,676***	***4,917***	***4,759***
SURMA VALLEY AND HILL DISTRICTS	...	...	...	***1,899***	***873***	***1,026***	...	...	...	***116***	***51***	***65***	***9,534***	***4,846***	***4,688***
Cachar	...	...	...	...	...	...	...	...	...	...	...	...	**828**	418	410
Sylhet	...	...	...	...	...	...	...	...	...	...	...	...	**8,121**	4,110	4,011
Khasi and Jaintia Hills	...	...	...	...	...	...	...	...	...	...	...	...	...	...	...
Naga Hills	...	...	...	**1,899**	873	1,026	...	...	...	...	...	...	...	...	...
Lushai Hills	...	...	...	...	...	...	...	...	...	**116**	51	65	**585**	318	267
ASSAM VALLEY DISTRICTS	...	...	...	***99***	***67***	***32***	***13***	***13***	...	...	...	...	***142***	***71***	***71***
Goalpara	...	...	...	...	...	...	...	...	...	...	...	...	...	...	...
Kamrup	...	...	...	...	...	...	...	...	...	...	...	...	...	...	...
Darrang	...	...	...	...	...	...	...	...	...	...	...	...	...	...	...
Nowgong	...	...	...	...	...	...	...	...	...	...	...	...	**142**	71	71
Sibsagar	...	...	...	**99**	67	32	**13**	13	...	...	...	...	...	...	...
Lakhimpur	...	...	...	...	...	...	...	...	...	...	...	...	...	...	...
Garo Hills	...	...	...	...	...	...	...	...	...	...	...	...	...	...	...
(2) Manipur State	***10,100***	***5,287***	***4,813***	...	...	...	***27,272***	***12,855***	***14,417***	***26,455***	***12,979***	***13,476***	...	...	...

District or State.	A.—VERNACULARS OF INDIA—continued. 2.—TIBETO-BURMAN—*concluded.* Vaiphei. Persons.	Vaiphei. Males.	Vaiphei. Females.	3.—SIAMESE-CHINESE. Khamti. Persons.	Khamti. Males.	Khamti. Females.	Shan. Persons.	Shan. Males.	Shan. Females.	4.—MON-KHMER. Khasi. Persons.	Khasi. Males.	Khasi. Females.	5.—MUNDA. Bhumij. Persons.	Bhumij. Males.	Bhumij. Females.
1	191	192	193	194	195	196	197	198	199	200	201	202	203	204	205
ASSAM	***2,303***	***1,035***	***1,268***	***2,063***	***1,142***	***921***	***1,029***	***541***	***488***	***200,802***	***94,418***	***106,384***	***5,342***	***2,668***	***2,674***
(1) British Territory	...	...	...	***2,063***	***1,142***	***921***	***1,029***	***541***	***488***	***200,795***	***94,417***	***106,378***	***5,342***	***2,668***	***2,674***
SURMA VALLEY AND HILL DISTRICTS	...	...	...	***17***	***17***	...	...	...	...	***199,993***	***93,962***	***106,031***	***274***	***122***	***152***
Cachar	...	...	...	**17**	17	...	...	...	...	**559**	303	256	**175**	70	105
Sylhet	...	...	...	...	...	...	...	...	...	**3,318**	1,651	1,667	**99**	52	47
Khasi and Jaintia Hills	...	...	...	...	...	...	...	...	...	**196,017**	91,942	104,075	...	...	...
Naga Hills	...	...	...	...	...	...	...	...	...	**44**	27	17	...	...	...
Lushai Hills	...	...	...	...	...	...	...	...	...	**55**	39	16	...	...	...
ASSAM VALLEY DISTRICTS	...	...	...	***2,046***	***1,125***	***921***	***1,029***	***541***	***488***	***802***	***455***	***347***	***5,068***	***2,546***	***2,522***
Goalpara	...	...	...	...	...	...	...	...	...	**4**	1	3	**5**	5	...
Kamrup	...	...	...	...	...	...	...	...	...	**594**	356	238	**3**	2	1
Darrang	...	...	...	**26**	26	...	**21**	21	...	**37**	23	14	**1,427**	768	650
Nowgong	...	...	...	...	...	...	...	...	...	**68**	34	34	**22**	11	11
Sibsagar	...	...	...	**110**	94	16	**1,000**	518	482	**19**	7	12	**3,292**	1,648	1,644
Lakhimpur	...	...	...	**1,910**	1,005	905	**8**	2	6	**76**	30	46	**319**	112	207
Garo Hills	...	...	...	...	...	...	...	...	...	**4**	4	...	...	...	...
(2) Manipur State	***2,303***	***1,035***	***1,268***	...	...	...	...	...	...	***7***	***1***	***6***	...	...	...

TABLE X.—LANGUAGE—continued.

A.—VERNACULARS OF INDIA—continued.

5.—MUNDA—continued.

District or State.	Kharia. Persons.	Kharia. Males.	Kharia. Females.	Korwa. Persons.	Korwa. Males.	Korwa. Females.	Kurku. Persons.	Kurku. Males.	Kurku. Females.	Mundari. Persons.	Mundari. Males.	Mundari. Females.	Santali. Persons.	Santali. Males.	Santali. Females.
1	206	207	208	209	210	211	212	213	214	215	216	217	218	219	220
ASSAM	*4,718*	*2,848*	*1,870*	*775*	*365*	*410*	*1,990*	*1,206*	*784*	*72,836*	*37,093*	*35,743*	*54,173*	*27,968*	*26,205*
(1) British Territory	*4,718*	*2,848*	*1,870*	*775*	*365*	*410*	*1,990*	*1,206*	*784*	*72,836*	*37,093*	*35,743*	*54,173*	*27,968*	*26,205*
SURMA VALLEY AND HILL DISTRICTS	*86*	*40*	*46*	*85*	*46*	*39*	*166*	*92*	*74*	*7,429*	*3,945*	*3,484*	*8,793*	*4.712*	*4,081*
Cachar	86	40	46	36	20	16	124	72	52	3.757	1,935	1,822	3 982	2,073	1,009
Sylhet	...	...	...	48	25	23	42	20	22	3,666	2,008	1,658	4.681	2,509	3,172
Khasi and Jaintia Hills	...	...	...	...	...	...	...	...	...	2	...	2	...	...	...
Naga Hills	...	...	...	1	1	...	...	...	...	4	2	2	...	...	...
Lushai Hills	...	...	...	...	...	...	...	...	...	...	...	...	130	130	...
ASSAM VALLEY DISTRICTS	*4,632*	*2,808*	*1.824*	*690*	*310*	*371*	*1,824*	*1,114*	*710*	*65,407*	*33,148*	*32,259*	*45,380*	*23,256*	*22,124*
Goalpara	...	...	...	...	...	...	...	...	...	124	67	57	8,687	4,733	3,954
Kamrup	...	...	...	...	...	...	...	...	...	474	239	235	461	250	211
Darrang	668	313	355	631	295	336	58	29	29	14.961	7,676	7,285	6,121	3,238	2,883
Nowgong	329	175	154	15	8	7	155	87	68	3 417	1,709	1,708	2,241	1,158	1,083
Sibsagar	562	284	278	19	9	10	205	98	107	13,912	7,082	6,830	14.469	7,437	7,032
Lakhimpur	3,073	2,036	1,037	25	7	18	1.406	900	506	32,519	16,375	16,144	13,401	6,440	6,961
Garo Hills	...	...	...	...	...	...	...	...	...	...	...	...	...	...	...
(2) Manipur State	...	...	...	...	...	...	...	...	...	...	...	...	...	...	...

A.—VERNACULARS OF INDIA—continued.

5.—MUNDA—concluded. / 6.—DRAVIDIAN.

District or State.	Savara. Persons.	Savara. Males.	Savara. Females.	Turi. Persons.	Turi. Males.	Turi. Females.	Gond. Persons.	Gond. Males.	Gond. Females.	Kandh or Kui. Persons.	Kandh or Kui. Males.	Kandh or Kui. Females.	Kurukh or Oraon. Persons.	Kurukh or Oraon. Males.	Kurukh or Oraon. Females.	Tamil. Persons.	Tamil. Males.	Tamil. Females.
1	221	222	223	224	225	226	227	228	229	230	231	232	233	234	235	236	237	238
ASSAM	*503*	*294*	*209*	*2,396*	*1,251*	*1,145*	*10,306*	*5,380*	*4,926*	*3,966*	*1,885*	*2,081*	*19,813*	*10,706*	*9,107*	*738*	*455*	*283*
(1) British Territory	*503*	*294*	*209*	*2,396*	*1,251*	*1,145*	*103 06*	*5,380*	*4,926*	*3,966*	*1,885*	*2,081*	*19,813*	*10,706*	*9,107*	*738*	*455*	*283*
SURMA VALLEY AND HILL DISTRICTS	*118*	*59*	*59*	*58*	*32*	*26*	*604*	*295*	*309*	*158*	*82*	*76*	*1,974*	*1,019*	*955*	*465*	*234*	*231*
Cachar	...	...	...	18	10	8	537	265	272	1	...	1	1,645	850	795	40	20	20
Sylhet	...	...	...	40	22	18	51	22	29	157	82	75	328	168	160	417	208	200
Khasi and Jaintia Hills	118	59	59	...	...	...	...	...	...	...	...	...	...	...	...	8	6	2
Naga Hills	...	...	...	...	...	...	16	8	8	...	...	...	1	1	...	...	...	...
Lushai Hills	...	...	...	...	...	...	...	...	...	...	...	...	...	...	...	...	...	...
ASSAM VALLEY DISTRICTS	*385*	*235*	*150*	*2,338*	*1,219*	*1,119*	*9,702*	*5,085*	*4,617*	*3,808*	*1,803*	*2,005*	*17,839*	*9,687*	*8,152*	*273*	*221*	*52*
Goalpara	...	...	...	...	...	...	1	1	...	...	...	...	127	74	53	...	...	...
Kamrup	...	...	...	...	...	...	...	...	...	...	...	...	86	47	39	...	...	...
Darrang	18	10	8	125	60	65	3,722	1,969	1,753	2,402	1,224	1,178	6 101	3,172	2,929	25	9	16
Nowgong	...	...	...	235	127	108	118	60	58	3	3	...	1 600	829	771	1	1	...
Sibsagar	7	...	7	1,972	1,031	941	3,115	1,538	1,577	175	97	78	2 636	1,333	1,303	...	...	...
Lakhimpur	360	225	135	6	1	5	2,746	1,517	1,229	1,226	479	740	7,287	4,232	3,055	247	211	36
Garo Hills	...	...	...	...	...	...	...	...	...	...	...	...	2	...	2	...	...	...
(2) Manipur State	...	...	...	...	...	...	...	...	...	...	...	...	...	...	...	...	...	...

TABLE X.—LANGUAGE—*concld.*

District or State.	A.—VERNACULARS OF INDIA—concld. 6.—DRAVIDIAN—concluded. Telugu or Andhra.			C.—EUROPEAN LANGUAGES. English.			C.—EUROPEAN LANGUAGES. Welsh.			OTHERS. (For details see Appendix I on following page.)		
	Persons.	Males.	Females.	Persons.	Males.	Females.	Persons.	Males.	Females.	Persons.	Males.	Females.
1	239	240	241	242	243	244	245	246	247	248	249	250
ASSAM	***20,750***	***11,076***	***9,674***	***2,606***	***1,814***	***792***	***3***	...	***3***	***5,831***	***3,634***	***2,197***
(1) British Territory	***20,742***	***11,072***	***9,670***	***2,569***	***1,780***	***780***	***3***	...	***3***	***4,598***	***2,976***	***1,622***
SURMA VALLEY AND HILL DISTRICTS	***4,472***	***2,199***	***2,273***	***1,121***	***736***	***385***	***3***	...	***3***	***1,545***	***968***	***577***
Cachar	1,310	677	633	271	193	78	...	...	...	218	143	75
Sylhet	3,142	1,508	1,634	478	342	136	...	...	...	428	269	159
Khasi and Jaintia Hills	12	8	4	310	159	151	3	...	3	93	74	19
Naga Hills	1	1	...	31	22	9	...	...	...	588	296	292
Lushai Hills	7	5	2	31	20	11	...	...	...	218	186	32
ASSAM VALLEY DISTRICTS	***16,970***	***8,873***	***7,397***	***1,448***	***1,053***	***395***	...	...	...	***3,053***	***2,008***	***1,045***
Goalpara	12	9	3	55	35	20	...	...	...	219	137	82
Kamrup	23	16	7	160	101	59	...	...	...	244	170	74
Darrang	3,812	2,122	1,690	215	162	53	...	...	...	214	160	54
Nowgong	560	305	255	118	77	41	...	...	...	21	20	1
Sibsagar	6,509	3,364	3,145	401	299	102	...	...	...	1,001	665	336
Lakhimpur	5,354	3,057	2,297	489	373	116	...	...	...	1,206	761	445
Garo Hills	...	...	...	10	6	4	...	...	...	148	95	53
(2) Manipur State...	***8***	***4***	***4***	***37***	***25***	***12***	...	...	...	***1,233***	***653***	***575***

TABLE X.

APPENDIX I.—*DETAILS OF LANGUAGES INCLUDED IN THE HEAD "OTHERS."*

Language.	Provincial Total. Persons.	Males.	Females.	Distribution.
1	2	3	4	5
A.—VERNACULARS OF INDIA—				
1.—Aryan—				
Baloch	109	96	13	Khasi and Jaintia Hills (22+1), Lakhimpur (74+12).
Central Pahari	70	68	2	Naga Hills (10+2), Lushai Hills (4+0), Sibsagar (54+0).
Gujrati	306	238	68	Cachar (36+6), Sylhet (24+0), Khasi and Jaintia Hills (20+9), Naga Hills (1+0), Goalpara (12+10), Kamrup (86+19), Darrang (6+2), Nowgong (1+0), Sibsagar (47+21), Lakhimpur (5+1).
Kashmiri	10	7	3	Sylhet.
Lahnda or Western Paujabi ...	2	2	...	Kamrup.
2.—Tibeto-Burman—				
Aimol	416	224	192	Manipur State.
Aka	35	34	1	Darrang.
Banjogi	2	2	...	Nowgong.
Bete	229	99	130	Naga Hills.
Burmese	151	87	64	Cachar (3+0), Sylhet (2+1), Naga Hills (1+0), Lushai Hills (1+1), Goalpara (1+0), Kamrup (23+9), Lakhimpur (1+0), Garo Hills 53+50), Manipur State (2+3).
Chote	193	134	59	Lushai Hills (4+9), Manipur State (130+50).
Dhimal	100	58	42	Cachar.
Hallam	367	218	149	Sylhet.
Hiroi-Lamgang	136	66	70	Manipur State.
Janggali	189	93	96	Lakhimpur.
Jimdar	48	38	10	Sibsagar.
Kami	111	63	48	Goalpara (24+28), Darrang (3+4), Sibsagar (13+3), Lakhimpur, (23+13).
Khami, Khweymi or Kumi ...	51	27	24	Cachar.
Kwoireng	369	176	193	Manipur State.
Manjhi	64	48	16	Goalpara (19+2), Kamrup (3+2), Darrang (4+0), Sibsagar (2+3), Lakhimpur (17+7), Garo Hills (3+2).
Mishmi	255	147	108	Lakhimpur.
Moran	24	6	18	Khasi and Jaintia Hills (0+1), Sibsagar (6+17).
Mru	43	33	10	Sylhet (1+0), Lushai Hills (32+10).
Namsangia	7	5	2	Sibsagar.
Rong or Lepcha	10	10	...	Goalpara (5+0), Nowgong (5+0).
Sunvar	52	38	14	Cachar (5+1), Lushai Hills (7+0), Goalpara (23+12), Darrang (3+1).
Tableng	299	163	136	Naga Hills (105+103), Sibsagar (58+33).
Tarau	100	51	49	Manipur State.
Tengsa	4	2	2	Naga Hills.
Thami	42	25	17	Cachar (5+0), Darrang (19+16), Sibsagar (1+1).
Toto	3	3	...	Sibsagar.
Yachumi	132	77	55	Naga Hills.
Yakha	390	336	54	Lushai Hills (138+12), Goalpara (89+29), Kamrup (0+3), Darrang (31+9), Sibsagar (79+0), Lakhimpur (10+0), Garo Hills (39+1).
3.—Siamese-Chinese—				
Aiton	412	233	179	Sibsagar.
Kob	27	9	18	Manipur State.
Phakial	361	182	179	Sibsagar (0+4), Lakhimpur (182+175).
4.—Mon-Khmer—				
Mon, Talaing or Peguan ...	1	1	...	Kamrup.
Wa	6	5	1	Sibsagar.
5.—Munda—				
Asuri	135	67	68	Darrang (12+16), Nowgong (1+0), Sibsagar (40+32), Lakhimpur (14+20).
Ho or Kol	122	76	46	Kamrup (41+40), Sibsagar (0+1), Lakhimpur (35+5).
Kora (Koda)	68	47	21	Nowgong (0+1), Sibsagar (46+20), Lakhimpur (1+0).
6.—Dravidian—				
Kanarese	5	4	1	Kamrup.
Kota	9	6	3	Sibsagar.
7.—Semitic—				
Arabic	17	17	...	Cachar (1+0), Sylhet (3+0), Goalpara (2+0), Darrang (1+0), Nowgong (1+0), Lakhimpur (9+0).
Unclassed Gipsy languages ...	3	3	...	Sibsagar.
B.—VERNACULARS OF ASIATIC COUNTRIES BEYOND INDIA—				
Armenian	1	1	...	Goalpara.
Chinese	244	237	7	Cachar (5+0), Sylhet (2+1), Khasi and Jaintia Hills (14+0), Naga Hills (1+0), Goalpara (2+0), Kamrup (2+0), Darrang (44+3), Nowgong (6+0), Sibsagar (13+0), Lakhimpur (148+3).
Mungi	4	4	...	Kamrup.
Persian	46	36	10	Cachar (3+2), Sylhet (4+3), Khasi and Jaintia Hills (3+0), Goalpara (5+0), Kamrup (4+0), Darrang (1+0), Nowgong (1+0), Sibsagar (13+4), Lakhimpur (2+1).
C.—EUROPEAN LANGUAGES—				
Danish	3	2	1	Goalpara.
French	2	...	2	Sibsagar.
German	20	8	12	Sylhet (4+0), Khasi and Jaintia Hills (2+8), Darrang (2+2), Lakhimpur (0+2).
Greek	2	2	...	Goalpara.
Portuguese	24	20	4	Sylhet (4+2), Khasi and Jaintia Hills (13+0), Nowgong (3+0), Lakhimpur (0+2).
TOTAL	*5,831*	*3,634*	*2,197*	

APPENDIX II.

NAGA UNCLASSED INCLUDES—	Males.	Females.
(1) Singtam	82	89
(2) Mongnyu	48	39
(3) Wanching	130	150
(4) Pullami	604	596
(5) Sohema	147	146
(6) Memi Naga	5	...
(7) Laphomi	1	...
(8) Temimi	60	34
(9) Yapi	1	1
TOTAL	*1,078*	*1,055*

TABLE XI.

BIRTHPLACE.

THIS Table contains the statistics of birthplace for the Province as a whole and for each District and Manipur State. In column 1 the birthplaces are arranged as follows:—

A. India { I. Assam.
II. Provinces or States beyond Assam—
(*a*) Adjacent Provinces or States.
(*b*) Non-adjacent Provinces or States.
(*c*) French and Portuguese Settlements.
(*d*) India unspecified.

B. Other Asiatic Countries.

C. Europe.

D. Africa.

E. America.

F. Australasia.

G. The Sea.

TABLE X.—LANGUAGE—*continued*.

TABLE XI.—BIRTHPLACE.—DISTRICTS AND STATES.

Birthplace.	District or State where enumerated.														
	Province.			Cachar.			Sylhet.			Khasi and Jaintia Hills.			Naga Hills.		
	Persons.	Males.	Females.	Persons.	Males.	Females.	Persons.	Males.	Females.	Persons.	Males.	Females.	Persons.	Males.	Females.
1	2	3	4	5	6	7	8	9	10	11	12	13	14	15	16
TOTAL POPULATION	*7,059,857*	*3,638,287*	*3,421,570*	*497,463*	*260,444*	*237,019*	*2,472,671*	*1,268,469*	*1,204,202*	*235,069*	*114,442*	*120,627*	*149,623*	*74,751*	*74,872*
A.—BORN IN INDIA	*7,008,907*	*3,603,632*	*3,405,275*	*496,173*	*259,416*	*236,757*	*2,471,952*	*1,267,870*	*1,204,082*	*231,888*	*111,927*	*119,961*	*148,651*	*74,028*	*74,623*
I.—BORN IN ASSAM	*6,177,789*	*3,139,115*	*3,038,674*	*413,943*	*215,379*	*198,564*	*2,315,153*	*1,182,570*	*1,132,583*	*228,130*	*109,048*	*119,082*	*147,876*	*73,394*	*74,482*
(1) British Territory	*5,835,472*	*2,970,763*	*2,864,709*	*412,669*	*214,511*	*198,158*	*2,314,617*	*1,182,150*	*1,132,467*	*228,005*	*108,975*	*119,030*	*147,373*	*73,022*	*74,351*
SURMA VALLEY AND HILL DISTRICTS ...	*3,200,989*	*1,625,723*	*1,575,266*	*412,155*	*214,103*	*198,052*	*2,314,139*	*1,181,804*	*1,132,335*	*225,751*	*107,724*	*118,027*	*146,911*	*72,643*	*74,268*
Cachar	395,188	201,605	193,583	336.956	196,904	190,052	4,030	2,230	1,800	728	361	307	815	367	448
Sylhet	2,337,342	1,198,752	1,138,590	24,284	16,695	7,589	2,309,215	1,178,948	1,130,267	1.384	1,129	255	30	22	8
Khasi and Jaintia Hills	226,810	108,152	118,658	611	340	271	890	622	268	223,558	106,176	117,382	52	29	93
Naga Hills	154,048	76,838	77,210	245	133	112	...	...	...	66	44	22	146,009	72,221	73,788
Lushai Hills	87,601	40,376	47,225	59	31	28	4	4	...	15	14	1	5	4	1
ASSAM VALLEY DISTRICTS	*2,634,483*	*1,345,040*	*1,289,443*	*514*	*408*	*106*	*478*	*346*	*132*	*2,254*	*1,251*	*1,003*	*462*	*379*	*83*
Goalpara	495,053	253,058	241,995	96	78	18	104	07	7	155	98	57	228	211	17
Kamrup	654,721	331,648	323,073	126	102	24	228	169	59	684	414	270	35	30	5
Darrang	258,721	132,363	126,358	22	15	7	43	27	16	13	8	5	...	...	...
Nowgong	278,309	138,847	139,462	84	60	24	35	20	15	678	343	335	81	53	28
Sibsagar	519,570	270,507	249,063	92	71	21	40	20	20	31	16	15	82	59	23
Lakhimpur	278,437	142,754	135,683	94	82	12	20	8	12	43	21	22	25	18	7
Garo Hills	148,748	75,309	73,439	...	...	...	8	5	3	650	351	299	11	8	3
Tribal areas beyond the inner line	924	554	370	...	...	...	...	...	...	...	...	...	...	...	...
(2) Manipur State	*341,786*	*167,932*	*173,854*	*1,243*	*849*	*394*	*76*	*44*	*32*	*113*	*63*	*50*	*503*	*372*	*131*
ASSAM UNSPECIFIED	*531*	*420*	*111*	*31*	*19*	*12*	*460*	*376*	*84*	*12*	*10*	*2*	...	...	...

TABLE XI.—Birthplace.—Districts and States—*continued.*

Birthplace.	Lushai Hills. Persons.	Lushai Hills. Males.	Lushai Hills. Females.	Goalpara. Persons.	Goalpara. Males.	Goalpara. Females.	Kamrup. Persons.	Kamrup. Males.	Kamrup. Females.	Darrang. Persons.	Darrang. Males.	Darrang. Females.	Nowgong. Persons.	Nowgong. Males.	Nowgong. Females.
	District or State where enumerated.														
1	17	18	19	20	21	22	23	24	25	26	27	28	29	30	31
TOTAL POPULATION	*91,204*	*43,028*	*48,176*	*600,643*	*318,475*	*282,168*	*667,828*	*339,398*	*328,430*	*377,314*	*198,581*	*178,733*	*303,596*	*154,938*	*148,658*
A.—BORN IN INDIA	*89,721*	*41,806*	*47,915*	*594,600*	*314,063*	*280,537*	*662,996*	*336,146*	*326,850*	*363,728*	*190,364*	*173,364*	*301,230*	*153,287*	*147,943*
I.—BORN IN ASSAM	*86,138*	*39,845*	*46,293*	*488,941*	*248,853*	*240,088*	*643,149*	*321,457*	*321,692*	*271,992*	*140,849*	*131,143*	*271,614*	*136,164*	*135,450*
(1) British Territory	*4,983*	*39,302*	*45,681*	*488,940*	*248,852*	*240,088*	*643,125*	*321,443*	*321,682*	*271,975*	*140,839*	*131,136*	*271,602*	*136,159*	*135,443*
SURMA VALLEY AND HILL DISTRICTS ...	*84,932*	*39,263*	*45,669*	*229*	*160*	*69*	*1,016*	*681*	*335*	*404*	*274*	*130*	*2,804*	*1,664*	*1,140*
Cachar	430	304	126	12	6	6	67	50	17	36	17	19	744	464	280
Sylhet	139	124	15	167	125	42	371	287	84	268	199	69	392	324	68
Khasi and Jaintia Hills	128	124	14	28	17	11	522	308	214	34	24	10	579	311	268
Naga Hills	3	3	...	18	11	7	54	35	19	59	28	31	1,088	564	524
Lushai Hills	84,222	38,708	45,514	4	1	3	2	1	1	7	6	1	1	1	...
ASSAM VALLEY DISTRICTS	*51*	*39*	*12*	*488,711*	*248,692*	*240,019*	*642,109*	*320,762*	*321,347*	*271,571*	*140,565*	*131,006*	*268,798*	*134,495*	*134,303*
Goalpara	42	31	11	482,410	244,825	237,585	3,185	2,040	1,145	1,219	973	246	727	463	264
Kamrup	4	3	1	4,209	2,622	1,587	636,255	317,300	318,955	5,548	4,148	1,400	1,550	1,299	251
Darrang	...	...	...	112	62	50	771	364	407	256,409	130,883	125,[illegible]	632	381	251
Nowgong	3	3	...	58	35	23	1,319	674	645	5,567	2,737	2,830	264,630	131,659	132,971
Sibsagar	1	1	...	68	44	24	289	200	89	1,994	1,065	929	1,024	541	483
Lakhimpur	1	1	...	86	71	15	182	116	66	991	583	408	197	133	64
Garo Hills	...	...	...	1,768	1,033	735	108	68	40	76	61	15	38	19	19
Tribal areas beyond the inner line	...	...	...	...	...	...	...	...	...	167	115	52	...	...	...
(2) Manipur State	*1,150*	*538*	*612*	*1*	*1*	...	*24*	*14*	*10*	*12*	*8*	*4*	*12*	*5*	*7*
ASSAM UNSPECIFIED	*5*	*5*	...	...	...	...	...	...	...	*5*	*2*	*3*	...	...	...

TABLE XI.—Birthplace.—Districts and States—*continued.*

Birthplace.	Sibsagar. Persons.	Sibsagar. Males.	Sibsagar. Females.	Lakhimpur. Persons.	Lakhimpur. Males.	Lakhimpur. Females.	Garo Hills. Persons.	Garo Hills. Males.	Garo Hills. Females.	Manipur. Persons.	Manipur. Males.	Manipur. Females.
	District or State where Enumerated.											
1	32	33	34	35	36	37	38	39	40	41	42	43
TOTAL POPULATION	*690,299*	*364,810*	*325,489*	*468,989*	*249,021*	*219,968*	*158,936*	*81,264*	*77,672*	*346,222*	*170,666*	*175,556*
A.—BORN IN INDIA	*685,973*	*361,822*	*324,151*	*459,362*	*242,639*	*216,730*	*157,592*	*80,384*	*77,208*	*345,041*	*169,887*	*175,154*
I.—BORN IN ASSAM	*530,242*	*278,123*	*252,119*	*285,953*	*148,269*	*137,684*	*151,654*	*76,919*	*74,735*	*343,004*	*168,245*	*174,759*
(1) British Territory	*529,930*	*277,845*	*252,085*	*285,823*	*148,163*	*137,660*	*151,654*	*76,919*	*74,735*	*4,776*	*2,583*	*2,193*
SURMA VALLEY AND HILL DISTRICTS ...	*6,954*	*4,131*	*2,823*	*845*	*673*	*172*	*166*	*90*	*76*	*4,683*	*2,513*	*2,170*
Cachar	148	101	47	100	83	17	8	4	4	1,114	714	400
Sylhet	574	479	95	396	321	75	31	23	8	91	76	15
Khasi and Jaintia Hills	79	38	41	136	70	66	126	62	64	57	31	26
Nága Hills	6,153	3,513	2,640	212	198	14	1	1	...	140	87	53
Lushai Hills	...	...	...	1	1	...	...	...	...	3,281	1,605	1,676
ASSAM VALLEY DISTRICTS	*522,976*	*273,714*	*249,262*	*284,978*	*147,490*	*137,488*	*151,488*	*76,829*	*74,659*	*93*	*70*	*23*
Goalpara	918	693	225	648	529	119	5,313	3,012	2,301	8	8	...
Kamrup	3,953	3,624	329	2,047	1,875	172	55	40	15	27	22	5
Darrang	464	281	183	651	338	313	1	1	...	3	3	...
Nowgong	5,369	2,957	2,412	471	302	169	2	...	2	12	4	8
Sibsagar	507,089	263,289	243,800	8,826	5,172	3,654	4	3	1	30	26	4
Lakhimpur	5,154	2,852	2,302	271,571	138,831	132,740	60	31	29	13	7	6
Garo Hills	29	18	11	7	4	3	146,053	73,742	72,311	...	...	...
Tribal areas beyond the inner line	...	...	...	757	439	318	...	...	...	...	...	...
(2) Manipur State	*312*	*278*	*34*	*113*	*99*	*14*	...	...	...	*338,227*	*165,661*	*172,566*
ASSAM UNSPECIFIED	...	...	...	*17*	*7*	*10*	...	...	...	*1*	*1*	...

TABLE XI.—Birthplace.—Districts and States—*continued.*

Birthplace.	District or State where enumerated.														
	Province.			Cachar.			Sylhet.			Khasi and Jaintia Hills.			Naga Hills.		
	Persons.	Males.	Females.	Persons.	Males.	Females.	Persons.	Males.	Females.	Persons.	Males.	Females.	Persons.	Males.	Females.
1	2	3	4	5	6	7	8	9	10	11	12	13	14	15	16
II.—BORN IN OTHER PARTS OF INDIA ...	*831,118*	*464,517*	*366,601*	*82,230*	*44,037*	*38,193*	*156,799*	*85,300*	*71,499*	*3,758*	*2,879*	*879*	*775*	*634*	*141*
(a) Provinces and States adjacent to Assam ...	*196,174*	*111,799*	*84,375*	*12,835*	*6,921*	*5,914*	*51,203*	*29,391*	*21,882*	*1,324*	*873*	*451*	*214*	*126*	*88*
(1) *British Territory*	*194,211*	*110,770*	*83,441*	*12,818*	*6,906*	*5,912*	*50,917*	*29,205*	*21,712*	*1,319*	*871*	*448*	*214*	*126*	*88*
1. *Bengal*	*191,912*	*109,658*	*82,254*	*12,814*	*6,902*	*5,912*	*50,906*	*29,200*	*21,706*	*1,311*	*867*	*444*	*214*	*126*	*88*
(i) *Contiguous Districts*	*94,036*	*51,643*	*42,393*	*789*	*530*	*259*	*32,611*	*17,056*	*15,555*	*143*	*98*	*45*	*6*	*4*	*2*
Jalpaiguri	1 869	1,025	844	...	...	...	6	4	2	2	2	...	1	...	1
Rangpur	16 692	9,430	7,262	9	7	2	235	222	13	7	4	3	1	1	...
Mymensingh	58 368	32,416	25,952	196	144	52	17,218	9,240	7,976	78	56	22	2	2	...
Tippera	16 303	8,347	7,956	584	379	205	15,153	7,589	7,564	56	36	20	2	1	1
Chittagong Hill Tracts	804	425	379	...	...	...	1	1	...	...	...	...	...	...	...
(ii) *Other Districts*	*97,876*	*58,015*	*39,861*	*12,025*	*6,372*	*5,53*	*18,295*	*12,144*	*6,151*	*1,168*	*769*	*399*	*208*	*122*	*86*
2. *Burma*	*2,299*	*1,112*	*1,187*	*4*	*4*	...	*1*	*5*	*6*	*8*	*4*	*4*	...	...	...
Contiguous District—Chin Hills ...	2,174	1,040	1,134	...	...	...	...	...	...	...	...	...	...	...	...
Other Districts	125	72	53	4	4	...	11	5	6	8	4	4	...	...	...
(2) *Feudatory States (Bengal)* ...	*1,963*	*1,029*	*934*	*17*	*15*	*2*	*286*	*116*	*170*	*5*	*2*	*3*	...	...	...
Cooch Behar	1.677	912	765	7	5	2	21	15	6	2	2	...	...	...	...
Hill Tippera	286	117	169	10	10	...	265	101	164	3	...	3	...	...	...
(b) Other Provinces and States in India ...	*634,833*	*352,659*	*282,174*	*69,392*	*37,113*	*32,279*	*105,560*	*55,966*	*49,594*	*2,416*	*1,995*	*421*	*560*	*507*	*53*
(1) *British Territory*	*603,008*	*333,044*	*269,964*	*68,231*	*36,507*	*31,724*	*103,171*	*54,678*	*48,493*	*2,170*	*1,788*	*382*	*481*	*439*	*42*
Ajmere-Merwara	46	22	24	15	8	7	12	1	11	2	2	...	1	1	...
Andamans and Nicobars ...	6	3	3	2	...	2	2	2	...	...	...	...	...	...	...
Bihar and Orissa	393,201	217,894	175,307	36,665	19,356	17,299	37,799	20,966	16,833	1,081	969	112	80	75	5
Baluchistan (Districts and Administered Territories).	190	164	26	20	20	...	...	...	...	...	...	...	...	...	...
Bombay (including Aden) ...	853	657	196	54	37	17	68	56	12	45	36	9	3	...	3
Central Provinces and Berar ...	72,491	36,975	35,516	11,566	5,805	5,761	9,770	4,688	5,082	145	95	50	25	18	7
Coorg	2	2	...	1	1	...	...	...	...	...	...	...	...	...	...
Madras (including Laccadives) ...	34,507	17,056	17,451	1,530	744	786	9,236	4,211	5,025	110	65	45	...	...	...
North-West Frontier Province (Districts and Administered Territories).	91	77	14	9	8	1	1	1	...	...	...	...	...	...	...
Punjab	3.396	2,569	737	191	160	31	156	123	33	167	130	37	205	201	4
United Provinces of Agra and Oudh ...	98,315	57,625	40,690	18,158	10,338	7,820	46,127	24,630	21,497	620	491	129	167	144	23

TABLE XI.—BIRTHPLACE.—DISTRICTS AND STATES—*continued.*

Birthplace.	DISTRICT OR STATE WHERE ENUMERATED.														
	Lushai Hills.			Goalpara.			Kamrup.			Darrang.			Nowgong.		
	Persons.	Males.	Females.	Persons.	Males.	Females.	Persons.	Males.	Females.	Persons.	Males.	Females.	Persons.	Males.	Females.
1	17	18	19	20	21	22	23	24	25	26	27	28	29	30	31
II.—BORN IN OTHER PARTS OF INDIA ...	*3,583*	*1,961*	*1,622*	*105,659*	*65,210*	*40,449*	*19,847*	*14,689*	*5,158*	*91,736*	*49,513*	*42,221*	*29,616*	*17,123*	*19,493*
(a) PROVINCES AND STATES ADJACENT TO ASSAM ...	*3,300*	*1,707*	*1,593*	*78,190*	*44,460*	*33,730*	*4,292*	*3,332*	*960*	*7,254*	*4,212*	*3,042*	*3,789*	*2,415*	*1,374*
(1) *British Territory* ...	*3,298*	*1,701*	*1,592*	*76,664*	*43,662*	*33,002*	*4,244*	*3,293*	*951*	*7,225*	*4,183*	*3,042*	*3,777*	*2,406*	*1,371*
1. *Bengal* ...	*1,110*	*659*	*451*	*76,663*	*43,661*	*33,002*	*4,234*	*3,285*	*949*	*7,217*	*4,179*	*3,038*	*3,774*	*2,405*	*1,369*
(i) *Contiguous Districts* ...	*875*	*464*	*411*	*51,367*	*28,447*	*22,920*	*1,230*	*1,000*	*230*	*719*	*479*	*240*	*853*	*551*	*301*
Jalpaiguri ...	...	...	...	1,818	994	824	14	9	5	14	8	6	3	1	2
Rangpur ...	...	...	...	15,304	8,388	6,916	350	312	38	78	65	13	39	36	3
Mymensingh ...	2	2	...	34,171	19,009	15,162	784	620	164	572	375	197	750	477	273
Tippera ...	70	38	32	74	56	8	82	59	23	55	32	23	60	37	23
Chittagong Hill Tracts ...	803	424	379	...	...	...	...	...	...	...	...	...	...	...	...
(ii) *Other Districts* ...	*235*	*195*	*40*	*25,296*	*15,214*	*10,082*	*3,004*	*2,285*	*719*	*6,498*	*3,700*	*2,798*	*2,922*	*1,854*	*1,068*
2. *Burma* ...	*2,183*	*1,042*	*1,141*	*1*	*1*	...	*10*	*8*	*2*	*8*	*4*	*4*	*3*	*1*	*2*
Contiguous District—Chin Hills ...	2,174	1,040	1,134	...	...	...	...	...	...	...	...	...	...	...	...
Other Districts ...	9	2	7	1	1	...	10	8	2	8	4	4	3	1	2
(2) *Feudatory States (Bengal)* ...	*7*	*6*	*1*	*1,526*	*798*	*728*	*48*	*39*	*9*	*29*	*29*	...	*12*	*9*	*3*
Cooch Behar ...	1	1	...	1,526	798	728	48	39	9	29	29	...	12	9	3
Hill Tippera ...	6	5	1	...	...	...	...	...	...	...	...	...	...	...	...
(b) OTHER PROVINCES AND STATES IN INDIA ...	*283*	*254*	*29*	*27,463*	*20,746*	*6,717*	*15,551*	*11,355*	*4,196*	*84,475*	*45,299*	*39,176*	*25,822*	*14,705*	*11,117*
(1) *British Territory* ...	*276*	*249*	*27*	*25,920*	*19,495*	*6,425*	*14,214*	*10,459*	*3,755*	*79,116*	*42,150*	*36,966*	*24,003*	*13,399*	*10,604*
Ajmere-Merwara ...	...	...	...	1	...	1	1	1	...	7	4	3	...	...	...
Andamans and Nicobars ...	...	...	...	...	...	...	2	1	1	...	...	...	...	...	...
Bihar and Orissa ...	88	85	3	18,254	13,825	4,429	8,357	6,368	1,989	57,859	31,099	26,760	15,564	8,782	6,782
Baluchistan (Districts and Administered Territories).	...	...	...	...	...	...	...	...	...	...	...	...	...	...	...
Bombay (including Aden) ...	1	1	...	21	20	1	109	93	16	141	66	75	37	23	14
Central Provinces and Berar ...	17	10	7	369	218	151	1,023	588	435	9,761	5,055	4,706	5,826	2,957	2,869
Coorg ...	...	...	...	...	...	...	1	1	...	...	...	...	...	...	...
Madras (including Laccadives) ...	16	12	4	23	17	6	70	42	28	6,916	3,302	3,551	881	470	411
North-West Frontier Province (Districts and Administered Territories).	...	...	...	1	1	...	6	6	...	14	11	3	15	14	1
Punjab ...	32	32	...	174	142	32	361	268	93	153	113	40	221	177	44
United Provinces of Agra and Oudh ...	122	109	13	7,077	5,272	1,805	4,284	3,091	1,193	4,265	2,440	1,825	1,459	976	483

TABLE XI.—BIRTHPLACE. DISTRICTS AND STATES.—*continued.*

Birthplace.	District or State where Enumerated.											
	Sibsagar.			Lakhimpur.			Garo Hills.			Manipur.		
	Persons.	Males.	Females.	Persons.	Males.	Females.	Persons.	Males.	Females.	Persons.	Males.	Females.
1	32	33	34	35	36	37	38	39	40	41	42	43
II.—BORN IN OTHER PARTS OF INDIA ...	*155,731*	*83,699*	*72,032*	*173,409*	*94,363*	*79,046*	*5,938*	*3,465*	*2,473*	*2,037*	*1,642*	*395*
(a) PROVINCES AND STATES ADJACENT TO ASSAM ...	*14,503*	*7,837*	*6,666*	*13,694*	*7,489*	*6,142*	*5,298*	*2,889*	*2,409*	*348*	*224*	*124*
(1) British Territory	*14,481*	*7,825*	*6,656*	*13,613*	*7,479*	*6,134*	*5,298*	*2,889*	*2,409*	*348*	*224*	*124*
1. Bengal	*14,468*	*7,813*	*6,655*	*13,603*	*7,474*	*6,129*	*5,298*	*2,889*	*2,409*	*300*	*198*	*102*
(i) Contiguous Districts	*260*	*191*	*69*	*321*	*240*	*81*	*4,830*	*2,555*	*2,275*	*33*	*28*	*5*
Jalpaiguri	7	5	2	3	1	2	1	1	...	...	...	...
Rangpur	32	16	16	58	39	19	578	339	239	1	1	...
Mymensingh	166	127	39	172	145	27	4,249	2,213	2,036	10	6	4
Tippera	55	43	12	88	55	33	2	2	...	22	21	1
Chittagong Hill Tracts	...	...	...	...	...	...	...	...	...	...	...	...
(ii) Other Districts	*14,208*	*7,622*	*6,586*	*13,282*	*7,234*	*6,048*	*468*	*334*	*134*	*267*	*170*	*97*
2. Burma	*13*	*12*	*1*	*10*	*5*	*5*	...	...	...	*48*	*26*	*22*
Contiguous District—Chin Hills ...	...	...	...	...	...	...	...	...	...	...	...	...
Other Districts	13	12	1	10	5	5	...	...	...	48	26	22
(2) Feudatory States (Bengal) ...	*22*	*12*	*10*	*11*	*3*	*8*	...	...	...	...	...	...
Cooch Behar	20	11	9	11	3	8	...	...	...	...	...	...
Hill Tippera	2	1	1	...	...	...	...	...	...	...	...	...
(b) OTHER PROVINCES AND STATES IN INDIA ...	*141,217*	*75,856*	*65,361*	*159,765*	*86,869*	*72,896*	*640*	*576*	*64*	*1,689*	*1,418*	*271*
(1) British Territory	*134,810*	*71,796*	*63,014*	*148,516*	*80,300*	*68,216*	*616*	*555*	*61*	*1,484*	*1,229*	*255*
Ajmere-Merwara	6	5	1	1	...	1	...	...	...	...	...	...
Andamans and Nicobars	...	...	...	...	...	...	...	...	...	...	...	...
Bihar and Orissa	102,099	54,355	47,744	114,394	61,182	53,212	438	400	38	503	402	101
Baluchistan (Districts and Administered Territories).	3	3	...	167	141	26	...	...	...	...	...	...
Bombay (including Aden)	62	48	14	297	266	31	3	2	1	12	9	3
Central Provinces and Berar ...	17,185	8,808	8,377	16,775	8,715	8,060	9	3	6	20	15	5
Coorg	...	...	...	...	...	...	...	...	...	...	...	...
Madras (including Laccadives) ...	8,415	4,162	4,253	7,300	3,964	3,336	...	...	...	10	7	3
North-West Frontier Province (Districts and Administered Territories).	26	21	5	14	13	1	...	...	...	5	2	3
Punjab	307	243	64	891	547	344	1	1	...	447	432	15
United Provinces of Agra and Oudh ...	6,707	4,151	2,556	8,677	5,472	3,205	165	149	16	487	362	125

TABLE XI.—Birthplace.—Districts and States—*continued.*

Birthplace.	District or State where enumerated.														
	Province.			Cachar.			Sylhet.			Khasi and Jaintia Hills.			Naga Hills.		
	Persons.	Males.	Females.	Persons.	Males.	Females.	Persons.	Males.	Females.	Persons.	Males.	Females.	Persons.	Males.	Females.
1	2	3	4	5	6	7	8	9	10	11	12	13	14	15	16
(2) *Feudatory States*	*31,825*	*19,615*	*12,210*	*1,161*	*606*	*555*	*2,389*	*1,288*	*1,101*	*246*	*207*	*39*	*79*	*68*	*11*
Bihar and Orissa States	6,166	3,067	3,099	45	31	14	104	51	53	...	...	...	...	...	...
Baluchistan (Agency Tracts)	17	15	2	...	...	...	...	...	...	17	15	2	...	...	...
Bombay States	1,710	931	779	11	10	1	1,503	764	739	40	39	1	1	1	...
Central India Agency	7,104	3,785	3,319	905	400	505	388	171	217	26	24	2	...	...	...
Central Provinces States	4,530	2,321	2,209	19	13	6	13	9	4	4	4	...	...	...	...
Hyderabad	119	81	38	14	8	6	28	14	14	...	...	...	...	...	...
Kashmir	19	12	7	1	1	...	10	5	5	4	3	1	...	...	...
Madras States (including Cochin and Travancore)	23	21	2	...	...	...	13	12	1	4	4	...	...	...	...
Cochin	7	6	1	...	...	...	1	...	1	2	2	...	...	...	...
Travancore	4	3	1	...	...	...	...	...	...	2	2	...	...	...	...
Mysore	141	82	59	6	1	5	58	38	20	17	10	7	2	2	...
North-West Frontier Province (Agencies and Tribal areas).	18	16	2	...	...	...	...	...	...	18	16	2	...	...	...
Punjab States	189	167	22	2	2	...	...	...	...	12	9	3	4	2	2
Rajputana Agency	11,620	9,026	2,594	145	136	9	265	219	46	96	77	19	72	63	9
Sikkim	52	30	22	...	...	...	...	...	...	6	4	2	...	...	...
United Provinces States	117	61	56	13	4	9	7	5	2	2	2	...	...	...	...
(c) French and Portuguese Settlements ...	*36*	*21*	*15*	*3*	*3*	...	*15*	*4*	*11*	*6*	*6*	...	...	...	...
(d) India unspecified	*75*	*38*	*37*	...	...	...	*21*	*9*	*12*	*12*	*5*	*7*	*1*	*1*	...
B.—BORN INOTHER ASIA TIC COUNTRIES	*49,353*	*33,490*	*15,933*	*1,086*	*866*	*220*	*463*	*387*	*75*	*3,069*	*2,456*	*613*	*953*	*710*	*243*
Afghanistan	667	651	16	90	89	1	159	159	...	38	33	5	1	1	...
Arabia	15	15	...	3	3	...	6	6	...	...	...	...	...	...	...
Bhutan	714	552	162	9	6	3	...	...	...	1	1	...	...	...	...
Ceylon	9	5	4	...	...	...	...	...	...	1	1	...	...	...	...
China	270	260	10	5	5	...	5	4	1	14	14	...	1	1	...
French Indo-China	1	...	1	...	...	...	...	...	...	1	...	1	...	...	...
Hong-Kong	1	1	...	...	...	...	1	1	...	...	...	...	...	...	...
Nepal	47,654	31,920	15,734	974	759	215	285	213	72	3,014	2,407	607	951	708	243
Persia	9	6	3	3	2	1	3	2	1	...	...	...	...	...	...
Russian Turkistan	4	2	2	...	...	...	...	...	...	...	...	...	...	...	...
Siam	1	1	...	1	1	...	...	...	...	...	...	...	...	...	...
Straits Settlements and Malaya	4	3	1	...	...	...	3	2	1	...	...	...	...	...	...
Tibet	3	3	...	1	1	...	...	...	...	...	...	...	...	...	...
Turkey in Asia	1	1	...	...	...	...	...	...	...	...	...	...	...	...	...

TABLE XI.—BIRTHPLACE.—DISTRICTS AND STATES—*continued.*

Birthplace.	DISTRICT OR STATE WHERE ENUMERATED.														
	Lushai Hills.			Goalpara.			Kamrup.			Darrang.			Nowgong.		
	Persons.	Males.	Females.	Persons.	Males.	Females.	Persons.	Males.	Females.	Persons.	Males.	Females.	Persons.	Males.	Females.
1	17	18	19	20	21	22	23	24	25	26	27	28	29	30	31
(2) *Feudatory States*	*7*	*5*	*2*	*1,543*	*1,251*	*292*	*1,337*	*896*	*441*	*5,359*	*3,149*	*2,210*	*1,819*	*1,306*	*513*
Bihar and Orissa States	1	...	1	3	3	...	43	26	17	780	317	463	2	2	...
Baluchistan (Agency Tracts) ...	...	...	...	...	...	...	...	...	...	...	...	...	...	...	...
Bombay States	...	...	...	4	2	2	17	7	10	21	7	14	2	2	...
Central India Agency	2	2	...	73	36	37	157	81	76	2,221	1,267	954	816	425	391
Central Provinces States	...	...	...	17	13	4	16	6	10	1,213	607	606	55	27	28
Hyderabad	...	...	...	...	...	...	...	...	...	...	...	...	...	...	...
Kashmir	...	...	...	1	1	...	...	...	...	1	1	...	...	...	...
Madras States (including Cochin and Travancore).	...	...	...	...	...	...	4	4	...	...	...	...	...	...	...
Cochin	...	...	...	...	...	...	4	4	...	...	...	...	...	...	...
Travancore	...	...	...	...	...	...	...	...	...	...	...	...	...	...	...
Mysore	...	...	...	1	1	...	2	2	...	19	8	11	5	4	1
North-West Frontier Province (Agencies and Tribal areas)	...	...	...	...	...	...	...	...	...	...	...	...	...	...	...
Punjab States	...	...	...	7	7	...	4	3	1	1	...	1	1	1	...
Rajputana Agency	4	3	1	1,397	1,169	228	1,062	744	318	1,083	932	151	938	845	93
Sikkim	...	...	...	35	18	17	1	...	1	1	...	1	...	...	...
United Provinces States	...	...	...	5	1	4	31	23	8	19	10	9	...	...	...
(c) French and Portuguese Settlements ...	...	...	...	...	...	...	*1*	...	*1*	*3*	*2*	*1*	*3*	*2*	*1*
(d) India unspecified	...	...	...	*6*	*4*	*2*	*3*	*2*	*1*	*4*	*2*	*2*	*2*	*1*	*1*
B.—BORN IN OTHER ASIATIC COUNTRIES	*1,469*	*1,213*	*256*	*6,021*	*4,398*	*1,623*	*4,754*	*3,200*	*1,554*	*13,425*	*8,088*	*5,337*	*2,312*	*1,607*	*705*
Afghanistan	...	...	...	35	35	...	37	37	...	53	53	...	33	32	1
Arabia	...	...	...	...	...	...	...	...	...	...	...	...	4	4	...
Bhutan	...	...	...	52	33	19	503	393	110	144	118	26	...	...	...
Ceylon	...	...	...	1	...	1	...	...	...	...	...	...	...	...	...
China	...	...	...	3	3	...	5	4	1	51	48	3	7	6	1
French Indo-China	...	...	...	...	...	...	...	...	...	...	...	...	...	...	...
Hong-Kong	...	...	...	...	...	...	...	...	...	...	...	...	...	...	...
Nepal	1,469	1,213	256	5,925	4,322	1,603	4,208	2,766	1,442	13,177	7,869	5,308	2,268	1,565	703
Persia	...	...	...	2	2	...	1	...	1	...	...	...	...	...	...
Russian Turkistan	...	...	...	1	1	...	...	...	...	...	...	...	...	...	...
Siam	...	...	...	...	...	...	...	...	...	...	...	...	...	...	...
Straits Settlements and Malaya ...	...	...	...	1	1	...	...	...	...	...	...	...	...	...	...
Tibet	...	...	...	1	1	...	...	...	...	...	...	...	...	...	...
Turkey in Asia	...	...	...	...	...	...	...	...	...	...	...	...	...	...	...

TABLE XI.—Birthplace.—Districts and States—*continued.*

Birthplace.	District or State where enumerated.											
	Sibsagar.			Lakhimpur.			Garo Hills.			Manipur.		
	Persons.	Males.	Females.	Persons.	Males.	Females.	Persons.	Males.	Females.	Persons.	Males.	Females.
1	32	33	34	35	36	37	38	39	40	41	42	43
(2) *Feudatory States*	*6,407*	*4,060*	*2,347*	*11,249*	*6,569*	*4,680*	*24*	*21*	*3*	*205*	*189*	*16*
Bihar and Orissa States	1,625	788	837	3,563		1,714	...		...	...	...	...
Baluchistan (Agency Tracts) ...	...	...	...	...	...	...	...	...	...	...	...	...
Bombay States	42	34	8	62	58	4	...	...	...	7	7	...
Central India Agency	1,295	689	606	1,219	688	531	...	...	...	2	2	...
Central Provinces States	461	231	230	2,732	1,411	1,321	...	...	...	...	...	...
Hyderabad	48	34	14	29	25	4	...	...	...	...	...	...
Kashmir	...	...	...	1	...	1	...	...	...	1	1	...
Madras States (including Cochin and Travancore).	...	...	...	2	1	1	...	...	...	...	...	...
Cochin	...	...	...	...	...	...	...	...	...	...	...	...
Travancore	...	...	...	2	1	1	...	...	...	...	...	...
Mysore	27	12	15	3	3	...	...	...	...	1	1	...
North-West Frontier Province (Agencies and Tribal areas).	...	...	...	...	...	...	...	...	...	...	...	...
Punjab States	22	16	6	61	53	8	...	...	...	75	74	1
Rajputana Agency	2,870	2,250	620	3,549	2,466	1,083	24	21	3	115	101	14
Sikkim	4	4	...	2	1	1	...	...	...	3	3	...
United Provinces States	13	2	11	26	14	12	...	...	...	1	...	1
(c) French and Portuguese Settlements ...	*4*	*3*	*1*	*1*	*1*	...	...	...	...	...	...	...
(d) India unspecified	*7*	*3*	*4*	*19*	*11*	*8*	...	...	...	...	...	...
B.—BORN IN OTHER ASIATIC COUNTRIES	*4,043*	*2,757*	*1,286*	*9,255*	*6,090*	*3,165*	*1,336*	*877*	*459*	*1,168*	*771*	*397*
Afghanistan	76	73	3	140	137	3	...	...	...	5	2	3
Arabia	2	2	...	...	...	...	...	...	...	...	...	...
Bhutan	4	1	3	...	...	...	1	...	1	...	...	...
Ceylon	4	1	3	3	3	...	...	...	...	...	...	...
China	15	15	...	164	160	4	...	...	...	...	...	...
French Indo-China	...	...	...	...	...	...	...	...	...	...	...	...
Hong-Kong	...	...	...	...	...	...	...	...	...	...	...	...
Nepal	3,939	2,664	1,275	8,946	5,788	3,158	1,335	877	458	1,163	769	394
Persia	...	...	...	...	...	...	...	...	...	...	...	...
Russian Turkistan	3	1	2	...	...	...	...	...	...	...	...	...
Siam	...	...	...	...	...	...	...	...	...	...	...	...
Straits Settlements and Malaya	...	...	...	...	...	...	...	...	...	...	...	...
Tibet	...	...	...	1	1	...	...	...	...	...	...	...
Turkey in Asia	...	...	...	1	1	...	...	...	...	...	...	...

TABLE XI.—Birthplace.—Districts and States—*contd.*

Birthplace.	Province. Persons.	Province. Males.	Province. Females.	Cachar. Persons.	Cachar. Males.	Cachar. Females.	Sylhet. Persons.	Sylhet. Males.	Sylhet. Females.	Khasi and Jaintia Hills. Persons.	Khasi and Jaintia Hills. Males.	Khasi and Jaintia Hills. Females.	Naga Hills. Persons.	Naga Hills. Males.	Naga Hills. Females.
1	2	3	4	5	6	7	8	9	10	11	12	13	14	15	16
C.—BORN IN EUROPE	*1,496*	*1,164*	*332*	*193*	*152*	*41*	*238*	*195*	*43*	*106*	*56*	*50*	*14*	*11*	*3*
United Kingdom	1,427	1,110	308	191	151	40	232	190	42	76	40	36	14	11	3
England and Wales	885	663	222	112	82	30	109	86	23	62	33	20	8	6	2
Scotland	443	381	62	60	54	6	108	91	17	7	5	2	2	2	...
Ireland	99	75	24	19	15	4	15	13	2	7	2	5	4	3	1
Austria-Hungary	1	1	...	...	...	...	...	...	...	...	...	...	...	...	...
Cyprus	1	1	...	...	...	...	...	...	...	...	...	...	...	...	...
Denmark	4	3	1	...	...	...	...	...	...	...	...	...	...	...	...
Germany	29	17	12	2	1	1	...	...	...	14	8	6	...	...	...
Gibraltar	1	1	...	...	...	...	1	1	...	...	...	...	...	...	...
Greece	2	2	...	...	...	...	2	2	...	...	...	...	...	...	...
Italy	16	8	8	...	...	...	1	...	1	15	8	7	...	...	...
Sweden	2	2	...	...	...	...	...	...	...	...	...	...	...	...	...
Portugal	1	1	...	...	...	...	1	1	...	...	...	...	...	...	...
Russia	6	6	...	...	...	...	...	...	...	...	...	...	...	...	...
Spain	1	1	...	...	...	...	...	...	...	...	...	...	...	...	...
Switzerland	3	1	2	...	...	...	...	...	...	...	...	...	...	...	...
Turkey in Europe	2	1	1	...	...	...	1	1	...	1	...	1	...	...	...
D.—BORN IN AFRICA	*14*	*13*	*1*	*1*	*1*	...	*8*	*7*	*1*	...	...	...	...	...	...
Cape Colony	1	1	...	...	...	...	...	...	...	...	...	...	...	...	...
Egypt	3	3	...	...	...	...	2	2	...	...	...	...	...	...	...
Natal	4	4	...	1	1	...	3	3	...	...	...	...	...	...	...
Africa unspecified	6	5	1	...	...	...	3	2	1	...	...	...	...	...	...
E.—BORN IN AMERICA	*58*	*33*	*25*	*2*	*2*	...	*8*	*7*	*1*	*4*	*2*	*2*	*5*	*2*	*3*
Argentine Republic	2	2	...	...	...	...		2	...	...	...	...	...	...	...
Bermudas	1	1	...	...	...	...	1	1	...	...	...	...	...	...	...
Brazil	2	2	...	...	...	...	2	2	...	...	...	...	...	...	...
Canada	9	6	3	1	1	...	1	1	...	2	2	...	...	...	...
Newfoundland	1	1	...	1	1	...	...	...	...	...	...	...	...	...	...
United States	18	...	18	...	...	...	...	...	...	...	...	...	3	...	3
America unspecified	25	21	4	...	...	...	2	1	1	2	...	2	2	2	...
F.—BORN IN AUSTRALASIA	*25*	*21*	*4*	*7*	*6*	*1*	*3*	*3*	...	*1*	...	*1*	...	...	...
Australia	14	12	2	2	2	...	3	3	...	1	...	1	...	...	...
Fiji	5	4	1	...	...	...	...	...	...	...	...	...	...	...	...
New Zealand	4	3	1	3	2	1	...	...	...	...	...	...	...	...	...
Tasmania	2	2	...	2	2	...	...	...	...	...	...	...	...	...	...
G.—BORN AT SEA	*4*	*4*	...	*1*	*1*	...	...	...	...	*1*	*1*	...	...	...	...

TABLE XI.—BIRTHPLACE.—DISTRICTS AND STATES—*continued.*

BIRTHPLACE.	DISTRICT OR STATE WHERE ENUMERATED.														
	LUSHAI HILLS.			GOALPARA.			KAMRUP.			DARRANG.			NOWGONG.		
	Persons.	Males.	Females.	Persons.	Males.	Females.	Persons.	Males.	Females.	Persons.	Males.	Females.	Persons.	Males.	Females.
1	17	18	19	20	21	22	23	24	25	26	27	28	29	30	31
C.—BORN IN EUROPE	*14*	*9*	*5*	*19*	*11*	*8*	*46*	*35*	*11*	*156*	*126*	*32*	*53*	*44*	*9*
United Kingdom	14	9	5	14	7	7	40	30	10	150	119	31	53	44	9
England and Wales	13	9	4	10	5	5	27	19	8	87	72	15	26	19	7
Scotland	1	...	1	2	...	2	10	9	1	54	42	12	23	22	1
Ireland	...	...	...	2	2	...	3	2	1	9	5	4	4	3	1
Austria-Hungary	...	...	...	1	1	...	...	...	...	...	...	...	...	...	...
Cyprus	...	...	...	1	1	...	...	...	...	...	...	...	...	...	...
Denmark	...	...	...	3	2	1	...	...	...	...	...	...	...	...	...
Germany	...	...	...	...	...	...	3	3	...	2	1	1	...	...	...
Gibraltar	...	...	...	...	...	...	...	...	...	...	...	...	...	...	...
Greece	...	...	...	...	...	...	...	...	...	...	...	...	...	...	...
Italy	...	...	...	...	...	...	...	...	...	...	...	...	...	...	...
Sweden	...	...	...	...	...	...	2	2	...	...	...	...	...	...	...
Portugal	...	...	...	...	...	...	...	...	...	...	...	...	...	...	...
Russia	...	...	...	...	...	...	...	...	...	5	5	...	...	...	...
Spain	...	...	...	...	...	...	...	...	...	...	...	...	...	...	...
Switzerland	...	...	...	...	...	...	1	...	1	1	1	...	...	...	...
Turkey in Europe	...	...	...	...	...	...	...	...	...	...	...	...	...	...	...
D.—BORN IN AFRICA	...	...	...	...	...	...	...	...	...	*1*	*1*	...	...	...	...
Cape Colony	...	...	...	...	...	...	...	...	...	...	...	...	...	...	...
Egypt	...	...	...	...	...	...	...	...	...	...	...	...	...	...	...
Natal	...	...	...	...	...	...	...	...	...	...	...	...	...	...	...
Africa unspecified	...	...	...	...	...	...	...	...	...	1	1	...	...	...	...
E.—BORN IN AMERICA	...	...	...	...	...	...	*31*	*16*	*15*	...	...	...	*1*	...	*1*
Argentine Republic	...	...	...	...	...	...	...	...	...	...	...	...	...	...	...
Bermudas	...	...	...	...	...	...	...	...	...	...	...	...	...	...	...
Brazil	...	...	...	...	...	...	...	...	...	...	...	...	...	...	...
Canada	...	...	...	...	...	...	1	...	1	...	...	...	1	...	1
Newfoundland	...	...	...	...	...	...	...	...	...	...	...	...	...	...	...
United States	...	...	...	...	...	...	14	...	14	...	...	...	...	...	...
America unspecified	...	...	...	...	...	...	16	16	...	...	...	...	...	...	...
F.—BORN IN AUSTRALASIA	...	...	...	*3*	*3*	...	*1*	*1*	...	*1*	*1*	...	...	...	...
Australia	...	...	...	3	3	...	...	...	...	1	1	...	...	...	...
Fiji	...	...	...	...	...	...	1	1	...	...	...	...	...	...	...
New Zealand	...	...	...	...	...	...	...	...	...	...	...	...	...	...	...
Tasmania	...	...	...	...	...	...	...	...	...	...	...	...	...	...	...
G.—BORN AT SEA	...	...	...	...	...	...	...	...	...	*1*	*1*	...	...	...	...

TABLE XI.—Birthplace.—Districts and States—*concluded*.

Birthplace.	District or State where enumerated.											
	Sibsagar.			Lakhimpur.			Garo Hills.			Manipur.		
	Persons.	Males.	Females.	Persons.	Males.	Females.	Persons.	Males.	Females.	Persons.	Males.	Females.
1	32	33	34	35	36	37	38	39	40	41	42	43
C.—BORN IN EUROPE	*272*	*222*	*50*	*365*	*292*	*73*	*5*	*3*	*2*	*13*	*8*	*5*
United Kingdom	269	219	50	359	289	70	3	2	1	12	8	4
{ *England and Wales*	163	128	35	257	198	59	2	1	1	9	5	4
{ *Scotland*	91	79	12	83	75	8	1	1	...	1	1	...
{ *Ireland*	15	12	3	19	16	3	...	...	...	2	2	...
Austria-Hungary	...	...	...	...	...	...	...	...	...	...	...	...
Cyprus	...	...	...	...	...	...	...	...	...	...	...	...
Denmark	1	1	...	...	...	...	...	...	...	...	...	...
Germany	...	...	...	5	3	2	2	1	1	1	...	1
Gibraltar	...	...	...	...	...	...	...	...	...	...	...	...
Greece	...	...	...	...	...	...	...	...	...	...	...	...
Italy	...	...	...	...	...	...	...	...	...	...	...	...
Sweden	...	...	...	...	...	...	...	...	...	...	...	...
Portugal	...	...	...	...	...	...	...	...	...	...	...	...
Russia	1	1	...	...	...	...	...	...	...	...	...	...
Spain	1	1	...	...	...	...	...	...	...	...	...	...
Switzerland	...	...	...	1	...	1	...	...	...	...	...	...
Turkey in Europe	...	...	...	...	...	...	...	...	...	...	...	...
D.—BORN IN AFRICA	*2*	*2*	...	*2*	*2*	...	...	...	...	...	...	...
Cape Colony	...	...	...	1	1	...	...	...	...	...	...	...
Egypt	...	...	...	1	1	...	...	...	...	...	...	...
Natal	...	...	...	...	...	...	...	...	...	...	...	...
Africa unspecified	2	2	...	...	...	...	...	...	...	...	...	...
E.—BORN IN AMERICA	*2*	*2*	...	*2*	*2*	...	*3*	...	*3*	...	...	...
Argentine Republic	...	...	...	...	...	...	...	...	...	...	...	...
Bermudas	...	...	...	...	...	...	...	...	...	...	...	...
Brazil	...	...	...	...	...	...	...	...	...	...	...	...
Canada	...	...	...	2	2	...	1	...	1	...	...	...
Newfoundland	...	...	...	...	...	...	...	...	...	...	...	...
United States	...	...	...	...	...	...	1	...	1	...	...	...
America unspecified	2	2	...	...	...	...	1	...	1	...	...	...
F.—BORN IN AUSTRALASIA	*7*	*5*	*2*	*2*	*2*	...	...	...	...	...	...	...
Australia	2	1	1	2	2	...	...	...	...	...	...	...
Fiji	4	3	1	...	...	...	...	...	...	...	...	...
New Zealand	1	1	...	...	...	...	...	...	...	...	...	...
Tasmania	...	...	...	...	...	...	...	...	...	...	...	...
G.—BORN AT SEA	...	...	...	*1*	*1*	...	...	...	...	...	...	...

TABLE XII.

INFIRMITIES.

THE infirmities recorded at the census were insanity, deaf-mutism, blindness and leprosy.

The Table is divided into two parts—Part I shows the distribution of the persons afflicted according to age, and Part II their distribution according to locality.

Some unfortunate persons were returned as suffering from more than one infirmity. In the Table they have been shown under each. This explains why the total afflicted in columns 2, 3 and 4 does not quite agree with the total of the figures for each separate infirmity. The following is a list of these multiple entries :—

—	Total.	Males.	Females.
Insane and blind	9	4	5
Insane and lepers	3	2	1
Insane and deaf-mutes	61	34	27
Deaf-mutes and blind	19	8	11
Deaf-mutes and lepers	4	2	2
Blind and lepers	12	8	4
Insane, deaf-mute and blind ...	2	1	1
Total	112	60	52

TABLE XII.—INFIRMITIES. PART I.—DISTRIBUTION BY AGE.

Age.	POPULATION AFFLICTED.			INSANE.			DEAF-MUTES.			BLIND.			LEPERS.		
	Persons.	Males.	Females.	Persons.	Males.	Females.	Persons.	Males.	Females.	Persons.	Males.	Females.	Persons.	Males.	Females.
1	2	3	4	5	6	7	8	9	10	11	12	13	14	15	16
Total	*19,183*	*11,628*	*7,555*	*3 116*	*1,840*	*1,276*	*5,399*	*3,152*	*2,247*	*6,408*	*3,417*	*2,991*	*4,372*	*3,279*	*1,093*
0—1	23	13	10	...	...	...	...	...	...	21	11	10	2	2	...
1—2	28	16	12	1	1	...	8	5	3	18	10	8	1	...	1
2—3	99	59	40	3	2	1	46	25	21	50	30	20	2	2	...
3—4	210	119	91	11	7	4	141	77	64	56	34	22	4	2	2
4—5	237	128	109	9	5	4	152	83	69	74	39	35	5	3	2
Total 0—5	*597*	*335*	*262*	*24*	*15*	*9*	*347*	*190*	*157*	*219*	*124*	*95*	*14*	*9*	*5*
5—10	1,283	782	501	123	69	57	846	512	334	291	187	104	38	24	14
10—15	1,479	871	608	172	89	83	891	527	364	283	174	109	147	90	57
15—20	1,339	767	[illegible]	244	126	118	643	365	278	250	141	109	212	131	81
20—25	[illegible]	[illegible]	607	314	187	127	606	341	265	261	141	120	298	199	97
25—30	1 786	1,107	679	433	279	159	590	351	239	312	166	146	456	315	141
30—35	1,836	1,194	[illegible]	474	284	190	451	262	189	395	218	177	584	436	148
35—40	[illegible]	1,010	[illegible]	345	220	125	308	194	114	337	181	156	524	418	106
40—45	1 653	1,090	563	308	185	123	247	141	106	451	232	219	654	536	118
45—50	1,049	[illegible]	368	187	112	75	127	78	49	373	202	171	368	293	75
50—55	[illegible]	848	543	209	125	84	134	82	52	630	316	314	423	328	95
55—60	625	357	268	75	41	34	59	26	29	342	174	168	161	117	44
60—65	1,314	709	60	112	55	57	77	40	37	856	394	462	271	220	51
65—70	371	215	156	28	18	10	20	13	7	260	135	125	66	50	16
70 and over	[illegible]	807	[illegible]	60	35	25	55	27	28	1,148	632	[illegible]	158	113	45

TABLE XII.—INFIRMITIES. PART II.—DISTRIBUTION BY DISTRICTS.

DISTRICT OR STATE.	POPULATION AFFLICTED.			INSANE.			DEAF-MUTES.			BLIND.			LEPERS.		
	Persons.	Males.	Females.	Persons.	Males.	Females.	Persons.	Males.	Females.	Persons.	Males.	Females.	Persons.	Males.	Females.
1	2	3	4	5	6	7	8	9	10	11	12	13	14	15	16
ASSAM	*19,183*	*11,628*	*7,555*	*3,116*	*1,840*	*1,276*	*5,399*	*3,159*	*2,247*	*6,408*	*3,417*	*2,991*	*4,372*	*3,976*	*1,093*
(1) British Territory	*18,975*	*11,512*	*7,463*	*3,068*	*1,818*	*1,250*	*5,365*	*3,132*	*2,233*	*6,291*	*3,351*	*2,940*	*4,359*	*3,268*	*1,091*
SURMA VALLEY AND HILL DISTRICTS ...	*9,982*	*6,051*	*3,931*	*1,658*	*917*	*741*	*2,799*	*1,654*	*1,145*	*3,537*	*1,905*	*1,632*	*2,040*	*1,602*	*438*
Cachar	1,345	768	577	243	122	121	335	192	143	458	224	234	326	237	89
Sylhet	6,589	4,251	2,338	978	607	371	1,565	994	571	2,467	1,368	1,099	1,612	1,301	311
Khasi and Jaintia Hills	426	239	187	74	34	40	115	66	49	177	102	75	62	38	24
Naga Hills	1,192	599	593	52	26	26	770	394	376	333	156	177	37	23	14
Lushai Hills	430	194	236	311	128	183	14	8	6	102	55	47	3	3	...
ASSAM VALLEY DISTRICTS	*8,993*	*5,461*	*3,532*	*1,410*	*901*	*509*	*2,566*	*1,478*	*1,088*	*2,754*	*1,446*	*1,308*	*2,319*	*1,666*	*653*
Goalpara	2,046	1,283	763	438	253	185	518	295	223	584	320	264	543	437	106
Kamrup	1,740	1,085	655	252	168	84	503	298	205	629	359	270	367	264	103
Darrang	987	625	362	286	227	59	302	164	138	216	108	108	183	126	57
Nowgong	862	493	369	83	46	37	247	141	106	307	145	162	225	161	64
Sibsagar	1,722	1,091	631	201	130	71	486	301	185	450	243	207	585	417	168
Lakhimpur	1,082	606	476	89	47	42	405	225	180	297	148	149	293	188	105
Garo Hills	554	278	276	61	30	31	105	54	51	271	123	148	123	73	50
(2) Manipur State	*208*	*116*	*92*	*48*	*22*	*26*	*34*	*20*	*14*	*117*	*66*	*51*	*13*	*11*	*2*

TABLE XII-A.

INFIRMITIES BY SELECTED CASTES, TRIBES OR RACES.

THE infirmites recorded in Table XII are shown here only for selected castes in the Province. In the column for "Population dealt with" have been shown the figures of each caste or tribe after classification given in Table XIII.

TABLE XII.-A.—INFIRMITIES BY SELECTED CASTES, TRIBES OR RACES.

CASTE, TRIBE OR RACE.	POPULATION DEALT WITH.			INSANE.			DEAF-MUTES.			BLIND.			LEPERS.		
	Persons.	Males.	Females.	Persons.	Males.	Females.	Persons.	Males.	Females.	Persons.	Males.	Females.	Persons.	Males.	Females.
1	2	3	4	5	6	7	8	9	10	11	12	13	14	15	16
Ahom	**197,444**	101,961	95,483	**100**	67	33	**218**	132	86	**137**	68	69	**257**	173	84
Baidya	**5 610**	3,049	2,561	...	...	...	**1**	1	...	**3**	3	...	...	...	...
Barui	**25 154**	12,986	12,168	**10**	5	5	**18**	10	8	**16**	6	10	**13**	11	2
Bhuinmali	**35 238**	18,313	16,925	**11**	6	5	**18**	14	4	**26**	13	13	**20**	17	3
Bhuiya	**66 665**	34,760	31,905	**11**	7	4	**17**	15	2	**42**	27	15	**43**	36	7
Brahman	**126,015**	69,396	56,619	**87**	67	20	**92**	54	38	**68**	42	26	**40**	32	8
Chamar	**54 234**	27,911	26,323	**4**	3	1	**8**	6	2	**53**	20	33	**13**	10	3
Chutita	**88,825**	45,603	43,222	**38**	29	9	**87**	45	42	**62**	34	28	**66**	43	23
Dhoba	**33 855**	17,569	16,286	**8**	7	1	**12**	7	5	**20**	12	8	**16**	14	2
Garo	**144 350**	72,569	71,781	**53**	26	27	**79**	41	38	**212**	98	114	**110**	66	44
Goala	**42 245**	23,950	18,295	**17**	10	7	**4**	16	8	**36**	21	15	**25**	16	9
Indian Christian	**63 837**	31,762	32,075	**10**	4	6	**22**	12	10	**27**	17	10	**20**	12	8
Jogi	**169,697**	86,171	83,926	**81**	42	39	**116**	77	39	**182**	80	102	**101**	74	27
Kachari	**230 102**	117,487	112,615	**63**	37	26	**194**	96	98	**164**	82	82	**182**	131	51
Kalita	**221 942**	115,506	106,436	**111**	72	39	**218**	115	103	**243**	125	118	**114**	80	3[illegible]
Kamar	**43 285**	21,923	21,362	**10**	7	3	**22**	14	8	**23**	14	9	**26**	20	6
Kayastha	**81 967**	44,377	37,590	**62**	44	18	**45**	25	20	**58**	36	22	**28**	22	6
Kewat	**94,777**	48,245	46,532	**21**	11	10	**73**	40	33	**67**	35	32	**45**	39	6
Khasi	**120,894**	57,328	63,566	**33**	11	22	**64**	39	25	**111**	65	46	**26**	14	12
Koch	**242,054**	123,187	118,867	**90**	54	36	**178**	102	76	**160**	85	75	**132**	87	45
Kshattriya	**250,541**	124,764	125,777	**70**	31	39	**43**	23	20	**74**	51	23	**49**	36	13
Manipuri	*20,015*	*9,871*	*10,144*	*47*	*20*	*27*	*25*	*11*	*14*	*26*	*16*	*10*	*41*	*30*	*11*
Kuki (total)	***69,819***	***34,625***	***35,194***	***19***	***9***	***10***	***7***	***2***	***5***	***27***	***17***	***10***	***3***	***3***	...
„ (unspecified)	**18.750**	9,228	9,522	**5**	3	2	**3**	1	2	**5**	3	2	**3**	3	...
„ Mhar	**4 963**	2,312	2,651	...	...	...	...	...	...	**1**	1	...	...	...	...
„ Kom	**2,245**	1,013	1,202	...	...	...	...	...	...	**2**	1	1	...	...	...
„ Paite	**7,202**	3,553	3,649	**4**	1	3	**1**	...	1	**4**	3	1	...	...	...
„ Rangte	**2,916**	1,484	1,432	...	...	...	...	...	...	**1**	1	...	...	...	...
„ Sakte	**4,911**	2,490	2,421	...	...	...	...	...	...	**2**	2	...	...	...	...
„ Thado	**25,402**	12,836	12,566	**10**	5	5	**2**	...	2	**11**	5	6	...	...	...
„ Vaiphei	**3,430**	1,679	1,751	...	...	...	**1**	1	...	**1**	1	...	...	...	...
Kumhar	**27,903**	14,418	13,485	**10**	7	3	**14**	8	6	**19**	9	10	**10**	8	2
Lakher	**3,647**	1,756	1,891	**17**	9	8	...	...	...	**5**	4	1	...	...	...

TABLE XII.-A.—Infirmities by selected Castes, Tribes or Races—*concluded.*

Caste, Tribe or Race.	Population dealt with.			Insane.			Deaf-mutes.			Blind.			Lepers.		
	Persons.	Males.	Females.	Persons.	Males.	Females.	Persons.	Males.	Females.	Persons.	Males.	Females.	Persons.	Males.	Females.
1	2	3	4	5	6	7	8	9	10	11	12	13	14	15	16
Lushai (total)	*15,749*	*7,333*	*9,416*	*80*	*29*	*51*	*2*	*2*	...	*12*	*7*	*5*	...	...	...
,, Fanai	3,631	1,680	1,951	17	5	12	...	...	...	3	3	...	...	...	...
,, Poi	10,884	5,067	5,817	62	24	38	2	2	...	8	3	5	...	...	...
,, Sailo	1,234	586	648	1	...	1	...	...	...	1	1	...	...	...	...
Malo	20,357	11,295	9,062	6	6	...	6	4	2	19	17	2	12	10	2
Mech	94,606	47,177	47,420	72	46	26	92	45	47	67	38	29	161	137	24
Mikir	105,077	53,642	51,435	30	18	12	55	21	34	131	73	58	188	130	58
Miri	57,792	29,335	28,457	10	10	...	60	35	25	22	11	11	88	61	27
Muchi	13,644	7,801	5,843	...	...	...	...	...	...	8	5	3	2	2	...
Munda	91,268	47,214	44,054	21	17	4	42	22	20	52	23	29	45	28	17
Nadiyal	68,350	34,891	33,459	22	12	10	69	35	34	37	16	21	23	13	10
Naga (total)	*201,290*	*97,692*	*103,598*	*56*	*26*	*30*	*743*	*381*	*362*	*364*	*165*	*199*	*33*	*21*	*12*
,, (unspecified)	12,876	6,070	6,806	2	2	...	...	...	...	...	...	...	3	3	...
,, Ao	27,360	12,987	14,373	20	13	7	81	45	36	57	33	24	3	1	2
,, Angami	39,805	19,990	19,815	6	...	6	212	112	100	19	7	12	5	2	3
,, Angwanku	208	105	103	...	...	...	...	...	...	1	...	1	...	...	...
,, Kachcha	14,167	6,905	7,262	4	...	4	5	3	2	5	5	...	9	7	2
,, Kabui	18,447	8,798	9,649	1	1	...	3	2	1	4	1	3	...	...	...
,, Lhota	19,511	9,448	10,063	10	3	7	174	77	67	174	70	104	12	7	5
,, Maram	2,718	1,319	1,399	...	...	...	1	...	1	1	1	...	...	...	...
,, Rengma	6,083	2,851	3,232	...	...	...	89	46	43	...	...	...	...	...	...
,, Sema	32,799	16,352	16,447	4	4	...	203	93	110	66	36	30	...	...	...
,, Tangkhul	27,316	12,867	14,449	9	3	6	5	3	2	37	12	25	1	1	...
Namasudra	172,753	89,347	83,406	101	65	36	129	76	53	179	97	82	96	79	17
Napit	36,868	19,144	17,724	14	10	4	21	15	6	24	12	12	13	11	2
Oraon	28,583	14,670	13,913	5	5	...	8	7	1	11	5	6	1	1	...
Patni	111,206	56,901	54,305	56	27	29	62	39	23	122	72	50	101	80	21
Rajbansi	133,078	68,584	64,494	114	69	45	112	73	39	144	77	67	152	118	34
Santal	59,068	30,382	28,686	15	11	4	9	7	2	22	16	6	23	18	5
Sudra	118,512	61,148	57,364	43	33	10	39	29	10	94	44	50	58	45	13
Sutradhar	15,982	8,368	7,614	10	9	1	8	5	3	21	10	11	7	6	1
Synteng	42,145	19,633	22,512	36	18	18	31	16	15	39	21	18	12	10	2
Tanti	41,236	20,466	20,770	...	...	...	6	3	3	6	4	2	2	2	...
Teli or Tili	38,757	20,399	18,358	17	12	5	16	10	6	28	17	11	16	16	...

TABLE XIII.

CASTE.

THIS Table is divided into two parts: Part A deals with the Castes and Tribes of Hindus, Animists, Buddhists, Jains, Sikhs and Brahmos, and Part B with those of Muhammadans. The figures for Christians are omitted from this Table, as they are specially dealt with in Tables XVII and XVIII. There are two appendices to the Table, (I) showing the details grouped together under 'Minor Castes' in the alphabetical arrangement, and (II) showing the individual tribes composing the totals of Kukis, Lushais and Nagas given in the Table.

As a rule, persons converted from Hinduism or Muhammadanism to Christianity were returned as "Deshi Christian" and their caste of origin was not mentioned in the Census Schedules. In the case of converts belonging to aboriginal tribes, however, the name of the tribes was frequently given, and the number so returned has been noted, wherever possible, for each tribe in the remarks column of the Table.

Where some members of a caste or tribe profess one religion and some another, separate figures have usually been given for each; but if the second religion was returned only in one or two districts, the figures for it have been added to those for the main religion, and the number so added has been noted in the column of remarks.

It is often very difficult to decide whether a group constitutes a separate caste or is a sub-caste of some other caste. The procedure that has been followed in each case is explained in the remarks column.

As far as possible, items that are not true castes have been eliminated from the return and added to the castes to which they appeared to belong after such enquiries, local and otherwise, as it was possible to make within the limited time available. The more important of these items are mentioned in the remarks column.

TABLE XIII.—Caste. Part A.—Hindus, Animists, Buddhists, Jains, Sikhs and Brahmos.

District or State.	Agaria. Hindu. Males.	Agaria. Hindu. Females.	Agarwala. Hindu. Males.	Agarwala. Hindu. Females.	Agarwala. Jain. Males.	Agarwala. Jain. Females.	Ahir. Hindu. Males.	Ahir. Hindu. Females.	Ahom. Hindu. Males.	Ahom. Hindu. Females.	Asur. Hindu. Males.	Asur. Hindu. Females.	Bagdi. Hindu. Males.	Bagdi. Hindu. Females.	Remarks.
1	2	3	4	5	6	7	8	9	10	11	12	13	14	15	16
ASSAM	*579*	*577*	*3,307*	*1,843*	*153*	*57*	*7,067*	*5,696*	*101,961*	*95,483*	*244*	*206*	*4,219*	*4,179*	Agaria includes 21 males and 15 females returned as Animists, *viz.*, Darrang (14+12), Sibsagar (4+2) and Lakhimpur (3+1). Ahir includes 9 males and 6 females returned as Animists, *viz.*, Sibsagar (6+2) and Lakhimpur (3+4). There are, besides, 6 males and 6 females returned as Christians, *viz.*, Sibsagar (8) and Lakhimpur (4). Ahom includes 2,044 males and 1,923 females returned as Chandaug, *viz.*, Sibsagar (3,956) and Lakhimpur (11); 2 males returned as Buddhists in Sibsagar, and 2 males and 2 females returned as Animists, *viz.*, Sibsagar (0+1) and Lakhimpur (2+1). There are, besides, 11 males and 2 females returned as Christians in Sibsagar. Asur includes 23 males and 22 females returned as Animists, *viz.*, Darrang (4+5), Nowgong (5+4) and Lakhimpur (14+13). Bagdi includes 8 males and 11 females returned as Animists, *viz.*, Sibsagar (6+9) and Lakhimpur (2+2). There is, besides, 1 female returned as Christian in Sibsagar.
(1) British Territory	*579*	*577*	*3,294*	*1,842*	*151*	*57*	*7,038*	*5,684*	*101,961*	*95,483*	*244*	*206*	*4,211*	*4,179*	
SURMA VALLEY AND HILL DISTRICTS	*219*	*237*	*49*	*45*	...	...	*5,198*	*4,561*	*87*	*17*	*48*	*33*	*2,118*	*2,123*	
Cachar	111	130	...	...	...	...	2,146	1,892	78	12	7	2	1,339	1,312	
Sylhet	108	107	21	27	...	...	2,948	2,648	...	...	41	31	779	810	
Khasi and Jaintia Hills	...	...	317	11	...	...	87	14	4	5	...	...	...	...	
Naga Hills	...	...	6	3	...	...	9	...	5	...	...	...	...	1	
Lushai Hills	...	...	5	4	...	...	8	7	...	...	...	...	...	...	
ASSAM VALLEY DISTRICTS	*353*	*340*	*3,245*	*1,797*	*151*	*57*	*1,840*	*1,123*	*101,874*	*95,466*	*196*	*173*	*2,093*	*2,056*	
Goalpara	...	...	250	133	45	17	78	11	33	1	2	...	7	...	
Kamrup	2	...	503	871	19	12	119	45	295	247	...	...	30	26	
Darrang	63	69	152	30	12	1	235	134	1,896	1,689	32	20	468	456	
Nowgong	8	6	201	54	3	...	91	44	1,863	1,896	9	12	129	132	
Sibsagar	206	202	1,107	854	25	5	645	482	66,943	62,407	132	115	879	876	
Lakhimpur	74	68	1,022	655	47	22	654	405	30,854	29,226	21	17	580	566	
Garo Hills	...	...	10	[illegible]	...	...	18	2	...	...	...	...	...	...	
(2) Manipur State	...	...	*13*	*1*	*2*	...	*29*	*19*	...	...	...	...	*1*	...	

District or State.	Baidya. Hindu. Males.	Baidya. Hindu. Females.	Baishnab (Bairagi). Hindu. Males.	Baishnab (Bairagi). Hindu. Females.	Baiti (Chunari). Hindu. Males.	Baiti (Chunari). Hindu. Females.	Barhi. Hindu. Males.	Barhi. Hindu. Females.	Barui. Hindu. Males.	Barui. Hindu. Females.	Bauri. Hindu. Males.	Bauri. Hindu. Females.	Bauri. Animist. Males.	Bauri. Animist. Females.	Remarks.
1	17	18	19	20	21	22	23	24	25	26	27	28	29	30	31
ASSAM	*3,049*	*2,561*	*5,182*	*6,162*	*551*	*584*	*521*	*190*	*12,986*	*12,168*	*21,020*	*22,204*	*349*	*379*	Baishnab (Bairagi) includes 5 males returned as Jains, *viz.*, Goalpara (2), Darrang (2) and Sibsagar (1). It also includes 4 males and 3 females returned as Animists, *viz.*, Darrang (0+1), Lakhimpur (1+1) and Garo Hills (3+1), and 3 males returned as Sikhs in Nowgong. Barhi includes 1 male returned as Animist in Darrang. Barui includes 4 males and 3 females returned as Animists in Nowgong.
(1) British Territory	*3,048*	*2,561*	*5,178*	*6,159*	*551*	*584*	*520*	*190*	*12,986*	*12,165*	*21,020*	*22,204*	*349*	*379*	
SURMA VALLEY AND HILL DISTRICTS...	*2,393*	*2,111*	*3,838*	*4,790*	*546*	*578*	*10*	...	*12,583*	*12,062*	*11,388*	*11,857*	...	...	
Cachar	333	215	886	465	22	...	...	...	1,279	1,047	7,331	7,329	...	...	
Sylhet	1,928	1,830	3,394	4,313	524	578	4	...	11,301	11,015	4,056	4,524	...	...	
Khasi and Jaintia Hills	102	43	33	1	...	...	5	...	3	...	1	3	...	...	
Naga Hills	3	1	25	11	...	...	...	...	...	...	...	1	...	...	
Lushai Hills	27	22	...	...	...	...	1	...	...	...	...	...	...	...	
ASSAM VALLEY DISTRICTS	*655*	*450*	*1,340*	*1,369*	*5*	*6*	*510*	*190*	*403*	*103*	*9,632*	*10,347*	*349*	*379*	
Goalpara	171	119	657	752	...	...	121	5	174	14	19	12	...	...	
Kamrup	170	137	16	19	...	...	114	17	17	5	74	75	...	...	
Darrang	51	26	117	113	4	6	96	44	10	...	1,634	1,789	18	34	
Nowgong	50	26	37	33	...	...	13	2	26	14	197	185	15	14	
Sibsagar	87	62	185	149	1	...	54	60	64	21	5,015	5,106	189	168	
Lakhimpur	121	76	290	283	...	...	107	62	103	49	2,693	3,180	127	163	
Garo Hills	5	4	38	20	...	...	5	...	...	...	...	...	...	...	
(2) Manipur State	*1*	...	*4*	*3*	...	...	*1*	...	...	*3*	...	...	...	...	

TABLE XIII.—Caste. Part A.—Hindus, Animists, Buddhists, Jains, Sikhs and Brahmos—*continued.*

District or State.	Bediya. Hindu. Males.	Bediya. Hindu. Females.	Behara. Hindu. Males.	Behara. Hindu. Females.	Beldar. Hindu. Males.	Beldar. Hindu. Females.	Besya. Hindu. Males.	Besya. Hindu. Females.	Bhar. Hindu. Males.	Bhar. Hindu. Females.	Bhat. Hindu. Males.	Bhat. Hindu. Females.	Bhil. Hindu. Males.	Bhil. Hindu. Females.
1	32	33	34	35	36	37	38	39	40	41	42	43	44	45
ASSAM	***902***	***877***	***128***	***72***	***146***	***124***	***33***	***1,375***	***7,331***	***6,938***	***514***	***455***	***528***	***321***
(1) *British Territory*	***902***	***877***	***128***	***72***	***146***	***124***	***33***	***1,375***	***7,331***	***6,938***	***514***	***455***	***528***	***321***
SURMA VALLEY AND HILL DISTRICTS	***120***	***82***	***69***	***44***	***18***	***25***	***33***	***1,291***	***6,783***	***6,582***	***465***	***427***	***463***	***279***
Cachar	48	49	...	...	16	22	...	9	2,131	1,758	62	38	252	256
Sylhet	70	33	56	40	2	3	31	1,282	4,645	4,824	400	389	211	23
Khasi and Jaintia Hills	1	...	...	...	...	...	2	...	6	...	1	...	...	...
Naga Hills	1	...	...	...	...	...	...	...	...	...	...	...	...	...
Lushai Hills	...	...	13	4	...	...	...	...	1	...	2	...	...	...
ASSAM VALLEY DISTRICTS	***782***	***795***	***59***	***28***	***128***	***99***	...	***84***	***548***	***356***	***49***	***28***	***65***	***42***
Goalpara	86	95	30	15	...	...	...	82	118	95	7	1	9	1
Kamrup	11	...	3	2	2	1	...	1	90	40	...	...	7	1
Darrang	45	43	...	...	70	63	...	...	31	23	7	6	22	19
Nowgong	7	1	...	...	4	2	...	...	37	25	5	1	3	1
Sibsagar	380	386	2	1	20	13	...	...	123	104	13	11	16	14
Lakhimpur	253	270	23	10	32	20	...	...	141	69	11	7	8	6
Garo Hills	...	...	1	...	...	...	...	1	8	...	6	2	...	...
(2) *Manipur State*	...	...	...	...	...	...	...	...	...	...	...	...	...	...

Remarks. (46)

Bediya includes 15 males and 13 females returned as Animists, *viz.*, Darrang (8 + 7) and Sibsagar (7 + 6).

Besya includes 3 females returned as Animists in Goalpara.

Bhar includes 4 males and 2 females returned as Animists, *viz.*, Lushai Hills (1 + 0) and Lakhimpur (3 + 2).

Bhat includes 5 males and 2 females returned as Animists, *viz.*, Sibsagar (4 + 2) and Garo Hills (1 + 0).

Bhat includes 37 males and 30 females returned as Animists, *viz.*, Darrang (22 + 17), Sibsagar (7 + 7) and Lakhimpur (8 + 6).

District or State.	Bhogta. Hindu. Males.	Bhogta. Hindu. Females.	Bhotia. Buddhist. Males.	Bhotia. Buddhist. Females.	Bhuinmali. Hindu. Males.	Bhuinmali. Hindu. Females.	Bhuiya. Hindu. Males.	Bhuiya. Hindu. Females.	Bhuiya. Animist. Males.	Bhuiya. Animist. Females.	Bhumij. Hindu. Males.	Bhumij. Hindu. Females.	Bhumij. Animist. Males.	Bhumij. Animist. Females.
1	47	48	49	50	51	52	53	54	55	56	57	58	59	60
ASSAM	***5,704***	***5,315***	***599***	***164***	***18,313***	***16,925***	***33,750***	***31,013***	***1,010***	***892***	***18,382***	***18,595***	***873***	***814***
(1) *British Territory*	***5,704***	***5,315***	***599***	***164***	***18,313***	***16,925***	***33,726***	***31,005***	***1,010***	***892***	***18,375***	***18,590***	***873***	***814***
SURMA VALLEY AND HILL DISTRICTS	***1,652***	***1,575***	***79***	***9***	***18,133***	***16,785***	***8,310***	***7,468***	...	...	***4,679***	***4,628***	...	...
Cachar	1,016	964	2	2	1,439	1,437	4,178	3,795	...	...	2,673	2,613	...	...
Sylhet	626	611	59	...	16,694	15,348	3,959	3,668	...	...	2,000	2,014	...	...
Khasi and Jaintia Hills	3	...	18	7	...	...	169	1	...	...	1	...	...	...
Naga Hills	...	...	...	...	...	...	4	...	...	...	5	1	...	...
Lushai Hills	7	...	...	...	...	...	2	4	...	...	...	...	...	...
ASSAM VALLEY DISTRICTS	***4,052***	***3,740***	***520***	***155***	***180***	***140***	***25,416***	***23,537***	***1,010***	***892***	***13,696***	***13,962***	***873***	***814***
Goalpara	6	...	21	16	146	112	198	86	...	...	42	36	...	...
Kamrup	302	273	379	105	3	...	446	331	...	...	257	224	...	...
Darrang	653	620	111	26	1	...	3,768	3,601	147	145	2,147	2,239	500	470
Nowgong	654	651	...	...	...	...	891	796	4	6	1,080	1,062	...	...
Sibsagar	1,463	1,335	1	...	1	...	13,272	12,381	672	573	5,305	5,297	69	60
Lakimpur	974	861	2	3	1	...	6,841	6,343	187	168	4,865	5,104	304	284
Garo Hills	...	...	6	5	28	28	...	...	...	...	...	...	...	...
(2) *Manipur State*	...	...	...	...	...	...	***24***	***8***	...	...	***7***	***5***	...	...

Remarks. (61)

Bhogta includes 48 males and 44 females returned as Animists, *viz.*, Darrang (0 + 1), Sibsagar (11 + 16) and Lakhimpur (37 + 27).

Bhotia includes 5 males and 3 females returned as Animists, *viz.*, Kamrup (4 + 0) and Lakhimpur (1 + 3). It also includes 77 males and 10 females returned as Hindus, *viz.*, Cachar (1 + 0), Sylhet (59 + 0), Khasi and Jaintia Hills (5 + 1), Goalpara (4 + 4), Kamrup (1 + 0), Sibsagar (1+0) and Garo Hills (6 +5).

Bhuiya (Hindu) includes 2 females returned as Jains in Sibsagar. There are, besides, 33 males and 26 females who have accepted Christianity, *viz.*, Darrang (1), Sibsagar (32) and Lakhimpur (26).

Bhumij (Hindu) includes 1 male returned as Buddhist in Sibsagar. There are, besides, 11 males and 23 females who have accepted Christianity, *viz.*, Sylhet (0), Sibsagar (15), and Lakhimpur (9).

TABLE XIII.—Caste. Part A.—Hindus, Animists, Buddhists, Jains, Sikhs, and Brahmos—*continued.*

District or State.	Bind. Hindu. Males.	Bind. Hindu. Females.	Binjhia. Hindu. Males.	Binjhia. Hindu. Females.	Birhor. Hindu. Males.	Birhor. Hindu. Females.	Boria. Hindu. Males.	Boria. Hindu. Females.	Brahman (Hindu). Brahman. Males.	Brahman (Hindu). Brahman. Females.	Brahman (Hindu). Agradani. Males.	Brahman (Hindu). Agradani. Females.	Brahman (Hindu). Barna. Males.	Brahman (Hindu). Barna. Females.
1	62	63	64	65	66	67	68	69	70	71	72	73	74	75
ASSAM	***2,088***	***1,172***	***438***	***435***	***239***	***222***	***10,994***	***10,519***	***69,396***	***56,619***	***131***	***86***	***2,694***	***2,371***
(1) British Territory	***2,088***	***1,172***	***438***	***435***	***232***	***222***	***10,994***	***10,519***	***65,342***	***52,663***	***131***	***86***	***2,693***	***2,371***
SURMA VALLEY AND HILL DISTRICTS ...	***1,246***	***1,006***	***12***	***31***	***35***	***51***	***10***	***8***	***25,583***	***20,998***	***115***	***71***	***2,242***	***1,918***
Cachar	131	206	5	24	20	38	4	...	3,085	1,879	3	6	114	102
Sylhet	1,065	800	7	7	15	13	6	8	21,320	18,716	112	65	2,128	1,816
Khasi and Jaintia Hills	...	...	...	...	...	...	...	...	800	308	...	...	...	...
Naga Hills	...	...	...	...	...	...	...	...	117	35	...	...	...	...
Lushai Hills	...	...	...	...	...	...	...	...	261	60	...	...	...	...
ASSAM VALLEY DISTRICTS	***849***	***166***	***426***	***404***	***197***	***171***	***10,984***	***10,511***	***39,759***	***31,665***	***16***	***15***	***451***	***453***
Goalpara	232	86	5	3	18	...	24	35	3,316	1,524	16	15	51	45
Kamrup	35	5	1	...	...	...	669	667	13,092	13,067	...	...	62	50
Darrang	112	10	190	188	11	9	2,088	2,055	6,047	4,737	...	...	168	191
Nowgong	4	1	85	31	8	12	4,433	4,478	8,084	2,085	...	...	139	151
Sibsagar	53	30	43	31	83	70	3,102	2,672	9,795	7,473	...	...	1	...
Lakhimpur	398	22	152	151	77	80	668	609	3,356	1,735	...	...	31	16
Garo Hills	8	3	...	...	...	...	...	...	469	194	...	...	...	...
(2) Manipur State	...	...	...	...	...	...	...	...	***4,054***	***3,956***	...	...	***1***	...

Remarks. (76)

Binjhia includes 47 males and 61 females returned as Animists *viz.*, Darrang (42+55), Nowgong (3+2) and Lakhimpur (2+4).

Birhor includes 18 males and 15 females returned as Animists, *viz.*, Sylhet (2+0), Darrang (2+0), Nowgong (0+4) and Lakhimpur (14+11).

Boria includes 1 female returned as Animist in Sibsagar.

Brahman includes 15 males and 15 females returned as Brahmos, *viz.*, Khasi and Jaintia Hills (9+12), Goalpara (2+3), Darrang (2+0) and Sibsagar (2+0). It also includes 2 males returned as Buddhists in Khasi and Jaintia Hills, and 177 males and 6 females returned as Jains, *viz.*, Naga Hills (3+0), Goalpara (57+2), Kamrup (6+0), Darrang (36+3), Nowgong (4+0), Sibsagar (25+0), Lakhimpur (24+0), Garo Hills (1+0) and Manipur (21+1), and 2 males and 2 females returned as Sikhs in Manipur.

District or State.	Brahmo (unspecified). Brahmo. Males.	Brahmo (unspecified). Brahmo. Females.	Brittial Baniya. Hindu. Males.	Brittial Baniya. Hindu. Females.	Buddhist (unspecified). Buddhist. Males.	Buddhist (unspecified). Buddhist. Females.	Chamar. Hindu. Males.	Chamar. Hindu. Females.	Chasa. Hindu. Males.	Chasa. Hindu. Females.	Chero. Hindu. Males.	Chero. Hindu. Females.	Chik (Baraik). Hindu. Males.	Chik (Baraik). Hindu. Females.
1	77	78	79	80	81	82	83	84	85	86	87	88	89	90
ASSAM	***104***	***74***	***4,563***	***4,591***	***252***	***138***	***27,911***	***26,323***	***2,281***	***2,169***	***701***	***544***	***2,954***	***2,749***
(1) British Territory	***104***	***74***	***4,563***	***4,521***	***252***	***138***	***27,904***	***26,312***	***2,281***	***2,169***	***701***	***544***	***2,952***	***2,749***
SURMA VALLEY AND HILL DISTRICTS...	***36***	***20***	***4***	...	***7***	...	***19,612***	***19,445***	***855***	***887***	***50***	***33***	***687***	***641***
Cachar	11	2	...	...	2	...	8,360	7,306	515	556	2	1	290	296
Sylhet	11	9	...	...	...	...	11,185	11,525	338	331	48	32	388	345
Khasi and Jaintia Hills	14	9	...	...	5	...	60	8	2	...	...	...	...	...
Naga Hills	...	...	4	...	...	...	7	6	...	...	...	...	...	...
Lushai Hills	...	...	...	...	...	...	...	...	...	...	...	...	...	...
ASSAM VALLEY DISTRICTS	***68***	***54***	***4,559***	***4,521***	***245***	***138***	***8,292***	***6,867***	***1,426***	***1,282***	***651***	***511***	***2,265***	***2,108***
Goalpara	35	27	...	...	7	...	417	145	12	6	...	...	84	15
Kamrup	6	5	1,415	1,511	9	1	836	371	5	...	...	...	7	6
Darrang	7	6	799	782	13	5	1,025	904	109	88	145	84	566	482
Nowgong	...	...	1,246	1,335	...	...	648	480	304	267	12	15	120	104
Sibsagar	...	...	627	516	9	1	3,637	3,473	699	650	369	264	637	634
Lakhimpur	20	16	472	377	207	131	1,715	1,486	297	271	125	148	851	867
Garo Hills	...	...	...	...	...	...	14	8	...	...	...	...	...	...
(2) Manipur State	...	...	...	...	...	...	***7***	***11***	...	...	...	...	***2***	...

Remarks. (91)

Brittial Baniya includes 1 female returned as Animist in Nowgong.

Chamar includes 168 males and 170 females returned as Animists, *viz.*, Kamrup (1+0), Darrang (0+3), Nowgong (17+15), Sibsagar (129+116) and Lakhimpur (19+36).

Chasa includes 16 males and 9 females returned as Animists, *viz.*, Sibsagar (7+5) and Lakhimpur (9+4).

Chero includes 7 males and 10 females returned as Animists, *viz.*, Nowgong (2+4), Sibsagar (5+3) and Lakhimpur (0+3).

Chik (Baraik) includes 58 males and 59 females returned as Animists, *viz.*, Darrang (5+5), Nowgong (4+7), Sibsagar (11+13) and Lakhimpur (38+34), and 1 male and 1 female returned as Buddhists in Goalpara.

TABLE XIII.—CASTE. PART A.—HINDUS, ANIMISTS, BUDDHISTS, JAINS, SIKHS AND BRAHMOS—*continued.*

District or State.	Chinese.		Chutiya.				Daflas.		Damai.		Darzi.		Dhanuk.		Remarks.
	Buddhist.		Hindu.		Animist.		Animist.		Hindu.		Hindu.		Hindu.		
	Males.	Females.	Males.	Females.	Males.	Females.	Males.	Females.	Males.	Females.	Males.	Females.	Males.	Females.	
1	92	93	94	95	96	97	98	99	100	101	102	103	104	105	106
ASSAM	***298***	***8***	***44,352***	***41,976***	***1,951***	***1,246***	***561***	***428***	***816***	***515***	***314***	***152***	***381***	***138***	Chutiya includes 869 males and 808 females returned as Deori in Sibsagar.
(1) British Territory	***298***	***8***	***44,359***	***41,976***	***1,251***	***1,246***	***561***	***428***	***786***	***488***	***314***	***150***	***381***	***138***	
SURMA VALLEY AND HILL DISTRICTS...	***15***	...	***514***	***456***	***1***	...	***5***	...	***103***	***62***	***16***	***11***	***99***	***28***	Dafla includes 2 males returned as Hindus in Lakhimpur.
Cachar	2	...	163	147	1	...	5	...	24	20	...	...	28	21	Damai includes 1 male returned as Buddhist in Darrang, and 12 males and 5 females returned as Animists, *viz.*, Lushai Hills (6+1) and Lakhimpur (6+4).
Sylhet	2	...	331	206	...	...	...	...	7	...	9	8	65	1	
Khasi and Jaintia Hills	11	...	...	...	...	...	...	...	21	13	4	3	6	6	
Naga Hills	...	...	20	13	...	...	...	...	49	28	3	...	...	...	
Lushai Hills	...	...	...	...	...	...	...	...	2	1	...	...	...	...	
ASSAM VALLEY DISTRICTS	***283***	***8***	***43,838***	***41,520***	***1,250***	***1,246***	***556***	***428***	***683***	***426***	***298***	***139***	***282***	***110***	
Goalpara	2	...	19	1	...	...	...	...	117	66	41	19	46	4	Darzi includes 6 males and 2 females returned as Buddhists, *viz.*, Sylhet (2+2) and Kamrup (4+0), and 4 males returned as Jains in Darrang. It also includes 12 males and 6 females returned as Animists, *viz.*, Kamrup (0+2) and Lakhimpur (12+4).
Kamrup	2	...	398	427	...	...	...	...	43	32	57	43	44	3	
Darrang	44	3	1,877	1,663	1	...	312	207	302	192	26	...	35	8	
Nowgong	6	...	3,485	3,580	...	...	...	...	59	26	1	...	12	...	
Sibsagar	15	...	29,574	27,754	65	51	7	...	23	27	35	16	81	52	
Lakhimpur	214	5	8,535	8,095	1,184	1,193	237	221	119	63	123	51	64	43	Dhanuk includes 1 male returned as Sikh in Goalpara.
Garo Hills	...	...	...	...	...	...	...	...	20	20	15	10	...	...	
(2) Manipur State	...	...	...	...	...	...	...	...	***30***	***27***	...	***2***	...	...	

District or State.	Dhenuar.		Dhimar.		Dhoba.		Dholi.		Dom.				Dosadh.		Remarks.
	Hindu.		Hindu.		Hindu.		Hindu.		Hindu.		Animist.		Hindu.		
	Males.	Females.	Males.	Females.	Males.	Females.	Males.	Females.	Males.	Females.	Males.	Females.	Males.	Females.	
1	107	108	109	110	111	112	113	114	115	116	117	118	119	120	121
ASSAM	***290***	***270***	***220***	***55***	***17,569***	***16,286***	***5,100***	***5,172***	***14,912***	***14,544***	***475***	***481***	***5,641***	***4,397***	Dhoba includes 3 males and 6 females returned as Animists, *viz.*, Sibsagar (2+1) and Lakhimpur (1+5).
(1) British Territory	***290***	***270***	***220***	***55***	***17,542***	***16,270***	***5,100***	***5,172***	***14,912***	***14,544***	***475***	***481***	***5,637***	***4,397***	
SURMA VALLEY AND HILL DISTRICTS...	***15***	***13***	...	...	***13,418***	***12,406***	***5,054***	***5,135***	***2,952***	***3,281***	***1***	...	***2,707***	***2,536***	Dom (Hindu) includes 1 female returned as Buddhist in Sibsagar.
Cachar	2	8	...	...	1,481	1,129	21	5	1,770	1,902	...	...	1,551	1,415	
Sylhet	13	5	...	...	11,870	11,234	5,083	5,130	1,182	1,379	1	...	1,090	1,094	
Khasi and Jaintia Hills	...	...	...	...	45	34	...	...	...	...	...	...	54	14	Dosadh includes 20 males and 8 females returned as Animists, *viz.*, Kamrup (8+0), Nowgong (2+1), Sibsagar (8+4) and Lakhimpur (2+3), and 2 males returned as Jains in Goalpara.
Naga Hills	...	...	...	...	10	2	...	...	...	...	...	...	1	...	
Lushai Hills	...	...	...	...	12	7	...	...	...	...	...	...	2	13	
ASSAM VALLEY DISTRICTS	***275***	***257***	***220***	***55***	***4,124***	***3,864***	***46***	***37***	***11,960***	***11,263***	***474***	***481***	***2,930***	***1,861***	
Goalpara	9	...	1	1	188	71	28	31	248	179	...	...	593	73	
Kamrup	...	6	...	...	1,865	2,128	...	...	210	112	...	...	270	92	
Darrang	24	37	28	3	251	151	...	...	1,871	1,811	4	3	292	182	
Nowgong	180	195	...	...	517	447	5	3	287	279	2	2	105	56	
Sibsagar	62	19	1	...	640	523	3	1	5,380	4,917	268	276	903	808	
Lakhimpur	...	...	100	51	640	544	10	2	3,954	3,963	200	200	746	650	
Garo Hills	...	...	...	...	14	...	...	...	10	2	...	...	21	...	
(2) Manipur State	...	...	...	...	***27***	***16***	...	...	...	...	...	...	***4***	...	

TABLE XIII.—CASTE. PART A.—HINDUS, ANIMISTS, BUDDHISTS, JAINS, SIKHS AND BRAHMOS—*continued.*

District or State.	Gandapal. Hindu. Males.	Gandapal. Hindu. Females.	Gandhabanik. Hindu. Males.	Gandhabanik. Hindu. Females.	Gareri. Hindu. Males.	Gareri. Hindu. Females.	Garo. Hindu. Males.	Garo. Hindu. Females.	Garo. Animist. Males.	Garo. Animist. Females.	Gaur. Hindu. Males.	Gaur. Hindu. Females.	Gaur. Animist. Males.	Gaur. Animist. Females.	Remarks.
1	122	123	124	125	126	127	128	129	130	131	132	133	134	135	136
ASSAM	***505***	***468***	***1,104***	***973***	***1,121***	***813***	***299***	***206***	***72,270***	***71,575***	***1,030***	***961***	***319***	***264***	Gareri includes 55 males and 26 females returned as Animists, *viz.*, Darrang (0+1), Nowgong (3+3), Sibsagar (50+17) and Lakhimpur (2+5).
(1) ***British Territory***	***505***	***468***	***1,104***	***973***	***1,121***	***813***	***299***	***206***	***72,270***	***71,575***	***1,028***	***961***	***319***	***264***	
SURMA VALLEY AND HILL DISTRICTS	***457***	***468***	***799***	***703***	***627***	***476***	***46***	***25***	***3,328***	***3,272***	***19***	...	...	...	
Cachar	...	...	15	11	343	260	4	8	...	...	...	...	...	...	Garo includes 15 males and 8 females returned as Barogharia in Khasi and Jaintia Hills. There are, besides, 540 males and 450 females returned as Christians, *viz.*, Sylhet (40), Khasi and Jaintia Hills (442), Naga Hills (3), Goalpara (15), Kamrup (97), Darrang (62), Sibsagar (108) and Garo Hills (223).
Sylhet	457	468	784	692	283	216	7	...	151	158	...	...	...	...	
Khasi and Jaintia Hills	...	...	...	...	1	...	11	8	3,135	3,090	19	...	...	...	
Naga Hills	...	...	...	...	...	...	22	7	42	24	...	...	...	...	
Lushai Hills	...	...	...	...	...	...	2	2	...	—	...	...	...	...	
ASSAM VALLEY DISTRICTS	***48***	...	***305***	***270***	***494***	***337***	***253***	***181***	***68,942***	***68,303***	***1,009***	***961***	***319***	***264***	
Goalpara	11	...	279	260	9	1	103	114	6,211	5,954	43	...	...	...	Gaur (Hindu) includes 1 male returned as Jain in Sibsagar.
Kamrup	22	...	...	—	29	6	...	...	2,311	2,458	10	12	...	...	
Darrang	...	...	3	4	113	96	2	1	227	220	401	373	14	14	
Nowgong	15	...	6	1	67	93	...	...	252	212	5	4	37	10	
Sibsagar	...	...	16	5	164	104	46	22	214	197	413	465	...	...	
Lakhimpur	...	...	1	...	110	37	89	44	19	16	107	108	268	240	
Garo Hills	...	...	...	...	2	...	13	...	59,708	59,246	...	...	...	...	
(2) ***Manipur State***	...	...	...	...	...	...	...	...	...	...	***2***	...	...	...	

District or State.	Gharti. Hindu. Males.	Gharti. Hindu. Females.	Gharti. Animist. Males.	Gharti. Animist. Females.	Ghasi. Hindu. Males.	Ghasi. Hindu. Females.	Ghasi. Animist. Males.	Ghasi. Animist. Females.	Ghatwal. Hindu. Males.	Ghatwal. Hindu. Females.	Goala. Hindu. Males.	Goala. Hindu. Females.	Remarks.
1	137	138	139	140	141	142	143	144	145	146	147	148	149
ASSAM	***175***	***96***	***2***	***1***	***6,906***	***6,820***	***674***	***714***	***2,000***	***2,068***	***23,950***	***18,295***	Goala includes 28 males and 25 females returned as Animists, *viz.*, Darrang (3+1), Nowgong (2+0), Sibsagar (8+3) and Lakhimpur (15+21). There are, besides, 23 males and 25 females returned as Christians, *viz.*, Sylhet (2), Kamrup (2), Nowgong (1), Sibsagar (22) and Lakhimpur (21).
(1) ***British Territory***	***165***	***90***	***2***	***1***	***6,906***	***6,820***	***674***	***714***	***2,000***	***2,068***	***23,930***	***18,277***	
SURMA VALLEY AND HILL DISTRICTS	***47***	***16***	***2***	***1***	***1,779***	***1,725***	...	...	***2,000***	***2,068***	***10,513***	***9,422***	
Cachar	2	...	...	...	1,066	1,069	...	...	1,193	1,238	2,930	2,462	
Sylhet	...	3	...	...	710	653	...	...	806	830	7,461	6,894	
Khasi and Jaintia Hills	11	2	...	...	3	3	...	...	...	...	98	62	
Naga Hills	5	1	...	...	...	...	...	...	...	...	8	3	
Lushai Hills	29	10	2	1	...	...	...	...	1	...	10	1	
ASSAM VALLEY DISTRICTS	***118***	***74***	...	...	***5,127***	***5,095***	***674***	***714***	...	...	***13,417***	***8,855***	
Goalpara	35	19	...	...	11	1	3	1	...	...	1,488	508	
Kamrup	7	2	...	...	15	4	...	...	...	...	890	254	
Darrang	48	43	...	...	1,022	1,047	17	24	...	...	2,420	1,534	
Nowgong	3	...	...	...	8	...	415	441	...	...	1,114	768	
Sibsagar	...	...	...	...	2,064	2,066	104	98	...	...	3,504	2,445	
Lakhimpur	18	8	...	...	2,007	1,977	135	150	...	...	3,969	3,346	
Garo Hills	7	2	...	...	...	...	...	...	...	...	32	...	
(2) ***Manipur State***	***10***	***6***	...	...	...	...	...	...	...	...	***20***	***18***	

TABLE XIII.—CASTE. PART A.—HINDUS, ANIMISTS, BUDDHISTS, JAINS, SIKHS AND BRAHMOS—*continued*.

District or State.	GOND (GONR). Hindu. Males.	Hindu. Females.	Animist. Males.	Animist. Females.	GORAIT. Hindu. Males.	Hindu. Females.	GOSAIN. Hindu. Males.	Hindu. Females.	GRAHABIPRA (GANAK). Hindu. Males.	Hindu. Females.	GURIA. Hindu. Males.	Hindu. Females.	GURUNG. Hindu. Males.	Hindu. Females.	Remarks.
1	150	151	152	153	154	155	156	157	158	159	160	161	162	163	164
ASSAM	***22,269***	***20,218***	***4,648***	***4,437***	***1,792***	***1,755***	***100***	***64***	***10,516***	***10,973***	***371***	***70***	***1,570***	***671***	Gond includes 17,298 males and 15,243 females returned as Gonr, *viz.*, Cachar (1,765), Sylhet (3,977), Khasi and Jaintia Hills (10), Naga Hills (24), Goalpara (411), Kamrup (727), Darrang (6,618), Nowgong (3,013), Sibsagar (6,177), Lakhimpur (9,904), Garo Hills (11) and Manipur (4). Gorait includes 111 males and 106 females returned as Animists, *viz.*, Darrang (17+28), Nowgong (0+1), Sibsagar (44+39) and Lakhimpur (50+38). It also includes 3 males and 6 females returned as Buddhists in Sibsagar. Gurung includes 17 males and 8 females returned as Buddhists, *viz.*, Kamrup (1+0), Darrang (4+3), Nowgong (11+4), Lakhimpur (1+1); it also includes 9 males and 2 females returned as Animists, *viz.*, Khasi and Jaintia Hills (2+0), Lushai Hills (5+1), and Garo Hills (2+1).
(1) British Territory	***22,266***	***20,217***	***4,648***	***4,437***	***1,792***	***1,755***	***97***	***58***	***10,516***	***10,973***	***371***	***70***	***1,501***	***624***	
SURMA VALLEY AND HILL DISTRICTS	***6,246***	***5,696***	***60***	***57***	***430***	***373***	***9***	***18***	***2,916***	***2,830***	***162***	***17***	***890***	***340***	
Cachar	13,340	3,225	60	57	208	205	5	18	90	32	111	...	100	13	
Sylhet	2,886	2,457	...	...	218	168	...	...	2,826	2,798	50	16	44	...	
Khasi and Jaintia Hills	5	5	...	...	...	...	...	...	...	...	1	1	523	196	
Naga Hills	15	9	...	...	...	...	4	...	...	...	...	...	88	54	
Lushai Hills	...	...	...	...	4	...	...	...	...	...	...	...	135	77	
ASSAM VALLEY DISTRICTS	***16,020***	***14,591***	***4,588***	***4,380***	***1,362***	***1,382***	***88***	***40***	***7,600***	***8,143***	***209***	***53***	***611***	***284***	
Goalpara	288	127	...	...	...	...	...	1	51	61	199	48	92	23	
Kamrup	410	295	15	...	1	...	60	39	3,070	3,510	...	1	44	20	
Darrang	2,947	2,768	1,688	1,508	191	193	...	...	2,913	3,006	5	3	50	28	
Nowgong	41	16	1,750	1,728	123	123	...	...	137	176	...	...	53	22	
Sibsagar	5,417	4,974	460	473	625	606	3	...	1,259	1,248	1	1	145	77	
Lakhimpur	6,874	6,341	666	671	422	460	25	...	170	142	4	...	180	88	
Garo Hills	13	...	...	...	...	...	...	...	...	...	...	...	47	31	
(2) Manipur State	***3***	***1***	...	...	...	...	***3***	***6***	...	...	...	...	***69***	***47***	

District or State.	HAJANG. Hindu. Males.	Hindu. Females.	HAJJAM. Hindu. Males.	Hindu. Females.	HALWAI. Hindu. Males.	Hindu. Females.	HARI. Hindu. Males.	Hindu. Females.	HIRA. Hindu. Males.	Hindu. Females.	JAIN (UNSPECIFIED). Jain. Males.	Jain. Females.	Remarks.
1	165	166	167	168	169	170	171	172	173	174	175	176	177
ASSAM	***4,324***	***3,964***	***1,043***	***669***	***1,010***	***320***	***2,732***	***2,856***	***8,063***	***8,288***	***296***	***38***	Hajjam includes 2 males returned as Jains, *viz.*, Goalpara (1) and Manipur (1). Halwai includes 1 male and 1 female returned as Animists in Lakhimpur. Hari includes 9 males and 5 females returned as Animists, *viz.*, Sibsagar (5+3) and Lakhimpur (4+2).
(1) British Territory	***4,324***	***3,964***	***1,039***	***667***	***985***	***314***	***2,552***	***2,613***	***8,063***	***8,288***	***251***	***36***	
SURMA VALLEY AND HILL DISTRICTS	***894***	***800***	***621***	***506***	***244***	***76***	***626***	***634***	...	...	***149***	***16***	
Cachar	...	...	47	50	109	62	358	392	...	...	13	6	
Sylhet	810	733	532	450	97	8	268	242	...	...	136	10	
Khasi and Jaintia Hills	84	67	26	1	27	5	...	...	...	...	...	...	
Naga Hills	...	...	1	...	3	1	...	...	...	...	...	...	
Lushai Hills	...	...	15	5	8	...	...	...	...	...	...	...	
ASSAM VALLEY DISTRICTS	***3,430***	***3,164***	***418***	***161***	***741***	***238***	***1,926***	***1,979***	***8,063***	***8,288***	***102***	***20***	
Goalpara	60	42	32	6	206	35	22	32	1,179	1,229	20	...	
Kamrup	...	...	9	...	97	9	317	333	2,823	2,877	2	...	
Darrang	...	...	23	5	69	33	331	348	662	743	24	...	
Nowgong	...	...	15	2	70	32	47	58	3,383	3,439	1	...	
Sibsagar	...	...	91	43	135	68	828	858	11	...	21	6	
Lakhimpur	...	...	240	105	164	61	381	350	2	...	34	14	
Garo Hills	3,370	3,122	8	...	...	...	...	...	3	...	...	...	
(2) Manipur State	...	...	***4***	***2***	***25***	***6***	***180***	***243***	...	...	***45***	***2***	

TABLE XIII.—CASTE. PART A.—HINDUS, ANIMISTS, BUDDHISTS, JAINS, SIKHS AND BRAHMOS—*continued.*

District or State.	Jaladha. Hindu. Males.	Jaladha. Hindu. Females.	Jaladha. Animist. Males.	Jaladha. Animist. Females.	Jat. Hindu. Males.	Jat. Hindu. Females.	Jhora. Hindu. Males.	Jhora. Hindu. Females.	Jogi (Jugi). Hindu. Males.	Jogi (Jugi). Hindu. Females.	Kachari. Hindu. Males.	Kachari. Hindu. Females.	Kachari. Animist. Males.	Kachari. Animist. Females.
1	178	179	180	181	182	183	184	185	186	187	188	189	190	191
ASSAM	***2,697***	***2,675***	***663***	***674***	***123***	***12***	***325***	***378***	***86,171***	***82,926***	***32,478***	***27,757***	***85,009***	***84,858***
(1) British Territory	***2,697***	***2,675***	***663***	***674***	***121***	***12***	***325***	***378***	***86,168***	***82,926***	***32,396***	***27,692***	***85,009***	***84,858***
SURMA VALLEY AND HILL DISTRICTS	***1***	...	...	...	***10***	...	***186***	***251***	***46,774***	***44,426***	***7,333***	***7,381***	***106***	***68***
Cachar	...	...	...	...	...	...	...	...	6,278	5,715	6,413	6,538	26	5
Sylhet	...	...	...	...	1	...	186	246	40,433	38,709	53	68	78	62
Khasi and Jaintia Hills	1	...	...	...	4	...	...	5	58	2	259	173	...	...
Naga Hills	...	...	...	...	1	...	...	...	...	...	583	590	...	...
Lushai Hills	...	...	...	...	4	...	...	...	5	...	25	12	2	1
ASSAM VALLEY DISTRICTS	***2,696***	***2,675***	***668***	***674***	***111***	***12***	***139***	***127***	***39,394***	***38,500***	***25,063***	***20,311***	***84,903***	***84,790***
Goalpara	2,598	2,581	...	...	14	...	...	...	8,302	7,914	159	159	...	...
Kamrup	93	82	407	403	22	4	1	...	9,389	9,447	1,570	950	46,210	49,506
Darrang	10	12	256	271	3	...	90	69	9,084	8,907	1,024	426	29,168	27,083
Nowgong	...	...	...		27	...	17	17	8,466	8,581	2	...	7,068	6,711
Sibsagar	...	...	...	...	18	4	...	18	3,351	2,973	8,842	6,396	1,189	525
Lakhimpur	...	...	...	...	26	4	31	23	788	678	13,408	12,345	1,248	952
Garo Hills	...	...	...	...	1	...	...	...	14	...	58	35	20	13
(2) Manipur State	...	...	...	...	***2***	...	...	...	***3***	...	***82***	***65***	...	...

Remarks (192).

Jat includes 2 males returned as Sikhs in Lushai Hills. It also includes 2 males returned as Jains, *viz.*, Darrang (1) and Garo Hills (1).

Jhora includes 4 males returned as Animists in Darrang.

Jogi includes 11 males returned as Animists in Sibsagar.

Kachari includes 2,922 males and 2,608 females returned as Thengals, *viz.*, Sibsagar (5,399) and Lakhimpur (131). Kachari (Hindu) includes 3 males returned as Buddhists in Darrang. There are, besides, 101 males and 92 females returned as Christians, *viz.*, Kamrup (1), Darrang (182) and Sibsagar (10).

District or State.	Kahar. Hindu. Males.	Kahar. Hindu. Females.	Kaibartta (Hindu). Kaibartta. Males.	Kaibartta (Hindu). Kaibartta. Females.	Kaibartta (Hindu). Chasi (Mahishya). Males.	Kaibartta (Hindu). Chasi (Mahishya). Females.	Kaibartta (Hindu). Jaliya. Males.	Kaibartta (Hindu). Jaliya. Females.	Kalita. Hindu. Males.	Kalita. Hindu. Females.	Kalu. Hindu. Males.	Kalu. Hindu. Females.	Kalwar. Hindu. Males.	Kalwar. Hindu. Females.
1	193	194	195	196	197	198	199	200	201	202	203	204	205	206
ASSAM	***6,524***	***5,182***	***10,624***	***10,219***	***34,304***	***31,008***	***23,331***	***21,767***	***115,506***	***106,436***	***1,354***	***672***	***1,451***	***1,039***
(1) British Territory	***6,489***	***5,170***	***10,624***	***10,219***	***34,304***	***31,008***	***23,331***	***21,767***	***115,496***	***106,432***	***1,342***	***672***	***1,448***	***1,039***
SURMA VALLEY AND HILL DISTRICTS	***4,073***	***3,887***	***21***	***1***	***33,741***	***30,454***	***22,638***	***21,085***	***116***	***68***	***530***	***403***	***444***	***390***
Cachar	792	680	...	...	499	282	50	76	6	8	224	212	263	187
Sylhet	3,191	3,181	...	...	33,180	30,158	22,588	21,009	55	54	306	191	174	208
Khasi and Jaintia Hills	70	23	20	1	52	14	...	...	35	1	...	...	5	...
Naga Hills	12	1	1	...	1	...	...	...	18	5	...	...	...	...
Lushai Hills	8	2	...	...	...	...	...	...	2	...	...	...	2	...
ASSAM VALLEY DISTRICTS	***2,416***	***1,283***	***10,603***	***10,218***	***563***	***554***	***693***	***682***	***115,380***	***106,364***	***812***	***269***	***1,004***	***649***
Goalpara	368	83	1,044	866	438	402	623	644	5,944	5,404	286	68	147	29
Kamrup	189	49	8,610	8,547	99	114	38	26	65,866	63,617	80	10	58	11
Darrang	298	158	93	67	...	7	...	1	8,694	7,582	93	32	54	30
Nowgong	160	100	37	25	15	12	18	11	8,613	8,335	14	...	24	20
Sibsagar	733	506	280	288	11	19	1	...	22,034	19,104	173	77	469	344
Lakhimpur	653	375	559	425	...	...	1	...	3,206	2,318	166	73	250	209
Garo Hills	15	3	...	...	...	...	12	...	23	4	...	...	7	...
(2) Manipur Satte	***3***	***12***	...	...	...	...	...	...	***10***	***4***	***12***	...	***3***	...

Remarks (207).

Kahar includes 1 male returned as Sikh in Khasi and Jaintia Hills, and 11 males and 6 females returned as Animists, *viz.*, Darrang (1+0), Nowgong (7+2), Sibsagar (2+4) and Lakhimpur (1+0).

Kaibartta includes 1 male returned as Animist in Kamrup.

Kaibartta (Jaliya) includes 1 male and 1 female returned as Animists, *viz.*, Nowgong (0+1) and Lakhimpur (1+0).

Kalita includes Nat Kalita (449), Kalita Dulia (233) and Kumhar Kalita (136) in Sibsagar. It also includes 1 male returned as Brahmo in Khasi and Jaintia Hills.

Kaln includes 1 male returned as Animist in Nowgong and 3 males returned as Jains in Manipur.

Kalwar includes 68 males and 57 females returned as Animists, *viz.*, Sibsagar (57+29) and Lakhimpur (11+28).

TABLE XIII.—CASTE. PART A.—HINDUS, ANIMISTS, BUDDHISTS, JAINS, SIKHS AND BRAHMOS—*continued.*

District or State.	KAMAR.				KAMI.		KANDH.				KANDU.		Remarks.
	Hindu.		Animist.		Hindu.		Hindu.		Animist.		Hindu.		
	Males.	Females.	Males.	Females.	Males.	Females.	Males.	Females.	Males.	Females.	Males.	Females.	
1	208	209	210	211	212	213	214	215	216	217	218	219	220
ASSAM	***21,622***	***21,078***	***301***	***284***	***795***	***543***	***1,895***	***1,847***	***762***	***634***	***1,296***	***762***	
(1) *British Territory*	***21,622***	***21,078***	***301***	***284***	***749***	***515***	***1,895***	***1,847***	***762***	***634***	***1,296***	***762***	Kami includes 9 males returned as Buddhists, *viz.*, Darrang (2) and Sibsagar (7).
SURMA VALLEY AND HILL DISTRICTS ...	***8,532***	***8,494***	...	...	***129***	***65***	***262***	***261***	...	...	***702***	***470***	
Cachar	2,702	2,553	...	...	81	12	150	159	...	...	76	82	
Sylhet	5,812	5,941	...	...	...	...	111	102	...	...	604	386	Kandu includes 5 males and 2 females returned as Animists in Sibsagar.
Khasi and Jaintia Hills	13	...	...	...	64	19	1	...	...	...	6	2	
Naga Hills	2	...	...	...	27	29	...	...	...	...	15	...	
Lushai Hills	3	...	...	...	7	5	...	...	...	...	1	...	
ASSAM VALLEY DISTRICTS	***13,090***	***12,584***	***301***	***284***	***620***	***450***	***1,633***	***1,586***	***762***	***634***	***594***	***299***	
Goalpara	305	171	...	...	88	60	1	...	...	...	65	33	
Kamrup	301	276	...	...	60	58	...	...	...	...	4	...	
Darrang	2,387	2,258	1	...	278	209	539	345	376	346	31	44	
Nowgong	463	505	5	...	10	10	34	22	...	...	36	18	
Sibsagar	4,922	4,706	141	144	28	14	301	414	39	35	261	176	
Lakhimpur	4,708	4,668	154	140	112	62	738	805	347	253	181	21	
Garo Hills	4	...	...	...	44	37	...	...	...	...	16	...	
(2) *Manipur State*	...	...	...	...	***46***	***28***	...	...	...	...	...	...	

District or State.	KANSARI.		KAORA.		KAPALI.		KAPUBIA.		KAUR.		KAYASTHA.		KEWAT.		Remarks.
	Hindu.		Hindu.		Hindu.		Hindu.		Hindu.		Hindu.		Hindu.		
	Males.	Females.	Males.	Females.	Males.	Females.	Males.	Females.	Males.	Females.	Males.	Females.	Males.	Females.	
1	221	222	223	224	225	226	227	228	229	230	231	232	233	234	235
ASSAM	***197***	***195***	***272***	***314***	***807***	***784***	***67***	***75***	***864***	***592***	***44,377***	***37,590***	***48,245***	***46,532***	
(1) *British Territory*	***197***	***195***	***272***	***314***	***807***	***784***	***67***	***75***	***864***	***590***	***44,289***	***37,538***	***48,242***	***46,530***	Kaora includes 2 males and 1 female returned as Animists, *viz.*, Darrang (2+0) and Nowgong (0+1).
SURMA VALLEY AND HILL DISTRICTS ...	***175***	***176***	***157***	***205***	***792***	***781***	***15***	***13***	***343***	***251***	***32,424***	***28,976***	***654***	***438***	
Cachar	...	...	157	205	...	6	...	...	206	118	3,181	1,659	201	175	Kaur includes 2 males and 8 females returned as Animists in Lakhimpur.
Sylhet	174	176	...	...	791	775	15	13	123	130	28,558	27,025	444	258	
Khasi and Jaintia Hills	...	...	...	...	1	...	...	...	9	...	600	269	3	...	
Naga Hills	1	...	...	...	...	...	...	...	5	3	40	11	6	5	
Lushai Hills	...	...	...	...	...	...	...	...	...	...	45	12	...	...	Kayastha includes 3 males returned as Brahmos in Darrang, and 1 male returned as Buddhist in Sibsagar.
ASSAM VALLEY DISTRICTS	***22***	***19***	***115***	***109***	***15***	***3***	***52***	***62***	***521***	***339***	***11,865***	***8,562***	***47,588***	***46,092***	
Goalpara	...	...	1	...	8	3	5	11	11	8	1,623	862	301	168	Kewat includes 11 males and 8 females returned as Animists, *viz.*, Nowgong (1+0), Sibsagar (4+0) and Lakhimpur (6+8).
Kamrup	...	...	...	...	...	...	...	10	...	...	2,690	2,203	17,275	17,969	
Darrang	15	16	70	89	...	...	1	...	144	107	1,202	818	6,897	6,554	
Nowgong	6	2	11	10	...	...	...	...	15	10	1,561	1,153	7,567	7,609	
Sibsagar	...	...	31	8	...	...	20	41	124	100	3,147	2,439	13,533	11,945	
Lakhimpur	1	1	2	2	7	...	26	...	227	119	1,573	978	2,003	1,847	
Garo Hills	...	...	...	...	...	...	...	...	...	...	69	19	12	...	
(2) *Manipur State*	...	...	...	...	...	...	...	...	...	***2***	***88***	***52***	***3***	***2***	

TABLE XIII.—Caste. Part A.—Hindus, Animists, Buddhists, Jains, Sikhs and Brahmos—*continued.*

District or State.	KHADAL. Hindu. Males.	KHADAL. Hindu. Females.	KHAIRA. Hindu. Males.	KHAIRA. Hindu. Females.	KHAMBU. Hindu. Males.	KHAMBU. Hindu. Females.	KHAMTI. Buddhist. Males.	KHAMTI. Buddhist. Females.	KHANDAIT. Hindu. Males.	KHANDAIT. Hindu. Females.	KHARIA. Hindu. Males.	KHARIA. Hindu. Females.	KHARIA. Animist. Males.	KHARIA. Animist. Females.
1	236	237	238	239	240	241	242	243	244	245	246	247	248	249
ASSAM	*2,085*	*2,181*	*515*	*425*	*2,445*	*807*	*1,014*	*854*	*780*	*547*	*5,233*	*4,818*	*1,184*	*1,122*
(1) British Territory	*2,085*	*2,181*	*515*	*425*	*2,279*	*739*	*1,014*	*854*	*780*	*547*	*5,233*	*4,818*	*1,184*	*1,122*
SURMA VALLEY AND HILL DISTRICTS	*725*	*815*	*192*	*190*	*591*	*217*	*17*	...	*228*	*135*	*1,279*	*1,148*	...	...
Cachar	...	...	102	96	48	28	17	...	83	53	670	613	...	...
Sylhet	725	815	90	94	...	...	...	...	145	82	607	520	...	...
Khasi and Jaintia Hills	...	...	...	...	46	15	...	...	...	...	2	15	...	...
Naga Hills	...	...	...	...	173	56	...	...	...	...	...	...	...	...
Lushai Hills	...	...	...	...	324	118	...	...	...	...	...	...	...	...
ASSAM VALLEY DISTRICTS	*1,360*	*1,366*	*323*	*235*	*1,688*	*522*	*997*	*854*	*552*	*412*	*3,954*	*3,670*	*1,184*	*1,122*
Goalpara	...	...	...	...	734	107	...	...	37	...	11	15	...	...
Kamrup	...	...	24	21	53	32	...	...	15	2	30	21	...	...
Darrang	1,039	1,036	73	60	184	71	46	...	169	148	848	840	208	229
Nowgong	1	...	7	1	8	3	...	...	69	59	3	4	227	188
Sibsagar	286	300	59	74	192	77	99	14	167	140	1,116	1,032	48	47
Lakhimpur	34	30	155	79	462	212	852	840	95	57	1,946	1,758	701	658
Garo Hills	...	...	...	...	55	20	...	...	...	...	...	...	...	...
(2) Manipur State	...	...	...	...	*166*	*68*	...	...	...	...	...	...	...	...

Remarks (250).

Khadal includes 45 males and 54 females returned as Animists, *viz.*, Darrang (41+49), Sibsagar (2+1) and Lakhimpur (2+4).

Khaira includes 8 males and 1 female returned as Animists, *viz.*, Darrang (7+0) and Sibsagar (1+1).

Khambu includes 7 males and 3 females returned as Animists, *viz.*, Naga Hills (0+1), Lakhimpur (3+2) and Garo Hills (4+0); it also includes 20 males and 4 females returned as Buddhists, *viz.*, Goalpara (3+0), Kamrup (5+4), Darrang (6+0), Sibsagar (2+0) and Lakhimpur (4+0).

Khamti includes 16 males returned as Animists, *viz.*, Cachar (8), Darrang (1) and Sibsagar (7). It also includes 2 males returned as Hindus in Lakhimpur.

Khandait includes 1 male returned as Animist in Lakhimpur.

Kharia.—There are 37 males and 11 females returned as Christians, *viz.*, Sibsagar (16) and Lakhimpur (32).

District or State.	KHARWAR. Hindu. Males.	KHARWAR. Hindu. Females.	KHAS. Hindu. Males.	KHAS. Hindu. Females.	KHASI. Hindu. Males.	KHASI. Hindu. Females.	KHASI. Animist. Males.	KHASI. Animist. Females.	KHATIK. Hindu. Males.	KHATIK. Hindu. Females.	KHAWAS. Hindu. Males.	KHAWAS. Hindu. Females.
1	251	252	253	254	255	256	257	258	259	260	261	262
ASSAM	*3,734*	*3,340*	*1,281*	*733*	*606*	*568*	*56,722*	*62,998*	*72*	*61*	*62*	*38*
(1) British Territory	*3,733*	*3,340*	*1,281*	*716*	*606*	*567*	*56,721*	*62,993*	*72*	*61*	*54*	*36*
SURMA VALLEY AND HILL DISTRICTS	*426*	*483*	*134*	*96*	*519*	*539*	*56,420*	*62,782*	*44*	*50*	*18*	*17*
Cachar	246	262	22	20	239	151	139	100	31	81	...	...
Sylhet	175	218	...	...	156	277	1,413	1,408	13	19	...	...
Khasi and Jaintia Hills	5	3	46	49	122	111	54,826	61,238	...	...	...	...
Naga Hills	...	...	...	1	1	...	21	22	...	...	18	17
Lushai Hills	...	...	56	26	1	...	30	14	...	...	...	...
ASSAM VALLEY DISTRICTS	*3,307*	*2,857*	*1,157*	*620*	*87*	*28*	*292*	*211*	*28*	*11*	*36*	*19*
Goalpara	4	4	24	8	...	...	1	...	9	...	17	9
Kamrup	3	8	1	3	2	...	232	149	4	10	1	...
Darrang	1,204	1,184	30	9	65	4	13	3	...	1	2	6
Nowgong	236	183	768	438	...	...	34	38	6	...	...	...
Sibsagar	688	629	273	127	4	9	3	6	9	...	1	...
Lakhimpur	1,169	844	38	27	16	15	9	15	...	...	10	2
Garo Hills	1	...	23	8	...	...	1	...	...	...	5	2
(2) Manipur State	*1*	...	...	*17*	...	*1*	*1*	*5*	...	...	*8*	*2*

Remarks (263).

Kharwar includes 23 males and 34 females returned as Animists, *viz.*, Darrang (15+20), Sibsagar (6+8) and Lakhimpur (2+6).

Khas includes 29 males and 22 females returned as Animists, *viz.*, Naga Hills (0+1), Lakhimpur (27+21) and Garo Hills (2+0). It also includes 6 males and 2 females returned as Buddhists in Nowgong.

Khasi (Animist) includes 2 females returned as Buddhists in Darrang.

Khasi (Hindu) includes 110 males and 97 females returned as Brahmos in Khasi and Jaintia Hills. There are, besides, 8,416 males and 9,114 females returned as Christians, *viz.*, Cachar (75), Sylhet (27), Khasi and Jaintia Hills (17,255), Lushai Hills (15), Kamrup (155) and Lakhimpur (3).

Khawas includes 1 male returned as Buddhist in Sibsagar.

TABLE XIII.—CASTE. PART A.—HINDUS, ANIMISTS, BUDDHISTS, JAINS, SIKHS AND BRAHMOS—*continued*.

District or State.	KOCH.				KOIRI.		KORA.		KORWA.				KSHATTRIYA (MANIPURI.)	
	Hindu.		Animist.		Hindu.		Hindu.		Hindu.		Animist.		Hindu.	
	Males.	Females.	Males.	Females.	Males.	Females.	Males.	Females.	Males.	Females.	Males.	Females.	Males.	Females.
1	264	265	266	267	268	269	270	271	272	273	274	275	276	277
ASSAM	*121,933*	*117,739*	*1,254*	*1,138*	*8,064*	*5,936*	*1,991*	*1,848*	*1,435*	*1,460*	*352*	*347*	*124,764*	*125,777*
(1) ***British Territory***	*121,933*	*117,739*	*1,254*	*1,128*	*8,051*	*5,933*	*1,989*	*1,848*	*1,432*	*1,460*	*352*	*347*	*40,597*	*38,242*
SURMA VALLEY AND HILL DISTRICTS...	*561*	*568*	...	...	*4,825*	*4,067*	*523*	*556*	*382*	*283*	...	...	*39,823*	*37,790*
Cachar	90	79	...	...	1,532	1,425	188	197	211	209	...	...	24,948	23,480
Sylhet	442	483	...	...	3,192	2,614	335	359	171	74	...	...	14,616	14,217
Khasi and Jaintia Hills	10	2	...	...	91	23	...	...	...	...	...	...	114	75
Naga Hills	15	1	...	...	3	...	...	...	...	...	...	...	102	8
Lushai Hills	4	3	...	...	7	5	...	...	...	...	...	...	43	10
ASSAM VALLEY DISTRICTS	*121,372*	*117,171*	*1,254*	*1,128*	*3,226*	*1,866*	*1,466*	*1,292*	*1,050*	*1,177*	*352*	*347*	*774*	*452*
Goalpara	5,717	5,370	2	...	342	48	...	...	...	...	...	...	...	...
Kamrup	51,005	50,238	733	654	201	56	6	8	4	5	...	...	37	32
Darrang	28,669	23,738	13	4	451	274	241	246	216	221	214	248	60	29
Nowgong	18,582	18,464	...	...	195	115	99	95	59	63	116	94	47	13
Sibsagar	16,281	14,901	...	...	1,108	829	820	752	338	385	...	...	347	230
Lakhimpur	4,002	3,375	...	3	913	544	300	191	433	503	22	5	280	123
Garo Hills	2,016	1,995	506	467	16	...	...	...	...	...	...	...	3	...
(2) ***Manipur State***	...	...	...	...	*13*	*3*	*2*	...	*3*	...	...	...	*84,167*	*87,535*

Remarks. (278)

Koch (Hindu) includes 3 males returned as Jains in Goalpara. It also includes 7,862 males and 7,409 females returned as (i) Madahi, *viz.*, Naga Hills (6), Goalpara (8,890), Kamrup (6,280), Darrang (91) and Sibsagar (4); 2,219 males and 2,262 females returned as (ii) Mahalia, *viz.*, Sylhet (761), Khasi and Jaintia Hills (2), Goalpara, (3), Kamrup (16), Darrang (3,684), and Lakhimpur (15); 457 males and 434 females returned as (iii) Matia, *viz.*, Goalpara (76), Kamrup (792), Darrang (2) and Lakhimpur (21), and 5,982 males and 6,240 females returned as (iv) Saraniya, *viz.*, Goalpara (951), Kamrup (10,565), Darrang (357), Sibsagar, (263) and Lakhimpur (86). There are, besides, 1 male and 6 females returned as Christians, *viz.*, Goalpara (1), Darrang (1) and Sibsagar (5).

Koiri includes 10 males and 22 females returned as Animists, *viz.*, Kamrup (1+0), Darrang (1+1), Sibsagar (3+5) and Lakhimpur (5+16), and 3 males returned as Jains in Manipur.

Kora includes 71 males and 35 females returned as Animists, *viz.*, Darrang (17+18), Nowgong (2+0), Sibsagar (16+11) and Lakhimpur (36+6).

Korwa (Hindu) includes 1 male returned as Buddhist in Sibsagar.

Kshattriya includes 9,871 males and 10,144 females returned as Manipuri, *viz.*, Cachar (10,544), Sylhet (8,866), Khasi and Jaintia Hills (56), Naga Hills (105), Lushai Hills (39), Kamrup (69), Nowgong (1), Sibsagar (21), Lakhimpur (174) and Manipur (140). It includes 2 males and 2 females returned as Buddhists in Sibsagar and 76 males and 76 females returned as Animists, *viz.*, Khasi and Jaintia Hills (1+0), Naga Hills (9+1), Nowgong (0+1) and Manipur (66+74), and 1 male returned as Brahmo and 2 males returned as Sikhs in Goalpara.

District or State.	KUKI (TOTAL).*				KUMHAR.		KURMI.		LALBEGI.		LALUNG.			
	Hindu.		Animist.		Hindu.		Hindu.		Hindu.		Hindu.		Animist.	
	Males.	Females.	Males.	Females.	Males.	Females.	Males.	Females.	Males.	Females.	Males.	Females.	Males.	Females.
1	279	280	281	282	283	284	285	286	287	288	289	290	291	292
ASSAM	*620*	*613*	*37,632*	*38,331*	*14,418*	*13,485*	*14,296*	*10,224*	*249*	*196*	*263*	*233*	*18,959*	*19,764*
(1) ***British Territory***	*620*	*613*	*6,076*	*6,533*	*14,416*	*13,482*	*14,264*	*10,218*	*247*	*194*	*263*	*233*	*18,959*	*19,764*
SURMA VALLEY AND HILL DISTRICTS...	*620*	*613*	*6,029*	*6,493*	*7,635*	*7,403*	*4,881*	*3,776*	*108*	*86*	*7*	*4*	*1,656*	*1,725*
Cachar	72	69	3,718	3,918	1,512	1,371	2,183	1,649	28	23	...	...	...	...
Sylhet	548	543	238	255	6,116	6,030	2,582	2,081	11	3	3	4	...	...
Khasi and Jaintia Hills	...	...	536	330	3	2	102	44	65	59	3	...	1,656	1,725
Naga Hills	...	...	1,552	1,783	2	...	4	...	–	...	1	–	...	...
Lushai Hills	...	...	185	207	2	...	10	3	4	1	...	...	...	...
ASSAM VALLEY DISTRICTS	...	*1*	*67*	*40*	*6,781*	*6,079*	*9,333*	*6,442*	*139*	*108*	*256*	*229*	*17,303*	*18,039*
Goalpara	...	...	...	...	590	222	1,185	250	33	15	...	...	...	...
Kamrup	...	...	...	...	3,760	3,681	418	127	...	3	4	...	861	898
Darrang	...	...	...	1	637	607	1,373	1,087	38	34	4	...	4	1
Nowgong	...	...	39	38	553	561	506	290	7	4	...	1	16,027	16,763
Sibsagar	...	1	8	1	581	499	3,193	2,558	15	14	91	81	3	8
Lakhimpur	...	...	...	...	531	420	2,645	2,125	46	38	157	147	408	369
Garo Hills	...	...	...	...	124	89	63	5	...	...	...	...	...	...
(2) ***Manipur State***	...	...	*31,556*	*31,798*	*2*	*3*	*32*	*6*	*2*	*2*	...	...	...	...

Remarks. (293)

*For details of Kuki see Appendix, Part I.

Kumhar includes 4 males and 14 females returned as Animists in Lakhimpur.

Kurmi includes 19 males and 18 females returned as Animists, *viz.*, Darrang (1+0), Nowgong (0+1), Sibsagar (6+5), Lakhimpur (10+12) and Garo Hills (2+0). It also includes 1 female returned as Sikh in Sibsagar.

Lalbegi includes 1 male returned as Sikh in Khasi and Jaintia Hills, and 2 males and 3 females returned as Animists in Sibsagar.

Lalung (Hindu) includes 4 males returned as Buddhists in Kamrup.

TABLE XIII.—Caste. Part A.—Hindus, Animists, Buddhists, Jains, Sikhs and Brahmos—*continued.*

District or State.	Limbu. Hindu. Males.	Limbu. Hindu. Females.	Limbu. Buddhist. Males.	Limbu. Buddhist. Females.	Lodha. Hindu. Males.	Lodha. Hindu. Females.	Lohar. Hindu. Males.	Lohar. Hindu. Females.	Lushai (Total).* Hindu. Males.	Lushai (Total).* Hindu. Females.	Lushai (Total).* Animist. Males.	Lushai (Total).* Animist. Females.	Remarks.
1	294	295	296	207	298	299	300	301	302	303	304	305	306
Assam	*1,823*	*748*	*242*	*106*	*617*	*543*	*6,390*	*5,801*	*34*	...	*36,724*	*43,667*	Limbu (Hindu) includes 8 males and 4 females returned as Animists, *viz.*, Lakhimpur (7+4) and Garo Hills (1+0).
(1) British Territory	*1,811*	*741*	*242*	*106*	*617*	*543*	*6,378*	*5,796*	*34*	...	*36,651*	*43,600*	
SURMA VALLEY AND HILL DISTRICTS ...	*442*	*215*	...	*3*	*291*	*302*	*1,636*	*1,479*	*34*	...	*36,651*	*43,600*	
Cachar	27	27	...	...	276	269	798	734	...	...	4	...	Lodha includes 36 males and 2 females returned as Animists in Sibsagar.
Sylhet	...	...	...	...	15	33	785	720	32	...	4	...	Lohar includes 74 males and 80 females returned as Animists, *viz.*, Darrang (5+0), Nowgong (4+3), Sibsagar (3+3) and Lakhimpur (62+74). It also includes 5 males and 5 females returned as Buddhists in Goalpara, and 4 males returned as Jains and 1 female returned as Sikh in Nowgong.
Khasi and Jaintia Hills	86	8	...	3	...	...	14	1	2	...	2	...	
Naga Hills	121	70	...	...	...	...	16	10	...	...	...	...	
Lushai Hills	208	110	...	...	...	...	23	14	...	...	36,641	43,600	
ASSAM VALLEY DISTRICTS	*1,369*	*526*	*242*	*103*	*396*	*241*	*4,742*	*4,317*	...	...	...	...	
Goalpara	507	142	183	64	11	1	177	43	...	...	...	...	* For Lushai details see Appendix, Part I. There are, besides, 664 males and 595 females returned as Christians in Lushai Hills.
Kamrup	83	58	...	...	7	2	106	28	...	...	...	...	
Darrang	349	123	59	39	58	24	448	422	...	...	...	...	
Nowgong	40	11	...	...	10	11	284	277	...	...	...	...	
Sibsagar	56	20	...	...	188	158	1,133	1,065	...	...	...	...	
Lakhimpur	173	58	...	...	52	45	2,590	2,479	...	...	...	...	
Garo Hills	161	105	...	...	...	...	4	3	...	...	...	...	
(2) Manipur State	*19*	*7*	...	...	...	...	*19*	*5*	...	...	*73*	*67*	

District or State.	Magh. Buddhist. Males.	Magh. Buddhist. Females.	Mahesri. Hindu. Males.	Mahesri. Hindu. Females.	Mahli. Hindu. Males.	Mahli. Hindu. Females.	Mahli. Animist. Males.	Mahli. Animist. Females.	Mal. Hindu. Males.	Mal. Hindu. Females.	Mal. Animist. Males.	Mal. Animist. Females.	Mali (Malakar). Hindu. Males.	Mali (Malakar). Hindu. Females.	Remarks.
1	307	308	309	310	311	312	313	314	315	316	317	318	319	320	321
Assam	*137*	*31*	*789*	*127*	*3,977*	*3,645*	*344*	*308*	*3,596*	*2,743*	*170*	*186*	*7,450*	*6,784*	Magh includes 18 males returned as Hindus, *viz.*, Sylhet (12), Khasi and Jaintia Hills (1), Lushai Hills (2), Sibsagar (1) and Lakhimpur (2). It also includes 2 males and 1 female returned as Animists, *viz.*, Lushai Hills (1+1) and Lakhimpur (1+0).
(1) British Territory	*136*	*31*	*789*	*127*	*3,976*	*3,615*	*344*	*308*	*3,596*	*2,743*	*170*	*186*	*7,448*	*6,784*	
SURMA VALLEY AND HILL DISTRICTS ...	*83*	*19*	...	...	*845*	*782*	...	...	*1,583*	*960*	...	...	*5,073*	*4,750*	
Cachar	11	1	...	...	779	730	...	...	1,582	960	...	...	745	651	Mahesri includes 58 males and 7 females returned as Jains, *viz.*, Goalpara (25+5), Darrang (4+0), Nowgong (3+0), Sibsagar (9+2), Lakhimpur (11+0) and Garo Hills (6+0).
Sylhet	16	2	...	...	66	52	...	...	...	...	...	...	4,317	4,099	
Khasi and Jaintia Hills	10	1	...	...	...	...	...	...	1	...	...	...	8	...	
Naga Hills	3	...	...	...	...	...	...	...	...	...	...	...	...	...	
Lushai Hills	43	15	...	...	...	...	...	...	...	...	...	...	3	...	
ASSAM VALLEY DISTRICTS	*53*	*12*	*789*	*127*	*3,131*	*2,863*	*344*	*308*	*2,013*	*1,783*	*170*	*186*	*2,375*	*2,034*	Mahli.—There are 22 males and 19 females returned as Christians in Sibsagar.
Goalpara	...	...	64	5	1	...	22	...	133	39	...	...	434	343	Mali (Malakar) includes 12 males and 1 female returned as Jains, *viz.*, Khasi and Jaintia Hills (1+0), Goalpara (2+0), Kamrup (1+0) and Darrang (8+1).
Kamrup	6	2	8	5	1	12	...	...	103	4	...	...	1,348	1,306	
Darrang	7	2	53	10	610	428	7	9	293	202	...	1	54	59	
Nowgong	2	...	188	19	5	1	81	93	109	113	...	...	39	19	
Sibsagar	12	4	340	68	1,303	1,238	208	176	984	995	32	33	189	64	
Lakhimpur	26	4	121	20	1,211	1,184	28	30	391	430	138	152	302	241	
Garo Hills	...	...	6	...	...	...	...	...	...	...	...	...	9	2	
(2) Manipur State	*1*	...	...	...	*1*	...	...	...	...	...	...	...	*2*	...	

TABLE XIII.—CASTE: PART A.—HINDUS, ANIMISTS, BUDDHISTS, JAINS, SIKHS AND BRAHMOS—*continued.*

DISTRICT OR STATE.	MALLAH.		MALO.		MALPAHARIA.				MANGAR.				MANJHI.		REMARKS.
	HINDU.		HINDU.		HINDU.		ANIMIST.		HINDU.		ANIMIST.		HINDU.		
	Males.	Females.	Males.	Females.	Males.	Females.	Males.	Females.	Males.	Females.	Males.	Females.	Males.	Females.	
1	322	323	324	325	326	327	328	329	330	331	332	333	334	335	336
ASSAM	***3,507***	***1,185***	***11,295***	***9,062***	***1,705***	***1,609***	***118***	***101***	***4,443***	***2,260***	***214***	***203***	***1,435***	***1,237***	Mallah includes 30 males and 19 females returned as Animists and 1 male returned as Sikh in Sibsagar. It also includes 43 males and 90 females returned as Gonhi, *viz.*, Sylhet (107), Khasi and Jaintia Hills (3), Lushai Hills (8), Goalpara (3) and Darrang (12).
(1) ***British Territory***	***3,506***	***1,185***	***11,295***	***9,062***	***1,705***	***1,609***	***118***	***101***	***4,398***	***2,258***	***214***	***203***	***1,420***	***1,233***	
SURMA VALLEY AND HILL DISTRICTS	***554***	***289***	***9,425***	***8,079***	***60***	***58***	...	...	***2,321***	***1,117***	***7***	***4***	***552***	***501***	
Cachar	39	8	414	751	...	...	...	...	91	34	...	...	315	300	Malo includes 3 males and 1 female returned as Animists in Sibsagar, and 2 males returned as Jains in Goalpara.
Sylhet	466	278	9,003	7,328	60	58	...	...	419	307	...	...	227	199	
Khasi and Jaintia Hills	40	3	...	...	...	...	...	...	1,298	511	2	...	6	1	
Naga Hills	1	...	...	...	...	...	...	...	261	153	...	...	3	1	
Lushai Hills	8	...	8	...	...	...	...	...	252	112	5	4	1	...	
ASSAM VALLEY DISTRICTS	***2,952***	***896***	***1,870***	***983***	***1,645***	***1,551***	***118***	***101***	***2,077***	***1,141***	***207***	***199***	***868***	***732***	Mangar (Hindu) includes 7 males returned as Buddhists, *viz.*, Kamrup (2), Darrang (1), Sibsagar (1) and Lakhimpur (3).
Goalpara	1,511	481	998	567	9	16	...	...	274	154	...	...	76	39	
Kamrup	256	24	308	4	45	48	...	...	346	162	3	3	27	23	Manjhi includes 5 males and 2 females returned as Buddhists in Kamrup, and 3 males and 8 females returned as Animists, *viz.*, Darrang (2+3) and Sibsagar (1+5). It also includes 6 males and 1 female returned as Sikhs in Khasi and Jaintia Hills.
Darrang	155	59	16	12	108	114	58	34	559	288	204	196	17	11	
Nowgong	83	4	109	7	264	282	2	2	34	19	...	...	3	2	
Sibsagar	355	126	234	236	191	98	22	17	184	75	...	...	303	297	
Lakhimpur	589	2.2	133	61	1,028	993	36	48	581	381	...	...	435	357	
Garo Hills	3	...	72	96	...	...	...	...	99	62	...	...	7	3	
(2) ***Manipur State***	***1***	...	...	...	...	...	...	...	***45***	***2***	...	...	***5***	***4***	

DISTRICT OR STATE.	MARWARI.		MAULIK (NAIYA).		MAYRA.		MECH.				MEHTAR.		REMARKS.
	HINDU.		HINDU.		HINDU.		HINDU.		ANIMIST.		HINDU.		
	Males.	Females.	Males.	Females.	Males.	Females.	Males.	Females.	Males.	Females.	Males.	Females.	
1	337	338	339	340	341	342	343	344	345	346	347	348	349
ASSAM	***159***	***65***	***2,193***	***2,034***	***1,033***	***1,153***	***34,908***	***34,992***	***12,269***	***12,437***	***375***	***280***	Marwari includes 28 males and 5 females returned as Jains, *viz.*, Goalpara (8+0), Sibsagar (4+0) and Lakhimpur (16+5).
(1) ***British Territory***	***159***	***65***	***2,192***	***2,034***	***1,030***	***1,153***	***34,902***	***34,992***	***12,266***	***12,436***	***375***	***279***	
SURMA VALLEY AND HILL DISTRICTS	***42***	***17***	***996***	***922***	***617***	***654***	***168***	***51***	...	...	***151***	***125***	Maulik includes 12 males and 4 females returned as Animists, *viz.*, Sibsagar (6+4) and Lakhimpur (6+0).
Cachar	4	1	932	880	78	16	24	13	...	...	25	11	
Sylhet	13	3	64	42	531	637	...	...	...	...	100	105	
Khasi and Jaintia Hills	25	13	...	...	8	1	3	...	...	...	16	6	Mayra includes 16 males and 12 females returned as Animists, *viz.*, Kamrup (1+0) and Sibsagar (15+12).
Naga Hills	...	...	...	...	...	...	125	33	...	...	6	3	
Lushai Hills	...	...	...	...	...	...	16	5	...	...	4	...	
ASSAM VALLEY DISTRICTS	***117***	***48***	***1,196***	***1,112***	***413***	***499***	***34,734***	***34,941***	***12,266***	***12,436***	***224***	***154***	Mech (Hindu) includes 5 males returned as Brahmos, *viz.*, Goalpara (1) and Darrang (4).
Goalpara	23	9	4	5	106	110	34,171	34,421	12,006	12,431	144	111	
Kamrup	7	2	146	122	8	37	22	23	142	2	26	16	
Darrang	7	...	102	66	22	9	4	...	30	1	9	4	
Nowgong	3	...	22	10	3	2	...	...	2	1	...	...	
Sibsagar	36	8	718	778	192	193	8	2	1	...	10	1	
Lakhimpur	41	20	204	131	55	117	62	50	...	...	34	22	
Garo Hills	...	...	...	...	27	31	467	445	85	1	1	...	
(2) ***Manipur State***	...	...	***1***	...	***3***	...	***6***	...	***3***	***1***	...	***1***	

TABLE XIII.—CASTE. PART A.—HINDUS, ANIMISTS, BUDDHISTS, JAINS, SIKHS AND BRAHMOS—*continued.*

DISTRICT OR STATE.	MIKIR.				MINOR CASTES.*		MIRI.				MUCHI.		MUKHI.		REMARKS.
	HINDU.		ANIMIST.		...		HINDU.		ANIMIST.		HINDU.		HINDU.		
	Males.	Females.	Males.	Females.	Males.	Females.	Males.	Females.	Males.	Females.	Males.	Females.	Males.	Females.	
1	350	351	352	353	354	355	356	357	358	359	360	361	362	363	364
ASSAM	***385***	***351***	***53,257***	***51,084***	***32,688***	***29,926***	***6,872***	***6,588***	***22,463***	***21,869***	***7,801***	***5,843***	***1,377***	***1,341***	
(1) British Territory	***385***	***351***	***53,257***	***51,084***	***23,757***	***20,603***	***6,872***	***6,588***	***22,463***	***21,869***	***7,785***	***5,829***	***1,377***	***1,341***	Mikir.—There are 615 males and 567 females returned as Christians, *viz.*, Cachar (49), Sylhet (43), Khasi and Jaintia Hills (1,078), Naga Hills (3) and Sibsagar (9).
SURMA VALLEY AND HILL DISTRICTS	***310***	***299***	***8,956***	***8,605***	***11,579***	***11,750***	***24***	...	***144***	***147***	***2,439***	***2,158***	***2***	...	
Cachar	303	290	970	969	2,349	2,096	24	...	5	...	2	4	2	...	*For details of Minor Castes see Appendix, Part I.
Sylhet	11	9	53	55	3,187	3,075	...	...	...	...	2,405	2,137	...	...	
Khasi and Jaintia Hills	5	...	7,323	7,580	3,967	4,542	...	...	...	...	20	15	...	...	Muchi includes 74 males and 61 females returned as Animists, *viz.*, Darrang (3+0), Nowgong (2+0), Sibsagar (64+57) and Lakhimpur (5+4).
Naga Hills	...	...	7	1	80	18	...	...	139	147	5	...	...	...	
Lushai Hills	...	...	1	...	1,996	2,019	...	...	...	...	7	2	...	...	
ASSAM VALLEY DISTRICTS	***66***	***52***	***44,301***	***42,479***	***12,178***	***8,853***	***6,848***	***6,588***	***22,319***	***21,722***	***5,346***	***3,671***	***1,375***	***1,341***	
Goalpara	2	...	...	...	675	545	...	...	...	...	1,601	806	...	...	
Kamrup	2	...	5,749	5,580	193	175	...	...	...	...	646	226	1,370	1,336	
Darrang	54	50	1,628	1,481	361	290	57	44	2,248	2,219	498	428	2	...	Mukhi includes 1 female returned as Animist in Lakhimpur.
Nowgong	1	...	24,064	23,262	146	55	...	...	...	...	333	159	2	...	
Sibsagar	3	...	12,859	12,147	1,579	1,393	6,695	6,459	4,770	4,561	1,551	1,377	...	2	
Lakhimpur	4	2	1	...	8,920	6,198	96	85	15,301	14,942	685	665	*1*	3	
Garo Hills	...	...	...	...	301	287	...	...	...	...	82	10	...	...	
(2) Manipur State	...	...	...	...	***8,931***	***9,323***	...	...	...	...	***16***	***14***	...	...	

DISTRICT OR STATE.	MUNDA.				MURIYARI.		MURMI.				MUSAHAR.		NADIYAL.		REMARKS.
	HINDU.		ANIMIST.		HINDU.		HINDU.		BUDDHIST.		HINDU.		HINDU.		
	Males.	Females.	Males.	Females.	Males.	Females.	Males.	Females.	Males.	Females.	Males.	Females.	Males.	Females.	
1	365	366	367	368	369	370	371	372	373	374	375	376	377	378	379
ASSAM	***31,746***	***29,360***	***15,468***	***14,694***	***555***	***472***	***1,062***	***500***	***734***	***658***	***7,555***	***6,729***	***34,891***	***33,459***	Munda (Hindu) includes 3 males returned as Buddhists in Sibsagar, and 1 male and 1 female returned as Brahmos in Goalpara. There are, besides, 2,267 males and 2,181 females returned as Christians, *viz.*, Cachar (109), Sylhet (79), Kamrup (12), Darrang (807), Sibsagar (2,634) and Lakhimpur (807).
(1) British Territory	***31,743***	***29,360***	***15,468***	***14,694***	***555***	***472***	***987***	***445***	***734***	***658***	***7,553***	***6,729***	***34,891***	***33,459***	
SURMA VALLEY AND HILL DISTRICTS	***7,046***	***6,537***	***178***	***173***	***10***	***7***	***315***	***112***	***9***	***7***	***5,573***	***5,253***	***12***	***11***	
Cachar	3,583	3,499	159	152	10	7	17	9	2	2	3,540	3,341	...	...	
Sylhet	3,452	3,024	19	20	..	...	134	5	...	...	2,033	1,912	10	10	
Khasi and Jaintia Hills	9	12	...	1	...	...	41	15	7	5	1	...	2	1	
Naga Hills	2	2	...	...	...	...	81	65	...	...	...	...	...	...	Muriyari includes 34 males and 42 females returned as Animists in Darrang. There are, besides, 25 males and 18 females returned as Christians, *viz.*, Darrang (2) and Sibsagar (41).
Lushai Hills	...	...	...	...	...	...	42	18	...	...	...	...	...	...	
ASSAM VALLEY DISTRICTS	***24,697***	***22,823***	***15,290***	***14,521***	***545***	***465***	***672***	***333***	***725***	***651***	***1,980***	***1,476***	***34,879***	***33,448***	
Goalpara	80	37	36	37	...	...	117	74	315	234	179	28	912	925	
Kamrup	474	342	61	41	12	11	64	37	11	3	200	106	5,893	5,877	Murmi (Buddhist) includes 2 males returned as Animists in Garo Hills.
Darrang	3,267	2,985	5,285	5,048	200	201	144	51	128	91	252	164	4,090	3,743	
Nowgong	2	4	1,536	1,707	2	...	2	...	5	5	35	10	10,440	10,477	
Sibsagar	8,037	7,681	1,401	1,225	331	253	141	63	31	22	814	775	9,421	8,483	Musahar includes 31 males and 19 females returned as Animists, *viz.*, Sylhet (0+1), Darrang (1+0), Sibsagar (16+13) and Lakhimpur (14+5).
Lakhimpur	12,837	11,774	6,931	6,469	...	...	194	104	218	286	500	393	4,119	3,943	
Garo Hills	...	...	...	...	...	...	10	4	17	10	...	...	4	...	
(2) Manipur State	***3***	...	...	...	...	...	***75***	***55***	...	...	***2***	...	...	...	

TABLE XIII.—Caste. Part A.—Hindus, Animists, Buddhists, Jains, Sikhs and Brahmos—*continued.*

District or State.	Naga (Total).* Hindu. Males.	Naga (Total).* Hindu. Females.	Naga (Total).* Animist. Males.	Naga (Total).* Animist. Females.	Nagesia. Hindu. Males.	Nagesia. Hindu. Females.	Nais. Hindu. Males.	Nais. Hindu. Females.	Namasudra. Hindu. Males.	Namasudra. Hindu. Females.	Napit. Hindu. Males.	Napit. Hindu. Females.	Nat. Hindu. Males.	Nat. Hindu. Females.
1	380	381	382	383	384	385	386	387	388	389	390	391	392	393
ASSAM	*58*	*12*	*108,517*	*111,446*	*623*	*623*	*300*	*240*	*89,347*	*83,406*	*19,144*	*17,724*	*2,556*	*2,586*
(1) ***British Territory***	*58*	*12*	*76,535*	*77,015*	*693*	*693*	*300*	*240*	*89,300*	*83,406*	*19,137*	*17,723*	*2,556*	*2,586*
SURMA VALLEY AND HILL DISTRICTS	...	*1*	*71,651*	*73,359*	*24*	*23*	*250*	*197*	*78,621*	*74,067*	*13,472*	*12,635*	*483*	*410*
Cachar	...	...	3,279	3,736	...	...	79	78	7,502	6,692	1,219	984	8	...
Sylhet	...	...	2	...	24	23	171	119	71,115	67,375	12,235	11,650	475	410
Khasi and Jaintia Hills	...	...	11	3	...	...	...	...	4	...	4	1	...	...
Naga Hills	...	1	68,331	69,581	...	...	...	...	...	...	14	...	...	...
Lushai Hills	...	...	28	32	...	...	...	...	...	...	...	...	...	...
ASSAM VALLEY AND HILL DISTRICTS	*58*	*11*	*4,884*	*3,663*	*599*	*600*	*50*	*43*	*10,679*	*9,339*	*5,665*	*5,088*	*2,073*	*2,176*
Goalpara	...	...	...	...	...	...	...	...	4,436	3,761	1,166	881	103	121
Kamrup	2	1	14	...	3	5	2	...	5,736	5,370	2,753	2,962	414	544
Darrang	...	...	26	...	133	190	15	16	124	22	764	636	135	119
Nowgong	...	1	8	2	20	26	1	...	41	36	117	52	364	396
Sibsagar	9	4	2,083	1,314	118	63	16	17	113	37	518	323	961	937
Lakhimpur	47	5	2,753	2,347	275	316	16	10	54	26	400	228	96	59
Garo Hills	...	...	...	...	...	...	...	...	175	87	7	6	...	...
(2) ***Manipur State***	...	...	*31,982*	*34,431*	...	...	...	...	*47*	...	*7*	*1*	...	...

Remarks. (394)

*For details of Naga see Appendix, Part I.

Nagesia includes 18 males and 11 females returned as Animists, *viz.*, Nowgong (1+0) and Lakhimpur (17+11).

Namasudra includes 1 male returned as Animist in Darrang.

Napit includes 521 males and 487 females returned as Bej in Darrang. It also includes 9 males and 4 females returned as Animists, *viz.*, Sibsagar (1+0) and Lakhimpur (8+4), and 2 males returned as Jains and 2 females returned as Sikhs in Sibsagar.

Nat includes 2 females returned as Animists in Lakhimpur.

District or State.	Nepali (Unspecified). Hindu. Males.	Nepali (Unspecified). Hindu. Females.	Nepali (Unspecified). Buddhist. Males.	Nepali (Unspecified). Buddhist. Females.	Newar. Hindu. Males.	Newar. Hindu. Females.	Nuniya. Hindu. Males.	Nuniya. Hindu. Females.	Oraon. Hindu. Males.	Oraon. Hindu. Females.	Oraon. Animist. Males.	Oraon. Animist. Females.	Oriya (Unspecified). Hindu. Males.	Oriya (Unspecified). Hindu. Females.
1	395	396	397	398	399	400	401	402	403	404	405	406	407	408
ASSAM	*1,214*	*496*	*339*	*241*	*1,092*	*685*	*9,232*	*5,136*	*7,865*	*7,321*	*6,805*	*6,592*	*3,237*	*2,727*
(1) ***British Territory***	*1,050*	*404*	*338*	*241*	*1,068*	*674*	*9,229*	*5,136*	*7,865*	*7,321*	*6,805*	*6,592*	*3,236*	*2,726*
SURMA VALLEY AND HILL DISTRICTS	*209*	*79*	*5*	*2*	*147*	*68*	*4,262*	*3,162*	*2,199*	*2,012*	*147*	*153*	*828*	*636*
Cachar	111	35	...	...	40	12	1,458	1,368	1,224	1,154	147	153	120	95
Sylhet	19	11	5	2	...	...	2,796	1,777	974	858	...	...	694	541
Khasi and Jaintia Hills	78	33	...	...	44	27	4	...	...	...	...	...	5	...
Naga Hills	...	...	...	...	42	26	2	1	...	...	...	...	5	...
Lushai Hills	1	...	...	...	21	3	2	1	1	...	...	...	4	...
ASSAM VALLEY AND HILL DISTRICTS	*841*	*325*	*333*	*239*	*921*	*606*	*4,957*	*1,974*	*5,666*	*5,339*	*6,658*	*6,439*	*2,408*	*2,090*
Goalpara	127	80	...	...	152	77	1,358	604	38	25	43	41	6	5
Kamrup	72	55	10	11	88	55	1,092	414	114	96	70	61	20	27
Darrang	9	4	1	...	219	155	571	93	785	738	2,064	2,592	22[illegible]	230
Nowgong	6	2	...	...	47	30	327	135	3	...	861	803	93	64
Sibsagar	50	35	4	...	69	79	1,089	437	1,993	1,874	548	548	516	395
Lakhimpur	565	147	318	225	308	175	509	282	2,733	2,574	2,472	2,393	1,541	1,369
Garo Hills	12	2	...	...	38	35	11	9	...	2	...	...	...	...
(2) ***Manipur State***	*164*	*92*	*1*	...	*24*	*11*	*3*	...	...	...	...	...	*1*	*1*

Remarks. (409)

Nepali (unspecified) (Hindu) includes 9 males and 7 females returned as Animists, *viz.*, Cachar (1+0), Khasi and Jaintia Hills (1+0), Goalpara (1+2), Kamrup (4+4) and Sibsagar (2+1).

Newar includes 13 males and 4 females returned as Buddhists, *viz.*, Goalpara (1+0), Kamrup (2+2), Darrang (6+1) and Lakhimpur (4+1). It also includes 8 males and 8 females returned as Animists, *viz.*, Darrang (6+7), Lakhimpur (1+0) and Garo Hills (1+1).

Nuniya includes 16 males returned as Animists, *viz.*, Darrang (5), Sibsagar (8), Lakhimpur (2), and Garo Hills (1), and 1 male and 2 females returned as Buddhists in Sibsagar.

Oraon.—There are 152 males and 87 females returned as Christians, *viz.*, Darrang (57), Sibsagar (83) and Lakhimpur (99).

Oriya includes 74 males and 78 females returned as Animists, *viz.*, Darrang (1+10), Nowgong (0+1), Sibsagar (37+54) and Lakhimpur (36+13).

TABLE XIII.—CASTE. PART A.—HINDUS, ANIMISTS, BUDDHISTS, JAINS, SIKHS AND BRAHMOS—*continued.*

DISTRICT OR STATE.	OSWAL.				PAN (PANIKA).				PASI.		PATIAL OR PATIKAR.		PATNI.		REMARKS.
	HINDU.		JAIN.		HINDU.		ANIMIST.		HINDU.		HINDU.		HINDU.		
	Males.	Females.	Males.	Females.	Males.	Females.	Males.	Females.	Males.	Females.	Males.	Females.	Males.	Females.	
1	410	411	412	413	414	415	416	417	418	419	420	421	422	423	424
ASSAM	***281***	***118***	***978***	***159***	***8,318***	***8,704***	***417***	***493***	***3,492***	***3,451***	***2,147***	***2,043***	***56,901***	***54,305***	Oswal (Jain) includes 10 males returned as Animists in Sylhet, and 2 males and 1 female returned as Sikhs in Darrang.
(1) British Territory	***281***	***118***	***978***	***159***	***8,316***	***8,704***	***417***	***493***	***3,488***	***3,449***	***2,147***	***2,043***	***56,856***	***54,288***	Oswal (Hindu) includes 4 females returned as Sikhs in Sibsagar.
SURMA VALLEY AND HILL DISTRICTS	***16***	...	***13***	...	***2,318***	***2,496***	...	...	***2,570***	***2,834***	***697***	***547***	***56,805***	***54,968***	
Cachar	...	...	...	...	881	931	...	...	590	659	...	...	20,482	19,231	Pasi includes 11 males and 13 females returned as Animists, *viz.*, Darrang (1+0), Sibsagar (0+2) and Lakhimpur (10+10).
Sylhet	14	...	10	...	1,430	1,564	...	...	1,976	2,175	697	547	38,307	35,036	
Khasi and Jaintia Hills	2	...	3	...	7	1	...	...	4	...	...	...	...	...	Patni includes 6 males and 5 females returned as Jains, *viz.*, Kamrup (5+5) and Manipur (1+0).
Naga Hills	...	...	...	...	1	...	...	...	...	...	...	...	...	...	
Lushai Hills	...	...	...	...	...	...	...	...	...	...	...	...	16	1	
ASSAM VALLEY DISTRICTS ...	***265***	***118***	***965***	***159***	***5,998***	***6,208***	***417***	***493***	***918***	***615***	***1,450***	***1,496***	***51***	***20***	
Goalpara	38	10	394	67	33	12	...	...	230	102	75	87	4	8	
Kamrup	27	9	45	11	75	92	...	...	71	61	41	53	6	5	
Darrang	4	...	208	30	1,129	1,169	1	2	65	39	80	86	...	...	
Nowgong	4	...	178	23	693	752	1	3	99	77	1,238	1,267	18	...	
Sibsagar	55	14	128	20	1,958	2,007	196	236	325	245	2	2	21	5	
Lakhimpur	136	85	5	2	2,110	2,176	219	252	120	83	14	1	2	2	
Garo Hills	1	...	7	6	...	...	...	...	8	9	...	...	...	...	
(2) Manipur State	...	...	...	...	***2***	...	...	...	***4***	***2***	...	...	***45***	***17***	

DISTRICT OR STATE.	PATOR.		PATWA.		PHAKIAL.		PORJA.				RABHA.				REMARKS.
	HINDU.		HINDU.		BUDDHIST.		HINDU.		ANIMIST.		HINDU.		ANIMIST.		
	Males.	Females.	Males.	Females.	Males.	Females.	Males.	Females.	Males.	Females.	Males.	Females.	Males.	Females.	
1	425	426	427	428	429	430	431	432	433	434	435	436	437	438	439
ASSAM	***628***	***375***	***674***	***564***	***253***	***253***	***1,955***	***1,833***	***1,077***	***996***	***17,556***	***17,365***	***21,948***	***22,153***	Pator includes 2 males and 3 females returned as Animists in Lakhimpur.
(1) British Territory	***628***	***375***	***674***	***564***	***253***	***253***	***1,955***	***1,833***	***1,077***	***996***	***17,556***	***17,365***	***21,948***	***22,153***	Phakial includes 1 male returned as Hindu in Lakhimpur. There are, besides, 36 males and 61 females returned as Christians, *viz.*, Kamrup (79), Darrang (16) and Sibsagar (2).
SURMA VALLEY AND HILL DISTRICTS	***61***	***59***	***31***	***21***	...	...	...	...	...	...	***217***	***137***	***2***	...	Rabha includes 3,684 males and 3,777 females returned as Totlas, *viz.*, Goalpara (24), Kamrup (7,228), Darrang (207) and Sibsagar (2).
Cachar	61	59	23	14	...	...	...	...	...	...	7	12	...	...	
Sylhet	...	...	8	7	...	...	...	...	...	...	2	3	...	...	
Khasi and Jaintia Hills	...	...	...	...	...	...	...	...	...	...	119	98	1	...	
Naga Hills	...	...	...	...	...	...	...	...	...	...	73	13	1	...	
Lushai Hills	...	...	...	...	...	...	...	...	...	...	16	11	...	...	
ASSAM VALLEY DISTRICTS	***567***	***316***	***643***	***543***	***253***	***253***	***1,955***	***1,833***	***1,077***	***996***	***17,339***	***17,228***	***21,946***	***22,153***	
Goalpara	...	...	17	4	...	...	1	...	...	...	14,106	14,171	2,024	1,905	
Kamrup	...	...	414	406	...	...	...	...	...	...	548	558	11,793	12,126	
Darrang	...	...	12	10	...	...	204	168	725	710	525	468	6,005	6,074	
Nowgong	...	...	42	29	...	...	...	...	...	...	...	...	51	37	
Sibsagar	...	...	93	62	3	6	231	218	38	38	29	27	5	4	
Lakhimpur	567	316	65	32	250	247	1,519	1,447	314	248	56	36	2	1	
Garo Hills	...	...	...	...	...	...	...	...	...	...	1,985	1,968	2,066	2,006	
(2) Manipur State	...	...	...	...	...	...	...	...	...	...	...	...	...	...	

TABLE XIII.—CASTE. PART A.—HINDUS, ANIMISTS, BUDDHISTS, JAINS, SIKHS AND BRAHMOS—*continued.*

District or State.	Rajbansi. Hindu. Males.	Rajbansi. Hindu. Females.	Rajbhar. Hindu. Males.	Rajbhar. Hindu. Females.	Rajput (Chattri). Hindu. Males.	Rajput (Chattri). Hindu. Females.	Rajput (Chattri). Sikh. Males.	Rajput (Chattri). Sikh. Females.	Rajwar. Hindu. Males.	Rajwar. Hindu. Females.	Rantia. Hindu. Males.	Rantia. Hindu. Females.	Sadgop. Hindu. Males.	Sadgop. Hindu. Females.	Remarks.
1	440	441	442	443	444	445	446	447	448	449	450	451	452	453	454
ASSAM	***68,584***	***64,494***	***1,792***	***1,703***	***16,896***	***9,964***	***187***	***163***	***4,291***	***4,047***	***2,700***	***2,145***	***1,197***	***695***	Rajbansi includes 2 males returned as Animists and 10 males returned as Jains in Goalpara. Rajbhar includes 42 males and 38 females returned as Animists in Darrang. Rajput (Chattri) (Hindu) includes 10 males and 8 females returned as Animists, *viz.*, Lushai Hills (2 + 0), Kamrup (1 + 0), Lakhimpur (7 + 8), and 44 males and 6 females returned as Jains, *viz.*, Naga Hills (4 + 0), Goalpara (15 + 1), Kamrup (0 + 3), Darrang (10 + 0), Sibsagar (9 + 2), Lakhimpur (5 + 0), and Manipur (1 + 0); *it also includes 12 males and 8 females* returned as Buddhists, *viz.*, Darrang (3 + 2) and Sibsagar (9 + 6). Rajwar includes 15 males and 22 females returned as Animists, *viz.*, Darrang (2 + 2), Nowgong (2 + 1), Sibsagar (7 + 11) and Lakhimpur (4 + 8). Rantia includes 29 males and 17 females returned as Animists, *viz.*, Darrang (8 + 2), Nowgong (1 + 0), Sibsagar (4 + 3) and Lakhimpur (10 + 12), and 2 males returned as Jains and 1 female returned as Sikh in Sibsagar.
(1) ***British Territory***	***68,579***	***64,494***	***1,791***	***1,703***	***16,617***	***9,821***	***186***	***163***	***4,291***	***4,047***	***2,700***	***2,145***	***1,197***	***695***	
SURMA VALLEY AND HILL DISTRICTS	***121***	***31***	***1,140***	***1,285***	***3,310***	***2,241***	***5***	...	***1,124***	***1,123***	***849***	***717***	***774***	***427***	
Cachar	22	4	315	499	1,237	1,179	...	...	816	632	461	474	...	...	
Sylhet	31	5	823	784	1,123	777	...	...	306	491	385	237	773	424	
Khasi and Jaintia Hills	13	9	2	2	365	87	5	...	1	...	3	6	1	3	
Naga Hills	42	5	...	...	345	129	...	...	...	...	...	...	...	...	
Lushai Hills	13	8	...	...	240	69	...	...	1	...	...	...	...	...	
ASSAM VALLEY DISTRICTS	***68,458***	***64,463***	***651***	***418***	***13,307***	***7,580***	***181***	***163***	***3,167***	***2,924***	***1,851***	***1,428***	***423***	***268***	
Goalpara	65,851	62,263	158	78	1,479	480	...	...	22	9	25	9	297	181	
Kamrup	1,603	1,471	94	25	1,981	886	3	...	28	12	11	8	5	5	
Darrang	71	26	114	88	3,481	2,385	1	...	593	574	796	481	10	10	
Nowgong	34	10	20	22	624	275	146	158	95	84	39	54	5	3	
Sibsagar	61	22	147	109	2,236	1,228	17	4	1,566	1,493	504	473	45	28	
Lakhimpur	147	89	117	96	3,071	2,112	14	1	863	752	475	403	60	41	
Garo Hills	691	582	1	...	435	220	...	...	...	...	1	...	1	...	
(2) ***Manipur State***	***5***	...	***1***	...	***279***	***143***	***1***	...	...	...	...	...	...	...	

District or State.	Saloi. Hindu. Males.	Saloi. Hindu. Females.	Sannyasi. Hindu. Males.	Sannyasi. Hindu. Females.	Santal. Hindu. Males.	Santal. Hindu. Females.	Santal. Animist. Males.	Santal. Animist. Females.	Saroagi. Hindu. Males.	Saroagi. Hindu. Females.	Saroagi. Jain. Males.	Saroagi. Jain. Females.	Sarki. Hindu. Males.	Sarki. Hindu. Females.	Remarks.
1	455	456	457	458	459	460	461	462	463	464	465	466	467	468	469
ASSAM	***4,651***	***4,683***	***335***	***179***	***14,007***	***13,770***	***16,315***	***14,916***	***487***	***201***	***331***	***4***	***360***	***217***	Sannyasi includes 3 males returned as Animists in Lakhimpur. Santal (Hindu) includes 1 male returned as Buddhist in Sylhet. There are, besides, 38 males and 38 females returned as Christians, *viz.*, Goalpara (8), Darrang (4), Sibsagar (57) and Lakhimpur (7). Sarki includes 12 males and 5 females returned as Buddhists in Goalpara.
(1) ***British Territory***	***4,651***	***4,683***	***333***	***179***	***14,007***	***13,769***	***16,315***	***14,916***	***463***	***200***	***309***	***82***	***360***	***217***	
SURMA VALLEY AND HILL DISTRICTS	...	...	***18***	***6***	***2,915***	***2,623***	***2,513***	***2,281***	***10***	***8***	***30***	...	***86***	***46***	
Cachar	...	...	2	1	1,890	1,654	959	937	...	...	...	...	...	...	
Sylhet	...	...	9	...	1,022	969	1,419	1,344	...	...	...	...	...	1	
Khasi and Jaintia Hills	...	...	5	5	1	...	...	...	9	8	...	...	47	15	
Naga Hills	...	...	1	...	2	...	...	...	1	...	30	...	24	27	
Lushai Hills	...	...	1	...	...	...	135	...	...	...	...	...	15	3	
ASSAM VALLEY DISTRICTS	***4,651***	***4,683***	***315***	***173***	***11,092***	***11,146***	***13,802***	***12,635***	***453***	***192***	***279***	***82***	***274***	***171***	
Goalpara	113	97	40	16	25	3	3,518	3,095	54	19	26	3	32	33	
Kamrup	4,096	4,127	19	8	249	198	25	28	39	16	100	53	18	7	
Darrang	420	440	93	73	703	619	2,886	2,601	13	9	28	3	140	94	
Nowgong	17	18	21	6	1	4	1,131	1,054	9	1	14	2	...	...	
Sibsagar	2	...	42	23	4,995	4,698	3,195	2,916	75	53	28	5	12	7	
Lakhimpur	3	1	76	39	5,119	5,622	3,047	2,941	263	94	83	16	67	26	
Garo Hills	...	...	24	8	...	2	...	...	...	...	...	...	5	4	
(2) ***Manipur State***	...	...	***2***	...	...	***1***	...	...	***24***	***1***	***22***	***2***	...	...	

TABLE XIII.—Caste. Part A.—Hindus, Animists, Buddhists, Jains, Sikhs and Brahmos—*continued*.

District or State.	Savara. Hindu. Males.	Savara. Hindu. Females.	Savara. Animist. Males.	Savara. Animist. Females.	Shaha. Hindu. Males.	Shaha. Hindu. Females.	Sikh. Sikh. Males.	Sikh. Sikh. Females.	Solanemia. Hindu. Males.	Solanemia. Hindu. Females.	Sonar. Hindu. Males.	Sonar. Hindu. Females.	Subarna Banik. Hindu. Males.	Subarna Banik. Hindu. Females.	Remarks.
1	470	471	472	473	474	475	476	477	478	479	480	481	482	483	484
ASSAM	***1,783***	***1,532***	***344***	***255***	***27,421***	***26,859***	***229***	***98***	***60***	***61***	***2,246***	***1,629***	***370***	***228***	Shaha includes 2 females returned as Animists in Lakhimpur.
(1) British Territory	*1,773*	*1,532*	*344*	*255*	*27,371*	*26,859*	*227*	*98*	*60*	*61*	*2,238*	*1,626*	*370*	*228*	Sikh includes 57 males and 20 females returned as Hindus, *viz.*, Cachar (10 + 6), Khasi and Jaintia Hills (38 + 11) and Sibsagar (9 + 3).
SURMA VALLEY AND HILL DISTRICTS	*468*	*614*	...	...	*18,681*	*18,420*	*89*	*28*	...	...	*305*	*221*	*313*	*215*	Sonar includes 219 males and 198 females returned as Animists in Sibsagar, and 3 males returned as Buddhists in Kamrup.
Cachar	49	70	...	...	627	299	26	11	...	...	207	124	104	25	
Sylhet	360	478	...	...	18,042	18,121	8	1	...	...	65	83	152	190	
Khasi and Jaintia Hills	59	57	...	...	8	...	44	16	...	...	29	12	57	...	
Naga Hills	...	...	...	...	2	...	2	1	...	...	4	2	...	...	
Lushai Hills	...	...	...	...	2	...	9	...	...	...	...	...	...	...	
ASSAM VALLEY DISTRICTS	*1,305*	*918*	*344*	*255*	*8,690*	*8,439*	*138*	*70*	*60*	*61*	*1,933*	*1405*	*57*	*13*	
Goalpara	24	4	...	...	639	377	18	11	...	...	145	60	49	7	
Kamrup	5	4	...	...	7,841	8,032	7	2	...	...	626	595	1	...	
Darrang	203	142	48	37	83	...	12	...	60	61	116	55	1	2	
Nowgong	19	2	...	...	44	15	12	6	...	...	55	22	...	...	
Sibsagar	138	199	...	...	32	10	25	13	...	...	542	387	...	...	
Lakhimpur	955	567	296	218	37	4	64	38	...	...	449	286	6	4	
Garo Hills	2	...	...	...	14	1	...	...	...	...	...	...	...	...	
(2) Manipur State	*10*	...	...	...	*50*	...	*2*	...	...	...	*8*	*3*	...	...	

District or State.	Sudra. Hindu. Males.	Sudra. Hindu. Females.	Sunri. Hindu. Males.	Sunri. Hindu. Females.	Sunwar. Hindu. Males.	Sunwar. Hindu. Females.	Surahiya. Hindu. Males.	Surahiya. Hindu. Females.	Sutradhar. Hindu. Males.	Sutradhar. Hindu. Females.	Swarnakar. Hindu. Males.	Swarnakar. Hindu. Females.	Synteng. Animist. Males.	Synteng. Animist. Females.	Remarks.
1	485	486	487	488	489	490	491	492	493	494	495	496	497	498	499
ASSAM	***61,148***	***57,364***	***1,446***	***1,903***	***165***	***111***	***588***	***198***	***8,368***	***7,614***	***411***	***365***	***19,633***	***22,512***	Sudra includes 5 males and 1 female returned as Jains in Manipur.
(1) British Territory	*60,929*	*57,114*	*1,446*	*1,903*	*162*	*108*	*588*	*198*	*8,368*	*7,614*	*411*	*365*	*19,633*	*22,512*	Sunri includes 2 males and 11 females returned as Animists, *viz.*, Darrang (0 + 6), Nowgong (1 + 1) and Lakhimpur (1 + 4).
SURMA VALLEY AND HILL DISTRICTS	*60,839*	*57,064*	*293*	*240*	*63*	*30*	*337*	*67*	*6,876*	*6,468*	*291*	*257*	*19,633*	*22,512*	Sunwar includes 5 males and 2 females returned as Animists, *viz.*, Lushai Hills (4 + 2) and Lakhimpur (1 + 0).
Cachar	1,235	694	12	7	13	2	...	...	65	81	...	...	2	2	
Sylhet	59,435	56,304	276	233	1	...	337	67	6,803	6,387	200	257	...	15	
Khasi and Jaintia Hills	146	63	5	...	1	7	...	...	1	...	...	...	19,630	22,495	
Naga Hills	4	...	...	...	5	5	...	...	7	...	...	...	1	...	
Lushai Hills	19	3	...	...	43	16	...	...	...	...	1	...	...	...	
ASSAM VALLEY DISTRICTS	*90*	*50*	*1,153*	*963*	*99*	*78*	*251*	*61*	*1,492*	*1,146*	*120*	*108*	...	...	Sutradhar includes 1 male returned as Animist in Goalpara, and 3 males returned as Jains in Darrang.
Goalpara	23	13	67	3	38	29	37	...	1,323	1,051	85	92	...	...	Synteng includes 1 male returned as Hindu in Khasi and Jaintia Hills. There are, besides, 4,959 males and 5,557 females returned as Christians, *viz.*, Cachar (4), Khasi and Jaintia Hills (10,507), and Naga Hills (5).
Kamrup	...	...	197	200	...	8	2	1	37	41	8	5	...	...	
Darrang	...	...	302	315	10	13	...	...	28	12	1	...	...	...	
Nowgong	...	...	348	280	6	1	...	...	7	1	11	8	...	...	
Sibsagar	18	3	55	46	4	3	155	42	29	16	11	3	...	...	
Lakhimpur	47	34	179	100	29	23	57	18	63	25	...	...	...	...	
Garo Hills	2	...	5	1	3	2	...	...	5	...	4	...	...	...	
(2) Manipur State	*219*	*250*	...	...	*3*	*3*	...	...	...	...	...	...	...	...	

TABLE XIII.—Caste. Part A.—Hindus, Animists, Buddhists, Jains, Sikhs and Brahmos—*continued.*

District or State.	Tanti.		Tatwa.		Teli or Tili.		Telinga.				Thakuri.		Remarks.
	Hindu.		Hindu.		Animist.		Hindu.		Animist.		Hindu.		
	Males.	Females.	Males.	Females.	Males.	Females.	Males.	Females.	Males.	Females.	Males.	Females.	
1	500	501	502	503	504	505	506	507	508	509	510	511	512
ASSAM	***20,466***	***20,770***	***223***	***69***	***20,399***	***18,358***	***3,437***	***3,136***	***1,395***	***1,163***	***354***	***273***	Tanti includes 78 males and 72 females returned as Animists, *viz.*, Darrang (7+7), Nowgong (5+3), Sibsagar (8+9) and Lakhimpur (58+53) and 1 male returned as Jain in Sibsagar. There are, besides, 23 males and 22 females returned as Christians, *viz.*, Darrang (3), Nowgong (1), Sibsagar (18) and Lakhimpur 23. Teli or Tili includes 13 males and 14 females returned as Animists, *viz.*, Darrang (0+1), Sibsagar (7+3) and Lakhimpur (6+10). Thakuri includes 3 males and 7 females returned as Buddhists in Lakhimpur.
(1) British Territory	*20,462*	*20,770*	*223*	*69*	*20,265*	*18,287*	*3,437*	*3,136*	*1,395*	*1,163*	*354*	*273*	
SURMA VALLEY AND HILL DISTRICTS	*4,172*	*4,530*	*45*	...	*15,705*	*14,732*	*684*	*783*	*20*	...	*190*	*171*	
Cachar	1,66	1,734	...	...	1,360	879	120	126	...	...	8	6	
Sylhet	2,52	2,792	43	...	14,313	13,843	561	655	20	...	117	124	
Khasi and Jaintia Hills	4	4	3	...	24	9	1	...	...	...	47	33	
Naga Hills	...	...	...	...	7	...	...	...	...	...	18	8	
Lushai Hills	...	...	...	...	1	1	2	2	...	...	...	...	
ASSAM VALLEY DISTRICTS	*16,290*	*16,240*	*178*	*69*	*4,560*	*3,555*	*2,753*	*2,353*	*1,375*	*1,163*	*164*	*102*	
Goalpara	117	44	66	33	457	268	7	3	...	...	7	...	
Kamrup	159	111	18	9	365	300	3	6	...	...	18	2	
Darrang	3,745	3,750	9	6	621	551	697	591	646	523	86	68	
Nowgong	528	521	39	15	211	132	8	4	291	251	8	...	
Sibsagar	4,497	4,572	20	4	1,492	1,177	1,350	1,201	240	218	25	22	
Lakhimpur...	7,243	7,242	14	2	1,384	1,119	688	548	198	171	17	10	
Garo Hills	1	...	3	...	30	8	...	...	...	...	3	...	
(2) Manipur State	*4*	...	...	...	*134*	*71*	...	...	...	...	...	...	

District or State.	Tharu.		Tipara.				Tiyor.		Tokar.		Turaha.		Remarks.
	Hindu.		Hindu.		Animist.		Hindu.		Hindu.		Hindu.		
	Males.	Females.	Males.	Females.	Males.	Females.	Males.	Females.	Males.	Females.	Males.	Females.	
1	513	514	515	516	517	518	519	520	521	522	523	524	525
ASSAM	***303***	***36***	***4,350***	***4,142***	***652***	***596***	***426***	***164***	***479***	***463***	***642***	***154***	Tharu includes 2 males returned as Animists in Garo Hills.
(1) British Territory	*300*	*34*	*4,350*	*4,142*	*652*	*596*	*426*	*164*	*479*	*463*	*642*	*154*	
SURMA VALLEY AND HILL DISTRICTS	*18*	*7*	*4,349*	*4,142*	*581*	*524*	*76*	*19*	...	...	*38*	*13*	
Cachar	7	3	216	208	257	221	...	...	...	...	...	...	
Sylhet	...	...	3,809	3,664	288	256	74	19	...	...	17	...	
Khasi and Jaintia Hills	10	2	...	...	...	...	2	...	...	...	21	13	
Naga Hills	1	2	...	...	33	43	...	...	...	...	...	...	
Lushai Hills	...	...	324	270	3	4	...	...	...	...	...	...	
ASSAM VALLEY DISTRICTS	*282*	*27*	*1*	...	*71*	*72*	*350*	*145*	*479*	*463*	*604*	*141*	
Goalpara	166	9	...	...	...	...	153	101	1	...	403	11	
Kamrup	25	5	...	...	...	...	47	10	417	427	32	1	
Darrang	47	...	...	...	...	...	31	15	60	36	19	3	
Nowgong	22	1	...	...	71	72	28	...	1	...	...	...	
Sibsagar	9	3	1	...	...	...	85	19	...	...	6	2	
Lakhimpur...	6	9	...	...	...	...	6	...	...	...	142	124	
Garo Hills	7	...	...	...	...	...	...	...	...	...	2	...	
(2) Manipur State	*3*	*2*	...	...	...	...	...	...	...	...	...	...	

TABLE XIII.—Caste. Part A.—Hindus, Animists, Buddhists, Jains, Sikhs and Brahmos—*concluded.*

District or State.	Turi.				Turung.		Vaisya.		Yakha.		Remarks.
	Hindu.		Animist.		Buddhist.		Hindu.		Hindu.		
	Males.	Females.	Males.	Females.	Males.	Females.	Males.	Females.	Males.	Females.	
1	526	527	528	529	530	531	532	533	534	535	536
ASSAM	***8,041***	***7,529***	***482***	***449***	***291***	***250***	***2,136***	***1,766***	***105***	***48***	
(1) British Territory	***8,041***	***7,529***	***482***	***449***	***291***	***250***	***2,103***	***1,747***	***105***	***48***	Turung includes 14 males and 12 females returned as Animists in Khasi and Jaintia Hills.
SURMA VALLEY AND HILL DISTRICTS ...	***2,679***	***2,568***	...	...	***14***	***12***	***15***	***5***	***4***	***6***	Vaisya includes 3 males and 2 females returned as Jains in Sibsagar.
Cachar	1,427	1,524	...	...	...	...	2	...	...	...	Yakha includes 1 male returned as Buddhist in Lakhimpur.
Sylhet	1,246	1,044	...	...	...	...	...	...	...	...	
Khasi and Jaintia Hills	5	...	...	...	14	12	7	4	4	6	
Naga Hills	...	...	...	...	...	...	6	1	...	...	
Lushai Hills	1	...	...	...	...	...	...	...	...	...	
ASSAM VALLEY DISTRICTS	***5,362***	***4,961***	***482***	***449***	***277***	***238***	***2,088***	***1,742***	***101***	***42***	
Goalpara	16	11	...	...	...	...	27	27	44	15	
Kamrup	13	9	1	2	...	...	1,727	1,585	1	7	
Darrang	671	651	7	4	...	...	42	9	35	18	
Nowgong	8	16	179	165	...	...	18	7	...	...	
Sibsagar	3,777	3,572	192	169	...	...	70	24	...	...	
Lakhimpur	877	702	103	109	277	238	202	90	21	2	
Garo Hills	...	...	...	...	...	...	2	...	...	...	
(2) Manipur State	...	...	...	...	...	...	***33***	***19***	...	...	

TABLE XIII.—CASTE. PART B.—MUSALMANS.

District or State.	Bediya. Males.	Bediya. Females.	Behara. Males.	Behara. Females.	Bhatiya. Males.	Bhatiya. Females.	Dai. Males.	Dai. Females.	Darzi. Males.	Darzi. Females.	Datiya. Males.	Datiya. Females.	Dhoba (Dhobi). Males.	Dhoba (Dhobi). Females.	Dholi. Males.	Dholi. Females.	Remarks.
1	2	3	4	5	6	7	8	9	10	11	12	13	14	15	16	17	18
ASSAM	***1,201***	***1,211***	***75***	***90***	***288***	***335***	***234***	***231***	***138***	***104***	***502***	***435***	***52***	***39***	***490***	***530***	
(1) British Territory	***1,201***	***1,211***	***75***	***90***	***288***	***335***	***234***	***231***	***138***	***104***	***502***	***435***	***52***	***39***	***490***	***530***	
SURMA VALLEY AND HILL DISTRICTS ...	***904***	***894***	***75***	***90***	...	...	***220***	***216***	...	...	...	...	***49***	***39***	***490***	***530***	
Cachar	122	123	75	90	...	...	...	...	...	...	...	...	4	...	...	...	
Sylhet	782	771	...	...	...	...	220	216	...	...	...	...	24	39	490	530	
Khasi and Jaintia Hills	...	...	...	...	...	...	...	...	...	...	...	...	20	...	...	...	
Naga Hills...	...	...	...	...	...	...	...	...	...	...	...	...	1	...	...	...	
Lushai Hills	...	...	...	...	...	...	...	...	...	...	...	...	...	...	...	...	
ASSAM VALLEY DISTRICTS	***297***	***317***	...	...	***288***	***335***	***14***	***15***	***138***	***104***	***502***	***435***	***3***	...	...	...	
Goalpara	297	315	...	...	288	335	...	...	...	...	502	435	...	...	...	...	
Kamrup	...	...	...	...	...	...	...	...	138	104	...	...	3	...	...	...	
Darrang	...	...	...	...	...	...	...	...	...	...	...	...	...	...	...	...	
Nowgong	...	...	...	...	...	...	...	...	...	...	...	...	...	...	...	...	
Sibsagar	...	...	...	...	...	...	...	...	...	...	...	...	...	...	...	...	
Lakhimpur	...	...	...	...	...	...	...	...	...	...	...	...	...	...	...	...	
Garo Hills	...	2	...	...	...	...	14	15	...	...	...	...	...	...	...	...	
(2) Manipur State	...	...	...	...	...	...	...	...	...	...	...	...	...	...	...	...	

District or State.	Dhunia (Dhunkar). Males.	Dhunia (Dhunkar). Females.	Fakir. Males.	Fakir. Females.	Hajjam. Males.	Hajjam. Females.	Jolaha. Males.	Jolaha. Females.	Kasbi. Males.	Kasbi. Females.	Khawandkar. Males.	Khawandkar. Females.	Kureshi. Males.	Kureshi. Females.	Mahimal. Males.	Mahimal. Females.	Remarks.
1	19	20	21	22	23	24	25	26	27	28	29	30	31	32	33	34	35
ASSAM	***62***	***25***	***55***	***53***	***638***	***563***	***3,728***	***3,407***	...	***86***	***63***	***61***	***197***	***135***	***39,102***	***38,277***	
(1) British Territory	***62***	***25***	***55***	***53***	***638***	***563***	***3,728***	***3,407***	...	***86***	***63***	***61***	***197***	***135***	***39,102***	***38,277***	
SURMA VALLEY AND HILL DISTRICTS ...	***34***	***20***	***31***	***34***	***621***	***559***	***1,901***	***1,817***	...	***40***	***54***	***57***	***197***	***135***	***39,102***	***38,277***	
Cachar	18	20	13	9	339	329	382	387	...	11	1	...	...	...	5,035	4,390	
Sylhet	16	...	18	25	282	230	1,505	1,425	...	29	53	57	160	135	34,067	33,887	
Khasi and Jaintia Hills	...	...	...	...	...	...	14	5	...	...	...	...	37	...	...	...	
Naga Hills	...	...	...	...	...	...	...	...	...	...	...	...	...	...	...	...	
Lushai Hills	...	...	...	...	...	...	...	...	...	...	...	...	...	...	...	...	
ASSAM VALLEY DISTRICTS	***28***	***5***	***24***	***19***	***17***	***4***	***1,827***	***1,590***	...	***46***	***9***	***4***	...	...	...	...	
Goalpara	13	...	1	...	9	...	1,054	893	...	27	5	4	...	...	...	...	
Kamrup	3	...	22	19	...	...	9	4	...	...	4	...	...	...	...	...	
Darrang	9	4	1	...	8	4	106	70	...	...	...	...	...	...	...	...	
Nowgong	8	1	...	...	...	...	1	6	...	...	...	...	...	...	...	...	
Sibsagar	...	...	...	...	...	...	657	617	...	...	...	...	...	...	...	...	
Lakhimpur	...	...	...	...	...	...	...	...	...	...	...	...	...	...	...	...	
Garo Hills	...	...	...	...	...	...	...	...	...	19	...	...	...	...	...	...	
(2) Manipur State	...	...	...	...	...	...	...	...	...	...	...	...	...	...	...	...	

TABLE XIII.—CASTE. PART B.—MUSALMANS—*concluded.*

DISTRICT OR STATE.	MANIPURI. Males.	MANIPURI. Females.	MINOR CASTES.* Males.	MINOR CASTES.* Females.	MIRSHIKARI. Males.	MIRSHIKARI. Females.	MOGHAL. Males.	MOGHAL. Females.	MORIA. Males.	MORIA. Females.	MUSALMAN (unspecified.) Males.	MUSALMAN (unspecified.) Females.	NAGARCHI. Males.	NAGARCHI. Females.	REMARKS.
1	36	37	38	39	40	41	42	43	44	45	46	47	48	49	50
ASSAM	*411*	*419*	*247*	*164*	*437*	*487*	*795*	*699*	*900*	*682*	*262*	*48*	*1,870*	*1,624*	
(1) British Territory	*411*	*419*	*231*	*164*	*437*	*487*	*795*	*695*	*900*	*682*	*262*	*48*	*1,870*	*1,624*	
SURMA VALLEY AND HILL DISTRICTS	*411*	*419*	*206*	*159*	*437*	*487*	*571*	*541*	...	...	*237*	*24*	*1,870*	*1,624*	
Cachar	32	29	63	64	27	26	73	49	...	...	...	...	198	124	* For details of minor castes see Appendix, Part I.
Sylhet	379	390	92	91	410	461	497	492	...	...	...	...	1,672	1,500	
Khasi and Jaintia Hills	...	...	51	4	...	...	1	...	...	...	...	...	...	...	
Naga Hills	...	...	...	...	...	...	...	...	...	...	237	24	...	...	
Lushai Hills	...	...	...	...	...	...	...	...	...	...	...	...	...	...	
ASSAM VALLEY DISTRICTS	...	...	*25*	*5*	...	...	*224*	*154*	*900*	*682*	*25*	*24*	...	...	
Goalpara	...	...	15	4	...	...	40	12	...	...	4	...	...	...	
Kamrup	...	...	5	1	...	...	5	1	1	...	...	...	...	...	
Darrang	...	...	5	...	...	...	7	1	263	192	...	...	...	...	
Nowgong	...	...	...	...	...	...	4	1	7	8	...	...	...	...	
Sibsagar	...	...	...	...	...	...	29	14	583	457	...	...	...	...	
Lakhimpur	...	...	...	...	...	...	139	125	46	25	21	24	...	...	
Garo Hills	...	...	...	...	...	...	...	...	...	...	...	...	...	...	
(2) Manipur State	...	...	*16*	...	...	...	...	*4*	...	...	...	...	...	...	

DISTRICT OR STATE.	NIKARI. Males.	NIKARI. Females.	PATHAN. Males.	PATHAN. Females.	RAJPUT. Males.	RAJPUT. Females.	SAIAD (SYED). Males.	SAIAD (SYED). Females.	SHEKH. Males.	SHEKH. Females.	SONAR. Males.	SONAR. Females.	SUNNI. Males.	SUNNI. Females.	REMARKS.
1	51	52	53	54	55	56	57	58	59	60	61	62	63	64	65
ASSAM	*810*	*821*	*7,916*	*5,723*	*453*	*7*	*7,435*	*6,575*	*916,488*	*853,178*	*45*	*46*	*74*	*9*	
(1) British Territory	*810*	*821*	*7,769*	*5,643*	*2*	...	*7,316*	*6,465*	*909,716*	*846,380*	*45*	*46*	*74*	*9*	
SURMA VALLEY AND HILL DISTRICTS	*782*	*821*	*5,410*	*4,399*	...	...	*4,607*	*4,028*	*725,465*	*683,960*	*45*	*46*	*53*	...	
Cachar	...	...	626	461	...	...	170	111	75,291	67,267	45	46	46	...	
Sylhet	782	821	4,639	3,906	...	...	4,375	3,888	649,007	616,376	...	...	...	...	
Khasi and Jaintia Hills	...	...	132	28	...	...	53	28	858	291	...	...	...	...	
Naga Hills	...	...	...	...	...	...	...	1	36	13	...	...	7	...	
Lushai Hills	...	...	13	4	...	...	9	...	273	14	...	...	...	...	
ASSAM VALLEY DISTRICTS	*28*	...	*2,359*	*1,244*	*2*	...	*2,709*	*2,437*	*184,251*	*162,420*	...	...	*21*	*9*	
Goalpara	28	...	616	367	...	...	197	160	108,833	97,084	...	...	15	9	
Kamrup	...	...	130	49	...	...	1,729	1,620	31,609	20,097	...	...	5	...	
Darrang	...	...	213	68	...	...	107	57	10,352	8,836	...	...	...	...	
Nowgong	...	...	166	79	2	...	138	128	7,844	7,308	...	...	...	...	
Sibsagar	...	...	408	283	...	...	401	381	14,273	11,570	...	...	1	...	
Lakhimpur	...	...	810	392	...	...	134	82	6,857	4,809	...	...	...	...	
Garo Hills	...	...	16	7	...	...	3	...	4,423	3,721	...	...	...	...	
(2) Manipur State	...	...	*147*	*80*	*451*	*7*	*119*	*110*	*6,772*	*6,798*	...	...	...	...	

APPENDIX I TO TABLE XIII.

DETAILS OF CASTES INCLUDED IN 'MINOR CASTES.' PART A.—HINDUS, BUDDHISTS, ANIMISTS, ETC.

Caste.	Religion.	Males.	Females.	Distribution.
1	2	3	4	5
Abor	Hindu	4	...	Sibsagar (3+0) and Lakhimpur (1+0).
Ditto	Animist	842	210	Lakhimpur.
Aguri	Hindu	6	...	Khasi and Jaintia Hills (3+0) and Kamrup (3+0).
Ditto	Animist	9	...	Sibsagar.
Aiton	Hindu	3	...	Darrang (2+0) and Lakhimpur (1+0).
Ditto	Buddhist	231	180	Sibsagar.
Aka	Animist	35	1	Darrang.
Amat	Hindu	1	...	Nowgong.
Arakanese	Animist	...	4	Lushai Hills.
Arya	Hindu	2	...	Khasi and Jaintia Hills (1+0) and Kamrup (1+0).
Assamese	Ditto	32	4	Cachar (6+0), Sylhet (15+0) and Lushai Hills (11+4).
Ditto	Animist	8	1	Sylhet (3+0) and Lushai Hills (5+1).
Atith	Hindu	83	90	Cachar (4+2), Sylhet (0+1), Khasi and Jaintia Hills (1+0), Goalpara (2+0), Kamrup (1+3) and Lakhimpur (75+84).
Babhan	Ditto	4	...	Sylhet (1+0) and Darrang (3+0).
Bahalia	Ditto	60	23	Sylhet (29+11), Goalpara (11+0), Kamrup (4+2), Nowgong (1+0), Sibsagar (10+4), Lakhimpur (0+1), Garo Hills (1+0) and Manipur (4+5).
Baiga	Ditto	15	34	Nowgong (6+0) and Lakhimpur (9+34).
Bais Baniya	Ditto	53	26	Cachar (5+0), Sylhet (4+0), Goalpara (10+14), Darrang (20+10), Nowgong (8+1) and Sibsagar (6+1).
Balija	Ditto	30	...	Cachar (29+0) and Khasi and Jaintia Hills (1+0).
Baniya	Ditto	122	78	Cachar (42+40) and Sylhet (80+38).
Banjogi	Ditto	5	5	Nowgong (2+0) and Lakhimpur (3+5).
Ditto	Brahmo	1	...	Kamrup.
Baola	Hindu	20	9	Goalpara (2+1) and Darrang (18+8).
Bari	Ditto	38	11	Cachar (8+0), Sylhet (6+0), Goalpara (9+2), Darrang (5+0) and Lakhimpur (10+9).
Ditto	Animist	4	4	Darrang (0+3) and Nowgong (4+1).
Barna Sankar	Hindu	9	7	Khasi and Jaintia Hills (1+0), Kamrup (1+0), Darrang (3+6), Nowgong (0+1) and Sibsagar (4+0).
Ditto	Animist	...	1	Nowgong.
Barnawar	Hindu	7	3	Lushai Hills (3+3) and Kamrup (4+0).
Barot	Jain	1	...	Darrang
Bengali	Hindu	6	5	Naga Hills (1+0), Kamrup (4+1) and Sibsagar (1+4).
Ditto	Animist	2	1	Sibsagar.
Bhabra	Hindu	1	...	Manipur.
Bhakat	Ditto	7	...	Lushai Hills.
Bhandari	Ditto	88	67	Sylhet (7+8), Naga Hills (3+0), Kamrup (0+1), Nowgong (10+5), Sibsagar (43+52) and Lakhimpur (25+1).
Bhaskar	Ditto	42	53	Kamrup (23+42), Darrang (0+5), Sibsagar (14+6) and Lakhimpur (5+0).
Bhatiya	Ditto	19	1	Goalpara (15+0), Kamrup (1+0), Darrang (0+1), Sibsagar (1+0) and Lakhimpur (2+0).
Binjhwar	Ditto	2	...	Lakhimpur.
Burmese	Buddhist	29	23	Lushai Hills (3+0), Goalpara (25+23) and Manipur (1+0).
Ditto	Animist	1	...	Kamrup.
Chain	Hindu	33	4	Sylhet (33+0), Kamrup (0+2) and Lakhimpur (0+2).
Chakma	Buddhist	159	96	Lushai Hills.
Dalu	Hindu	167	161	Darrang (0+2) and Garo Hills (167+159).
Ditto	Animist	1	...	Garo Hills.
Dehan	Hindu	613	539	Cachar (609+539) and Lakhimpur (4+0).
Dhangar	Ditto	22	...	Sylhet (19+0) and Manipur (3+0).
Dhari (Dharhi)	Animist	44	7	Darrang.
Dharkar	Hindu	...	3	Lakhimpur
Dhunia	Ditto	11	5	Khasi and Jaintia Hills (1+0), Goalpara (7+5) and Kamrup (3+0).
Doai (Daoyai)	Ditto	19	3	Sylhet (19+0) and Darrang (0+3).
Doania	Ditto	78	78	Cachar (1+0), Sibsagar (71+66) and Lakhimpur (6+12).
Ditto	Buddhist	982	709	Sibsagar (84+81) and Lakhimpur (898+628).
Dogara	Hindu	59	3	Naga Hills (43+1), Kamrup (4+2), Sibsagar (1+0), Lakhimpur (8+0) and Manipur (3+0).
Eruman	Ditto	3	2	Sibsagar.
Gain	Ditto	9	4	Khasi and Jaintia Hills (6+0), Kamrup (0+1), Darrang (1+0) and Nowgong (2+3).
Gangai (Ganesh)	Ditto	3	1	Sibsagar.
Ditto	Buddhist	3	...	Kamrup.
Gangauta	Hindu	3	1	Darrang (2+1) and Manipur (1+0.)
Ganjhu	Ditto	121	39	Cachar (6+0) and Sylhet (115+39).
Girgiria	Ditto	7	...	Cachar.
Gola	Ditto	20	15	Goalpara (3+3), Darrang (0+2), Sibsagar (15+10) and Lakhimpur (2+0).
Gujar	Ditto	8	13	Khasi and Jaintia Hills (1+0), Kamrup (1+0) and Sibsagar (6+13).
Gulgulia	Ditto	13	8	Goalpara (12+8) and Nowgong (1+0).
Guzrati	Ditto	15	...	Sylhet.
Halalkhor	Ditto	22	23	Goalpara (3+1), Kamrup (17+20) and Lakhimpur (2+2).
Hayu	Ditto	1	...	Goalpara.
Hindusthani (unspecified)	Ditto	40	36	Darrang (1+0) and Lakhimpur (39+36).
Hindu (unspecified)	Ditto	11	...	Khasi and Jaintia Hills (3+0), Goalpara (2+0), Kamrup (4+0) and Darrang (2+0).
Ho	Ditto	1	...	Darrang.
Jaisi	Ditto	14	6	Cachar.
Jatapu	Ditto	249	197	Sibsagar (14+14) and Lakhimpur (235+183).
Dito	Animist	170	137	Sibsagar (169+137) and Lakhimpur (1+0).
Jolaha	Hindu	35	37	Goalpara (2+0), Kamrup (1+0), Darrang (1+1), Sibsagar (23+13) and Lakhimpur (8+23).
Juang	Ditto	5	...	Lakhimpur.
Kachhi	Ditto	3	5	Nowgong.
Kadar	Ditto	50	44	Cachar (12+0), Sylhet (0+3), Kamrup (10+13), Darrang (2+0), Nowgong (4+0), Sibsagar (22+26) and Lakhimpur (0+2).
Ditto	Animist	...	1	Lakhimpur.
Kallar	Hindu	4	1	Goalpara (1+0), Nowgong (2+1) and Lakhimpur (1+0).
Ditto	Animist	...	5	Nowgong.
Kan	Hindu	32	5	Cachar (0+1), Darrang (27+0) and Manipur (5+4).
Kankar	Ditto	4	...	Goalpara.
Kanjar	Ditto	39	26	Khasi and Jaintia Hills (1+0), Kamrup (1+0), Darrang (5+0), Nowgong (1+0), Sibsagar (2+1) and Lakhimpur (29+25).
Kapu	Ditto	20	4	Sibsagar.
Karanga	Ditto	18	11	Kamrup (1+0), Darrang (11+4), Sibsagar (0+6), Lakhimpur (5+1) and Manipur (1+0).
Ditto	Animist	4	...	Lakhimpur.
Karni	Hindu	6	...	Cachar (3+0) and Sibsagar (3+0).
Kashmiri	Ditto	13	5	Kamrup (1+0), Darrang (10+5), Sibsagar (1+0) and Manipur (1+0).
Kawali	Ditto	24	13	Sylhet (19+12), Goalpara (3+1) and Lakhimpur (2+0).
Khandelwal	Ditto	66	54	Darrang.
Khatwe	Ditto	5	3	Goalpara (2+0) and Darrang (3+3).
Carried over	......	4,851	3,145	

APPENDIX I TO TABLE XIII—*continued.*

DETAILS OF CASTES INCLUDED IN 'MINOR CASTES'. PART A.—HINDUS, BUDDHISTS, ANIMISTS, ETC.—*concluded.*

Caste.	Religion.	Males.	Females.	Distribution.
1	2	3	4	5
	Brought forward ...	4,851	3,145	
Khyen	Hindu	482	501	Khasi and Jaintia Hills (1+0), Goalpara (413+422), Kamrup (65+79) and Sibsagar (3+0).
Kichak	Ditto	53	65	Goalpara (0+2), Darrang (4+0) and Sibsagar (49+63).
Kob	Animist	18	18	Manipur.
Kol	Hindu	1,895	2,003	Cachar (1,400+1,312), Sylhet (493+689) and Lushai Hills (2+2).
Koli	Ditto	9	...	Cachar.
Konai	Ditto	8	4	Cachar (6+0), Naga Hills (0+4) and Lakhimpur (2+0).
Koshta	Ditto	26	45	Sylhet (22+27) and Lakhimpur (4+18).
Kotal	Ditto	25	27	Sylhet (0+8), Goalpara (3+3), Kamrup (1+0), Darrang (1+1), Nowgong (4+2), Sibsagar (10+13) and Lakhimpur (6+0).
Ditto	Animist	1	2	Nowgong (1+0) and Lakhimpur (0+2).
Kusiari	Hindu	991	1,008	Sylhet (988+1,008) and Nowgong (3+0).
Kwi	Buddhist	1	2	Manipur.
Laheri	Hindu	19	18	Cachar (9+11), Sylhet (6+1), Goalpara (2+0), Kamrup (0+3) and Sibsagar (2+3).
Lai	Ditto	8,880	9,290	Manipur.
Lakher	Animist	1,756	1,891	Lushai Hills.
Lama	Hindu	25	15	Cachar (1+2) and Lushai Hills (24+13).
Lepcha	Buddhist	3	...	Cachar (1+0) and Goalpara (2+0).
Ditto	Hindu	4	...	Goalpara.
Lohait (Kurf)	Ditto	372	221	Sylhet (313+174), Goalpara (55+47) and Sibsagar (4+0).
Ditto	Jain	5	...	Goalpara.
Lyng-ngam	Animist	1,003	990	Khasi and Jaintia Hills.
Madgi (Madia)	Hindu	4	4	Manipur.
Madrasi	Ditto	84	67	Cachar (28+21) and Sylhet (56+46).
Mahanta	Ditto	9	7	Cachar (5+3) and Sylhet (4+4).
Mahar	Ditto	2	...	Manipur.
Maharu	Ditto	807	853	Cachar (3+0), Sylhet (797+849) and Lakhimpur (7+4).
Malar	Animist	3	3	Cachar.
Ditto	Hindu	19	2	Kamrup.
Male (Sauria)	Ditto	99	61	Darrang (1+0), Sibsagar (14+17) and Lakhimpur (84+44).
Man	Buddhist	132	128	Garo Hills.
Mar	Hindu	32	20	Sylhet (2+0), Goalpara (0+2), Kamrup (1+0), Darrang (2+4), Nowgong (13+2) and Sibsagar (14+12).
Maratha	Ditto	371	13	Cachar (5+13) and Lakhimpur (366+0).
Matak	Ditto	6,206	4,036	Lakhimpur.
Ditto	Buddhist	2	2	Ditto.
Mekuri	Hindu	6	10	Darrang.
Mishmi	Ditto	12	...	Lakhimpur.
Ditto	Animist	140	114	Ditto.
Ditto	Buddhist	3	2	Ditto.
Moran	Hindu	805	600	Sibsagar (311+268) and Lakhimpur (494+332).
Mudi	Ditto	69	71	Sylhet.
Murung	Animist	1	1	Lushai Hills.
Nagar	Hindu	5	2	Khasi and Jaintia Hills (1+1) and Nowgong (4+1).
Nagarchi	Ditto	55	39	Kamrup (1+0), Sibsagar (7+27) and Lakhimpur (47+12).
Nagesar	Ditto	3	...	Cachar.
Nagpuri	Ditto	13	17	Ditto.
Nahura	Ditto	1	...	Nowgong.
Nora	Ditto	5	4	Cachar (3+3), Darrang (2+0) and Lakhimpur (0+1).
Ditto	Buddhist	173	166	Sibsagar.
Ojali	Hindu	17	25	Darrang.
Pahari	Ditto	64	86	Cachar (47+77) and Naga Hills (17+9).
Paik	Ditto	...	3	Cachar.
Panjabi	Sikh	26	9	Khasi and Jaintia Hills.
Ditto	Hindu	10	...	Sibsagar (2+0), Lakhimpur (6+0) and Manipur (2+0).
Pankhu (Panika)	Ditto	4	3	Kamrup (3+3) and Sibsagar (1+0).
Parhaiya	Ditto	7	...	Kamrup.
Parwal	Ditto	3	...	Manipur.
Parwar	Ditto	49	...	Sibsagar (2+0) and Lakhimpur (47+0).
Patwari	Ditto	4	...	Cachar (2+0) and Kamrup (2+0).
Pod	Ditto	16	6	Sylhet (0+1), Goalpara (0+1), Darrang (1+0), Nowgong (8+0), Sibsagar (3+2) and Lakhimpur (4+2).
Ditto	Animist	...	1	Lakhimpur.
Prabhu	Hindu	1	...	Naga Hills.
Pradhan	Ditto	29	18	Sylhet (25+18) and Nowgong (4+0).
Pundari (Puro)	Ditto	65	8	Sylhet (6+0), Darrang (8+4), Nowgong (1+0), Sibsagar (6+3) and Lakhimpur (44+1).
Ditto	Animist	8	...	Darrang.
Rai	Hindu	35	45	Cachar (7+18) and Sylhet (28+27).
Ditto	Animist	3	4	Lushai Hills.
Rana	Hindu	...	1	Lakhimpur.
Rauniar (Nuniar)	Ditto	91	17	Goalpara (38+5), Kamrup (1+0), Darrang (2+0), Nowgong (6+7), Sibsagar (17+4) and Lakhimpur (25+1).
Raut	Ditto	2	19	Sylhet (0+19) and Lushai Hills (2+0).
Rewat	Ditto	25	3	Khasi and Jaintia Hills (12+0) and Naga Hills (13+3).
Relli	Ditto	4	...	Darrang (3+0) and Sibsagar (1+0).
Ditto	Animist	2	...	Darrang.
Sahar	Hindu	73	76	Sibsagar (5+0) and Lakhimpur (68+76).
Sankhari	Ditto	17	21	Sylhet (13+21) and Goalpara (4+0).
Sarak	Ditto	8	9	Darrang (2+2), Sibsagar (2+0) and Lakhimpur (4+7).
Ditto	Jain	2	...	Kamrup.
Sathawara	Hindu	1	...	Khasi and Jaintia Hills.
Shighora	Ditto	8	16	Darrang.
Singpho	Ditto	1	1	Lakhimpur.
Ditto	Animist	155	139	Ditto.
Ditto	Buddhist	90	68	Ditto.
Shan	Ditto	58	54	Ditto.
Siamese	Ditto	135	136	Sibsagar.
Taman	Ditto	35	4	Goalpara (33+4), Darrang (1+0) and Manipur (1+0).
Tamaria	Hindu	11	25	Sibsagar (8+15) and Lakhimpur (3+10).
Tambuli	Ditto	46	27	Cachar (2+3), Khasi and Jaintia Hills (1+0), Naga Hills (2+1), Goalpara (2+0), Kamrup (1+1), Darrang (14+3), Nowgong (0+1), Sibsagar (17+10) and Lakhimpur (7+8).
Ditto	Animist	3	...	Sibsagar (1+0) and Lakhimpur (2+0).
Tarkhan	Sikh	69	19	Lushai Hills (15+0) and Nowgong (54+19).
Thami	Hindu	31	20	Lushai Hills (2+0), Darrang (19+19), Sibsagar (1+1) and Lakhimpur (9+0).
Thapa	Ditto	59	22	Cachar (56+22) and Lushai Hills (3+0).
Thathera	Ditto	17	19	Sibsagar.
Tibetan	Buddhist	...	1	Goalpara.
Uppara	Hindu	13	12	Sibsagar.
War	Animist	2,903	3,542	Khasi and Jaintia Hills.
	Total	32,658	29,926	

APPENDIX I TO TABLE XIII—*concluded.*

DETAILS OF CASTES INCLUDED IN 'MINOR CASTES.' PART B.—MUSALMANS.

Caste.	Males.	Females.	Distribution.
1	2	3	4
Awan	9	...	Manipur.
Badyakar	3	...	Sylhet.
Bhuiya	5	...	Goalpara.
Biloch	7	1	Khasi and Jaintia Hills.
Dafali	1	...	Kamrup.
Dewan	2	...	Cachar.
Dogara	3	...	Manipur.
Gain	19	19	Cachar.
Ghazi	29	22	Sylhet.
Gujar	3	...	Manipur.
Halalkhor	3	...	Cachar.
Kalal	8	15	Cachar.
Kashmiri	2	1	Khasi and Jaintia Hills.
Kazi	2	...	Sylhet.
Khan	16	18	Sylhet (15+15), Khasi and Jaintia Hills (0+1) and Goalpara (1+2).
Kalu	2	3	Sylhet (0+3), Goalpara (1+0) and Darrang (1+0).
Kumhar	10	...	Sylhet.
Kunjra	...	3	Cachar.
Lalbegi	18	6	Cachar (11+5), Khasi and Jaintia Hills (6+1) and Goalpara (1+0).
Mahiferash	2	...	Cachar.
Mallah	4	...	Sylhet.
Mallik	21	19	Cachar (17+19), Khasi and Jaintia Hills (2+0) and Goalpara (2+0).
Mehtar	14	31	Cachar (1+0) and Sylhet (13+31).
Mewati	1	...	Manipur.
Mirdah	34	...	Khasi and Jaintia Hills.
Miyan	...	1	Sylhet.
Muchi	28	25	Cachar (0+3), Sylhet (16+19), Goalpara (4+2), Kamrup (4+1) and Darrang (4+0).
Nat	1	...	Goalpara.
Total	*247*	*164*	

APPENDIX II TO TABLE XIII.—DETAILS OF SUB-CASTES OF 'KUKI', 'LUSHAI', AND 'NAGA' SHEWN IN THE MAIN TABLE.

Caste.	Religion.	Males.	Females.	Distribution.
1	2	3	4	5
Kuki (Total)	***Hindu***	***620***	***613***	Cachar (72+69), Sylhet (548+543) and Sibsagar (0+1).
Kuki (Total)	***Animist***	***37,632***	***38,331***	Cachar (3,718+3,918), Sylhat (238+255), Khasi and Jaintia Hills (336+330), Naga Hills (1,552+1,783), Lushai Hills (185+2[illegible]7), Darrang (0+1), Nowgong (39+38), Sibsagar (8+1) and Manipur (31,556+31,798).
Kuki (unspecified)... ...	Hindu	176	155	Cachar (72+69), Sylhet (104+85) and Sibsagar (0+1).
" "	Animist	9,052	9,367	Cachar (3,718+3,918), Sylhet (238+254), Khasi and Jaintia Hills (336+330), Naga Hills (1,453+1,653), Darrang (0+1), Nowgong (39+38), Sibsagar (8+1) and Manipur (3,260+3,172).
" Thado	Ditto	12,836	12,566	Lushai Hills (158+176) and Manipur (12,678+12,390).
" Paite	Ditto	3,553	3,649	Manipur.
" Sakte	Ditto	2,490	2,421	Ditto.
" Mhar	Ditto	2,312	2,651	Ditto.
" Vaiphet	Ditto	1,679	1,751	Lushai Hills (1+0) and Manipur (1,678+1,751).
" Rengte	Ditto	1,484	1,432	Lushai Hills (5+6) and Manipur (1,479+1,426).
" Kom	Ditto	1,043	1,202	Manipur.
" Anal	Ditto	1,067	1,038	Ditto.
" Chiru	Ditto	592	706	Ditto.
" Hallam	Hindu	444	458	Sylhet.
" "	Animist	...	1	Ditto.
" Hirol Lamgang ...	Ditto	470	402	Manipur.
" Koireng or Kolren ...	Ditto	295	344	Ditto.
" Aimol	Ditto	225	196	Ditto.
" Old Kuki	Ditto	104	206	Ditto.
" Purum	Ditto	1[illegible]2	150	Ditto.
" Bete	Ditto	105	137	Naga Hills (90+130) and Lushai Hills (6+7).
" Chote	Ditto	42	68	Lushai Hills (15+18) and Manipur (27+50).
" Toran	Ditto	51	49	Manipur.
Lushai (Total)	***Hindu***	***34***	...	Sylhet (32+0) and Khasi and Jaintia Hills (2+0).
Lushai (Total)	***Animist***	***36,724***	***43,067***	Cachar (4+0), Sylhet (4+0), Khasi and Jaintia Hills (2+0), Lushai Hills (36,641+43,000) and Manipur (73+67).
Lushai (unspecified)... ...	Hindu	34	...	Sylhet (32+0) and Khasi and Jaintia Hills (2+0).
" "	Animist	14,935	18,086	Cachar (4+0), Sylhet (4+0), Khasi and Jaintia Hills (2+0), Lushai Hills (14,852+18,019) and Manipur (73+67).
" Ralte	Ditto	7,139	8,805	Lushai Hills.
" Mhar	Ditto	5,503	6,479	Ditto.
" Poi	Ditto	5,067	5,817	Ditto.
" Paite	Ditto	1,814	1,881	Ditto.
" Fanai	Ditto	1,680	1,951	Ditto.
" Sailo	Ditto	586	648	Ditto.
Naga (Total)	***Hindu***	***58***	***12***	Naga Hills (0+1), Kamrup (2+1), Nowgong (0+1), Sibsagar (9+4) and Lakhimpur (47+5).
Naga (Total)	***Animist***	***108,517***	***111,446***	Cachar (3,279+3,736), Sylhet (2+0), Khasi and Jaintia Hills (11+3), Naga Hills (68,331+69,581), Lushai Hills (28+32), Kamrup (14+0), Darrang (26+0), Nowgong (8+2), Sibsagar 2,083+1,314), Lakhimpur (2,753+2,347) and Manipur (31,982+34,431).
Naga (Unspecified)... ..	Hindu	56	11	Kamrup (0+1), Nowgong (0+1), Sibsagar (9+4) and Lakhimpur (47+5).
" "	Animist	6,014	4,259	Cachar (973+1,225), Sylhet (2+0), Khasi and Jaintia Hills (9+1), Naga Hills (942+93), Lushai Hills (2+4), Kamrup (4+0), Darrang (11+0), Nowgong (8+2), Sibsagar (1,105+387), Lakhimpur (2,753+2,347) and Manipur (205+200).
" Angami	Hindu	2	...	Kamrup.
" "	Animist	19,988	19,815	Khasi and Jaintia Hills (0+2), Naga Hills (19,875+19,797), Kamrup (8+0), Darrang (14+0), Sibsagar (57+12) and Manipur (34+4).
" Sema	Ditto	16,352	16,447	Naga Hills (16,304+16,422), Kamrup (1+0), Sibsagar (43+25) and Manipur (4+0).
" Ao	Ditto	12,987	14,373	Naga Hills (12,614+14,071), Sibsagar (29+12) and Manipur (344+290).
" Tankhul	Ditto	12,867	14,449	Lushai Hills (26+28), Kamrup (1+0), Sibsagar (14+0) and Manipur (12,826+14,421).
" Lhota	Ditto	9,448	10,063	Cachar (7+2), Khasi and Jaintia Hills (2+0), Naga Hills (9,437+10,061), Darrang (1+0) and Manipur (1+0).
" Kabui	Ditto	8,798	9,649	Naga Hills (12+6) and Manipur (8,786+9,643).
" Kachha	Hindu	...	1	Naga Hills.
" "	Animist	6,905	7,261	Cachar (2,299+2,509), Naga Hills (4,424+4,587) and Manipur (182+165).
" Sepvoma	Ditto	6,539	6,141	Manipur.
" Rengma	Ditto	2,851	3,232	Naga Hills (2,016+2,354) and Sibsagar (835+878).
" Kezhama	Ditto	2,600	2,085	Naga Hills.
" Maram	Ditto	1,319	1,399	Manipur.
" Maring	Ditto	1,206	1,500	Ditto.
" Khoirao	Ditto	431	540	Ditto.
" Kwoireng	Ditto	105	128	Ditto.
" Angwanka	Ditto	105	103	Naga Hills.
" Tengsa	Ditto	2	2	Ditto.

TABLE XIV.

CIVIL CONDITION BY AGE FOR SELECTED CASTES.

THIS Table, like Table IX, deals not with the whole population, but with certain selected castes in certain districts, or parts of districts, where they are specially numerous. This Table is intended to illustrate the relative prevalence of infant-marriage, etc. The strength of each caste or tribe is the same as given in Table IX and not as modified by classification for Table XIII.

TABLE XIV.—Civil Condition by Age for Selected Castes.

Caste, Tribe or Race.	Locality.	Sex.	Population dealt with.	Unmarried.							Married.							Widowed.						
				Total.	0—5	5—12	12—15	15—20	20—40	40 and over.	Total.	0—5	5-12	12—15	15—20	20—40	40 and over.	Total.	0—5	5—12	12—15	15—20	20—40	40 and over.
1	2	3	4	5	6	7	8	9	10	11	12	13	14	15	16	17	18	19	20	21	22	23	24	25
AHOM (Hindu)...	Brahmaputra Valley.	Male ...	99,418	60,262	16,124	21,622	6,074	7,334	8,717	391	33,285	...	49	64	431	19,988	12,753	5,871	...	3	10	33	2,159	3,673
		Female	93,142	48,976	16,993	20,717	5,079	5,179	960	48	33,024	...	80	365	3,340	23,210	6,129	11,149	...	9	11	106	2,988	8,028
BAIDYA (do.) ...	Province ...	Male ...	3,049	1,602	393	589	178	303	220	19	1,354	...	2	3	9	793	547	93	...	...	...	1	22	70
		Female	2,560	1,045	419	570	33	3	20	...	1,099	...	20	65	204	673	137	416	...	2	1	6	117	290
BARUI (do.) ...	Surma Valley	Male ...	12,504	6,765	1,525	2,375	733	880	1,115	137	4,989	...	6	15	134	2,836	1,991	757	...	...	...	...	157	600
		Female	12,038	3,617	1,596	1,928	53	19	15	6	5,103	...	297	524	1,030	2,827	416	3,318	...	11	23	179	1,217	1,988
BHUINMALI (do.)	Sylhet ...	Male ...	16,694	8,575	1,844	3,088	986	1,214	1,372	71	7,230	..	4	28	195	4,191	2,812	889	...	...	...	2	246	641
		Female	15,373	4,087	1,953	2,044	41	19	27	3	7,185	2	541	692	1,402	3,939	609	4,101	...	7	25	96	1,488	2,485
BHUIYA (do.) ...	Total ...	Male ...	28,399	13,193	3,471	5,333	1,475	1,132	1,624	158	12,760	...	64	124	359	7,560	4,653	9,446	...	...	5	48	1,252	1,141
		Female	26,278	9,778	3,599	4,661	842	428	226	22	12,896	4	181	392	1,111	9,226	1,982	3,604	...	7	21	67	1,958	2,251
	Surma Valley	Male ...	8,145	3,960	1,000	1,611	451	376	488	34	3,633	...	16	30	132	2,157	1,298	552	...	...	1	7	237	307
		Female	7,459	2,855	1,065	1,376	224	147	33	10	3,497	4	62	127	377	2,452	475	1,107	...	4	6	16	359	722
	Brahmaputra Valley.	Male ...	20,254	9,233	2,471	3,722	1,024	756	1,136	124	9,127	...	48	94	227	5,403	3,355	1,894	...	...	4	41	1,015	834
		Female	18,819	6,923	2,534	3,285	618	281	193	12	9,399	...	119	265	734	6,774	1,507	2,497	...	3	15	51	899	1,529
BHUIYA (Animist)	Ditto	Male ...	989	463	113	195	48	34	64	9	436	...	...	3	7	280	146	90	...	..	1	3	51	35
		Female	879	343	119	168	30	11	15	...	436	...	8	21	31	302	74	100	...	...	...	3	37	60
BRAHMAN (Hindu)	Province ...	Male ...	68,361	36,227	8,457	12,015	3,794	4,711	6,424	826	28,127	...	78	168	872	16,174	10,835	4,007	...	2	6	38	1,154	2,807
		Female	56,145	10,143	8,541	9,574	604	246	139	39	23,952	1	1,333	2,249	4,448	13,164	2,757	13,050	1	40	83	410	4,292	8,224
CHAMAR (do.)	Surma Valley	Male ...	19,541	9,026	2,511	3,621	898	836	1,097	63	9,303	1	38	159	423	5,732	2,950	1,212	...	3	8	24	594	583
		Female	19,428	6,367	2,579	3,089	433	169	85	12	9,374	7	317	440	1,069	6,380	1,161	3,687	...	17	23	75	1,344	2,228
CHUTIYA (do.)	Upper Brahmaputra Valley.	Male ...	49,359	25,019	6,448	8,927	2,529	3,093	3,803	219	14,631	...	28	32	198	8,494	5,879	9,709	...	...	4	25	978	2,702
		Female	39,805	19,568	6,581	8,782	1,971	1,759	438	37	14,931	...	55	112	1,657	10,376	2,731	5,306	...	6	5	41	1,296	3,958
CHUTIYA (Animist)	Ditto ...	Male ...	119	73	17	34	7	7	8	...	42	...	...	1	1	28	12	4	...	...	...	...	2	2
		Female	109	58	19	26	4	8	1	...	38	...	...	...	11	21	6	13	...	...	...	...	3	10
DHOBA (Hindu)	Sylhet ...	Male ...	11,870	6,475	1,251	2,162	691	309	1,412	150	4,612	...	6	8	86	2,595	1,917	783	...	...	1	...	204	578
		Female	11,223	3,115	1,369	1,638	62	22	26	8	4,659	1	282	445	977	2,554	400	3,449	...	14	16	134	1,287	1,998
GARO (do.) ...	Garo Hills and contiguous districts.	Male ...	118	51	15	20	5	4	7	...	61	...	...	...	1	34	26	6	...	...	...	...	2	4
		Female	114	51	20	14	10	6	1	...	55	...	...	6	9	27	13	8	...	...	...	...	...	8

TABLE XIV.—CIVIL CONDITION BY AGE FOR SELECTED CASTES—*contd.*

Caste, Tribe, or Race.	Locality.	Sex.	Population dealt with.	UNMARRIED. Total.	0–5	5–12	12–15	15–20	20–40	40 and over.	MARRIED. Total.	0–5	5–12	12–15	15–20	20–40	40 and over.	WIDOWED. Total.	0–5	5–12	12–15	15–20	20–40	40 and over.
1	2	3	4	5	6	7	8	9	10	11	12	13	14	15	16	17	18	19	20	21	22	23	24	25
GARO (Animist)	Garo Hills and contiguous districts.	Male ...	69,048	36,839	12,595	14,245	3,884	3,779	2,135	201	31,263	...	102	290	1,784	16,099	12,988	946	...	2	2	21	278	643
		Female	68,290	29,958	11,957	12,371	2,748	2,005	856	21	34,981	...	583	1,587	5,837	18,861	8,113	3,351	...	5	26	131	957	2,232
GOALA (Hindu) ...	Province ...	Male ...	22,800	10,156	2,238	2,947	926	1,048	2,713	284	10,634	1	49	91	252	6,424	3,817	2,010	...	1	2	28	987	992
		Female	18,058	5,671	2,348	2,659	327	195	122	20	8,912	2	336	369	1,064	6,044	1,097	3,475	...	7	16	72	1,421	1,959
INDIAN CHRISTIAN.	Ditto ...	Male ...	31,762	18,505	5,010	6,332	2,424	2,636	2,048	55	12,129	...	23	23	258	7,393	4,432	1,128	...	...	...	17	518	593
		Female	32,075	15,761	5,180	6,079	1,901	1,719	730	62	12,517	...	24	113	1,426	8,550	2,404	3,797	...	3	7	99	1,187	2,501
JOGI or JUGI (Hindu).	Ditto ...	Male ...	85,287	48,090	12,239	16,931	5,108	5,982	7,297	533	32,617	...	46	107	779	18,591	13,094	4,580	...	3	4	17	1,395	3,231
		Female...	82,234	29,375	12,632	14,259	1,311	840	277	56	33,479	1	1,617	2,449	5,817	19,756	3,839	19,380	...	35	103	497	6,772	11,973
KACHARI (do.) ...	Total ..	Male ...	28,487	16,245	4,606	5,336	1,678	1,905	2,523	197	10,385	...	11	20	209	6,435	3,710	1,857	...	...	2	21	750	1,084
		Female ..	23,892	12,414	4,465	4,691	1,558	1,389	297	14	8,934	...	31	129	955	6,088	1,731	2,544	1	3	7	51	768	1,714
	Cachar ...	Male ...	6,431	4,041	1,079	1,300	515	556	573	18	2,216	...	1	...	31	1,324	860	174	...	...	...	1	51	122
		Female...	6,538	3,410	1,197	1,326	542	358	69	8	2,254	...	18	58	435	1,471	272	874	1	1	2	31	308	531
	Brahmaputra Valley.	Male ...	22,056	12,234	3,527	4,036	1,163	1,349	1,950	179	8,169	...	10	20	178	5,111	2,850	1,683	...	...	2	20	639	962
		Female...	17,354	9,004	3,358	3,365	1,016	1,031	228	6	6,680	...	13	71	520	4,617	1,439	1,670	...	2	5	21	460	1,183
KACHARI (Animist).	Ditto	Male ...	84,277	46,645	16,737	17,323	4,435	3,676	4,220	254	33,857	...	72	221	1,078	19,951	12,535	3,775	...	5	6	32	1,342	2,390
		Female...	84,152	41,042	17,788	16,580	3,471	2,167	971	65	33,870	...	121	800	4,029	22,377	6,543	9,240	...	5	12	88	2,174	6,961
KAIBARTTA CHASI (Mahishya) (Hindu).	Province ...	Male ...	33,295	20,378	4,114	5,995	1,939	2,802	5,113	415	11,563	...	11	17	165	5,977	5,393	1,354	...	...	1	...	305	1,048
		Female...	30,257	10,487	4,424	5,606	329	49	58	21	11,420	1	440	888	2,334	6,851	906	8,350	...	22	28	197	3,060	5,043
KALITA (do.) ...	Brahmaputra Valley.	Male ...	114,886	68,356	17,911	23,117	7,303	8,700	10,671	654	41,023	...	84	106	678	21,960	18,195	5,507	...	2	9	20	1,510	3,966
		Female...	105,754	46,673	18,332	21,548	3,947	2,153	644	49	40,301	...	643	1,396	5,257	27,216	5,789	18,780	...	7	27	150	4,923	13,663
KAMAR (do.) ...	Province ...	Male ...	17,977	9,133	2,435	3,555	1,004	893	1,134	112	7,616	...	34	47	219	4,633	2,683	1,228	...	...	7	15	536	670
		Female...	17,656	6,500	2,466	3,064	519	298	139	14	8,211	...	226	373	1,047	5,598	967	2,945	...	5	15	108	1,132	1,685
KAYASTHA (do).	Ditto ...	Male ...	43,600	24,931	5,069	7,686	2,496	3,183	5,229	568	17,355	...	13	34	270	9,726	7,312	2,014	...	1	1	11	438	1,563
		Female...	37,577	13,266	5,376	7,014	520	210	133	13	15,008	1	506	1,189	3,010	8,783	1,519	9,303	...	11	28	171	3,069	6,024
KEWAT (do.)	Brahmaputra Valley.	Male ...	44,891	26,863	7,205	9,417	2,793	3,308	3,878	262	15,860	...	19	37	218	8,432	7,154	2,168	...	1	2	14	591	1,560
		Female...	43,156	19,536	7,311	9,056	1,726	1,100	320	23	16,136	...	172	350	1,841	11,206	2,567	7,484	...	3	12	63	1,897	5,509
KHASI (Animist)	Khasi and Jaintia Hills.	Male ...	54,627	30,497	9,653	10,387	3,116	3,968	3,195	178	21,199	...	4	31	483	12,154	8,527	2,931	...	...	5	58	1,136	1,732
		Female...	61,037	28,753	10,278	10,269	3,306	3,197	1,629	74	22,160	...	21	112	2,151	14,639	5,237	10,124	...	5	16	312	3,372	6,419

TABLE XIV.—Civil Condition by Age for Selected Castes—*contd.*

Caste, Tribe or Race.	Locality.	Sex.	Population dealt with.	UNMARRIED.							MARRIED.							WIDOWED.						
				Total.	0–5	5–12	12–15	15–20	20–40	40 and over.	Total.	0–5	5–12	12–15	15–20	20–40	40 and over.	Total.	0–5	5–12	12–15	15–20	20–40	40 and over.
1	2	3	4	5	6	7	8	9	10	11	12	13	14	15	16	17	18	19	20	21	22	23	24	25
KOCH (Hindu) ...	Brahmaputra Valley.	Male ...	103,960	62,097	16,610	21,886	6,478	7,523	9,056	544	36,694	1	37	77	446	20,227	15,906	5,169	...	...	3	36	1,588	3,542
		Female	99,815	45,838	17,062	20,672	4,114	3,024	902	64	37,272	...	273	709	4,535	25,998	5,757	16,705	...	3	19	159	4,371	19,153
KSHATTRIYA* (do.).	Total ...	Male ...	123,656	72.500	19,613	27,627	7,276	10,142	7,389	453	46,035	...	72	106	963	24,618	20,276	5.121	...	...	5	87	1,557	3,472
		Female...	124,623	57,054	19,541	26,611	6,488	3,547	712	155	47,686	6	225	863	7,171	28,393	11,028	19,883	...	28	48	683	5,364	13,760
	Cachar and Sylhet.	Male ...	39,564	23 404	6,015	8,239	2,287	3,063	3,598	209	14 361	...	19	27	152	8,113	6,050	1,799	...	...	3	44	497	1,255
		Female...	37,169	16,998	5,977	8,076	1,590	1,018	275	62	14,243	6	96	319	2,077	9,578	2,167	5,928	...	15	16	119	1,833	3,945
	Manipur ...	Male ...	84.092	49 096	13,598	19,395	4,980	7,079	3,791	244	31.674	...	53	79	811	16,505	14,226	3.322	...	...	2	43	1,060	2,217
		Female...	87,454	40,056	13,564	18,535	4,898	2,529	437	93	33,443	...	129	544	5,094	18,815	8,861	13,955	...	13	32	564	3,531	9,815
KUKI (Animist) ...	Province ...	Male ...	10,185	5,827	1,683	2,059	471	764	810	40	4,038	...	3	5	73	2,145	1,812	320	...	...	...	...	108	212
		Female	10,434	5,076	1,693	1,902	409	618	402	52	4,107	...	20	38	309	2,754	986	1,251	...	2	...	14	343	892
KUMHAR (Hindu)	Total ...	Male ...	9,927	5,516	1,291	1,840	575	678	1,050	82	3,750	...	6	10	98	2,110	1,596	661	...	...	...	5	163	493
		Female	9,711	3,199	1,267	1,650	136	95	48	3	3,756	...	195	263	616	2,327	355	2,756	...	3	10	73	998	1,672
	Sylhet ...	Male ...	6,167	3 396	670	1,011	318	444	784	79	2 356	...	5	9	73	1,359	910	505	...	...	...	4	131	370
		Female	6,030	1,618	674	904	22	5	10	3	2,395	...	179	226	449	1,375	166	2,017	...	2	9	67	825	1,114
	Kamrup ...	Male ...	3 760	2 210	621	829	257	234	266	3	1,394	...	1	1	25	751	616	156	...	...	...	1	32	123
		Female	3,681	1,581	593	746	114	90	38	...	1,361	...	16	37	167	952	189	739	...	1	1	6	173	558
LAKHER (Animist)	Lushai Hills	Male ...	1,751	1,088	309	364	122	141	145	7	612	...	...	...	4	342	266	51	...	...	...	...	23	28
		Female	1,888	933	276	351	89	124	78	15	695	...	...	3	35	497	160	260	...	...	2	4	66	188
LUSHAI (do.)	Ditto ...	Male ...	14,826	8,297	2,116	2,664	1,015	1,285	1,148	69	5,932	1	19	10	102	2,914	2,886	597	...	...	...	17	321	259
		Female	17,982	8,730	2,379	3,036	1,077	1,333	824	81	6,048	1	26	37	371	3,815	1,798	3,204	..	5	4	83	978	2,134
" MHAR (do.).	Ditto ...	Male ...	5,523	3,063	800	1,220	267	467	289	20	2,217	1	7	5	52	1,118	1,034	243	...	...	...	6	122	115
		Female	6,527	3,128	945	1,164	333	459	204	23	2,167	4	2	3	155	1,457	546	1,232	...	5	1	29	332	865
" PAITE (do).	Ditto ...	Male ...	1,822	1,046	266	345	80	155	188	12	708	...	1	...	8	298	401	68	...	...	...	1	24	43
		Female	1,864	902	254	332	88	124	88	16	673	1	1	1	48	402	220	289	2	3	...	13	69	202
" RALTE (do.).	Ditto ...	Male ...	7,136	3,969	938	1,416	421	632	541	21	2,853	...	5	3	47	1,321	1,477	314	...	1	1	11	161	140
		Female	8,795	4,123	1,103	1,475	418	652	444	31	2,959	2	5	5	152	1,910	885	1,713	1	7	...	33	506	1,166
" POI (do).	Ditto ...	Male ...	5.098	3,068	785	1,057	325	430	456	15	1,844	...	...	5	26	960	853	186	...	...	...	6	95	85
		Female	5,840	3,084	902	1,017	351	490	307	17	1,838	...	4	4	105	1,255	470	918	...	...	...	22	302	594

* KSHATTRIYA—Includes 19,410 persons who returned themselves as Manipuris.

TABLE XIV.—Civil Condition by Age for Selected Castes—*contd.*

Caste, Tribe or Race.	Locality.	Sex.	Population dealt with.	UNMARRIED.							MARRIED.							WIDOWED.						
				Total.	0—5	5—12	12—15	15—20	20—40	40 and over.	Total.	0—5	5—12	12—15	15—20	20—40	40 and over.	Total.	0—5	5—12	12—15	15—20	20—40	40 and over.
1	2	3	4	5	6	7	8	9	10	11	12	13	14	15	16	17	18	19	20	21	22	23	24	25
LUSHAI FANAI (do).	Lushai Hills	Male ...	1,681	981	189	341	126	177	143	5	620	1	2	3	13	288	313	80	...	...	...	3	43	34
		Female	1,950	1,010	228	362	109	196	110	5	617	...	...	3	36	384	194	323	...	1	1	10	126	185
" SAILO (do).	Ditto ...	Male ...	586	370	119	136	41	51	22	1	204	...	...	1	7	126	70	12	...	...	...	1	6	5
		Female	675	420	120	152	47	69	32	...	175	...	...	2	8	127	38	80	...	...	...	2	35	43
MALO (Hindu) ...	Sylhet ...	Male ...	7,002	4,005	709	1,093	369	498	1,315	121	2,621	...	6	14	55	1,428	1,118	376	...	...	1	...	89	286
		Female	6,458	1,902	834	1,005	35	9	16	3	2,644	...	153	202	463	1,604	222	1,912	...	5	15	50	796	1,046
MECH (do.) ...	Goalpara ...	Male ...	34,170	19,734	6,860	8,103	1,977	1,465	1,219	110	13,232	...	24	149	693	6,812	5,624	1,204	...	...	6	17	329	852
		Female	34,421	16,838	7,234	7,320	1,434	599	229	22	14,458	...	194	681	1,924	8,567	3,092	3,125	...	2	7	45	643	2,428
MECH (Animist)	Ditto ...	Male ...	12,006	6,692	2,493	2,619	566	491	487	36	4,914	..	7	45	209	2,437	2,216	400	...	...	...	...	124	276
		Female	12,431	5,968	2,657	2,518	476	221	92	4	5,374	...	50	234	687	3,180	1,223	1,089	...	...	3	16	166	904
MIKIR (do.) ...	Province ...	Male ...	52,180	29,769	9,775	10,770	2.555	3,321	3,128	220	20.856	...	67	92	539	10,942	9,216	1,555	...	...	3	22	531	999
		Female	50,032	25,621	10,178	9,921	2,207	2,348	879	88	20,289	...	92	281	1,847	12,687	5,382	4,122	...	3	9	76	972	3,062
MIRI (Hindu) ...	Sibsagar and Lakhimpur.	Male ...	6,753	4,410	1,476	1 615	348	489	446	36	2,149	...	...	...	23	1,277	849	194	...	...	...	1	70	123
		Female	6,503	3,860	1,462	1,398	358	443	195	4	2,154	...	1	4	213	1,460	476	489	...	...	...	7	104	378
MIRI (Animist) ...	Ditto ...	Male ...	19,357	12,033	3,820	4,293	1,113	1,333	1,374	100	6,753	...	17	29	173	4,111	2,423	571	...	...	...	12	241	318
		Female	18,114	10,409	3,953	3,888	979	1,136	428	25	6,307	...	8	83	584	4,298	1,334	1,398	...	...	1	35	373	989
MUCHI (Hindu) ...	Sylhet ...	Male ...	2,405	1,171	353	448	87	109	158	16	1,132	...	10	20	51	614	437	102	...	...	1	2	49	50
		Female	2,137	821	369	403	23	8	10	8	1,028	...	47	65	113	642	161	288	...	...	2	8	93	185
MUNDA (do.) ...	Total ...	Male ...	29,988	14,777	4,345	5 739	1,564	1 175	1,811	143	12,878	...	60	93	315	7,761	4,649	2,333	...	4	3	44	1,190	1,092
		Female	26,659	11,610	4,319	5,195	1,106	684	288	18	12,265	1	111	308	1,040	8,963	1,842	2,784	...	8	10	77	989	1,700
	Surma Valley	Male ...	6,438	3 435	919	1,363	365	324	437	27	2 586	...	9	9	63	1,570	935	417	...	...	1	3	152	261
		Female	6.186	2,781	959	1,292	294	153	76	7	2 664	1	31	84	302	1,913	333	741	...	2	3	19	228	489
	Darrang, Sibsagar and Lakhimpur.	Male ...	23 550	11 342	3,426	4,376	1,199	851	1,374	116	10 292	...	51	84	252	6,191	3,714	1,916	...	4	2	41	1,088	831
		Female	20,473	8,829	3,360	3,903	812	531	212	11	9,601	...	80	224	738	7,050	1,509	2,043	...	6	7	58	761	1,211
MUNDA Animist)	Total ...	Male ...	13,701	7,042	2,065	2,744	707	565	879	82	5,606	...	10	11	91	3,138	2,356	1,053	...	...	...	6	477	570
		Female	12,988	5,876	2,168	2,637	549	330	190	2	5,870	...	33	76	376	4,344	1,041	1,242	...	...	2	14	480	746
	Surma Valley	Male ...	174	97	26	32	17	11	11	...	62	...	1	...	2	32	27	15	...	...	...	...	6	9
		Female	170	86	30	45	5	5	1	...	65	...	1	...	12	50	2	19	...	...	...	...	7	12
	Darrang, Sibsagar and Lakhimpur.	Male ...	13 527	6,965	2,039	2,712	690	554	868	82	5 544	...	9	11	80	3,106	2,329	1,038	...	...	...	6	471	561
		Female	12,818	5,790	2,138	2,592	544	325	189	2	5,805	...	32	76	364	4,204	1,039	1,223	...	...	2	14	473	734

TABLE XIV.—Civil Condition by Age for Selected Castes—*contd.*

Caste, Tribe or Race.	Locality.	Sex.	Popu'at'on dealt with.	UNMARRIED. Total.	0–5	5–12	12–15	15–20	20–40	40 and over.	MARRIED. Total.	0–5	5–12	12–15	15–20	20–40	40 and over.	WIDOWED. Total.	0–5	5–12	12–15	15–20	20–40	40 and over.
1	2	3	4	5	6	7	8	9	10	11	12	13	14	15	16	17	18	19	20	21	22	23	24	25
NADIYAL (Hindu)	Brahmaputra Valley.	Male ...	32,026	19,041	5,420	6,969	1,999	2,186	2,334	133	11,084	...	11	20	152	6,505	4,396	1,901	...	...	2	20	766	1,113
		Female	31,255	15,183	5,822	6,911	1,248	874	305	23	11,476	...	25	131	1,538	8,052	1,730	4,596	...	3	7	96	1,458	3,032
NAGA, KACHHA (Animist).	Total ...	Male ...	4,581	2,636	816	901	227	311	362	19	1,672	...	...	...	20	873	779	273	...	...	...	1	68	204
		Female	4,726	2,416	899	924	235	266	88	4	1,710	...	2	18	67	1,074	549	600	...	...	...	7	147	446
	Manipur ...	Male ...	157	93	16	33	4	12	28	...	54	...	...	...	...	29	25	10	...	...	...	1	3	6
		Female	139	65	20	22	3	11	9	...	54	...	...	...	...	37	17	20	...	...	...	...	2	18
	Naga Hills ...	Male ...	4,424	2 543	800	868	223	299	334	19	1,618	...	...	...	20	844	754	263	...	...	...	...	65	198
		Female	4,587	2,351	879	902	232	255	79	4	1,656	...	2	18	67	1,037	532	580	...	...	...	7	145	428
" ANGAMI (do).	Ditto ...	Male ...	19,875	9,666	2,478	3,768	594	1,269	1,409	148	8,347	...	...	...	35	3,839	4,473	1,862	...	...	...	...	803	1,059
		Female	19,797	8,847	2,651	3,751	1,033	1,126	286	...	8,172	...	5	11	121	4,077	3,958	2,778	...	...	1	50	939	1,788
" KABUI (do).	Manipur ...	Male ...	5,930	3,419	852	1,325	310	359	556	17	2,240	...	1	2	36	1,172	1,029	261	...	...	...	2	66	193
		Female	6,515	3,304	966	1,306	381	391	233	27	2,306	...	4	5	128	1,394	775	905	...	...	...	8	194	703
" LHOTA (do).	Naga Hills...	Male ...	9,437	4,903	1,149	1,556	543	592	873	190	4,101	...	...	1	50	2,012	2,038	433	...	...	...	...	117	316
		Female	10,061	3,822	1,186	1,493	319	407	353	64	4,402	...	4	49	252	3,019	1,078	1,837	...	...	2	102	344	1,389
" SEMA (do.)	Ditto ...	Male ...	16,304	9,033	2,504	3,446	1,207	965	893	18	6,605	...	...	10	229	3,392	2,974	666	...	...	...	10	277	379
		Female	16,422	8,593	2,581	3,748	999	758	494	13	6,697	...	...	6	339	4,390	1,962	1,132	...	...	...	9	284	839
" TANGKHUL (do.).	Manipur ...	Male ...	12,506	6,537	2,720	2,131	496	662	471	57	5,404	...	18	22	270	3,052	2,042	565	...	...	...	16	178	371
		Female	14,071	6,760	3,005	2,209	565	704	277	...	5,704	...	5	34	363	3,379	1,923	1,607	...	...	1	9	438	1,159
" AO (do.)	Naga Hills	Male ...	12,533	6,418	1,555	2,266	904	783	867	43	5,989	...	...	2	17	2,965	3,005	896	...	...	...	4	295	597
		Female	13,972	6,272	1,734	2,476	784	684	535	59	5,222	...	...	26	273	2,976	1,947	2,478	...	...	2	62	706	1,708
" KEZHAMA (do.)	Ditto ...	Male ...	2,600	1,853	536	636	334	212	99	36	548	...	...	...	...	150	398	199	...	...	...	...	46	153
		Female	2,085	960	437	331	117	70	5	...	885	...	...	...	25	621	239	240	...	...	...	26	104	110
" RENGMA (do).	Ditto ...	Male ...	2,016	1,073	321	406	106	145	82	13	850	...	...	...	4	332	514	93	...	...	...	...	6	87
		Female	2,354	1,046	353	412	100	115	66	...	1,021	...	...	2	11	441	567	287	...	...	...	1	39	247
" UNSPECIFIED (do).	Ditto ...	Male ...	1,267	650	203	179	65	96	102	5	461	...	...	...	14	254	193	156	...	...	...	...	74	82
		Female	442	193	60	79	22	15	13	4	161	...	...	9	2	112	38	88	...	...	1	1	30	56

TABLE XIV.—Civil Condition by Age for Selected Castes—*contd.*

Caste, Tribe or Race.	Locality.	Sex.	Population dealt with.	Unmarried.							Married.							Widowed.						
				Total.	0—5	5—12	12—15	15—20	20—40	40 and over.	Total.	0—5	5—12	12—15	15—20	20—40	40 and over.	Total.	0—5	5—12	12—15	15—20	20—40	40 and over.
1.	2	3	4	5	6	7	8	9	10	11	12	13	14	15	16	17	18	19	20	21	22	23	24	25
NAMASUDRA (Hindu)	Total ...	Male ...	88,650	48,639	11,185	16,693	4,907	6,190	9,185	479	35,783	...	52	86	879	19,997	14,769	4,228	...	...	3	12	1,298	2,915
		Female	82,564	25,896	12,182	12,919	418	160	181	36	36,207	3	2,207	3,265	7,041	20,286	3,405	20,461	...	55	98	495	7,277	12,536
	Surma Valley	Male ...	78,635	42,939	9,626	14,703	4,300	5,465	8,401	442	31,856	...	50	71	791	17,773	13,171	3 840	...	...	2	11	1,172	2,655
		Female	74,967	22,464	10,609	11,314	263	92	153	33	32,866	3	2,053	3,066	6,557	18,240	2,947	18.737	...	51	84	463	6,730	11,409
	Goalpara, Kamrup and Nowgong.	Male ...	10.015	5.700	1,557	1,990	607	725	784	37	3,927	...	2	15	88	2,234	1,508	388	...	...	1	1	126	260
		Female	8,497	3,432	1,573	1,605	155	68	28	3	3,341	...	154	199	484	2,046	458	1,724	...	4	14	32	547	1,127
NAPIT (do.) ...	Total ...	Male ...	14,981	8,325	1,874	2,844	927	1,173	1,364	143	5,796	...	4	9	133	3,197	2,453	860	...	1	3	4	209	643
		Female	14,415	4,811	2.048	2,557	125	31	46	4	5,883	...	300	508	1,212	3,303	560	3,721	...	12	23	109	1,335	2,242
	Sylhet ...	Male ...	12.229	6,801	1,473	2,257	727	967	1,239	138	4,673	...	4	8	104	2,501	1,966	755	...	1	...	...	178	576
		Female	11,453	3,600	1,507	2,000	49	18	24	2	4,649	...	200	436	1,026	2,541	386	3,204	...	10	21	103	1,211	1,859
	Kamrup ...	Male ...	2,752	1.524	401	587	200	206	125	5	1.123	...	...	1	29	606	487	105	...	...	3	4	31	67
		Female	2,962	1,211	541	557	76	13	22	2	1.234	...	40	72	186	762	174	517	...	2	2	6	124	383
ORAON (do.) ...	Total ...	Male	6,665	3,546	974	1,388	421	325	401	37	2,641	...	7	10	66	1.533	1,025	478	...	...	1	6	240	231
		Female	6,240	2,810	999	1,291	274	181	63	2	2,743	...	35	74	207	1,964	463	687	..	...	2	24	265	396
	Cachar ...	Male	1,224	662	184	252	90	68	64	4	482	...	...	1	14	202	175	80	...	...	...	...	33	47
		Female	1,154	525	192	242	56	24	10	1	495	...	3	22	46	350	74	134	...	...	...	3	33	98
	Brahmaputra Valley.	Male	3,441	2.884	790	1,136	331	257	337	33	2,159	...	7	9	52	1.241	850	398	...	...	1	6	207	184
		Female	5,086	2,285	807	1,049	218	157	53	1	2,248	...	32	52	161	1,614	389	553	...	...	2	21	232	298
ORAON (Animist)	Total ...	Male	5,321	2,886	871	1,111	321	239	305	39	2,090	...	3	7	116	1,053	911	345	...	...	1	...	138	206
		Female	5,685	2,675	982	1,197	243	146	101	6	2,407	...	9	68	224	1,587	519	663	...	1	...	6	207	389
	Cachar ...	Male	147	76	23	35	10	2	6	...	63	...	...	...	2	44	17	8	...	...	...	...	3	5
		Female	153	72	28	28	5	4	2	5	64	...	2	4	9	49	...	17	...	...	...	...	7	10
	Brahmaputra Valley.	Male	5.174	2 810	848	1,076	311	237	299	39	2,027	...	3	7	114	1,009	894	337	...	...	1	...	135	201
		Female	5,532	2,603	954	1,169	238	142	99	1	2,343	...	7	64	215	1,538	519	566	...	1	...	6	200	379
PATNI (Hindu)	Surma Valley	Male	56,721	30,215	7,096	10,489	3,171	4,029	5,101	329	23,767	...	20	65	670	13,696	9,316	2,739	...	2	...	6	798	1,933
		Female	54,137	16,322	7,577	8,150	244	118	139	94	24,162	5	1,512	2,249	4,996	13,254	2,146	13,653	...	53	79	351	5,009	8,161
RAJBANSI (do.)	Goalpara ...	Male	65,747	37,235	9,798	13,917	3,565	4,592	5,719	344	25.442	...	49	119	755	13.742	10,777	3,070	...	2	3	13	871	2,181
		Female	62,199	21,830	10,477	10,071	749	376	143	14	27,378	3	1,652	2,273	5,052	14,179	4,219	19,991	...	70	117	497	5,091	7,216

TABLE XIV.—Civil Condition by Age for Selected Castes—*concld.*

Caste, Tribe, or Race.	Locality.	Sex.	Population dealt with.	Unmarried.							Married.							Widowed.						
				Total.	0—5	5—12	12—15	15—20	20—40	40 and over.	Total.	0—5	5—12	12—15	15—20	20—40	40 and over.	Total.	0—5	5—12	12—15	15—20	20—40	40 and over.
1	2	3	4	5	6	7	8	9	10	11	12	13	14	15	16	17	18	19	20	21	22	23	24	25
SANTAL (Hindu)...	Total ...	Male	13,659	6,504	1,867	2,492	586	552	932	75	5,961	...	14	39	112	3,523	2,280	1,194	...	...	4	18	616	556
		Female	13,280	5,301	1,938	2,485	472	271	124	11	6,424	...	72	145	504	4,859	844	1,555	...	1	2	24	669	859
	Surma Valley.	Male	2 911	1.519	379	586	129	159	234	13	1,176	...	1	2	19	705	449	216	...	...	1	1	81	133
		Female	2,623	1,103	373	549	102	50	22	7	1,152	...	16	53	137	811	135	368	...	1	1	7	113	247
	Brahmaputra Valley.	Male	10.748	4.985	1,488	1,906	457	394	678	62	4,785	...	13	30	93	2,318	1,831	978	...	...	3	17	535	423
		Female	10,657	4,198	1,565	1,936	370	221	102	4	5,272	...	56	92	367	4,048	709	1,187	...	...	1	17	557	612
SA TAL (Animist)	Total ...	Male	11,486	5,663	1,567	2,247	533	490	779	54	4,869	...	9	22	80	2,804	1,954	954	...	1	...	11	414	528
		Female	10,720	4,446	1,637	2,127	344	218	115	5	5,097	...	39	88	368	3,813	782	1,177	...	...	3	19	452	703
	Surma Valley	Male	2.360	1,236	309	503	126	126	163	9	975	...	1	4	18	588	364	149	...	...	...	2	48	99
		Female	2,270	1,002	342	489	94	59	15	3	1,013	...	5	21	110	730	147	255	...	...	1	3	79	172
	Brahmaputra Valley.	Male	9.126	4 427	1,238	1,744	407	364	609	45	3,894	...	9	18	62	2,216	1,590	895	...	1	...	9	366	429
		Female	8,459	3,444	1,295	1,638	250	159	100	2	4,084	...	34	67	258	3,083	642	922	...	...	2	16	373	531
SUDRA (Hindu) ...	Sylhet ...	Male ...	59,400	35,852	7,168	11,359	3,688	4,773	8,177	687	20,916	...	16	30	249	10.994	9,634	2,632	...	...	...	5	618	2,009
		Female...	55,741	18,707	7,586	10,400	488	124	87	22	21,225	...	881	1,696	4,265	19,419	1,964	15.809	...	38	67	386	5,752	9,566
SUTRADHAR (do.).	Total ...	Male ...	8,103	4,642	964	1,573	450	611	968	76	3,068	...	5	8	39	1,674	1,349	393	...	...	...	1	93	300
		Female...	7,321	2,389	962	1,336	54	16	19	2	3,016	2	127	285	619	1,718	265	1,916	...	2	12	61	708	1,133
	Sylhet ...	Male ...	6,803	3,904	742	1,314	385	539	849	75	2.568	...	1	3	28	1,404	1,132	331	...	...	...	1	76	254
		Female...	6,384	1,992	797	1,144	29	8	12	2	2,599	2	121	268	557	1,446	205	1,793	...	2	12	58	684	1,087
	Goalpara ...	Male ...	1,300	738	222	259	65	72	119	1	500	...	4	5	11	270	210	62	...	...	...	...	16	46
		Female...	937	397	165	192	25	8	7	...	417	...	6	17	62	272	60	123	...	...	...	3	24	96
SYNTENG (Animist)	Khasi and Jaintia Hills.	Male ...	19,629	10,758	3,707	3,833	1,264	1,318	570	66	7,609	...	4	20	417	4,587	2,581	1,962	...	1	1	54	604	602
		Female...	22,495	9,637	4,048	3,775	1,050	631	104	29	8,292	...	8	70	1,245	5,251	1,718	4,566	...	1	21	280	1,621	2,643
TANTI (Hindu) ...	Sibsagar and Lakhimpur.	Male ...	11,602	5,434	1,330	2,051	650	578	761	54	5,172	...	14	30	197	3.378	1,623	1,006	...	2	4	16	581	403
		Female...	11,773	4,366	1,572	1,948	488	234	117	7	5,814	...	55	133	510	4,506	610	1,593	...	2	11	38	759	783
TELI OR TILI (do.).	Sylhet ...	Male ...	14.368	7,782	1,725	2,499	871	985	1,554	148	5,702	...	4	10	118	3,280	2,290	884	...	...	...	2	220	662
		Female...	13,643	3,936	1,682	2,135	42	20	52	5	5,745	...	377	573	1,149	3,104	549	3,962	...	14	21	111	1,549	2,267

TABLE XV.

OCCUPATIONS.

For the purpose of this Table, a new scheme of classification of occupations, based on that drawn up by M. Bertillon, has been framed by the Census Commissioner. All occupations are divided, according to this scheme, into four main classes and subdivided into 12 sub-classes, 55 orders and 169 groups.

The Table is divided into four Parts, A, B, D and E. Part A is subdivided into two sections: the first section contains a general summary giving the total strength of each group, order, sub-class and class for (1) Assam, (2) British Territory and (3) Manipur State: the second section gives for each district and for Manipur State the total strength of each order and detailed statistics of those groups, the strength of which reaches 500 in any district except group 145, the strength of which in Manipur State is 370. Part B shows the subsidiary occupations of those persons whose main occupation is agriculture. Part C (combined occupations), which was optional, did not contain statistics of any importance and has been omitted for this province. Part D shows the distribution of occupations by religion. Part E embodies the results of the Industrial Census and its scope is explained in the title page prefixed to it.

TABLE XV.—Occupation or Means of Livelihood.

Group No.	Occupation.	Total workers and dependents.	Provincial Total. Actual workers. Total. Males.	Females.	Partially agriculturist. Males.	Females.	Dependents. Both sexes.
	1	2	3	4	5	6	7
	TOTAL POPULATION	*7,059,857*	*2,227,484*	*985,186*	*95,346*	*18,002*	*3,847,187*
	A.—PRODUCTION OF RAW MATERIALS.	*6,184,914*	*1,917,572*	*824,679*	*49,628*	*13,724*	*3,442,663*
	I.—EXPLOITATION OF THE SURFACE OF THE EARTH	*6,178,391*	*1,913,934*	*823,505*	*49,542*	*13,719*	*3,440,952*
	1.—PASTURE AND AGRICULTURE ...	*6,077,685*	*1,871,232*	*821,762*	*37,229*	*13,600*	*3,384,691*
	(a) *Ordinary cultivation*	*5,323,380*	*1,587,920*	*580,482*	*879*	...	*3,154,978*
1	Income from rent of agricultural land ...	137,106	18,286	4,195	...	...	114,625
2	Ordinary cultivators	5,092,771	1,525,888	566,322	...	...	3,000,561
2 (a)	Revenue-payers (included in total)	2,114,141	636,522	390,089	...	...	1,087,530
3	Agents, managers of landed estates (not planters), clerks, rent collectors, etc.	8,581	3,090	...	879	...	5,482
4	Farm servants and field labourers	84,922	40,647	9,965	...	...	34,310
	(b) *Growers of special products and market gardening.*	*702,793*	*246,281*	*238,142*	*34,353*	*13,506*	*218,370*
5	Tea, coffee, cinchona and indigo plantations ...	675,360	237,893	230,762	33,072	12,500	206,705
5 (a)	Tea plantations (included in total)	675,344	237,888	230,762	33,072	12,500	206,694
6	Fruit, flower, vegetable, betel, vine, areca nut, etc., growers	27,433	8,388	7,380	1,281	1,006	11,665
	(c) *Forestry*	*4,099*	*2,130*	*327*	*247*	*3*	*1,642*
7	Forest officers, rangers, guards, etc. ...	1,336	671	...	61	...	665
8	Wood-cutters; fire-wood, lac, catechu, rubber, etc., collectors, and charcoal burners ...	2,763	1,459	327	186	3	977
	(d) *Raising of farm stock*	*47,278*	*34,867*	*2,767*	*1,750*	*91*	*9,644*
9	Cattle and buffalo breeders and keepers ...	18,819	9,457	1,226	1,475	87	8,136
10	Sheep, goat and pig breeders	96	39	16	6	...	41
11	Breeders of other animals (horses, mules, camels, asses, etc.)	9	4	...	...	...	5
12	Herdsmen, shepherds, goatherds, etc. ...	28,354	25,367	1,525	269	4	1,462
	(e) *Raising of small animals*	*135*	*34*	*44*	...	...	*57*
13	(Birds, bees, silkworms, etc.)						
	2.—FISHING AND HUNTING	*100,706*	*42,702*	*1,743*	*12,313*	*119*	*56,261*
14	Fishing	100,102	42,459	1,716	12,281	118	55,927
15	Hunting	604	243	27	32	1	334
	II.—EXTRACTION OF MINERALS ...	*6,523*	*3,638*	*1,174*	*86*	*5*	*1,711*
	3.—MINES	*5,122*	*3,060*	*903*	*79*	*5*	*1,159*
16	Coal mines and petroleum wells	5,096	3,038	902	79	5	1,156
17	Mines and metallic minerals (gold, iron, manganese, etc.)	26	22	1	...	...	3
18	**4.—QUARRIES OF HARD ROCKS** ... ... [Other minerals (jade, diamonds, limestone, etc.]	*680*	*395*	*27*	*6*	...	*258*
18(a)	Limestone Quaries (included in total) ...	675	390	27	1	...	258
	5.—SALT, etc.	*721*	*183*	*244*	*1*	...	*294*
19	Rock, sea and marsh salt	712	183	237	1	...	292
20	Extraction of saltpetre, alum and other substances soluble in water	9	...	7	...	...	2
	B.—PREPARATION AND SUPPLY OF MATERIAL SUBSTANCES ...	*537,782*	*181,167*	*110,343*	*29,699*	*3,232*	*246,272*
	III.—INDUSTRY	*216,624*	*56,018*	*72,944*	*12,309*	*1,771*	*87,662*
	6.—TEXTILE	*59,419*	*2,914*	*44,736*	*90*	*1,033*	*11,769*
21	Cotton ginning, cleaning and pressing ...	46	21	...	...	...	25
22	Cotton spinning, sizing and weaving ...	56,295	2,019	43,467	748	1,023	10,809
23	Jute spinning, pressing and weaving ...	196	159	9	...	...	28
24	Rope, twine and string	1,085	425	372	142	6	288
26	Wool carders and spinners, weavers of woollen blankets, carpets, etc.	10	10	...	1	...	...
27	Silk spinners and weavers	1,717	249	876	8	3	592
30	Dyeing, bleaching, printing, preparation and sponging of textiles	44	13	10	...	1	21
31	Other (lace, crape, embroideries, fringes, etc.), and insufficiently described textile industries...	26	18	2	1	...	6
	7.—HIDES, SKINS AND HARD MATERIALS FROM THE ANIMAL KINGDOM.	*1,432*	*752*	*41*	*114*	*1*	*639*
32	Tanners, curriers, leather dressers and dyers, etc.	1,223	620	37	108	1	566
33	Makers of leather articles, such as trunks, water bags, etc.	83	46	3	...	...	34
34	Furriers...	113	79	1	6	...	33
35	Bone, ivory, horn, shell, etc., workers	13	7	...	...	...	6
	8.—WOOD	*34,029*	*12,071*	*7,552*	*2,739*	*87*	*14,406*
36	Sawyers, carpenters, turners and joiners, etc. ...	20,318	9,624	253	1,954	...	10,441
37	Basket makers and other industries of woody material, including leaves	13,711	2,447	7,299	785	87	3,965
	9.—METALS	*13,248*	*4,964*	*170*	*1,356*	*6*	*8,114*
38	Forging and rolling of iron and other metals ...	7	4	3	1	3	...
39	Plough and agricultural implement makers ...	220	78	...	53	...	142
40	Makers of arms, guns, etc.	40	16	...	...	...	24
41	Other workers in iron and makers of implements and tools, principally or exclusively of iron	7,880	3,209	48	1,016	3	4,603
42	Workers in brass, copper and bell metal ...	4,957	1,574	114	280	...	3,269
43	Workers in other metals (tin, zinc, lead, quick-silver, etc.	164	83	5	...	...	76

PART A.—GENERAL TABLE—PROVINCIAL SUMMARY.

BRITISH TERRITORY.						MANIPUR STATE.					
TOTAL WORKERS AND DEPENDENTS.	ACTUAL WORKERS.				DEPENDENTS.	TOTAL WORKERS AND DEPENDENTS.	ACTUAL WORKERS.				DEPENDENTS.
	Total.		Partially agriculturist.				Total.		Partially agriculturist.		
	Males.	Females.	Males.	Females.	Both sexes.		Males.	Females.	Males.	Females.	Both sexes.
8	9	10	11	12	13	14	15	16	17	18	19
6,713,635	*2,148,211*	*928,527*	*94,298*	*17,041*	*3,636,897*	*346,222*	*79,273*	*56,659*	*1,048*	*961*	*210,290*
5,913,575	*1,847,684*	*812,453*	*49,626*	*13,724*	*3,253,438*	*271,339*	*69,888*	*12,226*	*2*	...	*189,225*
5,907,789	*1,844,250*	*811,517*	*49,541*	*13,719*	*3,252,022*	*270,602*	*69,684*	*11,988*	*1*	...	*188,930*
5,807,234	*1,801,594*	*809,779*	*37,228*	*13,600*	*3,195,861*	*270,451*	*69,638*	*11,983*	*1*	...	*188,830*
5,054,324	*1,518,750*	*568,663*	*879*	...	*2,966,911*	*269,050*	*69,170*	*11,819*	...	...	*188,067*
137.104	18,286	4,193	...	...	114,625	2	...	2	...	...	...
4 824 061	1,456,873	554,520	...	...	2,812,668	268,710	69,015	11,802	...	...	187,893
1,845 463	567,515	378,288	...	...	899,660	268,678	69,007	11,801	...	...	187,870
8 543	3,091	...	879	...	5,452	38	8	...	...	...	30
84,616	40,500	9,950	...	...	34,166	306	147	15	...	...	144
702,695	*246,243*	*238,140*	*34,353*	*13,506*	*218,312*	*98*	*38*	*2*	...	...	*58*
675.359	237,893	230,762	33,072	12,500	206,704	1	...	...	...	...	1
675-344	237,888	230,762	33,072	12,500	206,694	...	...	...	...	...	...
27,336	8,350	7,378	1,281	1,006	11,608	97	38	2	...	...	57
3.857	*2,107*	*190*	*247*	*3*	*1.560*	*242*	*23*	*137*	...	...	*82*
1,323	667	...	61	...	656	13	4	...	...	...	9
2,534	1,440	190	186	3	904	229	19	137	...	...	73
46,931	*34,460*	*2,748*	*1,749*	*91*	*9,023*	*1,047*	*407*	*19*	*1*	...	*621*
16,018	9,240	1,211	1,474	87	7,567	801	217	15	1	...	569
96	39	16	6	...	41	...	...	...	...	...	...
3	3	...	...	...	...	6	1	...	...	...	5
28,114	25,178	1,521	269	4	1,415	240	189	4	...	...	47
197	*34*	*38*	...	...	*55*	*8*	...	*6*	...	...	*2*
100,555	*42,656*	*1,738*	*12,313*	*119*	*56,161*	*151*	*46*	*5*	...	...	*100*
99 951	42,413	1,711	12,281	118	55,827	151	46	5	...	...	100
604	243	27	32	1	334	...	...	...	...	...	...
5,786	*3.434*	*936*	*85*	*5*	*1,416*	*737*	*204*	*238*	*1*	...	*295*
5,097	*3,039*	*902*	*79*	*5*	*1,156*	*25*	*21*	*1*	...	...	*3*
5,096	3,038	902	79	5	1,156	...	...	...	...	...	...
1	1	...	...	...	...	25	21	1	...	...	3
680	*395*	*27*	*6*	...	*258*	...	...	...	...	...	...
675	390	27	1	...	258	...	...	...	...	...	...
9	...	*7*	...	...	*2*	*712*	*183*	*237*	*1*	...	*292*
...	...	...	...	...	...	712	183	237	1	...	292
9	...	7	...	...	2	...	...	...	...	...	...
474,581	*176,912*	*66,341*	*29,448*	*2,277*	*231,328*	*63,201*	*4,255*	*44,002*	*251*	*955*	*14,944*
168,193	*54,208*	*35,983*	*12,206*	*820*	*78,002*	*48,431*	*1,810*	*36,961*	*103*	*951*	*9,660*
15,673	*2,371*	*8,668*	*884*	*93*	*4,634*	*43,746*	*543*	*36,068*	*16*	*940*	*7,135*
45	21	...	...	...	24	1	...	...	...	...	1
13.185	1,66[illegible]	7,577	740	83	3,948	43,110	359	35,890	8	940	6,861
196	159	9	...	...	28	...	...	...	...	...	...
1.082	423	371	142	6	288	3	2	1	...	...	...
10	10	...	1	...	...	...	...	...	...	...	...
1,131	82	708	...	3	341	586	167	168	8	...	251
18	13	1	...	1	4	26	...	9	...	...	17
6	3	2	1	...	1	20	15	...	...	...	5
1,410	*743*	*40*	*114*	*1*	*627*	*22*	*2*	*1*	...	...	*12*
1,223	620	37	108	1	566	...	...	...	...	...	...
61	37	2	...	...	22	22	9	1	...	...	12
113	79	1	6	...	33	...	...	...	...	...	...
13	7	...	...	...	6	...	...	...	...	...	...
32,893	*11,687*	*7,532*	*2,720*	*87*	*13,674*	*1,136*	*384*	*20*	*19*	...	*732*
19,287	9,297	246	1,937	...	9,744	1,031	327	7	17	...	687
13.606	2,390	7,286	782	87	3,930	105	57	13	2	...	85
12,755	*4.783*	*97*	*1,331*	*6*	*7,875*	*49..*	*181*	*73*	*25*	...	*239*
7	4	3	1	3	...	...	...	...	...	...	...
220	78	...	53	...	142	...	...	...	...	...	...
40	16	...	...	...	24	...	...	...	...	...	...
7.561	3,095	28	901	3	4,438	299	114	20	25	...	165
4.763	1,507	61	286	...	3,195	194	67	53	...	...	74
164	83	5	...	...	76	...	...	...	...	...	...

TABLE XV.—Occupation or Means of Livelihood.

Group No.	Occupation.	Provincial Total. Total workers and dependents.	Actual workers. Total. Males.	Actual workers. Total. Females.	Actual workers. Partially agriculturist. Males.	Actual workers. Partially agriculturist. Females.	Dependents. Both sexes.
	1	2	3	4	5	6	7
	10.—CERAMICS	*16,795*	*4,415*	*5,513*	*1,042*	*916*	*6,867*
45	Makers of glass and crystal ware	4	...	...	...	...	4
46	Makers of porcelain and crockery	112	...	85	...	28	27
47	Potters and earthen pipe and bowl makers ...	15 677	3,817	5,295	1,015	188	6,565
48	Brick and tile makers	1,002	598	133	27	...	271
	11.—CHEMICAL PRODUCTS PROPERLY SO CALLED, AND ANALOGOUS.	*5,426*	*1,813*	*739*	*444*	*2*	*2,874*
50	Manufacture of matches and explosive materials	54	10	...	...	...	44
51	Manufacture of ærated and mineral waters ...	15	9	...	...	...	6
52	Manufacture of dyes, paints and ink	4	2	...	...	...	2
53	Manufacture and refining of vegetable and mineral oils	4,286	1,591	316	429	2	2,379
55	Others (soap, candles, lac, cutch, perfumes and miscellaneous drugs)	1,067	201	423	15	...	443
	12.—FOOD INDUSTRIES	*19,371*	*1,539*	*10,735*	*134*	*338*	*7,097*
56	Rice pounders and huskers and flour grinders ...	13,637	341	8,670	14	89	4,626
57	Bakers and biscuit makers	662	262	63	25	5	337
58	Grain parchers, etc.	1,023	55	620	1	13	848
59	Butchers	376	145	5	9	...	226
61	Butter, cheese and ghee makers	25	18	1	2	...	6
62	Makers of sugar, molasses and gur	45	25	3	5	...	17
63	Sweetmeat makers, preparers of jam and condiments, etc.	1.029	464	50	30	...	515
64	Brewers and distillers	2,516	187	1,323	47	251	1,006
65	Toddy drawers	16	14	...	...	...	2
66	Manufacturers of tobacco, opium and ganja ...	42	28	...	1	...	14
	13.—INDUSTRIES OF DRESS AND THE TOILET	*36,090*	*14,269*	*2,354*	*3,782*	*61*	*19,467*
67	Hat, cap and turban makers	3	...	...	...	...	3
68	Tailors, milliners, dress makers and darners, embroiderers on linen	10,018	4,153	791	283	19	5,074
69	Shoe, boot and sandal makers	1,852	835	28	67	1	989
70	Other industries pertaining to dress, gloves, socks, gaiters, belts, buttons, umbrellas, canes, etc.	308	131	16	4	...	161
71	Washing, cleaning and dyeing	8.956	3,320	1,437	1,140	40	4,199
72	Barbers, hairdressers and wig makers ...	14,949	5,829	79	2,288	1	9,041
73	Other industries connected with the toilet (tattooers, shampooers, bath houses, etc.) ...	4	1	3	...	...	...
	14.—FURNITURE INDUSTRIES	*73*	*45*	*4*	*2*	...	*24*
74	Cabinet makers, carriage painters, etc. ...	59	38	...	2	...	21
75	Upholsterers, tent makers, etc.	14	7	4	...	...	3
	15.—BUILDING INDUSTRIES	*8,958*	*4,582*	*414*	*701*	*11*	*3,962*
76	Lime burners, cement workers	749	169	154	4	3	426
77	Excavators, plinth builders and well-sinkers ...	3,004	1,780	203	427	8	1,021
78	Stone and marble workers, masons and bricklayers	3,044	1,507	10	170	...	1,527
79	Others (thatchers, building contractors, house painters, tilers, plumbers, locksmiths, etc.)...	2,161	1,126	47	100	...	988
	16.—CONSTRUCTION OF MEANS OF TRANSPORT	*640*	*356*	*5*	*27*	*1*	*279*
80	Cart, carriage, palki, etc., makers and wheelwrights	286	222	4	8	1	60
81	Saddlers, harness makers, whip and lash makers	6	5	...	...	...	1
82	Ship and boat builders	348	129	1	24	...	218
83	17.—PRODUCTION AND TRANSMISSION OF PHYSICAL FORCES (HEAT, LIGHT, ELECTRICITY, MOTIVE POWER, ETC.) (Gas works, electric light and ice factories) ...	*4*	*3*	...	...	...	*1*
	18.—INDUSTRIES OF LUXURY AND THOSE PERTAINING TO LITERATURE AND THE ARTS AND SCIENCES	*17,736*	*6,900*	*280*	*1,039*	*14*	*10,556*
84	Printers, lithographers, engravers, etc. ...	1,042	431	5	8	...	606
85	Newspaper and magazine managers and editors, journalists, etc....	5	3	...	...	...	2
86	Bookbinders and stitchers, envelope makers, etc.	73	47	...	6	...	26
87	Makers of musical instruments	82	50	1	5	...	31
88	Makers of watches and clocks and optical, photographic and surgical instruments ...	136	48	...	...	...	88
89	Workers in precious stones and metals, enamellers, imitation jewellery makers, gilders, etc.	15,647	5,985	212	995	13	9,450
90	Makers of bangles, rosaries, bead and other necklaces, spangles, lingams and sacred threads	350	119	56	16	1	175
91	Toy, kite, cage, fishing tackle, etc., makers, taxidermists, etc.	111	30	4	...	...	77
92	Others, including managers, persons other than performers employed in theatres and other places of public entertainment, employés of public societies, race course service, huntsmen, etc.	290	187	2	9	...	101
93	19.—INDUSTRIES CONCERNED WITH REFUSE MATTER (Sweepers, scavengers, dust and sweeping contractors)	*3,403*	*1,395*	*401*	*29*	*1*	*1,607*

PART A.—GENERAL TABLE—PROVINCIAL SUMMARY—*continued.*

BRITISH TERRITORY.						MANIPUR STATE.					
Total workers and dependents.	Actual workers.				Dependents.	Total workers and dependents.	Actual workers.				Dependents.
	Total.		Partially agriculturist.				Total.		Partially agriculturist.		
	Males.	Females.	Males.	Females.	Both sexes.		Males.	Females.	Males.	Females.	Both sexes.
8	9	10	11	12	13	14	15	16	17	18	19
16,202	*4,367*	*5,133*	*1,029*	*210*	*6,702*	*593*	*48*	*380*	*13*	*6*	*165*
4	...	...	...	...	4	...	...	...	...	...	...
112	...	85	...	28	27	...	...	...	...	...	...
15,165	3,801	4,915	1,015	182	6,449	512	16	380	...	6	116
921	566	133	14	...	222	81	32	...	13	...	49
5,312	*1,786*	*736*	*444*	*2*	*2,790*	*114*	*27*	*3*	...	...	*84*
54	10	...	...	...	44	...	...	...	...	...	...
15	9	...	...	...	6	...	...	...	...	...	...
4	2	...	...	...	2	...	...	...	...	...	...
4,172	1,564	313	429	2	2,295	114	27	3	...	...	84
1,067	201	423	15	...	443	...	...	...	...	...	...
19,135	*1,534*	*10,662*	*134*	*338*	*6,939*	*236*	*5*	*73*	...	...	*158*
13,635	340	8,670	14	89	4,625	2	1	...	...	...	1
651	259	62	25	5	330	11	3	1	...	...	7
876	54	598	1	13	224	147	1	22	...	...	124
376	145	5	9	...	226	...	...	...	...	...	...
25	18	1	2	...	6	...	...	...	...	...	...
45	25	3	5	...	17	...	...	...	...	...	...
1,029	464	50	30	...	515	...	...	...	...	...	...
2,440	187	1,273	47	231	980	76	...	50	...	...	26
16	14	...	...	...	2	...	...	...	...	...	...
42	28	...	1	...	14	...	...	...	...	...	...
35,090	*14,005*	*2,097*	*3,779*	*56*	*18,988*	*1,000*	*264*	*257*	*10*	*5*	*479*
3	...	...	...	...	3	...	...	...	...	...	...
9,166	3,941	540	273	14	4,676	852	212	242	10	5	398
1,797	820	20	67	1	957	55	15	8	...	...	32
278	125	11	4	...	142	30	6	5	...	...	19
8,968	3,300	1,435	1,140	40	4,173	48	20	2	...	...	26
14,934	5,818	70	2,288	1	9,037	15	11	...	...	...	4
4	1	3	...	...	...	...	...	...	...	...	...
69	*45*	...	*2*	...	*24*	*4*	...	*4*	...	...	...
59	38	...	2	...	21	...	...	...	...	...	...
10	7	...	...	...	3	4	...	4	...	...	...
8,912	*4,561*	*412*	*701*	*11*	*3,939*	*46*	*21*	*2*	...	...	*23*
738	165	154	4	3	419	11	4	...	...	...	7
3,004	1,780	203	427	8	1,021	...	...	...	...	...	...
3,026	1,498	9	170	...	1,519	18	9	1	...	...	8
2,144	1,118	46	100	...	980	17	8	1	...	...	8
608	*344*	*5*	*27*	*1*	*259*	*32*	*12*	...	...	...	*20*
260	214	4	3	1	42	26	8	...	...	...	18
1	1	...	...	...	...	5	4	...	...	...	1
347	129	1	24	...	217	1	...	...	...	...	1
4	*3*	...	...	...	*1*	...	...	...	...	...	...
17,067	*6,680*	*206*	*1,019*	*14*	*10,181*	*669*	*220*	*7*	*20*	...	*375*
1,041	430	5	8	...	606	1	1	...	...	...	...
5	3	...	...	...	2	...	...	...	...	...	...
73	47	...	6	...	26	...	...	...	...	...	...
76	47	1	5	...	28	6	3	...	...	...	3
132	49	...	...	...	87	4	3	...	...	...	1
15,184	6,854	152	988	13	9,178	463	131	60	7	...	272
161	41	42	3	1	78	189	78	14	13	...	97
111	30	4	...	...	77	...	...	...	...	...	...
284	183	2	9	...	99	6	4	...	...	...	2
3,063	*1,299*	*395*	*29*	*1*	*1,369*	*340*	*96*	*6*	...	...	*238*

TABLE XV.—OCCUPATION OR MEANS OF LIVELIHOOD.

Group No.	Occupation.	PROVINCIAL TOTAL.					
		Total workers and dependents.	Actual workers.				Dependents.
			Total.		Partially agriculturist.		
			Males.	Females.	Males.	Females.	Both sexes.
	1	2	3	4	5	6	7
	IV.—TRANSPORT	***76,600***	***44,685***	***4,029***	***4,480***	***379***	***27,886***
	20.—TRANSPORT BY WATER	***23,841***	***13,409***	***29***	***1,577***	***9***	***10,403***
94	Harbour works, dockyards and pilots ...	315	136	9	1	9	170
95	Ship owners and their employés, ship brokers, ships' officers, engineers, mariners and firemen	3,043	2,203	4	468	...	836
96	Persons employed on the maintenance of streams, rivers and canals (including construction)	3	2	...	...	...	1
97	Boat owners, boatmen and tow men... ...	20,480	11,068	16	1,108	...	9,396
	21.—TRANSPORT BY ROAD	***34,268***	***21,017***	***2,828***	***2,197***	***359***	***10,423***
98	Persons employed on the construction and maintenance of roads and bridges ...	13,967	10,342	954	970	25	2,671
99	Cart owners and drivers, coachmen, stable boys, tramway, mail carriage, etc., managers, and employés (excluding private servants)...	10,194	6,694	67	384	1	3,433
100	Palki, etc., bearers and owners	3,503	1,615	...	423	...	1,888
101	Pack elephant, camel, mule, ass and bullock owners and drivers	23	23	...	...	...	...
102	Porters and messengers	6,581	2,343	1,807	420	333	2,431
	22.—TRANSPORT BY RAIL	***13,877***	***7,927***	***1,179***	***419***	***11***	***4,778***
103	Railway employés of all kinds other than construction coolies	11,213	6,577	395	408	3	4,241
104	Labourers employed on railway construction...	2,664	1,350	777	11	8	537
105	**23.—POST OFFICE, TELEGRAPH AND TELEPHONE SERVICES.**	***4,614***	***2,332***	...	***287***	...	***2,282***
	V.—TRADE	***244,558***	***80,464***	***33,370***	***12,910***	***1,082***	***130,724***
106	**24.—BANKS, ESTABLISHMENTS OF CREDIT, EXCHANGE AND INSURANCE** (Bank managers, money-lenders, exchange and insurance agents, money changers and brokers and their employés).	***6,408***	***1,679***	***452***	***534***	***20***	***4,277***
107	**25.—BROKERAGE, COMMISSION AND EXPORT** (Brokers, commission agents, commercial travellers, warehouse owners and employés).	***413***	***187***	***3***	***4***	...	***223***
108	**26.—TRADE IN TEXTILES** (Trade in piece goods, wool, cotton, silk, hair and other textiles).	***15,323***	***5,730***	***3,258***	***638***	***32***	***6,335***
109	**27.—TRADE IN SKINS, LEATHER AND FURS** (Trade in skins, leather, furs, feathers, horn, etc.).	***8,049***	***3,403***	***128***	***512***	***21***	***4,518***
110	**28.—TRADE IN WOOD** [Trade in wood (not firewood), cork, bark, etc.].	***3,519***	***1,421***	***206***	***226***	***5***	***1892***
111	**29.—TRADE IN METALS** (Trade in metals, machinery, knife, tool, etc., sellers).	***659***	***319***	***44***	***9***	***1***	***296***
112	**30.—TRADE IN POTTERY ... ...**	***3,208***	***1,413***	***267***	***214***	***12***	***1,528***
113	**31.—TRADE IN CHEMICAL PRODUCTS** [Trade in chemical products (drugs, dyes, paints, petroleum, explosives, etc.)].	***1,811***	***687***	***228***	***60***	***2***	***896***
	32.—HOTELS, CAFES, RESTAURANTS, ETC.	***1,921***	***636***	***528***	***40***	***7***	***757***
114	Vendors of wine, liquors, ærated waters, etc....	1,246	314	517	12	7	415
115	Owners and managers of hotels, cookshops, sarais, etc., and their employés	675	322	11	28	...	342
	33.—OTHER TRADE IN FOOD STUFFS ...	***163,089***	***47,440***	***24,459***	***8,740***	***885***	***91,190***
116	Fish dealers	60,234	11,993	8,987	3,902	458	39,254
117	Grocers and sellers of vegetable oil, salt and other condiments	36,797	14,867	2,643	3,221	87	19,287
118	Sellers of milk, butter, ghee, poultry, eggs, etc.	11,043	5,024	1,082	265	49	4,937
119	Sellers of sweetmeats, sugar, gur and molasses	3,787	1,574	361	117	4	1,852
120	Cardamom, betel-leaf, vegetables, fruit and areca nut sellers	22,060	6,329	4,482	1,600	157	11,249
121	Grain and pulse dealers	26,551	6,710	6,610	522	126	13,231
122	Tobacco, opium, ganja, etc., sellers ...	2,360	838	248	112	3	1,274
123	Dealers in sheep, goats and pigs	157	58	35	1	1	64
124	Dealers in hay, grass and fodder	100	47	11	...	...	42
125	**34.—TRADE IN CLOTHING AND TOILET ARTICLES** [Trade in ready-made clothing and other articles of dress and the toilet (hats, umbrellas, socks, ready-made shoes, perfumes, etc.)].	***1,661***	***585***	***547***	***51***	–	***529***
	35.—TRADE IN FURNITURE	***3,800***	***1,773***	***408***	***350***	***22***	***1,619***
126	Trade in furniture, carpets, curtains and bedding	2,432	1,288	379	290	22	765
127	Hardware, cooking utensils, porcelain, crockery, glassware, bottles, articles for gardening, the cellar, etc.	1,368	485	29	60	...	854
128	**36.—TRADE IN BUILDING MATERIALS ...** [Trade in building materials (stones, bricks, plaster, cement, sand, tiles, thatch, etc.)].	***2,336***	***839***	***330***	***80***	***25***	***1,167***
129	**37.—TRADE IN MEANS OF TRANSPORT ...** [Dealers and hirers of elephants, camels, horses, cattle, asses, mules, etc., sellers (not makers) of carriages, saddlery, etc.].	***2,798***	***1,493***	***204***	***106***	***11***	***1,096***

PART A.—GENERAL TABLE—PROVINCIAL SUMMARY—*contd.*

BRITISH TERRITORY.						MANIPUR STATE.					
TOTAL WORKERS AND DEPENDENTS.	ACTUAL WORKERS.				DEPENDENTS.	TOTAL WORKERS AND DEPENDENTS.	ACTUAL WORKERS.				DEPENDENTS.
	Total.		*Partially agriculturist.*				*Total.*		*Partially agriculturist.*		
	Males.	Females.	Males.	Females.	Both sexes.		Males.	Females.	Males.	Females.	Both sexes.
8	9	10	11	12	13	14	15	16	17	18	19
75,128	*43,923*	*4,022*	*4,369*	*379*	*27,183*	*1,472*	*762*	*7*	*111*	...	*703*
23,831	*13,402*	*28*	*1,576*	*9*	*10,401*	*10*	*7*	*1*	*1*	...	*2*
315	136	9	1	9	170	...	...	...	...	...	...
3,043	2,203	4	468	...	836	...	...	...	...	...	...
2	1	...	...	...	1	1	1	...	...	...	...
20,471	11,062	15	1,107	...	9,394	9	6	1	1	...	2
32,882	*20,302*	*2,822*	*2,087*	*359*	*9,758*	*1,386*	*715*	*6*	*110*	...	605
13,880	10,303	953	970	25	2,624	87	89	1	...	...	47
9,053	6,074	62	276	1	2,917	1,141	620	5	108	...	516
3,499	1,611	...	423	...	1,888	4	4	...	...	...	...
23	23	...	...	...	...	...	...	...	...	...	...
6,427	2,291	1,807	418	333	2,329	154	52	...	2	...	102
13,877	*7,927*	*1,172*	*419*	*11*	*4,778*	...	...	...	...	...	...
11 213	6,577	395	408	3	4,241	...	...	...	...	...	...
2 664	1,350	777	11	8	537	...	...	...	...	...	...
4,538	*2,292*	...	*287*	...	*2,946*	*76*	*40*	...	...	...	*36*
231,260	*78,781*	*26,336*	*12,873*	*1,078*	*126,143*	*13,298*	*1,683*	*7,034*	*37*	*4*	*4,581*
6,409	*1,675*	*452*	*533*	*20*	*4,275*	*6*	*4*	...	*1*	...	*2*
412	*187*	*2*	*4*	...	*223*	*1*	...	*1*	...	...	...
11,779	*5,548*	*750*	*635*	*31*	*5,486*	*3,544*	*187*	*2,508*	*3*	*1*	*849*
8,046	*3,402*	*127*	*512*	*21*	*4,517*	*3*	*1*	*1*	...	...	*1*
3,184	*1,303*	*163*	*225*	*5*	*1,718*	*335*	*118*	43	*1*	...	*174*
624	*317*	*15*	*9*	*1*	*292*	*35*	*2*	*29*	...	...	*4*
3,170	*1,409*	*243*	*214*	*12*	*1,518*	*38*	*4*	*24*	...	...	*10*
1,790	*685*	*214*	*60*	*2*	*891*	*21*	*2*	*14*	...	...	*5*
1,377	*614*	*104*	*89*	*7*	*659*	*544*	*22*	*424*	*1*	...	*98*
733	302	94	12	7	337	513	12	423	...	...	78
644	312	10	27	...	322	31	10	1	1	...	20
155,503	*46,592*	*20,615*	*8,723*	*882*	*88,296*	*7,586*	*848*	*3,844*	*17*	*3*	*2,894*
58,908	11,378	8,270	3,898	458	33,760	1 326	115	717	4	...	494
36,105	14,802	2,252	2,221	87	19,051	692	65	391	...	...	236
10 857	4,962	1,044	264	49	4,851	186	62	33	1	...	86
3,759	1,572	344	117	4	1,843	28	2	17	...	...	9
19,785	6,091	3,245	1,501	155	10,449	2,275	238	1,237	9	2	800
23,669	6,349	5,296	519	125	12,024	2,282	861	1,814	3	1	1,207
2,178	833	125	112	3	1,220	182	5	123	...	...	54
144	58	30	1	1	56	13	...	5	...	...	8
98	47	9	...	...	42	2	...	2	...	...	...
1,642	*576*	*545*	*51*	...	*521*	*19*	*9*	2	...	...	*8*
3,785	*1,771*	*400*	*350*	*22*	*1,614*	*15*	*2*	*8*	...	...	*5*
2,424	1,267	375	290	22	762	8	1	4	...	...	3
1,361	484	25	60	...	852	7	1	4	...	...	2
2,290	*832*	*313*	*80*	*25*	*1,145*	*46*	*7*	*17*	...	...	*22*
2,528	*1,388*	*193*	*106*	*11*	*947*	*270*	*110*	*11*	...	...	*149*

TABLE XV.—OCCUPATION OR MEANS OF LIVELIHOOD.

Group No.	Occupation.	Total workers and dependents.	Provincial Total. Actual workers. Total. Males.	Females.	Partially agriculturist. Males.	Females.	Dependents. Both sexes.
	1	2	3	4	5	6	7
130	38.—TRADE IN FUEL ... (Dealers in firewood, charcoal, coal, cowdung, etc.)	*2,594*	*806*	*285*	*117*	*13*	*1,503*
	39.—TRADE IN ARTICLES OF LUXURY AND THOSE PERTAINING TO LETTERS AND THE ARTS AND SCIENCES.	*9,555*	*4,195*	*972*	*426*	*5*	*4,388*
131	Dealers in precious stones, jewellery (real and imitation), clocks, optical instruments, etc.)	463	163	123	25	...	177
132	Dealers in common bangles, bead necklaces, fans, small articles, toys, hunting and fishing tackle, flowers, etc. ...	8,858	3,917	846	399	5	4,095
133	Publishers, booksellers, stationers, dealers in music, pictures, musical instruments and curiosities ...	234	115	3	2	...	116
134	40.—TRADE IN REFUSE MATTER ... (Dealers in rags, stable refuse, etc.)	*3*	...	*3*	...	...	...
	41.—TRADE IN OTHER SORTS ...	*17,411*	*7,853*	*1,048*	*803*	*21*	*8,510*
135	Shop-keepers otherwise unspecified ...	15,356	6,845	933	710	19	7,578
136	Itinerant traders, pedlars, hawkers, etc. ...	139	34	42	...	2	63
137	Conjurors, acrobats, fortune-tellers, reciters, exhibitors of curiosities and wild animals ...	945	486	58	34	...	401
138	Other trades (including farmers of pounds, tolls and markets) ...	971	488	15	59	...	468
	C.—PUBLIC ADMINISTRATION AND LIBERAL ARTS.	*130,038*	*48,129*	*1,583*	*11,308*	*91*	*80,326*
	VI.—PUBLIC FORCE ...	*18,885*	*9,383*	...	*1,782*	...	*9,502*
	42.—ARMY ...	*3,122*	*2,170*	...	*584*	...	*952*
139	Army (Imperial) ...	3,105	2,155	...	584	...	950
140	Army (Native States) ...	17	15	...	...	...	2
	44.—POLICE ...	*15,763*	*7,213*	...	*1,198*	...	*8,550*
142	Police ...	10,770	5,442	...	516	...	5,328
143	Village watchmen ...	4,993	1,771	...	682	...	3,222
	VII.—(ORDER 45). *PUBLIC ADMINISTRATION* ...	*15,032*	*4,688*	*56*	*1,193*	...	*10,288*
144	Service of the State ...	9,126	2,846	...	589	...	6,280
145	Service of Native and Foreign States ...	545	203	20	24	...	322
146	Municipal and other local (not village) service...	1,160	439	36	59	...	685
147	Village officials and servants other than watchmen ...	4,201	1,200	...	521	...	3,001
	VIII.—PROFESSIONS AND LIBERAL ARTS.	*92,915*	*33,181*	*1,460*	*8,186*	*89*	*58,274*
	46.—RELIGION ...	*55,289*	*18,402*	*891*	*5,095*	*72*	*35,996*
148	Priests, ministers, etc. ...	48,309	15,460	639	4,729	66	32,210
149	Religious mendicants, inmates of monasteries, etc. ...	797	555	18	65	...	224
150	Catechists readers, church, and mission service	1,600	663	59	24	1	878
151	Temple, burial or burning ground service, pilgrim conductors, circumcisers ...	4,583	1,724	175	277	5	2,684
	47.—LAW ...	*5,118*	*1,323*	...	*415*	...	*3,795*
152	Lawyers of all kinds, including Kazis, law agents and mukhtiars ...	2,586	516	...	168	...	2,070
153	Lawyers' clerks, petition writers, etc. ...	2,532	807	...	247	...	1,725
	48.—MEDICINE ...	*10,886*	*3,992*	*264*	*592*	*6*	*6,630*
154	Medical practitioners of all kinds, including dentists, oculists and veterinary surgeons.	8,502	2,947	86	492	2	5,469
155	Midwives, vaccinators, compounders, nurses, masseurs, etc. ...	2,384	1,045	178	100	4	1,161
156	49.—INSTRUCTION [Professors and teachers of all kinds, (except law, medicine, music, dancing and drawing) and clerks and servants connected with education.]	*12,357*	*5,356*	*229*	*1,206*	*10*	*6,772*
	50.—LETTERS AND ARTS AND SCIENCES	*9,265*	*4,108*	*76*	*878*	*1*	*5,081*
158	Architects, surveyors, engineers, and their employés ...	2,716	1,401	...	263	...	1,315
159	Others (authors, photographers, artists, sculptors, astronomers, meteorologists, botanists, astrologers, etc.) ...	1,245	442	...	71	...	803
160	Music composers and masters, players on all kinds of musical instruments (not military), singers, actors, and dancers ...	5,304	2,265	76	544	1	2,963
161	*IX.*—(ORDER 51) *PERSONS LIVING PRINCIPALLY ON THEIR INCOME* [Proprietors (other than of agricultural land), fund and scholarship-holders and pensioners.]	*3,206*	*877*	*67*	*147*	*2*	*2,262*
	D.—MISCELLANEOUS ...	*207,123*	*80,616*	*48,581*	*4,711*	*955*	*77,926*
	X.—(ORDER 52). *DOMESTIC SERVICE* ...	*38,539*	*22,033*	*5,550*	*1,175*	*19*	*10,956*
162	Cooks, water carriers, door-keepers, watchmen and other in-door servants ...	35,389	20,228	5,526	1,095	19	9,635
163	Private grooms, coachmen, dog boys, etc. ...	3,150	1,805	24	80	...	1,321
	XI.—(ORDER 53) *INSUFFICIENTLY DESCRIBED OCCUPATIONS* (GENERAL TERMS WHICH DO NOT INDICATE A DEFINITE OCCUPATION)	*97,701*	*38,501*	*16,902*	*2,876*	*329*	*42,298*

PART A.—GENERAL TABLE—PROVINCIAL SUMMARY—*contd.*

BRITISH TERRITORY.						MANIPUR STATE.					
TOTAL WORKERS AND DEPENDENTS.	ACTUAL WORKERS.				DEPENDENTS.	TOTAL WORKERS AND DEPENDENTS.	ACTUAL WORKERS.				DEPENDENTS.
	Total.		*Partially agriculturist.*				*Total.*		*Partially agriculturist.*		
	Males.	Females.	Males.	Females.	Both sexes.		Males.	Females.	Males.	Females.	Both sexes.
8	9	10	11	12	13	14	15	16	17	18	19
2,461	781	220	117	13	1,460	133	25	65	...	...	43
9,445	4,168	959	425	5	4,318	110	27	13	1	...	70
456	163	120	25	...	173	7	...	3	...	...	4
8,755	3,890	836	398	5	4,029	103	27	10	1	...	66
234	115	3	2	...	116	...	...	...	...	...	...
3	...	3	...	...	...	...	...	...	...	...	...
16,819	7,538	1,018	790	21	8,263	592	315	30	13	...	247
14,846	6,563	903	702	19	7,380	510	282	30	8	...	196
139	34	42	...	2	63	...	...	...	...	...	...
916	477	58	32	...	381	29	9	...	2	...	20
916	464	15	56	...	439	53	24	...	3	...	29
120,998	44 287	1,321	10,554	85	75,390	9,040	3,849	269	754	6	4,936
17,594	8,480	...	1,320	...	9,114	1,291	903	...	462	...	388
2,495	1,620	...	139	...	875	627	550	...	445	...	77
2,495	1,620	...	139	...	875	610	535	...	445	...	75
...	...	...	...	...	...	17	15	...	...	...	2
15,099	6,860	...	1,181	...	8,239	664	353	...	17	...	311
10 252	5,146	...	514	...	5,106	518	296	...	2	...	222
4,847	1,714	...	667	...	3,133	146	57	...	15	...	89
14,313	4,405	37	1,122	...	9,871	710	283	19	71	...	417
8,907	2,772	...	578	...	6,135	219	74	...	11	...	145
175	76	1	17	...	98	370	127	19	7	...	224
1,157	437	36	59	...	684	3	2	...	...	...	1
4,074	1,120	...	468	...	2,954	127	80	...	53	...	47
86,150	30,588	1,224	7,967	83	54,338	6,765	2,593	236	219	6	3,936
50,708	16,757	708	4,938	66	33,243	4,581	1,645	183	157	6	2,753
47,456	15,195	612	4,719	66	31,049	853	265	27	10	...	561
795	554	17	65	...	224	2	1	1	...	...	...
942	359	52	11	...	531	658	304	7	13	1	347
1,515	649	27	143	...	839	3,068	1,075	148	134	5	1,845
5,107	1,318	...	415	...	3,789	11	5	...	...	...	6
2,586	516	...	168	...	2,070	...	...	...	...	...	...
2,521	802	...	247	...	1,719	11	5	...	...	...	...
10,335	3,737	225	568	6	6,373	551	255	39	24	...	257
8,017	2,702	78	468	2	5,237	485	245	8	24	...	232
2,318	1,035	147	100	4	1,136	66		31	...	...	25
11,798	5,123	226	1,192	10	6,449	559	233	8	14	...	323
8,202	3,653	65	854	1	4,484	1,063	455	11	24	...	597
2,560	1,343	...	262	...	1 217	156	58	...	1	...	98
1,116	391	...	66	...	725	129	51	...	5	...	73
4,526	1,919	65	526	1	2,542	778	346	11	18	...	421
2,941	814	60	145	2	2,067	265	63	7	2	...	195
204,481	79,328	48,412	4,670	955	76,741	2,642	288	169	41	...	1,185
37,490	21,526	5,510	1,158	19	10,454	1,049	1507	40	17	...	502
34 448	19,784	5,487	1,078	19	9.177	941	444	39	17	...	458
3,042	1,742	23	80	...	1.277	108	68	1	...	...	64
96,613	38,008	16,893	2,852	829	41,712	1,088	493	9	24	...	526

TABLE XV.—Occupation or Means of Livelihood.

Group No.	Occupation.	PROVINCIAL TOTAL.					
		Total workers and dependents.	Actual workers.				Dependents.
			Total.		Partially agriculturist.		
			Males.	Females.	Males.	Females.	Both sexes.
	1	2	3	4	5	6	7
164	Manufacturers, business men and contractors otherwise unspecified	1,899	740	...	64	...	1,159
165	Cashiers, accountants, book-keepers, clerks, and other employés in unspecified offices, warehouses and shops	9,898	6,208	114	318	...	3,576
166	Mechanics otherwise unspecified ...	2,124	10,73	...	93	...	1,051
167	Labourers and workmen otherwise unspecified	83,780	30,480	16,788	2,401	829	36,512
	XII.—UNPRODUCTIVE	***70,883***	***20,082***	***26,129***	***660***	***107***	***24,672***
168	**54.—INMATES OF JAILS, ASYLUMS AND HOSPITALS.**	***2,256***	***2,160***	***88***	***128***	...	***8***
169	**55.—BEGGARS, VAGRANTS, PROSTITUTES** (Beggars, vagrants, procurers, prostitutes, receivers of stolen goods, cattle poisoners).	***68,627***	***17,922***	***26,041***	***532***	***107***	***24,664***

Part A.—General Table.—Provincial Summary—*concld.*

British Territory.						Manipur State.					
Total workers and dependents.	Actual workers.				Dependents.	Total workers and dependents.	Actual workers.				Dependents.
	Total.		*Partially agriculturist.*				*Total.*		*Partially agriculturist.*		
	Males.	Females.	Males.	Females.	Both sexes.		Males.	Females.	Males.	Females.	Both sexes.
8	9	10	11	12	13	14	15	16	17	18	19
1,801	706	...	61	...	1,095	98	34	...	3	...	64
9,713	6,084	109	317	...	3,520	185	124	5	1		56
1 472	836	...	74	...	636	652	237	...	19	...	415
83,627	30,382	16,784	2,400	829	36,461	153	98	4	1	...	51
70,378	*19,794*	*26,009*	*660*	*107*	*24,575*	*505*	*288*	*190*	...	...	*97*
2,139	*2,043*	*88*	*128*	...	*8*	*117*	*117*	...	...	...	...
68,239	*17,751*	*25,921*	*532*	*107*	*24,567*	*388*	*171*	*190*	...	...	*97*

TABLE XV.—OCCUPATION OR MEANS OF LIVELIHOOD. PART A.—GENERAL TABLE—DETAILS FOR DISTRICTS.

Class and Sub-Class ...	CLASS A: SUB-CLASS I.—EXPLOITATION OF THE SURFACE OF THE EARTH.											
Order	1.—PASTURE AND AGRICULTURE :—(a) ORDINARY CULTIVATION.											
	TOTAL OF ORDER 1.						TOTAL OF ORDER 1(a).					
DISTRICT OR STATE.	TOTAL WORKERS AND DEPENDANTS.	ACTUAL WORKERS.				DEPENDANTS.	TOTAL WORKERS AND DEPENDANTS.	ACTUAL WORKERS.				DEPENDANTS.
		Total.		Partially agriculturist.				Total.		Partially agriculturist.		
		Males.	Females.	Males.	Females.	Both sexes.		Males.	Females.	Males.	Females.	Both sexes.
1	2	3	4	5	6	7	8	9	10	11	12	13
ASSAM ...	*6,077,685*	*1,871,232*	*821,762*	*37,229*	*13,600*	*3,384,691*	*5,323,380*	*1,587,990*	*580,482*	*879*	...	*3,154,978*
(1) British Territory ...	*5,807,234*	*1,801,594*	*809,779*	*37,228*	*13,600*	*3,195,861*	*5,054,324*	*1,518,750*	*568,663*	*879*	...	*2,966,911*
SURMA VALLEY AND HILL DISTRICTS ...	*2,895,475*	*874,832*	*212,751*	*15,280*	*2,988*	*1,807,892*	*2,601,548*	*773,754*	*117,728*	*483*	...	*1,710,066*
Cachar ...	448,729	141,450	54,569	7,454	986	252,717	327,941	99,470	15,865	11	...	212,606
Sylhet ...	2,635,763	613,042	73,621	6,540	1,011	1,349,040	1,894,814	566,414	25,507	470	...	1,302,893
Khasi and Jaintia Hills ...	184,689	55,163	53,677	1,268	991	75,849	153,267	43,128	45,516	1	...	64,623
Naga Hills ...	140,730	42,121	5,306	5	...	93,303	140,168	41,857	5,260	...	...	93,051
Lushai Hills ...	85,624	23,056	25,585	13	...	36,983	85,358	22,885	25,580	1	...	36,893
ASSAM VALLEY DISTRICTS ...	*2,911,759*	*926,762*	*597,028*	*21,948*	*10,612*	*1,387,969*	*2,452,776*	*744,996*	*450,935*	*396*	...	*1,256,845*
Goalpara ...	522,745	164,753	24,221	439	5	333,771	517,200	161,109	23,947	222	...	333,144
Kamrup ...	557,874	163,510	68,108	252	45	326,256	545,522	155,715	66,354	32	...	323,463
Darrang ...	348,812	123,901	100,030	2,847	844	124,881	261,474	85,574	72,925	39	...	102,975
Nowgong ...	279,475	82,852	72,394	962	521	124,229	258,461	73,[illegible]56	65,738	38	...	118,867
Sibsagar ...	634,913	293,890	169,018	9,215	4,295	262,005	466,824	142,980	115,316	37	...	208,528
Lakhimpur ...	414,124	141,063	122,922	8,197	4,897	150,139	250,242	79,508	66,360	24	...	104,374
Garo Hills ...	153,816	46,793	40,335	16	5	66,688	153,053	46,254	40,295	4	...	66,504
(2) Manipur State ...	*270,451*	*69,638*	*11,983*	*1*	...	*188,830*	*269,056*	*69,170*	*11,819*	...	...	*188,067*

Class and Sub-Class ...	CLASS A: SUB-CLASS I.—EXPLOITATION OF THE SURFACE OF THE EARTH.											
Order	1.—PASTURE AND AGRICULTURE: (a)—ORDINARY CULTIVATION.											
	1.—Income from rent of Agricultural land.						2.—Ordinary cultivators.					
DISTRICT OR STATE.	TOTAL WORKERS AND DEPENDANTS.	ACTUAL WORKERS.				DEPENDANTS.	TOTAL WORKERS AND DEPENDANTS.	ACTUAL WORKERS.				DEPENDANTS.
		Total.		Partially agriculturist.				Total.		Partially agriculturist.		
		Males.	Females.	Males.	Females.	Both sexes.		Males.	Females.	Males.	Females.	Both sexes.
1	14	15	16	17	18	19	20	21	22	23	24	25
ASSAM ...	*137,106*	*18,286*	*4,195*	...	...	*114,625*	*5,092,771*	*1,525,888*	*566,322*	...	...	*3,000,561*
(1) British Territory ...	*137,104*	*18,286*	*4,193*	...	...	*114,695*	*4,824,061*	*1,456,873*	*554,520*	...	...	*2,812,668*
SURMA VALLEY AND HILL DISTRICTS ...	*123,720*	*15,196*	*2,846*	...	...	*105,678*	*2,416,960*	*731,548*	*108,021*	...	...	*1,577,391*
Cachar ...	52,454	2,113	1,517	...	...	48,824	269,864	94,708	13,455	...	...	161,701
Sylhet ...	71,007	13,020	1,258	...	...	56,729	1,774,711	530,524	20,540	...	...	1,223,647
Khasi and Jaintia Hills ...	252	56	71	...	...	125	146,996	41,612	43,205	...	...	62,179
Naga Hills ...	3	3	...	...	...	...	140,061	41,832	5,241	...	...	92,988
Lushai Hills ...	4	4	...	...	...	...	85,328	22,872	25,580	...	...	36,876
ASSAM VALLEY DISTRICTS ...	*13,384*	*3,090*	*1,347*	...	...	*8,947*	*2,407,101*	*725,325*	*446,499*	...	...	*1,235,277*
Goalpara ...	3,521	986	98	...	...	2,437	499,944	153,607	23,010	...	...	323,327
Kamrup ...	8,491	1,768	1,018	...	...	5,705	526,684	148,940	64,044	...	...	313,700
Darrang ...	409	107	105	...	...	197	258,011	83,264	72,517	...	...	102,230
Nowgong ...	82	27	11	...	...	44	257,012	73,077	65,543	...	...	118,392
Sibsagar ...	719	141	87	...	...	491	464,222	141,587	115,123	...	...	207,512
Lakhimpur ...	102	49	23	...	...	30	249,402	79,079	66,260	...	...	104,063
Garo Hills ...	60	12	5	...	...	43	151,826	45,771	40,002	...	...	66,053
(2) Manipur State ...	*2*	...	*2*	...	...	...	*268,710*	*69,015*	*11,802*	...	...	*187,893*

TABLE XV.—OCCUPATION OR MEANS OF LIVELIHOOD. PART A.—GENERAL TABLE—DETAILS FOR DISTRICTS—*contd.*

Class and Sub-Class ...	*CLASS A : SUB-CLASS I.—EXPLOITATION OF THE SURFACE OF THE EARTH.*											
Order	1.—PASTURE AND AGRICULTURE :—(a) ORDINARY CULTIVATION.											
	2.—Ordinary cultivators.						*3.—Agents, managers of landed estates (not planters), clerks, rent collectors, etc.*					
	Revenue paying cultivators (included in total).											
DISTRICT OR STATE.	TOTAL WORKERS AND DEPENDANTS.	ACTUAL WORKERS.				DEPENDANTS.	TOTAL WORKERS AND DEPENDANTS.	ACTUAL WORKERS.				DEPENDANTS.
		Total.		*Partially agriculturist.*				*Total.*		*Partially agriculturist.*		
		Males.	Females.	Males.	Females.	Both sexes.		Males.	Females.	Males.	Females.	Both sexes.
1	26	27	28	29	30	31	32	33	34	35	36	37
ASSAM	***2,114,141***	***636,522***	***300,089***	...	...	***1,087,530***	***8,581***	***3,099***	...	***879***	...	***5,482***
(1) ***British Territory***	***1,845,463***	***567,515***	***378,288***	...	...	***899,660***	***8,543***	***3,091***	...	***879***	...	***5,452***
SURMA VALLEY AND HILL DISTRICTS	***207,411***	***72,654***	***12,845***	...	...	***121,912***	***4,415***	***1,666***	...	***483***	...	***2,749***
Cachar	128 876	49,946	1,084	...	...	77,246	189	63	...	11	...	126
Sylhet	43,130	12,673	522	...	...	20,935	4,183	1,588	...	470	...	2,595
Khasi and Jaintia Hills	35,401	10,035	10,638	...	...	14,728	23	7	...	1	...	16
Naga Hills	4	...	1	...	...	3	3	1	...	...	...	2
Lushai Hills	...	...	...	...	...	...	17	7	...	1	...	10
ASSAM VALLEY DISTRICTS	***1,638,052***	***494,861***	***365,443***	...	...	***777,748***	***4,128***	***1,425***	...	***396***	...	***2,703***
Goalpara	...	...	...	...	...	...	1,965	900	...	222	...	1,065
Kamrup	399,783	116,301	46,376	...	...	237,106	561	165	...	32	...	396
Darrang	218 024	68,529	63,009	...	...	86,486	353	94	...	89	...	259
Nowgong	251,996	71,429	64,136	...	...	116,431	326	67	...	38	...	259
Sibsagar	415,198	131,620	96,455	...	...	187,123	552	111	...	37	...	441
Lakhimpur	229 016	68,601	64,081	...	...	96,344	314	73	...	24	...	241
Garo Hills	124,035	38,391	31,386	...	...	54,258	57	15	...	4	...	42
(2) ***Manipur State***	***268,678***	***69,007***	***11,801***	...	...	***187,870***	***38***	***8***	...	...	...	***30***

Class and Sub-Class ...	*CLASS A : SUB-CLASS I.—EXPLOITATION OF THE SURFACE OF THE EARTH.*											
Order	1.—PASTURE AND AGRICULTURE :—(a) ORDINARY CULTIVATION.						(b) GROWERS OF SPECIAL PRODUCTS AND MARKET GARDENING.					
	4.—Farm servants and field labourers.						*TOTAL OF ORDER I(b).*					
DISTRICT OR STATE.	TOTAL WORKERS AND DEPENDANTS.	ACTUAL WORKERS.				DEPENDANTS.	TOTAL WORKERS AND DEPENDANTS.	ACTUAL WORKERS.				DEPENDANTS.
		Total.		*Partially agriculturist.*				*Total.*		*Partially agriculturist.*		
		Males.	Females.	Males.	Females.	Both sexes.		Males.	Females.	Males.	Females.	Both sexes.
1	38	39	40	41	42	43	44	45	46	47	48	49
ASSAM	***84,922***	***40,647***	***9,965***	...	...	***34,310***	***702,793***	***246,281***	***238,142***	***34,353***	***13,506***	***218,370***
(1) ***British Territory***	***84,616***	***40,500***	***9,950***	...	...	***34,166***	***702,695***	***246,243***	***238,140***	***34,353***	***13,506***	***218,312***
SURMA VALLEY AND HILL DISTRICTS	***56,453***	***25,344***	***6,861***	...	...	***24,248***	***275,650***	***89,166***	***93,721***	***13,550***	***2,972***	***92,763***
Cachar	5.434	2,584	893	...	...	1,965	119,358	40,968	18,587	7,391	984	39,803
Sylhet	44,913	21,282	3,709	...	...	19,922	130,307	40,289	47,959	4,905	1,002	42,059
Khasi and Jaintia Hills	5,996	1,453	2,240	...	...	2,303	25,854	7,833	7,167	1,253	986	10,854
Naga Hills	101	21	10	...	...	61	46	15	6	...	...	25
Lushai Hills	9	2	...	...	...	7	85	61	2	1	...	28
ASSAM VALLEY DISTRICTS	***28,163***	***15,156***	***3,089***	...	...	***9,918***	***427,045***	***157,077***	***144,419***	***20,803***	***10,534***	***125,549***
Goalpara	11,770	5,616	839	...	...	5,315	806	362	198	8	...	252
Kamrup	9,786	4,842	1,292	...	...	3,652	5,056	1,828	1,519	147	39	1,709
Darrang	2,701	2,109	303	...	...	289	78,316	29,583	26,234	2,511	784	20,499
Nowgong	1,041	685	184	...	...	172	17,962	6,435	6,547	875	519	5,009
Sibsagar	1,331	1,141	106	...	...	84	165,606	59,180	53,574	9,123	4,295	52,852
Lakhimpur	424	307	77	...	...	40	161,268	59,683	56,352	8,139	4,897	45,233
Garo Hills	1,110	456	288	...	...	366	11	6	1	...	...	4
(2) ***Manipur State***	***306***	***147***	***14***	...	...	***144***	***98***	***38***	***2***	...	...	***58***

TABLE XV.—OCCUPATION OR MEANS OF LIVELIHOOD. PART A.—GENERAL TABLE—DETAILS FOR DISTRICTS—*contd.*

Class and Sub-Class ... CLASS A : SUB-CLASS I.—EXPLOITATION OF THE SURFACE OF THE EARTH.

Order ... ... (b) GROWERS OF SPECIAL PRODUCTS AND MARKET GARDENING.

5.—Tea, coffee, cinchona and indigo plantations.

DISTRICT OR STATE.	TOTAL.						Tea plantations (included in total).					
	TOTAL WORKERS AND DEPENDANTS.	ACTUAL WORKERS. Total.		Partially agriculturist.		DEPENDANTS.	TOTAL WORKERS AND DEPENDANTS.	ACTUAL WORKERS. Total.		Partially agriculturist.		DEPENDANTS.
		Males.	Females.	Males.	Females.	Both sexes.		Males.	Females.	Males.	Females.	Both sexes.
1	50	51	52	53	54	55	56	57	58	59	60	61
ASSAM	*675,360*	*237,898*	*230,763*	*33,072*	*12,500*	*206,705*	*675,344*	*237,888*	*230,762*	*33,072*	*12,500*	*206,694*
(1) ***British Territory***	*675,359*	*237,893*	*230,762*	*33,072*	*12,500*	*206,704*	*675,344*	*237,888*	*230,762*	*33,072*	*12,500*	*206,694*
SURMA VALLEY AND HILL DISTRICTS	*249,257*	*81,299*	*86,453*	*12,296*	*1,973*	*81,512*	*240,242*	*81,287*	*86,453*	*12,296*	*1,973*	*81,502*
Cachar	119 347	40,967	38,577	7,391	982	39,893	119.347	40.967	38,577	7,391	982	30,803
Sylhet	129,830	40,266	47,876	4,904	991	41,688	129,823	40,263	47,876	4,904	991	41,684
Khasi and Jaintia Hills	8	2	...	...	...	6	...	...	...	...	...	...
Naga Hills	1	...	...	...	...	1	1	—	...	...	...	1
Lushai Hills	71	57	...	1	...	14	71	57	...	1	...	14
ASSAM VALLEY DISTRICTS	*426,102*	*156,601*	*144,309*	*20,776*	*10,527*	*125,192*	*426,109*	*156,601*	*144,300*	*20,776*	*10,527*	*125,192*
Goalpara	683	286	179	5	...	218	683	286	179	5	...	218
Kamrup	4,965	1,801	1,518	144	39	1,646	4 965	1,801	1,518	141	39	1,646
Darrang	76,275	29,565	26,234	2,511	784	20,476	76,275	29,565	26,234	2,511	784	20,476
Nowgong	17,965	6,426	6,547	875	519	4,992	17,965	6,426	6,547	875	519	4,992
Sibsagar	165,284	59,008	53,497	9,107	4,288	52,779	165 284	59,008	53,497	9,107	4,288	52,779
Lakhimpur	160,930	59,515	56,334	8,134	4,897	45,081	160,930	59,515	56,334	8,134	4,897	45,081
Garo Hills	...	...	...	...	...	...	...	...	...	...	...	...
(2) ***Manipur State***	1	...	...	...	...	1	...	...	...	...	...	...

Class and Sub-Class ... CLASS A : SUB-CLASS I.—EXPLOITATION OF THE SURFACE OF THE EARTH.

Order ... ... (b) GROWERS OF SPECIAL PRODUCTS AND MARKET GARDENING. | (c) FORESTRY.

DISTRICT OR STATE.	6.—Fruit, flower, vegetable, betel, vine, areca-nut, etc., growers.						TOTAL OF ORDER I(c).					
	TOTAL WORKERS AND DEPENDANTS.	ACTUAL WORKERS. Total.		Partially agriculturist.		DEPENDANTS.	TOTAL WORKERS AND DEPENDANTS.	ACTUAL WORKERS. Total.		Partially agriculturist.		DEPENDANTS.
		Males.	Females.	Males.	Females.	Both sexes.		Males.	Females.	Males.	Females.	Both sexes.
1	62	63	64	5	66	67	68	69	70	71	72	73
ASSAM	*27,433*	*8,388*	*7,380*	*1,281*	*1,006*	*11,665*	*4,099*	*2,130*	*327*	*247*	*3*	*1,649*
(1) ***British Territory***	*27,336*	*8,350*	*7,378*	*1,281*	*1,006*	*11,608*	*3,857*	*2,107*	*190*	*247*	*3*	*1,560*
SURMA VALLEY AND HILL DISTRICTS	*26,393*	*7,874*	*7,268*	*1,254*	*999*	*11,251*	*994*	*435*	*59*	*86*	*1*	*510*
Cachar	11	1	10	...	9	...	119	56	18	7	...	50
Sylhet	477	23	83	1	11	371	500	191	2	67	...	307
Khasi and Jaintia Hills	25,846	7,831	7,167	1,253	986	10,848	285	111	43	1	1	131
Naga Hills	45	15	6	...	...	24	30	23	1	...	...	6
Lushai Hills	14	4	2	...	...	8	60	44	...	11	...	16
ASSAM VALLEY DISTRICTS	*943*	*476*	*110*	*27*	*7*	*357*	*2,863*	*1,682*	*131*	*161*	*2*	*1,050*
Goalpara	123	76	13	3	...	34	770	434	18	116	...	318
Kamrup	91	27	1	3	...	63	928	440	91	14	2	397
Darrang	41	18	...	...	...	23	144	85	1	...	...	58
Nowgong	17	9	...	...	...	8	166	101	2	8	...	63
Sibsagar	322	172	77	16	7	73	239	149	2	19	...	88
Lakhimpur	338	168	18	5	...	152	519	419	10	4	...	90
Garo Hills	11	6	1	...	...	4	97	54	7	...	...	36
(2) ***Manipur State***	*97*	*38*	*2*	...	...	*57*	*242*	*23*	*137*	...	...	*82*

TABLE XV.—OCCUPATION OR MEANS OF LIVELIHOOD. PART A.—GENERAL TABLE—DETAILS FOR DISTRICTS—*contd.*

Class and Sub-Class ...	*CLASS A : SUB-CLASS I.—EXPLOITATION OF THE SURFACE OF THE EARTH.*											
Order ...	(c) FORESTRY.						(d) RAISING OF FARM STOCK.					
	8.—Wood-cutters; firewood, lac, catechu, rubber, etc., collectors, and charcoal burners.						*TOTAL OF ORDER 1 (d).*					
DISTRICT OR STATE.	TOTAL WORKERS AND DEPENDANTS.	ACTUAL WORKERS. Total. Males.	ACTUAL WORKERS. Total. Females.	ACTUAL WORKERS. *Partially agriculturist.* Males.	ACTUAL WORKERS. *Partially agriculturist.* Females.	DEPENDANTS. Both sexes.	TOTAL WORKERS AND DEPENDANTS.	ACTUAL WORKERS. Total. Males.	ACTUAL WORKERS. Total. Females.	ACTUAL WORKERS. *Partially agriculturist.* Males.	ACTUAL WORKERS. *Partially agriculturist.* Females.	DEPENDANTS. Both sexes.
1	74	75	76	77	78	79	80	81	82	83	84	85
ASSAM ...	*2,763*	*1,459*	*327*	*186*	*3*	*977*	*47,278*	*34,867*	*2,767*	*1,750*	*91*	*9,644*
(1) ***British Territory*** ...	*2,534*	*1,440*	*190*	*186*	*3*	*904*	*46,231*	*34,460*	*2,748*	*1,749*	*91*	*9,023*
SURMA VALLEY AND HILL DISTRICTS ...	*632*	*270*	*59*	*62*	*1*	*303*	*17,169*	*11,458*	*1,209*	*1,161*	*15*	*4,502*
Cachar ...	48	15	13	1	...	20	1 311	956	97	45	2	258
Sylhet ...	335	181	2	49	...	202	10 062	6,149	145	1,098	9	3,769
Khasi and Jaintia Hills ...	181	67	43	1	1	71	5 236	4,071	951	13	4	214
Naga Hills ...	30	23	1	...	...	6	445	223	13	5	...	209
Lushai Hills ...	38	34	...	11	...	4	115	60	3	...	...	52
ASSAM VALLEY DISTRICTS ...	*1,902*	*1,170*	*131*	*124*	*2*	*601*	*20,063*	*23,002*	*1,539*	*588*	*76*	*4,521*
Goalpara ...	580	295	18	94	...	267	3 969	2,848	64	93	5	1,057
Kamrup ...	695	341	91	11	2	263	6 366	5,527	142	59	4	697
Darrang ...	51	34	1	...	...	16	10 878	8,659	870	297	60	1,849
Nowgong ...	31	27	2	...	...	2	2 866	2,460	107	61	2	299
Sibsagar ...	103	87	2	16	...	14	2 237	1,579	125	36	...	533
Lakhimpur ...	418	376	10	3	...	32	2,091	1,450	199	30	...	442
Garo Hills ...	24	10	7	...	...	7	655	479	32	12	5	144
(2) ***Manipur State*** ...	*229*	*19*	*137*	...	...	*73*	*1,047*	*407*	*10*	*1*	...	*621*

Class and Sub-Class ...	*CLASS A : SUB-CLASS I—EXPLOITATION OF THE SURFACE OF THE EARTH.*											
Order ...	(d) RAISING OF FARM STOCK.											
	9.—Cattle and buffalo breeders and keepers.						*12.—Herdsmen, shepherds, goat herds, etc.*					
DISTRICT OR STATE.	TOTAL WORKERS AND DEPENDANTS.	ACTUAL WORKERS. Total. Males.	ACTUAL WORKERS. Total. Females.	ACTUAL WORKERS. *Partially agriculturist.* Males.	ACTUAL WORKERS. *Partially agriculturist.* Females.	DEPENDANTS. Both sexes.	TOTAL WORKERS AND DEPENDANTS.	ACTUAL WORKERS. Total. Males.	ACTUAL WORKERS. Total. Females.	ACTUAL WORKERS. *Partially agriculturist.* Males.	ACTUAL WORKERS. *Partially agriculturist.* Females.	DEPENDANTS. Both sexes.
1	86	87	88	89	90	91	92	93	94	95	96	97
ASSAM ...	*18,819*	*9,457*	*1,226*	*1,475*	*87*	*8,136*	*28,354*	*25,367*	*1,525*	*269*	*4*	*1,462*
(1) ***British Territory*** ...	*18,018*	*9,240*	*1,211*	*1,474*	*87*	*7,567*	*28,114*	*25,178*	*1,521*	*269*	*4*	*1,415*
SURMA VALLEY AND HILL DISTRICTS ...	*7,734*	*3,275*	*311*	*1,027*	*14*	*4,148*	*9,411*	*8,182*	*887*	*134*	*1*	*342*
Cachar ...	447	168	80	31	2	199	864	788	17	14	...	59
Sylhet... ...	6,399	2,646	136	983	9	3,617	3 662	3,502	9	115	...	151
Khasi and Jaintia Hills ...	490	269	87	8	3	134	4 732	3,802	867	5	1	73
Naga Hills ...	285	134	5	5	...	146	151	88	4	...	...	59
Lushai Hills ...	113	58	3	...	...	52	2	2	—	...	...	...
ASSAM VALLEY DISTRICTS ...	*10,284*	*5,965*	*900*	*447*	*73*	*3,419*	*18,703*	*16,996*	*634*	*135*	*3*	*1,073*
Goalpara ...	1,579	913	33	65	5	633	2 347	1,019	31	22	...	397
Kamrup ...	1 401	874	67	42	4	460	4 964	4,653	74	17	...	237
Darrang ...	3 914	2,170	557	236	57	1,187	6 964	6,489	313	61	3	162
Nowgong ...	981	705	24	56	2	252	1 879	1,754	80	5	...	45
Sibsagar ...	1,116	637	65	20	...	424	1 115	936	70	16	...	09
Lakhimpur ...	978	488	140	18	...	350	1,094	944	68	12	...	92
Garo Hills ...	315	178	24	10	5	113	340	301	8	2	...	31
(2) ***Manipur State*** ...	*801*	*217*	*15*	*1*	...	*560*	*240*	*189*	*4*	...	...	*47*

TABLE XV.—OCCUPATION OR MEANS OF LIVELIHOOD. PART A.—GENERAL TABLE—DETAILS FOR DISTRICTS—*contd.*

Class and Sub-Class ...	*CLASS A—SUB-CLASS I.—EXPLOITATION OF THE SURFACE OF THE EARTH.*											
Order	(e) RAISING OF SMALL ANIMALS.						2.—FISHING AND HUNTING.					
	13.—*Birds, bees, silkworms, etc.*						*TOTAL OF ORDER 2.*					
DISTRICT OR STATE.	TOTAL WORKERS AND DEPENDANTS.	ACTUAL WORKERS. Total.		Partially agriculturist.		DEPENDANTS.	TOTAL WORKERS AND DEPENDANTS.	ACTUAL WORKERS. Total.		Partially agriculturist.		DEPENDANTS.
		Males.	Females.	Males.	Females.	Both sexes.		Males.	Females.	Males.	Females.	Both sexes.
1	98	99	100	101	102	103	104	105	106	107	108	109
ASSAM	*135*	*34*	*44*	...	...	*57*	*100,706*	*42,702*	*1,743*	*12,313*	*119*	*56,261*
(1) ***British Territory***	*127*	*34*	*38*	...	...	*55*	*100,555*	*42,656*	*1,738*	*12,313*	*119*	*56,161*
SURMA VALLEY AND HILL DISTRICTS	*114*	*29*	*34*	...	...	*51*	*77,062*	*32,597*	*558*	*11,234*	*46*	*43,907*
Cachar	...	...	...	...	...	...	530	215	7	104	...	308
Sylhet	20	...	8	...	...	12	76,471	32,367	547	11,126	46	43,557
Khasi and Jaintia Hills	67	20	...	...	...	27	49	13	4	3	...	32
Naga Hills	41	3	26	...	...	12	12	2	...	1	...	10
Lushai Hills	6	5	...	...	...	...	...	...	...	...	...	...
ASSAM VALLEY DISTRICTS	*13*	*5*	*4*	...	...	*4*	*23,493*	*10,059*	*1,180*	*1,079*	*73*	*12,254*
Goalpara	...	...	...	...	...	...	7,654	3,330	216	147	...	4,108
Kamrup	2	...	2	...	...	...	9,101	3,508	721	247	8	4,872
Darrang	...	...	...	...	...	...	1,425	770	77	62	23	578
Nowgong	...	...	...	...	...	...	915	526	12	125	3	377
Sibsagar	7	2	1	...	...	4	2,675	1,170	109	396	32	1,396
Lakhimpur	4	3	1	...	...	...	1,519	643	42	96	6	834
Garo Hills	...	...	...	...	...	...	204	113	3	6	1	89
(2) ***Manipur State***	*8*	...	*6*	...	...	*2*	*151*	*46*	*5*	...	...	*100*

Class and Sub-Class ...	*CLASS A: SUB-CLASS I.—EXPLOITATION OF THE SURFACE OF THE EARTH.*						*CLASS A: SUB-CLASS II.—EXTRACTION OF MINERALS.*					
Order	2.—FISHING AND HUNTING.						3.—MINES.					
	14.—*Fishing.*						*TOTAL OF ORDER 3.*					
DISTRICT OR STATE.	TOTAL WORKERS AND DEPENDANTS.	ACTUAL WORKERS. Total.		Partially agriculturist.		DEPENDANTS.	TOTAL WORKERS AND DEPENDANTS.	ACTUAL WORKERS. Total.		Partially agriculturist.		DEPENDANTS.
		Males.	Females.	Males.	Females.	Both sexes.		Males.	Females.	Males.	Females.	Both sexes.
1	110	111	112	113	114	115	116	117	118	119	120	121
ASSAM ...	*100,102*	*42,459*	*1,716*	*12,281*	*118*	*55,927*	*5,122*	*3,060*	*903*	*79*	*5*	*1,159*
(1) ***British Territory***	*99,951*	*42,413*	*1,711*	*12,281*	*118*	*55,827*	*5,097*	*3,039*	*902*	*79*	*5*	*1,156*
SURMA VALLEY AND HILL DISTRICTS	*76,708*	*32,505*	*532*	*11,213*	*45*	*43,671*	*59*	*45*	*5*	...	...	*9*
Cachar	530	215	7	104	...	308	...	...	...	...	...	...
Sylhet	76,129	32,277	521	11,106	45	43,331	...	...	...	...	...	...
Khasi and Jaintia Hills	49	13	4	3	...	32	59	45	5	...	...	9
Naga Hills	...	...	...	...	...	...	...	...	...	...	...	...
Lushai Hills	...	...	...	...	...	...	...	...	...	...	...	...
ASSAM VALLEY DISTRICTS	*23,243*	*9,908*	*1,179*	*1,068*	*73*	*12,156*	*5,038*	*2,994*	*897*	*79*	*5*	*1,147*
Goalpara	7,630	3,314	216	142	...	4,100	...	...	...	...	...	...
Kamrup	9,039	3,485	721	245	8	4,833	...	...	...	...	...	...
Darrang	1,404	756	76	61	23	572	1	...	...	...	...	1
Nowgong	852	497	12	129	3	349	1	1	...	1	...	...
Sibsagar	2,636	1,133	109	395	32	1,388	2	2	...	...	...	...
Lakhimpur	1,478	611	42	96	6	825	5,034	2,991	897	78	5	1,146
Garo Hills	204	112	3	6	1	89	...	...	...	...	...	...
(2) ***Manipur State***	*151*	*46*	*5*	...	...	*100*	*25*	*21*	*1*	...	...	*3*

TABLE XV.—Occupation or means of Livelihood. Part A.—General Table.—Details for Districts—*contd.*

Class and Sub-Class ...	CLASS A : SUB-CLASS II.—EXTRACTION OF MINERALS.											
Order	3.—MINES.						4.—QUARRIES OF HARD ROCKS.					
	10.—Coal mines and petroleum wells.						13.—Other minerals (jade, diamonds, limestones, etc.). TOTAL.					
District or State.	Total workers and dependants.	Actual workers. Total. Males.	Actual workers. Total. Females.	Actual workers. Partially agriculturist. Males.	Actual workers. Partially agriculturist. Females.	Dependants. Both sexes.	Total workers and dependants.	Actual workers. Total. Males.	Actual workers. Total. Females.	Actual workers. Partially agriculturist. Males.	Actual workers. Partially agriculturist. Females.	Dependants. Both sexes.
1	122	123	124	125	126	127	128	129	130	131	132	133
ASSAM ...	***5,096***	***3,038***	***902***	***70***	***5***	***1,156***	***680***	***395***	***27***	***6***	...	***258***
(1) British Territory ...	*5,096*	*3,038*	*902*	*70*	*5*	*1,156*	*680*	*395*	*27*	*6*	...	*258*
SURMA VALLEY AND HILL DISTRICTS ...	*58*	*44*	*5*	...	...	*9*	*659*	*395*	*6*	*6*	...	*258*
Cachar ...	...	...	...	...	...	...	...	...	...	...	...	...
Sylhet ...	...	...	...	...	...	...	...	...	...	...	...	...
Khasi and Jaintia Hills ...	58	44	5	...	...	9	659	395	6	6	...	258
Naga Hills ...	...	...	...	...	...	...	...	...	...	...	...	...
Lushai Hills ...	...	...	...	...	...	...	...	...	...	...	...	...
ASSAM VALLEY DISTRICTS ...	*5,038*	*2,994*	*897*	*70*	*5*	*1,147*	*21*	...	*21*	...	...	...
Goalpara ...	...	...	...	...	...	...	...	...	...	...	...	...
Kamrup ...	...	...	...	...	...	...	...	...	...	...	...	...
Darrang ...	1	...	...	...	...	1	...	...	...	...	...	...
Nowgong ...	1	1	...	1	...	...	...	...	...	...	...	...
Sibsagar ...	2	2	...	...	...	...	...	...	...	...	...	...
Lakhimpur ...	5,034	2,991	897	78	5	1,146	21	...	21	...	...	...
Garo Hills ...	...	...	...	...	...	...	...	...	...	...	...	...
(2) Manipur State ...	...	...	...	...	...	...	...	...	...	...	...	...

Class and Sub-Class ...	CLASS A : SUB-CLASS II.—EXTRACTION OF MINERALS.											
Order	4.—QUARRIES OF HARD ROCKS.						5.—SALT, ETC.					
	Limestone quarries (included in total).						TOTAL OF ORDER 5.					
District or State.	Total workers and dependants.	Actual workers. Total. Males.	Actual workers. Total. Females.	Actual workers. Partially agriculturist. Males.	Actual workers. Partially agriculturist. Females.	Dependants. Both sexes.	Total workers and dependants.	Actual workers. Total. Males.	Actual workers. Total. Females.	Actual workers. Partially agriculturist. Males.	Actual workers. Partially agriculturist. Females.	Dependants. Both sexes.
1	134	135	136	137	138	139	140	141	142	143	144	145
ASSAM ...	***675***	***390***	***27***	***1***	...	***258***	***721***	***183***	***244***	***1***	...	***294***
(1) British Territory ...	*675*	*390*	*27*	*1*	...	*258*	*9*	...	*7*	...	...	*2*
SURMA VALLEY AND HILL DISTRICTS ...	*654*	*390*	*6*	*1*	...	*258*	...	...	...	...	...	...
Cachar ...	...	...	...	...	...	...	...	...	...	...	...	...
Sylhet ...	...	...	...	...	...	...	...	...	...	...	...	...
Khasi and Jaintia Hills ...	654	390	...	1	...	258	...	...	...	...	...	...
Naga Hills ...	...	...	...	...	...	...	...	...	...	...	...	...
Lushai Hills ...	...	...	...	...	...	...	...	...	...	...	...	...
ASSAM VALLEY DISTRICTS ...	*21*	...	*21*	...	...	...	*9*	...	*7*	...	...	*2*
Goalpara ...	...	...	...	...	...	...	...	...	...	...	...	...
Kamrup ...	...	...	...	...	...	...	...	...	...	...	...	...
Darrang ...	...	...	...	...	...	...	9	...	7	...	...	2
Nowgong ...	...	...	...	...	...	...	...	...	...	...	...	...
Sibsagar ...	...	...	...	...	...	...	...	...	...	...	...	...
Lakhimpur ...	21	...	21	...	...	...	...	...	...	...	...	...
Garo Hills ...	...	...	...	...	...	...	...	...	...	...	...	...
(2) Manipur State ...	...	...	...	...	...	...	*712*	*183*	*237*	*1*	...	*292*

TABLE XV.—Occupation or means of Livelihood. Part A.—General Table.—Details for Districts—*contd.*

Class and Sub-Class / Order / District or State	CLASS A: SUB-CLASS II.—EXTRACTION OF MINERALS. 5.—SALT, ETC. 19.—Rock, sea and marsh salt. Total workers and dependants.	Actual workers. Total. Males.	Females.	Partially agriculturist. Males.	Females.	Dependants. Both sexes.	CLASS B: SUB-CLASS III.—INDUSTRY. 6.—TEXTILES. TOTAL OF ORDER 6. Total workers and dependants.	Actual workers. Total. Males.	Females.	Partially agriculturist. Males.	Females.	Dependants. Both sexes.
1	146	147	148	149	150	151	152	153	154	155	156	157
ASSAM	*719*	*183*	*237*	*1*	...	*299*	*59,419*	*2,914*	*44,730*	*900*	*1,033*	*11,769*
(1) ***British Territory***	...	...	...	...	...	...	*15,673*	*2,871*	*8,668*	*884*	*93*	*4,634*
SURMA VALLEY AND HILL DISTRICTS	...	...	...	...	...	...	*10,713*	*1,987*	*5,505*	*880*	*62*	*3,221*
Cachar	...	...	...	...	...	...	1,550	43	1,402	3	24	105
Sylhet	...	...	...	...	...	...	8,329	1,941	3,397	877	35	2,991
Khasi and Jaintia Hills	...	...	...	...	...	...	784	3	661	...	3	120
Naga Hills	...	...	...	...	...	...	50	...	45	...	...	5
Lushai Hills	...	...	...	...	...	...	...	...	...	...	...	...
ASSAM VALLEY DISTRICTS	...	...	...	...	...	...	*4,960*	*884*	*3,163*	*4*	*31*	*1,413*
Goalpara	...	...	...	...	...	...	836	191	475	...	2	170
Kamrup	...	...	...	...	...	...	3,239	107	2,047	2	13	1,085
Darrang	...	...	...	...	...	...	178	29	92	...	4	57
Nowgong	...	...	...	...	...	...	488	10	425	...	6	58
Sibsagar	...	...	...	...	...	...	107	29	55	1	1	23
Lakhimpur	...	...	...	...	...	...	75	17	35	1	...	23
Garo Hills	...	...	...	...	...	...	37	1	34	...	...	3
(2) ***Manipur State***	*719*	*183*	*237*	*1*	...	*299*	*43,746*	*543*	*36,068*	*16*	*940*	*7,135*

Class and Sub-Class / Order / District or State	CLASS B: SUB-CLASS III.—INDUSTRY. 6.—TEXTILES. 22.—Cotton spinning, sizing and weaving. Total workers and dependants.	Actual workers. Total. Males.	Females.	Partially agriculturist. Males.	Females.	Dependants. Both sexes.	24.—Rope, twine and string. Total workers and dependants.	Actual workers. Total. Males.	Females.	Partially agriculturist. Males.	Females.	Dependants. Both sexes.
1	158	159	160	161	162	163	164	165	166	167	168	169
ASSAM	*56,295*	*2,019*	*43,467*	*748*	*1,023*	*10,809*	*1,085*	*425*	*372*	*142*	*6*	*288*
(1) ***British Territory***	*13,185*	*1,660*	*7,577*	*740*	*83*	*3,948*	*1,082*	*423*	*371*	*142*	*6*	*288*
SURMA VALLEY AND HILL DISTRICTS	*9,713*	*1,613*	*5,153*	*738*	*55*	*2,947*	*974*	*359*	*347*	*142*	*6*	*268*
Cachar	1,517	43	1,373	3	23	101	33	...	29	...	2	4
Sylhet	7,369	1,567	3,080	735	30	2,722	937	359	315	142	4	263
Khasi and Jaintia Hills	777	3	655	...	3	110	4	...	3	...	...	1
Naga Hills	50	...	45	...	...	5	...	...	...	...	...	...
Lushai Hills	...	...	...	...	...	...	...	...	...	...	...	...
ASSAM VALLEY DISTRICTS	*3,479*	*47*	*2,424*	*2*	*28*	*1,001*	*108*	*64*	*24*	...	...	*20*
Goalpara	606	11	454	...	2	141	32	18	11	...	...	3
Kamrup	2,300	11	1,555	1	16	734	23	5	11	...	...	7
Darrang	153	12	92	...	4	48	23	15	...	...	...	8
Nowgong	254	6	209	...	5	30	5	2	2	...	...	1
Sibsagar	71	6	45	1	1	21	24	23	...	...	...	1
Lakhimpur	53	2	35	...	...	16	...	...	...	...	...	...
Garo Hills	36	...	34	...	...	2	1	1	...	...	...	...
(2) ***Manipur State***	*43,110*	*359*	*35,890*	*8*	*940*	*6,861*	*3*	*2*	*1*	...	...	...

TABLE XV.—OCCUPATION OR MEANS OF LIVELIHOOD. PART A.—GENERAL TABLE—DETAILS FOR DISTRICTS—*contd.*

Class and Sub-Class ...	*CLASS B: SUB-CLASS III.—INDUSTRY.*											
Order	6.—TEXTILES.						7.—HIDES, SKINS AND HARD MATERIALS FROM THE ANIMAL KINGDOM.					
	27.—Silk spinners and weavers.						*TOTAL OF ORDER 7.*					
District or State.	Total workers and dependants.	Actual workers. Total. Males.	Actual workers. Total. Females.	Actual workers. Partially agriculturist. Males.	Actual workers. Partially agriculturist. Females.	Dependants. Both sexes.	Total workers and dependants.	Actual workers. Total. Males.	Actual workers. Total. Females.	Actual workers. Partially agriculturist. Males.	Actual workers. Partially agriculturist. Females.	Dependants. Both sexes.
1	170	171	172	173	174	175	176	177	178	179	180	181
ASSAM	*1,717*	*249*	*876*	*8*	*3*	*592*	*1,432*	*752*	*41*	*114*	*1*	*639*
(1) British Territory	*1,131*	*82*	*708*	...	*3*	*341*	*1,410*	*743*	*40*	*114*	*1*	*627*
SURMA VALLEY AND HILL DISTRICTS	*2*	...	*2*	...	...	...	*211*	*25*	*15*	*6*	...	*171*
Cachar	...	...	...	...	...	...	21	11	3		...	7
Sylhet	...	...	...	...	...	...	190	14	12	6	...	164
Khasi and Jaintia Hills	2	...	2	...	...	...	...	...	...	...	...	
Naga Hills	...	...	...	...	...	...	...	...	...	...	...	...
Lushai Hills	...	...	...	...	...	...	...	...	...	...	...	...
ASSAM VALLEY DISTRICTS	*1,129*	*82*	*706*	...	*3*	*341*	*1,199*	*718*	*25*	*108*	*1*	*456*
Goalpara	1	...	1	...		...	422	185	12	40	1	225
Kamrup	887	79	481	...	2	327	303	252	1	9		50
Darrang	1	1	...	...		...	73	45	5	...	...	23
Nowgong	229	2	214	...	1	13	260	183	4	57	...	73
Sibsagar	11	...	10	...	...	1	90	36	3	1	...	51
Lakhimpur	...	...	...	...	...	...	39	14	...	1	...	25
Garo Hills	...	...	...	...	...	...	12	3	...	...	...	9
(2) Manipur State	*586*	*167*	*168*	*8*	...	*251*	*22*	*9*	*1*	...	...	*12*

Class and Sub-Class ...	*CLASS B: SUB-CLASS III.—INDUSTRY.*											
Order	8. WOOD.											
	TOTAL OF ORDER 8.						*36.—Sawyers, carpenters, turners and joiners.*					
District or State.	Total workers and dependants.	Actual workers. Total. Males.	Actual workers. Total. Females.	Actual workers. Partially agriculturist. Males.	Actual workers. Partially agriculturist. Females.	Dependants. Both sexes.	Total workers and dependants.	Actual workers. Total. Males.	Actual workers. Total. Females.	Actual workers. Partially agriculturist. Males.	Actual workers. Partially agriculturist. Females.	Dependants. Both sexes.
1	182	183	184	185	186	187	188	189	190	191	192	193
ASSAM	*34,029*	*12,071*	*7,552*	*2,739*	*87*	*14,406*	*20,318*	*9,624*	*253*	*1,954*	...	*10,441*
(1) British Territory	*32,893*	*11,687*	*7,532*	*2,720*	*87*	*13,674*	*19,287*	*9,297*	*246*	*1,937*	...	*9,744*
SURMA VALLEY AND HILL DISTRICTS	*24,176*	*6,718*	*7,098*	*2,343*	*82*	*10,360*	*11,638*	*4,856*	*7*	*1,599*	...	*6,775*
Cachar	970	530	32	73	8	408	715	340	...	65	...	375
Sylhet	21,687	5,660	6,866	2,247	40	9,161	9,747	4,022	...	1,513	...	5,725
Khasi and Jaintia Hills	1,311	410	199	14	34	702	975	383	6	12	...	586
Naga Hills	100	46	1	1	...	53	93	39	1	1	...	53
Lushai Hills	108	72	...	8	...	36	108	72	...	8	...	36
ASSAM VALLEY DISTRICTS	*8,717*	*4,969*	*434*	*377*	*5*	*3,314*	*7,649*	*4,441*	*239*	*338*	...	*2,969*
Goalpara	2,122	1,607	56	221	1	459	1,969	1,557	4	210	...	408
Kamrup	2,063	745	82	36	1	1,236	1,710	627	8	17	...	1,075
Darrang	546	337	8	9	1	201	419	258	...	3	...	161
Nowgong	430	249	16	17	...	165	363	214	3	14	...	146
Sibsagar	1,353	871	59	51	2	423	1,099	668	38	44	...	393
Lakhimpur	2,135	1,105	212	43	...	818	2,025	1,064	186	41	...	775
Garo Hills	68	55	1	...	...	12	64	53	...	...	...	11
(2) Manipur State	*1,136*	*384*	*20*	*19*	...	*732*	*1,031*	*327*	*7*	*17*	...	*697*

TABLE XV.—OCCUPATION OR MEANS OF LIVELIHOOD. PART A.—GENERAL TABLE—DETAILS FOR DISTRICTS—contd.

Class and Sub-Class ...	CLASS B: SUB-CLASS III.—INDUSTRY.											
Order	8.—WOOD.						9.—METALS.					
	37.—Basket makers and other industries of woody material, including leaves.						TOTAL OF ORDER 9.					
DISTRICT OR STATE.	TOTAL WORKERS AND DEPENDANTS.	ACTUAL WORKERS. Total.		ACTUAL WORKERS. Partially agriculturist.		DEPENDANTS.	TOTAL WORKERS AND DEPENDANTS.	ACTUAL WORKERS. Total.		ACTUAL WORKERS. Partially agriculturist.		DEPENDANTS.
		Males.	Females.	Males.	Females.	Both sexes.		Males.	Females.	Males.	Females.	Both sexes.
1	194	195	196	197	198	199	200	201	202	203	204	205
ASSAM	*13,711*	*2,447*	*7,299*	*785*	*87*	*3,965*	*13,248*	*4,964*	*170*	*1,356*	*6*	*8,114*
(1) British Territory	*13,606*	*2,390*	*7,286*	*783*	*87*	*3,930*	*19,755*	*4,783*	*97*	*1,331*	*6*	*7,875*
SURMA VALLEY AND HILL DISTRICTS	*12,538*	*1,862*	*7,091*	*744*	*82*	*3,585*	*5,793*	*2,223*	*10*	*1,005*	*3*	*3,560*
Cachar	255	190	33	8	8	33	262	154	...	35	...	108
Sylhet	11,940	1,638	6,866	734	40	3,436	4,973	1,807	...	872	...	3,166
Khasi and Jaintia Hills	336	27	193	2	34	116	412	104	8	64	3	210
Naga Hills	7	7	...	...	...	...	40	14	2	3	...	24
Lushai Hills	...	...	...	...	...	...	106	54	...	31	...	52
ASSAM VALLEY DISTRICTS	*1,068*	*528*	*195*	*39*	*5*	*345*	*6,962*	*2,560*	*87*	*326*	*3*	*4,315*
Goalpara	153	50	52	2	1	51	489	291	5	25	...	193
Kamrup	353	118	74	19	1	161	4,049	1,189	59	109	...	2,801
Darrang	127	79	8	6	1	40	307	168	3	5	...	136
Nowgong	67	35	13	3	...	19	564	143	2	55	...	419
Sibsagar	254	203	21	7	2	30	965	436	10	116	3	519
Lakhimpur	110	41	26	2	...	43	544	312	5	15	...	227
Garo Hills	4	2	1	...	...	1	44	21	3	1	...	20
(2) Manipur State	*105*	*57*	*13*	*2*	...	*35*	*493*	*181*	*73*	*25*	...	*230*

Class and Sub-Class ...	CLASS B: SUB-CLASS III.—INDUSTRY.											
Order	9.—METALS.											
	41.—Other workers in iron and makers of implements and tools, principally or exclusively of iron.						42.—Workers in brass, copper and bell metal.					
DISTRICT OR STATE.	TOTAL WORKERS AND DEPENDANTS.	ACTUAL WORKERS. Total.		ACTUAL WORKERS. Partially agriculturist.		DEPENDANTS.	TOTAL WORKERS AND DEPENDANTS.	ACTUAL WORKERS. Total.		ACTUAL WORKERS. Partially agriculturist.		DEPENDANTS.
		Males.	Females.	Males.	Females.	Both sexes.		Males.	Females.	Males.	Females.	Both sexes.
1	206	207	208	209	210	211	212	213	214	215	216	217
ASSAM	*7,800*	*3,209*	*48*	*1,016*	*3*	*4,003*	*4,957*	*1,574*	*114*	*286*	...	*3,269*
(1) British Territory	*7,561*	*3,095*	*28*	*991*	*3*	*4,438*	*4,763*	*1,507*	*61*	*286*	...	*3,195*
SURMA VALLEY AND HILL DISTRICTS	*5,320*	*2,093*	*7*	*915*	...	*3,399*	*190*	*103*	...	*87*	...	*87*
Cachar	258	150	...	34	...	108	4	4	...	1	...	...
Sylhet	4,745	1,694	...	836	...	3,051	178	96	...	36	...	82
Khasi and Jaintia Hills	181	112	5	11	...	64	7	2	...	...	...	5
Naga Hills	39	13	2	3	...	24	1	1	...	...	...	...
Lushai Hills	106	54	...	31	...	52	...	...	...	...	...	...
ASSAM VALLEY DISTRICTS	*2,233*	*1,079*	*21*	*76*	*3*	*1,139*	*4,573*	*1,404*	*61*	*249*	...	*3,108*
Goalpara	404	251	5	22	...	148	68	30	...	3	...	38
Kamrup	878	280	4	19	...	594	3,129	887	51	90	...	2,191
Darrang	134	92	...	1	...	42	165	69	3	2	...	93
Nowgong	118	64	...	4	...	54	442	76	2	52	...	364
Sibsagar	235	126	5	16	3	104	698	298	4	100	...	396
Lakhimpur	433	244	4	12	...	185	71	44	1	3	...	26
Garo Hills	30	15	3	...	...	12	...	...	...	...	...	...
(2) Manipur State	*299*	*114*	*20*	*25*	...	*165*	*194*	*67*	*53*	...	...	*74*

TABLE XV.—Occupation or Means of Livelihood. Part A.—General Table—Details for Districts—*contd.*

Class and Sub-Class ... CLASS B: SUB-CLASS III.—INDUSTRY.

Order ... 10.—CERAMICS.

District or State.	TOTAL OF ORDER 10. Total workers and dependants.	Actual workers. Total. Males.	Actual workers. Total. Females.	Actual workers. Partially agriculturist. Males.	Actual workers. Partially agriculturist. Females.	Dependants. Both sexes.	47.—Potters and earthen pipe and bowl makers. Total workers and dependants.	Actual workers. Total. Males.	Actual workers. Total. Females.	Actual workers. Partially agriculturist. Males.	Actual workers. Partially agriculturist. Females.	Dependants. Both sexes.
1	218	219	220	221	222	223	224	225	226	227	228	229
ASSAM	*16,795*	*4,415*	*5,513*	*1,042*	*216*	*6,867*	*15,677*	*3,817*	*5,295*	*1,015*	*188*	*6,565*
(1) British Territory ...	*16,202*	*4,367*	*5,133*	*1,029*	*210*	*6,702*	*15,165*	*3,801*	*4,915*	*1,015*	*182*	*6,449*
SURMA VALLEY AND HILL DISTRICTS ...	*6,009*	*1,890*	*1,348*	*780*	*26*	*2,765*	*5,940*	*1,846*	*1,346*	*778*	*26*	*2,748*
Cachar ...	287	79	163	23	5	45	270	68	163	21	5	39
Sylhet ...	5,646	1,801	1,154	757	9	2,691	5,594	1,762	1,152	757	9	2,680
Khasi and Jaintia Hills ...	70	16	26	...	12	28	70	16	26	...	12	28
Naga Hills ...	6	...	5	...	...	1	6	...	5	...	...	1
Lushai Hills ...	...	...	...	...	...	...	...	...	...	...	...	......
ASSAM VALLEY DISTRICTS ...	*10,193*	*2,471*	*3,785*	*249*	*184*	*3,937*	*9,225*	*1,955*	*3,569*	*237*	*156*	*3,701*
Goalpara ...	1,809	520	629	40	...	660	1,715	469	616	40	...	630
Kamrup ...	4,164	768	1,850	49	35	1,546	3,870	648	1,742	49	7	1,480
Darrang ...	570	174	208	20	14	188	553	162	206	19	14	185
Nowgong ...	523	117	307	21	64	99	433	59	293	16	64	81
Sibsagar ...	2,397	497	648	108	71	1,252	2,302	414	643	108	71	1,245
Lakhimpur ...	509	291	74	11	...	144	131	99	...	5	...	32
Garo Hills ...	221	104	69	...	...	48	221	104	69	...	...	48
(2) Manipur State ...	*593*	*48*	*380*	*13*	*6*	*165*	*512*	*16*	*380*	...	*6*	*116*

Class and Sub-Class ... CLASS B: SUB-CLASS III.—INDUSTRY.

Order ... 11.—CHEMICAL PRODUCTS PROPERLY SO-CALLED, AND ANALOGOUS.

District or State.	TOTAL OF ORDER 11. Total workers and dependants.	Actual workers. Total. Males.	Actual workers. Total. Females.	Actual workers. Partially agriculturist. Males.	Actual workers. Partially agriculturist. Females.	Dependants. Both sexes.	53.—Manufacture and refining of vegetable and mineral oils. Total workers and dependants.	Actual workers. Total. Males.	Actual workers. Total. Females.	Actual workers. Partially agriculturist. Males.	Actual workers. Partially agriculturist. Females.	Dependants. Both sexes.
1	230	231	232	233	234	235	236	237	238	239	240	241
ASSAM ...	*5,496*	*1,813*	*739*	*444*	*2*	*2,874*	*4,286*	*1,591*	*316*	*429*	*2*	*2,379*
(1) British Territory ...	*5,312*	*1,786*	*736*	*444*	*2*	*2,790*	*4,172*	*1,564*	*313*	*429*	*2*	*2,295*
SURMA VALLEY AND HILL DISTRICTS ...	*3,487*	*1,082*	*505*	*403*	*2*	*1,900*	*2,429*	*883*	*102*	*388*	*2*	*1,444*
Cachar ...	1	1	...	...	...	...	1	1	...	...	...	...
Sylhet ...	3,483	1,079	505	403	2	1,899	2,427	881	102	388	2	1,444
Khasi and Jaintia Hills ...	2	1	...	...	...	1	...	...	...	...	...	...
Naga Hills ...	1	1	...	...	...	...	1	1	...	...	...	...
Lushai Hills ...	...	...	...	...	...	...	...	...	...	...	...	...
ASSAM VALLEY DISTRICTS ...	*1,825*	*704*	*231*	*41*	...	*890*	*1,743*	*681*	*211*	*41*	...	*851*
Goalpara ...	215	66	36	6	...	113	202	62	33	6	...	107
Kamrup ...	517	204	54	1	...	259	468	192	43	1	...	233
Darrang ...	189	73	12	18	...	104	186	72	12	18	...	102
Nowgong ...	147	73	4	10	...	70	143	73	2	10	...	68
Sibsagar ...	428	168	106	4	...	154	425	166	106	4	...	153
Lakhimpur ...	310	115	11	2	...	184	301	111	8	2	...	182
Garo Hills ...	19	5	8	...	...	6	18	5	7	...	...	6
(2) Manipur State ...	*114*	*27*	*3*	...	...	*84*	*114*	*27*	*3*	...	...	*84*

TABLE XV.—OCCUPATION OR MEANS OF LIVELIHOOD. PART A.—GENERAL TABLE.—DETAILS FOR DISTRICTS—*contd.*

Class and Sub-Class ... / Order	CLASS B : SUB-CLASS III.—INDUSTRY.											
	11.—CHEMICAL PRODUCTS PROPERLY SO-CALLED, AND ANALOGOUS.						12.—FOOD INDUSTRIES.					
	55.—*Others (soap, candles, lac, cutch, perfumes and miscellaneous drugs).*						*TOTAL OF ORDER 12.*					
DISTRICT OR STATE.	TOTAL WORKERS AND DEPENDANTS.	ACTUAL WORKERS. Total. Males.	ACTUAL WORKERS. Total. Females.	ACTUAL WORKERS. *Partially agriculturist.* Males.	ACTUAL WORKERS. *Partially agriculturist.* Females.	DEPENDANTS. Both sexes.	TOTAL WORKERS AND DEPENDANTS.	ACTUAL WORKERS. Total. Males.	ACTUAL WORKERS. Total. Females.	ACTUAL WORKERS. *Partially agriculturist.* Males.	ACTUAL WORKERS. *Partially agriculturist.* Females.	DEPENDANTS. Both sexes.
1	242	243	244	245	246	247	248	249	250	251	252	253
ASSAM	*1,067*	*201*	*423*	*15*	...	*443*	*19,371*	*1,539*	*10,735*	*134*	*338*	*7,097*
(1) British Territory	*1,067*	*201*	*423*	*15*	...	*443*	*19,135*	*1,534*	*10,662*	*134*	*338*	*6,939*
SURMA VALLEY AND HILL DISTRICTS	*1,036*	*195*	*403*	*15*	...	*438*	*14,365*	*805*	*8,468*	*118*	*322*	*5,092*
Cachar	...	...	...	...	...	...	984	98	567	15	5	319
Sylhet	1,036	195	403	15	...	438	10,670	474	6,574	49	81	3,622
Khasi and Jaintia Hills	...	...	...	...	...	...	2,704	229	1,337	54	236	1,148
Naga Hills	...	...	...	...	...	...	6	3	...	...	...	3
Lushai Hills	...	...	...	...	...	...	1	1	...	...	...	...
ASSAM VALLEY DISTRICTS	*31*	*6*	*20*	...	...	*5*	*4,770*	*729*	*2,194*	*16*	*16*	*1,847*
Goalpara	3	...	3	...	...	...	2,691	171	1,537	5	11	913
Kamrup	19	5	11	...	...	2	731	91	338	...	1	302
Darrang	...	...	...	...	...	...	103	51	18	1	...	34
Nowgong	4	...	2	...	...	2	246	59	74	3	2	113
Sibsagar + ...	1	1	...	...	...	...	316	149	59	3	...	115
Lakhimpur	3	...	8	...	...	...	629	201	95	3	2	333
Garo Hills	1	...	1	...	...	...	124	14	73	1	...	37
(2) Manipur State	...	...	...	...	...	...	*236*	*5*	*73*	...	...	*158*

Class and Sub-Class ... / Order	CLASS B : SUB-CLASS III.—INDUSTRY.											
	12.—FOOD INDUSTRIES.											
	56.—*Rice pounders and huskers and flour grinders.*						64.—*Brewers and distillers.*					
DISTRICT OR STATE.	TOTAL WORKERS AND DEPENDANTS.	ACTUAL WORKERS. Total. Males.	ACTUAL WORKERS. Total. Females.	ACTUAL WORKERS. *Partially agriculturist.* Males.	ACTUAL WORKERS. *Partially agriculturist.* Females.	DEPENDANTS. Both sexes.	TOTAL WORKERS AND DEPENDANTS.	ACTUAL WORKERS. Total. Males.	ACTUAL WORKERS. Total. Females.	ACTUAL WORKERS. *Partially agriculturist.* Males.	ACTUAL WORKERS. *Partially agriculturist.* Females.	DEPENDANTS. Both sexes.
1	254	255	256	257	258	259	260	261	262	263	264	265
ASSAM	*13,637*	*341*	*8,670*	*14*	*89*	*4,626*	*9,516*	*187*	*1,323*	*47*	*231*	*1,006*
(1) British Territory	*13,635*	*340*	*8,670*	*14*	*89*	*4,625*	*9,440*	*187*	*1,273*	*47*	*231*	*980*
SURMA VALLEY AND HILL DISTRICTS	*10,330*	*136*	*6,865*	*12*	*76*	*3,329*	*9,395*	*152*	*1,273*	*46*	*231*	*970*
Cachar	791	12	517	...	5	262	...	...	...	...	...	...
Sylhet	9,507	121	6,334	12	71	3,052	...	...	...	...	...	...
Khasi and Jaintia Hills	32	3	14	...	...	15	2,394	151	1,272	46	231	970
Naga Hills	...	...	...	...	...	...	1	1	...	...	...	...
Lushai Hills	...	...	...	...	...	...	...	...	...	...	...	...
ASSAM VALLEY DISTRICTS	*3,305*	*204*	*2,805*	*2*	*13*	*1,296*	*45*	*35*	...	*2*	...	*10*
Goalpara	2,114	25	1,336	...	10	753	...	...	...	...	...	...
Kamrup	538	20	306	...	1	212	...	...	...	...	...	...
Darrang	11	1	8	...	...	2	10	9	...	...	...	1
Nowgong	181	38	59	1	2	84	...	...	...	...	...	...
Sibsagar	59	10	22	...	...	27	31	24	...	1	...	7
Lakhimpur	381	108	60	1	...	213	3	1	...	...	...	2
Garo Hills	21	2	14	...	...	5	1	1	...	...	...	...
(2) Manipur State	*2*	*1*	...	...	...	*1*	*76*	...	*50*	...	...	*96*

TABLE XV.—Occupation or means of Livelihood. Part A.—General Table—Details for Districts—*contd.*

Class and Sub-Class …	CLASS B: SUB-CLASS III.—INDUSTRY.											
Order …	13.—INDUSTRIES OF DRESS AND THE TOILET.											
	TOTAL OF ORDER 13.						68.—Tailors, milliners, dress makers and darners, embroiderers on linen.					
District or State.	Total workers and dependants.	Actual workers. Total.		Actual workers. Partially agriculturist.		Dependants.	Total workers and dependants.	Actual workers. Total.		Actual workers. Partially agriculturist.		Dependants.
		Males.	Females.	Males.	Females.	Both sexes.		Males.	Females.	Males.	Females.	Both sexes.
1	266	267	268	269	270	271	272	273	274	275	276	277
ASSAM	*36,090*	*14,269*	*2,354*	*3,782*	*61*	*19,467*	*10,018*	*4,153*	*791*	*283*	*19*	*5,074*
(1) ***British Territory***	*35,090*	*14,005*	*2,097*	*3,772*	*56*	*18,938*	*9,166*	*3,941*	*549*	*273*	*14*	*4,676*
SURMA VALLEY AND HILL DISTRICTS	*23,839*	*8,689*	*1,505*	*3,438*	*42*	*13,645*	*4,053*	*1,620*	*324*	*140*	*6*	*2,109*
Cachar	2,671	1,303	201	183	3	1,267	63	314	36	49	...	213
Sylhet	19,964	6,994	1,084	3,252	33	11,886	2,598	987	90	89	...	1,521
Khasi and Jaintia Hills	1,015	390	214	2	6	411	837	285	195	2	6	347
Naga Hills	128	58	5	1	...	65	47	17	2	...	...	28
Lushai Hills	61	44	1	...	...	16	18	17	1	...	...	...
ASSAM VALLEY DISTRICTS	*11,251*	*5,316*	*592*	*334*	*14*	*5,343*	*5,113*	*2,321*	*225*	*133*	*8*	*2,567*
Goalpara	2,373	1,167	26	119	...	1,180	586	322	16	21	...	248
Kamrup	2,139	766	100	38	2	1,273	854	313	45	16	2	496
Darrang	882	400	85	35	6	335	541	239	50	20	4	252
Nowgong	836	360	46	22	1	430	473	191	15	13	1	267
Sibsagar	2,540	1,244	158	80	2	1,138	1,418	626	32	49	...	760
Lakhimpur	2,396	1,260	173	40	3	963	1,181	592	63	14	1	526
Garo Hills	87	59	4	...	...	24	60	38	4	...	...	18
(2) ***Manipur State***	*1,000*	*264*	*257*	*10*	*5*	*479*	*852*	*212*	*242*	*10*	*5*	*398*

Class and Sub-Class …	CLASS B: SUB-CLASS III.—INDUSTRY.											
Order …	13.—INDUSTRIES OF DRESS AND THE TOILET.											
	69.—Shoe, boot and sandal makers.						71.—Washing, cleaning and dyeing.					
District or State.	Total workers and dependants.	Actual workers. Total.		Actual workers. Partially agriculturist.		Dependants.	Total workers and dependants.	Actual workers. Total.		Actual workers. Partially agriculturist.		Dependants.
		Males.	Females.	Males.	Females.	Both sexes.		Males.	Females.	Males.	Females.	Both sexes.
1	278	279	280	281	282	283	284	285	286	287	288	289
ASSAM	*1,852*	*835*	*28*	*67*	*1*	*989*	*8,956*	*3,320*	*1,437*	*1,140*	*40*	*4,199*
(1) ***British Territory***	*1,797*	*820*	*20*	*67*	*1*	*957*	*8,908*	*3,300*	*1,435*	*1,140*	*40*	*4,173*
SURMA VALLEY AND HILL DISTRICTS	*958*	*396*	*14*	*48*	...	*548*	*7,188*	*2,450*	*1,009*	*1,110*	*35*	*3,639*
Cachar	245	85	14	13	...	136	719	277	144	21	3	208
Sylhet	622	268	...	34	...	356	6,308	2,078	941	1,080	32	3,238
Khasi and Jaintia Hills	34	17	...	...	...	17	121	63	13	...	...	45
Naga Hills	46	14	...	1	...	32	18	14	...	...	...	4
Lushai Hills	11	4	...	...	...	7	22	18	...	...	...	4
ASSAM VALLEY DISTRICTS	*839*	*424*	*6*	*19*	*1*	*409*	*1,720*	*850*	*336*	*30*	*5*	*534*
Goalpara	141	100	...	2	...	41	191	98	9	1	...	84
Kamrup	211	103	2	2	...	106	194	91	50	1	...	53
Darrang	29	25	1	2	...	3	158	77	30	...	2	51
Nowgong	109	46	1	4	...	62	149	62	30	1	...	57
Sibsagar	136	68	2	6	1	66	499	235	111	17	1	153
Lakhimpur	208	78	...	3	...	130	521	279	106	10	2	136
Garo Hills	5	4	...	...	...	1	8	8	...	...	...	...
(2) ***Manipur State***	*55*	*15*	*3*	...	...	*32*	*48*	*20*	*2*	...	...	*26*

TABLE XV.—Occupation or means of Livelihood. Part A.—General Table—Details for Districts—*contd.*

Class and Sub-Class ... / Order ...	CLASS B: SUB-CLASS III.—INDUSTRY.											
	13.—INDUSTRIES OF DRESS AND THE TOILET.						14.—FURNITURE INDUSTRIES.					
	72.—*Barbers, hairdressers and wig makers.*						*TOTAL OF ORDER 14.*					
District or State.	Total workers and dependants.	Actual workers. Total.		Actual workers. Partially agriculturist.		Dependants.	Total workers and dependants.	Actual workers. Total.		Actual workers. Partially agriculturist.		Dependants.
		Males.	Females.	Males.	Females.	Both sexes.		Males.	Females.	Males.	Females.	Both sexes.
1	290	291	292	293	294	295	296	297	298	299	300	301
ASSAM ...	***14,949***	***5,329***	***79***	***2,288***	***1***	***9,041***	***73***	***45***	***4***	***2***	...	***24***
(1) British Territory ...	***14,934***	***5,818***	***79***	***2,288***	***1***	***9,037***	***69***	***45***	...	***2***	...	***24***
SURMA VALLEY AND HILL DISTRICTS ...	***11,411***	***4,124***	***57***	***2,136***	***1***	***7,230***	***25***	***9***	...	...	...	***16***
Cachar ...	1,144	517	7	100	...	620	1	1	...	...	...	...
Sylhet ...	10,220	3,565	50	2,036	1	6,605	24	8	...	...	...	16
Khasi and Jaintia Hills ...	24	24	...	...	...	...	...	...	...	...	...	...
Naga Hills ...	13	13	...	...	...	...	...	...	...	...	...	...
Lushai Hills ...	10	5	...	...	...	5	...	...	...	...	...	...
ASSAM VALLEY DISTRICTS ...	***3,523***	***1,694***	***22***	***152***	...	***1,807***	***44***	***36***	...	***2***	...	***8***
Goalpara ...	1,442	640	1	95	...	801	24	23	...	...	...	1
Kamrup ...	870	257	2	19	...	611	7	4	...	...	...	3
Darrang ...	148	116	3	3	...	29	...	...	...	...	...	...
Nowgong ...	89	54	...	4	...	35	...	...	...	...	...	...
Sibsagar ...	481	309	13	18	...	159	11	7	...	2	...	4
Lakhimpur ...	479	309	3	13	...	167	2	2	...	...	...	...
Garo Hills ...	14	9	...	...	...	5	...	...	...	...	...	...
(2) Manipur State ...	***15***	***11***	...	...	...	***4***	***4***	...	***4***	...	...	...

Class and Sub-Class ... / Order ...	CLASS B: SUB-CLASS III.—INDUSTRY.											
	15.—BUILDING INDUSTRIES.											
	TOTAL OF ORDER 15.						76.—*Lime burners, cement workers.*					
District or State.	Total workers and dependants.	Actual workers. Total.		Actual workers. Partially agriculturist.		Dependants.	Total workers and dependants.	Actual workers. Total.		Actual workers. Partially agriculturist.		Dependants
		Males.	Females.	Males.	Females.	Both sexes.		Males.	Females.	Males.	Females.	Both sexes.
1	302	303	304	305	306	307	308	309	310	311	312	313
ASSAM ...	***8,958***	***4,582***	***414***	***701***	***11***	***3,962***	***749***	***169***	***154***	***4***	***3***	***426***
(1) British Territory ...	***8,912***	***4,561***	***412***	***701***	***11***	***3,939***	***738***	***165***	***154***	***4***	***3***	***419***
SURMA VALLEY AND HILL DISTRICTS ...	***5,599***	***2,892***	***200***	***627***	***8***	***2,507***	***53***	***26***	***10***	***2***	...	***17***
Cachar ...	776	337	59	69	1	380	...	...	...	...	...	...
Sylhet ...	4,423	2,380	131	552	7	1,912	...	...	...	...	...	...
Khasi and Jaintia Hills ...	326	136	10	6	...	180	53	26	10	2	...	17
Naga Hills ...	40	23	...	...	...	17	...	...	...	...	...	...
Lushai Hills ...	34	16	...	...	...	18	...	...	...	...	...	...
ASSAM VALLEY DISTRICTS ...	***3,313***	***1,669***	***212***	***74***	***3***	***1,432***	***685***	***139***	***144***	***2***	***3***	***402***
Goalpara ...	584	332	22	9	...	230	65	17	12	...	...	36
Kamrup ...	1,159	405	125	40	2	629	566	115	106	2	2	345
Darrang ...	227	167	1	2	...	39	...	...	...	...	...	...
Nowgong ...	124	47	23	4	...	54	26	2	18	...	...	6
Sibsagar ...	239	156	10	3	...	73	6	1	4	...	...	1
Lakhimpur ...	966	530	31	16	1	405	22	4	4	...	1	14
Garo Hills ...	14	12	...	...	...	2	...	...	...	...	...	...
(2) Manipur State ...	***46***	***21***	***2***	...	...	***23***	***11***	***4***	...	...	...	***7***

TABLE XV.—OCCUPATION OR MEANS OF LIVELIHOOD. PART A.—GENERAL TABLE—DETAILS FOR DISTRICTS—*contd.*

Class and Sub-Class ... CLASS B: SUB-CLASS III.—INDUSTRY.

Order ... 15.—BUILDING INDUSTRIES.

District or State.	77.—Excavators, plinth builders and well sinkers. Total workers and dependants.	Actual workers. Total. Males.	Total. Females.	Partially agriculturist. Males.	Partially agriculturist. Females.	Dependants. Both sexes.
1	314	315	316	317	318	319
ASSAM	*3,004*	*1,780*	*203*	*427*	*8*	*1,021*
(1) British Territory	*3,004*	*1,780*	*203*	*427*	*8*	*1,021*
SURMA VALLEY AND HILL DISTRICTS	*2,864*	*1,658*	*188*	*427*	*8*	*1,018*
Cachar	619	217	59	43	1	343
Sylhet	2,245	1,441	129	384	7	675
Khasi and Jaintia Hills	...	...	...	...	...	...
Naga Hills	...	...	...	...	...	...
Lushai Hills	...	...	...	...	...	...
ASSAM VALLEY DISTRICTS	*140*	*122*	*15*	...	...	*3*
Goalpara	10	10	...	...	...	...
Kamrup	42	26	14	...	...	2
Darrang	80	80	...	...	...	...
Nowgong	...	...	...	...	...	...
Sibsagar	5	3	1	...	...	1
Lakhimpur	...	...	...	...	...	...
Garo Hills	3	3	...	...	...	...
(2) Manipur State	...	...	...	...	...	...

District or State.	78.—Stone and marble workers, masons and bricklayers. Total workers and dependants.	Actual workers. Total. Males.	Total. Females.	Partially agriculturist. Males.	Partially agriculturist. Females.	Dependants. Both sexes.
1	320	321	322	323	324	325
ASSAM	*3,044*	*1,507*	*10*	*170*	...	*1,527*
(1) British Territory	*3,026*	*1,498*	*9*	*170*	...	*1,19*
SURMA VALLEY AND HILL DISTRICTS	*1,840*	*823*	...	*128*	...	*1,017*
Cachar	124	94	...	19	...	80
Sylhet	1,371	582	...	105	...	789
Khasi and Jaintia Hills	273	110	...	4	...	163
Naga Hills	40	23	...	...	...	17
Lushai Hills	32	14	...	...	...	18
ASSAM VALLEY DISTRICTS	*1,186*	*675*	*9*	*42*	...	*509*
Goalpara	198	117	1	3	...	80
Kamrup	232	116	...	27	...	116
Darrang	123	84	1	2	...	38
Nowgong	81	89	5	2	...	37
Sibsagar	169	114	1	2	...	54
Lakhimpur	376	198	1	6	...	177
Garo Hills	7	7	...	...	...	...
(2) Manipur State	*18*	*9*	*1*	...	...	*8*

Class and Sub-Class ... CLASS B: SUB-CLASS III.—INDUSTRY.

Order ... 15.—BUILDING INDUSTRIES. 16.—CONSTRUCTION OF MEANS OF TRANSPORT.

District or State.	79.—Others (thatchers, building contractors, house painters, tilers, plumbers, locksmiths, etc.). Total workers and dependants.	Actual workers. Total. Males.	Total. Females.	Partially agriculturist. Males.	Partially agriculturist. Females.	Dependants. Both sexes.
1	326	327	328	329	330	331
ASSAM	*2,161*	*1,126*	*47*	*100*	...	*988*
(1) British Territory	*2,144*	*1,118*	*46*	*100*	...	*980*
SURMA VALLEY AND HILL DISTRICTS	*842*	*385*	*2*	*70*	...	*455*
Cachar	33	26	...	7	...	7
Sylhet	807	357	2	63	...	448
Khasi and Jaintia Hills	...	...	...	...	...	...
Naga Hills	...	...	...	...	...	...
Lushai Hills	2	2	...	...	...	...
ASSAM VALLEY DISTRICTS	*1,302*	*733*	*44*	*30*	...	*525*
Goalpara	311	188	9	6	...	114
Kamrup	319	148	5	11	...	166
Darrang	24	23	...	...	...	1
Nowgong	17	6	...	2	...	11
Sibsagar	56	38	4	1	...	17
Lakhimpur	568	328	26	10	...	214
Garo Hills	4	2	...	...	...	2
(2) Manipur State	*17*	*8*	*1*	...	...	*8*

District or State.	TOTAL OF ORDER 16. Total workers and dependants.	Actual workers. Total. Males.	Total. Females.	Partially agriculturist. Males.	Partially agriculturist. Females.	Dependants. Both sexes.
1	332	333	334	335	336	337
ASSAM	*640*	*356*	*5*	*27*	*1*	*279*
(1) British Territory	*608*	*344*	*5*	*27*	*1*	*259*
SURMA VALLEY AND HILL DISTRICTS	*160*	*87*	*3*	*20*	*1*	*70*
Cachar	...	...	...	...	...	...
Sylhet	125	61	...	20	...	64
Khasi and Jaintia Hills	35	26	3	...	1	6
Naga Hills	...	...	...	...	...	...
Lushai Hills	...	...	...	...	...	...
ASSAM VALLEY DISTRICTS	*448*	*257*	*2*	*7*	...	*189*
Goalpara	94	90	...	4	...	4
Kamrup	228	74	1	1	...	153
Darrang	37	34	...	...	...	3
Nowgong	25	16	...	2	...	9
Sibsagar	53	36	...	...	...	17
Lakhimpur	8	5	1	...	...	2
Garo Hills	3	2	...	...	...	1
(2) Manipur State	*32*	*12*	...	...	...	*20*

TABLE XV.—Occupation or Means of Livelihood. Part A.—General Table—Details for Districts—*contd.*

Class and Sub-Class ... Order ... District or State.	CLASS B: SUB-CLASS III.—INDUSTRY. 17.—Production and transmission of physical forces (heat, light, electricity, motive power, etc.) 83.—*Gas works, electric light and ice factories.* Total workers and dependants.	Actual workers. Total. Males.	Actual workers. Total. Females.	Actual workers. Partially agriculturist. Males.	Actual workers. Partially agriculturist. Females.	Dependants. Both sexes.	18.—Industries of luxury and those pertaining to literature and the arts and sciences. TOTAL OF ORDER 18. Total workers and dependants.	Actual workers. Total. Males.	Actual workers. Total. Females.	Actual workers. Partially agriculturist. Males.	Actual workers. Partially agriculturist. Females.	Dependants. Both sexes.
1	338	339	340	341	342	343	344	345	346	347	348	349
ASSAM	*4*	*3*	...	...	...	*1*	*17,736*	*6,900*	*280*	*1,039*	*14*	*10,556*
(1) British Territory	*4*	*3*	...	...	...	*1*	*17,067*	*6,680*	*206*	*1,019*	*14*	*10,181*
SURMA VALLEY AND HILL DISTRICTS	...	...	...	...	...	...	*8,673*	*3,433*	*16*	*555*	...	*5,224*
Cachar	...	...	...	...	...	...	697	356	...	29	...	251
Sylhet	...	...	...	...	...	...	6,845	2,538	8	522	...	4,299
Khasi and Jaintia Hills	...	...	...	...	...	...	1,203	534	8	4	...	661
Naga Hills	...	...	...	...	...	...	17	4	...	...	...	13
Lushai Hills	...	...	...	...	...	...	1	1	...	...	...	...
ASSAM VALLEY DISTRICTS	*4*	*3*	...	...	...	*1*	*8,394*	*3,247*	*190*	*464*	*14*	*4,957*
Goalpara	3	2	...	...	...	1	1,539	644	23	51	1	872
Kamrup	...	...	...	...	...	...	3,535	1,157	53	90	5	2,3[illegible]5
Darrang	...	...	...	...	...	...	687	300	37	73	6	350
Nowgong	1	1	...	...	...	...	550	213	36	100	...	301
Sibsagar	...	...	...	...	...	...	1,235	505	26	125	2	704
Lakhimpur	...	...	...	...	...	...	804	404	15	25	...	385
Garo Hills	...	...	...	...	...	...	44	24	...	...	...	20
(2) Manipur State	...	...	...	...	...	...	*669*	*290*	*74*	*20*	...	*375*

Class and Sub-Class ... Order ... District or State.	CLASS B: SUB-CLASS III.—INDUSTRY. 18.—Industries of luxury and those pertaining to literature and the arts and sciences. 84.—*Printers, lithographers, engravers, etc.* Total workers and dependants.	Actual workers. Total. Males.	Actual workers. Total. Females.	Actual workers. Partially agriculturist. Males.	Actual workers. Partially agriculturist. Females.	Dependants. Both sexes.	89.—*Workers in precious stones and metals, enamellers, immitation jewelery makers, gilders, etc.* Total workers and dependants.	Actual workers. Total. Males.	Actual workers. Total. Females.	Actual workers. Partially agriculturist. Males.	Actual workers. Partially agriculturist. Females.	Dependants. Both sexes.
1	350	351	352	353	354	355	356	357	358	359	360	361
ASSAM	*1,042*	*431*	*5*	*8*	...	*606*	*15,647*	*5,985*	*212*	*995*	*13*	*9,450*
(1) British Territory	*1,041*	*430*	*5*	*8*	...	*606*	*15,184*	*5,854*	*152*	*988*	*13*	*9,178*
SURMA VALLEY AND HILL DISTRICTS	*861*	*358*	*5*	*7*	...	*498*	*7,409*	*2,910*	*3*	*535*	...	*4,496*
Cachar	...	...	...	...	...	...	596	350	...	27	...	246
Sylhet	63	29	...	5	...	34	6,445	2,373	...	506	...	4,072
Khasi and Jaintia Hills	798	329	5	2	...	464	350	182	3	2	...	165
Naga Hills	...	...	...	...	...	...	17	4	...	...	...	13
Lushai Hills	...	...	...	...	...	...	7	1	...	...	...	...
ASSAM VALLEY DISTRICTS	*180*	*72*	...	*1*	...	*108*	*7,775*	*2,944*	*149*	*453*	*13*	*4,682*
Goalpara	15	5	...	...	...	10	1,401	572	11	47	1	818
Kamrup	19	11	...	...	...	8	3,400	1,103	33	87	4	2,264
Darrang	15	7	...	...	...	8	624	275	30	71	6	319
Nowgong	8	3	...	1	...	5	529	199	36	99	...	294
Sibsagar	23	8	...	...	...	15	1,161	456	25	124	2	680
Lakhimpur	100	38	...	...	...	62	618	317	14	25	...	287
Garo Hills	...	...	...	...	...	...	42	22	...	...	...	20
(2) Manipur State	*1*	*1*	...	...	...	...	*463*	*131*	*60*	*7*	...	*272*

TABLE XV.—OCCUPATION OR MEANS OF LIVELIHOOD. PART A.—GENERAL TABLE—DETAILS FOR DISTRICTS—*contd.*

Class and Sub-Class ...	*CLASS B : SUB-CLASS III.—INDUSTRY.*						*CLASS B : SUB-CLASS IV.—TRANSPORT.*					
Order	10.—INDUSTRIES CONCERNED WITH REFUSE MATTER.						20.—TRANSPORT BY WATER.					
	93.—Sweepers, scavengers, dust and sweeping contractors.						*TOTAL OF ORDER 20.*					
District or State.	Total workers and dependants.	Actual workers. Total. Males.	Actual workers. Total. Females.	Partially agriculturist. Males.	Partially agriculturist. Females.	Dependants. Both sexes.	Total workers and dependants.	Actual workers. Total. Males.	Actual workers. Total. Females.	Partially agriculturist. Males.	Partially agriculturist. Females.	Dependants. Both sexes.
1	362	363	364	365	366	367	368	369	370	371	372	373
ASSAM	***3,403***	***1,395***	***401***	***29***	***1***	***1,607***	***23,841***	***13,409***	***29***	***1,577***	***9***	***10,403***
(1) British Territory	***3,063***	***1,299***	***305***	***29***	***1***	***1,369***	***23,831***	***13,402***	***28***	***1,576***	***9***	***10,401***
SURMA VALLEY AND HILL DISTRICTS	*1,157*	*486*	*156*	*11*	*1*	*515*	*16,781*	*8,000*	*5*	*1,232*	...	*8,776*
Cachar	209	98	40	4	...	71	684	492	...	32	...	192
Sylhet	486	170	79	2	1	237	16,030	7,452	5	1,183	...	8,573
Khasi and Jaintia Hills	246	132	33	...	...	81	22	17	...	...	...	5
Naga Hills	62	38	1	...	...	23	...	...	...	...	...	...
Lushai Hills	154	48	3	5	...	103	45	39	...	17	...	6
ASSAM VALLEY DISTRICTS...	*1,906*	*813*	*239*	*18*	...	*854*	*7,050*	*5,402*	*23*	*344*	*9*	*1,625*
Goalpara	582	231	42	7	...	309	3,234	2,494	4	81	...	736
Kamrup	341	125	41	1	...	175	1,089	714	...	37	...	375
Darrang	133	63	25	...	...	45	541	382	...	56	...	159
Nowgong	171	74	23	2	...	74	282	249	9	42	9	24
Sibsagar	252	117	35	...	...	100	799	658	5	41	...	136
Lakhimpur	413	202	73	8	...	138	1,094	896	5	87	...	193
Garo Hills	14	11	...	...	...	3	11	9	...	...	...	2
(2) Manipur State	***340***	***96***	***6***	...	...	***238***	***10***	***7***	***1***	***1***	...	***2***

Class and Sub-Class ...	*CLASS B: SUB-CLASS IV.—TRANSPORT.*											
Order	20.—TRANSPORT BY WATER.											
	95.—Ship owners and their employés, ship brokers, ships' officers, engineers, mariners and firemen.						*97.—Boat owners, boatmen and towmen.*					
District or State.	Total workers and dependants.	Actual workers. Total. Males.	Actual workers. Total. Females.	Partially agriculturist. Males.	Partially agriculturist. Females.	Dependants. Both sexes.	Total workers and dependants.	Actual workers. Total. Males.	Actual workers. Total. Females.	Partially agriculturist. Males.	Partially agriculturist. Females.	Dependants. Both sexes.
1	374	375	376	377	378	379	380	381	382	383	384	385
ASSAM	***3,043***	***2,203***	***4***	***468***	...	***836***	***20,480***	***11,068***	***16***	***1,108***	...	***9,396***
(1) British Territory	***3,043***	***2,203***	***4***	***468***	...	***836***	***20,471***	***11,062***	***15***	***1,107***	...	***9,394***
SURMA VALLEY AND HILL DISTRICTS	*1,059*	*656*	...	*204*	...	*403*	*15,722*	*7,344*	*5*	*1,028*	...	*8,378*
Cachar	72	67	...	18	...	5	612	425	...	64	...	187
Sylhet	980	584	...	186	...	396	15,050	6,868	5	947	...	8,177
Khasi and Jaintia Hills	7	5	...	...	...	2	15	12	...	...	...	3
Naga Hills	...	...	...	...	...	...	...	...	...	...	...	...
Lushai Hills	...	...	...	...	...	...	45	39	...	17	...	6
ASSAM VALLEY DISTRICTS	*1,984*	*1,547*	*4*	*264*	...	*433*	*4,749*	*3,718*	*10*	*79*	...	*1,021*
Goalpara	455	378	...	33	...	77	2,670	2,087	4	48	...	579
Kamrup	354	225	...	26	...	129	692	468	...	11	...	224
Darrang	352	256	...	52	...	96	110	95	...	4	...	15
Nowgong	100	88	...	42	...	12	146	138	...	...	...	8
Sibsagar	344	299	...	32	...	45	413	332	5	9	...	76
Lakhimpur	379	301	4	79	...	74	707	589	1	7	...	117
Garo Hills	...	...	...	...	...	...	11	9	...	...	...	2
(2) Manipur State	...	...	...	...	...	...	***9***	***6***	***1***	***1***	...	***2***

TABLE XV.—OCCUPATION OR MEANS OF LIVELIHOOD. PART A.—GENERAL TABLE—DETAILS FOR DISTRICTS—*contd.*

Class and Sub-Class ...	* CLASS B: SUB-CLASS IV.—TRANSPORT.											
Order	21.—TRANSPORT BY ROAD.											
	TOTAL OF ORDER 21.						98.—Persons employed on the construction and maintenance of roads and bridges.					
DISTRICT OR STATE.	TOTAL WORKERS AND DEPENDANTS.	ACTUAL WORKERS. Total. Males.	ACTUAL WORKERS. Total. Females.	ACTUAL WORKERS. Partially agriculturist. Males.	ACTUAL WORKERS. Partially agriculturist. Females.	DEPENDANTS. Both sexes.	TOTAL WORKERS AND DEPENDANTS.	ACTUAL WORKERS. Total. Males.	ACTUAL WORKERS. Total. Females.	ACTUAL WORKERS. Partially agriculturist. Males.	ACTUAL WORKERS. Partially agriculturist. Females.	DEPENDANTS. Both sexes.
1	386	387	388	389	390	391	392	393	394	395	396	397
ASSAM ...	*34,268*	*21,017*	*2,828*	*2,197*	*359*	*10,423*	*13,967*	*10,342*	*954*	*970*	*25*	*2,671*
(1) *British Territory* ...	*32,882*	*20,302*	*2,822*	*2,087*	*359*	*9,758*	*13,880*	*10,303*	*953*	*970*	*25*	*2,624*
SURMA VALLEY AND HILL DISTRICTS ...	*15,131*	*7,216*	*2,016*	*1,300*	*340*	*5,899*	*4,726*	*3,003*	*228*	*406*	*7*	*1,495*
Cachar ...	1,022	506	54	22	...	462	571	275	54	7	...	242
Sylhet ...	7,446	4,077	185	844	8	3,184	3,716	2,400	160	342	7	1,096
Khasi and Jaintia Hills ...	6,157	2,197	1,776	401	332	2,184	336	237	13	54	...	136
Naga Hills ...	336	307	1	24	...	28	32	18	1	...	...	13
Lushai Hills ...	170	129	...	9	...	41	21	13	...	3	...	8
ASSAM VALLEY DISTRICTS ...	*17,751*	*13,086*	*806*	*787*	*19*	*3,859*	*9,154*	*7,300*	*725*	*564*	*18*	*1,129*
Goalpara ...	5,137	4,654	222	146	...	861	3,168	2,523	211	91	...	434
Kamrup ...	4,854	3,181	394	208	18	1,279	2,686	1,945	367	180	18	374
Darrang ...	2,017	1,610	17	295	...	390	850	826	6	272	...	18
Nowgong ...	1,488	1,088	48	29	...	357	590	466	35	6	...	89
Sibsagar ...	2,287	1,847	78	64	...	362	1,244	1,051	73	9	...	170
Lakhimpur ...	1,793	1,174	44	43	1	575	547	434	31	5	...	82
Garo Hills ...	175	137	3	2	...	35	69	55	2	1	...	12
(2) *Manipur State* ...	*1,386*	*715*	*6*	*110*	...	*665*	*87*	*39*	*1*	...	...	*47*

Class and Sub-Class ...	CLASS B: SUB-CLASS IV.—TRANSPORT.											
Order ...	21.—TRANSPORT BY ROAD.											
	99.—Cart owners and drivers, coachmen, stable boys, tramway, mail carriage, etc., managers and employés, (excluding private servants).						100.—Palki, etc., bearers and owners.					
DISTRICT OR STATE.	TOTAL WORKERS AND DEPENDANTS.	ACTUAL WORKERS. Total. Males.	ACTUAL WORKERS. Total. Females.	ACTUAL WORKERS. Partially agriculturist. Males.	ACTUAL WORKERS. Partially agriculturist. Females.	DEPENDANTS. Both sexes.	TOTAL WORKERS AND DEPENDANTS.	ACTUAL WORKERS. Total. Males.	ACTUAL WORKERS. Total. Females.	ACTUAL WORKERS. Partially agriculturist. Males.	ACTUAL WORKERS. Partially agriculturist. Females.	DEPENDANTS. Both sexes.
1	398	399	400	401	402	403	404	405	406	407	408	409
ASSAM ...	*10,194*	*6,694*	*67*	*384*	*1*	*3,433*	*3,503*	*1,615*	...	*423*	...	*1,888*
(1) *British Territory* ...	*9,053*	*6,074*	*62*	*276*	*1*	*2,917*	*3,499*	*1,611*	...	*423*	...	*1,888*
SURMA VALLEY AND HILL DISTRICTS ...	*1,932*	*1,256*	*8*	*106*	...	*668*	*3,075*	*1,273*	...	*404*	...	*1,802*
Cachar ...	403	201	...	13	...	202	47	30	...	2	...	17
Sylhet ...	514	255	...	21	...	259	3,023	1,240	...	402	...	1,783
Khasi and Jaintia Hills ...	634	450	8	45	...	176	5	3	...	...	...	2
Naga Hills ...	275	274	...	23	...	1	...	...	...	...	...	...
Lushai Hills ...	106	76	...	4	...	30	...	...	...	...	...	...
ASSAM VALLEY DISTRICTS ...	*7,121*	*4,818*	*54*	*170*	*1*	*2,249*	*424*	*338*	...	*19*	...	*86*
Goalpara ...	1,564	1,170	7	37	...	387	329	298	...	16	...	31
Kamrup ...	1,527	911	19	11	...	597	70	25	...	1	...	45
Darrang ...	1,091	719	11	22	...	361	...	...	...	...	...	...
Nowgong ...	839	583	6	23	...	250	1	1	...	...	...	...
Sibsagar ...	926	722	5	46	...	199	9	4	...	2	...	5
Lakhimpur ...	1,074	636	5	30	1	433	11	6	...	...	...	5
Garo Hills ...	100	77	1	1	...	23	4	4	...	...	...	...
(2) *Manipur State* ...	*1,141*	*620*	*5*	*108*	...	*516*	*4*	*4*	...	...	...	...

TABLE XV.—Occupation or Means of Livelihood. Part A.—General Table—Details for Districts—*contd.*

Class and Sub-Class … CLASS B: SUB-CLASS IV.—TRANSPORT.

Order …

District or State.	21.—Transport by road. 102.—Porters and messengers. Total workers and dependants.	Actual workers. Total. Males.	Total. Females.	Partially agriculturist. Males.	Partially agriculturist. Females.	Dependants. Both sexes.	22.—Transport by rail. Total of Order 22. Total workers and dependants.	Actual workers. Total. Males.	Total. Females.	Partially agriculturist. Males.	Partially agriculturist. Females.	Dependants. Both sexes.
1	410	411	412	413	414	415	416	417	418	419	420	421
ASSAM	*6,581*	*2,343*	*1,807*	*420*	*333*	*2,431*	*13,877*	*7,927*	*1,179*	*419*	*11*	*4,778*
(1) British Territory	*6,427*	*2,291*	*1,807*	*418*	*333*	*2,329*	*13,877*	*7,927*	*1,179*	*419*	*11*	*4,778*
SURMA VALLEY AND HILL DISTRICTS	*5,375*	*1,661*	*1,780*	*384*	*333*	*1,034*	*3,777*	*1,918*	*575*	*215*	*8*	*1,284*
Cachar	1	…	…	…	…	1	1,896	940	375	46	…	591
Sylhet	103	122	25	79	1	46	1,860	805	296	155	8	669
Khasi and Jaintia Hills	5,132	1,507	1,755	302	332	1,870	111	83	…	14	…	24
Naga Hills	20	15	…	1	…	14	…	…	…	…	…	…
Lushai Hills	20	17	…	2	…	3	…	…	…	…	…	…
ASSAM VALLEY DISTRICTS	*1,052*	*630*	*27*	*34*	…	*395*	*10,100*	*6,009*	*597*	*204*	*3*	*3,494*
Goalpara	76	63	4	[illegible]	…	9	2,016	1,303	223	26	…	490
Kamrup	571	300	8	16	…	263	2,164	1,297	191	51	…	676
Darrang	70	65	…	1	…	11	306	165	8	28	…	133
Nowgong	58	33	7	…	…	18	1,898	1,146	29	16	1	640
Sibsagar	198	70	…	[illegible]	…	38	1,438	897	74	29	…	467
Lakhimpur	161	98	8	8	…	55	2,387	1,201	79	54	2	1,087
Garo Hills	2	1	…	…	…	1	1	…	…	…	…	1
(2) Manipur State	*154*	*59*	…	*2*	…	*109*	…	…	…	…	…	…

Class and Sub-Class … CLASS B: SUB-CLASS IV. TRANSPORT.

Order … 22.—TRANSPORT BY RAIL.

District or State.	103.—Railway employés of all kinds other than construction coolies. Total workers and dependants.	Actual workers. Total. Males.	Total. Females.	Partially agriculturist. Males.	Partially agriculturist. Females.	Dependants. Both sexes.	104.—Labourers employed on railway construction. Total workers and dependants.	Actual workers. Total. Males.	Total. Females.	Partially agriculturist. Males.	Partially agriculturist. Females.	Dependants. Both sexes.
1	422	423	424	425	426	427	428	429	430	431	432	433
ASSAM	*11,213*	*6,577*	*395*	*408*	*3*	*4,241*	*2,664*	*1,350*	*777*	*11*	*8*	*557*
(1) British Territory	*11,213*	*6,577*	*395*	*408*	*3*	*4,241*	*2,664*	*1,350*	*777*	*11*	*8*	*537*
SURMA VALLEY AND HILL DISTRICTS	*2,029*	*1,178*	*5*	*205*	…	*846*	*1,748*	*740*	*570*	*10*	*8*	*438*
Cachar	793	446	…	45	…	347	1,013	494	275	1	…	244
Sylhet	1,125	649	1	146	…	475	735	246	295	9	8	194
Khasi and Jaintia Hills	111	83	4	14	…	24	…	…	…	…	…	…
Naga Hills	…	…	…	…	…	…	…	…	…	…	…	…
Lushai Hills	…	…	…	…	…	…	…	…	…	…	…	…
ASSAM VALLEY DISTRICTS	*9,184*	*5,399*	*390*	*203*	*3*	*3,395*	*916*	*610*	*207*	*1*	…	*99*
Goalpara	1,199	754	33	26	…	412	617	549	190	…	…	78
Kamrup	2,122	1,280	181	51	…	661	42	17	10	…	…	15
Darrang	290	131	1	28	…	128	46	34	7	…	…	5
Nowgong	1,808	1,146	22	13	1	640	…	…	…	…	…	…
Sibsagar	1,427	887	74	28	…	466	11	10	…	…	…	…
Lakhimpur	2,367	1,201	79	54	2	1,087	…	…	…	1	…	1
Garo Hills	1	…	…	…	…	1	…	…	…	…	…	…
(2) Manipur State	…	…	…	…	…	…	…	…	…	…	…	…

TABLE XV.—Occupation or means of Livelihood. Part A.—General Table—Details for Districts—*contd.*

Class and Sub-Class ...	CLASS B: SUB-CLASS IV.—TRANSPORT.						CLASS B: SUB-CLASS V.—TRADE.					
Order	23.—POST OFFICE, TELEGRAPH AND TELEPHONE SERVICES.						24.—BANKS, ESTABLISHMENTS OF CREDIT, EXCHANGE AND INSURANCE.					
	105.—Post Office, Telegraph and Telephone services.						*106.—Bank managers, money lenders, exchange and insurance agents, money changers and brokers and their employés.*					
District or State.	Total workers and dependants.	Actual workers. Total. Males.	Actual workers. Total. Females.	Actual workers. Partially agriculturist. Males.	Actual workers. Partially agriculturist. Females.	Dependants. Both sexes.	Total workers and dependants.	Actual workers. Total. Males.	Actual workers. Total. Females.	Actual workers. Partially agriculturist. Males.	Actual workers. Partially agriculturist. Females.	Dependants. Both sexes.
1	434	435	436	437	438	439	440	441	442	443	444	445
ASSAM	*4,614*	*2,332*	...	*287*	...	*2,282*	*6,408*	*1,679*	*452*	*534*	*20*	*4,277*
(1) British Territory	*4,538*	*2,292*	...	*287*	...	*2,246*	*6,402*	*1,675*	*452*	*533*	*20*	*4,275*
SURMA VALLEY AND HILL DISTRICTS	*2,093*	*1,003*	...	*184*	...	*1,090*	*5,175*	*1,169*	*349*	*476*	*13*	*3,657*
Cachar	634	273	...	65	...	361	261	73	17	15	2	171
Sylhet	989	444	...	113	...	545	4,373	1,088	314	461	10	3,471
Khasi and Jaintia Hills	170	94	...	1	...	76	37	7	17	...	1	13
Naga Hills	149	90	...	2	...	59	3	...	1	...	...	2
Lushai Hills	151	102	...	3	...	49	1	1	...	...	...	...
ASSAM VALLEY DISTRICTS	*2,445*	*1,289*	...	*103*	...	*1,156*	*1,227*	*506*	*103*	*57*	*7*	*618*
Goalpara	392	188	...	15	...	204	850	406	56	44	4	388
Kamrup	630	251	...	14	...	379	309	72	39	12	1	198
Darrang	200	132	...	9	...	68	9	6	1	...	1	2
Nowgong	279	190	...	21	...	89	13	2	2	1	1	9
Sibsagar	495	289	...	30	...	206	14	5	4	...	...	5
Lakhimpur	412	223	...	14	...	189	11	5	...	...	...	6
Garo Hills	37	16	...	...	...	21	21	10	1	...	...	10
(2) Manipur State	*76*	*40*	...	...	...	*36*	*6*	*4*	...	*1*	...	*2*

Class and Sub-Class ...	CLASS B: SUB-CLASS V.—TRADE.											
Order	25.—BROKERAGE, COMMISSION AND EXPORT.						26.—TRADE IN TEXTILES.					
	107.—Brokers, commission agents, commercial travellers, warehouse owners and employés.						*108.—Trade in piece-goods, wool, cotton, silk, hair and other textiles.*					
District or State.	Total workers and dependants.	Actual workers. Total. Males.	Actual workers. Total. Females.	Actual workers. Partially agriculturist. Males.	Actual workers. Partially agriculturist. Females.	Dependants. Both sexes.	Total workers and dependants.	Actual workers. Total. Males.	Actual workers. Total. Females.	Actual workers. Partially agriculturist. Males.	Actual workers. Partially agriculturist. Females.	Dependants. Both sexes.
1	446	447	448	449	450	451	452	453	454	455	456	457
ASSAM	*413*	*187*	*3*	*4*	...	*223*	*15,323*	*5,730*	*3,258*	*638*	*32*	*6,335*
(1) British Territory	*412*	*187*	*2*	*4*	...	*223*	*11,779*	*5,543*	*750*	*635*	*31*	*5,486*
SURMA VALLEY AND HILL DISTRICTS	*227*	*92*	*1*	...	...	*134*	*7,282*	*3,057*	*638*	*532*	*28*	*3,587*
Cachar	2	2	...	...	...	...	1,207	688	167	44	...	352
Sylhet	223	88	1	...	...	134	4,896	2,056	271	443	2	2,569
Khasi and Jaintia Hills	2	2	...	...	...	...	1,168	305	199	45	26	664
Naga Hills	...	...	...	...	...	...	11	8	1	...	...	2
Lushai Hills	...	...	...	...	...	...	...	...	...	...	...	...
ASSAM VALLEY DISTRICTS	*185*	*95*	*1*	*4*	...	*89*	*4,497*	*2,486*	*112*	*103*	*3*	*1,899*
Goalpara	106	43	...	3	...	63	1,352	792	9	37	...	551
Kamrup	29	11	...	1	...	18	1,165	427	29	38	...	709
Darrang	7	5	...	...	...	2	253	200	5	12	1	48
Nowgong	16	15	...	...	...	1	254	156	1	3	...	97
Sibsagar	22	17	1	...	...	4	863	530	43	8	1	290
Lakhimpur	2	1	...	...	...	1	551	338	25	3	1	188
Garo Hills	3	3	...	...	...	...	59	43	...	2	...	16
(2) Manipur State	*1*	...	*1*	...	...	...	*3,544*	*187*	*2,508*	*3*	*1*	*849*

TABLE XV.—OCCUPATION OR MEANS OF LIVELIHOOD. PART A.—GENERAL TABLE—DETAILS FOR DISTRICTS—*contd.*

Class and Sub-Class ...	*CLASS B : SUB-CLASS V.—TRADE.*											
Order	27.—TRADE IN SKINS, LEATHER AND FURS.						28.—TRADE IN WOOD.					
	109.—Trade in skins, leather, furs, feathers, horn, etc.						*110.—Trade in wood (not firewood), cork, bark, etc.*					
DISTRICT OR STATE.	TOTAL WORKERS AND DEPENDANTS.	ACTUAL WORKERS. Total. Males.	ACTUAL WORKERS. Total. Females.	ACTUAL WORKERS. *Partially agriculturist.* Males.	ACTUAL WORKERS. *Partially agriculturist.* Females.	DEPENDANTS. Both sexes.	TOTAL WORKERS AND DEPENDANTS.	ACTUAL WORKERS. Total. Males.	ACTUAL WORKERS. Total. Females.	ACTUAL WORKERS. *Partially agriculturist.* Males.	ACTUAL WORKERS. *Partially agriculturist.* Females.	DEPENDANTS. Both sexes.
1	458	459	460	461	462	463	464	465	466	467	468	469
ASSAM ...	*8,049*	*3,403*	*128*	*513*	*21*	*4,518*	*3,510*	*1,421*	*206*	*226*	*5*	*1,892*
(1) ***British Territory***	*8,046*	*3,402*	*127*	*512*	*21*	*4,517*	*3,184*	*1,303*	*163*	*225*	*5*	*1,718*
SURMA VALLEY AND HILL DISTRICTS	*6,308*	*2,370*	*65*	*373*	*6*	*3,873*	*2,389*	*961*	*110*	*190*	*1*	*1,318*
Cachar ...	412	154	6	48	1	252	179	60	52	17	...	67
Sylhet ...	5,887	2,214	57	324	5	3,616	2,045	822	36	163	...	1,187
Khasi and Jaintia Hills	9	2	2	1	...	5	99	40	18	6	...	41
Naga Hills ...	...	...	...	...	...	...	5	4	...	...	...	1
Lushai Hills ...	...	...	...	...	...	...	61	35	4	4	1	22
ASSAM VALLEY DISTRICTS ...	*1,738*	*1,032*	*62*	*139*	*15*	*644*	*795*	*342*	*53*	*35*	*4*	*400*
Goalpara ...	887	518	9	77	...	360	305	115	13	22	...	177
Kamrup ...	253	187	15	36	14	51	176	62	3	9	1	111
Darrang ...	175	108	10	7	...	57	56	1	20	...	3	35
Nowgong ...	107	57	1	6	...	49	7	...	2	...	...	5
Sibsagar ...	281	140	25	13	1	116	139	87	12	4	...	40
Lakhimpur ...	22	15	2	...	...	5	107	73	3	...	...	31
Garo Hills ...	13	7	...	...	...	6	5	4	...	...	...	1
(2) ***Manipur State***	*3*	*1*	*1*	...	...	*1*	*335*	*118*	*43*	*1*	...	*174*

Class and Sub-Class ...	*CLASS B : SUB-CLASS V.—TRADE.*											
Order	29.—TRADE IN METALS.						30.—TRADE IN POTTERY.					
	111.—Trade in metals, machinery, knife, tool, etc., sellers.						*112.—Trade in pottery.*					
DISTRICT OR STATE.	TOTAL WORKERS AND DEPENDANTS.	ACTUAL WORKERS. Total. Males.	ACTUAL WORKERS. Total. Females.	ACTUAL WORKERS. *Partially agriculturist.* Males.	ACTUAL WORKERS. *Partially agriculturist.* Females.	DEPENDANTS. Both sexes.	TOTAL WORKERS AND DEPENDANTS.	ACTUAL WORKERS. Total. Males.	ACTUAL WORKERS. Total. Females.	ACTUAL WORKERS. *Partially agriculturist.* Males.	ACTUAL WORKERS. *Partially agriculturist.* Females.	DEPENDANTS. Both sexes.
1	470	471	472	473	474	475	476	477	478	479	480	481
ASSAM ...	*659*	*319*	*44*	*9*	*1*	*296*	*3,208*	*1,413*	*267*	*214*	*12*	*1,528*
(1) ***British Territory***	*624*	*317*	*15*	*9*	*1*	*292*	*3,170*	*1,409*	*243*	*214*	*12*	*1,518*
SURMA VALLEY AND HILL DISTRICTS	*38*	*11*	*7*	*1*	*1*	*20*	*598*	*275*	*58*	*152*	*1*	*265*
Cachar ...	...	...	...	...	...	...	67	54	...	22	...	13
Sylhet ...	12	3	4	...	...	5	511	216	56	125	1	239
Khasi and Jaintia Hills	26	8	3	1	1	15	7	5	...	5	...	2
Naga Hills ...	...	...	...	...	...	...	3	...	1	...	...	2
Lushai Hills ...	...	...	...	...	...	...	10	...	1	...	...	9
ASSAM VALLEY DISTRICTS	*586*	*306*	*8*	*8*	...	*272*	*2,572*	*1,134*	*185*	*62*	*11*	*1,253*
Goalpara ...	117	66	4	4	...	47	1,114	440	109	18	...	565
Kamrup ...	322	142	...	1	...	180	1,257	585	44	23	...	623
Darrang ...	39	29	...	1	...	10	44	34	8	3	7	2
Nowgong ...	12	9	...	...	...	3	44	3	1	...	...	2
Sibsagar ...	54	39	2	2	...	13	6	59	21	17	4	48
Lakhimpur ...	40	20	2	...	...	18	128	13	2	1	...	8
Garo Hills ...	2	1	...	...	...	1	23	...	...	...	...	...
(2) ***Manipur State***	*35*	*2*	*29*	...	...	*4*	*38*	*4*	*24*	...	...	*10*

TABLE XV.—Occupation or Means of Livelihood. Part A.—General Table—Details for Districts—*contd.*

Class and Sub-class ...	CLASS B : SUB-CLASS V.—TRADE.											
Order	31.—TRADE IN CHEMICAL PRODUCTS.						32.—HOTELS, CAFES, RESTAURANTS, ETC.					
	113.—Trade in Chemical products (drugs, dyes, paints, petroleum, explosives, etc.)						TOTAL OF ORDER 32.					
District or State.	Total workers and dependants.	Actual workers. Total. Males.	Actual workers. Total. Females.	Actual workers. Partially agriculturist. Males.	Actual workers. Partially agriculturist. Females.	Dependants. Both sexes.	Total workers and dependants.	Actual workers. Total. Males.	Actual workers. Total. Females.	Actual workers. Partially agriculturist. Males.	Actual workers. Partially agriculturist. Females.	Dependants. Both sexes.
1	482	483	484	485	486	487	488	489	490	491	492	493
ASSAM	*1,811*	*687*	*228*	*60*	*2*	*896*	*1,921*	*636*	*528*	*40*	*7*	*757*
(1) British Territory	*1,790*	*685*	*214*	*60*	*2*	*891*	*1,377*	*614*	*104*	*39*	*7*	*650*
SURMA VALLEY AND HILL DISTRICTS	*789*	*224*	*181*	*43*	*2*	*384*	*667*	*201*	*94*	*21*	*6*	*372*
Cachar	104	12	64	...	...	28	33	21	...	1	...	12
Sylhet	527	127	100	35	1	201	371	126	...	16	...	245
Khasi and Jaintia Hills	158	85	8	8	1	65	220	35	93	2	6	92
Naga Hills	...	...	...	...	...	...	20	7	1	2	...	18
Lushai Hills	...	...	...	...	...	...	23	12	...	...	...	11
ASSAM VALLEY DISTRICTS	*1,001*	*461*	*33*	*17*	...	*507*	*710*	*413*	*10*	*18*	*1*	*287*
Goalpara	319	114	16	2	...	189	158	81	4	5	...	73
Kamrup	259	130	5	5	...	124	82	45	...	...	...	37
Darrang	35	27	2	...	...	6	53	40	...	2	...	13
Nowgong	289	141	5	7	...	143	63	42	1	3	...	20
Sibsagar	46	19	5	1	...	22	148	106	4	5	...	38
Lakhimpur	36	13	...	2	...	23	194	91	1	3	1	102
Garo Hills	17	17	...	...	...	...	12	8	...	...	...	4
(2) Manipur State	*21*	*2*	*14*	...	...	*5*	*544*	*22*	*424*	*1*	...	*98*

Class and Sub-class ...	CLASS B : SUB-CLASS V.—TRADE.											
Order	33.—OTHER TRADE IN FOOD STUFFS.											
	TOTAL OF ORDER 33.						116.—Fish dealers.					
District or State.	Total workers and dependants.	Actual workers. Total. Males.	Actual workers. Total. Females.	Actual workers. Partially agriculturist. Males.	Actual workers. Partially agriculturist. Females.	Dependants. Both sexes.	Total workers and dependants.	Actual workers. Total. Males.	Actual workers. Total. Females.	Actual workers. Partially agriculturist. Males.	Actual workers. Partially agriculturist. Females.	Dependants. Both sexes.
1	494	495	496	497	498	499	500	501	502	503	504	505
ASSAM	*163,089*	*47,440*	*24,459*	*8,740*	*885*	*91,190*	*60,234*	*11,993*	*8,987*	*3,902*	*458*	*39,254*
(1) British Territory	*155,503*	*46,592*	*20,615*	*8,723*	*882*	*88,296*	*58,908*	*11,878*	*8,270*	*3,898*	*458*	*38,760*
SURMA VALLEY AND HILL DISTRICTS	*94,638*	*26,129*	*8,671*	*7,795*	*488*	*59.838*	*45,537*	*9,736*	*2,544*	*3,761*	*201*	*33,257*
Cachar	9 872	3,776	3,021	610	43	3,075	1.698	834	84	198	8	780
Sylhet	79.996	21,340	3,937	6,971	230	54,731	43,052	8,759	2,121	3,544	161	32,172
Khasi and Jaintia Hills	4,672	980	1,680	213	215	2 012	787	143	339	19	32	305
Naga Hills	90	27	33	1	...	30	...	...	...	...	...	...
Lushai Hills	6	6	...	...	...	...	...	...	...	...	...	...
ASSAM VALLEY DISTRICTS...	*60,865*	*20,463*	*11,944*	*928*	*394*	*28,458*	*13,371*	*2,142*	*5,726*	*137*	*257*	*5,503*
Goalpara	12 817	4,255	2,007	141	14	5,055	3 315	702	1,202	11	1	1,321
Kamrup	21 022	5,609	2,042	193	18	13,071	4 153	482	1,829	42	...	1,842
Darrang	3 757	1,717	850	83	68	1,190	796	56	489	2	50	251
Nowgong	4 173	1.595	1,262	134	82	1,316	598	38	417	7	28	143
Sibsagar	10.127	3.822	2,365	102	137	3,940	3.013	473	1,222	65	117	1,318
Lakhimpur	6 803	2,742	1,367	169	74	2,694	1.370	248	562	8	63	560
Garo Hills	1.566	723	251	16	1	592	126	53	5	2	...	68
(2) Manipur State	*7,586*	*848*	*3,844*	*17*	*3*	*2,894*	*1,326*	*115*	*717*	*4*	...	*494*

TABLE XV.—Occupation or Means of Livelihood. Part A.—General Table—Details for Districts—*contd.*

Class and Sub-class: *CLASS B: SUB-CLASS V.—TRADE.*

Order: 33.—OTHER TRADE IN FOOD STUFFS.

District or State.	117.—*Grocers and sellers of vegetable oil, salt, and other condiments.* Total workers and dependants.	Actual workers. Total. Males.	Actual workers. Total. Females.	Actual workers. *Partially agriculturist.* Males.	Actual workers. *Partially agriculturist.* Females.	Dependants. Both sexes.	118.—*Sellers of milk, butter, ghee, poultry, eggs, etc.* Total workers and dependants.	Actual workers. Total. Males.	Actual workers. Total. Females.	Actual workers. *Partially agriculturist.* Males.	Actual workers. *Partially agriculturist.* Females.	Dependants. Both sexes.
1	506	507	508	509	510	511	512	513	514	515	516	517
ASSAM	***36 797***	***14,867***	***2,643***	***2,221***	***87***	***19,287***	***11,043***	***5,024***	***1,082***	***265***	***49***	***4,937***
(1) British Territory	***36,105***	***14,802***	***2,252***	***2,221***	***87***	***19,051***	***10,857***	***4,962***	***1,044***	***264***	***49***	***4,851***
SURMA VALLEY AND HILL DISTRICTS	***22,564***	***8,358***	***969***	***1,887***	***69***	***13,237***	***1,255***	***332***	***149***	***39***	***13***	***774***
Cachar	2 685	1,547	113	239	2	1,025	179	118	12	15	1	49
Sylhet	18.559	6,578	403	1,597	25	11,578	673	44	42	6	2	587
Khasi and Jaintia Hills	1,319	232	453	51	42	634	391	162	93	18	10	136
Naga Hills	1	1	...	...	...	...	6	2	2	...	...	2
Lushai Hills	...	...	...	...	...	...	6	6	...	...	...	...
ASSAM VALLEY DISTRICTS	***13,541***	***6,444***	***1,283***	***334***	***18***	***5,814***	***9,602***	***4,630***	***895***	***225***	***36***	***4,077***
Goalpara	2.174	974	218	34	...	982	1.912	794	68	41	2	1,060
Kamrup	3.773	1,347	322	60	...	2,104	2,332	1,096	117	34	7	1,120
Darrang	916	538	87	29	1	291	971	583	97	37	14	291
Nowgong	985	553	82	63	6	350	1,186	633	226	22	4	327
Sibsagar	3.628	1,880	376	85	9	1,372	1 139	521	118	22	6	500
Lakhimpur	2.015	1,115	197	63	2	703	972	481	115	62	3	376
Garo Hills	50	37	1	...	...	12	1,090	523	164	7	...	403
(2) Manipur State	***692***	***65***	***391***	...	...	***236***	***186***	***62***	***38***	***1***	...	***86***

Class and Sub-class: *CLASS B: SUB-CLASS V.—TRADE.*

Order: 33.—OTHER TRADE IN FOOD STUFFS.

District or State.	119.—*Sellers of sweetmeats, sugar, gur and molasses.* Total workers and dependants.	Actual workers. Total. Males.	Actual workers. Total. Females.	Actual workers. *Partially agriculturist.* Males.	Actual workers. *Partially agriculturist.* Females.	Dependants. Both sexes.	120.—*Cardamom, betel-leaf, vegetables, fruit and areca nut sellers.* Total workers and dependants.	Actual workers. Total. Males.	Actual workers. Total. Females.	Actual workers. *Partially agriculturist.* Males.	Actual workers. *Partially agriculturist.* Females.	Dependants. Both sexes.
1	518	519	520	521	522	523	524	525	526	527	528	529
ASSAM	***3,787***	***1,574***	***361***	***117***	***4***	***1,852***	***22,060***	***6,329***	***4,482***	***1,600***	***157***	***11,249***
(1) British Territory	***3,759***	***1,572***	***344***	***117***	***4***	***1,843***	***19,785***	***6,091***	***3,245***	***1,591***	***155***	***10,449***
SURMA VALLEY AND HILL DISTRICTS	***1,656***	***691***	***29***	***92***	...	***936***	***13,663***	***4,505***	***1,434***	***1,535***	***137***	***7,724***
Cachar	103	49	9	2	...	45	1,087	560	208	59	6	220
Sylhet	1,464	595	2	90	...	867	11 412	3,683	710	1,376	23	7,019
Khasi and Jaintia Hills	58	44	2	...	...	12	1,146	253	424	99	108	469
Naga Hills	31	3	16	...	...	12	18	9	2	1	...	7
Lushai Hills	...	...	...	...	...	...	...	...	...	...	...	...
ASSAM VALLEY DISTRICTS	***2,103***	***881***	***315***	***25***	***4***	***907***	***6,122***	***1,586***	***1,811***	***56***	***18***	***2,725***
Goalpara	502	285	28	6	...	189	1.744	463	486	16	1	795
Kamrup	349	89	54	4	...	206	2.137	460	431	10	1	1,246
Darrang	126	64	24	1	1	38	242	67	74	1	...	101
Nowgong	81	43	6	4	1	32	647	67	401	2	11	179
Sibsagar	354	178	49	4	...	127	698	239	269	5	4	190
Lakhimpur	654	197	152	4	2	305	592	278	132	22	1	182
Garo Hills	37	25	2	...	...	10	62	12	18	...	...	32
(2) Manipur State	***28***	***2***	***17***	...	...	***9***	***2,275***	***238***	***1,237***	***9***	***2***	***800***

TABLE XV.—Occupation or Means of Livelihood. Part A.—General Table—Details for Districts—contd.

Class and Sub-class … / Order …	CLASS B: SUB-CLASS V.—TRADE.											
	33.—OTHER TRADE IN FOOD STUFFS.						34.—TRADE IN CLOTHING AND TOILET ARTICLES.					
	121.—Grain and pulse dealers.						125.—Trade in ready-made clothing and other articles of dress and the toilet hats, umbrellas, socks, ready-made shoes, perfumes, etc.).					
District or State.	Total workers and dependants.	Actual workers. Total.		Actual workers. Partially agriculturist.		Dependants.	Total workers and dependants.	Actual workers. Total.		Actual workers. Partially agriculturist.		Dependants.
		Males.	Females.	Males.	Females.	Both sexes.		Males.	Females.	Males.	Females.	Both sexes.
1	530	53	532	533	534	535	536	537	538	539	540	541
ASSAM …	*96,551*	*6,710*	*6,610*	*522*	*126*	*13,231*	*1,661*	*585*	*547*	*51*	…	*529*
(1) ***British Territory*** …	*23,669*	*6,349*	*5,296*	*519*	*125*	*12,024*	*1,642*	*576*	*545*	*51*	…	*521*
SURMA VALLEY AND HILL DISTRICTS …	*8,683*	*9,131*	*3,460*	*393*	*66*	*3,092*	*1,198*	*275*	*516*	*44*	…	*407*
Cachar …	**4,035**	636	2,505	92	26	894	**27**	16	…	…	…	11
Sylhet …	**3,779**	1,358	630	276	19	1,791	**1,156**	256	509	44	…	391
Khasi and Jaintia Hills …	**857**	129	325	25	21	403	**14**	3	6	…	…	5
Naga Hills …	**12**	8	…	…	…	4	**1**	…	1	…	…	…
Lushai Hills …	…	…	…	…	…	…	…	…	…	…	…	…
ASSAM VALLEY DISTRICTS …	*14,986*	*4,218*	*1,836*	*126*	*59*	*8,939*	*444*	*301*	*29*	*7*	…	*114*
Goalpara …	**2 882**	833	899	25	10	1,150	**206**	108	29	…	…	60
Kamrup …	**8 749**	2,070	180	39	10	6,499	**18**	11	…	…	…	7
Darrang …	**576**	339	64	10	2	173	**45**	43	…	…	…	2
Nowgong …	**604**	221	120	33	33	263	**8**	4	…	…	…	4
Sibsagar …	**1,033**	389	320	5	…	324	**65**	48	…	1	…	17
Lakhimpur …	**964**	305	194	7	3	465	**101**	86	…	6	…	15
Garo Hills …	**178**	61	59	7	1	58	**1**	1	…	…	…	…
(2) ***Manipur State*** …	*2,882*	*361*	*1,314*	*3*	*1*	*1,207*	*19*	*9*	*2*	…	…	*8*

Class and Sub-class … / Order …	CLASS B: SUB-CLASS V.—TRADE.											
	35.—TRADE IN FURNITURE.											
	TOTAL OF ORDER 35.						126.—Trade in furniture, carpets, curtains and bedding.					
District or State.	Total workers and dependants.	Actual workers. Total.		Actual workers. Partially agriculturist.		Dependants.	Total workers and dependants.	Actual workers. Total.		Actual workers. Partially agriculturist.		Dependants.
		Males.	Females.	Males.	Females.	Both sexes.		Males.	Females.	Males.	Females.	Both sexes.
1	542	543	544	545	546	547	548	549	550	551	552	553
ASSAM …	*3,800*	*1,773*	*408*	*350*	*29*	*1,619*	*2,432*	*1,288*	*379*	*290*	*22*	*765*
(1) ***British Territory*** …	*3,785*	*1,771*	*400*	*350*	*29*	*1,614*	*2,424*	*1,287*	*375*	*290*	*22*	*762*
SURMA VALLEY AND HILL DISTRICTS …	*3,159*	*1,460*	*390*	*330*	*22*	*1,309*	*2,347*	*1,227*	*371*	*290*	*22*	*749*
Cachar …	**192**	59	86	7	17	47	**149**	33	86	…	17	30
Sylhet …	**2,938**	1,400	289	323	3	1,249	**2,169**	1,193	270	290	3	706
Khasi and Jaintia Hills …	**29**	1	15	…	2	13	**29**	1	15	…	2	13
Naga Hills …	…	…	…	…	…	…	…	…	…	…	…	…
Lushai Hills …	…	…	…	…	…	…	…	…	…	…	…	…
ASSAM VALLEY DISTRICTS …	*626*	*311*	*10*	*20*	…	*305*	*77*	*60*	*4*	…	…	*13*
Goalpara …	**165**	99	…	5	…	66	**17**	8	…	…	…	9
Kamrup …	**280**	91	3	4	…	186	**27**	22	1	…	…	4
Darrang …	**29**	19	6	…	…	4	**21**	18	3	…	…	…
Nowgong …	**40**	19	…	1	…	21	…	…	…	…	…	…
Sibsagar …	**73**	57	…	10	…	16	**9**	9	…	…	…	…
Lakhimpur …	**30**	17	1	…	…	12	…	…	…	…	…	…
Garo Hills …	**9**	9	…	…	…	…	**3**	3	…	…	…	…
(2) ***Manipur State*** …	*15*	*9*	*8*	…	…	*5*	*8*	*1*	*4*	…	…	*3*

TABLE XV.—OCCUPATION OR MEANS OF LIVELIHOOD. PART A.—GENERAL TABLE—DETAILS FOR DISTRICTS—*contd.*

Class and Sub-class ... / Order ...	CLASS B: SUB-CLASS V.—TRADE.											
	36.—TRADE IN BUILDING MATERIALS.						37.—TRADE IN MEANS OF TRANSPORT					
	128.—*Trade in building materials (stones, bricks, plaster, cement, sand, tiles, thatch, etc.).*						129.—*Dealers and hirers of elephants, camels, horses, cattle, asses, mules, etc., sellers (not makers) of carriages, saddlery, etc.*					
DISTRICT OR STATE.	TOTAL WORKERS AND DEPENDANTS.	ACTUAL WORKERS. Total. Males.	Total. Females.	Partially agriculturist. Males.	Partially agriculturist. Females.	DEPENDANTS. Both sexes.	TOTAL WORKERS AND DEPENDANTS.	ACTUAL WORKERS. Total. Males.	Total. Females.	Partially agriculturist. Males.	Partially agriculturist. Females.	DEPENDANTS. Both sexes.
1	554	555	556	557	558	559	560	561	562	563	564	565
ASSAM ...	*2,336*	*839*	*330*	*80*	*25*	*1,167*	*2,798*	*1,498*	*204*	*106*	*11*	*1,096*
(1) ***British Territory*** ...	*2,290*	*832*	*313*	*80*	*25*	*1,145*	*2,528*	*1,388*	*193*	*106*	*11*	*947*
SURMA VALLEY AND HILL DISTRICTS ...	*1,208*	*532*	*43*	*63*	*3*	*633*	*528*	*208*	*15*	*25*	*4*	*305*
Cachar ...	6	4	...	...	...	2	31	18	...	2	...	13
Sylhet ...	886	359	2	60	...	525	328	142	...	1	...	216
Khasi and Jaintia Hills ...	316	169	41	3	3	106	149	74	10	22	4	68
Naga Hills ...	...	...	...	...	...	...	20	4	5	...	...	11
Lushai Hills ...	...	...	...	...	...	...	...	...	...	...	...	...
ASSAM VALLEY AND HILL DISTRICTS ...	*1,082*	*300*	*270*	*17*	*22*	*512*	*2,000*	*1,180*	*178*	*81*	*7*	*642*
Goalpara ...	42	17	1	2	...	24	275	145	17	3	...	113
Kamrup ...	449	138	73	8	2	238	391	202	42	23	2	147
Darrang ...	51	16	22	...	1	13	740	306	79	47	3	265
Nowgong ...	71	10	39	1	4	22	290	193	31	5	2	66
Sibsagar ...	217	33	97	6	15	87	146	132	2	2	...	12
Lakhimpur ...	252	86	33	...	...	128	138	103	6	1	...	29
Garo Hills ...	...	...	...	...	...	...	20	9	1	...	...	10
(2) ***Manipur State*** ...	*46*	*7*	*17*	...	...	*22*	*270*	*110*	*11*	...	...	*149*

Class and Sub-class ... / Order ...	CLASS B: SUB-CLASS V.—TRADE.											
	38.—TRADE IN FUEL.						39.—TRADE IN ARTICLES OF LUXURY AND THOSE PERTAINING TO LETTERS AND THE ARTS AND SCIENCES.					
	130.—*Dealers in firewood, charcoal, coal, cowdung, etc.*						*TOTAL OF ORDER 39.*					
DISTRICT AND STATE.	TOTAL WORKERS AND DEPENDANTS.	ACTUAL WORKERS. Total. Males.	Total. Females.	Partially agriculturist. Males.	Partially agriculturist. Females.	DEPENDANTS. Both sexes.	TOTAL WORKERS AND DEPENDANTS.	ACTUAL WORKERS. Total. Males.	Total. Females.	Partially agriculturist. Males.	Partially agriculturist. Females.	DEPENDANTS. Both sexes.
1	566	567	568	569	570	571	572	573	574	575	576	577
ASSAM ...	*2,594*	*806*	*285*	*117*	*13*	*1,503*	*9,555*	*4,195*	*972*	*426*	*5*	*4,388*
(1) ***British Territory*** ...	*2,461*	*781*	*220*	*117*	*13*	*1,460*	*9,445*	*4,168*	*959*	*425*	*5*	*4,318*
SURMA VALLEY AND HILL DISTRICTS ...	*2,004*	*535*	*180*	*116*	*13*	*1,289*	*5,990*	*2,067*	*452*	*393*	*1*	*2,871*
Cachar ...	221	77	4	28	...	140	600	415	12	40	...	173
Sylhet ...	1,666	422	156	81	13	1,088	5,330	2,226	435	338	1	2,669
Khasi and Jaintia Hills ...	105	34	13	7	...	53	57	23	5	6	...	29
Naga Hills ...	12	2	2	...	...	8	3	3	...	...	...	...
Lushai Hills ...	...	...	...	...	...	...	...	...	...	...	...	...
ASSAM VALLEY DISTRICTS ...	*457*	*246*	*40*	*1*	...	*171*	*3,455*	*1,501*	*507*	*32*	*4*	*1,447*
Goalpara ...	63	37	6	...	...	30	1,714	664	308	10	...	742
Kamrup ...	120	106	1	...	...	13	392	165	38	7	...	189
Darrang ...	24	7	1	...	...	16	241	81	69	2	1	92
Nowgong ...	16	5	3	1	...	8	233	81	31	5	3	121
Sibsagar ...	32	9	4	...	...	19	347	191	30	1	...	126
Lakhimpur ...	195	79	24	...	...	92	433	257	21	4	...	155
Garo Hills ...	7	3	1	...	...	3	95	62	11	3	...	22
(2) ***Manipur State*** ...	*133*	*25*	*65*	...	...	*43*	*110*	*27*	*13*	*1*	...	*70*

TABLE XV.—Occupation or Means of Livelihood. Part A.—General Table—Details for Districts—*contd.*

Class and Sub-class ... / Order ...	CLASS B: SUB-CLASS V.—TRADE.											
	39.—TRADE IN ARTICLES OF LUXURY AND THOSE PERTAINING TO LETTERS AND THE ARTS AND SCIENCES.						40.—TRADE IN REFUSE MATTER.					
	132.—Dealers in common bangles, bead necklaces, fans, small articles, toys, hunting and fishing tackle, flowers, etc.						*134.—Dealers in rags, stable refuse, etc.*					
District or State.	Total workers and dependants.	Actual workers. Total.		Actual workers. *Partially agriculturist.*		Dependants.	Total workers and dependants.	Actual workers. Total.		Actual workers. *Partially agriculturist.*		Dependants.
		Males.	Females.	Males.	Females.	Both sexes.		Males.	Females.	Males.	Females.	Both sexes.
1	578	579	580	581	582	583	584	585	586	587	588	589
ASSAM	*8,858*	*3,917*	*846*	*399*	*5*	*4,095*	*3*	...	*3*	...	...	...
(1) ***British Territory***	*8,755*	*3,890*	*836*	*398*	*5*	*4,029*	*3*	...	*3*	...	...	...
SURMA VALLEY AND HILL DISTRICTS	*5,468*	*2,479*	*346*	*368*	*1*	*2,643*	*3*	...	*3*	...	...	...
Cachar	490	358	11	49	...	121	...	...	...	...	...	...
Sylhet	4,964	2,113	335	318	1	2,516	3	...	3	...	...	...
Khasi and Jaintia Hills	11	5	...	1	...	6	...	...	...	...	...	...
Naga Hills	3	3	...	...	...	...	...	...	...	...	...	...
Lushai Hills	...	...	...	...	...	...	...	...	...	...	...	...
ASSAM VALLEY DISTRICTS	*3,287*	*1,411*	*490*	*30*	*4*	*1,386*	...	...	...	...	...	...
Goalpara	1,687	645	307	8	...	735	...	...	...	...	...	...
Kamrup	354	148	37	7	...	169	...	...	...	...	...	...
Darrang	236	60	66	2	1	[illegible]	...	...	...	...	...	...
Nowgong	228	80	31	5	3	117	...	...	...	...	...	...
Sibsagar	322	178	24	1	...	120	...	...	...	...	...	...
Lakhimpur	363	218	14	4	...	131	...	...	...	...	...	...
Garo Hills	95	62	11	3	...	22	...	...	...	...	...	...
(2) ***Manipur State***	*103*	*27*	*10*	*1*	...	*66*	...	...	...	...	...	...

Class and Sub-class ... / Order ...	CLASS B: SUB-CLASS V.—TRADE.											
	41.—TRADE OF OTHER SORTS.											
	TOTAL OF ORDER 41.						*135.—Shop-keepers otherwise unspecified.*					
District or State.	Total workers and dependants.	Actual workers. Total.		Actual workers. *Partially agriculturist.*		Dependants.	Total workers and dependants.	Actual workers. Total.		Actual workers. *Partially agriculturist.*		Dependants.
		Males.	Females.	Males.	Females.	Both sexes.		Males.	Females.	Males.	Females.	Both sexes.
1	590	591	592	593	594	595	596	597	598	599	600	601
ASSAM	*17,411*	*7,853*	*1,048*	*803*	*21*	*8,510*	*15,356*	*6,845*	*933*	*710*	*19*	*7,578*
(1) ***British Territory***	*16,819*	*7,538*	*1,018*	*790*	*21*	*8,263*	*14,846*	*6,563*	*903*	*702*	*19*	*7,380*
SURMA VALLEY AND HILL DISTRICTS	*6,070*	*2,654*	*167*	*573*	*1*	*3,249*	*5,323*	*2,340*	*147*	*538*	*1*	*2,836*
Cachar	244	130	16	15	...	98	232	120	16	13	...	96
Sylhet	5,207	2,246	69	514	1	2,892	4,553	1,990	53	515	1	2,510
Khasi and Jaintia Hills	461	187	63	10	...	211	385	141	60	6	...	184
Naga Hills	88	40	19	1	...	29	23	38	18	1	...	27
Lushai Hills	70	51	...	3	...	19	70	51	...	3	...	19
ASSAM VALLEY DISTRICTS	*10,749*	*4,884*	*851*	*217*	*20*	*5,014*	*9,523*	*4,223*	*756*	*164*	*18*	*4,544*
Goalpara	1,179	599	27	43	...	553	953	482	14	32	...	457
Kamrup	1,975	685	51	17	1	[illegible]	1,709	573	43	14	1	1,093
Darrang	1,136	705	98	29	2	333	1,043	652	92	24	2	299
Nowgong	445	207	49	25	3	189	363	161	44	19	...	158
Sibsagar	2,467	1,079	217	58	3	1,171	2,102	867	174	37	2	1,061
Lakhimpur	3,489	1,584	409	44	13	1,496	3,324	1,474	389	38	13	1,461
Garo Hills	58	25	...	2	...	33	29	14	...	...	...	15
(2) ***Manipur State***	*592*	*315*	*30*	*13*	...	*247*	*510*	*282*	*30*	*8*	...	*198*

TABLE XV.—OCCUPATION OR MEANS OF LIVELIHOOD. PART A.—GENERAL TABLE—DETAILS FOR DISTRICTS—*contd.*

Class and Sub-class / Order	CLASS B: SUB-CLASS V.—TRADE. 41.—TRADE OF OTHER SORTS. 137.—Conjurors, acrobats, fortune tellers, reciters, exhibitors of curiosities and wild animals.						CLASS C: SUB-CLASS VI.—PUBLIC FORCE. 42.—ARMY. TOTAL OF ORDER 42.					
District or State.	Total workers and dependants.	Actual workers. Total. Males.	Actual workers. Total. Females.	Actual workers. Partially agriculturist. Males.	Actual workers. Partially agriculturist. Females.	Dependants. Both sexes.	Total workers and dependants.	Actual workers. Total. Males.	Actual workers. Total. Females.	Actual workers. Partially agriculturist. Males.	Actual workers. Partially agriculturist. Females.	Dependants. Both sexes.
1	602	603	604	605	606	607	608	609	610	611	612	613
ASSAM	*945*	*486*	*58*	*34*	...	*401*	*3,122*	*2,170*	...	*584*	...	*952*
(1) *British Territory*	*916*	*477*	*58*	*32*	...	*381*	*2,495*	*1,620*	...	*139*	...	*875*
SURMA VALLEY AND HILL DISTRICTS	*618*	*235*	*10*	*25*	...	*344*	*1,859*	*1,074*	...	*136*	...	*785*
Cachar	3	3	...	...	...	...	10	3	...	...	...	7
Sylhet	563	318	16	22	...	329	2	1	...	...	...	1
Khasi and Jaintia Hills	47	32	2	3	...	13	1,652	905	...	...	...	748
Naga Hills	5	2	1	...	...	2	179	163	...	136	...	16
Lushai Hills	...	...	...	...	...	...	15	2	...	...	...	13
ASSAM VALLEY DISTRICTS	*298*	*222*	*39*	*7*	...	*87*	*636*	*546*	...	*3*	...	*90*
Goalpara	49	33	9	4	...	7	10	6	...	2	...	4
Kamrup	7	6	...	...	...	1	23	25	...	...	...	3
Darrang	17	10	1	...	...	6	54	36	...	...	...	18
Nowgong	8	5	...	...	...	3	5	2	...	...	...	3
Sibsagar	126	98	13	3	...	15	10	7	...	1	...	3
Lakhimpur	91	70	16	...	...	5	526	468	...	...	...	58
Garo Hills	...	...	...	...	...	...	3	2	...	...	...	1
(2) *Manipur State*	*20*	*9*	...	*2*	...	*20*	*627*	*550*	...	*445*	...	*77*

Class and Sub-class / Order	CLASS C: SUB-CLASS VI.—PUBLIC FORCE. 42.—ARMY. 139.—Army (Imperial).						44.—POLICE. TOTAL OF ORDER 44.					
District or State.	Total workers and dependants.	Actual workers. Total. Males.	Actual workers. Total. Females.	Actual workers. Partially agriculturist. Males.	Actual workers. Partially agriculturist. Females.	Dependants. Both sexes.	Total workers and dependants.	Actual workers. Total. Males.	Actual workers. Total. Females.	Actual workers. Partially agriculturist. Males.	Actual workers. Partially agriculturist. Females.	Dependants. Both sexes.
1	614	615	616	617	618	619	620	621	622	623	624	625
ASSAM	*3,105*	*2,155*	...	*584*	...	*950*	*15,763*	*7,213*	...	*1,198*	...	*8,550*
(1) *British Territory*	*2,495*	*1,620*	...	*139*	...	*875*	*15,099*	*6,860*	...	*1,181*	...	*8,239*
SURMA VALLEY AND HILL DISTRICTS	*1,859*	*1,074*	...	*136*	...	*785*	*10,040*	*4,369*	...	*979*	...	*5,671*
Cachar	10	3	...	...	...	7	1,704	894	...	256	...	810
Sylhet	2	1	...	...	...	1	5,115	1,813	...	687	...	3,302
Khasi and Jaintia Hills	1,653	905	...	...	...	748	278	162	...	8	...	116
Naga Hills	179	163	...	136	...	16	1,278	696	...	17	...	582
Lushai Hills	15	2	...	...	...	13	1,665	804	...	11	...	861
ASSAM VALLEY DISTRICTS	*636*	*546*	...	*3*	...	*90*	*5,059*	*2,491*	...	*202*	...	*2,568*
Goalpara	10	6	...	2	...	4	1,023	428	...	124	...	595
Kamrup	28	25	...	...	...	3	698	309	...	16	...	384
Darrang	54	36	...	...	...	18	491	269	...	2	...	238
Nowgong	5	2	...	...	...	3	381	183	...	46	...	198
Sibsagar	10	7	...	1	...	3	618	336	...	13	...	283
Lakhimpur	526	468	...	...	...	58	1,482	801	...	2	...	681
Garo Hills	3	2	...	...	...	1	371	165	...	...	...	206
(2) *Manipur State*	*610*	*535*	...	*445*	...	*75*	*664*	*353*	...	*17*	...	*311*

TABLE XV.—Occupation or Means of Livelihood. Part A.—General Table—Details for Districts—*contd.*

Class and Sub-class ...	CLASS C; SUB-CLASS VI.—POLICE FORCE.										
Order ...	44.—POLICE.										
	142.—Police.						*143.—Village watchmen.*				
District or State.	Total workers and dependants.	Actual workers. Total.		Actual workers. Partially agriculturist.		Dependants.	Total workers and dependants.	Actual workers. Total.		Actual workers. Partially agriculturist.		Dependants.
		Males.	Females.	Males.	Females.	Both sexes.		Males.	Females.	Males.	Females.	Both sexes.
1	626	627	628	629	630	631	632	633	634	635	636	637
ASSAM	***10,770***	***5,442***	...	***516***	...	***5,328***	***4,993***	***1,771***	...	***682***	...	***3,222***
(1) British Territory	***10,252***	***5,146***	...	***514***	...	***5,106***	***4,847***	***1,714***	...	***667***	...	***3,133***
ASSAM VALLEY AND HILL DISTRICTS	***5,690***	***2,804***	...	***372***	...	***2,886***	***4,350***	***1,565***	...	***607***	...	***2,785***
Cachar	929	536	...	106	...	393	775	358	...	150	...	417
Sylhet	1,661	654	...	241	...	1,007	3,454	1,159	...	446	...	2,295
Khasi and Jaintia Hills	278	162	...	8	...	116	...	...	...	...	...	...
Naga Hills	1 278	696	...	17	...	582	...	...	...	...	...	...
Lushai Hills	1 544	756	...	...	...	788	121	48	...	11	...	73
ASSAM VALLEY DISTRICTS	***4,562***	***2,342***	...	***142***	...	***2,220***	***497***	***149***	...	***60***	...	***348***
Goalpara	526	279	...	64	...	247	497	149	...	60	...	348
Kamrup	693	309	...	16	...	384	...	...	...	...	...	...
Darrang	491	269	...	2	...	222	...	...	...	...	...	...
Nowgong	381	183	...	46	...	198	...	...	...	...	...	...
Sibsagar	618	336	...	12	...	282	...	...	...	...	...	...
Lakhimpur	1,482	801	...	2	...	681	...	...	...	...	...	...
Garo Hills	371	165	...	...	...	206	...	...	...	...	...	...
(2) Manipur State	***518***	***296***	...	***2***	...	***222***	***146***	***57***	...	***15***	...	***89***

Class and Sub-class ...	CLASS C; SUB-CLASS VII.—PUBLIC ADMINISTRATION.										
Order ...	45.—PUBLIC ADMINISTRATION.										
	TOTAL OF ORDER 45.						*144.—Service of the State.*				
District or State.	Total workers and dependants.	Actual workers. Total.		Actual workers. Partially agriculturist.		Dependants.	Total workers and dependants.	Actual workers. Total.		Actual workers. Partially agriculturist.		Dependants.
		Males.	Females.	Males.	Females.	Both sexes.		Males.	Females.	Males.	Females.	Both sexes.
1	638	639	640	641	642	643	644	645	646	647	648	649
ASSAM	***15,032***	***4,688***	***56***	***1,193***	...	***10,288***	***9,126***	***2,846***	...	***589***	...	***6,280***
(1) British Territory	***14,313***	***4,405***	***37***	***1,122***	...	***9,871***	***8,907***	***2,772***	...	***578***	...	***6,135***
ASSAM VALLEY AND HILL DISTRICTS	***7,278***	***2,154***	***1***	***457***	...	***5,123***	***5,306***	***1,712***	...	***382***	...	***3,594***
Cachar	692	254	...	47	...	438	585	199	...	34	...	886
Sylhet	3,257	1,038	...	352	...	2,219	3,065	967	...	339	...	2,098
Khasi and Jaintia Hills	1,517	537	1	20	...	979	1,289	432	...	...	...	857
Naga Hills	135	50	...	6	...	85	127	47	...	5	...	80
Lushai Hills	1,677	275	...	32	...	1,402	240	67	...	4	...	173
ASSAM VALLEY DISTRICTS	***7,035***	***2,251***	***36***	***665***	...	***4,748***	***3,601***	***1,060***	...	***196***	...	***2,541***
Goalpara	653	215	...	43	...	438	487	144	...	25	...	343
Kamrup	1 947	555	...	130	...	1,392	965	253	...	45	...	712
Darrang	938	316	1	115	...	621	436	135	...	30	...	301
Nowgong	977	332	...	183	...	645	387	112	...	42	...	275
Sibsagar	1,554	460	...	131	...	1,094	738	204	...	33	...	534
Lakhimpur	845	321	35	52	...	489	509	179	...	19	...	330
Garo Hills	121	52	...	11	...	69	79	33	...	2	...	46
(2) Manipur State	***719***	***283***	***19***	***71***	...	***417***	***219***	***74***	...	***11***	...	***145***

Class and Sub-class ...	CLASS C: SUB-CLASS VII.—PUBLIC ADMINISTRATION.											
Order	45.—PUBLIC ADMINISTRATION.											
	145.—Service of the Native and Foreign States.						147.—Village officials and servants other than watchmen.					
District or State.	Total workers and dependants.	Actual workers. Total. Males.	Actual workers. Total. Females.	Actual workers. Partially agriculturist. Males.	Actual workers. Partially agriculturist. Females.	Dependants. Both sexes.	Total workers and dependants.	Actual workers. Total. Males.	Actual workers. Total. Females.	Actual workers. Partially agriculturist. Males.	Actual workers. Partially agriculturist. Females.	Dependants. Both sexes.
1	650	651	652	653	654	655	656	657	658	659	660	661
ASSAM ...	***545***	***203***	***20***	***24***	...	***329***	***4,201***	***1,200***	...	***591***	...	***3,001***
(1) British Territory ...	***175***	***76***	***1***	***17***	...	***98***	***4 074***	***1,120***	...	***468***	...	***2,954***
SURMA VALLEY AND HILL DISTRICTS ...	***157***	***60***	***1***	***16***	...	***96***	***1,507***	***243***	...	***32***	...	***1,264***
Cachar ...	...	...	...	...	...	...	...	...	...	...	...	...
Sylhet ...	...	...	...	...	...	...	16	...	...	...	...	16
Khasi and Jaintia Hills ...	157	60	1	16	...	96	50	35	...	3	...	15
Naga Hills ...	...	...	...	...	...	...	6	2	...	1	...	4
Lushai Hills ...	...	...	...	...	...	...	1,435	206	...	28	...	1,229
ASSAM VALLEY DISTRICTS ...	***18***	***16***	...	***1***	...	***2***	***2,567***	***877***	...	***436***	...	***1,690***
Goalpara ...	1	...	...	...	...	1	77	38	...	18	...	39
Kamrup ...	4	3	...	...	...	1	799	285	...	79	...	564
Darrang ...	10	10	...	...	...	...	375	128	...	76	...	247
Nowgong ...	...	...	...	...	...	...	494	172	...	137	...	322
Sibsagar ...	1	1	...	1	...	...	639	195	...	89	...	435
Lakhimpur ...	2	2	...	...	...	...	151	91	...	28	...	60
Garo Hills ...	...	...	...	...	...	...	41	18	...	9	...	23
(2) Manipur State ...	***370***	***127***	***19***	***7***	...	***224***	***127***	***80***	...	***53***	...	***47***

Class and Sub-class ...	CLASS C: SUB-CLASS VIII.—PROFESSIONS AND LIBERAL ARTS.											
Order	46.—RELIGION.											
	TOTAL OF ORDER 46.						148.—Priests, ministers, etc.					
District or State.	Total workers and dependants.	Actual workers. Total. Males.	Actual workers. Total. Females.	Actual workers. Partially agriculturist. Males.	Actual workers. Partially agriculturist. Females.	Dependants. Both sexes.	Total workers and dependants.	Actual workers. Total. Males.	Actual workers. Total. Females.	Actual workers. Partially agriculturist. Males.	Actual workers. Partially agriculturist. Females.	Dependants. Both sexes.
1	662	663	664	665	666	667	668	669	670	671	672	673
ASSAM ...	***55,289***	***18,402***	***891***	***5,095***	***72***	***35,996***	***48,309***	***15,460***	***639***	***4,729***	***66***	***32,210***
(1) British Territory ...	***50,708***	***16,757***	***708***	***4,938***	***66***	***33,243***	***47,456***	***15,195***	***612***	***4,719***	***66***	***31,649***
SURMA VALLEY AND HILL DISTRICTS ...	***36,279***	***11,633***	***518***	***3,598***	***49***	***24,128***	***35,449***	***11,293***	***475***	***3,524***	***49***	***23,681***
Cachar ...	2,002	797	50	187	4	1,155	1 963	781	48	187	4	1,134
Sylhet ...	33,726	10,639	439	3,384	45	22,648	33 270	10,400	425	3,313	45	22,445
Khasi and Jaintia Hills ...	265	63	20	1	...	176	86	36	1	1	...	49
Naga Hills ...	48	31	1	1	...	16	19	9	...	...	...	10
Lushai Hills ...	238	103	2	25	...	139	111	67	1	23	...	43
ASSAM VALLEY DISTRICTS ...	***14,429***	***5,124***	***190***	***1,340***	***17***	***9,115***	***12,007***	***3,909***	***137***	***1,195***	***17***	***7,968***
Goalpara ...	1 672	784	20	154	4	868	1.535	692	20	140	4	823
Kamrup ...	7 929	2,426	88	697	8	5,415	6,951	2,079	58	808	8	4,814
Darrang ...	767	290	20	110	4	457	641	218	15	100	4	408
Nowgong ...	903	262	8	148	...	633	853	228	7	144	...	618
Sibsagar ...	2,382	973	41	211	1	1,368	1,618	500	31	187	1	1,087
Lakhimpur ...	723	362	11	20	...	350	376	168	6	16	...	204
Garo Hills ...	53	27	2	...	...	24	33	19	...	...	...	14
(2) Manipur State ...	***4,581***	***1,645***	***183***	***157***	***6***	***2,753***	***853***	***265***	***27***	***10***	...	***561***

TABLE XV.—Occupation or Means of Livelihood. Part A.—General Table—Details for Districts—*contd.*

Class and Sub-class ...	CLASS C: SUB-CLASS VIII.—PROFESSIONS AND LIBERAL ARTS.											
Order	46.—RELIGION.						47.—LAW.					
	151.—Temple, burial or burning ground service, pilgrim conductors, circumcisers.						*TOTAL OF ORDER 47.*					
District or State.	Total workers and dependants.	Actual workers. Total. Males.	Actual workers. Total. Females.	Actual workers. Partially agriculturist. Males.	Actual workers. Partially agriculturist. Females.	Dependants. Both sexes.	Total workers and dependants.	Actual workers. Total. Males.	Actual workers. Total. Females.	Actual workers. Partially agriculturist. Males.	Actual workers. Partially agriculturist. Females.	Dependants. Both sexes.
1	674	675	676	677	678	679	680	681	682	683	684	685
ASSAM	*4,583*	*1,724*	*175*	*277*	*5*	*2,684*	*5,118*	*1,393*	...	*415*	...	*3,795*
(1) British Territory	*1,515*	*649*	*27*	*143*	...	*839*	*5,107*	*1,318*	...	*415*	...	*3,789*
SURMA VALLEY AND HILL DISTRICTS	*111*	*69*	*1*	*13*	...	*41*	*3,264*	*934*	...	*339*	...	*2,330*
Cachar	7	4	...	...	...	3	337	65	...	24	...	272
Sylhet	77	45	...	12	...	32	2,863	850	...	311	...	2,013
Khasi and Jaintia Hills	...	...	...	...	...	...	62	17	...	2	...	45
Naga Hills	27	20	1	1	...	6	...	...	...	...	...	...
Lushai Hills	...	...	...	...	...	...	2	2	...	2	...	...
ASSAM VALLEY DISTRICTS	*1,404*	*580*	*26*	*130*	...	*798*	*1,843*	*384*	...	*76*	...	*1,459*
Goalpara	113	76	...	13	...	37	332	69	...	2	...	263
Kamrup	841	290	23	87	...	528	428	99	...	20	...	329
Darrang	73	36	...	8	...	37	136	36	...	11	...	100
Nowgong	29	20	1	4	...	8	187	33	...	17	...	154
Sibsagar	225	92	1	17	...	132	488	93	...	21	...	390
Lakhimpur	122	65	1	1	...	56	258	47	...	5	...	211
Garo Hills	1	1	...	...	...	...	14	2	...	...	...	12
(2) Manipur State	*3,068*	*1,075*	*148*	*134*	*5*	*1,845*	*11*	*5*	...	...	...	*6*

Class and Sub-class ...	CLASS C: SUB-CLASS VIII.—PROFESSIONS AND LIBERAL ARTS.											
Order	47.—LAW.											
	152.—Lawyers of all kinds, including Kazis, law agents and mukhtiars.						*153.—Lawyers' clerks, petition writers, etc.*					
District or State.	Total workers and dependants.	Actual workers. Total. Males.	Actual workers. Total. Females.	Actual workers. Partially agriculturist. Males.	Actual workers. Partially agriculturist. Females.	Dependants. Both sexes.	Total workers and dependants.	Actual workers. Total. Males.	Actual workers. Total. Females.	Actual workers. Partially agriculturist. Males.	Actual workers. Partially agriculturist. Females.	Dependants. Both sexes.
1	686	687	688	689	690	691	692	693	694	695	696	697
ASSAM	*2,586*	*516*	...	*168*	...	*2,070*	*2,532*	*807*	...	*247*	...	*1,725*
(1) British Territory	*2,586*	*516*	...	*168*	...	*2,070*	*2,521*	*802*	...	*247*	...	*1,719*
SURMA VALLEY AND HILL DISTRICTS	*1,747*	*381*	...	*144*	...	*1,366*	*1,517*	*553*	...	*195*	...	*964*
Cachar	261	50	...	19	...	211	76	15	...	5	...	61
Sylhet	1.453	324	...	125	...	1,129	1.410	526	...	186	...	884
Khasi and Jaintia Hills	33	7	...	...	...	26	29	10	...	2	...	19
Naga Hills	...	...	...	...	...	...	...	...	...	...	...	...
Lushai Hills	...	...	...	...	...	...	2	2	...	2	...	...
ASSAM VALLEY DISTRICTS	*839*	*135*	...	*24*	...	*704*	*1,004*	*249*	...	*52*	...	*755*
Goalpara	196	32	...	1	...	164	136	37	...	1	...	99
Kamrup	229	37	...	10	...	192	199	62	...	10	...	137
Darrang	31	6	...	2	...	25	105	30	...	9	...	75
Nowgong	69	10	...	2	...	59	118	23	...	15	...	95
Sibsagar	181	31	...	6	...	150	367	67	...	15	...	240
Lakhimpur	133	19	...	3	...	114	125	28	...	2	...	97
Garo Hills	...	...	...	...	...	...	14	2	...	...	...	12
(2) Manipur State	...	...	...	...	...	...	*11*	*5*	...	...	...	*6*

TABLE XV.—Occupation or Means of Livelihood. Part A.—General Table—Details for Districts—*contd.*

Class and Sub-class ...	CLASS C: SUB-CLASS VIII.—PROFESSIONS AND LIBERAL ARTS.											
Order	48.—MEDICINE.											
	TOTAL OF ORDER 48.						154.—Medical practitioners of all kinds, including dentists, oculists, and veterinary surgeons.					
District or State.	Total workers and dependants.	Actual workers. Total. Males.	Actual workers. Total. Females.	Partially agriculturist. Males.	Partially agriculturist. Females.	Dependants. Both sexes.	Total workers and dependants.	Actual workers. Total. Males.	Actual workers. Total. Females.	Partially agriculturist. Males.	Partially agriculturist. Females.	Dependants. Both sexes.
1	698	639	700	701	702	703	704	705	706	707	708	709
ASSAM ...	*10,836*	*3,992*	*264*	*599*	*6*	*6,630*	*8,502*	*2,947*	*86*	*492*	*2*	*5,460*
(1) *British Territory*	*10,335*	*3,737*	*225*	*568*	*6*	*6,373*	*8,017*	*2,702*	*78*	*468*	*2*	*5,237*
SURMA VALLEY AND HILL DISTRICTS	*5,147*	*1,796*	*113*	*414*	*5*	*3,238*	*4,418*	*1,509*	*50*	*370*	*2*	*2,859*
Cachar ...	690	354	9	100	1	327	600	307	1	92	...	292
Sylhet ...	4,068	1,202	88	307	3	2,658	3,625	1,125	48	276	2	2,452
Khasi and Jaintia Hills	280	102	12	4	1	166	134	48	...	1	...	86
Naga Hills	76	31	4	...	...	41	29	14	1	...	...	14
Lushai Hills	93	47	...	3	...	46	30	15	...	1	...	15
ASSAM VALLEY DISTRICTS	*5,188*	*1,941*	*112*	*154*	*1*	*3,135*	*3,509*	*1,193*	*28*	*98*	...	*2,378*
Goalpara	811	267	20	28	...	524	648	208	9	24	...	431
Kamrup	1,463	493	41	32	...	929	1,027	340	11	23	...	676
Darrang	476	240	13	19	...	223	303	146	1	14	...	156
Nowgong	305	129	6	19	...	170	200	73	...	11	...	128
Sibsagar	1,169	390	22	39	1	757	860	225	6	18	...	629
Lakhimpur	912	401	9	15	...	502	543	106	1	7	...	346
Garo Hills	52	21	1	2	...	30	18	6	...	1	...	12
(2) *Manipur State*	*551*	*255*	*39*	*24*	...	*257*	*485*	*243*	*8*	*24*	...	*232*

Class and Sub-class ...	CLASS C: SUB-CLASS VIII.—PROFESSIONS AND LIBERAL ARTS.											
Order	49.—INSTRUCTION.						50.—LETTERS AND ARTS AND SCIENCES.					
	156.—Professors and teachers of all kinds (except law, medicine, music, dancing and drawing) and clerks and servants connected with education.						TOTAL OF ORDER 50.					
District or State.	Total workers and dependants.	Actual workers. Total. Males.	Actual workers. Total. Females.	Partially agriculturist. Males.	Partially agriculturist. Females.	Dependants. Both sexes.	Total workers and dependants.	Actual workers. Total. Males.	Actual workers. Total. Females.	Partially agriculturist. Males.	Partially agriculturist. Females.	Dependants. Both sexes.
1	710	711	712	713	714	715	716	717	718	719	720	731
ASSAM ...	*12,357*	*5,356*	*229*	*1,206*	*10*	*6,772*	*9,265*	*4,108*	*76*	*878*	*1*	*5,081*
(1) *British Territory*	*11,798*	*5,123*	*226*	*1,192*	*10*	*6,449*	*8,202*	*3,653*	*65*	*854*	*1*	*4,484*
SURMA VALLEY AND HILL DISTRICTS	*6,630*	*2,858*	*161*	*639*	*9*	*3,611*	*5,251*	*2,233*	*14*	*735*	*1*	*3,004*
Cachar ...	783	421	13	116	1	346	112	52	5	3	...	55
Sylhet ...	4,207	1,903	33	444	3	2,271	4,130	1,553	8	546	1	2,569
Khasi and Jaintia Hills	1,443	461	109	76	5	873	890	565	...	182	...	325
Naga Hills	108	31	3	...	...	74	73	33	1	3	...	39
Lushai Hills	89	39	3	3	...	47	46	30	...	1	...	16
ASSAM VALLEY DISTRICTS	*5,168*	*2,265*	*65*	*553*	*1*	*2,838*	*2,951*	*1,420*	*51*	*119*	...	*1,480*
Goalpara	681	326	11	62	...	344	929	458	5	63	...	466
Kamrup	1,513	580	16	88	...	917	736	236	10	24	...	490
Darrang	353	165	6	49	...	182	221	99	8	4	...	114
Nowgong	590	230	7	109	1	353	142	76	3	4	...	63
Sibsagar	1,354	594	11	167	...	749	404	204	12	14	...	188
Lakhimpur	597	321	11	71	...	265	427	272	13	5	...	142
Garo Hills	80	49	3	7	...	28	92	75	...	5	...	17
(2) *Manipur State*	*559*	*233*	*3*	*14*	...	*323*	*1,063*	*455*	*11*	*24*	...	*597*

TABLE XV.— OCCUPATION OR MEANS OF LIVELIHOOD. PART A.—GENERAL TABLE—DETAILS FOR DISTRICTS—*contd.*

Class and Sub-class ... Order	*CLASS C: SUB-CLASS VIII.—PROFESSIONS AND LIBERAL ARTS.* 50.—LETTERS AND ARTS AND SCIENCES. *158.—Architects, surveyors, engineers and their employés.*						*160.—Music composers and masters, players on all kinds of musical instruments (not military), singers, actors and dancers.*					
District or State.	Total workers and dependants.	Actual workers. Total. Males.	Actual workers. Total. Females.	Partially agriculturist. Males.	Partially agriculturist. Females.	Dependants. Both sexes.	Total workers and dependants.	Actual workers. Total. Males.	Actual workers. Total. Females.	Partially agriculturist. Males.	Partially agriculturist. Females.	Dependants. Both sexes.
1	722	723	724	725	726	727	728	729	730	731	732	733
ASSAM	*2,716*	*1,401*	...	*263*	...	*1,315*	*5,304*	*2,365*	*76*	*544*	*1*	*2,963*
(1) British Territory	*2,560*	*1,343*	...	*262*	...	*1,217*	*4,526*	*1,919*	*65*	*526*	*1*	*2,542*
SURMA VALLEY AND HILL DISTRICTS	*1,210*	*685*	...	*216*	...	*525*	*3,423*	*1,331*	*14*	*485*	*1*	*2,078*
Cachar	45	11	...	3	...	34	49	26	5	...	...	18
Sylhet	292	108	...	29	...	184	3 363	1,298	8	485	1	2,057
Khasi and Jaintia Hills	787	516	...	182	...	271	6	6	...	...	...	...
Naga Hills	42	22	...	1	...	20	4	...	1	...	...	3
Lushai Hills	44	28	...	1	...	16	1	1	...	...	...	...
ASSAM VALLEY DISTRICTS...	*1,350*	*658*	...	*46*	...	*692*	*1,103*	*588*	*51*	*41*	...	*464*
Goalpara	178	104	...	15	...	74	649	317	5	35	...	327
Kamrup	287	112	...	11	...	175	147	48	10	1	...	89
Darrang	154	59	...	1	...	95	50	30	8	...	...	12
Nowgong	116	55	...	4	...	61	13	10	3	...	...	...
Sibsagar	276	120	...	12	...	156	106	73	12	1	...	21
Lakhimpur	276	149	...	3	...	127	110	95	13	...	...	2
Garo Hills	63	59	...	...	...	4	28	15	...	4	...	13
(2) Manipur State	*156*	*58*	...	*1*	...	*98*	*778*	*346*	*11*	*18*	...	*421*

Class and Sub-class ... Order	*CLASS C: SUB-CLASS IX.—PERSONS LIVING ON THEIR INCOME.* 51.—PERSONS LIVING PRINCIPALLY ON THEIR INCOME. *161.—Proprietors (other than of agricultural land), fund and scholarship-holders and pensioners.*						*CLASS D: SUB-CLASS X.—DOMESTIC SERVICE.* 52.—DOMESTIC SERVICE. *TOTAL OF ORDER 52.*					
District or State.	Total workers and dependants.	Actual workers. Total. Males.	Actual workers. Total. Females.	Partially agriculturist. Males.	Partially agriculturist. Females.	Dependants. Both sexes.	Total workers and dependants.	Actual workers. Total. Males.	Actual workers. Total. Females.	Partially agriculturist. Males.	Partially agriculturist. Females.	Dependants. Both sexes.
1	734	735	736	737	738	739	740	741	742	743	744	745
ASSAM	*3,206*	*877*	*67*	*147*	*2*	*2,263*	*38,539*	*22,033*	*5,550*	*1,175*	*19*	*10,956*
(1) British Territory	*2,041*	*814*	*60*	*145*	*2*	*2,067*	*37,490*	*21,526*	*5,510*	*1,158*	*19*	*10,454*
SURMA VALLEY AND HILL DISTRICTS	*1,341*	*403*	*10*	*60*	...	*998*	*18,204*	*9,403*	*2,952*	*845*	*12*	*5,849*
Cachar	137	20	...	2	...	117	2,158	1,509	210	111	1	439
Sylhet	345	109	...	37	...	236	13,739	6,671	2,418	716	10	4,650
Khasi and Jaintia Hills	532	167	7	5	...	358	1,535	677	309	8	1	549
Naga Hills	182	77	2	2	...	103	499	344	12	7	...	143
Lushai Hills	145	30	1	14	...	114	273	202	3	3	...	68
ASSAM VALLEY DISTRICTS	*1,600*	*411*	*50*	*85*	*2*	*1,139*	*19,286*	*12,123*	*2,558*	*313*	*7*	*4,605*
Goalpara	186	54	12	17	1	120	3 472	2,356	408	132	...	708
Kamrup	367	94	16	24	...	257	3,763	2,079	584	27	...	1,100
Darrang	123	37	4	16	...	82	2 518	1,618	403	35	3	497
Nowgong	120	35	2	12	...	83	1,364	855	220	12	1	289
Sibsagar	292	63	7	13	1	222	4,255	2,866	535	51	3	854
Lakhimpur	498	122	9	3	...	367	3,791	2,253	400	55	...	1,138
Garo Hills	14	6	...	...	...	8	123	96	8	1	...	19
(2) Manipur State	*265*	*63*	*7*	*2*	...	*195*	*1,049*	*507*	*40*	*17*	...	*502*

TABLE XV.—Occupation or Means of Livelihood. Part A.—General Table—Details for Districts—*contd.*

Class and Sub-class ... CLASS D: SUB-CLASS X.—DOMESTIC SERVICE.

Order ... 52.—DOMESTIC SERVICE.

District or State.	162.—Cooks, water carriers, doorkeepers, watchmen and other in-door servants. Total workers and dependants.	Actual workers. Total. Males.	Actual workers. Total. Females.	Actual workers. Partially agriculturist. Males.	Actual workers. Partially agriculturist. Females.	Dependants. Both sexes.	163.—Private grooms, coachmen, dog boys, etc. Total workers and dependants.	Actual workers. Total. Males.	Actual workers. Total. Females.	Actual workers. Partially agriculturist. Males.	Actual workers. Partially agriculturist. Females.	Dependants. Both sexes.
1	746	747	748	749	750	751	752	753	754	755	756	757
ASSAM	*35,389*	*20,228*	*5,526*	*1,09*	*19*	*9,635*	*3,150*	*1,805*	*24*	*80*	...	*1,321*
(1) British Territory	*34,448*	*19,784*	*5,487*	*1,078*	*19*	*9,177*	*3,049*	*1,749*	*23*	*80*	...	*1,277*
SURMA VALLEY AND HILL DISTRICTS	*17,300*	*9,009*	*2,938*	*816*	*12*	*5,253*	*1,004*	*394*	*14*	*29*	...	*596*
Cachar	1,932	1,802	210	100	1	330	226	117	...	11	...	109
Sylhet	13,238	6,572	2,418	698	10	4,278	471	99	...	18	...	872
Khasi and Jaintia Hills	1,261	510	295	8	1	447	274	158	14	...	...	102
Naga Hills	436	324	12	7	...	130	33	20	...	...	...	13
Lushai Hills	273	202	3	3	...	68	...	...	...	...	...	...
ASSAM VALLEY DISTRICTS	*17,948*	*10,775*	*2,549*	*262*	*7*	*3,924*	*2,038*	*1,348*	*9*	*51*	...	*681*
Goalpara	3,111	2,118	403	124	...	585	361	238	...	8	...	123
Kamrup	3,410	1,846	583	22	...	981	353	233	1	5	...	119
Darrang	2,275	1,435	402	20	3	438	243	183	1	15	...	59
Nowgong	1,197	730	219	11	1	248	167	125	1	1	...	41
Sibsagar	3,832	2,635	552	43	3	715	373	231	3	8	...	189
Lakhimpur	3,265	1,929	397	41	...	939	526	324	3	14	...	199
Garo Hills	163	83	8	1	...	18	15	14	...	...	...	1
(2) Manipur State	*941*	*444*	*39*	*17*	...	*458*	*108*	*63*	*1*	...	...	*44*

Class and Sub-class ... CLASS D: SUB-CLASS XI.—INSUFFICIENTLY DESCRIBED OCCUPATIONS.

Order ... 53.—GENERAL TERMS WHICH DO NOT INDICATE A DEFINITE OCCUPATION.

District or State.	TOTAL OF ORDER 53. Total workers and dependants.	Actual workers. Total. Males.	Actual workers. Total. Females.	Actual workers. Partially agriculturist. Males.	Actual workers. Partially agriculturist. Females.	Dependants. Both sexes.	165.—Cashiers, accountants, book-keepers, clerks and other employes in unspecified offices, warehouses and shops. Total workers and dependants.	Actual workers. Total. Males.	Actual workers. Total. Females.	Actual workers. Partially agriculturist. Males.	Actual workers. Partially agriculturist. Females.	Dependants. Both sexes.
1	758	759	760	761	762	763	764	765	766	767	768	769
ASSAM	*97,701*	*38,501*	*16,902*	*2,876*	*829*	*42,298*	*9,898*	*6,208*	*114*	*318*	...	*3,576*
(1) British Territory	*96,613*	*38,008*	*16,893*	*2,852*	*829*	*41,712*	*9,713*	*6,084*	*109*	*317*	...	*3,520*
SURMA VALLEY AND HILL DISTRICTS	*62,254*	*22,173*	*11,128*	*2,241*	*714*	*28,953*	*3,765*	*2,004*	*2*	*234*	...	*1,759*
Cachar	8,732	3,578	1,039	342	71	3,205	68	52	...	2	...	16
Sylhet	30,523	12,327	1,865	1,420	33	16,354	3,297	1,686	...	222	...	1,612
Khasi and Jaintia Hills	16,999	4,896	6,737	461	610	7,837	152	85	2	1	...	65
Naga Hills	3,768	1,208	588	6	...	1,973	114	68	...	1	...	46
Lushai Hills	323	234	9	12	...	85	134	114	...	8	...	40
ASSAM VALLEY DISTRICTS	*34,359*	*15,835*	*5,765*	*611*	*115*	*12,759*	*5,948*	*4,080*	*107*	*83*	...	*1,761*
Goalpara	5,929	3,163	494	139	1	2,332	1,012	816	...	31	...	196
Kamrup	6,025	2,856	447	67	1	2,722	1,068	698	27	6	...	348
Darrang	3,091	1,761	490	66	1	840	815	624	50	14	...	141
Nowgong	2,432	1,251	480	31	7	701	639	548	11	18	...	89
Sibsagar	6,458	3,091	1,100	149	39	2,267	983	670	13	6	...	801
Lakhimpur	9,534	3,374	2,607	159	66	3,553	1,391	688	7	8	...	696
Garo Hills	890	839	207	...	...	344	40	38	...	...	...	4
(2) Manipur State	*1,088*	*493*	*9*	*24*	...	*586*	*185*	*124*	*5*	*1*	...	*56*

TABLE XV.—OCCUPATION OR MEANS OF LIVELIHOOD. PART A.—GENERAL TABLE—DETAILS FOR DISTRICTS—*concld.*

Class and Sub-class ... *CLASS D: SUB-CLASS XI.—INSUFFICIENTLY DESCRIBED OCCUPATIONS.*

Order ... 53.—GENERAL TERMS WHICH DO NOT INDICATE A DEFINITE OCCUPATION.

166.—*Mechanics otherwise unspecified.*

District or State.	Total workers and dependants.	Actual workers. Total. Males.	Actual workers. Total. Females.	Actual workers. Partially agriculturist. Males.	Actual workers. Partially agriculturist. Females.	Dependants. Both sexes.
1	770	771	772	773	774	775
ASSAM	*2,124*	*1,073*	...	*93*	...	*1,051*
(1) ***British Territory***	*1,472*	*836*	...	*74*	...	*636*
SURMA VALLEY AND HILL DISTRICTS	*54*	*14*	...	*9*	...	*40*
Cachar	...	...	...	...	...	...
Sylhet	...	...	...	...	...	...
Khasi and Jaintia Hills	17	3	...	2	...	14
Naga Hills	37	11	...	...	...	26
Lushai Hills	...	...	...	...	...	...
ASSAM VALLEY DISTRICTS	*1,418*	*822*	...	*72*	...	*596*
Goalpara	62	45	...	13	...	17
Kamrup	162	111	...	17	...	51
Darrang	153	113	...	19	...	40
Nowgong	33	16	...	...	...	17
Sibsagar	140	94	...	4	...	46
Lakhimpur	864	439	...	19	...	425
Garo Hills	4	4	...	...	...	...
(2) ***Manipur State***	*652*	*237*	...	*19*	...	*415*

167.—*Labourers and workmen otherwise unspecified.*

District or State.	Total workers and dependants.	Actual workers. Total. Males.	Actual workers. Total. Females.	Actual workers. Partially agriculturist. Males.	Actual workers. Partially agriculturist. Females.	Dependants. Both sexes.
1	776	777	778	779	780	781
ASSAM	*83,780*	*30,480*	*16,788*	*2,401*	*829*	*36,512*
(1) ***British Territory***	*83,627*	*30,382*	*16,784*	*2,400*	*829*	*36,461*
SURMA VALLEY AND HILL DISTRICTS	*57,998*	*20,029*	*11,126*	*1,988*	*714*	*26,843*
Cachar	8 611	3,514	1,930	333	71	3,158
Sylhet	27 070	10,606	1,855	1,190	33	14 609
Khasi and Jaintia Hills	18 596	4,696	6,735	452	610	7,165
Naga Hills	3 543	1,096	588	4	...	1,859
Lushai Hills	178	117	9	4	...	52
ASSAM VALLEY DISTRICTS	*25,629*	*10,353*	*5,658*	*412*	*115*	*9,618*
Goalpara	4 669	2,227	434	91	1	2,008
Kamrup	4,529	1,938	420	37	1	2,162
Darrang	2 023	986	440	24	1	597
Nowgong	1 654	637	469	9	7	548
Sibsagar	5 011	2,163	1,088	136	39	1,760
Lakhimpur	6 915	2,106	2,604	115	66	2,209
Garo Hills	837	206	207	...	...	334
(2) ***Manipur State***	*153*	*98*	*4*	*1*	...	*51*

Class and Sub-class ... *CLASS D:—SUB-CLASS XII.—UNPRODUCTIVE.*

Order ... 54.—INMATES OF JAILS, ASYLUMS AND HOSPITALS. / 55.—BEGGARS, VAGRANTS, PROSTITUTES.

168.—*Inmates of Jails, Asylums and Hospitals.*

District or State.	Total workers and dependants.	Actual workers. Total. Males.	Actual workers. Total. Females.	Actual workers. Partially agriculturist. Males.	Actual workers. Partially agriculturist. Females.	Dependants. Both sexes.
1	782	783	784	785	786	787
ASSAM	*2,256*	*2,160*	*88*	*128*	...	*8*
(1) ***British Territory***	*2,139*	*2,043*	*88*	*128*	...	*8*
SURMA VALLEY AND HILL DISTRICTS	*948*	*926*	*17*	*128*	...	*5*
Cachar	78	78	...	...	...	...
Sylhet	783	767	14	123	...	5
Khasi and Jaintia Hills	55	52	3	...	...	...
Naga Hills	25	25	...	...	...	...
Lushai Hills	4	4	...	...	...	...
ASSAM VALLEY DISTRICTS	*1,191*	*1,117*	*71*	...	...	*3*
Goalpara	30	30	...	...	...	...
Kamrup	324	321	3	...	...	...
Darrang	551	500	48	...	...	3
Nowgong	48	48	...	...	...	...
Sibsagar	92	77	15	...	...	...
Lakhimpur	135	130	5	...	...	...
Garo Hills	11	11	...	...	...	...
(2) ***Manipur State***	*117*	*117*	...	...	...	...

169.—*Beggars, vagrants, procurers, prostitutes, receivers of stolen goods, cattle poisoners.*

District or State.	Total workers and dependants.	Actual workers. Total. Males.	Actual workers. Total. Females.	Actual workers. Partially agriculturist. Males.	Actual workers. Partially agriculturist. Females.	Dependants. Both sexes.
1	788	789	790	791	792	793
ASSAM	*68,627*	*17,922*	*26,041*	*532*	*107*	*24,664*
(1) ***British Territory***	*68,239*	*17,751*	*25,921*	*532*	*107*	*24,567*
SURMA VALLEY AND HILL DISTRICTS	*34,020*	*10,175*	*11,066*	*466*	*54*	*12,779*
Cachar	4 836	1,628	1,630	57	15	1,578
Sylhet	27,756	8,214	8,637	409	39	10,905
Khasi and Jaintia Hills	106	35	41	...	...	30
Naga Hills	1,319	296	757	...	...	266
Lushai Hills	3	2	1	...	...	...
ASSAM VALLEY DISTRICTS	*34,219*	*7,576*	*14,855*	*66*	*53*	*11,788*
Goalpara	8 355	1,962	3,186	35	3	3,207
Kamrup	15 317	2,432	6,925	6	50	5,960
Darrang	3 069	794	1,906	18	...	969
Nowgong	1 486	275	844	1	...	367
Sibsagar	3 459	1,356	1,245	6	...	858
Lakhimpur	1,640	678	633	...	...	329
Garo Hills	293	79	116	...	...	98
(2) ***Manipur State***	*388*	*171*	*120*	...	...	*97*

TABLE XV.—OCCUPATION OR MEANS OF LIVELIHOOD. PART B.—SUBSIDIARY OCCUPATIONS OF AGRICULTURISTS—ACTUAL WORKERS ONLY.

(1) RENT-RECEIVERS.

District or State.	Total number of rent-receivers (actual workers).		Number of actual workers who returned subsidiary occupation. (a) Agricultural.		(b) Non-agricultural.		Details of subsidiary occupations returned. Rent-payers.		Agricultural labourers.		Government servants of all kinds.		Money lenders and grain dealers.		Other traders of all kinds.	
	Males.	Females.	Males.	Females.	Males.	Females.	Males.	Females.	Males.	Females.	Males.	Females.	Males.	Females.	Males.	Females.
1	2	3	4	5	6	7	8	9	10	11	12	13	14	15	16	17
ASSAM	*18,286*	*4,195*	*4,179*	*272*	*6,370*	*335*	*4,039*	*248*	*140*	*24*	*222*	*1*	*710*	*54*	*1,942*	*45*
(1) British Territory	*18,286*	*4,193*	*4,179*	*272*	*6,370*	*335*	*4,039*	*248*	*140*	*24*	*222*	*1*	*710*	*54*	*1,942*	*45*
SURMA VALLEY AND HILL DISTRICTS	*15,196*	*2,846*	*3,874*	*193*	*5,398*	*163*	*3,750*	*178*	*124*	*15*	*196*	*1*	*694*	*53*	*1,810*	*29*
Cachar	2,113	1,517	206	83	685	78	287	78	9	5	62	...	93	29	180	16
Sylhet	13,020	1,258	3,577	108	4,697	75	3,463	99	114	9	134	1	601	24	1,638	13
Khasi and Jaintia Hills	56	71	1	2	13	10	...	1	1	1	...	...	...	...	1	...
Naga Hills	3	...	...	...	...	...	...	...	...	...	...	...	...	...	...	...
Lushai Hills	4	...	...	...	3	...	...	...	...	...	...	...	...	...	...	...
ASSAM VALLEY DISTRICTS	*3,090*	*1,347*	*305*	*79*	*972*	*172*	*289*	*70*	*16*	*9*	*26*	...	*16*	*1*	*133*	*16*
Goalpara	986	98	235	12	182	11	234	12	1	...	12	...	3	...	41	2
Kamrup	1,768	1,018	45	26	659	128	43	18	2	8	10	...	13	...	65	13
Darrang	107	105	7	9	56	24	4	9	3	...	1	...	...	...	2	...
Nowgong	27	11	...	1	4	3	...	1	...	...	...	...	...	...	...	...
Sibsagar	141	87	16	30	57	2	6	30	10	...	2	...	...	...	12	1
Lakhimpur	49	23	...	...	10	3	...	...	...	...	...	...	...	...	...	...
Garo Hills	12	5	2	1	4	1	2	...	...	1	1	...	...	1	8	...
(2) Manipur State...	...	*2*	...	...	...	...	...	...	...	...	...	...	...	...	...	...

District or State.	Details of subsidiary occupations returned—*concld.* Priests.		Clerks of all kinds (not Government).		School masters.		Lawyers.		Estate agents and managers.		Medical practitioners.		Artisans.		Other occupations.	
	Males.	Females.	Males.	Females.	Males.	Females.	Males.	Females.	Males.	Females.	Males.	Females.	Males.	Females.	Males.	Females.
1	18	19	20	21	22	23	24	25	26	27	28	29	30	31	32	33
ASSAM	*898*	*31*	*362*	...	*297*	*2*	*74*	...	*92*	...	*161*	*1*	*179*	*13*	*1,433*	*188*
(1) British Territory	*898*	*31*	*362*	...	*297*	*2*	*74*	...	*92*	...	*161*	*1*	*179*	*13*	*1,433*	*188*
SURMA VALLEY AND HILL DISTRICTS	*599*	*24*	*338*	...	*285*	*2*	*73*	...	*89*	...	*131*	*1*	*112*	*5*	*1,062*	*48*
Cachar	22	9	28	...	25	...	23	...	...	...	28	...	21	4	203	20
Sylhet	577	15	310	...	260	2	50	...	80	...	103	1	91	1	844	18
Khasi and Jaintia Hills	...	...	...	...	...	...	...	...	...	...	...	...	...	...	12	10
Naga Hills	...	...	...	...	...	...	...	...	...	...	...	...	...	...	...	...
Lushai Hills	...	...	...	...	...	...	...	...	...	...	...	...	...	...	3	...
ASSAM VALLEY DISTRICTS	*299*	*7*	*24*	...	*12*	...	*1*	...	*3*	...	*30*	...	*67*	*8*	*371*	*140*
Goalpara	7	1	21	...	2	...	1	...	3	...	10	...	32	...	50	8
Kamrup	290	6	1	...	10	...	...	...	...	...	19	...	20	8	231	101
Darrang	...	...	1	...	...	...	...	...	...	...	1	...	...	...	51	24
Nowgong	2	...	...	...	...	...	...	...	...	...	...	...	...	...	2	3
Sibsagar	...	...	1	...	...	...	...	...	...	...	...	...	15	...	27	1
Lakhimpur	...	...	...	...	...	...	...	...	...	...	...	...	...	...	10	3
Garo Hills	...	...	...	...	...	...	...	...	...	...	...	...	...	...	...	...
(2) Manipur State	...	...	...	...	...	...	...	...	...	...	...	...	...	...	...	...

TABLE XV.—Occupation or Means of Livelihood. Part B.—Subsidiary Occupations of Agriculturists—Actual Workers only—*contd.*

(2) RENT-PAYERS.

District or State.	Total number of rent-payers (actual workers). Males.	Females.	Number of actual workers who returned subsidiary occupations. (a) Agricultural. Males.	Females.	(b) Non-agricultural. Males.	Females.	Details of subsidiary occupations returned. Rent-receivers. Males.	Females.	Agricultural labourers. Males.	Females.	General labourers. Males.	Females.	Government servants of all kinds. Males.	Females.	Money-lenders and grain dealers. Males.	Females.	Other traders of all kinds. Males.	Females.
1	2	3	4	5	6	7	8	9	10	11	12	13	14	15	16	17	18	19
ASSAM	*1,525,888*	*566,329*	*19,781*	*3,034*	*237,571*	*43,282*	*11,719*	*598*	*8,062*	*2,436*	*59,403*	*13,065*	*1,594*	*4*	*4,257*	*382*	*49,166*	*4,871*
(1) British Territory	*1,456,873*	*554,520*	*19,736*	*3,030*	*221,835*	*39,839*	*11,719*	*598*	*8,017*	*2,432*	*45,699*	*12,334*	*1,565*	*4*	*4,257*	*377*	*48,200*	*4,830*
SURMA VALLEY AND HILL DISTRICTS	*731,548*	*108,021*	*12,746*	*2,603*	*137,140*	*13,675*	*7,558*	*244*	*5,188*	*2,359*	*24,290*	*4,331*	*232*	*4*	*3,604*	*293*	*34,589*	*1,661*
Cachar	94,708	13,455	1,634	71	11,176	1,199	1,462	47	222	24	3,553	592	19	...	440	94	3,243	182
Sylhet	530,524	20,040	9,343	220	113,926	2,348	6,018	152	3,325	68	17,584	511	191	4	3,148	181	20,817	399
Khasi and Jaintia Hills	45,612	43,205	1,719	2,312	10,222	10,109	78	45	1,641	2,267	2,951	3,227	1	...	7	18	1,478	1,080
Naga Hills	41,832	5,241	...	...	107	2	...	...	...	...	5	...	...	...	...	...	3	...
Lushai Hills	28,872	25,580	...	...	1,709	17	...	...	...	...	197	1	21	...	...	...	48	...
ASSAM VALLEY DISTRICTS	*725,325*	*446,499*	*6,990*	*427*	*84,695*	*26,164*	*4,161*	*354*	*2,829*	*73*	*21,409*	*8,003*	*1,333*	...	*653*	*84*	*13,611*	*3,169*
Goalpara	153,667	23,010	4,009	44	12,429	4,481	3,589	32	420	12	3,746	21	230	...	203	5	2,060	148
Kamrup	148,940	62,044	1,468	128	23,214	3,021	427	98	1,041	30	2,237	265	202	...	288	31	2,383	280
Darrang	83,564	72,517	11	7	7,238	2,309	6	6	6	1	1,117	294	127	...	17	...	841	112
Nowgong	73,077	65,563	11	12	7,284	4,252	3	2	8	10	1,685	1,173	348	...	5	4	1,349	729
Sibsagar	141,587	115,123	1,378	213	21,244	7,631	44	209	1,314	4	7,473	3,755	233	...	129	40	3,132	1,688
Lakhimpur	70,079	66,260	37	2	9,873	3,016	3	...	34	2	5,125	2,495	98	...	...	...	1,281	175
Garo Hills	45,771	40,002	96	21	3,383	554	90	7	6	14	46	...	5	...	11	4	2,565	37
(2) Manipur State	*69,015*	*11,802*	*45*	*4*	*15,736*	*3,443*	...	...	*45*	*4*	*13,704*	*731*	*29*	...	...	*5*	*966*	*41*

DETAILS OF SUBSIDIARY OCCUPATIONS RETURNED—*concld.*

District or State.	Fishermen and boatmen. Males.	Females.	Cattle breeders and milkmen. Males.	Females.	Village watchmen. Males.	Females.	Weavers. Males.	Females.	Barbers. Males.	Females.	Oil-pressers. Males.	Females.	Washermen. Males.	Females.	Potters. Males.	Females.	Blacksmiths and carpenters. Males.	Females.	Other occupations. Males.	Females.
1	20	21	22	23	24	25	26	27	28	29	30	31	32	33	34	35	36	37	38	39
ASSAM	*30,892*	*2,459*	*3,815*	*150*	*5,308*	...	*2,004*	*10,088*	*2,999*	*25*	*1,684*	*37*	*2,225*	*83*	*2,191*	*1,197*	*7,661*	*18*	*64,372*	*10,903*
(1) British Territory	*30,841*	*2,459*	*3,812*	*150*	*5,291*	...	*1,999*	*7,432*	*2,999*	*25*	*1,684*	*37*	*2,225*	*83*	*2,048*	*1,195*	*7,592*	*17*	*63,623*	*10,896*
SURMA VALLEY AND HILL DISTRICTS	*24,585*	*324*	*1,331*	*43*	*2,821*	...	*1,863*	*1,059*	*2,717*	*17*	*1,228*	*34*	*2,201*	*71*	*998*	*88*	*4,737*	*12*	*31,944*	*5,738*
Cachar	656	5	47	13	250	...	3	10	107	1	...	...	43	1	14	...	246	...	2,546	301
Sylhet	23,862	261	1,252	3	2,471	...	1,841	171	2,610	16	1,228	34	2,158	70	830	70	4,159	12	22,875	616
Khasi and Jaintia Hills	4	58	29	26	...	...	19	878	...	...	...	...	...	...	151	18	190	...	5,392	4,804
Naga Hills	...	...	3	...	39	...	...	...	...	...	...	...	...	...	3	...	20	...	85	2
Lushai Hills	63	...	1	1	61	...	...	...	...	...	...	...	...	...	...	...	222	...	1,096	15
ASSAM VALLEY DISTRICTS	*6,256*	*2,135*	*2,481*	*107*	*2,470*	...	*136*	*6,373*	*282*	*8*	*456*	*3*	*24*	*12*	*1,050*	*1,107*	*2,855*	*5*	*31,679*	*5,158*
Goalpara	342	130	391	5	341	...	98	4,116	25	...	377	1	9	...	41	1	913	...	3,668	54
Kamrup	774	143	397	8	706	...	17	180	193	4	61	...	5	...	414	194	504	...	14,883	2,816
Darrang	779	208	373	73	461	...	16	856	17	...	...	...	1	4	24	260	170	1	3,205	432
Nowgong	1,676	766	242	1	114	...	...	468	9	...	1	1	2	3	230	507	141	...	1,502	600
Sibsagar	2,125	776	946	16	572	...	1	260	82	3	2	...	7	5	340	136	549	1	5,652	951
Lakhimpur	514	68	106	4	264	...	1	...	5	1	...	...	...	...	1	...	225	...	2,223	289
Garo Hills	16	...	36	...	12	...	8	498	...	...	15	1	...	...	...	...	213	3	456	16
(2) Manipur State	*51*	...	*3*	...	*17*	...	*5*	*2,656*	...	...	...	...	...	...	*143*	*2*	*69*	*1*	*749*	*7*

TABLE XV.—OCCUPATION OR MEANS OF LIVELIHOOD. PART B.—SUBSIDIARY OCCUPATIONS OF AGRICULTURISTS—ACTUAL WORKERS ONLY

(3) AGRICULTURAL LABOURERS.

District or State.	Total number of agricultural labourers (actual workers).		Number of actual workers who returned subsidiary occupations. (a) Agricultural.		(b) Non-Agricultural.		Details of subsidiary occupations returned. Rent-receivers.		Rent-payers.		General labourers.		Village watchmen.		Cattle breeders and milkmen.		Mill hands.	
	Males.	Females.	Males.	Females.	Males.	Females.	Males.	Females.	Males.	Females.	Males.	Females.	Males.	Females.	Males.	Females.	Males.	Females.
1	2	3	4	5	6	7	8	9	10	11	12	13	14	15	16	17	18	19
ASSAM	*40,647*	*9,965*	*700*	*56*	*2,182*	*927*	*52*	*9*	*648*	*47*	*790*	*91*	*12*	...	*52*	*2*	*14*	...
(1) ***British Territory***	*40,500*	*9,950*	*700*	*56*	*2,179*	*925*	*52*	*9*	*648*	*47*	*790*	*89*	*12*	...	*52*	*2*	*14*	...
SURMA VALLEY AND HILL DISTRICTS	*25,344*	*6,861*	*681*	*54*	*1,869*	*738*	*45*	*9*	*636*	*45*	*671*	*81*	*9*	...	*50*	*2*	...	...
Cachar	2,586	893	64	5	239	235	18	1	46	4	81	28	1	...	9	...	...	...
Sylhet	21,282	3,709	585	19	1,437	275	26	7	559	12	590	52	8	...	41	2	...	...
Khasi and Jaintia Hills	1,453	2,240	32	30	193	228	1	1	31	29	...	1	...	...	...	...	...	...
Naga Hills	21	19	...	...	...	...	...	...	...	...	...	...	...	...	...	...	...	...
Lushai Hills	2	...	...	...	...	...	...	...	...	...	...	...	...	...	...	...	...	...
ASSAM VALLEY DISTRICTS	*15,156*	*3,089*	*19*	*2*	*310*	*187*	*7*	...	*12*	*2*	*119*	*8*	*3*	...	*2*	...	*14*	...
Goalpara	5,616	839	6	...	168	156	1	...	5	...	69	2	3	...	...	...	13	...
Kamrup	4,842	1,292	10	2	95	9	6	...	4	...	40	...	...	...	...	...	...	...
Darrang	2,109	303	1	...	23	3	...	...	1	...	1	...	...	...	2	...	...	...
Nowgong	685	184	...	...	9	8	...	...	...	...	1	...	...	...	...	...	...	...
Sibsagar	1,141	106	...	...	6	2	...	...	...	...	6	2	...	...	...	...	...	...
Lakhimpur	307	77	...	...	2	...	...	...	...	...	...	...	...	...	...	...	1	...
Garo Hills	456	288	2	...	7	9	...	...	2	...	2	4	...	...	...	...	...	...
(2) ***Manipur State***	*147*	*15*	...	...	*3*	*2*	...	...	...	...	...	*2*	...	...	...	...	...	...

DETAILS OF SUBSIDIARY OCCUPATIONS RETURNED—*concld.*

District or State.	Fishermen and boatmen.		Rice pounders.		Traders of all kinds.		Oil-pressers.		Weavers.		Potters.		Leather workers.		Washermen.		Blacksmiths and carpenters.		Other occupations.	
	Males.	Females.	Males.	Females.	Males.	Females.	Males.	Females.	Males.	Females.	Males.	Females.	Males.	Females.	Males.	Females.	Males.	Females.	Males.	Females.
1	20	21	22	23	24	25	26	27	28	29	30	31	32	33	34	35	36	37	38	39
ASSAM	*376*	*30*	*1*	*36*	*61*	*6*	*2*	...	*24*	*228*	*6*	*1*	*24*	*5*	*27*	...	*21*	...	*772*	*528*
(1) ***British Territory***	*376*	*30*	*1*	*36*	*61*	*6*	*2*	...	*24*	*228*	*6*	*1*	*24*	*5*	*27*	...	*21*	...	*769*	*528*
SURMA VALLEY AND HILL DISTRICTS	*365*	*24*	*1*	*36*	*35*	*5*	*1*	...	*20*	*76*	*6*	...	*22*	*5*	*27*	...	*9*	...	*653*	*509*
Cachar	13	1	...	18	10	2	...	...	...	6	...	...	22	5	...	...	2	...	101	175
Sylhet	352	23	1	18	24	2	1	...	20	69	6	...	...	...	27	...	6	...	361	109
Khasi and Jaintia Hills	...	...	...	...	1	1	...	...	...	1	...	...	...	...	...	...	1	...	191	225
Naga Hills	...	...	...	...	...	...	...	...	...	...	...	...	...	...	...	...	...	...	...	...
Lushai Hills	...	...	...	...	...	...	...	...	...	...	...	...	...	...	...	...	...	...	...	...
ASSAM VALLEY DISTRICTS	*11*	*6*	...	...	*26*	*1*	*1*	...	*4*	*152*	...	*1*	*2*	...	...	...	*12*	...	*116*	*19*
Goalpara	1	...	...	...	22	1	1	...	4	148	...	...	...	...	...	...	11	...	44	5
Kamrup	4	...	...	...	3	...	...	...	...	...	...	...	2	...	...	...	...	...	46	9
Darrang	...	...	...	...	...	...	...	...	...	...	...	...	...	...	...	...	...	...	20	3
Nowgong	6	6	...	...	...	...	...	...	...	...	...	1	...	...	...	...	...	...	2	1
Sibsagar	...	...	...	...	...	...	...	...	...	...	...	...	...	...	...	...	...	...	...	...
Lakhimpur	...	...	...	...	...	...	...	...	...	...	...	...	...	...	...	...	...	...	1	...
Garo Hills	...	...	...	...	1	...	...	...	...	4	...	...	...	...	...	...	1	...	3	1
(2) ***Manipur State***	...	...	...	...	...	...	...	...	...	...	...	...	...	...	...	...	...	...	*3*	...

TABLE XV.—Occupation or Means of Livelihood.

Part D.—Distribution by Religion.

Group No.	Occupation.	Total number of workers and dependants.	Distribution by Religion.					
			Hindus.	Musalmans.	Christians.	Buddhists.	Animists.	Others.
	1	2	3	4	5	6	7	8
	TOTAL POPULATION ...	*7,059,857*	*3,838,769*	*1,901,032*	*66,562*	*10,513*	*1,239,280*	*3,701*
	A.—PRODUCTION OF RAW MATERIALS.	*6,184,914*	*3,217,114*	*1,725,955*	*55,555*	*8,916*	*1,176,810*	*564*
	I.—EXPLOITATION OF THE SURFACE OF THE EARTH	*6,178,391*	*3,212,443*	*1,725,255*	*55,450*	*8,723*	*1,175,980*	*540*
	1.—PASTURE AND AGRICULTURE ...	*6,077,685*	*3,150,477*	*1,686,726*	*55,498*	*8,707*	*1,175,812*	*535*
	(a) *Ordinary Cultivation* ...	*5,323,380*	*2,518,817*	*1,669,069*	*45,198*	*8,269*	*1,081,734*	*370*
1	Income from rent of agricultural land ...	137,106	42,306	90,568	88	1	4,142	1
2	Ordinary cultivators	5,092,771	2,426,123	1,547,060	43,923	8,218	1,067,089	363
3	Agents, managers of landed estates (not planters), clerks, rent collectors, etc.	8,581	7,185	1,227	35	8	120	6
4	Farm servants and field labourers ...	84 922	48,203	30,214	1,082	40	10,383	...
	(b) *Growers of special products and market gardening.*	*702,793*	*596,644*	*12,273*	*9,295*	*166*	*84,268*	*147*
5	Tea, coffee, cinchona and indigo plantations.	675,360	595,259	12,195	5,544	121	62,176	65
6	Fruit, flower, vegetable, betel, vine, areca nut, etc., growers.	27,433	1,385	78	3,751	45	22,092	82
	(c) *Forestry*	*4,099*	*2,685*	*410*	*102*	*21*	*874*	*7*
7	Forest officers, rangers, guards, etc. ...	1,336	996	107	67	6	154	6
8	Wood-cutters, firewood, lac, catechu, rubber, etc., collectors, and charcoal burners.	2,763	1,689	303	35	15	720	1
	(d) *Raising of farm stock* ...	*47,278*	*32,316*	*4,949*	*899*	*258*	*8,845*	*11*
9	Cattle and buffalo breeders and keepers	18,819	17,565	472	28	113	641	...
10	Sheep, goat and pig breeders.	96	64	11	3	...	18	...
11	Breeders of other animals (horses, mules, camels, asses, etc.).	9	6	3	...	...	...	...
12	Herdsmen, shepherds, goat-herds, etc. ...	28,354	14,681	4,463	868	145	8,186	11
13	(e) *Raising of small animals* (Birds, bees, silkworms, etc.).	*135*	*15*	*25*	*4*	...	*91*	...
	2.—FISHING AND HUNTING ...	*100,706*	*61,966*	*38,529*	*22*	*16*	*168*	*5*
14	Fishing	100,102	61,600	38,364	21	...	117	...
15	Hunting	604	366	165	1	16	51	5
	II.—EXTRACTION OF MINERALS.	*6,523*	*4,671*	*700*	*105*	*193*	*830*	*24*
	3.—MINES	*5,122*	*4,206*	*607*	*56*	*191*	*57*	*5*
16	Coal mines and petroleum wells ...	5,096	4,181	607	55	191	57	5
17	Mines and metallic minerals (gold, iron, manganese, etc.).	26	25	...	1	...	...	...
18	4.—QUARRIES OF HARD ROCKS (other minerals) (jade, diamonds, limestones, etc.).	*680*	*162*	*92*	*49*	*2*	*356*	*19*
	5.—SALT, ETC.	*721*	*303*	*1*	...	...	*417*	...
19	Rock, sea and marsh salt	712	295	...	...	...	417	...
20	Extraction of saltpetre, alum and other substances soluble in water.	9	8	1	...	...	...	...
	B.—PREPARATION AND SUPPLY OF MATERIAL SUBSTANCES.	*537,782*	*408,706*	*96,327*	*3,270*	*874*	*26,309*	*2,296*
	III.—INDUSTRY	*216,624*	*176,197*	*27,770*	*1,114*	*258*	*11,061*	*224*
	6.—TEXTILES	*59,419*	*53,854*	*1,820*	*98*	*6*	*3,641*	...
21	Cotton ginning, cleaning and pressing...	46	1	45	...	...	...	...
22	Cotton spinning, sizing and weaving ...	56 285	51,350	1,388	98	6	3,453	...
23	Jute spinning, pressing and weaving ...	196	183	63	...	...	...	...
24	Rope, twine and string	1,085	793	285	...	...	7	...
26	Wool carders and spinners, weavers of woolen blankets, carpets, etc.	16	10	...	...	...	...	...
27	Silk spinners and weavers	1,717	1,509	28	...	...	180	...
30	Dyeing, bleaching, printing, preparation and sponging of textiles.	44	33	11	...	...	...	...
31	Other (lace, crape, embroideries, fringes, etc.), and insufficiently described textile industries.	26	25	...	...	...	1	...

TABLE XV.—Occupation or Means of Livelihood.

Part D.—Distribution by Religion—*continued*.

Group No.	Occupation.	Total number of workers and dependants.	Distribution by Religion.					
			Hindus.	Musalmans.	Christians.	Buddhists.	Animists.	Others.
	1	2	3	4	5	6	7	8
	7.—HIDES, SKINS AND HARD MATERIALS FROM THE ANIMAL KINGDOM.	*1,432*	*1,372*	*49*	...	*5*	*13*	...
32	Tanners, curriers, leather dressers and dyers, etc.	1,223	1,169	36	...	5	13	...
33	Makers of leather articles, such as trunks, water bags, etc.	83	83	...	...	...	...	...
34	Furriers	113	112	1	...	...	...	...
35	Bone, ivory, horn, shell, etc., workers...	13	8	5	...	...	...	...
	8.—WOOD	*34,029*	*29,829*	*2,094*	*351*	*178*	*1,413*	*164*
36	Sawyers, carpenters, turners and joiners, etc.	20 318	17,359	1,363	346	178	908	164
37	Basket makers and other industries of woody material, including leaves.	13 711	12,470	731	5	...	505	...
	9.—METALS	*13,248*	*10,560*	*2,161*	*27*	*15*	*483*	*2*
38	Forging and rolling of iron and other metals.	7	...	...	...	...	7	...
39	Plough and agricultural implement makers.	220	3	9	...	...	208	...
40	Makers of arms, guns, etc.	40	13	27	...	...	...	...
41	Other workers in iron and makers of implements and tools, principally or exclusively of iron.	7,860	7,325	244	21	15	253	2
42	Workers in brass, copper and bell metal	4,957	3,136	1,810	2	...	9	...
43	Workers in other metals (tin, zinc, lead, quick-silver, etc.).	164	83	71	4	...	6	...
	10.—CERAMICS	*16,795*	*16,450*	*249*	*9*	...	*87*	...
45	Makers of glass and crystal ware ...	4	4	...	...	...	...	...
46	Makers of porcelain and crockery ...	112	112	...	...	...	...	...
47	Potters and earthen pipe and bowl makers.	15,677	15,436	158	6	...	77	...
48	Brick and tile makers	1,002	898	91	3	...	10	...
	11.—CHEMICAL PRODUCTS PROPERLY SO CALLED, AND ANALOGOUS.	*5,426*	*4,047*	*1,371*	...	...	*8*	...
50	Manufacture of matches and explosive materials.	54	31	23	...	...	...	...
51	Manufacture of ærated and mineral waters.	15	12	2	...	...	1	...
52	Manufacture of dyes, paint and ink ...	4	3	...	...	...	1	...
53	Manufacture and refining of vegetable and mineral oils.	4,286	3,957	323	...	...	6	...
55	Others (soap, candles, lac, cutch, perfumes and miscellaneous drugs).	1,067	44	1,023	...	...	...	...
	12.—FOOD INDUSTRIES	*19,371*	*9,050*	*7,368*	*36*	*1*	*2,908*	*6*
56	Rice pounders and huskers and flour grinders.	13,637	6,842	6,508	15	1	271	...
57	Bakers and biscuit makers	662	175	337	6	...	144	...
58	Grain parchers, etc.	1,023	977	46	...	...	...	...
59	Butchers	376	10	281	11	...	74	...
61	Butter, cheese and ghee makers ...	25	18	...	...	...	7	...
62	Makers of sugar, molasses and gur ...	45	38	7	...	...	...	...
63	Sweetmeat makers, preparers of jam and condiments, etc.	1,029	843	182	1	...	...	3
64	Brewers and distillers	2,516	95	1	5	...	2,412	3
65	Toddy drawers	16	10	6	...	...	...	...
66	Manufacturers of tobacco, opium and ganja.	42	42	...	...	...	...	...
	13.—INDUSTRIES OF DRESS AND THE TOILET.	*36,090*	*27,139*	*7,963*	*211*	*13*	*739*	*25*
67	Hat, cap and turban makers ...	3	...	3	...	...	...	...
68	Tailors, milliners, dress makers and darners, embroiderers on linen.	10,018	2,516	6,630	202	10	646	14
69	Shoe, boot and sandal makers ...	1,852	1,757	18	...	3	74	...
70	Other industries pertaining to dress—gloves, socks, gaiters, belts, buttons, umbrellas, canes, etc.	308	58	244	...	...	6	...
71	Washing, cleaning and dyeing ...	8 956	8,450	496	7	...	3	...
72	Barbers, hairdressers and wig makers...	14,949	14,356	572	2	...	8	11
73	Other industries connected with the toilet (tattooers, shampooers, bath houses, etc.).	4	2	...	...	...	2	...
	14.—FURNITURE INDUSTRIES ...	*73*	*61*	*11*	...	...	*1*	...
74	Cabinet makers, carriage painters, etc....	59	55	4	...	...	...	...
75	Upholsterers, tent makers, etc. ...	14	6	7	...	...	1	...
	15.—BUILDING INDUSTRIES ...	*8,958*	*5,718*	*2,678*	*54*	*1*	*500*	*7*
76	Lime burners, cement workers ...	749	689	27	1	...	32	...
77	Excavators, plinth builders and well-sinkers.	3,004	2,564	357	3	...	80	...
78	Stone and marble workers, masons and bricklayers.	3,044	1,126	1,551	37	1	322	7
79	Others (thatchers, building contractors, house painters, tilers, plumbers, locksmiths, etc.).	2,161	1,339	743	13	...	66	...

TABLE XV.—Occupation or Means of Livelihood.

Part D.—Distribution by Religion—*continued.*

Group No.	Occupation.	Total number of workers and dependants.	Distribution by Religion.					
			Hindus.	Musalmans.	Christians.	Buddhists.	Animists.	Others.
	1	2	3	4	5	6	7	8
	16.—CONSTRUCTION OF MEANS OF TRANSPORT.	*640*	*550*	*19*	*3*	...		...
80	Cart, carriage, palki, etc., makers and wheelwrights.	286	236	16	3	...	31	...
81	Saddlers, harness makers, whip and lash makers.	6	6	...	...	...	...	...
82	Ship and boat builders	348	308	3	...	...	37	...
83	**17.—PRODUCTION AND TRANSMISSION OF PHYSICAL FORCES (HEAT, LIGHT, ELECTRICITY, MOTIVE POWER, etc.).** (Gas works, electric light and ice factories.)	*4*	*3*	...	...	...	...	*1*
	18.—INDUSTRIES OF LUXURY AND THOSE PERTAINING TO LITERATURE AND THE ARTS AND SCIENCES.	*17,736*	*14,971*	*1,843*	*296*	*39*	*580*	*7*
84	Printers, lithographers, engravers, etc....	1,042	347	114	251	1	322	7
85	Newspaper and magazine managers and editors, journalists, etc.	5	5	...	...	...	...	...
86	Bookbinders and stitchers, envelope makers, etc.	73	18	52	1	2	...	...
87	Makers of musical instruments ...	82	76	1	...	...	5	...
88	Makers of watches and clocks and optical, photographic and surgical instruments.	136	93	35	...	...	8	...
89	Workers in precious stones and metals, enamellers, imitation jewellery makers, gilders, etc.	15,647	13,840	1,489	41	34	243	...
90	Makers of bangles, rosaries, bead and other necklaces, spangles, lingams and sacred threads.	350	632	18	...	...	...	...
91	Toy, kite, cage, fishing tackle, etc., makers, taxidermists, etc.	111	42	67	2	...	...	...
92	Others, including managers, persons other than performers employed in theatres and other places of public entertainment, employés of public societies, race course service, huntsmen, etc.	290	218	67	1	2	2	...
93	**19.—INDUSTRIES CONCERNED WITH REFUSE MATTER.** (Sweepers, scavengers, dust and sweeping contractors.)	*3,403*	*2,593*	*151*	*27*	...	*620*	*12*
	IV.—TRANSPORT	*76,600*	*56,247*	*12,505*	*1,091*	*54*	*6,602*	*101*
	20.—TRANSPORT BY WATER ...	*23,841*	*16,468*	*7,235*	*51*	*12*	*75*	...
94	Harbour works, dockyards and pilots.	315	275	35	1	...	4	...
95	Ship owners and their employés, ship brokers, ships' officers, engineers, mariners and firemen.	3,043	803	2,194	40	...	6	...
96	Persons employed on the maintenance of streams, rivers and canals (including construction).	3	1	2	...	...	...	...
97	Boat owners, boat men and tow men ...	20,480	15,389	5,004	10	12	65	...
	21.—TRANSPORT BY ROAD... ...	*34,268*	*24,861*	*3,065*	*499*	*19*	*5,783*	*41*
98	Persons employed on the construction and maintenance of roads and bridges.	13,967	12,302	1,227	34	3	392	9
99	Cart owners and drivers, coachmen, stable boys, tramway, mail carriage, etc., managers and employés (excluding private servants).	10,194	7,723	1,612	111	15	712	21
100	Palki, etc., bearers and owners ...	3,503	3,489	13	...	...	1	...
101	Pack elephant, camel, mule, ass and bullock owners and drivers.	23	15	7	...	...	1	...
102	Porters and messengers	6,581	1,332	206	354	1	4,677	11
	22.—TRANSPORT BY RAIL ...	*13,877*	*11,235*	*1,689*	*436*	*13*	*444*	*60*
103	Railway employés of all kinds other than construction coolies.	11,213	8,874	1,405	436	13	425	60
104	Labourers employed on railway construction.	2,664	2,361	284	...	...	19	...
105	**23.—POST OFFICE, TELEGRAPH AND TELEPHONE SERVICES.**	*4,614*	*3,683*	*516*	*105*	*10*	*300*	...
	V.—TRADE	*244,558*	*176,262*	*56,052*	*1,065*	*562*	*8,646*	*1,371*
106	**24.—BANKS, ESTABLISHMENTS OF CREDIT, EXCHANGE AND INSURANCE.** (Bank managers, money lenders, exchange and insurance agents, money changers and brokers and their employés).	*6,408*	*5,564*	*678*	*15*	...	*6*[illegible]	*33*
107	**25.—BROKERAGE, COMMISSION AND EXPORT.** (Brokers, commission agents, commercial travellers, warehouse owners and employés)	*413*	*325*	*83*	*1*	...	*2*	*2*

TABLE XV.—Occupation or Means of Livelihood.

Part D.—Distribution by Religion—*continued.*

Group No.	Occupation.	Total number of workers and dependants.	Distribution by Religion. Hindus.	Musalmans.	Christians.	Buddhists.	Animists.	Others.
	1	2	3	4	5	6	7	8
108	**26.—TRADE IN TEXTILES** (Trade in piece goods, wool, cotton, silk, hair and other textiles).	*15,323*	*11,317*	*2,093*	*308*	*3*	*902*	*700*
109	**27.—TRADE IN SKINS, LEATHER, AND FURS** (Trade in skins, leather, furs, feathers, horn, etc.).	*8,049*	*6,880*	*1,151*	*3*	...	*15*	...
110	**28.—TRADE IN WOOD** [Trade in wood (not firewood), cork, bark, etc.].	*3,519*	*1,966*	*1,199*	*5*	*10*	*338*	*1*
111	**29.—TRADE IN METALS** (Trade in metals, machinery, knife, tool, etc., sellers).	*659*	*543*	*89*	*7*	*1*	*20*	...
112	**30.—TRADE IN POTTERY**	*3,208*	*3,091*	*97*	...	...	*20*	...
113	**31.—TRADE IN CHEMICAL PRODUCTS** [Trade in chemical products (drugs, dyes, paints, petroleum, explosives, etc.)].	*1,811*	*988*	*581*	*21*	*31*	*168*	*22*
	32.—HOTELS, CAFES, RESTAURANTS, ETC.	*1,921*	*961*	*364*	*20*	...	*576*	...
114	Vendors of wine, liquors, ærated waters, etc.	**1,246**	708	23	11	...	504	...
115	Owners and managers of hotels, cook-shops, sarais, etc., and their employés.	**675**	253	341	9	...	72	...
	33.—OTHER TRADE IN FOOD STUFFS	*163,089*	*119,863*	*36,758*	*543*	*364*	*2,078*	*483*
116	Fish dealers	**60,234**	39,095	21,190	107	...	839	3
117	Grocers and sellers of vegetable oil, salt and other condiments.	**36,797**	28,306	6,605	152	236	1,193	305
118	Sellers of milk, butter, ghee, poultry, eggs, etc.	**11,043**	10,111	5[illegible]9	32	116	264	1
119	Sellers of sweetmeats, sugar, gur and molasses.	**3,787**	3,506	241	1	...	38	1
120	Cardamom, betel-leaf, vegetables, fruit and areca nut sellers.	**22,060**	16,485	3,728	126	12	1,708	1
121	Grain and pulse dealers	**26,551**	21,741	3,6[illegible]3	110	...	897	151
122	Tobacco, opium, ganja, etc., sellers ...	**2,360**	1,479	766	14	...	80	21
123	Dealers in sheep, goats and pigs ...	**157**	57	39	2	...	59	...
124	Dealers in hay, grass and fodder ...	**100**	83	17	...	...	...	...
125	**34.—TRADE IN CLOTHING AND TOILET ARTICLES** [Trade in ready-made clothing and other articles of dress and the toilet (hats, umbrellas, socks, ready-made shoes, perfumes, etc.)].	*1,661*	*129*	*1,505*	*24*	...	*1*	*2*
	35.—TRADE IN FURNITURE ...	*3,800*	*3,325*	*391*	*2*	*49*	*26*	*7*
126	Trade in furniture, carpets, curtains and bedding.	**2,432**	2,160	201	2	28	26	5
127	Hardware, cooking utensils, porcelain, crockery, glassware, bottles, articles for gardening, the cellar, etc.	**1,363**	1,163	190	...	11	...	2
128	**36.—TRADE IN BUILDING MATERIALS** [Trade in building materials (stones, bricks, plaster, cement, sand, tiles, thatch, etc.)].	*2,336*	*1,339*	*733*	*11*	...	*243*	*10*
129	**37.—TRADE IN MEANS OF TRANSPORT** [Dealers and hirers of elephants, camels, horses, cattle, asses, mules, etc., sellers (not makers) of carriages, saddlery, etc.)].	*2,798*	*1,808*	*714*	*28*	*17*	*231*	*6*
130	**38.—TRADE IN FUEL** (Dealers in fire-wood, charcoal, coal, cowdung, etc.).	*2,594*	*1,090*	*1,150*	*14*	*6*	*334*	...
	39.—TRADE IN ARTICLES OF LUXURY AND THOSE PERTAINING TO LETTERS AND THE ARTS AND SCIENCES.	*9,555*	*3,677*	*5,630*	*18*	*2*	*212*	*16*
131	Dealers in precious stones, jewellery (real and imitation), clocks, optical instruments, etc.	**463**	287	23	15	...	184	4
132	Dealers in common bangles, bead necklaces, fans, small articles, toys, hunting and fishing tackle, flowers, etc.	**8,856**	3,349	5,464	3	2	28	12
133	Publishers, book-sellers, stationers, dealers in music, pictures, musical instruments and curiosities.	**234**	91	143	...	...	...	...
134	**40.—TRADE IN REFUSE MATTER** (Dealers in rags, stable refuse, etc.).	*3*	*3*	...	...	...	...	...

TABLE XV.—OCCUPATION OR MEANS OF LIVELIHOOD.

PART D.—DISTRIBUTION BY RELIGION—*continued*.

Group No.	Occupation.	Total number of workers and dependants.	Distribution by Religion. Hindus.	Musalmans.	Christians.	Buddhists.	Animists.	Others.
	1	2	3	4	5	6	7	8
	41.—TRADE OF OTHER SORTS ...	*17,411*	*13,394*	*2,836*	*45*	*85*	*412*	*639*
135	Shopkeepers otherwise unspecified ...	**15,356**	11,829	2,457	35	85	311	639
136	Itinerant traders, pedlars, hawkers, etc.	**139**	86	50	1	...	2	...
137	Conjurors, acrobats, fortune tellers, reciters, exhibitors of curiosities and wild animals.	**945**	677	202	...	...	66	...
138	Other trades (including farmers of pounds, tolls and markets).	**971**	802	127	9	...	33	...
	C.—PUBLIC ADMINISTRATION AND LIBERAL ARTS.	*130,038*	*104,405*	*16,936*	*4,266*	*290*	*3,925*	*216*
	VI.—PUBLIC FORCE	*18,885*	*13,397*	*4,116*	*238*	*165*	*964*	*5*
	42.—ARMY	*3,122*	*2,157*	*747*	*130*	*20*	*66*	*2*
139	Army (Imperial)	**3,105**	2,140	747	130	20	66	2
140	Army (Native States)	**17**	17	...	...	...	...	...
	44.—POLICE	*15,763*	*11,240*	*3,369*	*108*	*145*	*898*	*3*
142	Police	**10,770**	8,402	1,210	102	144	819	3
143	Village watchmen	**4,993**	2,748	2,159	6	1	79	...
	VII.—(ORDER 45) PUBLIC ADMINISTRATION.	*15,032*	*10,616*	*1,711*	*487*	*15*	*2,141*	*62*
144	Service of the State	**9,126**	6,962	1,397	381	1	328	57
145	Service of Native and Foreign States ...	**545**	333	15	31	12	154	...
146	Municipal and other local (not village) service.	**1,160**	900	227	22	...	11	...
147	Village officials and servants other than watchmen.	**4,201**	2,421	72	53	2	1,648	5
	VIII.—PROFESSIONS AND LIBERAL ARTS.	*99,915*	*77,073*	*10,754*	*3,294*	*102*	*647*	*145*
	46.—RELIGION	*55,289*	*50,090*	*4,184*	*806*	*90*	*102*	*17*
148	Priests, ministers, etc.	**48,309**	44,029	3,938	211	52	76	3
149	Religious mendicants, inmates of monasteries, etc.	**797**	667	92	9	26	...	3
150	Catechists, readers, church and mission service.	**1,600**	948	40	583	12	11	6
151	Temple, burial or burning ground service, pilgrim conductors, circumcisers.	**4,583**	4,446	114	3	...	15	5
	47.—LAW	*5,118*	*4,411*	*638*	*84*	...	*31*	*4*
152	Lawyers of all kinds, including Kazis, law agents and mukhtiars.	**2,586**	2,258	301	16	...	7	4
153	Lawyers' clerks, petition writers, etc. ...	**2,532**	2,153	337	18	...	24	...
	48.—MEDICINE	*10,886*	*7,883*	*2,360*	*348*	*6*	*261*	*23*
154	Medical practitioners of all kinds, including dentists, oculists and veterinary surgeons.	**8,502**	6,369	1,806	216	1	88	22
155	Midwives, vaccinators, compounders, nurses, masseurs, etc.	**2,384**	1,519	554	132	5	173	1
156	**49.—INSTRUCTION** [Professors and teachers of all kinds (except law, medicine, music, dancing and drawing) and clerks and servants connected with education].	*12,357*	*8,097*	*2,300*	*1,784*	*3*	*104*	*69*
	50.—LETTERS AND ARTS AND SCIENCES.	*9,265*	*7,487*	*1,272*	*322*	*3*	*149*	*32*
158	Architects, surveyors, engineers, and their employés.	**2,716**	1,970	324	297	3	100	22
159	Others (authors, photographers, artists, sculptors, astronomers, meteorologists, botanists, astrologers, etc.).	**1,245**	1,098	92	8	...	37	10
160	Music composers and masters, players on all kinds of musical instruments (not military), singers, actors and dancers.	**5,304**	4,419	856	17	...	12	...
161	***IX.—(ORDER 51) PERSONS LIVING ON THEIR INCOME*** [Proprietors (other than of agricultural land), fund and scholarship-holders and pensioners].	*3,206*	*2,419*	*355*	*247*	*8*	*173*	*4*
	D.—MISCELLANEOUS ...	*207,123*	*108,544*	*61,814*	*3,471*	*433*	*32,236*	*625*
	X.—(ORDER 52) DOMESTIC SERVICE.	*38,539*	*22,826*	*11,885*	*763*	*189*	*2,775*	*101*
162	Cooks, water carriers, doorkeepers, watchmen and other indoor servants.	**35,389**	21,007	10,928	724	180	2,449	101
163	Private grooms, coachmen, dog boys, etc.	**3,150**	1,819	957	39	9	326	...

TABLE XV.—Occupation or Means of Livelihood.

Part D.—Distribution by Religion—*concluded.*

Group No.	Occupation.	Total number of workers and dependants.	Distribution by Religion.					
			Hindus.	Musalmans.	Christians.	Buddhists.	Animists.	Others.
	1	2	3	4	5	6	7	8
	XI.—(ORDER 53) *INSUFFICIENTLY DESCRIBED OCCUPATIONS* (GENERAL TERMS WHICH DO NOT INDICATE A DIFINITE OCCUPATION).	*97,701*	*47,098*	*24,085*	*2,540*	*151*	*23,316*	*511*
164	Manufacturers, business men and contractors otherwise unspecified.	1.899	1,388	354	48	8	85	16
165	Cashiers, accountants, book-keepers, clerks and other employés in unspecified offices, warehouses and shops.	9.898	8,160	952	68	29	243	446
166	Mechanics otherwise unspecified ...	2.124	1,740	269	37	30	35	13
167	Labourers and workmen otherwise unspecified.	83.780	35,810	22,510	2,387	84	22,953	36
	XII.—UNPRODUCTIVE ...	*70,883*	*38,620*	*25,844*	*168*	*93*	*6,145*	*13*
168	54.—INMATES OF JAILS, ASYLUMS AND HOSPITALS.	*2,256*	*1,176*	*820*	*6*	*1*	*253*	...
169	55.—BEGGARS, VAGRANTS, PROSTITUTES (Beggars, vagrants, procurers, prostitutes, receivers of stolen goods, cattle poisoners).	*68,627*	*37,444*	*25,024*	*162*	*92*	*5,892*	*13*

TABLE XV-E.

STATISTICS OF INDUSTRIES.

THIS Table furnishes statistics of industrial concerns, such as tea-gardens, mines, mills, factories, etc., in which twenty persons or more were employed on the day of the census. It is divided into four parts. Part I shows for the Province as a whole the number of persons employed in each kind of industry distinguishing between industrial concerns in which mechanical power is used and those in which it is not, and classifying them according to the number of persons employed. Part II gives for each district the number of persons employed in each industry without these details. Part III and IV show the castes and races of the owners and managers of industries that are of special importance, *i.e.*, tea, coal and oil, in Assam.

TABLE XV-E.—STATISTICS OF INDUSTRIES. PART I.—PROVINCIAL SUMMARY.

Description of Factory, Mine, etc.	Classification of Factory, etc., according to number of persons employed (including management).	Number of Factories.	Total number of persons employed.		Classification of persons employed. Direction, Supervision and Clerical Work. Europeans and Anglo-Indians.		Direction, Supervision and Clerical Work. Indians.		Skilled Workmen. Europeans and Anglo-Indians.		Skilled Workmen. Indians.		Unskilled Labourers. Age 14 and over.		Unskilled Labourers. Under 14.		Remarks. * (1) Much brisker than usual. (2) Brisker than usual. (3) Somewhat brisker than usual. (4) Normal. (5) Somewhat slacker than usual. (6) Slacker than usual. (7) Much slacker than usual.
			Males.	Females.	Males.	Females.	Males.	Females.	Males.	Females.	Males.	Females.	Males.	Females.	Males.	Females.	
1	2	3	4	5	6	7	8	9	10	11	12	13	14	15	16	17	18
TOTAL	......	*650*	*262,334*	*239,272*	*802*	*3*	*4,459*	*54*	*187*	...	*6,810*	*261*	*202,265*	*195,794*	*47,811*	*43,160*	
GROWING OF SPECIAL PRODUCTS.	......	*612*	*256,263*	*237,498*	*749*	*3*	*4,256*	*54*	*139*	...	*4,923*	*260*	*198,554*	*194,108*	*47,642*	*43,073*	Details of mechanical power— Steam ... ... 460 Steam and water ... 10 Oil ... ... 1 Steam and oil... ... 4 475
Tea	......	*609*	*256,048*	*237,435*	*748*	*3*	*4,240*	*54*	*139*	...	*4,837*	*260*	*198,448*	*194,051*	*47,636*	*43,067*	
With mechanical power ...	*Total*	*475*	*229,796*	*212,336*	*686*	*3*	*3,754*	*43*	*135*	...	*4,674*	*235*	*178,278*	*173,654*	*42,209*	*38,401*	* Condition of business at the time of the census— (1) ... ... 14 (2) ... ... 112 (3) ... ... 48 (4) ... ... 278 (5) ... ... 4 (6) ... ... 14 (7) ... ... 5 475 The figure 4,674 in column 12 includes 38 Chinese.
	From 20 to 50 ...	6	130	53	3	...	10	...	9	...	8	3	72	42	28	8	
	„ 50 to 100 ...	7	286	284	...	...	17	...	...	...	28	10	222	194	29	30	
	„ 100 to 200 ...	20	1,688	1,355	4	...	75	...	2	...	73	9	1,223	1,044	311	302	
	„ 200 to 400 ...	69	11,376	9,679	40	...	309	7	5	...	433	7	8,710	8,070	1,879	1,595	
	400 and over ...	373	216,366	201,015	639	3	3,343	36	119	...	4,132	206	168,051	164,304	40,022	36,466	
Without mechanical power ...	*Total*	*134*	*26,252*	*25,099*	*62*	...	*486*	*11*	*4*	...	*163*	*25*	*20,170*	*20,397*	*5,367*	*4,666*	* Condition of business at the time of the census— (1) ... ... 15 (2) ... ... 33 (3) ... ... 8 (4) ... ... 76 (7) ... ... 2 134 The figure 486 in column 8 includes 1 Chinese.
	From 20 to 50 ...	10	260	172	3	...	20	...	...	...	43	24	148	127	46	21	
	„ 50 to 100 ...	9	381	287	4	...	16	5	...	...	1	...	286	235	74	47	
	„ 100 to 200 ...	27	2,123	2,173	8	...	58	...	...	...	18	1	1,718	1,878	321	294	
	„ 200 to 400 ...	37	5,723	5,142	19	...	145	4	...	...	23	...	4,329	4,188	1,207	955	
	400 and over ...	51	17,765	17,325	28	...	247	2	4	...	78	...	13,680	13,974	3,719	3,349	
Rubber—																	
Without mechanical power ...	From 100 to 200 ...	1	124	...	1	...	10	...	...	...	84	...	25	...	4	...	* Condition of business at the time of the census— (4) 1

TABLE XV-E.—Statistics of Industries. Part I.—Provincial Summary—*contd.*

Description of Factory, Mine, etc.	Classification of Factory, etc., according to number of persons employed (including management).	Number of Factories.	Total number of persons employed.		Classification of Persons Employed. Direction, Supervision and Clerical Work. Europeans and Anglo-Indians.		Direction, Supervision and Clerical Work. Indians.		Skilled Workmen. Europeans and Anglo-Indians.		Skilled Workmen. Indians.		Unskilled Labourers. Age 14 and over.		Unskilled Labourers. Under 14.		Remarks. (1) Much brisker than usual. (2) Brisker than usual. (3) Somewhat brisker than usual. * (4) Normal. (5) Somewhat slacker than usual. (6) Slacker than usual. (7) Much slacker than usual.
			Males.	Females.	Males.	Females.	Males.	Females.	Males.	Females.	Males.	Females.	Males.	Females.	Males.	Females.	
1	2	3	4	5	6	7	8	9	10	11	12	13	14	15	16	17	18
Sugarcane	...	*2*	*91*	*63*	...	...	*6*	...	...	...	*2*	...	*81*	*57*	*2*	*6*	Details of mechanical power— Steam 1
With mechanical power ...	From 100 to 200 ...	1	70	55	...	...	4	...	...	...	...	...	64	49	2	6	* Condition of business at the time of the census— (3) 1
Without mechanical power ...	From 20 to 50 ...	1	21	8	...	...	2	...	...	...	2	...	17	8	...	...	* Condition of business at the time of the census— (4) 1
MINES	......	*8*	*2,884*	*995*	*30*	...	*53*	...	*1*	...	*599*	...	*2,138*	*981*	*63*	*14*	Details of mechanical power— Steam 5
Collieries	......	*6*	*2,023*	*787*	*15*	...	*17*	...	*1*	...	*312*	...	*1,638*	*778*	*40*	*9*	* Condition of business at the time of the census— (4) 5
With mechanical power ...	*Total* ...	*5*	*1,868*	*739*	*14*	...	*15*	...	*1*	...	*299*	...	*1,501*	*730*	*38*	*9*	The figure 1,501 in column 14 includes 71 Chinese.
	From 50 to 100 ...	2	132	15	1	...	5	...	...	...	63	...	56	15	7	...	
	400 and over ...	3	1,736	724	13	...	10	...	1	...	236	...	1,445	715	31	9	
Without mechanical power ...	From 200 to 400 ...	1	155	48	1	...	2	...	...	...	13	...	137	48	2	...	* Condition of business at the time of the census— (4) ... ... 1 The figure 2 in column 8 and the figure 137 in column 14 include 1 and 112 Chinese respectively.
Petroleum wells—																	
With mechanical power ...	400 and over ...	1	803	207	15	...	32	...	...	...	260	...	473	202	23	5	Details of mechanical power— Steam, oil and electric current 1 * Condition of business at the time of the census— (4) 1
Copper Mines—																	
Without mechanical power ...	From 50 to 100 ...	1	58	1	...	...	4	...	...	...	27	...	27	1	...	...	* Condition of business at the time of the census— (2) 1
TEXTILE INDUSTRIES.																	
Sisal—	*Total*	*4*	*513*	*409*	*4*	...	*9*	...	...	...	*17*	...	*438*	*371*	*45*	*38*	Details of mechanical power— Steam 4
With mechanical power ...	From 50 to 100 ...	1	30	27	2	...	1	...	...	...	2	...	17	27	8	...	* Condition of business at the time of the census—
	„ 100 to 200 ...	1	88	65	1	...	1	...	...	...	8	...	70	54	8	11	(2) 1
	„ 200 to 400 ...	1	164	163	...	...	1	...	...	...	3	...	150	96	10	7	(4) 1
	400 and over ...	1	231	214	1	...	6	...	...	...	4	...	201	194	19	20	(6) 2
																	4

TABLE XV-E.—STATISTICS OF INDUSTRIES. PART I.—PROVINCIAL SUMMARY—*contd.*

Description of Factory, Mine, etc.	Classification of Factory, etc., according to numbers of persons employed (including management).	Number of Factories.	Total number of persons employed.		Classification of persons employed. Direction, Supervision and Clerical work. Europeans and Anglo-Indians.		Direction, Supervision and Clerical work. Indians.		Skilled workmen. Europeans and Anglo-Indians.		Skilled workmen. Indians.		Unskilled labourers. Age 14 and over.		Unskilled labourers. Under 14.		Remarks. (1) Much brisker than usual. (2) Brisker than usual. (3) Somewhat brisker than usual. * (4) Normal. (5) Somewhat slacker than usual. (6) Slacker than usual. (7) Much slacker than usual.
			Males.	Females.	Males.	Females.	Males.	Females.	Males.	Females.	Males.	Females.	Males.	Females.	Males.	Females.	
1	2	3	4	5	6	7	8	9	10	11	12	13	14	15	16	17	18
WOOD, ETC., INDUSTRIES ...	......	*11*	*849*	*323*	*10*	...	*41*	...	*2*	...	*155*	*1*	*590*	*290*	*51*	*32*	
Carpentry works—																	
Without mechanical power ...	From 20 to 50 ...	1	21	1	2	...	...	...	1	...	3	1	11	...	4	...	* Condition of business at the time of the census— (4) 1
Saw Mills—																	
	Total	*10*	*828*	*322*	*8*	...	*41*	...	*1*	...	*152*	...	*579*	*290*	*47*	*32*	Details of mechanical power— Steam ... ... 10 * Condition of business at the time of the census— (2) ... ... 1 (3) ... ... 1 (4) ... ... 5 (5) 2 (6) 1
With mechanical power ...	From 20 to 50 ...	2	68	12	1	...	4	...	...	...	7	...	56	12	...	...	
	" 50 to 100 ...	3	203	63	2	...	15	...	1	...	49	...	124	57	12	6	
	" 100 to 200 ...	3	242	79	1	...	11	...	...	...	57	...	166	70	7	9	
	" 200 to 400 ...	2	315	168	4	...	11	...	...	...	39	...	233	151	28	17	
METAL INDUSTRIES.																	
Engineering Workshops ...	......	*2*	*72*	...	...	...	*5*	...	...	...	*40*	...	*27*	...	...	...	Details of mechanical power— 10 Steam 1
With mechanical power ...	From 50 to 100 ...	1	50	...	...	...	4	...	...	...	34	...	12	...	...	...	* Condition of business at the time of the census— (4) 1
Without mechanical power ...	From 20 to 50 ...	1	22	...	...	...	1	...	...	...	6	...	15	...	...	...	* Condition of business at the time of the census— (4) 1
GLASS AND EARTHEN WARE INDUSTRIES.																	
Brick and Tile Factories—																	
With mechanical power ...	From 100 to 200 ...	*1*	*101*	*35*	*1*	...	*2*	...	...	...	*17*	...	*90*	*39*	*1*	*3*	Details of mechanical power— Steam ... ... 1 * Condition of business at the time of the census— (4) 1
INDUSTRIES CONNECTED WITH CHEMICAL PRODUCTS.																	
Oil Mills—																	
With mechanical power ...	From 20 to 50 ...	*4*	*131*	*4*	...	...	*12*	...	...	...	*38*	...	*81*	*4*	...	...	Details of mechanical power— Steam ... ... 2 Steam and water ... ... 2 4 * Condition of business at the time of the census— (4) ... ... 1 (5) ... ... 1 (6) 2 4

TABLE XV-E.—Statistics of Industries. Part I.—Provincial Summary—*concld.*

Description of factory, mine, etc.	Classification of factory, etc., according to number of persons employed (including management).	Number of factories.	Total number of persons employed.		Classification of persons employed. Direction, supervision and clerical work. Europeans and Anglo-Indians.		Direction, supervision and clerical work. Indians.		Skilled workmen. Europeans and Anglo-Indians.		Skilled workmen. Indians.		Unskilled labourers. Age 14 and over.		Unskilled labourers. Under 14.		Remarks. (1) Much brisker than usual. (2) Brisker than usual. (3) Somewhat brisker than usual. (4) Normal. (5) Somewhat slacker than usual. (6) Slacker than usual. (7) Much slacker than usual.
			Males.	Females.	Males.	Females.	Males.	Females.	Males.	Females.	Males.	Females.	Males.	Females.	Males.	Females.	
1	2	3	4	5	6	7	8	9	10	11	12	13	14	15	16	17	18
FOOD INDUSTRIES.																	
Distilleries—																	
With mechanical power ...	From 50 to 100 ...	1	62	4	...	...	9	...	...	...	19	...	34	4	...	...	Details of mechanical power— Steam ... ... 1 * Condition of business at the time of the census— (4) 1
CONSTRUCTION OF MEANS OF TRANSPORT.																	
Railway Workshops—																	
With mechanical power ...	*Total*	5	999	4	6	...	27	...	39	...	693	...	225	4	9	...	Details of mechanical power— Steam ... ... 4 Steam, oil and gas 1 5
	From 20 to 50 ...	2	98	...	...	...	3	...	1	...	86	...	8	...	...	...	* Condition of business at the time of the census— (2) ... ... 1 (3) ... ... 2 (4) 2 5
	" 100 to 200 ...	1	141	...	...	...	4	...	2	...	90	...	45	...	...	...	
	" 200 to 400 ...	1	283	...	3	...	9	...	30	...	93	...	139	...	9	...	
	400 and over ...	1	477	4	3	...	11	...	6	...	424	...	33	4	...	...	
INDUSTRIES OF LUXURY ...	......	9	460	...	2	...	45	...	6	...	319	...	88	...	...	...	
Printing Presses—																	
With mechanical power ...	From 200 to 400 ...	1	298	...	1	...	32	...	5	...	239	...	21	...	...	...	Details of mechanical power— Oil ... ... 1 * Condition of business at the time of the census— (6) 1
Map Reproduction Factories																	
With mechanical power ...	From 100 to 200 ...	1	162	...	1	...	13	...	1	...	80	...	67	...	...	...	Details of mechanical power— Oil ... ... 1 * Condition of business at the time of the census— (2) 1

TABLE XV-E.—Statistics of Industries. Part II.—Distribution by Districts.

Description of factory, mine, etc.	District.	Number of Factories.	Total number of persons employed. Males.	Total number of persons employed. Females.	Direction, Supervision and Clerical work. Europeans and Anglo-Indians. Males.	Direction, Supervision and Clerical work. Europeans and Anglo-Indians. Females.	Direction, Supervision and Clerical work. Indians. Males.	Direction, Supervision and Clerical work. Indians. Females.	Skilled workmen. Europeans and Anglo-Indians. Males.	Skilled workmen. Europeans and Anglo-Indians. Females.	Skilled workmen. Indians. Males.	Skilled workmen. Indians. Females.	Unskilled Labourers. Age 14 and over. Males.	Unskilled Labourers. Age 14 and over. Females.	Unskilled Labourers. Under 14. Males.	Unskilled Labourers. Under 14. Females.
1	2	3	4	5	6	7	8	9	10	11	12	13	14	15	16	17
TOTAL	......	*650*	*262,334*	*239,272*	*802*	*3*	*4,459*	*54*	*187*	...	*6,810*	*261*	*202,265*	*195,794*	*47,811*	*43,160*
GROWING OF SPECIAL PRODUCTS.	......	*612*	*256,263*	*237,498*	*749*	*3*	*4,256*	*54*	*139*	...	*4,923*	*260*	*198,554*	*194,108*	*47,642*	*43,073*
Tea	Total	609	256,048	237,435	748	3	4,240	54	139	...	4,837	260	198,448	194,051	47,636	43,067
	Cachar	111	37,278	35,628	120	...	615	17	13	...	837	68	28,676	29,330	7,017	6,213
	Sylhet	127	50,293	51,148	117	...	588	12	31	...	685	53	36,927	40,505	11,945	10,778
	Goalpara	3	245	198	3	...	6	...	...	...	1	...	174	132	61	66
	Kamrup	10	1,764	1,323	4	...	43	1	...	...	47	6	1,483	1,128	187	188
	Darrang	65	33,065	28,856	83	...	495	...	16	...	508	...	27,150	24,400	4,813	4,456
	Nowgong	34	6,296	5,637	45	...	170	13	19	...	97	11	4,841	4,588	1,124	1,025
	Sibsagar	152	65,235	58,053	186	1	1,335	9	22	...	1,096	89	49,481	45,968	13,115	11,986
	Lakhimpur	106	61,872	56,592	190	2	988	3	38	...	1,566	32	49,716	48,200	9,374	8,355
Rubber	Darrang	1	124	...	1	...	10	...	...	...	84	...	25	...	4	...
Sugarcane	Sibsagar	2	91	63	...	...	6	...	...	...	2	...	81	57	2	6
MINES	......	*8*	*2,884*	*995*	*30*	...	*53*	...	*1*	...	*599*	...	*2.138*	*981*	*63*	*14*
Collieries	Lakhimpur	6	2,023	787	15	...	17	...	1	...	312	...	1,638	778	40	9
Petroleum wells	Ditto	1	803	207	15	...	32	...	...	...	260	...	473	202	23	5
Copper mines	Manipur State	1	58	1	...	...	4	...	...	...	27	...	27	1	...	...
TEXTILE INDUSTRIES—																
Sisal	Sylhet	4	513	409	4	...	9	...	...	...	17	...	438	371	45	38
WOOD, ETC., INDUSTRIES ...	......	*11*	*849*	*323*	*10*	...	*41*	...	*2*	...	*155*	*1*	*590*	*290*	*51*	*32*
Carpentry works	Sibsagar	1	21	1	2	...	...	...	1	...	3	1	11	...	4	...
Saw mills	Total	10	828	322	8	...	41	...	1	...	152	...	579	290	47	32
	Cachar	1	61	37	...	...	5	...	...	...	16	...	35	85	5	2
	Sylhet	1	74	6	1	...	6	...	...	...	25	...	42	6	...	...
	Kamrup	1	32	...	...	...	2	...	...	...	6	...	24	...	...	...
	Darrang	1	36	12	1	...	2	...	...	...	1	...	32	12	...	...
	Sibsagar	1	68	20	1	...	4	...	1	...	8	...	47	16	7	4
	Lakhimpur	5	557	247	5	...	22	...	...	...	96	...	399	221	35	26

TABLE XV-E.—STATISTICS OF INDUSTRIES. PART II.—DISTRIBUTION BY DISTRICTS—*concld.*

Description of factory, mine, etc.	District.	Number of factories.	Total number of persons employed.		Classification of persons employed.											
					Direction, supervision and clerical work.				Skilled workmen.				Unskilled labourers.			
					Europeans and Anglo-Indians.		Indians.		Europeans and Anglo-Indians.		Indians.		Age 14 and over.		Under 14.	
			Males.	Females.	Males.	Females.	Males.	Females.	Males.	Females.	Males.	Females.	Males.	Females.	Males.	Females.
1	2	3	4	5	6	7	8	9	10	11	12	13	14	15	16	17
METAL INDUSTRIES—																
Engineering workshops ...	***Total***	***2***	***79***	...	...	...	***5***	...	...	...	***40***	...	***27***	...	...	...
	Sylhet	1	50	...	...	...	4	...	...	...	34	...	12	...	...	...
	Sibsagar	1	22	...	...	...	1	...	...	...	6	...	15	...	...	...
GLASS AND EARTHENWARE INDUSTRIES—																
Brick and tile factories ...	Lakhimpur	1	101	35	1	...	2	...	...	...	7	...	90	32	1	3
INDUSTRIES CONNECTED WITH CHEMICAL PRODUCTS—																
Oil-mills	***Total***	***4***	***131***	***4***	...	...	***12***	...	...	...	***38***	...	***81***	***4***	...	...
	Kamrup	1	35	...	...	...	4	...	...	...	5	...	26		...	...
	Nowgong	1	34	...	...	...	2	...	...	...	12	...	20	...	...	...
	Lakhimpur	2	62	4	...	...	6	...	...	...	21	...	35	4	...	...
FOOD INDUSTRIES—																
Distilleries	Sibsagar	1	62	4	...	...	9	...	...	...	19	...	34	4	...	...
CONSTRUCTION OF MEANS OF TRANSPORT—																
Railway workshops ...	***Total***	***5***	***999***	***4***	***6***	...	***27***	...	***30***	...	***698***	...	***225***	***4***	***9***	...
	Sylhet	1	283	...	3	...	9	...	30	...	93	...	139		9	...
	Darrang	1	49	...	...	...	2	...	1	...	41	...	5	...		...
	Nowgong	1	141	...	...	...	4	...	2	...	90	...	45	...	...	...
	Sibsagar	1	49	...	...	...	1	...	...	...	45	...	3	...	...	...
	Lakhimpur	1	477	4	3	...	11	...	6	...	424	...	33	4	...	...
INDUSTRIES OF LUXURY ...	......	***2***	***460***	...	***2***	...	***45***	...	***6***	...	***319***	...	***88***	...	...	...
Printing Presses ...	Khasi and Jaintia Hills ...	1	298	...	1	...	32	...	5	...	239	...	21	...	...	...
Map reproduction factories ...	Ditto ...	1	162	...	1	...	13	...	1	...	80	...	67	...	...	...

TABLE XV-E.—Statistics of Industries. Part III.—Particulars as to ownership of factories, etc.

Description of factory, etc.	Number of factories.	Number owned by companies of which the Directors are: Europeans and Anglo-Indians.	Indians.	Of both races.	Number privately owned by: Europeans and Anglo-Indians.	Indians: Total.	Agarwala.	Ahom.	Baidya.	Brahman.	Kalita.	Kayastha.	Musalman.	Native Christian.	Shaha.	Tambuli.	Castes (unspecified).	Remarks.
1	2	3	4	5	6	7	8	9	10	11	12	13	14	15	16	17	18	19
Tea	609	494	12	...	55	48	1	1	2	15	2	11	8	1	3	1	5	One factory is owned by a Baidya and a Kayastha shown separately in columns 10 and 13, respectively; another is owned by a Brahman and an Indian Christian shown separately in columns 11 and 15, respectively. The total of columns 8 to 18 therefore, exceeds the figure in column 7 by 2.
Coal	6	6	...	...	...	...	...	...	...	...	...	...	...	...	...	...	...	
Oil mills	4	...	1	...	...	3	1	...	...	...	...	...	...	...	...	...	2	

TABLE XV-E.—Statistics of Industries. Part IV.—Caste or Race of Managers of factories, etc.

Description of factory, etc.	Number of factories.	Number managed by: Europeans or Anglo-Indians.	Indians: Total.	Agarwala.	Ahom.	Baidya.	Brahman.	Kalita.	Kayastha.	Musalman.	Shaha.	Castes (unspecified).
1	2	3	4	5	6	7	8	9	10	11	12	13
Tea	609	536	73	1	2	5	27	3	19	8	...	8
Coal	6	6	...	...	...	...	...	...	...	...	...	...
Oil mills	4	...	4	3	...	...	...	...	...	...	1	...

TABLE XVI.

OCCUPATION

BY SELECTED CASTES, TRIBES OR RACES.

In this Table statistics are given of the occupations of selected castes and races in areas where they are especially numerous or otherwise important. The occupations are arranged under 13 main heads corresponding to the sub-classes of the scheme of classification adopted in Table XV-A : these heads have been subdivided, where necessary, in order to distinguish between different occupations. Columns 7 to 10 are intended to throw light on the extent to which traditional caste occupations are followed, while columns 11 and 12 are designed to make it possible to discount the tendency of functional castes to return their traditional occupations as their means of livelihood. The figures in the subsequent columns are exclusive of the number shown in columns 7 and 8 as following the traditional occupation.

The appendix at the end of the table shows, for a few important occupations, the distribution by caste of Hindus and by religion of members of other religions, who were returned as actual workers.

TABLE XVI.—Occupation by Selected

Serial No.	Caste, Tribe or Race and Locality.	Traditional Occupation.	Population dealt with. Actual Workers. Males.	Population dealt with. Actual Workers. Females.	Population dealt with. Dependants. Males.	Population dealt with. Dependants. Females.	Number of actual workers whose traditional caste occupation was returned as their Principal means of livelihood. Males.	Principal means of livelihood. Females.	Subsidiary means of livelihood. Males.	Subsidiary means of livelihood. Females.	Number of actual workers returning their traditional occupation as their principal means of livelihood who had some subsidiary occupation. Males.	Females.
	1	2	3	4	5	6	7	8	9	10	11	12
1	AHOM—Brahmaputra Valley ...	Cultivators ...	58,693	49,479	40,725	43,663	54,976	47,916	400	4	3,713	287
2	ANGLO-INDIAN (Christian)—Province	Nil	175	17	97	186	...	...	...	...	...	...
3	ARMENIAN (Christian)—Province	Nil	4	...	...	1	...	...	...	...	...	...
4	BAIDYA—Province	Physicians ...	1,608	120	1,441	2,440	150	1	18	...	43	...
5	BARUI—Surma Valley	Betel-leaf growers ...	8,011	1,276	4,493	10,762	2,026	576	3,131	87	1,478	64
6	BHUINMALI—Sylhet	Scavengers ...	11,089	1,342	5,605	14,031	393	8	31	...	130	1
7	BRAHMAN—Province	Priests	41,365	8,169	26,993	47,976	11,030	467	5,040	62	4,511	90
8	CHAMAR—Surma Valley	Hide dressers and cobblers.	13,260	10,808	6,281	8,620	1,405	43	294	27	339	7
9	DHOBA—Sylhet	Washermen ...	7,881	1,487	3,989	9,736	2,057	886	2,553	80	1,225	43
10	EUROPEAN AND OTHER ALLIED RACES (Christian)—Province	Nil	1,460	89	134	564	...	...	...	...	...	...
11	GOALA—Province	Herdsmen and milkmen.	71,235	7,965	5,565	10.093	2,963	209	680	51	980	30
12	INDIAN CHRISTIAN—Province	Nil	18,655	15.512	13.167	16,563	...	...	...	...	...	...
13	JOGI OR JUGI—Province	Weavers ...	53,041	18,169	32 246	64.045	1,630	1,226	2,518	767	903	36
14	KAIBARTTA CHASI (Mahishya)—Province	Cultivators ...	21,541	1.329	11.754	28,928	18,062	524	464	4	2,549	41
15	KALITA—Brahmaputra Valley ...	Ditto ...	68.309	32.024	46,577	73.730	56,624	28,150	1,239	79	4,805	655
16	KAMAR—Province	Blacksmiths ...	11,821	8,626	6.156	9.030	1,510	25	559	8	711	9
17	KAYASTHA—Province	Writers	26.280	2.372	17,320	35.205	1,851	5	411	3	602	1
18	KEWAT—Brahmaputra Valley ...	Fishermen ...	26,565	16,471	18.326	26.685	21,842	14,253	278	14	1,572	381
19	KHASI (Animist)—Khasi and Jaintia Hills ...	Cultivators ...	33,554	36,121	21.073	24 916	24,576	26,761	1,248	1,519	6,998	8, 632
	KSHATTRIYA†	*TOTAL* ...	*69,152*	*45,436*	*61,504*	*79,187*	*47,640*	*2,412*	*987*	*183*	*2,474*	*382*
20	Cachar and Sylhet	Cultivators ...	21.839	7 263	17,725	29.906	12,860	1,347	693	57	1,645	360
21	Manipur	Ditto ...	40,313	38.173	43,779	49,281	34,780	1,065	294	126	829	22
	KUMHAR	*TOTAL* ...	*6,330*	*2,844*	*3,597*	*6,867*	*1,567*	*1,503*	*1,782*	*282*	*914*	*109*
23	Sylhet	Potters	4 240	1 683	1 927	4 347	1,431	1,149	1,428	67	775	15
28	Kamrup	Ditto	2,090	1,161	1,670	2.520	136	354	354	215	139	94
	MALO—											
24	Sylhet	Fishermen ...	5 131	468	1,871	5,992	1,432	105	697	4	683	14

* Exclusive of the number shown in.

† Kshattriya includes 19,410 who returned themselves as Manipuris.

Castes, Tribes or Races.

Recorded principal occupation of actual workers.																				
I.—Exploitation of the surface of the soil.												II.—Extraction of minerals.				III.—Industries.				
Income from rent of land.		Cultivators of all kinds.		Agents and managers of landed estates, planters, forest officers and their clerks, rent collectors, etc.		Field labourers, wood-cutters etc.		Raisers of live-stock, milkmen and herdsmen.		Fishing and hunting.		Owners, managers, clerks, etc.		Labourers.		Owners, managers, clerks, etc.		Artisans and other workmen.		
Males.	Females.	Males.	Females.	Males.	Females.	Males.	Females.	Males.	Females.	Males.	Females.	Males.	Females.	Males.	Females.	Males.	Females.	Males.	Females.	Serial No.
13	14	15	16	17	18	19	20	21	22	23	24	25	26	27	28	29	30	31	32	
19	17	9*	770*	767	...	331	101	206	18	4	...	1	...	47	1	7	...	281	62	1
...	...	1	2	7	...	...	...	...	...	...	...	1	...	2	...	2	...	7	3	2
...	...	...	...	...	...	...	...	...	...	...	...	...	...	...	...	...	...	...	...	3
501	52	176	35	156	...	11	11	1	...	...	...	3	...	...	...	1	...	9	1	4
774	44	4,455*	284*	10	...	276	249	61	1	...	...	...	...	2	...	...	...	34	26	5
15	16	7,826	313	5	...	426	192	125.	1	80	14	...	...	28	...	...	...	774*	295*	6
2,865	365	12,742	4,031	1,277	...	612	362	1,970	384	...	...	11	...	42	1	11	...	177	1,332	7
137	54	1,691	286	4	...	9,136	10,076	114	1	...	3	...	...	...	...	...	...	140*	55*	8
82	3	5,002	163	17	...	441	308	45	...	1	...	...	...	...	...	...	...	33*	59*	9
2	...	4	...	914	7	...	...	...	...	...	...	8	...	10	...	4	...	2	2	10
387	64	3,917	1,513	52	1	5,998	5,263	57*	10*	...	...	2	...	123	70	...	...	489	111	11
16	23	13,479	11,726	37	181	1,757	1,580	739	122	2	...	...	...	40	8	21	...	287	195	12
2,513	177	43,330	14,140	54	...	1,216	359	639	27	...	...	4	...	1	...	1	...	399*	538*	13
1,043	83	8*	90*	60	...	404	56	55	...	64	1	...	...	2	7	2	...	188	218	14
425	335	19*	16*	380	1	1,176	142	1,352	15	...	...	1	...	48	1	4	...	1,687	1,317	15
206	9	2,355	1,270	94	1	6,671	6,954	53	2	...	...	1	...	31	31	3	...	306*	74*	16
3,274	313	10,946	1,148	635	...	387	276	40	6	...	...	5	...	20	3	22	...	997	103	17
38	55	7	371	97	...	833	539	799	17	36*	31*	...	...	...	...	...	...	523	320	18
9	17	...*	...*	4	...	945	1,431	1,794	591	8	...	7	3	165	1	...	...	664	894	19
6,580	*482*	*432**	*25**	*97*	*1*	*524*	*244*	*69*	*5*	*49*	*33*	...	...	*17*	...	*6*	...	*1,971*	*33,494*	
6,580	482	422*	25*	20	...	409	234	52	...	...	...	...	...	...	...	...	...	469	2,565	20
...	...	10*	...*	7	1	115	10	17	5	49	33	...	...	17	...	6	...	1,502	30,929	21
52	*11*	*3,836*	*777*	*2*	...	*371*	*343*	*29*	—	...	...	...	...	...	...	...	...	*44**	*46**	
40	1	2,136	118	2	...	336	330	8	...	...	...	...	...	...	...	...	...	24*	25*	22
12	10	1,700	659	...	—	35	13	21	...	...	...	...	...	...	...	...	—	20*	21*	23
2	...	2,187	28	...	...	218	263	17	...	...*	...*	...	...	...	...	...	...	3	15	24

columns 7 and 8 as following the traditional occupation of the caste.

TABLE XVI.—Occupation by selected

Serial No.	Caste, Tribe or Race and Locality.	Traditional Occupation.	RECORDED PRINCIPAL OCCUPATION: IV.—Transport. Owners, managers, ships' officers, etc. Males.	IV.—Transport. Owners, managers, ships' officers, etc. Females.	IV.—Transport. Labourers, boatmen, carters, palki-bearers, etc. Males.	IV.—Transport. Labourers, boatmen, carters, palki-bearers, etc. Females.	V.—Trade. Males.	V.—Trade. Females.	VI.—Public Force. Commissioned and Gazetted Officers. Males.	VI.—Public Force. Commissioned and Gazetted Officers. Females.	VI.—Public Force. Others.* Males.	VI.—Public Force. Others.* Females.
	1	2	33	34	35	36	37	38	39	40	41	42
1	AHOM— Brahmaputra Valley ...	Cultivators ...	37	...	342	...	246	12	...	...	105	...
2	ANGLO-INDIAN (Christian)— Province...	Nil	88	...	4	...	2	...	1	...	12	...
3	ARMENIAN (Christian)— Province	Nil	4	...	...	...	...	...	...	...	...	...
4	BAIDYA— Province...	Physicians ...	99	...	5	...	88	9	2	...	32	...
5	BARUI— Surma Valley	Betel-leaf growers ...	1	...	10	...	165	9	...	...	11	...
6	BHUINMALI— Sylhet	Scavengers ...	2	...	370	3	424	222	1	...	57	...
7	BRAHMAN— Province	Priests	488	...	412	4	3,090	580	10	...	314	...
8	CHAMAR— Surma Valley	Hide dressers and Cobblers.	1	...	155	45	61	30	...	...	13	...
9	DHOBA— Sylhet	Washermen ...	1	...	9	...	42	4	...	...	27	...
10	EUROPEAN AND OTHER ALLIED RACES (Christian)— Province	Nil	94	...	11	...	26	1	60	...	10	...
11	GOALA— Province	Herdsmen and milkmen.	21	...	883	31	511	123	...	...	68	...
12	INDIAN CHRISTIAN— Province	Nil	51	...	128	126	210	290	...	...	38	...
13	JOGI OR JUGI— Province...	Weavers ...	16	...	100	2	798	124	...	...	124	...
14	KAIBARTTA CHASI (Mahishya)— Province	Cultivators ...	16	...	41	...	574	23	...	...	63	...
15	KALITA— Brahmaputra Valley ...	Ditto ...	104	...	542	1	2,559	180	...	...	70	...
16	KAMAR— Province	Blacksmiths ...	2	...	83	20	130	29	1	...	...	...
17	KAYASTHA— Province	Writers	590	...	216	2	3,183	141	17	...	228	...
18	KEWAT— Brahmaputra Valley ...	Fishermen ...	22	...	304	16	1,007	166	...	...	33	...
19	KHASI (Animist)— Khasi and Jaintia Hills ...	Cultivators ...	1	...	1,241	1,368	896	1,406	...	...	23	...
	KSHATTRIYA†	TOTAL ...	*15*	*1*	*549*	*2*	*1,714*	*8,431*	*21*	...	*355*	...
20	Cachar and Sylhet	Cultivators ...	12	...	32	...	415	2,478	21	...	43	...
21	Manipur	Ditto ...	3	1	517	2	1,299	5,953	...	...	312	...
	KUMHAR	TOTAL ...	*1*	...	*23*	...	*236*	*51*	...	...	*4*	...
22	Sylhet	Potters	...	...	9	...	165	20	...	...	4	...
23	Kamrup	Ditto ...	1	...	14	...	71	31	...	...	...	...
24	MALO— Sylhet	Fishermen ...	...	...	666	...	555	10	...	...	1	...

* Exclusive of the number as shown in columns 7 and 8

† Kshatriya includes 19,410 who returned themselves as Manipuris.

CASTES, TRIBES OR RACES—*continued.*

OF ACTUAL WORKERS.

VII.—Public Administration.				VIII.—Arts and professions.						IX.—Persons living on their income.		X.—Domestic service.		XI.—Contractors, clerks, cashiers, etc., otherwise unspecified.		XII.—Labourers, unspecified.		XIII.—Beggars, prostitutes, criminals and inmates of jails and asylums.		
Gazetted Officers.		Others.		Religions.		Lawyers, doctors and teachers.		Others.												
Males.	Females.	Males.	Females.	Males.	Females.	Males.	Females.	Males.	Females.	Males.	Females.	Males	Females.	Males.	Females.	Males.	Females.	Males.	Females.	Serial No.
43	44	45	46	47	48	49	50	51	52	53	54	55	56	57	58	59	60	61	62	
1	...	178	...	10	...	147	2	42	...	7	1	288	91	52	...	318	132	282	356	1
2	...	15	...	1	...	3	3	22	8	3	...	1	...	1	...	...	...	...	1	2
...	...	...	...	...	...	...	...	...	...	...	...	...	...	...	...	...	...	...	...	3
10	...	145	...	2	...	146*	5*	35	...	13	...	6	1	9	...	4	2	4	3	4
...	...	8	...	2	...	43	...	1	...	...	...	43	2	...	...	33	5	56	80	5
...	...	8	...	5	...	4	1	8	2	1	...	171	50	...	...	304	128	53	97	6
12	...	511	...	1,372*	117*	1,400	11	512	11	78	6	1,000	21	134	...	348	44	938	433	7
...	...	...	...	...	...	2	...	4	7	...	3	83	4	2	...	266	143	46	58	8
...	...	4	...	4	...	2	...	6	1	...	...	36	4	...	...	54	10	18	49	9
36	...	13	...	70	39	68	13	123	16	5	5	...	5	5	1	...	...	...	...	10
...	...	15	...	7	1	19	...	23	4	1	...	722	161	12	1	888	300	137	103	11
4	...	68	...	161	18	616	129	89	12	72	1	279	129	33	...	497	930	81	83	12
...	...	90	...	601	34	176	7	71	4	14	...	234	45	6	...	475	98	500	1,408	13
...	...	55	...	6	...	147	1	11	3	6	...	505	150	1	...	104	19	104	160	14
1	...	891	...	185	7	464	5	157	5	17	...	859	110	64	...	594	34	586	1,705	15
...	...	1	...	2	...	14	...	5	...	...	...	95	14	1	...	201	146	56	51	16
37	...	440	...	484	33	1,391	18	305	5	63	1	513	70	170*	2*	146	20	230	226	17
1	...	134	...	83	...	121	...	52	1	12	1	178	56	15	1	261	45	167	599	18
11	1	45	...	2	...	12	...	52	5	7	...	124	136	33	...	2,890	3,490	45	17	19
1	...	*193*	*19*	*240*	*33*	*480*	*12*	*472*	*39*	*29*	*7*	*364*	*32*	*38*	*1*	*175*	*75*	*191*	*88*	
...	...	11	...	62	8	110	4	76	4	7	...	35	8	5	...	131	75	67	35	20
1	...	152	19	178	25	370	8	396	35	22	7	329	28	33	1	44	...	124	53	21
...	...	*3*	...	*2*	*1*	*21*	...	*2*	...	...	...	*71*	*6*	*2*	..	*31*	*12*	*33*	*94*	
...	...	...	...	1	...	12	...	...	...	...	...	41	4	...	...	19	12	12	24	22
...	...	3	...	1	1	9	...	2	...	...	...	30	2	2	...	12	...	21	70	23
...	...	...	...	...	...		...	1	1	...	...	23	14	...	...	23	2	2	8	24

as following the traditional occupation of the caste.

TABLE XVI.—OCCUPATION BY SELECTED

Serial No.	Caste, Tribe or Race and Locality.	Traditional Occupation.	Population dealt with. Actual workers. Males.	Actual workers. Females.	Dependants. Males.	Dependants. Females.	Number of actual workers whose traditional caste occupation was returned as their Principal means of livelihood. Males.	Principal means. Females.	Subsidiary means of livelihood. Males.	Subsidiary means. Females.	Number of actual workers returning their traditional occupation as their principal means of livelihood who had some subsidiary occupation. Males.	Females.
	1	2	3	4	5	6	7	8	9	10	11	12
25	MUCHI— Sylhet	Shoe-makers and cobblers.	1,526	364	879	1,773	624	31	80	...	108	1
26	NADIYAL— Brahmaputra Valley ...	Fishermen ...	18 592	15.243	13,434	16,012	4,243	3,251	4,914	2,017	1,021	332
	NAMASUDRA	TOTAL ...	*58,588*	*12,921*	*30,062*	*69,643*	*37,960*	*1,313*	*4,630*	*81*	*24,378*	*292*
27	Surma Valley	Cultivators and boatmen.	52.425	10,284	26.210	63.783	36,387	1,130	4,387	79	23,813	258
28	Goalpara, Kamrup and Nowgong	Ditto ...	6.163	2,637	3 852	5,860	1,573	183	243	2	565	34
	NAPIT	TOTAL ...	*9,332*	*1,097*	*5.649*	*13,318*	*3,551*	*44*	*2,837*	*16*	*2,105*	*2*
29	Sylhet	Barbers	7.718	519	4 511	10 943	3,313	41	2,626	15	2,067	2
30	Kamrup	Ditto	1 614	587	1,138	2.375	238	3	211	1	38	...
31	PATNI— Surma Valley	Boatmen ...	37,111	5,343	19.610	48,794	4,848	149	2,715	12	2,134	15
32	RAJBANSI— Goalpara	Cultivators ...	41,634	4,783	24 713	57.416	36,664	2,327	910	16	3,137	374
	RAJPUT (Chhatri)	TOTAL ...	*3,216*	*1,254*	*1,074*	*1,515*	*22*	...	...	...	...	...
33	Cachar	Military service ...	742	301	312	676	2	...	...	...	...	...
34	Nowgong and Lakhimpur ...	Ditto ...	2,474	953	762	839	20	...	...	...	...	...
	SANTAL (Hindu)	TOTAL ...	*9,396*	*8,296*	*4,263*	*5,054*	*2,712*	*1,664*	*708*	*460*	*858*	*389*
35	Surma Valley	Cultivators ...	1.939	1.218	972	1.405	578	94	168	12	149	17
36	Brahmaputra Valley ...	Ditto	7,457	7,008	3,291	3,649	2,134	1,570	540	448	709	372
	SANTAL (Animist)	TOTAL ...	*7,756*	*6,507*	*3,730*	*4,213*	*2,603*	*1,820*	*899*	*291*	*731*	*321*
37	Surma Valley	Cultivators ...	1,564	1 321	796	949	240	62	160	10	101	18
38	Brahmaputra Valley ...	Ditto	6 192	5,186	2.934	3,264	2,363	1,758	739	281	630	303
39	SUDRA— Sylhet	Indoor servants ...	37,487	2,634	21.913	53,107	1,237	231	174	2	180	3
	SUTRADHAR	TOTAL ...	*5,030*	*377*	*3,073*	*6,944*	*2,957*	*16*	*1,946*	*6*	*1,961*	*9*
40	Sylhet	Carpenters ...	4,315	257	2,488	6,127	2,143	16	1,505	5	1,254	2
41	Goalpara...	Ditto	715	120	585	817	114	...	441	1	7	...
42	SYNTENG (Animist)— Khasi and Jaintia Hills ...	Cultivators ...	11.825	12,469	7,804	10,026	8,822	8,457	85	118	912	1,335
43	TANTI— Sibsagar and Lakhimpur ...	Weavers ...	8,435	8,182	3,167	13,591	1	1	...	72	...	1
44	TELI OR TILI— Sylhet	Oil-pressers ...	9,254	1.194	5,114	12,449	1,443	146	2,234	31	872	20

* Exclusive of the number shown in columns 7 and 8

CASTES, TRIBES OR RACES—*continued.*

RECORDED PRINCIPAL OCCUPATION OF ACTUAL WORKERS.																				
I.—Exploitation of the surface of the soil.												II.—Extraction of minerals.				III.—Industries.				
Income from rent of land.		Cultivators of all kinds.		Agents and managers of landed estates, planters, forest officers and their clerks, rent collectors, etc.		Field labourers, wood-cutters, etc.		Raisers of live-stock, milkmen and herdsmen.		Fishing and hunting.		Owners, managers, clerks, etc.		Labourers.		Owners, managers, clerk, etc.		Artisans and other workmen.		
Males.	Females.	Males.	Females.	Males.	Females.	Males.	Females.	Males.	Females.	Males.	Females.	Males.	Females.	Males.	Females.	Males.	Females.	Males.	Females.	Serial No.
13	14	15	16	17	18	19	20	21	22	23	24	25	26	27	28	29	30	31	32	
4	...	160	18	9	...	239	249	...	...	...	...	...	...	...	...	...	...	62*	17*	25
6	13	12,365	9,867	8	...	224	56	356	31	11*	86*	...	...	2	...	5	...	315	295	26
1,919	*76*	*1682**	*153**	*9*	...	*1,028*	*147*	*369*	...	*6,686*	*1,012*	...	...	*37*	...	*2*	...	*3,498*	*7,827*	
1,916	76	650*	153*	4	...	953	141	298	...	3,109	29	...	...	37	...	2	...	3,158	7,442	27
3	...	32*	...*	5	...	75	6	71	...	3,577	983	...	...	...	...	...	...	340	385	28
168	*17*	*5,052*	*694*	*15*	*1*	*131*	*122*	*49*	*2*	...	...	...	...	...	...	*1*	...	*46**	*75**	
166	8	3,829	222	14	1	117	109	17	2	...	...	...	...	...	...	...	...	36*	62*	29
2	9	1,223	472	1	...	14	13	32	...	...	...	...	...	...	...	1	...	10*	13*	30
5,139	311	15,346	729	1	20	1,285	1,396	309	17	3,967	217	...	...	53	...	2	...	179	637	31
388	27	14*	7*	281	...	1,107	101	419	1	177	...	...	...	...	...	...	...	228	868	32
86	*16*	*1,291*	*539*	*6*	...	*727*	*391*	*313*	*46*	...	...	...	...	*23*	*6*	*1*	...	*58*	*146*	
77	16	134	15	1	...	339	112	2	...	...	...	...	...	...	...	...	...	1	139	33
9	...	1,157	524	5	...	388	279	311	46	...	...	...	...	23	6	1	...	57	7	34
70	*9*	*39**	*12**	*14*	*1*	*5,901*	*6,211*	*140*	*1*	...	...	...	...	*34*	*24*	...	...	*64*	*27*	
68	8	36*	2*	...	1	1,025	1,006	88	...	...	...	...	...	...	...	...	...	20	18	35
2	1	3*	10*	14	...	4,876	5,205	52	1	...	...	...	...	34	24	...	...	44	9	36
13	*5*	*782**	*754**	*172*	...	*3,860*	*3,792*	*103*	*10*	...	...	...	...	*7*	*8*	...	...	*19*	*1*	
13	5	769*	741*	12	...	488	502	4	...	...	...	...	...	...	...	...	...	1	...	37
...	...	18*	13*	160	...	3,372	3,290	99	10	...	...	...	...	7	8	...	...	18	1	38
970	61	30,477	1,315	273	...	621	21	40	...	2	...	...	...	6	...	3	...	1,307	554	39
29	*2*	*2,517*	*213*	*4*	...	*51*	*8*	...	...	...	...	...	...	...	...	...	...	*66**	*72**	
29	1	1,990	121	...	...	22	4	...	...	...	...	...	...	...	...	...	...	64*	72*	40
...	1	527	92	4	...	29	4	...	...	...	...	...	...	...	...	...	...	2*	...*	41
23	30	...*	...*	1	...	302	473	1,081	148	...	...	...	1	3	...	...	...	327	912	42
...	...	1,040	767	12	...	6,775	7,063	39	2	...	1	5	...	29	30	1	...	105*	18*	43
277	26	5,423	343	17	...	552	488	16	...	...	...	...	...	...	...	...	...	31*	58*	44

as following the traditional occupation of the caste.

TABLE XVI.—Occupation by selected

RECORDED PRINCIPAL

Serial No.	Caste, Tribe or Race and Locality.	Traditional occupation.	IV.—Transport. Owners, managers, ships' officers, etc. Males.	IV.—Transport. Owners, managers, ships' officers, etc. Females.	IV.—Transport. Labourers, boatmen, carters, palki-bearers, etc. Males.	IV.—Transport. Labourers, boatmen, carters, palki-bearers, etc. Females.	V.—Trade. Males.	V.—Trade. Females.	VI.—Public Force. Commissioned and Gazetted Officers. Males.	VI.—Public Force. Commissioned and Gazetted Officers. Females.	VI.—Public Force. Others. Males.	VI.—Public Force. Others. Females.
	1	2	33	34	35	36	37	38	39	40	41	42
25	MUCHI— Sylhet	Shoe-makers and cobblers.	1	...	41	...	286	4	...	...	4	...
26	NADIYAL— Brahmaputra Valley ...	Fishermen ...	30	...	165	3	372	1,315	...	...	9	...
	NAMASUDRA	**TOTAL ...**	***16***	...	***711****	***14****	***3,481***	***1,380***	***1***	...	***107***	...
27	Surma Valley	Cultivators and boat men.	15	...	700*	14*	3,158	466	1	...	105	...
28	Goalpara, Kamrup and Nowgong.	Ditto ...	1	...	11*	...*	323	914	...	...	2	...
	NAPIT	**TOTAL ...**	***2***	...	***18***	...	***120***	***15***	...	...	***11***	...
29	Sylhet	Barbers ...	1	...	9	...	88	13	...	...	10	...
30	Kamrup	Ditto ...	1	...	9	...	32	2	...	...	1	...
31	PATNI— Surma Valley	Boatmen ...	17	...	84*	8*	3,921	1,036	...	...	105	...
32	RAJBANSI— Goalpara	Cultivators ...	5	...	87	1	409	543	2	...	84	...
	RAJPUT (Chhatri)	**TOTAL ...**	***11***	...	***136***	***3***	***294***	***66***	...	...	***61****	...*
33	Cachar	Military service ...	2	...	38	2	69	4	...	...	50*	...*
34	Nowgong and Lakhimpur ...	Ditto ...	9	...	98	1	225	62	...	...	11*	...*
	SANTAL (Hindu)	**TOTAL ...**	***4***	...	***69***	***5***	***38***	***10***	...	...	***4***	...
35	Surma Valley	Cultivators ...	...	...	18	...	2	...	...	...	4	...
36	Brahmaputra Valley ...	Ditto ...	4	...	51	5	36	10	...	...	...	...
	SANTAL (Animist)	**TOTAL ...**	...	...	***19***	...	***11***	***1***	...	...	...	...
37	Surma Valley	Cultivators ...	...	...	5	...	...	...	...	...	...	...
38	Brahmaputra Valley ...	Ditto ...	...	...	14	...	11	1	...	...	...	...
39	SUDRA— Sylhet	Indoor servants ...	11	...	117	...	1,459	93	...	...	177	...
	SUTRADHAR	**TOTAL ...**	***2***	...	***5***	...	***47***	***16***	...	...	***1***	...
40	Sylhet	Carpenters ...	2	...	1	...	34	12	...	...	...	...
41	Goalpara	Ditto ...	...	...	4	...	13	4	...	...	1	...
42	SYNTENG (Animist)— Khasi and Jaintia Hills ...	Cultivators ...	...	...	80	90	316	437	...	...	1	...
43	TANTI— Sibsagar and Lakhimpur ...	Weavers ...	6	...	70	9	35	61	...	...	...	...
44	TELI OR TILI— Sylhet	Oil-pressers ...	9	...	5	...	1,232	40	3	...	7	...

* Exclusive of the number shown in columns 7 and 8 as

CASTES, TRIBES OR RACES—*concluded.*

OCUPATION OF ACTUAL WORKERS.																				
VII.—PUBLIC ADMINISTRATION.				VIII.—ARTS AND PROFESSIONS.						IX.—PERSONS LIVING ON THEIR INCOME.		X.—DOMESTIC SERVICE.		XI.—CONTRACTORS, CLERKS, CASHIERS, ETC., OTHERWISE UNSPECIFIED.		XII.—LABOURERS, UNSPECIFIED.		XIII.—BEGGARS, PROSTITUTES, CRIMINALS AND INMATES OF JAILS AND ASYLUMS.		
Gazetted Officers.		Others.		Religious.		Lawyers, doctors and teachers.		Others.												
Males.	Females.	Males.	Females.	Males.	Females.	Males.	Females.	Males.	Females.	Males.	Females.	Males.	Females.	Males.	Females.	Males.	Females.	Males.	Females.	Serial No.
43	44	45	46	47	48	49	50	51	52	53	54	55	56	57	58	59	60	61	62	
...	...	...	...	1	...	...	...	2	1	...	...	12	5	...	...	74	31	7	8	25
...	...	29	...	3	...	15	1	21	...	14	3	79	19	3	...	123	65	194	239	26
...	...	*9*	...	*59*	*1*	*32*	*2*	*64*	*1*	...	...	*559*	*75*	*18*	...	*970*	*338*	*371*	*582*	
...	...	4	...	54	...	23	3	56	1	...	...	526	71	16	...	947	337	306	422	27
...	...	5	...	5	1	9	...	8	...	...	...	33	4	2	...	23	1	65	160	28
...	...	*11*	...	*2*	*2*	*41*	*2*	*9*	*2*	*1*	...	*47*	*9*	*2*	...	*18*	*8*	*37*	*104*	
...	...	8	...	...	...	36	1	6	...	1	...	39	6	...	...	11	7	17	38	29
...	...	3	...	2	2	5	1	3	2	...	...	8	3	2	...	7	1	20	66	30
...	...	24	...	25	2	44	6	3	1	2	...	579	40	2	1	851	385	325	408	31
...	...	21	...	92	1	111	2	22	3	10	9	361	242	4	...	241	30	307	612	32
...	...	*2*	...	*3*	...	*4*	...	*18*	*2*	*5*	*2*	*46*	*13*	*10*	...	*64*	*15*	*35*	*9*	
...	...	...	...	1	...	3	...	...	...	1	...	14	4	...	...	2	6	7	3	33
...	...	2	...	2	...	2	...	18	2	4	2	32	9	10	...	62	9	28	6	34
...	...	...	...	...	...	*1*	...	*2*	...	*1*	...	*61*	*10*	*1*	...	*207*	*224*	*34*	*28*	
...	...	...	...	...	...	...	...	...	...	...	...	8	1	...	...	86	82	6	6	35
...	...	...	...	...	...	1	...	2	...	1	...	63	9	1	...	121	142	28	22	36
...	...	...	...	...	...	...	...	...	...	...	...	*34*	*12*	...	...	*113*	*84*	*20*	*20*	
...	...	...	...	...	...	...	...	...	...	...	...	2	...	...	...	30	10	...	1	37
...	...	...	...	...	...	...	...	...	...	...	...	32	12	...	...	83	74	20	19	38
...	...	175	...	19	1	179	4	22	7	13	...	34*	57*	18	...	209	94	118	196	39
...	...	*2*	...	...	...	*3*	*1*	...	...	...	...	*21*	*13*	*2*	...	*8*	*6*	*15*	*30*	
...	...	1	...	...	...	3	1	...	...	...	...	11	10	...	...	7	2	8	18	40
...	...	1	...	...	...	...	...	...	...	...	...	10	3	2	...	1	4	7	12	41
...	...	52	...	...	...	3	...	3	...	...	...	17	40	...	...	786	1,869	8	13	42
...	...	3	...	...	...	3	...	4	...	...	...	107	12	7	...	163	189	31	29	43
...	...	5	...	2	...	51	1	8	...	...	...	104	12	...	...	30	32	34	48	44

following the traditional occupation of the caste.

APPENDIX TO TABLE XVI.

Distribution of actual workers in certain groups (by caste for Hindus, by race for Christians and by religion for members of other religions).

Group 3.—Agents, managers (not planters), clerks of all landed estates, rent collectors.

Caste.	Assam.	Surma Valley Division.	Assam Valley Division.	Manipur State.	Caste.	Assam.	Surma Valley Division.	Assam Valley Division.	Manipur State.
1	2	3	4	5	1	2	3	4	5
Ahom	50	...	50	...	Kayastha	822	661	158	3
Animist (unspecified)	29	2	27	...	Kewat	34	...	34	...
Baidya	55	41	14	...	Koch	43	...	43	...
Brahman	472	235	236	1	Musalman	275	138	137	...
Chhatri	52	...	52	...	Rajbansi	268	...	268	...
Goala	34	4	30	...	Shaha	89	89	...	...
Jugi	32	7	25	...	Sudra	90	90	...	...
Kaibartta Chasi (Mahishya) ...	31	30	1	...	Teli	20	20	...	...
Kalita	104	...	104	...	Others	258	84	170	4
Kalwar	59	...	59	...	Grand Total	2,817	1,401	1,408	8

Group 105.—Post Office, Telegraph, excluding peons and linesmen.

Caste.	Assam.	Surma Valley Division.	Assam Valley Division.	Manipur State.	Caste.	Assam.	Surma Valley Division.	Assam Valley Division.	Manipur State.
Baidya	48	28	20	...	Kayastha	283	181	102	...
Brahman	176	82	92	2	Musalman	85	44	41	...
Eurasian	20	4	15	1	Others	190	61	128	1
Kalita	46	...	46	...	Grand Total	848	400	444	4

Group 142.—Police Superintendents, Assistant and Deputy Superintendents, Inspectors, Sub-Inspectors and Head Constables.

Caste.	Assam.	Surma Valley Division.	Assam Valley Division.	Manipur State.	Caste.	Assam.	Surma Valley Division.	Assam Valley Division.	Manipur State.
Ahom	26	...	26	...	Khas	5	2	3	...
Animist (unspecified)	32	6	12	14	Koch	20	...	20	...
Baidya	23	13	10	...	Kshattriya (Manipuri)	45	9	2	34
Brahman	78	38	40	...	Limbu	17	16	1	...
Brittal Baniya	10	...	10	...	Marhatta	12	...	12	...
Buddhist (unspecified)	7	...	7	...	Mech	9	7	2	...
Chutia	9	...	9	...	Mangar	51	41	10	...
European	13	5	8	...	Musalman (unspecified)	113	62	51	...
Grahabipra (Ganak)	5	...	5	...	Nadiyal	5	...	5	...
Gurung	16	16	...	...	Newar	5	4	1	...
Indian Christian	12	8	4	...	Rabha	7	3	4	...
Kachari	19	7	12	...	Rai	13	13	...	...
Kalita	20	1	19	...	Rajbansi	7	1	6	...
Kayastha	116	61	55	...	Rajput (Chhatri)	44	28	13	3
Kewat	6	...	6	...	Shaha	5	4	1	...
Khambu	21	8	13	...	Others	62	36	24	2
					Grand Total	833	389	391	53

Group 142.—Police constables.

Caste.	Assam.	Surma Valley Division.	Assam Valley Division.	Manipur State.	Caste.	Assam.	Surma Valley Division.	Assam Valley Division.	Manipur State.
Ahom	118	38	80	...	Kayastha	119	99	20	...
Animist (unspecified)	235	90	142	3	Kewat	27	...	27	...
Bhuinya	22	12	10	...	Khambu	191	70	118	3
Boria	26	...	26	...	Koch	150	2	148	...
Brahman	177	79	98	...	Kshattriya (Manipuri)	239	30	6	203
Buddhist (unspecified)	45	2	43	...	Limbu	202	183	19	...
Chutiya	51	7	44	...	Mangar	210	137	72	1
Damai	20	19	1	...	Mech	98	79	19	...
Dhoba	23	20	3	...	Murmi	50	39	11	...
Dogra	29	29	...	...	Musalman (unspecified) ...	435	371	60	4
Goala	35	8	27	...	Nepali (unspecified)	212	49	161	2
Gurung	122	101	18	3	Rabha	91	57	34	...
Indian Christian	22	13	9	...	Rai	194	194	...	...
Jugi	35	9	26	...	Rajbansi	153	68	84	1
Kachari	211	92	119	...	Rajput (Chhatri)	342	169	165	8
Kaibartta Chasi (Mahishya) ...	43	43	...	...	Sudra	80	73	7	...
Kalita	53	2	51	...	Others	423	208	209	6
Kandu	31	8	23	...	Grand Total	4,514	2,400	1,880	234

Group 144.—Public administration—Gazetted Officers.

Caste.	Assam.	Surma Valley Division.	Assam Valley Division.	Manipur State.	Caste.	Assam.	Surma Valley Division.	Assam Valley Division.	Manipur State.
Animist (unspecified)	15	12	3	...	Kayastha	23	14	9	...
Baidya	10	8	2	...	Musalman (unspecified)	14	8	6	...
Brahman	12	6	6	...	Others	15	6	8	1
European	38	18	19	1	Grand Total	127	72	53	2

APPENDIX TO TABLE XVI—*concluded.*

GROUP 144.—PUBLIC ADMINISTRATION—OTHERS.

Caste.	Assam.	Surma Valley Division.	Assam Valley Division.	Manipur State.	Caste.	Assam.	Surma Valley Division.	Assam Valley Division.	Manipur State.
1	2	3	4	5	1	2	3	4	5
Ahom	182	...	182	...	Kalita	395	3	392	...
Animist (unspecified)	307	149	94	64	Kayastha	529	312	211	6
Baidya	139	117	21	1	Kewat	140	...	140	...
Baria	25	...	25	...	Koch	215	...	215	...
Brahman	460	233	221	6	Kshattriya (Manipuri)	248	42	5	201
Brahmo (unspecified)	44	14	30	...	Musalman (unspecified)	427	255	165	7
Chutiya	81	...	81	...	Nadiyal	29	...	29	...
Grahabipra (Ganak)	48	13	35	...	Rajbansi	35	1	34	...
Indian Christian	64	51	13	...	Shaha	60	49	10	1
Jugi	75	24	51	...	Sudra	81	76	1	4
Kachari	26	...	24	2	Others	324	119	195	10
Kaibartta Chasi (Mahishya) ...	39	37	2	...	Grand Total	3,973	1,495	2,176	302

GROUP 152.—LAWYERS OF ALL KINDS (EXCLUDING KAZIS), LAW AGENTS, MUKHTIARS.

Caste.	Assam.	Surma Valley Division.	Assam Valley Division.	Manipur State.	Caste.	Assam.	Surma Valley Division.	Assam Valley Division.	Manipur State.
Baidya	42	25	17	...	Kewat	8	1	7	...
Brahman	97	69	28	...	Musalman (unspecified)	49	35	14	...
Kaibartta Chasi (Mahishya) ...	20	20	...	...	Shaha	15	14	1	...
Kayastha	214	174	40	...	Others	46	19	27	...
					Grand Total	491	357	134	...

GROUP 154.—MEDICAL PRACTITIONERS OF ALL KINDS (INCLUDING DENTISTS, OCULISTS AND VETERINARY SURGEONS).

Caste.	Assam.	Surma Valley Division.	Assam Valley Division.	Manipur State.	Caste.	Assam.	Surma Valley Division.	Assam Valley Division.	Manipur State.
Animist (unspecified)	54	18	15	21	Kayastha	625	345	278	2
Baidya	140	76	64	...	Koch	33	...	33	...
Brahman	448	291	151	6	Kshattriya (Manipuri)	278	54	9	215
European	52	21	31	...	Musalman (unspecified)	504	239	265	...
Grahabipra (Ganak)	176	132	44	...	Napit	37	25	12	...
Indian Christian	33	21	12	...	Rajbansi	46	...	46	...
Jugi	57	40	17	...	Shaha	82	72	10	...
Kaibartta Chasi (Mahishya) ...	30	30	...	...	Sudra	41	41	...	...
Kalita	71	1	70	...	Others	305	132	164	9
					Grand Total	3,012	1,538	1,221	253

GROUP 156.—PROFESSORS, TEACHERS AND INSPECTING STAFF OF SCHOOLS AND COLLEGES (OMITTING CLERKS AND SERVANTS CONNECTED WITH EDUCATION).

Caste.	Assam.	Surma Valley Division.	Assam Valley Division.	Manipur State.	Caste.	Assam.	Surma Valley Division.	Assam Valley Division.	Manipur State.
Ahom	141	...	141	...	Kaibartta (Jalia)	31	5	26	...
Animist (unspecified)	50	15	28	7	Kalita	391	...	391	...
Baidya	65	46	19	...	Kayastha	586	392	191	3
Barui	24	24	...	...	Kewat	105	...	105	...
Bhat	24	24	...	...	Koch	132	...	132	...
Boria	23	...	23	...	Kshattriya (Manipuri)	211	51	1	159
Brahman	816	338	447	31	Musalman (unspecified)	1,082	921	151	10
Brahmo (unspecified)	27	5	22	...	Napit	23	18	5	...
Chutiya	69	...	69	...	Patni	43	43	...	...
European	20	17	3	...	Rajbansi	82	1	81	...
Grahabipra (Ganak)	36	11	25	...	Shaha	61	47	14	...
Indian Christian	708	594	108	6	Sudra	99	99	...	...
Jugi	118	58	60	...	Toli	42	40	2	...
Kaibartta Chasi (Mahishya) ...	87	97	...	...	Others	225	94	126	5
					Grand Total	5,821	2,930	2,170	221

GROUP 168.—INMATES OF JAILS.

Caste.	Assam.	Surma Valley Division.	Assam Valley Division.	Manipur State.	Caste.	Assam.	Surma Valley Division.	Assam Valley Division.	Manipur State.
Ahom	25	...	25	...	Koch	33	2	31	...
Animist (unspecified)	159	80	79	...	Kurmi	23	13	10	...
Brahman	32	10	22	...	Musalman (unspecified)	785	573	212	...
Goala	21	7	14	...	Nadiyal	34	...	34	...
Kaibartta Chasi (Mahishya) ...	32	32	...	...	Namasudra	27	27	...	...
Kayastha	40	28	12	...	Tanti	20	2	18	...
Kshattriya (Manipuri)	31	24	7	...	Others	401	140	261	...
					Grand Total	1,663	938	725	...

TABLE XVII.

CHRISTIANS BY SECT AND RACE.

THIS Table shows the sects of Christians of all races. Armenians have been classed under the head "European and allied races": they are shown separately in Table XVIII. The Feringis of Assam, who have been treated as Anglo-Indians for the purpose of this Table, number 5 (4 males and 1 female): they are Roman Catholics and were enumerated in Sylhet district.

TABLE XVII.—TERRITORIAL DISTRIBUTION OF THE CHRISTIAN POPULATION BY SECT AND RACE.

District or State.	ALL DENOMINATIONS.									ANGLICAN COMMUNION.								
	Total.			Distribution by Race.						Total.			Distribution by Race.					
				European and allied races.		Anglo-Indians.		Indians.					European and allied races.		Anglo-Indians.		Indians.	
	Persons.	Males.	Females.	Males.	Females.	Males.	Females.	Males.	Females.	Persons.	Males.	Females.	Males.	Females.	Males.	Females.	Males.	Females.
1	2	3	4	5	6	7	8	9	10	11	12	13	14	15	16	17	18	19
ASSAM	***66,562***	***33,632***	***32,930***	***1,598***	***652***	***276***	***204***	***31,758***	***32,074***	***5,019***	***2,820***	***2,199***	***1,001***	***404***	***123***	***83***	***1,696***	***1,712***
(1) British Territory	***66,430***	***33,548***	***32,882***	***1,583***	***647***	***254***	***183***	***31,711***	***32,052***	***4,985***	***2,797***	***2,188***	***988***	***400***	***113***	***76***	***1,696***	***1,712***
SURMA VALLEY AND HILL DISTRICTS	***39,710***	***19,184***	***20,535***	***615***	***302***	***145***	***110***	***18,424***	***20,123***	***1,180***	***647***	***533***	***328***	***161***	***53***	***47***	***266***	***325***
Cachar	1,181	649	532	189	75	8	12	452	445	244	148	96	117	53	6	5	26	38
Sylhet	1,512	863	649	288	93	63	47	512	500	229	146	83	128	38	16	16	2	29
Khasi and Jaintia Hills	31 257	14,855	16,402	97	114	69	46	14,689	16,242	670	327	343	57	59	32	26	238	258
Naga Hills	3 308	1,554	1,754	22	8	...	1	1,532	1,745	22	17	5	17	5	...	...	...	...
Lushai Hills	2,461	1,263	1,198	19	12	5	4	1,239	1,182	15	9	6	9	6	...	...	...	...
ASSAM VALLEY DISTRICTS	***26,711***	***14,364***	***12,347***	***968***	***345***	***109***	***73***	***13,287***	***11,929***	***3,805***	***2,150***	***1,655***	***660***	***239***	***60***	***29***	***1,430***	***1,387***
Goalpara	5,252	2,731	2,521	29	13	12	8	2,690	2,500	57	36	21	22	12	6	4	8	5
Kamrup	2,535	1.373	1,162	84	49	20	10	1,269	1,103	67	49	18	44	16	5	...	...	2
Darrang	1,913	1,028	885	156	50	9	8	863	827	1,025	536	489	101	38	5	5	430	446
Nowgong	1,373	707	666	61	27	18	14	628	625	223	121	102	37	21	9	5	75	76
Sibsagar	5 410	2,933	2,477	278	91	31	24	2,624	2,368	565	359	206	208	67	21	8	130	131
Lakhimpur	4.789	2,647	2,142	354	111	19	9	2,274	2,022	1,862	1,044	818	243	84	14	7	787	727
Garo Hills	5,439	2,945	2,494	6	4	...	...	2,939	2,490	6	5	1	5	1	...	...	...	...
(2) Manipur State	***132***	***84***	***48***	***15***	***5***	***22***	***21***	***47***	***22***	***34***	***23***	***11***	***13***	***4***	***10***	***7***	...	...

TABLE XVII.—Territorial Distribution of the Christian Population by Sect and Race—*contd.*

District or State.	Armenian.									Baptist.								
	Total.			Distribution by Race.						Total.			Distribution by Race.					
				European and Allied Races.		Anglo-Indians.		Indians.					European and Allied Races.		Anglo-Indians.		Indians.	
	Persons.	Males.	Females.	Males.	Females.	Males.	Females.	Males.	Females.	Persons.	Males.	Females.	Males.	Females.	Males.	Females.	Males.	Females.
1	20	21	22	23	24	25	26	27	28	29	30	31	32	33	34	35	36	37
ASSAM	*2*	*1*	*1*	*1*	*1*	...	...	...	...	*21,479*	*11,080*	*10,399*	*50*	*33*	*8*	*16*	*11,022*	*10,350*
(1) ***British Territory***	*2*	*1*	*1*	*1*	*1*	...	...	...	...	*21,408*	*11,032*	*10,376*	*49*	*32*	*8*	*16*	*10,975*	*10,328*
SURMA VALLEY AND HILL DISTRICTS	*1*	...	*1*	...	*1*	...	...	...	...	*5,076*	*2,474*	*2,602*	*13*	*9*	*1*	...	*2,460*	*2,593*
Cachar	...	...	...	...	...	...	...	...	...	502	268	234	...	...	...	...	268	234
Sylhet	...	...	...	...	...	...	...	...	...	139	75	64	7	3	...	...	68	61
Khasi and Jaintia Hills	1	...	1	...	1	...	...	...	...	440	250	190	...	2	...	...	250	188
Naga Hills	...	...	...	...	...	...	...	...	...	3,277	1,520	1,748	2	3	...	...	1,527	1,745
Lushai Hills	...	...	...	...	...	...	...	...	...	718	352	366	4	1	1	...	347	365
ASSAM VALLEY DISTRICTS	*1*	*1*	...	*1*	...	...	...	...	...	*16,332*	*8,558*	*7,774*	*36*	*23*	*7*	*16*	*8,515*	*7,735*
Goalpara	1	1	...	1	...	...	...	...	...	2,735	1,408	1,327	...	...	...	...	1,408	1,327
Kamrup	...	...	...	...	...	...	...	...	...	2,163	1,158	1,005	26	18	4	3	1,128	984
Darrang	...	...	...	...	...	...	...	...	...	222	123	99	1	...	...	...	122	99
Nowgong	...	...	...	...	...	...	...	...	...	929	468	461	1	1	3	3	464	457
Sibsagar	...	...	...	...	...	...	...	...	...	4,197	2,209	1,988	4	1	...	10	2,205	1,977
Lakhimpur	...	...	...	...	...	...	...	...	...	851	419	433	3	...	...	...	416	433
Garo Hills	...	...	...	...	...	...	...	...	...	5,235	2,773	2,462	1	3	...	...	2,772	2,459
(2) ***Manipur State***	...	...	...	...	...	...	...	...	...	*71*	*48*	*23*	*1*	*1*	...	...	*47*	*22*

TABLE XVII.—Territorial Distribution of the Christian Population by Sect and Race—*contd.*

District or State.	*Congregationalist.* Total. Persons.	Total. Males.	Total. Females.	Distribution by Race. European and Allied Races. Males.	European and Allied Races. Females.	Anglo-Indians. Males.	Anglo-Indians. Females.	Indians. Males.	Indians. Females.	*Greek.* Total. Persons.	Total. Males.	Total. Females.	Distribution by Race. European and Allied Races. Males.	European and Allied Races. Females.	Anglo-Indians. Males.	Anglo-Indians. Females.	Indians. Males.	Indians. Females.
1	38	39	40	41	42	43	44	45	46	47	48	49	50	51	52	53	54	55
ASSAM	*29*	*23*	*6*	*15*	*6*	...	...	*8*	...	*3*	*3*	...	*3*	...	...	...	...	...
(1) British Territory	*29*	*23*	*6*	*15*	*6*	...	...	*8*	...	*3*	*3*	...	*3*	...	...	...	...	...
SURMA VALLEY AND HILL DISTRICTS	*16*	*13*	*3*	*5*	*3*	...	...	*8*	...	*1*	*1*	...	*1*	...	...	...	...	...
Cachar	2	1	1	1	1	...	...	...	...	...	...	...	...	...	...	...	...	...
Sylhet	3	3	...	3	...	...	...	...	...	1	1	...	1	...	...	...	...	...
Khasi and Jaintia Hills	7	7	...	...	...	...	...	7	...	...	...	...	...	...	...	...	...	...
Naga Hills	...	...	...	...	...	...	...	...	...	...	...	...	...	...	...	...	...	...
Lushai Hills	4	2	2	1	2	...	...	1	...	...	...	...	...	...	...	...	...	...
ASSAM VALLEY DISTRICTS	*13*	*10*	*3*	*10*	*3*	...	...	...	...	*2*	*2*	...	*2*	...	...	...	...	...
Goalpara	...	...	...	...	...	...	...	...	...	2	2	...	2	...	...	...	...	...
Kamrup	...	...	...	...	...	...	...	...	...	...	...	...	...	...	...	...	...	...
Darrang	5	4	1	4	1	...	...	...	...	...	...	...	...	...	...	...	...	...
Nowgong	...	...	...	...	...	...	...	...	...	...	...	...	...	...	...	...	...	...
Sibsagar	5	3	2	3	2	...	...	...	...	...	...	...	...	...	...	...	...	...
Lakhimpur	3	3	...	3	...	...	...	...	...	...	...	...	...	...	...	...	...	...
Garo Hills	...	...	...	...	...	...	...	...	...	...	...	...	...	...	...	...	...	...
(2) Manipur State	...	...	...	...	...	...	...	...	...	...	...	...	...	...	...	...	...	...

TABLE XVII.—TERRITORIAL DISTRIBUTION OF THE CHRISTIAN POPULATION BY SECT AND RACE—*contd.*

District or State.	*LUTHERN.*									*METHODIST.*								
	Total.			Distribution by Race.						Total.			Distribution by Race.					
				European and Allied Races.		Anglo-Indians.		Indians.					European and Allied Races.		Anglo-Indians.		Indians.	
	Persons.	Males.	Females.	Males.	Females.	Males.	Females.	Males.	Females.	Persons.	Males.	Females.	Males.	Females.	Males.	Females.	Males.	Females.
1	56	57	58	59	60	61	62	63	64	65	66	67	68	69	70	71	72	73
ASSAM	***3,752***	***1,941***	***1,811***	***6***	***7***	...	...	***1,935***	***1,804***	***30***	***19***	***11***	***7***	***4***	***2***	...	***10***	***7***
(1) *British Territory*	***3,752***	***1,941***	***1,811***	***6***	***7***	...	...	***1,935***	***1,804***	***30***	***10***	***11***	***7***	***4***	***2***	...	***10***	***7***
SURMA VALLEY AND HILL DISTRICTS	...	...	...	...	...	...	...	...	...	***23***	***13***	***10***	***3***	***4***	...	...	***10***	***6***
Cachar	...	...	...	...	...	...	...	...	...	19	10	9	2	3	...	...	8	6
Sylhet	...	...	...	...	...	...	...	...	...	1	...	1	...	1	...	...	...	...
Khasi and Jaintia Hills	...	...	...	...	...	...	...	...	...	1	1	...	...	...	...	...	1	...
Naga Hills	...	...	...	...	...	...	...	...	...	1	1	...	...	...	...	...	1	...
Lushai Hills	...	...	...	...	...	...	...	...	...	1	1	...	1	...	...	...	...	...
ASSAM VALLEY DISTRICTS	***3,752***	***1,941***	***1,811***	***6***	***7***	...	...	***1,935***	***1,804***	***7***	***6***	***1***	***4***	...	***2***	...	...	***1***
Goalpara	2,399	1,246	1,153	2	1	...	...	1,244	1,152	1	...	1	...	...	...	...	...	1
Kamrup	64	33	31	1	2	...	...	32	29	2	2	...	...	...	2	...	...	...
Darrang	435	222	213	2	2	...	...	220	211	...	...	...	...	...	...	...	...	...
Nowgong	129	68	61	...	...	...	...	68	61	1	1	...	1	...	...	...	...	...
Sibsagar	254	129	125	...	...	...	...	129	125	...	...	...	...	...	...	...	...	...
Lakhimpur	471	243	228	1	2	...	...	242	226	3	3	...	3	...	...	...	...	...
Garo Hills	...	...	...	...	...	...	...	...	...	...	...	...	...	...	...	...	...	...
(2) *Manipur State*	...	...	...	...	...	...	...	...	...	...	...	...	...	...	...	...	...	...

TABLE XVII.—Territorial Distribution of the Christian Population by Sect and Race—*contd.*

District or State.	Minor Protestant Denominations. Total. Persons.	Total. Males.	Total. Females.	Distribution by Race. European and Allied Races. Males.	European and Allied Races. Females.	Anglo-Indians. Males.	Anglo-Indians. Females.	Indians. Males.	Indians. Females.	Presbyterian. Total. Persons.	Total. Males.	Total. Females.	Distribution by Race. European and Allied Races. Males.	European and Allied Races. Females.	Anglo-Indians. Males.	Anglo-Indians. Females.	Indians. Males.	Indians. Females.
1	74	75	76	77	78	79	80	81	82	83	84	85	86	87	88	89	90	91
ASSAM	*162*	*72*	*90*	...	*1*	*1*	...	*71*	*89*	*31,184*	*14,999*	*16,185*	*379*	*93*	*27*	*17*	*14,593*	*16,075*
(1) ***British Territory***	*162*	*72*	*90*	...	*1*	*1*	...	*71*	*89*	*31,184*	*14,999*	*16,185*	*379*	*93*	*27*	*17*	*14,593*	*16,075*
SURMA VALLEY AND HILL DISTRICTS	*151*	*68*	*83*	...	*1*	*1*	...	*67*	*82*	*30,916*	*14,775*	*16,141*	*198*	*57*	*22*	*12*	*14,560*	*16,072*
Cachar	...	...	...	...	...	...	...	...	...	168	99	69	53	9	...	...	46	60
Sylhet	...	...	...	...	...	...	...	...	...	735	391	344	121	36	1	3	269	305
Khasi and Jaintia Hills	151	68	83	...	1	1	...	67	83	28,290	13,386	14,904	14	9	17	5	13,355	14,890
Naga Hills	...	...	...	...	...	...	...	...	...	2	2	...	2	...	...	...	...	...
Lushai Hills	...	...	...	...	...	...	...	...	...	1,721	897	824	3	3	4	4	890	817
ASSAM VALLEY DISTRICTS	*11*	*4*	*7*	...	...	...	...	*4*	*7*	*268*	*224*	*44*	*186*	*36*	*5*	*5*	*33*	*3*
Goalpara	...	...	...	...	...	...	...	...	...	5	2	3	...	...	1	...	1	3
Kamrup	...	...	...	...	...	...	...	...	...	29	23	6	1	2	2	4	20	...
Darrang	4	4	...	...	...	...	...	4	...	44	36	8	36	8	...	...	...	...
Nowgong	...	...	...	...	...	...	...	...	...	19	17	2	17	2	...	...	...	...
Sibsagar	7	...	7	...	...	...	...	...	7	66	52	14	48	13	1	1	3	...
Lakhimpur	...	...	...	...	...	...	...	...	...	105	94	11	84	11	1	...	9	...
Garo Hills	...	...	...	...	...	...	...	...	...	...	...	...	...	...	...	...	...	...
(2) ***Manipur State***	...	...	...	...	...	...	...	...	...	...	...	...	...	...	...	...	...	...

TABLE XVII.—Territorial Distribution of the Christian Population by Sect and Race—*contd.*

District or State.	PROTESTANT (UNSECTARIAN OR SECT NOT SPECIFIED).									ROMAN CATHOLIC.								
	Total.			Distribution by Race.						Total.			Distribution by Race.					
				European and Allied Races.		Anglo-Indians.		Indians.					European and Allied Races.		Anglo-Indians.		Indians.	
	Persons.	Males.	Females.	Males.	Females.	Males.	Females.	Males.	Females.	Persons.	Males.	Females.	Males.	Females.	Males.	Females.	Males.	Females.
1	92	93	94	95	96	97	98	99	100	101	102	103	104	105	106	107	108	109
ASSAM	***1,701***	***1,014***	***687***	***9***	***5***	***3***	***1***	***1,002***	***681***	***2,783***	***1,450***	***1,333***	***95***	***93***	***111***	***87***	***1,244***	***1,153***
(1) ***British Territory***	***1,701***	***1,014***	***687***	***9***	***5***	***3***	***1***	***1,002***	***681***	***2,756***	***1,437***	***1,319***	***94***	***93***	***99***	***73***	***1,244***	***1,153***
SURMA VALLEY AND HILL DISTRICTS	***43***	***24***	***19***	***9***	***5***	***3***	***1***	***12***	***13***	***1,976***	***1,009***	***967***	***55***	***61***	***64***	***50***	***890***	***856***
Cachar	4	2	2	2	2	...	...	...	...	236	115	121	8	7	3	7	104	107
Sylhet	39	22	17	7	3	3	1	12	13	363	223	140	19	12	43	27	161	101
Khasi and Jaintia Hills	...	...	...	...	...	...	...	...	...	1,363	664	705	26	42	18	15	620	648
Naga Hills	...	...	...	...	...	...	...	...	...	6	5	1	1	...	...	1	4	...
Lushai Hills	...	...	...	...	...	...	...	...	...	2	2	...	1	...	...	...	1	...
ASSAM VALLEY DISTRICTS	***1,658***	***990***	***668***	...	...	...	...	***990***	***668***	***780***	***428***	***352***	***39***	***32***	***35***	***23***	***354***	***297***
Goalpara	37	26	11	...	...	...	...	26	11	14	9	5	1	...	5	4	3	1
Kamrup	165	84	81	...	...	...	...	84	81	40	19	21	7	11	7	3	5	7
Darrang	20	9	11	...	...	...	...	9	11	151	87	64	6	1	4	3	77	60
Nowgong	...	...	...	...	...	...	...	...	...	72	32	40	5	3	6	6	21	31
Sibsagar	5	...	5	...	...	...	...	...	5	247	148	99	7	4	9	5	132	90
Lakhimpur	1,233	704	529	...	...	...	...	704	529	256	153	123	13	13	4	2	116	108
Garo Hills	198	167	31	...	...	...	...	107	31	...	...	...	...	...	...	...	...	...
(2) ***Manipur State***	...	...	...	...	...	...	...	...	...	***27***	***13***	***14***	***1***	...	***12***	***14***	...	...

TABLE XVII.—TERRITORIAL DISTRIBUTION OF THE CHRISTIAN POPULATION BY SECT AND RACE—*concld.*

District or State.	*Sect not returned.*									*Indefinite beliefs.*								
	Total.			Distribution by race.						Total.			Distribution by race.					
				European and allied races.		Anglo-Indians.		Indians.					European and allied races.		Anglo-Indians.		Indians.	
	Persons.	Males.	Females.	Males.	Females.	Males.	Females.	Males.	Females.	Persons.	Males.	Females.	Males.	Females.	Males.	Females.	Males.	Females.
1	110	111	112	113	114	115	116	117	118	119	120	121	122	123	124	125	126	127
ASSAM	*16*	*12*	*4*	*11*	*4*	*1*	...	...	...	*402*	*198*	*204*	*21*	*1*	...	...	*177*	*203*
(*1*) ***British Territory***	*16*	*12*	*4*	*11*	*4*	*1*	...	...	...	*402*	*198*	*204*	*21*	*1*	...	...	*177*	*203*
SURMA VALLEY AND HILL DISTRICTS	*1*	*1*	...	...	...	*1*	...	...	...	*335*	*159*	*176*	*8*	...	...	...	*151*	*176*
Cachar	...	...	...	...	...	...	...	...	...	6	6	...	6	...	...	...	...	...
Sylhet	...	...	...	...	...	...	...	...	...	2	2	...	2	...	...	...	...	...
Khasi and Jaintia Hills	1	1	...	...	...	1	...	...	...	327	151	176	...	...	...	...	151	176
Naga Hills	...	...	...	...	...	...	...	...	...	...	...	...	...	...	...	...	...	...
Lushai Hills	...	...	...	...	...	...	...	...	...	...	...	...	...	...	...	...	...	...
ASSAM VALLEY DISTRICTS	*15*	*11*	*4*	*11*	*4*	...	...	...	...	*67*	*39*	*28*	*13*	*1*	...	...	*26*	*27*
Goalpara	1	1	...	1	...	...	...	...	...	...	...	...	...	...	...	...	...	...
Kamrup	5	5	...	5	...	...	...	...	...	...	...	...	...	...	...	...	...	...
Darrang	2	2	...	2	...	...	...	...	...	5	5	...	4	...	...	...	1	...
Nowgong	...	...	...	...	...	...	...	...	...	...	...	...	...	...	...	...	...	...
Sibsagar	3	...	3	...	3	...	...	...	...	61	33	28	8	1	...	...	25	27
Lakhimpur	4	3	1	3	1	...	...	...	...	1	1	...	1	...	...	...	...	...
Garo Hills	...	...	...	...	...	...	...	...	...	...	...	...	...	...	...	...	...	...
(*2*) ***Manipur State***	...	...	...	...	...	...	...	...	...	...	...	...	...	...	...	...	...	...

TABLE XVIII.

EUROPEANS, ARMENIANS AND ANGLO-INDIANS BY RACE AND AGE.

The Feringis (males 4, female 1) have been excluded from the figures for Anglo-Indians in this Table.

TABLE XVIII.—EUROPEANS, ARMENIANS AND ANGLO-INDIANS BY RACE AND AGE.

District or State.	TOTAL.			EUROPEAN AND ALLIED RACES.																									
				BRITISH SUBJECTS.													OTHERS.												
				All ages.			0–12.		12–15.		15–30.		30–50.		50 and over.		All ages.			0–12.		12–15.		15–30.		30–50.		50 and over.	
	Total.	Males.	Females.	Total.	Males.	Females.	Males.	Females.	Males.	Females.	Males.	Females.	Males.	Females.	Males.	Females.	Total.	Males.	Females.	Males.	Females.	Males.	Females.	Males.	Females.	Males.	Females.	Males.	Females.
1	2	3	4	5	6	7	8	9	10	11	12	13	14	15	16	17	18	19	20	21	22	23	24	25	26	27	28	29	30
ASSAM	*2,725*	*1,870*	*855*	*2,172*	*1,556*	*616*	*122*	*131*	*2*	*12*	*486*	*167*	*796*	*280*	*150*	*26*	*73*	*38*	*35*	*2*	*6*	...	*1*	*3*	*5*	*28*	*16*	*5*	*7*
(1) British Territory	*2,662*	*1,833*	*829*	*2,153*	*1,542*	*611*	*122*	*130*	*2*	*12*	*482*	*167*	*789*	*277*	*147*	*25*	*73*	*38*	*35*	*2*	*6*	...	*1*	*3*	*5*	*28*	*16*	*5*	*7*
SURMA VALLEY AND HILL DISTRICTS	*1,167*	*756*	*411*	*874*	*596*	*278*	*48*	*66*	*1*	*8*	*175*	*75*	*305*	*113*	*67*	*16*	*41*	*18*	*23*	...	*3*	...	*1*	...	*3*	*16*	*12*	*2*	*4*
Cachar	284	197	87	260	187	73	9	12	...	...	60	24	99	35	19	2	4	2	2	...	...	...	...	...	1	2	1	...	...
Sylhet	486	347	139	380	288	92	16	25	1	1	90	26	151	38	30	4	1	...	1	...	...	...	...	...	...	...	1	...	...
Khasi and Jaintia Hills	326	166	160	173	80	93	14	25	...	7	13	19	38	33	15	9	36	16	20	...	3	...	1	...	2	14	10	2	4
Naga Hills	31	22	9	30	22	8	4	1	...	...	7	5	9	2	2	...	...	...	...	...	...	...	...	...	...	...	...	...	...
Lushai Hills	40	24	16	31	19	12	5	3	...	...	5	1	8	7	1	1	...	...	...	...	...	...	...	...	...	...	...	...	...
ASSAM VALLEY DISTRICTS	*1,495*	*1,077*	*418*	*1,279*	*946*	*333*	*74*	*64*	*1*	*4*	*307*	*92*	*484*	*164*	*80*	*9*	*32*	*20*	*12*	*2*	*3*	...	...	*3*	*2*	*12*	*4*	*3*	*3*
Goalpara	62	41	21	36	24	12	3	2	...	...	5	4	14	6	2	...	4	3	1	...	...	...	...	1	...	2	...	...	1
Kamrup	163	104	59	126	78	43	12	14	...	...	18	13	34	19	14	2	7	6	1	...	...	...	...	1	...	5	1	...	...
Darrang	223	165	58	201	153	48	13	8	...	...	47	12	82	27	11	1	5	3	2	1	1	...	...	...	...	1	1	1	...
Nowgong	120	79	41	85	58	27	3	7	...	...	23	6	25	10	7	2	3	3	...	...	...	...	...	1	...	2	...	...	...
Sibsagar	424	309	115	367	277	90	19	16	...	1	99	21	136	50	23	2	2	1	1	...	...	...	...	...	...	1	1	...	...
Lakhimpur	493	373	120	454	350	104	24	17	1	8	113	33	189	49	23	2	11	4	7	1	2	...	...	...	2	1	1	2	2
Garo Hills	10	6	4	10	6	4	...	...	...	...	2	1	4	3	...	...	...	...	...	...	...	...	...	...	...	...	...	...	...
(2) Manipur State	*63*	*37*	*26*	*19*	*14*	*5*	...	*1*	...	...	*4*	...	*7*	*3*	*3*	*1*	...	...	...	...	...	...	...	...	...	...	...	...	...

TABLE XVIII.—Europeans, Armenians and Anglo-Indians by Race and Age—*concld.*

District or State.	Armenians.													Anglo-Indians.												
	All ages.			0–12.		12–15.		15–30.		30–50.		50 and over.		All ages.			0–12.		12–15.		15–30.		30–50.		50 and over.	
	Total.	Males.	Females.	Males.	Females.	Males.	Females.	Males.	Females.	Males.	Females.	Males.	Females.	Total.	Males.	Females.	Males.	Females.	Males.	Females.	Males.	Females.	Males.	Females.	Males.	Females.
1	31	32	33	34	35	36	37	38	39	40	41	42	43	44	45	46	47	48	49	50	51	52	53	54	55	56
ASSAM	*5*	*4*	*1*	...	...	...	...	...	...	*3*	*1*	*1*	...	*475*	*272*	*203*	*75*	*63*	*6*	*8*	*87*	*81*	*85*	*43*	*19*	*8*
(1) ***British Territory***	*4*	*3*	*1*	...	...	...	...	...	...	*2*	*1*	*1*	...	*432*	*250*	*182*	*67*	*51*	*5*	*8*	*84*	*77*	*78*	*39*	*16*	*7*
SURMA VALLEY AND HILL DISTRICTS	*2*	*1*	*1*	...	...	...	...	...	...	*1*	*1*	...	...	*250*	*141*	*109*	*43*	*29*	*3*	*5*	*44*	*45*	*44*	*34*	*7*	*6*
Cachar	...	...	...	...	...	...	...	...	...	...	...	...	...	20	6	12	4	2	1	...	2	7	1	3	...	...
Sylhet	...	...	...	...	...	...	...	...	...	...	...	...	...	105	59	46	18	15	1	1	17	20	22	7	1	3
Khasi and Jaintia Hills	2	1	1	...	...	...	...	...	...	1	1	...	...	115	69	46	18	11	1	3	24	15	20	14	6	3
Naga Hills	...	...	...	...	...	...	...	...	...	...	...	...	...	1	...	1	...	...	...	...	...	1	...	...	...	...
Lushai Hills	...	...	...	...	...	...	...	...	...	...	...	...	...	9	5	4	3	1	...	1	1	2	1	...	...	...
ASSAM VALLEY DISTRICTS	*2*	*2*	...	...	...	...	...	...	...	*1*	...	*1*	...	*182*	*109*	*73*	*24*	*22*	*3*	*2*	*40*	*32*	*34*	*15*	*9*	*1*
Goalpara	2	2	...	...	...	...	...	...	...	1	...	1	...	20	12	8	5	4	...	...	3	2	8	1	1	...
Kamrup	...	...	...	...	...	...	...	...	...	...	...	...	...	30	20	10	3	2	...	...	13	6	3	2	1	...
Darrang	...	...	...	...	...	...	...	...	...	...	...	...	...	17	9	8	3	3	...	...	4	2	1	3	1	...
Nowgong	...	...	...	...	...	...	...	...	...	...	...	...	...	32	18	14	2	5	...	1	11	6	4	2	1	1
Sibsagar	...	...	...	...	...	...	...	...	...	...	...	...	...	55	31	24	6	4	1	2	8	13	13	5	3	...
Lakhimpur	...	...	...	...	...	...	...	...	...	...	...	...	...	26	19	9	7	4	1	...	2	3	7	2	2	...
Garo Hills	...	...	...	...	...	...	...	...	...	...	...	...	...	...	...	...	...	...	...	...	...	...	...	...	...	...
(2) ***Manipur State***	*1*	*1*	...	...	...	...	...	...	...	*1*	...	...	...	*43*	*22*	*21*	*8*	*19*	*1*	...	*3*	*6*	*7*	*4*	*3*	*1*

PROVINCIAL TABLE I.

AREA AND POPULATION OF THANAS, MAUZAS, ETC.

In all districts the district figures and those of subdivisions where they exist have been given. Thanas or out-posts have been shown in the Surma Valley and Goalpara, except in the Eastern Duars of the latter district where each Duar is shown: in the remaining districts of the Assam Valley mauzas have been shown thanawari under the orders of Government. Of the hill districts, in Khasi and Jaintia Hills separate figures have been given for the areas under Seims, Lyngdohs, Wahadadars, Dolois and Sirdars, while mauza figures have been given in the case of Garo Hills: in Lushai Hills and Naga Hills only subdivisions are shown. In Manipur State the Valley and Hill sections have been shown separately and are divided into panahs and lams. The areas of the districts have been taken from the District Gazetteers under the orders of Government (*vide* title page of Imperial Table I): those of lesser units have been supplied by the local authorities and their totals do not necessarily agree with the district figures.

All districts and the State of Manipur have been supplied with Village Census Tables in manuscript showing the population by sex and religion of every village, arranged according to the local unit of administration.

PROVINCIAL TABLE I.—AREA AND POPULATION OF THANAS, MAUZAS, ETC.

Thana, Mauza or other local unit.	Area in square miles.	Number of: Towns.	Number of: Villages.	Number of occupied houses.	Population 1911: Persons.	Population 1911: Males.	Population 1911: Females.	Population 1901 (Both sexes).	Percentage of variation: 1901 to 1911.	Percentage of variation: 1891 to 1901.	Number of persons per square mile in 1911.
1	2	3	4	5	6	7	8	9	10	11	12
ASSAM	*61,471*	*21*	*29,352*	*1,521,510*	*7,059,857*	*3,638,287*	*3,421,570*	*6,126,343*	*+15·24*	*+ 11·85*	*115*
(I) ***British Territory***	*53,015*	*20*	*27,875*	*1,452,019*	*6,713,635*	*3,467,621*	*3,246,014*	*5,841,878*	*+14·92*	*+ 6·66*	*127*
SURMA VALLEY AND HILL DISTRICTS ...	*25,277*	*9*	*15,112*	*760,478*	*3,446,030*	*1,761,134*	*1,684,896*	*3,084,527*	*+ 11·72*	*+ 7·13*	*136*
CACHAR DISTRICT	3,565	2	1,413	115,442	497,463	260,444	237,019	455,593	+ 9·19	+17·88	140
Sadar Subdivision...	*1,649·00*	*1*	*829*	*79,694*	*339,107*	*177,901*	*161,206*	*301,884*	*+12·33*	*+12·78*	*205*
Silchar	719·00	1	524	53,413	221,145	116,693	104,452	194,269	+ 13·83	+ 38·31	308
Lakhipur	266·91	...	148	16,157	65 607	34,143	31,464	57,889	+ 13·33	— 20·74	246
Katigora	661·85	...	157	10,124	52,355	27,065	25,290	49,726	+ 5·29	— 8·21	79
Hailakandi Subdivision (Hailakandi) ...	*414·00*	*1*	*272*	*28,529*	*131,060*	*68,304*	*62,756*	*112,897*	*+16·88*	*+13·05*	*317*
North Cachar Subdivision (North Cachar)	*1,706·00*	...	*312*	*7,219*	*27,296*	*14,239*	*13,057*	*40,812*	*—33·12*	*+115·46*	*16*
SYLHET DISTRICT	5,388	5	10,776	547,655	2,472,671	1,268,469	1,204,202	2,241,848	+10·29	+4·05	459
North Sylhet Subdivision...	*863·50*	*1*	*2,470*	*120,985*	*523,931*	*266,170*	*257,761*	*463,477*	*+13·04*	*—3·91*	*506*
Sylhet (Sadar)	583·28	1	1,038	62,330	278,877	142,207	136,670	241,811	+ 15·33	— 5·19	478
Kanairghat	220·60	...	469	21,665	82,240	42,510	39,730	79,677	+ 3·22	— 3·96	372
Balaganj	230·66	...	963	37,090	162,814	81,453	81,361	141,989	+ 14·67	— 1·61	706
Sunamganj Subdivision	*1,450·00*	1	*2,573*	*98,290*	*479,523*	*254,427*	*225,096*	*433,752*	*+10·55*	*+ 4·93*	*335*
Sunamganj	440·95	1	718	25,587	124 364	66,887	57,477	113,088	+ 9·97	+ 5·17	282
Chhatak	273·91	...	626	22,632	102 295	54,009	48,286	90,683	+ 12·85	+ 2·23	373
Dirai	393·64	...	773	32,287	165 566	86,584	78,982	151,020	+ 9·63	+ 4·85	421
Dharmapasa	322·90	...	456	17,584	87,298	46,947	40,351	78,961	+ 10·56	+ 7·99	270
Habiganj Subdivision	*999·00*	*1*	*2,525*	*137,050*	*597,056*	*304,252*	*292,804*	*555,001*	*+7·58*	*+9·99*	*604*
Habiganj	362·05	1	1,169	54,472	229 123	116,756	112,367	214,710	+ 6·71	+ 8·05	633
Baniachung	273·97	...	498	29,591	140,741	72,562	68,179	130,198	+ 8·09	+ 13·42	514
Madhabpur	185·42	...	424	29,821	129 017	64,913	64,104	119,153	+ 8·28	+ 10·29	696
Nabiganj	167·04	...	434	23,166	98,175	50,021	48,154	90,940	+ 7·96	+ 11·89	588
South Sylhet Subdivision...	*1,064·00*	*1*	*1,643*	*87,306*	*408,002*	*206,884*	*201,118*	*379,158*	*+ 7·60*	*+2·57*	*475*
Maulvi Bazar	606·74	1	1,218	58,826	294,146	148·340	145,806	276,592	+ 6·35	+ 3·27	485
Kulaura	251·76	...	425	28,480	113,856	58,544	55,312	102,566	+11·008	+ 0·75	452

PROVINCIAL TABLE I.—Area and Population of Thanas, Mauzas, etc.—*continued.*

Thana, mauza or other local unit.	Area in square miles.	Number of Towns.	Number of Villages.	Number of occupied houses.	Population 1911 Persons.	Population 1911 Males.	Population 1911 Females.	Population 1901 (Both sexes.)	Percentage of variation 1901 to 1911.	Percentage of variation 1891 to 1901.	Number of persons per square mile in 1911.
1	2	3	4	5	6	7	8	9	10	11	12
Karimganj Subdivision	*1,066·00*	*1*	*1,565*	*104,024*	*464,159*	*236,736*	*227,423*	*410,460*	*+13·08*	*+6·71*	*434*
Karimganj	820·78	1	1,086	71,629	318,055	163,805	154,250	281,565	+ 12·96	+ 8·61	388
Jaldhup	247·77	...	479	32,395	146,104	72,931	73,173	128,805	+ 13·35	+ 2·79	590
KHASI AND JAINTIA HILLS DISTRICT	6,027	1	2,140	37,816	235,069	114,442	120,627	202,250	+16·23	+2·20	39
Shillong Subdivision	*3,941*	*1*	*1,311*	*26,241*	*157,202*	*77,331*	*79,871*	*134,329*	*+17·03*	*+0·71*	*40*
Shillong town		1	...	2,962	13,639	7,762	5,877	8,384	+62·68	+ 24·76	
Seimships—											
Khyrim	Areas are not available.	...	296	6,518	20,940	10,687	10,253	31,327	+ 14·73	+3·98	
Mylliem		...	282	3,449	21,398	10,591	10,807	17,863	+ 19·70	+4·83	
Cherra		...	85	1,140	9,198	4,321	4,877	8,155	+ 12·79	−17·64	
Nongstoin		...	169	1,014	9,162	4,358	4,804	9,606	+ 0·58	+4·30	
Maharam		...	67	1,228	10,387	5,026	5,361	8,464	+ 22·72	−5·40	
Nongkhlao		...	66	1,368	10,716	5,171	5,545	9,715	+ 10·30	+8·84	
Marriaw		...	17	617	2,579	1,253	1,326	2,289	+ 12·67	−14·08	
Rambrai		...	28	646	2,680	1,321	1,359	2,697	+ 0·63	−16·34	
Maoiang		...	19	524	2,371	1,165	1,206	1,856	+ 27·75	−3·98	
Langrin		...	25	266	1,174	591	583	1,138	+ 3·16	−14·44	
Nobosophoh		...	14	379	1,650	745	905	1,555	+ 6·11	+4·86	
Maosanram		...	7	277	1,656	773	883	1,414	+ 17·11	+9·95	
Malaisohmat		...	9	111	493	244	249	491	+ 0·41	+21·84	
Bhowal		...	12	159	686	323	363	865	− 20·69	+39·52	
Nongspung		...	19	516	2,368	1,192	1,176	1,859	+ 27·38	+13·28	
Lyngdohships—											
Sohlong		...	23	542	2,534	1,197	1,337	2,014	+ 25·83	−20·08	
Maoflang		...	11	236	1,173	551	622	947	+ 23·86	+4·87	
Langiong		...	5	166	764	349	415	596	+ 28·19	+9·96	
Wahadadarships—											
Shella		...	32	1,098	4,085	1,977	2,108	4,358	− 6·26	−31·46	
Jirngam		...	6	179	1,028	545	483	723	+ 42·18	−3·47	
Maolong		...	15	515	2,010	1,108	902	1,472	+ 36·55	−6·18	
Maodon		...	5	106	389	169	220	296	+ 31·42	+15·18	
Dwara Nongtyrmen...		...	5	110	373	178	195	362	+ 3·04	−2·69	
Nonglwai		...	4	94	416	199	217	169	+146·15	+24·26	
Pamsanngut		...	5	80	372	190	182	288	+ 29·17	+35·85	
British villages		...	*135*	*1,884*	*17,195*	*8,579*	*8,616*	*15,426*	*+11·47*	*+7·81*	
1 to 16 Survey Camp		...	...	58	181	181	...	...	...	...	
16 to 27 Survey Camp		...	...		85	85	...	...	...	...	

PROVINCIAL TABLE I.—Area and Population of Thanas, Mauzas, etc.—*continued.*

Thana, mauza or other local unit.	Area in square miles.	Number of Towns.	Number of Villages.	Number of occupied houses.	Population 1911 Persons.	Population 1911 Males.	Population 1911 Females.	Population 1901 (Both sexes).	Percentage of variation 1901 to 1911.	Percentage of variation 1891 to 1901.	Number of persons per square mile in 1911.
1	2	3	4	5	6	7	8	9	10	11	12
Jowai Subdivision	2,086	...	829	11,575	77,867	37,111	40,756	67,921	+ 14·63	+ 0·05	37
Doloiships—											
Jowai	Areas are not available.	...	41	1,670	10,496	4,797	5,690	9,107	+ 15·25	+ 4·97	
Nartiang		...	63	1,002	4,617	2,185	2,432	4,466	+ 3·38	− 33·55	
Raliang		...	78	1,643	8,100	3,889	4,211	6,870	+ 17·90	+ 19·12	
Bhoi		...	217	985	11,615	5,925	5,690	9,649	+ 20·37	+ 76·75	
Shangpung		...	20	432	4,142	2,011	2,131	3,647	+ 13·57	+ 3·11	
Nongtalang		...	19	678	5,805	2,600	3,145	5,105	+ 13·76	− 12·96	
Nonglwai (Nongbob)		...	12	327	2,724	1,261	1,463	2,300	+ 18·44	+ 5·89	
Maskut		...	2	28	114	56	58	98	+ 16·33	− 10·09	
Nongjngi		...	36	528	2,8[illegible]9	1,209	1,510	2,497	+ 12·49	+ 10·68	
Mynso		...	18	289	1,496	676	820	1,327	+ 12·74	+ 2·23	
Shiliang Myntang		...	23	364	2,423	1,179	1,244	2,348	+ 3·19	+ 3·66	
Nongphymut		...	44	465	2,232	1,087	1,145	2,120	+ 5·28	+ 0·14	
Sutnga		...	27	625	4,060	1,960	2,100	4,156	− 2·31	+ 10·27	
Nongkhlieh		...	7	189	947	462	485	824	+ 14·93	− 1·90	
Narpuh		...	28	342	1,934	939	995	1,801	+ 7·36	− 3·17	
Satpator		...	24	476	2,584	1,174	1,410	2,412	+ 5·81	+ 2·05	
Lakadong		...	6	121	665	270	395	742	− 10·38	− 24·59	
Rymbai		...	22	309	3,472	1,588	1,934	3,061	+ 13·43	− 7·38	
Amwi		...	8	336	2,053	1,003	1,050	1,541	+ 33·23	+ 9·06	
Darang		...	6	204	1,120	521	599	1,117	+ 0·27	− 11·49	
Sirdarships—											
Mynriang } Langsoh }		...	120	356	3,651	1,812	1,839	2,339	+ 56·09	+ 29·44	
Saipung		...	8	125	808	407	401	366	+ 120·77	− 43·52	
NAGA HILLS DISTRICT	3,070	1	407	41,232	149,623	74,751	74,872	102,402	+ 46·13	+ 17·24	49
Kohima Subdivision	Areas are not available.	1	264	23,186	86,597	44,617	41,980	58,544	+ 47·92	...	
Mokokchang Subdivision		...	143	18,046	63,026	30,134	32,892	43,858	+ 43·70	...	
LUSHAI HILLS DISTRICT... ...	7,227	...	376	18,333	91,204	43,028	48,176	82,434	+ 10·64	Not censused in 1891.	13
Aijal Subdivision	4,701	...	211	16,121	65,215	30,778	34,437	56,305	+ 15·82		14
Lungleh Subdivision	2,526	...	165	2,212	25,989	12,250	13,739	26,129	− 0·54		10

PROVINCIAL TABLE I.—Area and Population of Thanas, Mauzas, etc.—*continued.*

Thana, Mauza or other local unit.	Area in square miles.	Number of: Towns.	Number of: Villages.	Number of occupied houses.	Population 1911: Persons.	Population 1911: Males.	Population 1911: Females.	Population 1901 (Both sexes.)	Percentage of variation: 1901 to 1911.	Percentage of variation: 1891 to 1901.	Number of persons per square mile in 1911.
1	2	3	4	5	6	7	8	9	10	11	12
ASSAM VALLEY DISTRICTS	*27,738*	*11*	*12,763*	*691,541*	*3,267,605*	*1,706,487*	*1,561,118*	*2,757,351*	+ *18·51*	+ *6·13*	*118*
GOALPARA DISTRICT	3,954	2	2,135	112,298	600,643	318,475	282,168	462,052	+ 29·99	+ 2·05	152
Dhubri Subdivision	*2,865*	*1*	*1,310*	*81,861*	*443,238*	*236,235*	*207,003*	*330,844*	+ *33·97*	+ *3·69*	*255*
Dhubri	180	1	143	11,232	62,035	33,509	28,526	52,770	+ 17·56	− 8·27	345
Bilasipara	545	...	270	17,869	95,896	51,684	44,212	69,162	+ 38·65	+ 35·67	176
South Salmara	365	...	312	18,048	107,063	57,179	49,884	62,921	+ 70·15	− 13·14	298
Golakganj	205	...	82	17,759	86,652	45,512	41,140	77,078	+ 11·12	+ 6·20	423
Eastern Duars	1,570	...	503	16,953	91,592	48,351	43,241	68,913	+ 32·91	+ 5·11	58
Ripu	242	...	64	2,186	14,349	8,044	6,305	5,456	+ 162·99	+ 6·19	59
Guma	98	...	44	1,765	8,795	5,091	3,704	5,342	+ 64·64	+ 6·20	90
Sidli	361	...	211	6,878	38,697	19,733	18,964	31,461	+ 22·99	+ 4·95	107
Bijni	374	...	180	6,093	29,341	15,263	14,078	25,859	+ 13·46	+ 4·05	78
Chirang	495	...	4	101	410	220	190	795	− 48·43	+ 5·02	1
Goalpara Subdivision	*1,089*	*1*	*825*	*30,437*	*157,405*	*82,240*	*75,165*	*131,208*	+ *19·97*	− *1·52*	*145*
Goalpara	214	1	179	7,639	35,463	19,071	16,392	31,256	+ 13·46	+ 4·93	166
Dudhni	265	...	317	7,223	36,676	18,506	18,170	31111	+ 17·80	+ 9·62	138
Lakhipur	277	...	260	5,776	35,924	19,426	16,498	22,201	+ 61·81	− 15·29	130
North Salmara	333	...	60	9,799	49,342	25,237	24,105	46,640	+ 5·79	− 4·55	148
KAMRUP DISTRICT	3,858	2	1,952	131,493	667,828	339,398	328,430	589,187	+ 13·35	− 7·10	173
Gauhati Subdivision	*2,584·00*	*1*	*1,521*	*103,446*	*528,679*	*267,095*	*261,584*	*473,252*	+ *11·71*	− *5·07*	*227*
Gauhati Thana	*555·05*	*1*	*148*	*10,317*	*52,095*	*28,581*	*23,514*	*46,981*	+ *10·89*	− *4·89*	*94*
Panbari including town	91·71	1	38	4,766	24,980	14,239	10,041	22,680	+ 7·05	...	265
Beltola	45·67	...	39	1,885	8,333	4,301	4,029	6,921	+ 20·36	...	182
Demoria	149·15	...	54	1,909	10,245	5,197	5,048	10,198	+ 0·46	...	69
Ramsarani (16 villages)	22·55	...	16	1,109	5,774	2,958	2,816	4,598	+ 25·58	...	256
North Gauhati (Sila Sundari Ghopa Mauza) ...	1·48	...	1	648	2,947	1,476	1,471	2,581	+ 14·05	...	1,991
Brahmaputra River	244·49	...	...	...	519	410	109	...	...	...	2
Palasbari Thana	*152·75*	...	*121*	*10,361*	*50,356*	*24,508*	*25,848*	*48,123*	+ *4·64*	− *9·68*	*330*
Ramsarani (12 villages)	14·96	...	12	1,614	7,530	3,691	3,839	6,851	+ 9·91	...	503
Dakuin Rani	43·86	...	30	1,085	5,043	2,515	2,528	5,278	− 4·45	...	115
Chayani	26·98	...	28	3,265	15,889	7,745	8,184	14,856	+ 6·95	...	589
Dhakhin Saru Bangsar	66·95	...	51	4,297	21,894	10,547	11,347	21,138	+ 3·58	...	327
Chhaygaon Outpost	*175·94*	...	*113*	*3,940*	*19,320*	*10,487*	*8,842*	*18,380*	+ *5·11*	− *4·07*	*110*
Chhaygaon Pantan	91·30	...	43	1,989	9,095	5,150	3,945	8,695	+ 4·60	...	100
Barduar	84·64	...	70	1,951	10,234	5,337	4,897	9,694	+ 5·57	...	121

PROVINCIAL TABLE I.—AREA AND POPULATION OF THANAS, MAUZAS, etc.—*continued.*

THANA, MAUZA OR OTHER LOCAL UNIT.	Area in square miles.	NUMBER OF		Number of occupied houses.	POPULATION.				PERCENTAGE OF VARIATION.		Number of persons per square mile in 1911.
		Towns.	Villages.		1911. Persons.	1911. Males.	1911. Females.	1901 (Both sexes).	1901 to 1911.	1891 to 1901.	
1	2	3	4	5	6	7	8	9	10	11	12
Boko Outpost	*431·66*	...	*223*	*6,800*	*34,292*	*17,596*	*16,696*	*30,839*	*+11·19*	*−7·36*	*79*
Bongaon	117·21	...	71	1,693	8 987	4,547	4,440	7,453	+20·58	...	77
Boko	35·67	...	33	994	5.414	2,764	2,650	4,845	+11·56	...	153
Luki	92·01	...	53	2,164	11 441	5,672	5,769	9,950	+14·98	...	124
Chamaria	186 77	...	66	1,949	8 450	4,613	3,837	8,591	− 1·64	...	45
Nalbari Thana	*257·95*	...	*220*	*25,561*	*127,903*	*62,093*	*65,810*	*116,529*	*+ 9 76*	*+2·82*	*496*
Banyjani...	17·95	...	35	4,178	15 163	7,189	7,974	14,976	+ 1·25	...	845
Khata	18 67	...	42	4,095	15 158	7,415	7,743	14,862	+ 1·99	...	812
Pakowa	22·24	...	23	3.077	17 061	8,159	8,902	13,798	+23·65	...	767
Dharmapur —	43·67	...	36	4,945	26 899	13,260	13,639	22,850	+17 72	...	616
Batasgila	30·75	...	19	1,416	11 533	5,565	5,968	10,245	+12·57	...	375
Namati	29·71	...	24	2,332	12 293	5,966	6,327	11,950	+ 2·87	...	414
Namborbhag	30·23	...	19	8,458	17.663	8.702	8,961	15,925	+10·91	...	584
Paschim Baska	64·73	...	22	2,060	12,133	5.837	6,296	11,923	+ 1·76	...	187
Ranjia Thana	*615·10*	...	*313*	*18,067*	*99,394*	*50,603*	*48,791*	*89,851*	*+10·6 2*	*+0·51*	*162*
Pub Borigog	21·56	...	29	2,039	8.876	4.439	4,437	10.100	−12·20	...	413
Paschim Borigog	23·04	...	35	2,627	16 992	8,394	8,598	12,446	+36·53	...	738
Pub Kachari Mahal...	57·44	...	32	2,393	14 194	7,328	6,866	11,178	+26·98	...	247
Panduri	34·56	...	38	1,821	10.045	5,440	4,605	8.833	+13·72	...	291
Pub Banbhag	23·21	...	42	2,102	10,205	5,0 8	5,177	9,258	+10·23	...	439
Paschim Banbhag	33·72	...	33	1,763	9 690	4,707	4,983	9,966	− 2·77	...	287
Pub Baska	73·67	...	26	1,485	8 548	4,318	4,230	8,641	− 1·08	...	116
Uttar Baska	203·36	...	28	1,654	8 113	4,334	3,779	8,459	− 4 09	...	40
Betna	144·57	...	60	2,233	12,731	6,615	6,116	10,961	+16 15	...	88
Kamalpur Outpost	*161·43*	...	*167*	*10,902*	*63,102*	*32,397*	*30,705*	*53,851*	*+17·18*	*−4·54*	*391*
Patidarang	30·67	...	31	1,750	9 039	4,731	4,308	7,600	+18·93	...	295
Barbangsar	25·25	...	26	1,205	10 403	5,270	5,183	9,626	+ 8·07	...	412
Silasundari Ghopa (excluding N. Gauhati) ...	28·11	...	25	1,035	8 606	4 610	3,996	5,771	+49·12	...	306
Karara	16·81	...	21	1,893	10,544	5,382	5,162	9,127	+15·81	...	627
Madartola	30·54	...	24	1,552	8 446	4,247	4,199	7,298	+15·73	...	277
Pubpar...	30·05	...	40	2,867	16,064	8,157	7,907	14,419	+11·41	...	535
Hajo Outpost	*226·27*	...	*216*	*17,498*	*82,208*	*40,830*	*41,378*	*68,689*	*+19·68*	*−18 49*	*363*
Hajo	72·79	...	44	5,728	27 060	13,631	13,429	21,588	+25·35	...	372
Uttar Saru Bangsar...	55·70	...	56	3,817	18 555	8,951	9,604	16.222	+14·38	...	333
Upar Barbhag	23·67	...	46	4.485	21 554	10,125	11,429	19,877	+ 8·44	...	911
Barkhetri	74·11	...	70	3,408	15,039	8,123	6,916	11,002	+36·69	...	203
Barpeta Subdivision	*1,274·00*	*1*	*431*	*28,047*	*139,149*	*72,303*	*66,846*	*115,935*	*+20·02*	*−14·57*	*114*
Barpeta Thana	*566·72*	*1*	*188*	*10,080*	*46,188*	*24,616*	*21,572*	*37,100*	*+24·50*	...	*82*
Barpeta	120·65	1	40	4,549	19 507	9,782	9,725	15,550	+25·45	...	162
Chenga and Bagribari	227·43	...	37	1,394	6.103	3,613	2,490	5,694	+ 7·18	...	27
Sarukhetri	109·65	...	68	2,383	11.999	6,549	5,450	8,420	+42·51	...	109
Bhowanipur (part)	108·99	...	43	1,754	8,579	4,672	3,907	7,436	+15·37	...	79

PROVINCIAL TABLE I.—Area and Population of Thanas, Mauzas, etc.—*continued.*

Thana, mauza or other local unit.	Area in square miles.	Number of — Towns.	Number of — Villages.	Number of occupied houses.	Population. 1911. Persons.	Population. 1911. Males.	Population. 1911. Females.	Population. 1901 (Both sexes).	Percentage of variation. 1901 to 1911.	Percentage of variation. 1891 to 1901.	Number of persons per square mile in 1911.
1	2	3	4	5	6	7	8	9	10	11	12
Sorbhog Outpost	*422·15*	...	*112*	*7,370*	*36,242*	*18,856*	*17,386*	*28,578*	*+26·83*	...	*86*
Rupasi	98·12	...	31	1,392	6 494	3,522	2,972	5,965	+ 8·87	...	66
Damk. chakabansi	38·39	...	29	2,782	12 732	6,733	5,999	10,129	+25·70	...	333
Bijni	285·64	...	52	3,196	17 016	8,601	8,415	12,484	+36·30	...	60
Bajali Outpost	*230·13*	...	*131*	*10,597*	*53,719*	*28,831*	*27,388*	*50,257*	*+12·86*	+ 6·38	*246*
Chapaguri	110·44	...	36	2,213	12 576	6,419	6,157	10,437	+20·49	...	114
Sariha	26·22	...	26	2,121	11.878	5,984	5,894	10 610	+11·95	...	453
Manikpur	19·37	...	15	1,616	8 348	4,279	4,069	6 931	+20·44	...	431
Uttar Bajali	22·58	...	19	2,465	13 134	6,643	6,491	11,704	+12·22	...	581
Pub Bajali	16·92	...	20	1,619	7 910	3,947	3,963	7,743	+ 2·16	...	467
Bhowanipur (part)	34·60	...	15	563	2,873	1,559	1,314	2,832	+ 1·45	...	83
DARRANG DISTRICT	3,418	1	1,405	87,517	377,314	198,581	178,733	337,313	+11·84	+ 9·72	110
Tezpur Subdivision...	*2,041*	*1*	*646*	*51,794*	*207,155*	*111,189*	*95,966*	*166,733*	*+24·24*	*+39·54*	*101*
Tezpur Thana	*936*	*1*	*327*	*27,782*	*109,530*	*58,931*	*50,599*	*92,495*	*+18·42*	...	*117*
Tezpur town	1	1	...	1.264	5 355	3.759	1,596	5,067	+ 5·68	...	5,355
Barchola	290	...	54	2,746	12,053	6,671	5,382	6 980	+72·68	...	42
Bargaon	154	...	80	3,181	15 038	8,071	6,967	8,758	+71·71	...	98
Bausbari	81	...	37	5,939	19.717	10.120	9,597	19,081	+ 3·33	...	243
Bihaguri	53	...	28	1,597	7.132	3,833	3,299	6,421	+11·07	...	135
Halleswar	73	...	51	4,875	18 605	9,862	8,743	19,415	− 4·17	...	255
Mahabhairab	100	...	28	1,958	9 231	4,949	4,282	7,457	+23·79	...	92
Balipara	184	...	49	6,722	22 399	11,666	10,733	19,316	+15·96	...	122
Sootea Thana	*515*	...	*155*	*13,107*	*51,766*	*27,463*	*24,303*	*43,639*	*+ 18·62*	...	*101*
Chilabandha	164	...	31	1,574	6,931	3.717	3,214	5,434	+ 27·55	...	42
Barbhogia	22	...	20	1.518	6.254	3,249	3,005	5,870	+ 6·54	...	284
Sootea	111	...	46	3,985	16.262	8,713	7,489	14,267	+ 13·56	...	146
Bishnath (part)	218	...	58	6,030	22.279	11,784	10,505	18,068	+ 23·86	...	103
Behali Thana	*312*	...	*96*	*7,510*	*30,927*	*16,640*	*14,287*	*16,875*	*+ 82·19*	...	*99*
Bishnath (part)	82	...	27	2,264	9 019	4.891	4,128	5,193	+ 73·68	...	110
Behali (part)	230	...	60	5,246	21,908	11,749	10,159	11,782	+ 85·94	...	95
Gohpur Thana	*278*	...	*68*	*3,395*	*14,932*	*8,155*	*6,777*	*13,624*	*+ 9·60*	...	*54*
Behali (part)	62	...	13	916	3.301	1,846	1,455	2,832	+ 16·56	...	53
Gohpur	216	...	55	2,479	11.631	6,309	5,322	10,792	+ 7·77	...	54

PROVINCIAL TABLE I.—AREA AND POPULATION OF THANAS, MAUZAS, etc.—*continued.*

THANA, MAUZA OR OTHER LOCAL UNIT.	Area in square miles.	NUMBER OF Towns.	NUMBER OF Villages.	Number of occupied houses.	POPULATION. 1911. Persons.	POPULATION. 1911. Males.	POPULATION. 1911. Females.	POPULATION. 1901 (Both sexes).	PERCENTAGE OF VARIATION. 1901 to 1911.	PERCENTAGE OF VARIATION. 1891 to 1901.	Number of persons per square mile in 1911.
1	2	3	4	5	6	7	8	9	10	11	12
Mangaldai Subdivision	*1,377*	...	*759*	*35,723*	*170,159*	*87,392*	*82,767*	*170,580*	—0·25	— 9·24	*124*
Mangaldai Thana	*344*	...	*262*	*15,260*	*74,455*	*37,865*	*36,590*	*64,652*	+ 15·16	- 21·13	*216*
Bangamati	100	...	38	2,448	11,447	5,853	5,505	10,419	+ 9·87	...	114
Dahi	15	...	19	1,213	5,970	2,943	3,027	5,417	+ 10·21	...	398
Chopai	33	...	37	1,865	8 597	4,531	4,066	8,890	— 3·30	...	261
Dhula (Samabari)	27	...	38	1,455	8 138	4,396	3,742	3,719	+117·07	...	301
Hindughopa	11	...	13	1,421	7 409	3,453	3,956	6,602	+ 12·22	...	674
Sipajhar	77	...	43	2,143	9 790	5,144	4,646	8,253	+ 18·62	...	127
Lokrai	24	...	26	1,714	8 187	4,018	4,169	8,181	+ 0·07	...	341
Rainakuchi	8	...	10	1,003	5 561	2,686	2,875	4,955	+ 12·23	...	695
Dipila	40	...	34	1,409	6,500	3,410	3,090	5,229	+ 24·31	...	162
Lorakuchi (Sarabari)	9	...	9	569	2 856	1,432	1,424	2,957	- 3·42	...	317
Kalaigaon Thana	*189*	...	*168*	*5,802*	*29,462*	*15,079*	*14,383*	*36,428*	— 10·12	...	*156*
Sarabari (part)	16	...	20	1,063	5 260	2 654	2,606	5,678	- 7·36	...	329
Chinakona	49	...	52	1,348	7 626	3,916	3,710	9,759	- 21·86	...	156
Kalaigaon	43	...	41	1,693	7,606	3,955	3,651	7,914	- 3·89	...	177
Samabari (part)	40	...	7	134	993	490	503	4,861	- 79·57	...	25
Silpota	41	...	48	1,544	7,977	4,064	3,913	8,217	- 2·92	...	195
Panery Thana	*320*	...	*174*	*10,760*	*44,379*	*23,318*	*21,061*	*46,078*	— 3·69	...	*139*
Majikuchi	37	...	39	1,224	6 979	3,506	3,473	8,430	- 17·21	...	189
Dakua	28	...	34	1,304	6 389	3,244	3,145	7,302	- 12·50	...	228
Sekhar	131	...	42	3,586	12 374	6,641	5,733	11,010	+ 12·39	...	94
Harisinga	89	...	42	3,877	14 715	8,036	6,679	14,775	- 0·41	...	165
Ambagaon (part)	35	...	17	679	3,922	1,891	2,031	4,561	- 14·01	...	112
Koriapara Outpost	*524*	...	*155*	*3,901*	*21,863*	*11,130*	*10,733*	*23,422*	— 6·66	— 6·73	*42*
Orang	340	...	61	2,170	11 415	5,947	5,468	11,325	+ 0·88	...	34
Barsilajhar	154	...	52	1,133	7.127	3,567	3,560	7,954	- 10·40	...	46
Ambagaon (part)	30	...	22	593	3,321	1,616	1,705	4,143	- 19·84	...	111
NOWGONG DISTRICT	3,843	1	1,494	62,159	303,596	154,938	148,658	261,160	+16·25	— 24·78	79
Sadar Thana	*527·94*	*1*	*294*	*16,823*	*81,797*	*41,397*	*40,400*	*68,548*	+ 19·33	...	*155*
Nowgong town	2·03	1	...	1,223	5,433	3,145	2,288	4,430	+ 22·64	...	2,676
Nijsahar	15·87	...	18	1,533	7 300	3,631	3,669	6,011	+ 21·44	...	460
Pakhimoria (part)	24·61	...	24	1,904	9 729	4,785	4,944	8,269	+ 17·66	...	395
Singia Patoni	21·37	...	25	1,735	8,137	3,930	4,207	7,379	+ 10·29	...	381
Chalchali (part)	19·37	...	20	1,701	8 247	4,078	4,169	6,590	+ 25·14	...	426
Barkandali	24·43	...	27	1,561	7.185	3,573	3,612	7,216	- 0·43	...	294
Kachamari	28·04	...	31	1,680	7,189	3,557	3,632	6,116	+ 17·54	...	256
Hatichong (part)	17·96	...	16	1,957	10 281	5,156	5,125	8,963	+ 14·70	...	572
Juria	121·34	...	33	900	3 641	2,102	1,539	2,723	+ 33·71	...	29
Dhing	109·93	...	47	1,992	10 377	5,263	5,114	9,116	+ 13·83	...	94
Duar Bamuni	139·99	...	53	577	4,278	2,177	2,101	1,736	+146·43	...	31

PROVINCIAL TABLE I.—AREA AND POPULATION OF THANAS, MAUZAS, ETC.—*continued.*

THANA, MAUZA OR OTHER LOCAL UNIT.	Area in square miles.	NUMBER OF		Number of occupied houses.	POPULATION.				PERCENTAGE OF VARIATION.		Number of persons per square mile in 1911.
		Towns.	Villages.		1911.			1901 (Both sexes).	1901 to 1911.	1891 to 1901.	
					Persons.	Males.	Females.				
1	2	3	4	5	6	7	8	9	10	11	12
Samaguri Thana	*374·60*	...	*130*	*9,069*	*36,875*	*18,830*	*18,045*	*31,643*	+ *16·53*	...	*98*
Bhelauguri	55·36	...	45	3,542	13 981	7,129	6,852	12,172	+ 14·86	...	253
Chalchali (part)	11·60	...	16	1,891	5,325	2,735	2,590	4,647	+ 14·59	...	459
Khotwal ...	58·09	...	30	1,968	8 236	4,204	4,032	7,230	+ 13·91	...	142
Duar Salana	249·55	...	39	2,188	9,333	4,762	4,571	7,594	+ 22·90	...	37
Kaliabor Outpost	*300·39*	...	*85*	*5,936*	*23,836*	*12,569*	*11,267*	*22,190*	+ *7·42*	+ *3·49*	*79*
Duar Bagari	209 55	...	19	490	2.557	1,406	1,151	2,483	+ 2·98	...	12
Pubtheria	48·42	...	23	1,672	6.869	3,786	3,023	6,034	+ 12·84	...	141
Chatial	12·44	...	15	1,711	6,724	3,455	3,269	5,777	+ 16·39	...	541
Barbhagia	29·98	...	29	2,063	7,746	3,922	3,824	7,896	− 1·90	...	256
Baha Thana	*234·96*	...	*153*	*10,191*	*52,684*	*26,071*	*26,613*	*46,877*	+ *12·39*	...	*224*
Jagial	25·01	...	19	1,831	9,516	4,600	4,916	9,225	+ 3·15	...	380
Barapujia	34·99	...	25	2,397	12,545	6,042	6,503	11,708	+ 7·15	...	359
Mikir Bheta	63·22	...	44	2,499	12,775	6.488	6,287	11,394	+ 12·12	...	202
Charaibahi	19·91	...	14	1,282	7,147	3.504	3,643	5,359	+ 33·36	...	359
Sahari	84·40	...	44	1,684	8 064	4,191	3,873	6,733	+ 19·77	...	95
Pakhimoria (part)	3·60	...	4	101	597	287	310	424	+ 40·80	...	166
Hatichong (part)	3·74	...	3	397	2 040	959	1,081	2,034	+ 0·29	...	545
Jagi Road Outpost	*654·09*	...	*314*	*9,716*	*53,060*	*26,911*	*26,158*	*48,410*	+ *9·62*	...	*81*
Dandua	25·17	...	16	1,520	8 400	4.112	4.288	6.509	+ 29·05	...	334
Uttarkhola	53·16	...	45	2,173	10 289	5.209	5,080	8,858	+ 16·15	...	194
Nij Tetelia	43·33	...	85	1,310	6 922	3.415	3,507	5,831	+ 18·71	...	160
Mayang	118·64	...	50	987	5 319	2,764	2.555	4.706	+ 13·03	...	45
Ghugua	66·16	...	45	1,061	6 362	3.173	3,189	5,550	+ 14·63	...	96
Gerua Bokoni	219·45	...	93	1,363	7 742	4,086	3,656	9,901	− 21·81	...	35
Gobha ...	33·33	...	20	618	2 887	1,570	1,317	2,956	− 2·33	...	87
Duar Amla	94·05	...	10	744	5,148	2,582	2,566	4,099	+ 25·59	...	54
Jamunamukh Thana	*425·15*	...	*113*	*4,651*	*23,237*	*11,954*	*11,283*	*16,824*	+ *38·12*	− *35·93*	*55*
Kathiatoli	17·50	...	19	861	3.715	1,918	1,797	2,900	+ 28·10	...	219
Kampur ...	19·75	...	14	1,155	5 996	2,996	3,000	4,611	+ 30·04	...	304
Jamunamukh	40·28	...	32	1,266	5.552	2,967	2,585	3,993	+ 39·04	...	138
Garubat ...	85·90	...	37	1,006	5,082	2,574	2,508	3,727	+ 36·36	...	59
Duar Kathiatoli	68·02	...	12	122	951	499	452	844	+ 12·68	...	14
Duar Dikharu	193·70	...	4	221	1,941	1,000	941	740	+150·15	...	10
Lumding Outpost	*1,374·51*	...	*400*	*6,758*	*32,098*	*17,206*	*14,892*	*26,568*	+ *20·86*	− *14·98*	*93*
Namati ...	338·09	...	43	1,006	5.140	2,781	2,359	4,684	+ 9·74	...	15
Rangkhang	470·09	...	236	2,550	17,186	8,837	8,349	12,500	+ 37·49	...	37
Lumding Kachari	566·33 (for Lumding Kachari to Langpher)	...	11	132	502	252	250	424	+ 18·40	...	17 (for Lumding Kachari to Langpher)
" Kuki		...	3	80	230	135	95	278	− 17·27	...	
" Mikir		...	29	176	1 390	785	605	4,065	− 65·81	...	
" Town		...	1	897	2,318	1,570	748	1,414	+ 63·93	...	
Jamunapar		...	86	470	2,841	1,482	1,359	2,044	+ 38·99	...	
Langpher		...	11	512	2,491	1,364	1,127	1,259	+ 97·86	...	

PROVINCIAL TABLE I.—Area and Population of Thanas, Mauzas, etc.—*continued.*

Thana, Mauza or other local unit.	Area in square miles.	Number of Towns.	Number of Villages.	Number of occupied houses.	Population 1911 Persons.	Population 1911 Males.	Population 1911 Females.	Population 1901 (Both sexes).	Percentage of variation 1901 to 1911.	Percentage of variation 1891 to 1901.	Number of persons per square mile in 1911.
1	2	3	4	5	6	7	8	9	10	11	12
SIBSAGAR DISTRICT	4,996·00	4	2,139	150,803	690,299	364,810	325,489	597,969	+15·44	+24·41	138
Sibsagar Subdivision	*1,162·00*	*2*	*68*	*54,843*	*240,158*	*126,710*	*113,448*	*211,764*	*+13·41*	*+32·10*	*236*
Sibsagar Thana	*401·75*	*1*	*261*	*18,840*	*97,670*	*51,444*	*46,226*	...	...	...	*243*
Sibsagar town	3·04	1	...	1,166	5,764	3,228	2,536	5,712	+0·91	...	1,896
Sibsagar Nagarmahal (including Meteka Bongaon) ...	15·68	...	23	1,275	6 975	3,637	3,338	...	...	...	445
Jakaichuk	35·47	...	32	1,392	7,783	4,264	3,519	...	...	...	219
Kowarpur	59·21	...	37	2,093	12 205	6,583	5,622	...	...	...	206
Morabazar	24·83	...	24	1,930	10,711	5,435	5,276	...	...	...	432
Solaguri	32·92	...	20	1,690	8,924	4,559	4,365	...	...	...	271
Hahchara	13·77	...	15	1,004	5,318	2,760	2,558	...	...	...	386
Bakata	36·10	...	33	2,374	11 078	5,707	5,371	...	...	...	307
Thaura	} 153·59	...	28	2,543	9.401	5,002	4,399	...	...	...	} 127
Panidihing		...	48	1,694	10,170	5,481	4,689	...	...	...	
Betbari	27·15	...	23	1,679	9,341	4,788	4,553	...	...	...	344
Bortola Thana	*216·50*	*1*	*156*	*18,561*	*75,976*	*40,002*	*35,974*	...	...	...	*351*
Nazira	15·55	1	16	3,327	11 952	6,180	5,772	...	...	...	769
Joktali	18·98	...	20	2,282	9 711	5,132	4,579	...	...	...	512
Athkhel Golaki	74·92	...	32	4,539	17.257	9,029	8,228	...	...	...	230
Dhopabar	43·18	...	33	3,650	14,057	7,529	6,528	...	...	...	326
Silakuti	53·92	...	44	3,754	17.180	9.088	8,092	...	...	...	319
Dopdar (part)	9·95	...	11	1,009	5,819	3,044	2,775	...	...	...	585
Sonari Outpost	*334·11*	...	*186*	*12,568*	*47,419*	*25,289*	*22,130*	*36,267*	*+30·75*	*+37·91*	*142*
Abhaipur	219·95	...	107	7,947	29 845	16,113	13,732	21,632	+37·97	...	136
Khalaighogora	114·16	...	79	4,621	17,574	9,176	8,398	14,635	+20·08	...	154
Selleng Outpost (part)	*63·25*	...	*45*	*4,874*	*19,093*	*9,975*	*9,118*	...	...	...	*302*
Godhulibazar	24·93	...	26	2,450	10,535	5,532	5,003	...	...	...	423
Dopdar (part)	38·32	...	19	2,424	8·558	4,443	4,115	...	...	...	223
Jorhat Subdivision	*1,032·91*	*1*	*65*	*58,487*	*254,645*	*134,880*	*119,765*	*219,137*	*+16·20*	*+20·97*	*247*
Jorhat Thana	*583·85*	*1*	*494*	*48,447*	*203,559*	*107,561*	*95,998*	...	...	...	*349*
Jorhat town	1·81	1	...	1,200	5 231	3,225	2,006	2,899	+80·44	...	2,890
Garamur	11·92	...	9	1,157	4.104	2,299	1,805	...	...	...	344
Karangaon	10·70	...	37	3,5[illegible]7	12.237	6,513	5,724	...	...	...	621
Charaibahi	23·33	...	26	2,102	9 879	5,122	4,757	...	...	...	423
Khangia	28·79	...	37	4,917	19,691	9,919	9,772	...	...	...	684
Thengal	23·80	...	24	1,864	9 239	4,713	4,526	...	...	...	388
Titabar	35·56	...	37	3,398	14 203	7,491	6,712	...	...	...	399
Churamani or Simaluguri	26·10	...	26	1,823	9 538	4,968	4,570	...	...	...	365
Chowkat	37·03	...	39	2,063	9 527	4,959	4,568	...	...	...	257
Tiok	35 07	...	35	1,532	7 858	4,177	3,681	...	...	...	224
Holongapar	61·61	...	46	5,032	19,922	10,447	9,475	...	...	...	323
Kotohagar Charigaon	19·64	...	20	2,596	13.265	6,704	6,561	...	...	...	675
Hazari	37·17	...	22	2,063	8 704	4,913	3,791	...	...	...	234
Baligaon	30·58	...	24	1,882	9.038	4,938	4,100	...	...	...	296
Parbatia	24·50	...	22	1,724	7,058	3,645	3,413	...	...	...	288
Amguri Kharikatia	118·39	...	83	7,820	30.310	16,208	14,102	...	...	...	256
Nakachari (part)	38·50	...	21	2,764	9 720	5,211	4.509	...	...	...	252
Gakhirkhowa (part)	9·35	...	16	983	4,035	2,109	1,926	...	...	...	432

PROVINCIAL TABLE I.—AREA AND POPULATION OF THANAS, MAUZA, ETC.—*continued*.

Thana, Mauza or other local unit.	Area in square miles.	Number of: Towns.	Number of: Villages.	Number of occupied houses.	Population 1911: Persons.	Population 1911: Males.	Population 1911: Females.	Population 1901 (Both sexes).	Percentage of variation: 1901 to 1911.	Percentage of variation: 1891 to 1901.	Number of persons per square mile in 1911.
1	2	3	4	5	6	7	8	9	10	11	12
Selleng Outpost (part) ...	100·59	...	54	4,569	18,191	9,504	8,687	...	...	...	181
Nabachari (part) ...	37·08	...	12	613	2,607	1,384	1,223	...	...	...	70
Gakhirkhowa (part) ...	8·29	...	11	542	2,473	1,297	1,176	...	...	...	298
Lahing ...	55·32	...	81	3,404	13,111	6,833	6,278	...	...	...	237
Kamalabari (Majuli) Outpost (Salmora) ...	349·47	...	137	6,471	32,895	17,815	15,080	26,591	+23·71	...	94
Golaghat Subdivision ...	*3,014·83*	*1*	*776*	*49,341*	*195,496*	*103,220*	*92,276*	*167,068*	*+17·02*	*+20·01*	*65*
Dergaon Outpost ...	214·79	...	119	13,991	40,049	21,114	18,935	31,809	+25·90	+12·00	186
Ahatguri ...	135·60	...	58	1,709	11,274	5,988	5,286	8,594	+31·18	...	83
Michamara ...	} 68·56	...	36	3,065	13,133	7,039	6,094	} 19,040	} +29·33	...	} 370
Dergaon ...		...	13	7,596	11,491	5,965	5,524				
Naharani ...	12·63	...	5	831	4,151	2,122	2,029	4,175	−0·57	...	329
Golaghat Thana ...	*	1	239	46,859	121,893	64,002	57,891	113,544	+7·35	+18·75	...
Golaghat town ...	0·78	1	...	845	2,236	1,360	876	2,859	−5·21	...	2,867
Rangamati ...	100·90	...	48	3,789	15,684	8,265	7,419	13,016	+20·50	...	155
Gurjogania ...	27·62	...	17	3,240	10,430	5,396	5,034	} 45,887	} +11·17	...	386
Marangi ...	89·60	...	32	3,017	11,413	5,912	5,501				128
Dhekial ...	21·48	...	24	1,948	8,734	4,591	4,148				407
Mowkhowa ...	44·95	...	18	2,579	6,952	3,633	3,319				158
Khumtai ...	22·90	...	29	3,350	13,485	6,974	6,511				607
Dakhinhengra ...	28·70	...	24	3,660	11,004	5,672	5,332	} 33,488	} +10·94	...	388
Kacharihat ...	9·82	...	13	1,195	5,593	2,893	2,700				487
Ghiladhari ...	88·71	...	49	3,532	14,367	7,644	6,723				163
Athgaon ...	24·05	...	18	1,846	6,187	3,218	2,969				257
Barpathar ...	*	...	22	678	3,137	1,842	1,295	} 3,200	} +29·84	...	
Kardaiguri ...	*	...	8	234	1,018	714	804				
Rengma ...	*	...	37	1,746	11,653	5,888	5,765	15,594	−25·27	...	
Bokakhat Outpost ...	423·69	..	171	5,739	23,517	12,428	11,089	15,811	+47·74	+25·48	56
Namdayang ...	221·60	...	55	4,914	16,977	9,024	7,953	13,135	+29·25	...	77
Duar Bagari ...	208·09	...	116	525	6,549	3,404	3,136	2,676	+144·39	...	32
Dimapur Outpost ...	*	..	154	1,588	10,087	5,676	4,361	5,904	+70·00	...	
Dimapur ...	*	...	17	675	2,168	1,603	565	568	+283·00	...	
Duardisha ...	*	...	78	583	4,320	2,234	2,086	3,139	+37·62	...	
Barjan ...	*	...	59	424	3,549	1,839	1,710	2,199	+61·39	...	

* Area is not available

PROVINCIAL TABLE I.—AREA AND POPULATION OF THANAS, MAUZAS, ETC.—*continued.*

Thana, Mauza or other local unit.	Area in square mile.	Number of		Number of occupied houses.	Population.				Percentage of variation.		Number of persons per square mile in 1911.
		Towns.	Villages.		1911.			1901 (Both sexes).	1901 to 1911.	1891 to 1901.	
					Persons.	Males.	Females.				
1	2	3	4	5	6	7	8	9	10	11	12
LAKHIMPUR DISTRICT	4,529	1	1,701	114,498	468,989	249,021	219,968	371,396	+26·28	+46·19	104
Sadar Subdivision	3,033·00	*1*	*1,252*	*94,162*	*369,738*	*197,069*	*172,669*	*286,572*	+29·09	+50·34	*143*
Dibrugarh Thana	*	*1*	*348*	*31,198*	*197,460*	*68,306*	*59,154*	...	...	...	...
Dibrugarh town	2·59	1	...	3,390	14,563	8,896	5,667	11,297	+29·71	+19·68	+5,622
Dibrugarh	29·28	...	51	4,271	20,060	11,058	9,002	...	...	...	685
Jamira	21·30	...	56	2,948	12,241	6,539	5,702	...	...	...	575
Larua	97·86	...	34	2,071	10,130	5,286	4,844	...	...	...	104
Lahoal	54·68	...	54	6,262	22,232	11,466	10,766	...	...	...	407
Mankata Khonikar	51·25	...	35	2,431	10,528	5,510	5,018	...	...	...	205
Madarkhat	38·66	...	43	3,733	13,430	6,984	6,446	...	...	...	347
Rohmoria	47·81	...	37	3,445	13,126	6,832	6,294	...	...	...	275
Tengakhat (part)	*	...	22	944	4,669	2,435	2,234	...	...	...	...
Bogdung (part)	*	...	15	879	3,730	1,907	1,823	...	...	...	...
Chabua Polonga (part)	*	...	1	824	2,751	1,393	1,358	...	...	...	...
Tinsukia Thana	*	...	*210*	*17,590*	*68,430*	*36,135*	*32,295*	...	...	...	...
Chabua Polonga (part)	*	...	12	515	2,345	1,249	1,096	...	...	...	...
Bangagora	109·91	...	53	4,163	14,727	8,037	6,690	...	...	...	134
Gharbondi	57·60	...	64	3,304	12,962	6,755	6,207	...	...	...	225
Tipling (part)	*	...	22	1,932	6,540	3,536	3,004	...	...	...	...
Ujonnakhankhola (part)	*	...	18	2,193	7,582	4,040	3,542	...	...	...	...
Bogdung (part)	*	...	43	4,444	16,366	8,437	7,929	...	...	...	...
Tengakhat (part)	*	...	27	1,548	7,908	4,081	3,827	...	...	...	...
Dumduma Thana	*	...	*127*	*21,603*	*69,413*	*36,026*	*33,387*	...	...	...	...
Buridihing	*	...	25	287	1,436	751	685	...	...	...	...
Ujonnakhankhola (part)	*	...	79	18,215	57,603	30,024	27,579	...	...	...	...
Saikhoa (part)	*	...	23	3,101	10,374	5,251	5,123	...	...	...	...
Jaipur Outpost	*	...	*107*	*5,527*	*20,883*	*11,211*	*9,672*	...	...	...	...
Jaipur (part)	*	...	99	5,295	19,963	10,709	9,254	...	...	...	...
Jaipur Khiraj (Phakial)	320·70	...	3	85	374	207	167	...	...	...	1
Tipling (part) (Chapitola)	*	...		Jungle (no population)			Jungle (no population.)			...	
Tipling Khiraj (Phakial)	136·41	...	5	147	546	295	251	...	...	...	4
Makum (part)	...	...	...	Jungle (no population)							
Margherita Outpost	*	...	*74*	*6,097*	*22,937*	*12,687*	*16,250*	...	...	...	...
Phakial	29·76	...	9	239	1,137	619	518	...	...	...	38
Makum (part)	*	...	65	5,858	21,800	12,068	9,732	...	...	...	...
Moran Outpost	*	...	*109*	*5,053*	*23,953*	*12,620*	*11,333*	...	...	...	...
Khowang...	155·94	...	75	4,172	19,817	10,405	9,412	...	...	...	128
Jaipur (part)	*	...	34	881	4,136	2,215	1,921	...	...	...	...
Sadiya Outpost	*	...	*159*	*4,489*	*22,753*	*12,768*	*9,985*	...	...	...	...
Sadiya	75·08	...	101	2,405	13,561	7,821	5,740	...	...	...	174
Saikhoa (part)	*	...	58	1,987	9,192	4,947	4,245	...	...	...	...

* Area is not available.

PROVINCIAL TABLE I.—Area and Population of Thanas, Mauzas, etc.—*concluded.*

Thana, Mauza or other local unit.	Area in square miles.	Number of: Towns.	Number of: Villages.	Number of occupied houses.	Population 1911: Persons.	Population 1911: Males.	Population 1911: Females.	Population 1901 (Both sexes).	Percentage of variation: 1901 to 1911.	Percentage of variation: 1891 to 1901.	Number of persons per square mile in 1911.
1	2	3	4	5	6	7	8	9	10	11	12
Dhemaji Outpost	*401·45*	...	*88*	*2,603*	*13,909*	*7,316*	*6,593*	*10,836*	+ *28·36*	+ *·38*	*35*
Dhemaji	153·96	...	54	1,470	7,838	4,001	3,835	6,435	+ 21·77	...	51
Sissi	247·49	...	34	1,133	6,073	3,315	2,758	4,401	+ 37·90	...	25
North Lakhimpur Subdivision... ...	*1,174·00*	...	*449*	*230,336*	*99,251*	*51,952*	*47,299*	*84,824*	+ *17·01*	+ *33·72*	*85*
North Lakhimpur Thana	*732·22*	...	*328*	*15,428*	*69,866*	*36,666*	*33,200*	*59,293*	+ *17·83*	+ *34·07*	*95*
Narayanpur and Khirajkhat	133·54	...	60	1,741	10,126	5,205	4,921	...	...	...	76
Laluk	167·95	...	56	2,267	13,347	7,067	6,280	...	...	...	79
Naobaicha	68·17	...	36	2,020	4,967	2,661	2,306	...	...	...	73
Telahi (Beteri)	93·52	...	37	1,437	7,671	4,056	3,615	...	...	...	82
Lakhimpur and Khirajkhat	66·19	...	33	1,589	7,467	4,032	3,435	...	...	...	113
Kamalbari	11·09	...	19	813	4,163	2,157	2,006	...	...	...	375
Noakari	37·25	...	37	2,798	10,045	5,310	4,735	...	...	...	270
Kadam	154·51	...	50	2,754	12,080	6,178	5,902	...	...	...	78
Dhakuakhana Outpost...	*434·39*	...	*121*	*4,908*	*29,385*	*15,286*	*14,099*	*25,531*	+ *15·10*	+ *32·92*	*68*
Bardalani	115·97	...	27	1,145	6,104	3,070	3,034	...	...	...	53
Gohaingaon	133·55	...	51	1,930	11,431	6,017	5,414	...	...	...	86
Dhakuakhana	184·87	...	43	1,833	11,850	6,199	5,651	...	...	...	64
GARO HILLS DISTRICT	3,140	...	1,937	32,773	158,936	81,264	77,672	138,274	+ 14·94	+ 13·74	51
Mauza No. I	Separate area is not available.	...	450	4,647	23,222	11,744	11,478	21,249	+ 9·29	+ 7·90	
" II		...	410	5,746	27,633	13,906	13,727	21,097	+ 30·98	+ 21·42	
" III		...	406	7,109	33,191	16,872	16,319	30,366	+ 9·30	+ 1·25	
" IV		...	346	6,332	30,089	14,997	15,092	26,946	+ 11·66	+ 8·43	
" V		...	90	13,191	15,723	8,023	7,700	10,916	+ 41·04	...	
" VI		...	59	1,931	9,951	5,356	4,595	11,763	— 15·40	...	
" VII		...	40	1,078	5,338	2,776	2,562	4,286	+ 24·55	...	
" VIII		...	126	2,441	12,203	6,398	5,805	10,276	+ 18·75	...	
" IX (Tura town)		...	1	298	1,586	1,192	394	1,375	+ 15·35	— 36·05	
(2) Manipur State	*8,456*	*1*	*1,477*	*69,491*	*346,222*	*170,666*	*175,556*	*284,465*	+ *21·71*	†	*41*
Valley Section	Separate area is not available.	1	418	42,962	222,917	110,223	112,694	191,065	+ 16·67		
Imphal Panah		1	...	15,322	74,650	36,393	38,257	72,234	+ 3·34		
Naharup "		...	104	6,261	28,809	14,924	13,885	18,241	+ 57·94		
Ahalup "		...	92	7,620	43,186	21,339	21,847	37,651	+ 14·70		
Laifam "		...	91	7,933	46,775	22,952	23,823 }	62,153	+ 20·82		
Khabum "		...	115	5,473	28,318	13,860	14,458 }				
Taluk Cachar Road...		...	1	...	148	124	24	786	— 81·17		
Thana Jhirighat Panah		...	15	353	1,031	631	400		Newly formed in 1911.		
Hill Section		...	1,059	26,529	123,305	60,443	62,862	93,400	+ 31·68		
Awang Lam		...	153	5,512	23,254	11,651	11,603	15,148	+ 53·51		
Sekta "		...	140	5,577	22,888	10,924	11,964	19,576	+ 16·92		
Nangpak "		...	261	4,252	20,464	10,163	10,301	14,408	+ 41·20		
Mairang "		...	208	5,618	28,534	14,080	14,454	16,823	+ 69·61		
Nongchup "		...	220	3,908	18,340	8,996	9,344	19,724	— 7·02		
Cachar Road		...	68	1,662	9,825	4,629	5,196	7,636	+ 28·67		

†The Census papers of 1891 were destroyed in the rising.

PROVINCIAL TABLE II.

POPULATION OF THANAS, ETC., BY RELIGION AND EDUCATION.

In this Table thanas and outposts have been shown except in the hill districts and Manipur : in the latter subdivisions have been shown except in Garo Hills, where mauzas have been given, and Manipur, where figures for panahs and lams have been exhibited.

It should be noted that totals of the figures for those literate and literate in English in minor divisions do not equal the totals of the districts, because only the latter include Christians, Buddhists and "other" religions, while the former include Hindus, Muhammadans and Animists only.

Village population by religion has been given in the Village Census Tables supplied in manuscript to each district and the State of Manipur.

PROVINCIAL TABLE II.—POPULATION OF THANAS, ETC. BY RELIGION AND EDUCATION.

THANA.	DISTRIBUTION BY RELIGION.										NUMBER OF PERSONS.			
	HINDUS.		MUSALMANS.		CHRISTIANS.		ANIMISTS.		OTHERS.		LITERATE.		LITERATE IN ENGLISH.	
	Males.	Females.	Males.	Females.	Males.	Females.	Males.	Females.	Males.	Females.	Males.	Females.	Males.	Females.
1	2	3	4	5	6	7	8	9	10	11	12	13	14	15
ASSAM	***1,997,724***	***1,841,045***	***984,968***	***916,064***	***33,632***	***32,930***	***619,899***	***626,381***	***9,064***	***5,150***	***312,910***	***20,753***	***34,333***	***1,529***
(1) British Territory	***1,808,460***	***1,738,940***	***977,463***	***909,065***	***33,548***	***32,882***	***549,200***	***559,987***	***8,950***	***5,140***	***306,030***	***20,536***	***33,799***	***1,504***
SURMA VALLEY AND HILL DISTRICTS ...	*743,597*	*692,637*	*783,772*	*739,216*	*19,184*	*20,535*	*213,843*	*232,206*	*738*	*309*	*166,496*	*13,350*	*16,035*	*889*
CACHAR DISTRICT ...	67,424	152,680	82,560	73,536	649	532	9,743	10,253	68	18	27,738	1,751	2,726	118
Sadar Subdivision	*122,258*	*111,245*	*51,224*	*45,464*	*556*	*486*	*3,833*	*4,002*	*30*	*9*	*20,243*	*1,206*	*1,947*	*29*
Silchar	78,806	70,776	34,809	30,628	402	347	2,593	2,693	23	8	14,089	1,022	1,615	29
Lakhipur	26,760	24,004	6,467	6,879	60	44	850	936	6	1	3,586	120	204	...
Katigora	16,692	15,865	9,858	8,957	94	95	390	373	1	...	2,568	64	128	...
Hailakandi Subdivision ...	*36,992*	*34,540*	*31,015*	*27,950*	*53*	*22*	*230*	*240*	*14*	*4*	*6,550*	*362*	*432*	*3*
Hailakandi	36,992	34,540	31,015	27,950	53	22	230	240	14	4	6,550	362	432	3
North Cachar Subdivision ...	*8,174*	*6,895*	*321*	*122*	*40*	*24*	*5,680*	*6,011*	*24*	*5*	*648*	*51*	*136*	*3*
North Cachar	8,174	6,895	321	122	40	24	5,680	6,011	24	5	648	51	136	3
SYLHET DISTRICT ...	564,266	534,684	699,470	665,269	863	649	3,701	3,574	169	26	124,785	7,710	10,789	241
North Sylhet Subdivision ...	*81,025*	*75,627*	*183,233*	*180,283*	*184*	*174*	*1,696*	*1,665*	*32*	*12*	*26,275*	*1,926*	*2,795*	*56*
Sylhet (Sadar)	41,768	38,331	99,050	97,083	150	151	1,209	1,093	30	12	14,254	1,164	2,104	46
Kanairghat	10,986	10,160	31,003	28,975	33	23	487	572	1	...	2,544	128	94	1
Balaganj	28,271	27,136	53,180	54,225	1	...	...	...	1	...	9,477	634	597	9
Sunamganj Subdivision ...	*109,149*	*93,015*	*145,049*	*131,863*	*52*	*47*	*171*	*171*	*6*	*...*	*17,954*	*834*	*1,118*	*3*
Sunamganj	25,921	20,970	40,799	36,349	7	...	155	158	5	...	4,337	366	516	3
Chhatak	11,267	11,504	30,725	36,768	1	1	16	13	...	...	3,459	157	211	...
Dirai	45,856	41,166	40,728	37,816	...	...	...	...	...	...	6,905	185	271	...
Dharmapasa	23,105	19,375	23,797	20,930	44	46	...	...	1	...	2,653	126	120	...
Habiganj Subdivision ...	*134,474*	*131,693*	*168,750*	*160,181*	*70*	*30*	*951*	*900*	*7*	*...*	*34,098*	*2,109*	*2,755*	*20*
Habiganj	48,442	47,295	67,516	64,356	51	24	741	692	6	...	13,154	897	1,405	6
Baniachung	34,572	32,912	37,990	35,267	...	...	...	...	...	...	8,534	370	646	7
Madhabpur	29,491	30,214	35,192	33,676	19	6	210	208	1	...	6,267	561	422	5
Nabiganj	21,969	21,272	28,052	26,882	...	...	...	...	...	...	6,143	281	282	2

N. B.—The figures in columns 12 to 15 against thanas and subdivisions include Hindus, Muhammadans and Animists only. The totals in the same columns for the province, divisions and districts include other religions as well.

PROVINCIAL TABLE II.—Population of Thanas, etc., by Religion and Education—*continued.*

Thana.	Distribution by Religion.										Number of Persons			
	Hindus.		Musalmans.		Christians.		Animists.		Others.		Literate.		Literate in English.	
	Males.	Females.	Males.	Females.	Males.	Females.	Males.	Females.	Males.	Females.	Males.	Females.	Males.	Females.
1	2	3	4	5	6	7	8	9	10	11	12	13	14	15
South Sylhet Subdivision ...	*119,535*	*118,594*	*86,342*	*81,690*	*275*	*187*	*662*	*635*	*70*	*12*	*24,054*	*1,582*	*1,921*	*14*
Maulvi Bazar	85,300	86,198	62,329	59,054	240	174	411	372	60	8	17,660	1,177	1,384	9
Kulaura	34,235	32,308	24,018	22,636	35	13	251	263	10	4	6,394	405	537	5
Karimganj Subdivision ...	*120,083*	*115,755*	*116,096*	*111,252*	*282*	*211*	*221*	*203*	*54*	*2*	*21,846*	*1,083*	*1,776*	*15*
Karimganj	86,790	82,834	76,609	71,122	271	210	81	82	54	2	14,036	712	1,276	10
Jaldhup	33,293	32,921	39,487	40,130	11	1	140	121	...	...	7,810	371	500	5
KHASI AND JAINTIA HILLS DISTRICT.	6,738	2,716	1,172	356	14,855	16,402	91,447	101,006	230	147	9,242	3,698	2,216	501
Shillong Subdivision ...	*6,621*	*2,673*	*1,120*	*355*	*8,826*	*9,842*	*60,534*	*66,854*	*230*	*147*	*4,889*	*931*	*1,217*	*60*
Jowai Subdivision ...	*117*	*43*	*52*	*1*	*6,039*	*6,560*	*30,913*	*34,152*	...	...	*222*	*19*	*9*	*2*
NAGA HILLS DISTRICT ...	2,737	1,476	281	37	1,554	1,754	70,136	71,604	43	1	1,233	54	169	15
Kohima Subdivision ...	*2,320*	*1,257*	*270*	*36*	*112*	*82*	*41,875*	*40,605*	*40*	...	*897*	*18*	*105*	*1*
Mokokchang Subdivision ...	*417*	*219*	*11*	*1*	*1,442*	*1,672*	*28,261*	*30,999*	*3*	*1*	*201*	...	*19*	...
LUSHAI HILLS DISTRICT	2,432	1,081	289	18	1,263	1,198	38,816	45,769	228	110	3,498	137	186	14
Aijal Subdivision ...	*1,875*	*730*	*220*	*15*	*903*	*826*	*27,760*	*32,865*	*20*	*1*	*2,483*	*39*	*80*	...
Lungleh Subdivision ...	*557*	*351*	*69*	*3*	*360*	*372*	*11,056*	*12,904*	*208*	*109*	*385*	*12*	*25*	...
ASSAM VALLEY DISTRICTS...	***1,154,863***	***1,046,303***	***193,691***	***169,849***	***14,364***	***12,347***	***335,357***	***327,781***	***8,212***	***4,838***	***139,534***	***7,186***	***17,757***	***615***
GOALPARA DISTRICT ...	178,673	156,047	111,917	99,645	2,731	2,521	23,870	23,469	1,284	486	23,523	1,130	2,097	54
Dhubri Subdivision ...	*118,683*	*100,206*	*96,644*	*86,894*	*1,337*	*1,225*	*18,411*	*18,216*	*1,160*	*462*	*13,633*	*558*	*1,179*	*4*
Dhubri	13,977	10,762	18,498	16,873	16	17	941	830	142	44	3,358	331	583	4
Bilasipara	33,145	27,784	15,065	12,970	34	34	3,383	3,277	168	67	3,109	129	276	...
South Salmara	9,299	6,333	47,441	43,226	5	1	257	259	177	65	2,669	39	150	...
Golakganj	29,501	26,963	13,704	12,276	1,122	1,033	1,043	946	142	23	3,614	55	130	...
Eastern Duars	32,761	28,364	2,061	1,549	160	140	12,838	12,904	531	284	883	4	40	...
Goalpara Subdivision ...	*59,990*	*55,841*	*15,273*	*12,751*	*1,394*	*1,296*	*5,459*	*5,253*	*124*	*24*	*8,873*	*420*	*765*	*7*
Goalpara	13,270	11,349	3,117	2,455	632	558	2,027	2,025	85	5	2,505	170	340	1
Lakhipur	14,590	14,576	603	495	748	733	2,548	2,361	17	5	1,146	31	57	...
Lakhipur	9,736	8,563	8,892	7,464	5	4	780	765	10	3	756	30	38	...
North Salmara	22,454	21,653	2,661	2,337	6	1	104	102	12	13	4,466	189	330	6

N.B.—The figures in columns 12 to 15 against thanas and subdivisions include Hindus, Muhammadans and Animists only. The totals in the same columns for the province, divisions and districts include other religions as well.

PROVINCIAL TABLE II.—Population of Thanas, etc., by Religion and Education—*continued.*

Thana.	Distribution by Religion.										Number of Persons.			
	Hindus.		Musalmans.		Christians.		Animists.		Others.		Literate.		Literate in English.	
	Males.	Females.	Males.	Females.	Males.	Females.	Males.	Females.	Males.	Females.	Males.	Females.	Males.	Females.
1	2	3	4	5	6	7	8	9	10	11	12	13	14	15
KAMRUP DISTRICT ...	235,014	224,213	33,723	30,904	1,373	1,162	68,649	7,927	639	224	34,580	1,614	2,993	101
Gauhati Subdivision ...	*179,956*	*174,570*	*30,042*	*27,976*	*1,371*	*1,162*	*55,179*	*57,668*	*547*	*208*	*26,108*	*1,199*	*2,316*	*39*
Gauhati	15,641	11,715	3,178	2,319	201	142	9,512	9,324	49	14	4,984	659	1,431	37
Palasbari	20,778	22,124	1,676	1,620	84	80	1,854	1,859	116	65	2,752	93	168	...
Chhaygaon	6,259	4,6 2	209	132	181	162	3,837	3,716	1	...	782	21	39	...
Boko	6,476	5,900	1,087	951	885	768	9,143	9,075	5	1	1,171	25	32	...
Nalbari	46,604	48,538	6,143	6,126	1	...	9,289	11,123	56	23	5,953	104	217	2
Rangia	26,321	23,843	5,673	5,537	8	6	18,301	19 3ı1	300	94	3,300	71	119	...
Kamalpur	24,626	23,316	5,604	5,354	11	4	2,147	2,129	9	2	3,412	88	171	...
Hajo	33,251	34,302	6,472	5,936	...	...	1,096	1,131	11	9	3,754	108	139	...
Barpeta Subdivision ...	*55,058*	*49,643*	*3,681*	*2,928*	*2*	...	*13,470*	*14,259*	*92*	*16*	*7,911*	*245*	*546*	*3*
Barpeta	21,481	19,101	1,653	1,140	...	...	1,473	1,330	9	1	3,663	113	357	...
Sarbhog	11,403	9,671	871	728	2	...	6,549	6,982	31	5	1,325	41	72	2
Bajali	22,174	20,871	1,157	1,060	...	...	5,448	5,947	52	10	2,923	91	117	1
DARRANG DISTRICT ...	120,631	115,710	11,073	9,232	1,028	885	56,043	52,688	806	218	12,210	515	1,569	62
Tezpur Subdivision ...	*81,135*	*70,194*	*3,107*	*1,864*	*715*	*571*	*25,727*	*23,177*	*505*	*160*	*7,860*	*389*	*1,054*	*9*
Tezpur	41,277	35,727	1,941	1,094	562	470	14,910	13,259	241	49	4,416	265	704	7
Sootea	21,685	19,252	814	635	67	36	4,826	4,354	91	26	1,767	79	130	1
Behali	11,440	9,713	258	89	47	23	4,752	4,377	143	65	800	16	98	...
Gohpur	6,733	5,502	94	46	59	42	1,239	1,187	30	...	877	29	32	1
Mangaldai Subdivision ...	*48,496*	*45,516*	*7,966*	*7,368*	*313*	*314*	*30,316*	*29,511*	*301*	*58*	*3,851*	*49*	*325*	*2*
Mangaldai	28,166	27,611	7, 020	6,669	11	6	2,594	2,293	74	11	2,352		179	3
Kalaigaon	7,151	6,507	708	613	27	31	7,166	7,280	27	3	659	...	41	...
Panery	8,997	7,981	172	71	249	257	13,784	12,729	116	23	549	10	90	...
Kariapara	4,182	3,417	66	15	26	20	6,772	7,259	84	23	291	...	15	...
NOWGONG DISTRICT ...	91,313	86,582	8,163	7,526	707	666	54,403	53,664	452	220	14,654	747	1,427	48
Sadr Thana	30,653	29,654	3,192	3,137	115	148	7,324	7,240	113	31	5,690	351	536	9
Samaguri	11,177	10,734	532	417	417	387	6,693	6,507	11	...	1,254	81	136	...
Kaliabor	9,334	8,358	528	499	27	13	2,655	2,400	25	2	1,605	47	160	...
Raha	17,607	17,816	1,793	1,739	7	6	6,494	6,910	180	152	2,051	75	97	...
Jagi Road	13,900	13,104	1,475	1,408	6	2	11,512	11,644	18	5	1,419	32	60	1
Jamunamukh	5,768	6,297	2.3	111	52	49	5,920	5,836	8	...	1,262	31	61	...
Lumding	2,790	1,434	481	240	33	61	13,805	13,127	97	30	945	56	249	3

N.B.—The figures in columns 12 to 15 against thanas and subdivisions include Hindus, Mahammadans and Animists only. The totals in the same columns for the province, divisions and districts include other religions as well.

PROVINCIAL TABLE II.—POPULATION OF THANAS, ETC., BY RELIGION AND EDUCATION—*continued.*

THANA.	DISTRIBUTION BY RELIGION.										NUMBER OF PERSONS.			
	HINDUS.		MUSALMANS.		CHRISTIANS.		ANIMISTS.		OTHERS.		LITERATE.		LITERATE IN ENGLISH.	
	Males.	Females.	Males.	Females.	Males.	Females.	Males.	Females.	Males.	Females.	Males.	Females.	Males.	Females.
1	2	3	4	5	6	7	8	9	10	11	12	13	14	15
SIBSAGAR DISTRICT ...	313,748	281,518	16,373	13,345	2,933	2,477	30,362	27,218	1,394	931	32,978	1,821	5,529	162
Sibsagar Subdivision	*116,643*	*105,41 8*	*7,079*	*5,941*	*1,148*	*974*	*1,481*	*851*	*359*	*264*	*11,298*	*543*	*1,887*	*20*
Sibsagar	47,303	42,801	3,516	2,935	368	230	304	234	63	26	5,918	353	904	1
Barhola	35,794	32,554	3,751	1,388	598	521	629	325	230	186	2,651	96	520	11
Sonari	24,007	21,334	538	381	368	215	400	148	75	52	1,719	66	270	6
Selleng part	9,530	8,729	274	237	14	8	148	144	...	...	1,010	28	193	2
Jorhat Subdivision	*119,518*	*106,847*	*4,626*	*3,665*	*1,339*	*1,130*	*8,894*	*7,755*	*503*	*368*	*13,417*	*708*	*2,117*	*27*
Jorhat	94,551	85,158	4,279	3,464	1,230	1,039	7,007	5,973	494	365	12,036	688	2,083	27
Selleng part	7,345	6,701	199	138	109	91	1,851	1,757	...	...	...	...	...	...
Kamalbari (Majuli)	17,622	14,988	148	63	...	...	36	26	9	3	1,381	20	34	...
Golaghat Subdivision ...	*77,587*	*69,253*	*4,668*	*3,739*	*446*	*373*	*19,987*	*18,612*	*532*	*299*	*7,432*	*411*	*1,151*	*13*
Dergaon	17,381	15,656	1,411	1,123	46	31	2,276	2,125	...	...	1,555	55	148	2
Golaghat	50,795	45,831	2,895	2,424	298	257	9,577	9,086	437	293	5,145	319	873	10
Bokakhat	8,390	7,478	200	107	95	84	3,738	3,417	5	3	499	27	88	...
Dimapur	1,021	288	162	85	7	1	4,396	3,984	90	3	233	10	43	1
LAKHIMPUR DISTRICT ...	195,291	172,699	7,986	5,433	2,647	2,142	39,622	37,079	3,475	2,615	19,892	1,190	3,995	177
Sadr Subdivision	*164,894*	*145,553*	*6,548*	*4,378*	*2,117*	*1,691*	*20,400*	*18,861*	*3,110*	*2,186*	*15,451*	*924*	*3,287*	*55*
Dibrugarh	58,541	49,215	3,911	2,853	1,050	899	6,265	5,861	539	326	7,546	479	1,845	46
Tinsukia	32,737	29,512	617	384	377	271	2,323	2,091	81	37	2,439	56	465	1
Dumduma...	31,276	29,206	508	275	296	235	3,260	3,090	686	581	1,106	57	360	7
Jaipur	9,928	8,775	205	152	41	20	750	553	227	173	738	25	122	1
Margherita...	8,871	7,120	703	406	112	63	3,176	3,152	826	509	612	46	234	...
Moran	11,824	10,677	200	151	131	113	458	387	7	5	993	20	133	...
Sadiya	8,270	6,169	272	116	107	89	3,434	3,118	685	493	1,120	28	93	...
Dhemaji	5,447	4,879	73	41	3	1	1,734	1,609	59	63	697	13	35	...
North Lakhimpur Subdivision ...	*30,397*	*27,146*	*1,438*	*1,055*	*530*	*451*	*19,222*	*18,218*	*365*	*429*	*3,257*	*79*	*266*	...
North Lakhimpur	19,253	16,984	1,345	1,025	528	450	15,243	14,343	297	398	2,169	64	200	...
Dhakuakhana	11,144	10,162	93	30	2	1	3,979	3,875	68	31	1,088	15	66	...

N.B.—The figures in columns 1 to 15 against thanas and subdivisions include Hindus, Muhammadans and Animists only. The totals in the same columns for the province, divisions and districts include other religions as well.

PROVINCIAL TABLE II.—POPULATION OF THANAS, ETC., BY RELIGION AND EDUCATION—*concluded.*

THANA.	DISTRIBUTION BY RELIGION.										NUMBER OF PERSONS.			
	HINDUS.		MUSALMANS.		CHRISTIANS.		ANIMISTS.		OTHERS.		LITERATE.		LITERATE IN ENGLISH.	
	Males.	Females.	Males.	Females.	Males.	Females.	Males.	Females.	Males.	Females.	Males.	Females.	Males.	Females.
1	2	3	4	5	6	7	8	9	10	11	12	13	14	15
GARO HILLS DISTRICT ...	11,293	9,534	4,436	3,764	2,945	2,494	62,408	61,736	162	144	1,667	169	147	11
Mauza No. I	84	40	1	1	571	510	11,088	10,927	...	...	...	...	...	...
Ditto No. II	332	179	2	...	366	299	13,192	13,239	15	10	...	...	...	...
Ditto No. III	411	197	...	...	42	25	16,419	16,097	...	...	...	...	...	...
Ditto No. IV	59	11	1	...	418	396	14,519	14,665	...	...	...	...	...	...
Ditto No. V	2,557	2,458	53	10	931	900	4,493	4,323	...	...	...	...	...	...
Ditto No. VI	1,454	1,141	2,766	2,401	62	52	944	873	130	128	...	...	...	...
Ditto No. VII	2,416	2,245	102	78	31	34	227	205	...	...	...	...	...	...
Ditto No. VIII	3,350	3,034	1,398	1,254	248	209	1,396	1,302	11	6	...	...	...	...
Ditto No. IX (Tura)	630	229	140	11	236	69	130	85	6	...	...	...	...	...
(9) *Manipur State*	*99,264*	*102,105*	*7,505*	*6,999*	*84*	*48*	*63,699*	*66,394*	*114*	*10*	*6,389*	*217*	*541*	*18*
Valley Section	99,168	102,075	7,503	6,996	40	25	3,390	3,590	113	8	...	...	...	...
Imphal Panah	34,262	31,806	1,377	685	39	25	708	733	107	8	4,244	125	333	...
Nalarup „	13,889	18,023	878	839	1	...	656	623	...	...	...	...	...	...
Abalup „	19,037	19,957	736	729	...	...	963	1,161	...	...	...	...	...	...
Laifam „	19,309	20,051	3,108	3,394	...	...	447	488	3	...	...	...	...	...
Khabum „	11,457	11,919	1,898	1,955	...	...	507	584	3	...	...	...	...	...
Taluk Cachar Road	77	2	3	4	...	...	42	18	...	...	...	...	...	...
Thana Jhirighat Panah	537	317	21	...	...	...	73	88	...	...	...	...	...	...
Hill Section	96	30	2	3	44	23	60,300	62,804	1	2	...	...	...	...
Awang Lam	...	...	...	...	...	...	11,651	11,603	...	...	...	...	...	...
Sekta „	14	...	...	...	44	23	10,866	11,941	...	...	...	...	...	...
Nangpak „	65	26	...	...	...	...	10,097	10,273	1	2	...	...	...	...
Mairang „	11	...	...	...	...	...	14,069	14,454	...	...	...	...	...	...
Nongchup „	...	...	...	...	...	...	8,996	9,344	...	...	...	...	...	...
Cachar Road	6	4	2	3	...	...	4,621	5,189	...	...	...	...	...	...

N. B.—The figures in columns 12 to 15 against thanas and subdivisions include Hindus, Muhammadans and Animists only. The totals in the same columns for the province, divisions and districts include other religions as well.

PROVINCIAL TABLE III.

TEA-GARDEN POPULATION BY LANGUAGE.

THIS and the two following Tables deal with the tea-garden population of each district.

This Table has been arranged on the same principles as Imperial Table X and has a similar appendix showing the details included under the head of 'other' languages.

PROVINCIAL TABLE III.—TEA-GARDEN POPULATION BY LANGUAGE.

District or State.	Population.			A.—Vernaculars of India. 1.—Aryan. Assamese.			Bengali.			Hindi.			Marathi.		
	Persons.	Males.	Females.	Persons.	Males.	Females.	Persons.	Males.	Females.	Persons.	Males.	Females.	Persons.	Males.	Females.
1	2	3	4	5	6	7	8	9	10	11	12	13	14	15	16
ASSAM	*702,034*	*361,916*	*340,118*	*16,061*	*10,645*	*5,416*	*258,909*	*130,870*	*128,039*	*239,906*	*122,774*	*117,132*	*112*	*69*	*3*
SURMA VALLEY AND HILL DISTRICTS	*273,582*	*139,786*	*133,796*	*315*	*129*	*186*	*89,834*	*47,436*	*42,398*	*147,865*	*74,408*	*73,457*	*11*	*8*	*3*
Cachar	**130 832**	67,572	63,260	**226**	108	118	**54.618**	28,308	26,310	**62.68**	32,307	30,361	**8**	5	3
Sylhet	**142,750**	72,214	70,536	**89**	21	68	**35,216**	19,128	16,088	**85,97**	42,101	43,096	**3**	3	...
ASSAM VALLEY DISTRICTS	*428,452*	*222,130*	*206,322*	*15,746*	*10,516*	*5,230*	*169,075*	*83,434*	*85,641*	*92,041*	*48,366*	*43,675*	*101*	*61*	*40*
Goalpara	**565**	307	258	...	...	...	**134**	77	57	**153**	87	66	...	...	...
Kamrup	**4,459**	2,400	2,059	**1,022**	573	449	**1,751**	875	876	**367**	192	175	...	...	...
Darrang	**79,665**	41,660	37,405	**1,658**	1,241	417	**36,781**	18,152	18,629	**8 785**	4,809	3,976	...	...	...
Nowgong	**18,169**	9,134	9,035	**624**	338	286	**4 811**	2,387	2,424	**6 108**	3,010	3,098	...	...	...
Sibsagar	**163,623**	84,993	78,630	**8,407**	5,565	2,842	**79.319**	39,780	39 539	**29.118**	15,209	13,909	**73**	35	38
Lakhimpur	**162,571**	83,636	78,935	**4,035**	2,799	1,236	**46,279**	22,163	24,116	**47,510**	25,059	22,451	**28**	26	2

District or State.	A.—Vernaculars of India—contd. 1.—Aryan—concld. Naipali.			Oriya.			Panjabi.			Pashto.			Rajasthani.		
	Persons.	Males.	Females.	Persons.	Males.	Females.	Persons.	Males.	Females.	Person.	Males.	Females.	Persons.	Males.	Females.
1	17	18	19	20	21	22	23	24	25	26	27	28	29	30	31
ASSAM	*1,037*	*745*	*292*	*51,759*	*25,307*	*26,452*	*156*	*145*	*11*	*37*	*37*	...	*1,938*	*1,475*	*463*
SURMA VALLEY AND HILL DISTRICTS	*322*	*245*	*77*	*12,827*	*5,992*	*6,835*	...	...	...	*29*	*29*	...	*436*	*239*	*197*
Cachar	**166**	102	64	**2.601**	1,223	1,378	...	...	...	**10**	10	...	**10**	5	5
Sylhet	**156**	143	13	**10,226**	4,769	5,457	...	...	...	**19**	19	...	**426**	234	192
ASSAM VALLEY DISTRICTS	*715*	*500*	*215*	*38,939*	*19,315*	*19,617*	*156*	*145*	*11*	*8*	*8*	...	*1,502*	*1,236*	*266*
Goalpara	...	...	...	**1**	1	...	...	...	...	...	...	...	...	...	...
Kamrup	**152**	85	67	**106**	63	43	...	...	...	...	...	...	**6**	4	2
Darrang	**234**	168	66	**7.764**	3,820	3,944	**10**	7	3	**7**	7	...	**160**	154	6
Nowgong	**28**	20	8	**1 965**	976	905	...	...	...	**1**	1	...	**22**	22	...
Sibsagar	**115**	94	21	**12,783**	6,284	6,499	**26**	22	4	...	...	...	**785**	625	160
Lakhimpur	**186**	133	53	**16,313**	8,177	8,136	**120**	116	4	...	...	...	**529**	431	98

PROVINCIAL TABLE III.—TEA-GARDEN POPULATION BY LANGUAGE—*continued.*

District or State.	A.—VERNACULARS OF INDIA—contd. 2.—TIBETO-BURMAN. Angami. Persons.	Angami. Males.	Angami. Females.	Ao. Persons.	Ao. Males.	Ao. Females.	Bhotia of Bhutan. Persons.	Bhotia of Bhutan. Males.	Bhotia of Bhutan. Females.	Bhotia of Tibet. Persons.	Bhotia of Tibet. Males.	Bhotia of Tibet. Females.	Bodo, Mech or Plains Kachari. Persons.	Bodo, Mech or Plains Kachari. Males.	Bodo, Mech or Plains Kachari. Females.
1	32	33	34	35	36	37	38	39	40	41	42	43	44	45	46
ASSAM	*99*	*88*	*11*	*39*	*35*	*4*	*1*	...	*1*	*18*	*9*	*9*	*7,115*	*5,789*	*1,326*
SURMA VALLEY AND HILL DISTRICTS	...	...	...	...	...	...	*1*	...	*1*	...	...	...	*148*	*119*	*29*
Cachar	...	...	...	...	...	...	1	...	1	...	...	...	61	32	29
Sylhet	...	...	...	...	...	...	...	...	...	...	...	...	87	87	...
ASSAM VALLEY DISTRICTS	*99*	*88*	*11*	*39*	*35*	*4*	...	...	...	*18*	*9*	*9*	*6,967*	*5,670*	*1,297*
Goalpara	...	...	...	...	...	...	...	...	...	...	...	...	1	1	...
Kamrup	...	...	...	...	...	...	...	...	...	...	...	...	391	230	161
Darrang	...	...	...	...	...	...	...	...	...	7	5	2	4,108	3,195	913
Nowgong	...	...	...	...	...	...	...	...	...	...	...	...	382	265	117
Sibsagar	99	88	11	10	6	4	...	...	...	...	...	...	1,532	1,432	100
Lakhimpur	...	...	...	29	29	...	...	...	...	11	4	7	553	547	6

District or State.	A.—VERNACULARS OF INDIA—contd. 2.—TIBETO-BURMAN—contd. Dapla. Persons.	Dapla. Males.	Dapla. Females.	Dimasa. Persons.	Dimasa. Males.	Dimasa. Females.	Garo. Persons.	Garo. Males.	Garo. Females.	Gurung. Persons.	Gurung. Males.	Gurung. Females.	Khambu. Persons.	Khambu. Males.	Khambu. Females.
1	47	48	49	50	51	52	53	54	55	56	57	58	59	60	61
ASSAM	*21*	*19*	*2*	*383*	*202*	*181*	*1,172*	*525*	*647*	*12*	*10*	*2*	*22*	*22*	...
SURMA VALLEY AND HILL DISTRICTS	...	...	...	*383*	*202*	*181*	...	...	...	...	...	...	...	...	...
Cachar	...	...	...	383	202	181	...	...	...	...	...	...	...	...	...
Sylhet	...	...	...	...	...	...	...	...	...	...	...	...	...	...	...
ASSAM VALLEY DISTRICTS	*21*	*19*	*2*	...	...	...	*1,172*	*525*	*647*	*12*	*10*	*2*	*22*	*22*	...
Goalpara	...	...	...	...	...	...	5	5	...	...	...	...	...	...	...
Kamrup	...	...	...	...	...	...	99	47	52	...	...	...	...	...	...
Darrang	21	19	2	...	...	...	261	139	122	6	4	2	...	...	...
Nowgong	...	...	...	...	...	...	285	148	137	6	6	...	...	...	...
Sibsagar	...	...	...	...	...	...	501	186	315	...	...	...	...	...	...
Lakhimpur	...	...	...	...	...	...	21	...	21	...	...	...	22	22	...

PROVINCIAL TABLE III.—Tea-Garden Population by Language—*continued.*

District or State.	A.—*VERNACULARS OF INDIA*—contd.														
	2.—TIBETO-BURMAN—*contd.*														
	Koch.			Kuki (unspecified).			Lalung.			Limbu.			Mangar.		
	Persons.	Males.	Females.	Persons.	Males.	Females.	Persons.	Males.	Females.	Persons.	Males.	Females.	Persons.	Males.	Females.
1	62	63	64	65	66	67	68	69	70	71	72	73	74	75	76
ASSAM	*1*	*1*	...	*288*	*154*	*134*	*26*	*22*	*4*	*5*	*5*	...	*74*	*65*	*9*
SURMA VALLEY AND HILL DISTRICTS ...	...	...	...	*288*	*154*	*134*	...	...	...	...	...	...	...	...	...
Cachar	...	...	...	287	154	133	...	...	...	...	...	...	...	...	...
Sylhet	...	...	...	1	...	1	...	...	...	...	...	...	...	...	...
ASSAM VALLEY DISTRICTS	*1*	*1*	...	...	...	...	*26*	*22*	*4*	*5*	*5*	...	*74*	*65*	*9*
Goalpara	...	...	...	...	...	...	...	...	...	...	...	...	...	...	...
Kamrup	...	...	...	...	...	...	23	22	1	...	...	...	...	...	...
Darrang	...	...	...	...	...	...	...	...	...	...	...	...	40	31	9
Nowgong	...	...	...	...	...	...	...	...	...	5	5	...	...	...	...
Sibsagar	1	1	...	...	...	...	3	...	3	...	...	...	9	9	...
Lakhimpur	...	...	...	...	...	...	...	...	...	...	...	...	25	25	...

District or State.	A.—*VERNACULARS OF INDIA*—contd.														
	2.—TIBETO-BURMAN—*contd.*														
	Manipuri, Meithei, Kathe or Ponnu.			Mikir.			Miri.			Mojung.			Murmi.		
	Persons.	Males.	Females.	Persons.	Males.	Females.	Persons.	Males.	Females.	Persons.	Males.	Females.	Persons.	Males.	Females.
1	77	78	79	80	81	82	83	84	85	86	87	88	89	90	91
ASSAM	*619*	*407*	*212*	*1,521*	*809*	*712*	*16*	*6*	*10*	*7*	*5*	*2*	*11*	*7*	*4*
SURMA VALLEY AND HILL DISTRICTS...	*537*	*352*	*185*	*458*	*231*	*227*	...	...	...	...	...	...	*11*	*7*	*4*
Cachar	499	319	180	458	231	227	...	...	...	...	...	...	11	7	4
Sylhet	38	33	5	...	...	...	...	...	...	...	...	...	...	...	...
ASSAM VALLEY DISTRICTS	*82*	*55*	*27*	*1,063*	*578*	*485*	*16*	*6*	*10*	*7*	*5*	*2*	...	...	...
Goalpara	...	...	...	...	...	...	...	...	...	...	...	...	...	...	...
Kamrup	...	...	...	126	93	33	...	...	...	...	...	...	...	...	...
Darrang	1	...	1	212	116	96	...	...	...	...	...	...	...	...	...
Nowgong	...	...	...	691	347	344	...	...	...	...	...	...	...	...	...
Sibsagar	16	13	3	34	22	12	4	1	3	7	5	2	...	...	...
Lakhimpur	65	42	23	...	...	...	12	5	7	...	...	...	...	...	...

PROVINCIAL TABLE III.—Tea-Garden Population by Language—*continued.*

A.—VERNACULARS OF INDIA—contd.

2.—TIBETO-BURMAN—concld.

District or State.	Naga (unspecified).			Newari.			Pahri.			Rabha.			Tipura or Mrung.		
	Persons.	Males.	Females.	Persons.	Males.	Females.	Persons.	Males.	Females.	Persons.	Males.	Females.	Persons.	Males.	Females.
1	92	93	94	95	96	97	98	99	100	101	102	103	104	105	106
ASSAM	*423*	*330*	*84*	*75*	*31*	*44*	*1,023*	*553*	*470*	*12*	*8*	*4*	*149*	*73*	*76*
SURMA VALLEY AND HILL DISTRICTS...	*71*	*33*	*38*	...	...	...	*2*	...	*2*	...	...	...	*149*	*73*	*76*
Cachar	71	33	38	...	...	...	2	...	2	...	...	...	81	38	43
Sylhet	...	...	...	...	...	...	...	...	...	...	...	...	68	35	33
ASSAM VALLEY DISTRICTS	*352*	*306*	*46*	*75*	*31*	*44*	*1,021*	*553*	*468*	*12*	*8*	*4*	...	...	...
Goalpara	...	...	...	...	...	...	12	6	6	...	...	...	...	...	...
Kamrup	...	...	...	52	25	27	63	32	31	9	6	3	...	...	...
Darrang	...	...	...	19	5	14	2	2	...	3	2	1	...	...	...
Nowgong	...	...	...	1	1	...	...	...	...	...	...	...	...	...	...
Sibsagar	206	162	44	3	...	3	301	175	126	...	...	...	...	...	...
Lakhimpur	146	144	2	...	...	...	643	338	305	...	...	...	...	...	...

A.—VERNACULARS OF INDIA—contd.

District or State.	4.—MON-KHMER.			5.—MUNDA.											
	Khasi.			Bhumij.			Kharia.			K[illegible]wa.			Kurku.		
	Persons.	Males.	Females.	Persons.	Males.	Females.	Persons.	Males.	Females.	Persons.	Males.	Females.	Persons.	Males.	Females.
1	107	108	109	110	111	112	113	114	115	116	117	118	119	120	121
ASSAM	*658*	*323*	*335*	*1,933*	*901*	*1,032*	*3,699*	*2,385*	*1,314*	*564*	*269*	*295*	*1,855*	*1,130*	*725*
SURMA VALLEY AND HILL DISTRICTS...	*616*	*305*	*311*	*11*	*5*	*6*	*76*	*34*	*42*	*83*	*44*	*39*	*166*	*92*	*74*
Cachar	143	76	67	...	...	...	76	34	42	35	19	16	124	72	52
Sylhet	473	229	244	11	5	6	...	...	...	48	25	23	42	20	22
ASSAM VALLEY DISTRICTS	*42*	*18*	*24*	*1,922*	*896*	*1,026*	*3,623*	*2,351*	*1,272*	*481*	*225*	*256*	*1,689*	*1,038*	*651*
Goalpara	...	...	...	...	...	...	...	...	...	...	...	...	...	...	...
Kamrup	1	1	...	...	...	...	...	...	...	...	...	...	...	...	...
Darrang	13	11	2	32	16	16	513	239	274	442	212	230	58	29	29
Nowgong	4	1	3	10	6	4	156	82	74	...	...	...	25	14	11
Sibsagar	6	...	6	1,742	856	886	427	213	214	14	6	8	200	95	105
Lakhimpur	18	5	13	138	18	120	2,527	1,817	710	25	7	18	1,406	900	506

PROVINCIAL TABLE III.—TEA-GARDEN POPULATION BY LANGUAGE—*concluded.*

District or State.	*A.—VERNACULARS OF INDIA.*—contd. 5.—MUNDA.—*concld.* Mundari. Persons.	Mundari. Males.	Mundari. Females.	Santali. Persons.	Santali. Males.	Santali. Females.	Savara. Persons.	Savara. Males.	Savara. Females.	Turi. Persons.	Turi. Males.	Turi. Females.	6. DRAVIDIAN. Gond. Persons.	Gond. Males.	Gond. Females.
1	122	123	124	125	126	127	128	129	130	131	132	133	134	135	136
ASSAM	*39,637*	*19,277*	*20,360*	*29,118*	*14,297*	*14,821*	*275*	*160*	*115*	*1,459*	*738*	*721*	*6,277*	*3,151*	*3,126*
SURMA VALLEY AND HILL DISTRICTS...	*5,272*	*2,630*	*2,642*	*6,513*	*3,351*	*3,162*	...	...	...	*10*	*6*	*4*	*298*	*124*	*174*
Cachar	2,644	1,363	1,281	2,672	1,370	1,302	...	...	...	...	...	...	247	103	145
Sylhet	2,628	1,267	1,361	3,841	1,981	1,860	...	...	...	10	6	4	51	22	29
ASSAM VALLEY DISTRICTS	*34,365*	*16,647*	*17,718*	*22,605*	*10,946*	*11,659*	*275*	*160*	*115*	*1,449*	*732*	*717*	*5,979*	*3,027*	*2,952*
Goalpara	101	54	47	141	62	79	...	...	...	...	...	...	1	1	...
Kamrup	151	78	73	61	26	35	...	...	...	...	...	...	...	...	...
Darrang	6,671	3,295	3,376	2,707	1,391	1,316	...	...	...	41	19	22	1,383	705	678
Nowgong	1,139	554	585	727	329	398	...	...	...	77	41	36	117	60	57
Sibsagar	7,277	3,567	3,710	9,048	4,545	4,503	7	...	7	1,331	672	659	2,394	1,168	1,226
Lakhimpur	19,026	9,099	9,927	9,921	4,593	5,328	268	160	108	...	...	...	2,084	1,093	991

District or State.	*A.—VERNACULARS OF INDIA*—concld. 6.—DRAVIDIAN—*concld.* Kandh or Kui. Persons.	Kandh or Kui. Males.	Kandh or Kui. Females.	Kurukh or Oraon. Persons.	Kurukh or Oraon. Males.	Kurukh or Oraon. Females.	Tamil. Persons.	Tamil. Males.	Tamil. Females.	Telugu or Andhra. Persons.	Telugu or Andhra. Males.	Telugu or Andhra. Females.	*C.—EUROPEAN LANGUAGES.* English. Persons.	English. Males.	English. Females.	*OTHERS.* (For details see Appendix on following page.) Persons.	Others. Males.	Others. Females.
1	137	138	139	140	141	142	143	144	145	146	147	148	149	150	151	152	153	154
ASSAM	*3,773*	*1,773*	*2,000*	*7,571*	*4,001*	*3,570*	*655*	*410*	*245*	*19,684*	*10,502*	*9,182*	*1,338*	*1,044*	*294*	*491*	*304*	*187*
SURMA VALLEY AND HILL DISTRICTS...	*157*	*82*	*75*	*1,510*	*769*	*741*	*411*	*203*	*208*	*4,280*	*2,101*	*2,179*	*482*	*374*	*108*	*10*	*9*	*1*
Cachar	1	...	1	1,254	639	615	...	...	...	1,265	653	612	203	153	50	7	7	...
Sylhet	156	82	74	256	130	126	411	203	208	3,015	1,448	1,567	279	221	58	3	2	1
ASSAM VALLEY DISTRICTS	*3,616*	*1,691*	*1,925*	*6,061*	*3,232*	*2,829*	*244*	*207*	*37*	*15,404*	*8,401*	*7,003*	*856*	*670*	*186*	*481*	*295*	*186*
Goalpara	...	...	...	7	6	1	...	...	...	3	3	...	6	4	2	...	...	...
Kamrup	...	...	...	14	8	6	...	...	...	...	...	...	11	9	2	54	31	23
Darrang	2,212	1,114	1,008	1,016	539	477	2	...	2	3,674	2,035	1,639	168	132	36	54	47	7
Nowgong	3	3	...	420	209	211	...	...	...	509	276	233	47	33	14	6	6	...
Sibsagar	175	97	78	1,143	585	558	...	...	...	6,066	3,145	2,921	321	249	72	132	93	39
Lakhimpur	1,226	477	749	3,461	1,885	1,576	242	207	35	5,152	2,942	2,210	363	243	60	235	118	117

APPENDIX TO PROVINCIAL TABLE III.—PROVINCIAL TOTALS AND DISTRIBUTION BY DISTRICTS OF LANGUAGES INCLUDED IN THE HEAD "OTHERS."

Language.	Provincial Total.			Distribution.
	Persons.	Males.	Females.	
1	2	3	4	5
A.—VERNACULARS OF INDIA—				
1. ARYAN—				
Gujrati	28	15	13	Cachar (1+0), Kamrup (11+7), Sibsagar (3+6).
2. TIBETO-BURMAN—				
Burmese	2	2	...	Cachar (1+0), Lakhimpur (1+0).
Jauggai	171	85	86	Lakhimpur.
Jimdar	16	16	...	Sibsagar.
Kami	4	...	4	Darrang.
Maujhi	13	6	7	Lakhimpur.
Moran	23	6	17	Sibsagar.
5. MUNDA—				
Asuri	37	18	19	Darrang (4+0), Lakhimpur (14+19).
Ho or Kol	55	33	22	Kamrup (20+16), Sibsagar (0+1), Lakhimpur (13+5).
Kora (Koda)	49	39	10	Sibsagar (38+10), Lakhimpur (1+0).
6. DRAVIDIAN—				
Kota	9	6	3	Sibsagar.
B.—VERNACULARS OF ASIATIC COUNTRIES BEYOND INDIA.				
Chinese	82	78	4	Cachar (5+0), Sylhet (2+1), Darrang (43+3), Nowgong (6+0), Sibsagar (12+0), Lakhimpur (10+0).
C.—EUROPEAN LANGUAGES—				
French	2	...	2	Sibsagar.
Total	491	304	187	

PROVINCIAL TABLE IV.

TEA-GARDEN POPULATION BY BIRTH-PLACE.

THIS Table and the previous and the following Table deal with the Tea-garden population of each district.

This Table has been arranged on the principles adopted for Imperial Table XI, the title page of which may be referred to.

PROVINCIAL TABLE IV.—Tea-garden Population by Birth-place.

Birth place.	Province.			Districts where enumerated.								
				Cachar.			Sylhet.			Goalpara.		
	Persons.	Males.	Females.	Persons.	Males.	Females.	Persons.	Males.	Females.	Persons.	Males.	Females.
1	2	3	4	5	6	7	8	9	10	11	12	13
TOTAL POPULATION	*703,034*	*361,916*	*340,118*	*130,839*	*67,572*	*63,260*	*142,750*	*72,214*	*70,536*	*565*	*307*	*258*
A.—BORN IN INDIA	*696,455*	*358,398*	*338,057*	*130,489*	*67,301*	*63,188*	*142,466*	*71,986*	*70,480*	*545*	*289*	*256*
I.—BORN IN ASSAM	*260,812*	*138,553*	*122,259*	*72,969*	*37,962*	*35,000*	*56,187*	*30,097*	*26,090*	*155*	*82*	*73*
(1) *British Territory*	*260,673*	*138,463*	*122,210*	*72,916*	*37,931*	*34,985*	*56,149*	*30,078*	*26,071*	*155*	*82*	*73*
SURMA VALLEY AND HILL DISTRICTS...	*129,466*	*68,304*	*61,162*	*72,863*	*37,898*	*34,965*	*55,917*	*29,908*	*26,009*	...	...	...
Cachar	71,280	36,043	35,237	69,357	35,093	34,264	1,833	899	934	...	...	...
Sylhet	57,305	31,575	25,730	3,331	2,710	621	53,797	28,780	25,067	...	...	...
Khasi and Jaintia Hills	511	392	119	174	94	80	287	279	8	...	...	...
Naga Hills	370	294	76	1	1	...	...	...	...	...	...	...
Lushai Hills	...	...	...	...	...	...	...	...	...	...	...	...
ASSAM VALLEY DISTRICTS	*131,207*	*70,159*	*61,048*	*53*	*33*	*20*	*232*	*170*	*62*	*155*	*82*	*73*
Goalpara	1,634	1,271	363	...	...	...	5	5	...	154	81	73
Kamrup	7,262	5,850	1,412	32	21	11	183	140	43	...	...	...
Darrang	17,982	9,974	8,008	7	5	2	29	17	12	...	...	...
Nowgong	5,268	2,649	2,619	4	...	4	5	5	...	...	...	...
Sibsagar	53,951	28,092	25,859	3	2	1	2	1	1	...	...	...
Lakhimpur	45,047	22,283	22,764	7	5	2	8	2	6	1	1	...
Garo Hills	63	40	23	...	...	...	...	...	...	...	...	...
(2) *Manipur State*	*67*	*52*	*15*	*17*	*14*	*3*	*7*	*4*	*3*	...	...	...
ASSAM UNSPECIFIED	*72*	*38*	*34*	*29*	*17*	*12*	*31*	*15*	*16*	...	...	...
II.—BORN IN OTHER PARTS OF INDIA...	*435,643*	*219,845*	*215,798*	*57,527*	*29,339*	*28,188*	*86,279*	*41,889*	*44,390*	*390*	*207*	*183*
(a) PROVINCES AND STATES ADJACENT TO ASSAM.	*34,917*	*16,768*	*18,149*	*8,210*	*3,894*	*4,316*	*6,234*	*3,039*	*3,195*	*22*	*15*	*7*
(1) *British Territory* ...	*34,886*	*16,754*	*18,132*	*8,207*	*3,891*	*4,316*	*6,227*	*3,035*	*3,192*	*22*	*15*	*7*
1. *Bengal*	*34,870*	*16,743*	*18,127*	*8,207*	*3,891*	*4,316*	*6,225*	*3,033*	*3,192*	*22*	*15*	*7*
(i) *Contiguous Districts* ...	*670*	*510*	*160*	*155*	*113*	*42*	*323*	*292*	*31*	*6*	*4*	*2*
Jalpaiguri	17	5	12	...	...	...	1	1	...	2	...	2
Rangpur	215	192	23	2	2	...	166	165	1	3	3	...
Mymensingh	165	117	48	45	31	14	42	35	7	...	...	...
Tippera	273	196	77	108	80	28	114	91	23	1	1	...
(ii) *Other Districts*	*34,200*	*16,233*	*17,967*	*8,052*	*3,778*	*4,274*	*5,902*	*2,741*	*3,161*	*16*	*11*	*5*
2. *Burma (other Districts)* ...	*16*	*11*	*5*	...	...	...	*2*	*2*	...	...	...	...
(ii) *Cooch Behar State* ...	*31*	*14*	*17*	*3*	*3*	...	*7*	*4*	*3*	...	...	...

PROVINCIAL TABLE IV.—Tea-garden Population by Birth-place—*continued.*

Birth-place.	Kamrup. Persons.	Kamrup. Males.	Kamrup. Females.	Darrang. Persons.	Darrang. Males.	Darrang. Females.	Nowgong. Persons.	Nowgong. Males.	Nowgong. Females.	Sibsagar. Persons.	Sibsagar. Males.	Sibsagar. Females.	Lakhimpur. Persons.	Lakhimpur. Males.	Lakhimpur. Females.
	DISTRICTS WHERE ENUMERATED.														
1	14	15	16	17	18	19	20	21	22	23	24	25	26	27	28
TOTAL POPULATION	*4,459*	*2,400*	*2,059*	*79,065*	*41,660*	*37,405*	*18,109*	*9,134*	*9,035*	*163,623*	*84,993*	*78,630*	*162,571*	*83,636*	*78,935*
A.—BORN IN INDIA	*4,304*	*2,311*	*1,993*	*77,046*	*40,489*	*36,557*	*17,971*	*9,007*	*8,964*	*162,548*	*84,276*	*78,272*	*161,086*	*82,739*	*78,347*
I.—BORN IN ASSAM	*2,683*	*1,494*	*1,189*	*20,426*	*11,969*	*8,457*	*5,669*	*2,982*	*2,687*	*56,266*	*30,357*	*25,909*	*46,464*	*23,610*	*22,854*
(1) *British Territory*	*2,683*	*1,494*	*1,189*	*20,421*	*11,966*	*8,455*	*5,669*	*2,982*	*2,687*	*56,257*	*30,350*	*25,907*	*46,423*	*23,580*	*22,843*
SURMA VALLEY AND HILL DISTRICTS	*10*	*9*	*1*	*57*	*30*	*27*	*60*	*41*	*19*	*444*	*330*	*114*	*115*	*88*	*27*
Cachar	3	3	...	22	9	13	17	11	6	38	20	18	10	8	2
Sylhet	2	1	1	31	21	10	18	16	2	62	48	14	64	49	15
Khasi and Jaintia Hills	4	4	...	4	...	4	12	6	6	13	2	11	17	7	10
Naga Hills	1	1	...	...	...	...	13	8	5	331	260	71	24	24	...
Lushai Hills	...	...	...	...	...	...	...	...	...	...	...	...	...	...	...
ASSAM VALLEY DISTRICTS	*2,673*	*1,485*	*1,188*	*20,364*	*11,936*	*8,428*	*5,609*	*2,941*	*2,668*	*55,813*	*30,020*	*25,793*	*46,308*	*23,492*	*22,816*
Goalpara	71	35	36	594	509	85	179	122	57	392	317	75	239	202	37
Kamrup	2,434	1,362	1,072	1,411	1,252	159	272	231	41	2,072	2,000	72	858	844	14
Darrang	82	36	46	17,719	9,827	7,892	79	41	38	39	26	13	27	22	5
Nowgong	62	34	28	180	106	74	4,944	2,469	2,475	42	24	18	31	11	20
Sibsagar	10	4	6	254	134	120	85	49	36	52,776	27,406	25,370	821	496	325
Lakhimpur	14	14	...	185	93	92	32	19	13	470	234	236	44,330	21,915	22,415
Garo Hills	...	...	...	21	15	6	18	10	8	22	13	9	2	2	...
(2) *Manipur State*	...	...	...	*2*	*1*	*1*	...	...	...	*9*	*7*	*2*	*32*	*26*	*6*
ASSAM UNSPECIFIED	...	...	...	*3*	*2*	*1*	...	...	...	...	...	...	*9*	*4*	*5*
II.—BORN IN OTHER PARTS OF INDIA	*1,621*	*817*	*804*	*56,620*	*28,520*	*28,100*	*12,302*	*6,025*	*6,277*	*106.282*	*53,919*	*52,363*	*114,622*	*59,129*	*55,493*
(a) Provinces and States adjacent to Assam.	*182*	*93*	*89*	*3,443*	*1,652*	*1,791*	*853*	*405*	*448*	*8,685*	*4,112*	*4,573*	*7,288*	*3,558*	*3,730*
(1) *British Territory*	*182*	*93*	*89*	*3,442*	*1,651*	*1,791*	*850*	*404*	*446*	*8,674*	*4,108*	*4,566*	*7,282*	*3,557*	*3,725*
1. *Bengal*	*181*	*92*	*89*	*3,441*	*1,650*	*1,791*	*849*	*403*	*446*	*8,669*	*4,103*	*4,566*	*7,276*	*3,556*	*3,720*
(i) *Contiguous Districts* ...	...	...	...	*51*	*21*	*30*	*6*	*4*	*2*	*62*	*34*	*28*	*67*	*42*	*25*
Jalpaiguri	...	...	...	10	4	6	...	...	...	2	...	2	2	...	2
Rangpur	...	...	...	5	1	4	2	2	...	17	7	10	20	12	8
Mymensingh	...	...	...	21	10	11	3	1	2	24	17	7	30	23	7
Tippera	...	...	...	15	6	9	1	1	...	19	10	9	15	7	8
(ii) *Other Districts*	*181*	*92*	*89*	*3,390*	*1,629*	*1,761*	*843*	*399*	*444*	*8,607*	*4,069*	*4,538*	*7,209*	*3,514*	*3,695*
2. *Burma (other Districts)* ...	*1*	*1*	...	*1*	*1*	...	*1*	*1*	...	*5*	*5*	...	*6*	*1*	*5*
(ii) *Cooch Behar State* ...	...	...	...	*1*	*1*	...	*3*	*1*	*2*	*11*	*4*	*7*	*6*	*1*	*5*

PROVINCIAL TABLE IV.—TEA-GARDEN POPULATION BY BIRTH-PLACE—*continued.*

Birth place.	Province.			Districts where enumerated. Cachar.			Sylhet.			Goalpara.		
	Persons.	Males.	Females.	Persons.	Males.	Females.	Persons.	Males.	Females.	Persons.	Males.	Females.
1	2	3	4	5	6	7	8	9	10	11	12	13
(b) OTHER PROVINCES AND STATES IN INDIA	*400,697*	*203,067*	*197,630*	*49,316*	*25,444*	*23,872*	*80,034*	*38,848*	*41,186*	*368*	*192*	*176*
(1) ***British Territory***	*381,695*	*193,055*	*188,640*	*48,345*	*24,992*	*23,353*	*78,113*	*37,862*	*40,251*	*367*	*191*	*176*
Ajmere-Merwara	14	14	...	...	...	...	...	...	...	...	...	...
Bihar and Orissa	245,251	125,080	120,171	26,369	13,569	12,800	28,200	14,002	14,198	351	180	171
Bombay (including Aden) ...	192	103	89	32	17	15	60	43	17	...	...	...
Central Provinces and Berar ...	51,024	25,049	25,975	9,539	4,687	4,852	8,493	3,937	4,556	5	8	2
Coorg	1	1	...	1	1	...	...	...	...	...	...	...
Madras (including Laccadives) ...	31,070	15,214	15,856	1,350	657	693	8,469	3,829	4,640	...	...	...
North-West Frontier Province (Districts and Administered Territories).	11	8	3	...	...	...	1	1	...	...	...	...
Punjab	722	386	336	12	10	2	71	47	24	9	7	2
United Provinces of Agra and Oudh ...	53,410	27,200	26,210	11,042	6,051	4,991	32,819	16,003	16,816	2	1	1
(2) ***Feudatory States***	*19,009*	*10,019*	*8,990*	*971*	*452*	*519*	*1,921*	*986*	*935*	*1*	*1*	...
Bihar and Orissa States	5,998	2,956	3,042	17	9	8	102	51	51	...	...	...
Bombay States	1,405	736	669	...	...	...	1,393	726	667	...	...	...
Central India Agency	5,295	2,697	2,598	765	318	447	294	113	181	...	...	...
Central Provinces States	3,532	1,734	1,798	19	13	6	9	5	4	...	...	...
Kashmir	2	1	1	...	...	...	1	...	1	1	1	...
Madras States	69	29	40	66	27	39	3	2	1	...	...	...
Mysore	168	59	49	4	1	3	56	36	20	...	...	...
Punjab States	13	13	...	...	...	...	...	...	...	...	...	...
Rajputana Agency	2,538	1,770	768	88	80	8	59	50	9	...	...	...
United Provinces States	42	17	25	12	4	8	4	3	1	...	...	...
(c) FRENCH AND PORTUGUESE SETTLEMENTS	*4*	*2*	*2*	...	...	...	...	...	...	...	...	...
(d) INDIA UNSPECIFIED	*25*	*8*	*17*	*1*	*1*	...	*11*	*9*	*2*	...	...	...
B.—BORN IN OTHER ASIATIC COUNTRIES.	*4,593*	*2,698*	*1,895*	*176*	*130*	*46*	*83*	*56*	*27*	*17*	*15*	*2*
Afghanistan	53	53	...	14	14	...	20	20	...	...	...	...
Bhotan	13	5	8	4	1	3	...	...	...	...	...	...
Ceylon	6	3	3	...	...	...	...	...	...	...	...	...
China	86	83	3	5	5	...	2	2	...	...	...	...
Nepal	4,364	2,483	1,881	152	109	43	61	34	27	17	15	2
Tibet	1	1	...	1	1	...	...	...	...	...	...	...
C.—BORN IN EUROPE	*1,020*	*857*	*163*	*158*	*132*	*26*	*192*	*163*	*29*	*1*	*1*	...
United Kingdom	1,011	851	160	154	130	24	190	162	28	1	1	...
England and Wales	564	465	99	81	66	15	79	67	12	...	...	...
Scotland	382	336	46	55	50	5	101	88	13	...	...	...
Ireland	65	50	15	18	14	4	10	7	3	1	1	...
Denmark	2	1	1	2	1	1	...	...	...	...	...	...
Germany	3	2	1	2	1	1	...	...	...	...	...	...
Gibraltar	*1*	*1*	...	...	...	...	*1*	*1*	...	...	...	...
Italy	*1*	...	1	...	...	...	*1*	...	*1*	...	...	...
Russia	1	1	...	...	...	...	...	...	...	...	...	...
Switzerland	1	1	...	...	...	...	...	...	...	...	...	...
D.—BORN IN AFRICA	*4*	*4*	...	*1*	*1*	...	*2*	*2*	...	...	...	...
Natal	2	2	...	1	1	...	1	1	...	...	...	...
Africa Unspecified	2	2	...	...	...	...	1	1	...	...	...	...

PROVINCIAL TABLE IV.—TEA-GARDEN POPULATION BY BIRTH-PLACE.—*continued.*

Birth-Place.	Kamrup. Persons.	Kamrup. Males.	Kamrup. Females.	Darrang. Persons.	Darrang. Males.	Darrang. Females.	Nowgong. Persons.	Nowgong. Males.	Nowgong. Females.	Sibsagar. Persons.	Sibsagar. Males.	Sibsagar. Females.	Lakhimpur. Persons.	Lakhimpur. Males.	Lakhimpur. Females.
	Districts where enumerated.														
1	14	15	16	17	18	19	20	21	22	23	24	25	26	27	28
(b) Other Provinces and States in India	*1,438*	*724*	*714*	*53,170*	*26,864*	*26,306*	*11,449*	*5,620*	*5,829*	*97,593*	*49,806*	*47,787*	*107,329*	*55,569*	*51,760*
(1) ***British Territory***	*1,294*	*652*	*642*	*49,542*	*24,989*	*24,553*	*10,655*	*5,210*	*5,445*	*93,704*	*47,671*	*46,033*	*99,675*	*51,488*	*48,187*
Ajmere-Merwara	...	...	...	2	2	...	...	...	...	5	5	...	7	7	...
Bihar and Orissa	1,139	575	564	33,873	17,143	16,730	6,908	3,384	3,524	69,879	35,650	34,229	78,532	40,577	37,955
Bombay (including Aden)... ...	16	2	14	32	14	18	8	3	5	19	11	8	25	13	12
Central Provinces and Berar ...	75	34	41	6,499	3,304	3,186	2,750	1,281	1,469	12,947	6,441	6,506	10,725	5,362	5,363
Coorg	...	...	...	...	...	...	...	...	...	...	...	...	...	...	...
Madras (including Laccadives) ...	12	12	...	6,131	2,949	3,182	735	374	361	7,641	3,756	3,885	6,732	3,637	3,095
North-West Frontier Provinces (Districts and Administered Territories).	...	...	...	10	7	3	...	...	...	...	...	...	...	...	...
Punjab	1	...	1	73	42	31	15	11	4	101	69	32	440	200	240
United Provinces of Agra and Oudh ...	51	29	22	2,931	1,528	1,403	239	157	82	3,112	1,739	1,373	3,214	1,692	1,522
(2) ***Feudatory States***	*144*	*72*	*72*	*3,628*	*1,875*	*1,753*	*794*	*410*	*384*	*3,889*	*2,135*	*1,754*	*7,654*	*4,081*	*3,573*
Bihar and Orissa States	...	...	...	764	306	458	1	1	...	1,603	782	821	3,511	1,807	1,704
Bombay States	...	...	...	2	...	2	...	...	...	8	8	...	2	2	...
Central India Agency	133	66	67	1,475	811	664	690	348	342	1,189	625	564	749	416	333
Central Provinces States	5	1	4	1,055	519	536	39	19	20	380	181	199	2,025	996	1,029
Kashmir	...	...	...	...	...	...	...	...	...	...	...	...	...	...	...
Madras States	...	...	...	...	...	...	...	...	...	...	...	...	...	...	...
Maysore	...	...	...	19	8	11	...	...	...	26	11	15	3	3	...
Punjab States...	...	...	...	...	...	...	...	...	...	1	1	...	12	12	...
Rajputana Agency	6	5	1	300	227	73	64	42	22	680	527	153	1,341	839	502
United Provinces States	...	...	...	13	4	9	...	...	...	2	...	2	11	6	5
(c) French and Portuguese Settlements	...	...	...	*3*	*2*	*1*	...	...	...	*1*	...	*1*	...	...	...
(d) India Unspecified	*1*	...	*1*	*4*	*2*	*2*	...	...	...	*3*	*1*	*2*	*5*	*2*	*3*
B.—BORN IN OTHER ASIATIC COUNTRIES.	*148*	*83*	*65*	*1,887*	*1,064*	*823*	*163*	*97*	*66*	*816*	*501*	*315*	*1,233*	*682*	*551*
Afghanistan	...	...	...	9	9	...	2	2	...	4	4	...	4	4	...
Bhotan	...	...	...	6	4	2	...	...	...	3	...	3	...	...	...
Ceylon	...	...	...	...	...	...	...	...	...	4	1	3	2	2	...
China	1	1	...	50	47	3	6	6	...	13	13	...	9	9	...
Nepal	147	82	65	1,822	1,004	818	155	89	66	792	483	309	1,218	667	551
Tibet	...	...	...	...	...	...	...	...	...	...	...	...	...	...	...
C.—BORN IN EUROPE	*7*	*6*	*1*	*129*	*104*	*25*	*35*	*30*	*5*	*249*	*209*	*40*	*245*	*212*	*37*
United Kingdom	7	6	1	128	103	25	35	30	5	248	208	40	248	211	37
England and Wales	5	4	1	71	61	10	14	10	4	150	121	29	164	136	28
Scotland	2	2	...	51	39	12	21	20	1	84	75	9	68	62	6
Ireland	...	...	...	6	3	3	...	...	...	14	12	2	16	13	3
Denmark	...	...	...	...	...	...	...	...	...	...	...	...	...	...	...
Germany	...	...	...	...	...	...	...	...	...	...	...	...	...	...	...
Gibraltar	...	...	...	...	...	...	...	...	...	...	...	...	1	1	...
Italy	...	...	...	...	...	...	...	...	...	...	...	...	...	...	...
Russia	...	...	...	...	...	...	...	...	...	...	...	...	...	...	...
Switzerland	...	...	...	1	1	...	...	...	...	1	1	...	...	...	...
D.—BORN IN AFRICA	...	...	...	*1*	*1*	...	...	...	...	...	...	...	...	...	...
Natal	...	...	...	...	...	...	...	...	...	...	...	...	...	...	...
Africa Unspecified	...	...	...	1	1	...	...	...	...	...	...	...	...	...	...

PROVINCIAL TABLE IV.—Tea-garden Population by Birth-place—*concluded.*

Birth-place.	Province.			Districts where enumerated. Cachar.			Sylhet.			Goalpara.		
	Persons.	Males.	Females.	Persons.	Males.	Females.	Persons.	Males.	Females.	Persons.	Males.	Females.
1	2	3	4	5	6	7	8	9	10	11	12	13
E.—BORN IN AMERICA	*10*	*10*	...	*3*	*3*	...	*5*	*5*	...	...	...	...
Argentine Republic	1	1	...	...	...	...	1	1	...	...	...	...
Canada	1	1	...	...	...	...	1	1	...	...	...	...
Newfoundland	2	2	...	2	2	...	...	...	...	...	...	...
America Unspecified	6	6	...	1	1	...	3	3	...	...	...	...
F.—BORN IN AUSTRALASIA	*20*	*17*	*3*	*5*	*5*	...	*2*	*2*	...	*2*	*2*	...
Australia	12	10	2	2	2	...	2	2	...	2	2	...
Fizi	4	3	1	...	...	...	...	...	...	...	...	...
New Zealand	2	2	...	1	1	...	...	...	...	...	...	...
Tasmania	2	2	...	2	2	...	...	...	...	...	...	...
G.—BORN AT SEA	*2*	*2*	...	...	...	...	...	...	...	...	...	...

Birth-place.	Districts where enumerated. Kamrup.			Darrang.			Nowgong.			Sibsagar.			Lakhimpur.		
	Persons.	Males.	Females.	Persons.	Males.	Females.	Persons.	Males.	Females.	Persons.	Males.	Females.	Persons.	Males.	Females.
1	14	15	16	17	18	19	20	21	22	23	24	25	26	27	28
E.—BORN IN AMERICA	...	...	...	...	...	...	...	...	...	*2*	*2*	...	...	...	...
Argentine Republic	...	...	...	...	...	...	...	...	...	...	...	...	...	...	...
Canada	...	...	...	...	...	...	...	...	...	...	...	...	...	...	...
Newfoundland	...	...	...	...	...	...	...	...	...	...	...	...	...	...	...
America Unspecified	...	...	...	...	...	...	...	...	...	2	2	...	...	...	...
F.—BORN IN AUSTRALASIA	...	...	...	*1*	*1*	...	...	...	...	*8*	*5*	*3*	*2*	*2*	...
Australia	...	...	...	1	1	...	...	...	...	3	1	2	2	2	...
Fizi	...	...	...	...	...	...	...	...	...	4	3	1	...	...	...
New Zealand	...	...	...	...	...	...	...	...	...	1	1	...	...	...	...
Tasmania	...	...	...	...	...	...	...	...	...	...	...	...	...	...	...
G.—BORN AT SEA	...	...	...	*1*	*1*	...	...	...	...	...	...	...	*1*	*1*	...

PROVINCIAL TABLE V.

TEA-GARDEN POPULATION BY CASTE.

THIS Table and the two previous Tables deal with the tea-garden population of each district.

This Table has been arranged in the same manner as Imperial Table XIII, and is divided into two parts, of which Part A includes all castes except Muhammadans and Part B contains Muhammadans only: Christians have not been included. In the appendix are shown the details of 'Minor Castes' grouped together in the alphabetical arrangement of the Table.

PROVINCIAL TABLE V.—TEA-GARDEN POPULATION BY CASTE. PART A.—HINDUS, ANIMISTS BUDDHISTS, ETC.

Province or District.	Population.			Agaria.		Agarwala.				Ahir.		Ahom.		Remarks.
				Hindu.		Hindu.		Jain.		Hindu.		Hindu.		
	Persons.	Males.	Females.	Males.	Females.	Males.	Females.	Males.	Females.	Males.	Females.	Males.	Females.	
1	2	3	4	5	6	7	8	9	10	11	12	13	14	15
ASSAM	*683,829*	*351,035*	*332,794*	*385*	*391*	*541*	*281*	*18*	*4*	*5,573*	*4,948*	*1,981*	*689*	Agaria includes (1+0) Animist in Lakhimpur. Agarwala (Hindu) includes (1+0) Animist in Lakhimpur. Ahir includes (19+6) Animists, *viz.*, Darrang (1+0), Nowgong (2+0), Sibsagar (8+5) and Lakhimpur (8+1). Ahom includes (1+0) Animist in Lakhimpur.
SURMA VALLEY DISTRICTS	*262,344*	*132,823*	*129,521*	*213*	*236*	...	...	...	...	*4,551*	*4,224*	...	...	
Cachar	125,315	64,165	61,150	109	130	...	...	...	...	1,905	1,734	...	...	
Sylhet	137,029	68,658	68,371	104	106	...	...	...	...	2,646	2,490	...	...	
ASSAM VALLEY DISTRICTS	*421,485*	*218,212*	*203,273*	*172*	*155*	*541*	*281*	*18*	*4*	*1,022*	*724*	*1,981*	*689*	
Goalpara	524	282	242	...	...	...	...	...	...	...	...	...	...	
Kamrup	4 420	2,372	2,048	...	...	3	3	...	...	2	4	...	...	
Darrang	78.287	41,147	37,140	25	16	32	2	3	3	139	97	16	5	
Nowgong	17.944	9,004	8.940	...	...	6	...	...	...	47	26	4	3	
Sibsagar	159,162	82,600	76,562	138	131	253	122	12	1	375	241	1,062	309	
Lakhimpur	161,148	82,807	78,341	9	8	247	154	3	...	459	356	899	381	

Province or District.	Asur.		Bagdi.		Baidya.		Baishnab (Bairagi).		Baniya.		Barhi.		Bari.		Remarks.
	Hindu.		Hindu.		Hindu.		Hindu.		Hindu.		Hindu.		Hindu.		
	Males.	Females.	Males.	Females.	Males.	Females.	Males.	Females.	Males.	Females.	Males.	Females.	Males.	Females.	
1	16	17	18	19	20	21	22	23	24	25	26	27	28	29	30
ASSAM	*111*	*78*	*2,926*	*3,140*	*296*	*172*	*809*	*861*	*63*	*65*	*79*	*71*	*6*	*8*	Asur includes (15+9) Animists, *viz.*, Darrang (2+1) and Lakhimpur (13+8). Bagdi includes (7+9) Animists, *viz.*, Sibsagar (5+8) and Lakhimpur (2+1). Baishnab (Bairagi) includes (0+1) Animist in Darrang and 1 Jain male in Sibsagar. Barhi includes (1+0) Animist in Darrang. Bari includes (0+3) Animists in Darrang.
SURMA VALLEY DISTRICTS	*43*	*19*	*1,743*	*1,814*	*206*	*117*	*475*	*509*	*63*	*65*	...	...	...	...	
Cachar	2	2	1,012	1,065	79	39	74	78	21	40	...	...	...	...	
Sylhet	41	17	731	749	127	78	401	431	42	25	...	...	...	...	
ASSAM VALLEY DISTRICTS	*68*	*59*	*1,183*	*1,326*	*90*	*55*	*327*	*352*	...	...	*79*	*71*	*6*	*8*	
Goalpara	...	...	...	...	...	...	...	...	...	...	...	...	...	...	
Kamrup	...	...	19	16	...	...	1	...	...	...	...	...	...	...	
Darrang	15	12	244	273	26	16	70	68	...	...	30	22	5	3	
Nowgong	4	8	50	65	10	2	9	17	...	...	2	2	...	...	
Sibsagar	29	27	552	581	32	25	120	130	...	...	23	26	...	...	
Lakhimpur	20	12	318	391	22	12	127	137	...	...	24	21	1	5	

PROVINCIAL TABLE V.—Tea-garden Population by Caste. Part A.—Hindus, Animists, Buddhists, etc.—*continued*.

Province or District.	Babui. Hindu. Males.	Babui. Hindu. Females.	Bauri. Hindu. Males.	Bauri. Hindu. Females.	Bauri. Animist. Males.	Bauri. Animist. Females.	Bediya. Hindu. Males.	Bediya. Hindu. Females.	Behara. Hindu. Males.	Behara. Hindu. Females.	Beldar. Hindu. Males.	Beldar. Hindu. Females.	Besya. Hindu. Males.	Besya. Hindu. Females.	Remarks.
1	31	32	33	34	35	36	37	38	39	40	41	42	43	44	45
ASSAM	***456***	***365***	***16,593***	***18,407***	***254***	***306***	***318***	***370***	***13***	***3***	***80***	***79***	...	***250***	
SURMA VALLEY DISTRICTS	***341***	***318***	***10,102***	***10,941***	...	...	***17***	***27***	***12***	...	***16***	***25***	...	***250***	
Cachar	94	78	6,313	6,538	...	...	11	11	...	...	16	22	...	...	Bediya includes (7+8) Animists, *viz.*, Darrang (0+2) and Sibsagar (7+6).
Sylhet	247	240	3,789	4,403	...	...	6	16	12	...	...	3	...	250	
ASSAM VALLEY DISTRICTS	***115***	***47***	***6,491***	***7,460***	***254***	***306***	***301***	***343***	***1***	***3***	***64***	***54***	...	...	
Goalpara	...	...	...	...	...	...	...	...	...	...	...	...	...	...	
Kamrup	...	...	51	55	...	...	...	...	...	...	...	...	...	...	
Darrang	19	...	829	1,129	17	33	8	13	...	...	34	43	...	...	
Nowgong	...	1	126	123	4	4	...	1	...	...	1	1	...	...	
Sibsagar	10	4	3,608	3,667	121	116	160	190	...	...	7	7	...	...	
Lakhimpur	86	42	1,877	2,292	112	153	133	139	1	3	22	3	...	...	

Province or District.	Bhar. Hindu. Males.	Bhar. Hindu. Females.	Bhat. Hindu. Males.	Bhat. Hindu. Females.	Bhatiya. Hindu. Males.	Bhatiya. Hindu. Females.	Bhil. Hindu. Males.	Bhil. Hindu. Females.	Bhogta. Hindu. Males.	Bhogta. Hindu. Females.	Bhotia. Buddhist. Males.	Bhotia. Buddhist. Females.	Remarks.
1	46	47	48	49	50	51	52	53	54	55	56	57	58
ASSAM	***4,669***	***5,036***	***39***	***57***	***2***	***1***	***135***	***123***	***3,404***	***3,245***	***8***	***7***	Bhar includes (3+2) Animists in Lakhimpur. Bhat includes (4+3) Animists in Sibsagar. Bhil includes (10+11) Animists, *viz.*, Sibsagar (6+7) and Lakhimpur (4+6). Bhogta includes (18+19) Animists, *viz.*, Sibsagar (11+16) and Lakhimpur (7+3). Bhotia includes (1+3) Animists in Lakhimpur.
SURMA VALLEY DISTRICTS ...	***4,555***	***4,942***	***17***	***42***	...	...	***123***	***106***	***1,363***	***1,311***	***1***	***2***	
Cachar	1,203	1,082	...	37	...	...	118	93	791	758	1	2	
Sylhet	3,352	3,860	17	5	...	...	5	13	572	553	...	...	
ASSAM VALLEY DISTRICTS	***114***	***94***	***22***	***15***	***2***	***1***	***12***	***17***	***2,041***	***1,934***	***7***	***5***	
Goalpara	...	...	...	...	...	...	...	...	...	...	...	...	
Kamrup	...	1	...	...	1	...	...	...	156	135	...	...	
Darrang	9	16	7	4	...	1	...	2	267	256	...	...	
Nowgong	10	11	2	1	...	...	...	...	299	313	5	2	
Sibsagar	62	48	4	3	...	...	8	9	917	876	...	...	
Lakhimpur	33	18	9	7	1	...	4	6	402	354	2	3	

PROVINCIAL TABLE V.—TEA-GARDEN POPULATION BY CASTE. PART A.—HINDUS, ANIMISTS, BUDDHISTS, etc.—*continued.*

Province or District.	Bhuiya.				Bhumij.				Bind.		Binjhia.		Birhor.		Remarks.
	Hindu.		Animist.		Hindu.		Animist.		Hindu.		Hindu.		Hindu.		
	Males.	Females.	Males.	Females.	Males.	Females.	Males.	Females.	Males.	Females.	Males.	Females.	Males.	Females.	
1	59	60	61	62	63	64	65	66	67	68	69	70	71	72	73
Assam	***21,874***	***21,140***	***577***	***525***	***11,513***	***12,659***	***194***	***201***	***776***	***897***	***285***	***308***	***108***	***121***	Binjhia includes (43+58) Animists, *viz.*, Darrang (42+55) and Lakhimpur (1+3). Birhor includes (9+7) Animists, *viz.*, Sylhet (2+0), Nowgong (0+4) and Lakhimpur (7+3).
Surma Valley Districts	***6,450***	***16,055***	...	...	***3,396***	***3,523***	...	...	***703***	***883***	***9***	***27***	***7***	***22***	
Cachar	3,1[illegible]8	2,9[illegible]6	...	...	1,7[illegible]9	1,797	...	...	72	147	4	23	3	14	
Sylhet	3,3[illegible]2	3,1[illegible]9	...	...	1,[illegible]87	1,7[illegible]	...	...	631	736	5	4	4	8	
Assam Valley Districts	***15,424***	***15,085***	***577***	***525***	***8,117***	***9,124***	***194***	***201***	***73***	***14***	***276***	***281***	***101***	***99***	
Goalpara	11	10	...	...	12	10	...	...	...	...	...	...	...	...	
Kamrup	67	102	...	...	93	101	...	...	1	...	...	...	...	...	
Darrang	2,059	2,080	143	148	1,1[illegible]6	1,414	50	59	37	3	121	1[illegible]3	...	4	
Nowgong	368	4[illegible]7	...	...	368	452	...	...	...	...	19	20	...	5	
Sibsagar	8,475	8,267	344	311	3,2[illegible]9	3,424	53	39	13	8	36	20	34	19	
Lakhimpur	4,403	4,189	90	7[illegible]	3,2[illegible]9	3,723	91	103	23	3	100	118	67	71	

Province or District.	Boria.		Brahman.		Chamar.				Chasa.		Chero.		Chik (Baraik).		Remarks.
	Hindu.		Hindu.		Hindu.		Animist.		Hindu.		Hindu.		Hindu.		
	Males.	Females.	Males.	Females.	Males.	Females.	Males.	Females.	Males.	Females.	Males.	Females.	Males.	Females.	
1	74	75	76	77	78	79	80	81	82	83	84	85	86	87	88
Assam	***18***	***17***	***2,949***	***1,301***	***17,799***	***18,652***	***139***	***143***	***1,820***	***1,778***	***539***	***422***	***1,787***	***1,774***	Boria includes (0+1) Animist in Sibsagar. Brahman includes (2+1) Sikhs in Darrang and (15+1) Jains, *viz.*, Darrang (8+0) and Sibsagar (7+0). Chasa includes (10+3) Animists, *viz.*, Sibsagar (3+3) and Lakhimpur (7+0). Chero includes (5+5) Animists, *viz.*, Sibsagar (5+3) and Lakhimpur (0+2). Chik (Baraik) includes (19+21) Animists, *viz.*, Darrang (3+5), Nowgong (1+0), Sibsagar (8+11) and Lakhimpur, 7+5
Surma Valley Districts	...	...	***1,335***	***714***	***13,414***	***14,465***	...	...	***711***	***716***	***35***	***32***	***507***	***488***	
Cachar	...	...	642	295	5,063	4,990	...	...	386	394	...	...	244	234	
Sylhet	...	...	693	419	8,351	9,475	...	...	325	322	35	32	263	254	
Assam Valley Districts	***18***	***17***	***1,614***	***587***	***4,385***	***4,187***	***139***	***143***	***1,109***	***1,062***	***504***	***390***	***1,280***	***1,286***	
Goalpara	...	...	2	3	...	...	...	...	...	...	...	...	...	1	
Kamrup	...	...	6	5	16	...	...	...	...	...	...	...	2	6	
Darrang	10	12	245	82	682	639	...	1	98	85	81	56	340	277	
Nowgong	1	...	63	25	224	205	1	...	285	252	6	4	46	39	
Sibsagar	5	4	863	371	2,599	2,602	123	110	500	530	327	219	346	378	
Lakhimpur	2	1	435	101	864	741	15	32	217	195	90	111	546	585	

PROVINCIAL TABLE V.—Tea-Garden Population by Caste. Part A.—Hindus, Animists, Buddhists, etc.—*continued.*

Province or District.	Chinese. Buddhist. Males.	Chinese. Buddhist. Females.	Chutiya. Hindu. Males.	Chutiya. Hindu. Females.	Dhanuk. Hindu. Males.	Dhanuk. Hindu. Females.	Dhenwar. Hindu. Males.	Dhenwar. Hindu. Females.	Dhoba. Hindu. Males.	Dhoba. Hindu. Females.	Dom. Hindu. Males.	Dom. Hindu. Females.	Dom. Animist. Males.	Dom. Animist. Females.	Remarks.
1	89	90	91	92	93	94	95	96	97	98	99	100	101	102	03
ASSAM	*73*	*3*	*451*	*164*	*76*	*69*	*226*	*225*	*1,953*	*1,665*	*7,036*	*7,236*	*447*	*464*	Dhoba includes (0+2) Animists in Lakhimpur.
SURMA VALLEY DISTRICTS ...	*4*	...	*1*	...	*35*	*22*	*2*	*9*	*1,035*	*866*	*2,297*	*2,275*	...	...	
Cachar	2	...	...	...	28	21	2	8	405	344	1,366	1,486	...	...	
Sylhet	2	...	1	...	7	1	...	1	630	522	861	789	...	...	
ASSAM VALLEY DISTRICTS	*69*	*3*	*450*	*164*	*41*	*47*	*224*	*216*	*918*	*799*	*4,799*	*4,961*	*447*	*464*	
Goalpara	...	...	...	...	...	...	...	...	1	...	4	2	...	...	
Kamrup	...	...	...	...	...	1	...	...	8	4	11	...	...	...	
Darrang	43	3	11	2	1	1	10	34	182	74	812	819	2	3	
Nowgong	6	...	6	4	6	...	101	131	[illegible]	38	144	143	...	...	
Sibsagar	14	...	240	49	21	36	57	15	444	361	1,547	1.602	263	272	
Lakhimpur	6	...	193	109	13	9	47	36	[illegible]	322	2,281	2,305	182	189	

Province or District.	Dosadh. Hindu. Males.	Dosadh. Hindu. Females.	Gareri. Hindu. Males.	Gareri. Hindu. Females.	Garo. Hindu. Males.	Garo. Hindu. Females.	Garo. Animist. Males.	Garo. Animist. Females.	Gaur. Hindu. Males.	Gaur. Hindu. Females.	Gaur. Animist. Males.	Gaur. Animist. Females.	Remarks.
1	104	105	106	107	108	109	110	111	112	113	114	115	116
ASSAM	*2,801*	*2,831*	*661*	*491*	*40*	*8*	*483*	*454*	*850*	*863*	*151*	*156*	
SURMA VALLEY DISTRICTS ...	*1,936*	*1,961*	*435*	*340*	*4*	*8*	...	...	...	...	...	...	Dosadh includes (1+5) Animists, *viz.*, Sibsagar (0+3) and Lakhimpur 1+2). Gareri includes (50+18) Animists, *viz.*, Darrang (0+1) and Sibsagar (50+17).
Cachar	1,049	994	198	202	4	8	...	...	...	...	...	...	
Sylhet	887	967	237	138	...	...	...	...	...	...	...	...	
ASSAM VALLEY DISTRICTS ...	*865*	*870*	*226*	*151*	*36*	...	*483*	*454*	*850*	*863*	*151*	*156*	
Goalpara	...	...	...	...	...	...	5	...	...	...	...	...	
Kamrup	...	2	...	...	...	...	82	83	...	12	...	...	
Darrang	93	82	18	18	...	...	135	132	401	372	...	...	
Nowgong	13	7	15	59	...	...	138	125	...	2	14	14	
Sibsagar	541	598	129	61	24	...	123	114	416	437	13	...	
Lakhimpur	218	181	64	13	12	...	...	...	33	40	124	142	

PROVINCIAL TABLE V.—TEA-GARDEN POPULATION BY CASTE. PART A.—HINDUS, ANIMISTS, BUDDHISTS, etc.—*continued.*

PROVINCE OR DISTRICT.	GHASI.				GHATWAL.		GOALA.		GOND (GONR).				GORAIT.		REMARKS.
	HINDU.		ANIMIST.		HINDU.		HINDU.		HINDU.		ANIMIST.		HINDU.		
	Males.	Females.	Males.	Females.	Males.	Females.	Males.	Females.	Males.	Females.	Males.	Females.	Males.	Females.	
1	117	118	119	120	121	122	123	124	125	126	127	128	129	130	131
ASSAM	*5,170*	*5,286*	*394*	*469*	*1,694*	*1,736*	*8,227*	*7,705*	*15,829*	*15,258*	*1,949*	*2,092*	*1,266*	*1,324*	Gorait includes (78+81) Animists, *viz.*, Darrang (17+28), Nowgong (0+1), Sibsagar (25+19) and Lakhimpur (36+33).
SURMA VALLEY DISTRICTS ...	*1,585*	*1,544*	...	...	*1,694*	*1,736*	*2,402*	*2,545*	*5,096*	*4,785*	*60*	*57*	*380*	*347*	
Cachar	909	917	...	...	1,001	1,053	990	945	2,691	2,588	60	57	170	179	
Sylhet	676	627	...	...	693	683	1,412	1,600	2,405	2,197	...	...	210	168	
ASSAM VALLEY DISTRICTS ...	*3,585*	*3,742*	*394*	*469*	...	...	*5,825*	*5,160*	*10,733*	*10,473*	*1,889*	*2,035*	*886*	*977*	
Goalpara	4	...	...	...	...	...	6	2	1	...	...	...	...	...	
Kamrup	...	1	...	...	...	...	26	19	54	55	...	...	...	...	
Darrang	478	557	14	24	...	...	1,026	923	2,188	2,263	388	402	97	104	
Nowgong	6	...	209	246	...	...	234	316	28	1	853	945	78	100	
Sibsagar	1,624	1,719	74	72	...	...	2,158	1,847	3,830	3,764	225	258	394	400	
Lakhimpur	1,473	1,465	97	127	...	...	2,2.5	2,053	4,632	4,370	423	430	317	373	

PROVINCE OR DISTRICT.	GRAHABIPRA (GANAK).		HAJJAM.		HALWAI.		HARI.		JHORA.		JOGI (JUGI).		REMARKS.
	HINDU.		HINDU.		HINDU.		HINDU.		HINDU.		HINDU.		
	Males.	Females.	Males.	Females.	Males.	Females.	Males.	Females.	Males.	Females.	Males.	Females.	
1	132	133	134	135	136	137	138	139	140	141	142	143	144
ASSAM	*47*	*15*	*160*	*100*	*145*	*88*	*1,234*	*1,346*	*306*	*306*	*622*	*430*	
SURMA VALLEY DISTRICTS ...	*2*	*9*	*38*	*50*	*48*	*30*	*451*	*497*	*178*	*189*	*331*	*194*	Halwai includes (2+1) Animists, *viz.*, Nowgong (2+0) and Lakhimpur (0+1).
Cachar	2	4	38	50	43	23	348	376	...	...	126	113	Hari includes (5+4) Animists, *viz.*, Sibsagar (5+3) and Lakhimpur (0+1).
Sylhet	...	5	...	...	5	7	103	121	178	189	205	81	
ASSAM VALLEY DISTRICTS ...	*45*	*6*	*122*	*50*	*97*	*58*	*783*	*849*	*128*	*117*	*291*	*236*	Jhora includes (4+0) Animists in Darrang.
Goalpara	...	...	...	...	...	...	...	...	...	...	...	...	
Kamrup	1	...	1	...	...	...	1	1	...	...	1	3	
Darrang	22	...	13	4	17	14	182	209	90	69	92	84	
Nowgong	...	...	...	...	13	6	34	46	14	15	10	7	
Sibsagar	22	6	44	21	34	15	280	323	...	14	86	66	
Lakhimpur	...	...	64	25	33	23	286	270	24	19	102	76	

PROVINCIAL TABLE V.—Tea-garden Population by Caste. Part A.—Hindus, Animists, Buddhists, etc.—*continued.*

Province or District.	Kachari. Hindu. Males.	Kachari. Hindu. Females.	Kachari. Animist. Males.	Kachari. Animist. Females.	Kahar. Hindu. Males.	Kahar. Hindu. Females.	Kaibartta. Hindu. Males.	Kaibartta. Hindu. Females.	Kalita. Hindu. Males.	Kalita. Hindu. Females.	Kalu. Hindu. Males.	Kalu. Hindu. Females.	Kalwar. Hindu. Males.	Kalwar. Hindu. Females.	Remarks.
1	145	146	141	148	149	150	151	152	153	154	155	156	157	158	159
ASSAM	***3,673***	***910***	***3,952***	***1,006***	***1,987***	***1,716***	***603***	***528***	***764***	***166***	***446***	***379***	***740***	***645***	Kahari includes (4+2) Animists, *viz.*, Darrang (1+0), Nowgong (1+0), Sibsagar (1+2) and Lakhimpur (1+0).
SURMA VALLEY DISTRICTS ...	*135*	*96*	*28*	*1*	*1,128*	*1,163*	*271*	*148*	*3*	*3*	*399*	*361*	*369*	*363*	Kaibartta includes Kaibartta Chasi (Mahishya) (265+140) and Kaibartta Jaliya (297+341).
Cachar	105	96	2	...	531	532	106	58	...	3	193	194	210	160	Kalu includes (1+0) Animists in Nowgong.
Sylhet	30	...	26	1	607	681	165	90	3	...	206	167	159	203	
ASSAM VALLEY DISTRICTS	*3,538*	*814*	*3,924*	*1,005*	*859*	*553*	*332*	*380*	*761*	*163*	*47*	*18*	*371*	*282*	Kalwar includes (59+27) Animists, *viz.*, Sibsagar (56+27) and Lakhimpur 3+0).
Goalpara	...	...	...	...	...	...	...	...	...	...	...	...	...	...	
Kamrup	2	5	179	107	...	3	4	10	11	...	...	...	...	...	
Darrang	549	101	2,783	750	151	63	35	35	170	40	11	1	20	16	
Nowgong	...	...	298	119	44	27	11	12	61	19	2	...	8	10	
Sibsagar	1,725	275	455	28	386	285	237	200	383	75	7	8	209	223	
Lakhimpur...	1,262	483	219	1	278	175	45	33	136	29	27	9	44	33	

Province or District.	Kamar. Hindu. Males.	Kamar. Hindu. Females.	Kamar. Animist. Males.	Kamar. Animist. Females.	Kami. Hindu. Males.	Kami. Hindu. Females.	Kandh. Hindu. Males.	Kandh. Hindu. Females.	Kandh. Animist. Males.	Kandh. Animist. Females.	Kora. Hindu. Males.	Kora. Hindu. Females.	Kandu. Hindu. Males.	Kandu. Hindu. Females.	Remarks.
1	160	161	162	163	164	165	166	167	168	169	170	171	172	173	174
ASSAM	***11,862***	***11,892***	***204***	***200***	***22***	***18***	***1,674***	***1,704***	***723***	***621***	***880***	***494***	***180***	***230***	Kami includes (4+0) Buddhists, *viz.*, Darrang (2+0) and Sibsagar (2+0).
SURMA VALLEY DISTRICTS ...	*3,596*	*3,675*	*11*	*7*	...	...	*216*	*225*	...	...	*544*	*370*	*150*	*205*	Kandu includes (5+2) Animists in Sibsagar.
Cachar	1,878	1,765	...	...	...	...	149	159	...	...	76	68	150	205	Kaora includes (2+0) Animists in Darrang.
Sylhet	1,718	1,920	11	7	...	...	67	66	...	...	468	302	...	...	
ASSAM VALLEY DISTRICTS	*8,266*	*8,217*	*193*	*193*	*22*	*18*	*1,458*	*1,479*	*723*	*621*	*336*	*124*	*30*	*25*	
Goalpara	28	35	...	...	...	...	...	...	...	...	...	...	...	...	
Kamrup	94	75	...	...	...	...	...	...	...	...	...	...	...	...	
Darrang	1,308	1,392	...	...	14	12	452	282	343	333	...	40	2	16	
Nowgong	197	251	1	...	...	...	34	22	...	...	5	4	...	...	
Sibsagar	3,320	3,212	70	82	2	...	272	384	39	35	156	79	28	8	
Lakhimpur...	3,223	3,252	122	111	6	6	700	791	341	253	175	1	...	1	

PROVINCIAL TABLE V.—TEA-GARDEN POPULATION BY CASTE. PART A.—HINDUS, ANIMISTS, BUDDHISTS, ETC.—*continued.*

Province or District.	Kaur. Hindu. Males.	Kaur. Hindu. Females.	Kayastha. Hindu. Males.	Kayastha. Hindu. Females.	Kewat. Hindu. Males.	Kewat. Hindu. Females.	Khadal. Hindu. Males.	Khadal. Hindu. Females.	Khaira. Hindu. Males.	Khaira. Hindu. Females.	Khambu. Hindu. Males.	Khambu. Hindu. Females.	Khandait. Hindu. Males.	Khandait. Hindu. Females.	Remarks.
1	175	176	177	178	179	180	181	182	183	184	185	186	187	188	189
ASSAM	***468***	***426***	***2,395***	***1,259***	***1,418***	***1,399***	***1,545***	***1,705***	***290***	***44***	***88***	***41***	***606***	***507***	Kayastha includes (3+0) Brahmos in Darrang.
SURMA VALLEY DISTRICTS	***212***	***231***	***1,551***	***783***	***329***	***360***	***690***	***780***	***90***	***94***	...	...	***225***	***177***	Kewat includes (7+3) Animists, *viz.*, Nowgong (1+0), Sibsagar (4+0) and Lakhimpur (2+3).
Cachar	98	118	863	397	177	161	...	...	...	...	...	...	80	108	Khadal includes (43+54) Animists, *viz.*, Darrang (41+49), Sibsagar (2+1) and Lakhimpur (0+4).
Sylhet	114	113	688	386	152	199	690	780	90	94	...	...	145	69	Khaira includes (7+0) Animists in Darrang.
ASSAM VALLEY DISTRICTS	***256***	***195***	***844***	***476***	***1,089***	***1,039***	***855***	***925***	***200***	***150***	***88***	***41***	***381***	***330***	Khambu includes (6+0) Buddhists, *viz.*, Sibsagar (2+0) and Lakhimpur (4+0).
Goalpara	...	...	3	...	2	1	...	...	...	...	...	...	...	...	
Kamrup	...	...	15	10	4	2	...	...	23	10	1	1	1	...	
Darrang	106	86	169	83	194	150	623	609	22	18	4	2	147	119	
Nowgong	2	1	85	37	65	55	...	...	...	...	...	...	30	31	
Sibsagar	84	74	281	203	487	399	206	294	39	71	42	19	131	131	
Lakhimpur	64	34	291	143	337	432	26	22	116	48	41	19	72	49	

Province or District.	Kharia. Hindu. Males.	Kharia. Hindu. Females.	Kharia. Animist. Males.	Kharia. Animist. Females.	Kharwar. Hindu. Males.	Kharwar. Hindu. Females.	Khasi. Hindu. Males.	Khasi. Hindu. Females.	Khasi. Animist. Males.	Khasi. Animist. Females.	Koch. Hindu. Males.	Koch. Hindu. Females.	Koiri. Hindu. Males.	Koiri. Hindu. Females.	Remarks.
1	190	191	192	193	194	195	196	197	198	199	200	201	202	203	204
ASSAM	***3,536***	***3,497***	***637***	***641***	***2,094***	***2,067***	***98***	***60***	***106***	***91***	***1,488***	***1,058***	***4,108***	***2,868***	Kharwar includes (19+29) Animists, *viz.*, Darrang (15+20), Sibsagar (2+3) and Lakhimpur (2+6).
SURMA VALLEY DISTRICTS	***1,166***	***1,067***	...	...	***359***	***440***	***41***	***49***	***105***	***87***	***560***	***594***	***2,859***	***2,019***	Koiri includes (3+4) Animists, *viz.*, Darrang (0+1), Sibsagar (2+2) and Lakhimpur (0+1).
Cachar	648	607	...	...	203	232	21	18	76	60	204	219	760	708	
Sylhet	518	460	...	...	156	208	20	31	29	27	356	375	2,099	1,311	
ASSAM VALLEY DISTRICTS	***2,370***	***2,430***	***637***	***641***	***1,735***	***1,627***	***57***	***11***	***1***	***4***	***928***	***464***	***1,249***	***849***	
Goalpara	...	...	...	...	...	...	...	...	...	...	...	...	2	...	
Kamrup	12	6	...	...	2	...	2	...	...	...	247	189	4	4	
Darrang	451	490	206	227	590	646	53	3	...	...	265	175	148	112	
Nowgong	1	4	116	99	20	23	...	...	1	2	60	16	79	66	
Sibsagar	633	655	43	43	403	376	...	6	...	2	245	39	639	507	
Lakhimpur	1,273	1,275	272	272	720	582	2	2	...	...	111	45	377	160	

PROVINCIAL TABLE V.—TEA-GARDEN POPULATION BY CASTE. PART A.—HINDUS, ANIMISTS, BUDDHISTS, ETC.—*continued.*

PROVINCE OR DISTRICT.	KOL.		KORA.		KORWA.				KSHATTRIYA (MANIPUR).		KUMHAR.		KURMI.		REMARKS.
	HINDU.		HINDU.		HINDU.		ANIMIST.		HINDU.		HINDU.		HINDU.		
	Males.	Females.	Males.	Females.	Males.	Females.	Males.	Females.	Males.	Females.	Males.	Females.	Males.	Females.	
1	205	206	207	208	209	210	211	212	213	214	215	216	217	218	219
ASSAM	***1,669***	***1,640***	***1,366***	***1,986***	***1,150***	***1,146***	***219***	***248***	***751***	***532***	***1,411***	***1,294***	***6,091***	***5,422***	
SURMA VALLEY DISTRICTS	***1,669***	***1,640***	***398***	***1,150***	***341***	***245***	...	...	***647***	***479***	***911***	***866***	***2,861***	***2,528***	
Cachar	1,166	1,042	165	180	202	193	...	...	568	438	365	365	1,208	1,009	Kora includes (35+32) Animists, *viz.*, Darrang (12+16), Sibsagar (13+11) and Lakhimpur (10+5).
Sylhet	503	598	233	970	139	52	...	...	79	41	546	501	1,653	1,519	Kshattriya includes (1+0) Sikh in Lakhimpur.
ASSAM VALLEY DISTRICTS	...	...	***968***	***836***	***809***	***901***	***219***	***248***	***104***	***53***	***500***	***428***	***3,230***	***2,894***	
Goalpara	...	...	...	...	...	...	...	...	...	...	...	3	2	...	Kumhar includes (0+3) Animists in Lakhimpur.
Kamrup	...	...	6	8	...	...	...	...	...	...	4	1	...	3	Kurmi includes (8+8) Animist, *viz.*, Darrang (1+0), Nowgong (0+1), Sibsagar, (2+4) and Lakhimpur (5+3).
Darrang	...	...	86	74	130	134	200	237	13	8	71	98	445	363	
Nowgong	...	...	26	16	49	59	16	11	3	1	32	14	98	85	
Sibsagar	...	...	617	595	276	324	...	...	24	5	149	132	1,454	1,340	
Lakhimpur	...	...	233	143	354	384	3	...	64	39	244	180	1,231	1,103	

PROVINCE OR DISTRICT.	LIMBU.		LODHA.		LOHAR.		MAHESRI.		MAHLI.				MAL.		REMARKS.
	HINDU.		HINDU.		HINDU.		HINDU.		HINDU.		ANIMIST.		HINDU.		
	Males.	Females.	Males.	Females.	Males.	Females.	Males.	Females.	Males.	Females.	Males.	Females.	Males.	Females.	
1	220	221	222	223	224	225	226	227	228	229	230	231	232	233	234
ASSAM	***94***	***29***	***530***	***486***	***4,169***	***4,203***	***149***	***22***	***2,545***	***2,361***	***54***	***150***	***2,571***	***2,213***	Lodha includes (0+2) Animists in Sibsagar.
SURMA VALLEY DISTRICTS	...	...	***311***	***296***	***1,274***	***1,160***	...	...	***430***	***419***	***2***	***1***	***1,290***	***765***	Lohar includes (43+52) Animists, *viz.*, Darrang (2+0), Sibsagar (3+2) and Lakhimpur (38+50).
Cachar	...	...	271	265	597	565	...	...	368	367	...	...	1,290	765	Mahesri includes (4+0) Jains, *viz.*, Sibsagar (3+0) and Lakhimpur (1+0).
Sylhet	...	...	40	31	677	505	...	...	62	52	2	1	...	...	
ASSAM VALLEY DISTRICTS	***94***	***29***	***219***	***190***	***2,895***	***3,043***	***149***	***22***	***2,115***	***1,942***	***52***	***149***	***1,281***	***1,448***	Mal includes (189+195) Animists, *viz.*, Sibsagar (52+49) and Lakhimpur (137+146).
Goalpara	...	...	...	...	4	4	...	...	...	...	...	...	1	...	
Kamrup	1	2	5	2	4	8	...	...	...	2	...	...	1	2	
Darrang	42	11	42	18	281	303	14	4	414	265	1	5	138	122	
Nowgong	5	...	6	8	159	181	3	...	...	...	40	50	55	62	
Sibsagar	...	...	133	135	708	725	104	18	868	827	...	81	661	780	
Lakhimpur	46	16	33	27	1,739	1,822	28	...	833	848	11	13	425	482	

PROVINCIAL TABLE V.—Tea-garden Population by Caste. Part A.—Hindus, Animists, Buddhists, etc.—*continued.*

Province or District.	Mali (Malakar). Hindu. Males.	Mali (Malakar). Hindu. Females.	Mallah. Hindu. Males.	Mallah. Hindu. Females.	Malo. Hindu. Males.	Malo. Hindu. Females.	Malpaharia. Hindu. Males.	Malpaharia. Hindu. Females.	Malpaharia. Animist. Males.	Malpaharia. Animist. Females.	Mangar. Hindu. Males.	Mangar. Hindu. Females.	Mangar. Animist. Males.	Mangar. Animist. Females.	Remarks.
1	235	236	237	238	239	240	241	242	243	244	245	246	247	248	249
ASSAM	*702*	*789*	*336*	*300*	*856*	*1,346*	*1,438*	*1,469*	*107*	*99*	*101*	*31*	*204*	*196*	Malo includes (3+0) Animists in Sibsagar.
SURMA VALLEY DISTRICTS	*395*	*495*	*140*	*126*	*500*	*1,041*	*60*	*58*	...	...	...	...	...	...	
Cachar	196	242	3	2	161	603	...	...	...	...	...	...	...	...	
Sylhet	199	253	137	124	339	438	60	56	...	...	...	...	...	...	
ASSAM VALLEY DISTRICTS	*307*	*294*	*196*	*174*	*356*	*305*	*1,378*	*1,406*	*107*	*99*	*101*	*31*	*204*	*196*	
Goalpara	...	...	...	...	...	...	7	12	...	...	...	...	...	...	
Kamrup	...	1	...	...	...	...	35	46	...	...	2	2	...	...	
Darrang	31	41	21	26	...	10	74	82	48	32	47	10	204	196	
Nowgong	11	11	...	1	...	1	250	270	2	2	...	...	...	...	
Sibsagar	107	49	58	68	232	233	153	96	22	17	41	...	...	...	
Lakhimpur...	158	192	117	79	124	61	850	900	35	48	11	19	...	...	

Province or District.	Manjhi. Hindu. Males.	Manjhi. Hindu. Females.	Marwari. Hindu. Males.	Marwari. Hindu. Females.	Maulik (Naiya). Hindu. Males.	Maulik (Naiya). Hindu. Females.	Mayra. Hindu. Males.	Mayra. Hindu. Females.	Mech. Hindu. Males.	Mech. Hindu. Females.	Mech. Animist. Males.	Mech. Animist. Females.	Mehtar. Hindu. Males.	Mehtar. Hindu. Females	Remarks.
1	250	251	252	253	254	255	256	257	258	259	260	261	262	263	264
ASSAM	*656*	*625*	*51*	*27*	*1,898*	*1,818*	*159*	*146*	*46*	*28*	*33*	*2*	*26*	*36*	Manjhi includes (2+3) Animists in Darrang.
SURMA VALLEY DISTRICTS	*357*	*312*	*4*	*4*	*889*	*847*	*30*	*18*	...	...	...	...	*14*	*31*	Maulik (Naiya) includes (2+0) Animists in Lakhimpur.
Cachar	276	256	4	1	870	826	26	16	...	...	...	...	...	11	Mayra includes (1+0) Animist in Kamrup.
Sylhet	81	56	...	3	19	21	4	2	...	...	...	...	14	20	
ASSAM VALLEY DISTRICTS	*299*	*313*	*47*	*23*	*1,009*	*971*	*129*	*128*	*46*	*28*	*33*	*2*	*12*	*5*	Mech (Hindu) includes (4+0) Brahmos in Darrang.
Goalpara	...	...	...	...	...	...	...	...	...	...	...	...	...	...	
Kamrup	...	...	...	...	146	121	1	...	...	...	...	...	7	3	
Darrang	5	4	7	...	53	31	13	8	4	...	30	1	...	...	
Nowgong	...	...	2	...	12	4	...	2	...	...	2	1	...	...	
Sibsagar	20	63	22	5	640	703	69	58	2	...	1	...	...	...	
Lakhimpur	274	256	16	18	158	112	46	60	40	28	...	...	5	2	

PROVINCIAL TABLE V.—Tea-garden Population by Caste.—Part A.—Hindus, Animists, Buddhists, etc.—*continued.*

Province or District.	Mikir. Hindu. Males.	Mikir. Hindu. Females.	Mikir. Animist. Males.	Mikir. Animist. Females.	Minor Castes.* Males.	Minor Castes.* Females.	Muchi. Hindu. Males.	Muchi. Hindu. Females.	Muchi. Animist. Males.	Muchi. Animist. Females.	Munda. Hindu. Males.	Munda. Hindu. Females.	Munda. Animist. Males.	Munda. Animist. Females.	Remarks.
1	265	266	267	268	269	270	271	272	273	274	275	276	277	278	279
ASSAM	*191*	*184*	*649*	*536*	*6,231*	*4,533*	*1,267*	*1,294*	*43*	*33*	*19,717*	*19,023*	*7,117*	*7,252*	* For details of minor castes see Appendix.
SURMA VALLEY DISTRICTS ...	*133*	*133*	*90*	*86*	*2,054*	*1,429*	*367*	*347*	...	...	*4,930*	*4,572*	*173*	*170*	
Cachar	133	133	90	86	872	745	...	...	...	...	2,279	2,203	158	152	
Sylhet	...	...	...	...	1,182	684	367	347	...	...	2,651	2,369	15	18	
ASSAM VALLEY DISTRICTS	*58*	*51*	*559*	*450*	*4,177*	*3,104*	*900*	*947*	*43*	*33*	*14,787*	*14,451*	*6,944*	*7,082*	
Goalpara	...	...	...	...	64	52	...	...	...	...	18	12	30	32	
Kamrup	...	...	110	46	115	94	7	5	...	...	127	104	...	...	
Darrang	54	49	64	48	793	516	169	168	3	...	1,837	1,722	2,396	2,524	
Nowgong	...	...	369	344	270	123	5	6	...	...	...	4	544	577	
Sibsagar	...	...	16	12	1,062	999	554	538	36	29	4,774	4,814	577	583	
Lakhimpur	4	2	...	...	1,926	1,318	165	230	4	4	8,031	7,795	3,397	3,366	

Province or District.	Muriyari. Hindu. Males.	Muriyari. Hindu. Females.	Murmi. Hindu. Males.	Murmi. Hindu. Females.	Mushar. Hindu. Males.	Mushar. Hindu. Females.	Nadiyal. Hindu. Males.	Nadiyal. Hindu. Females.	Naga (Total). Animist. Males.	Naga (Total). Animist. Females.	Nagesia. Hindu. Males.	Nagesia. Hindu. Females.	Naik. Hindu. Males.	Naik. Hindu. Females.	Remarks.
1	280	281	282	283	284	285	286	287	288	289	290	291	292	293	294
ASSAM	*350*	*304*	*56*	*11*	*4,869*	*4,712*	*55*	*30*	*415*	*101*	*367*	*384*	*237*	*194*	Muriyari includes (34+42) Animists in Darrang. Murmi includes (6+2) Buddhists, *viz.*, Cachar (2+2) and Lakhimpur (4+0). Mushar includes (9+2) Animists, *viz.*, Sylhet (0+1), Sibsagar (0+1) and Lakhimpur (9+0). Nagesia includes (1+0) Animist in Lakhimpur.
SURMA VALLEY DISTRICTS	...	...	*2*	*7*	*3,795*	*3,685*	...	...	*33*	*38*	...	...	*219*	*172*	
Cachar	...	...	2	2	2,316	2,187	...	...	33	38	...	...	79	78	
Sylhet	...	...	...	5	1,479	1,498	...	...	...	...	...	...	140	94	
ASSAM VALLEY DISTRICTS	*350*	*304*	*54*	*4*	*1,074*	*1,027*	*55*	*30*	*382*	*63*	*367*	*384*	*18*	*22*	
Goalpara	...	...	...	...	1	...	...	...	...	...	...	...	...	...	
Kamrup	10	11	2	...	58	62	1	6	1	...	2	3	...	...	
Darrang	194	201	20	1	119	123	7	...	...	...	83	105	8	7	
Nowgong	...	...	...	...	5	2	1	5	...	...	8	9	1	...	
Sibsagar	146	92	6	2	703	680	25	11	249	63	72	48	8	12	
Lakhimpur	...	...	26	1	188	160	21	8	132	...	202	219	1	3	

PROVINCIAL TABLE V.—TEA-GARDEN POPULATION BY CASTE. PART A.—HINDUS, ANIMISTS, BUDDHISTS, etc.—*continued*.

Province or District.	NAMASUDRA. Hindu. Males.	NAMASUDRA. Hindu. Females.	NAPIT. Hindu. Males.	NAPIT. Hindu. Females.	NEPALI (UNSPECIFIED). Hindu. Males.	NEPALI (UNSPECIFIED). Hindu. Females.	NEPALI (UNSPECIFIED). Buddhist. Males.	NEPALI (UNSPECIFIED). Buddhist. Females.	NEWAR. Hindu. Males.	NEWAR. Hindu. Females.	NUNIYA. Hindu. Males.	NUNIYA. Hindu. Females.	Remarks.
1	295	296	297	298	299	300	301	302	303	304	305	306	307
ASSAM	***429***	***153***	***1,319***	***952***	***90***	***54***	***35***	***9***	***57***	***70***	***2,253***	***1,911***	Nepali (unspecified) (Hindu) includes (4+0) Animists, *viz.*, Cachar (1+0), Sibsagar (1+0) and Lakhimpur (2+0).
SURMA VALLEY DISTRICTS	***354***	***97***	***698***	***538***	***5***	***8***	***5***	***2***	...	***23***	***1,677***	***1,730***	
Cachar	311	90	301	288	5	8	...	...	...	...	882	901	Nuniya includes (1+0) Animist in Darrang.
Sylhet	43	7	307	250	...	...	5	2	...	23	795	829	
ASSAM VALLEY DISTRICTS	***75***	***56***	***621***	***414***	***85***	***46***	***30***	***7***	***57***	***47***	***576***	***181***	
Goalpara	3	...	...	...	...	...	...	...	...	...	1	1	
Kamrup	...	3	...	1	1	...	...	...	40	37	...	...	
Darrang	13	...	108	76	...	...	...	...	6	8	80	6	
Nowgong	1	32	16	12	...	1	...	...	...	...	9	...	
Sibsagar	17	...	301	195	18	10	4	...	3	2	375	125	
Lakhimpur	41	21	196	130	66	35	26	7	9	...	111	29	

Province or District.	ORAON. Hindu. Males.	ORAON. Hindu. Females.	ORAON. Animist. Males.	ORAON. Animist. Females.	ORIYA (UNSPECIFIED) Hindu. Males.	ORIYA (UNSPECIFIED) Hindu. Females.	OSWAL. Hindu. Males.	OSWAL. Hindu. Females.	OSWAL. Jain. Males.	OSWAL. Jain. Females.	PAN (PANIKA). Hindu. Males.	PAN (PANIKA). Hindu. Females.	PAN (PANIKA). Animist. Males.	PAN (PANIKA). Animist. Females.	Remarks.
1	308	309	310	311	312	313	314	315	316	317	318	319	320	321	322
ASSAM	***3,837***	***3,873***	***1,872***	***2,016***	***2,228***	***2,057***	***36***	***5***	***63***	***1***	***6,611***	***7,141***	***352***	***452***	
SURMA VALLEY DISTRICTS	***1,373***	***1,286***	***147***	***153***	***536***	***420***	...	...	...	...	***2,189***	***2,318***	...	...	Oriya (unspecified) includes (62+65) Animists, *viz.*, Darrang (1+0), Sibsagar (33+52) and Lakhimpur (28+13).
Cachar	750	769	147	153	96	85	...	...	...	...	824	891	...	...	
Sylhet	623	517	...	...	440	335	...	...	...	...	1,365	1,427	...	...	
ASSAM VALLEY DISTRICTS	***2,464***	***2,587***	***1,725***	***1,863***	***1,692***	***1,637***	***36***	***5***	***63***	***1***	***4,429***	***4,823***	***352***	***452***	
Goalpara	3	...	3	1	...	...	...	...	...	...	1	...	...	...	
Kamrup	27	35	5	9	17	16	...	...	...	...	38	49	...	...	
Darrang	253	287	490	551	186	210	...	...	34	...	835	898	1	2	
Nowgong	...	...	242	251	24	28	...	...	...	...	421	514	1	3	
Sibsagar	787	794	283	288	346	321	16	1	29	1	1,617	1,734	184	230	
Lakhimpur	1,394	1,471	702	763	1,119	1,062	30	4	...	...	1,510	1,638	166	217	

PROVINCIAL TABLE V.—TEA-GARDEN POPULATION BY CASTE. PART A.—HINDUS, ANIMISTS, BUDDHISTS, etc.—*continued.*

PROVINCE OR DISTRICT.	PASI.		PATNI.		PATWA.		POROJA.				PUNDARI (PURO).		REMARKS.
	HINDU.		HINDU.		HINDU.		HINDU.		ANIMIST.		HINDU.		
	Males.	Females.	Males.	Females.	Males.	Females.	Males.	Females.	Males.	Females.	Males.	Females.	
1	323	324	325	326	327	328	329	330	331	332	333	334	335
ASSAM	*2,354*	*2,440*	*485*	*294*	*102*	*73*	*1,927*	*1,823*	*1,073*	*992*	*54*	*4*	Pasi includes (8+8) Animists, *viz.*, Sibsagar (0+2) and Lakhimpur (8+6). Pundari (Puro) includes (8+0) Animists in Darrang.
SURMA VALLEY DISTRICTS ...	*1,996*	*2,205*	*473*	*290*	*9*	*7*	...	...	...	...	*1*	...	
Cachar	399	370	333	208	1	...	...	...	...	...	...	...	
Sylhet	1,597	1,835	140	82	8	7	...	...	...	...	1	...	
ASSAM VALLEY DISTRICTS ...	*358*	*235*	*12*	..	*93*	*66*	*1,927*	*1,823*	*1,073*	*992*	*53*	*4*	
Goalpara	...	...	...	...	...	...	...	...	...	...	...	...	
Kamrup	10	7	...	...	...	7	...	...	...	...	...	...	
Darrang	33	27	...	...	4	5	208	168	725	706	8	1	
Nowgong	11	5	...	...	4	...	...	...	...	...	...	...	
Sibsagar	263	171	12	4	59	28	231	218	38	38	5	3	
Lakhimpur	41	25	...	...	36	26	1,494	1,437	310	248	40	...	

PROVINCE OR DISTRICT.	RABHA.				RAJBANSI.		RAJBHAR.		RAJPUT (CHHATTRI).		RAJWAR.		REMARKS.
	HINDU.		ANIMIST.		HINDU.		HINDU.		HINDU.		HINDU.		
	Males.	Females.	Males.	Females.	Males.	Females.	Males.	Females.	Males.	Females.	Males.	Females.	
	336	337	338	339	340	341	342	343	344	345	346	347	348
ASSAM	*79*	*26*	*264*	*219*	*85*	*58*	*1,027*	*1,184*	*2,211*	*1,760*	*2,613*	*2,464*	Rajbhar includes (42+38) Animists in Darrang. Rajput (Chhattri) includes (2+2) Animists in Lakhimpur. Rajwar includes (4+10) Animists, *viz.*, Darrang (0+2), Sibsagar (1+2) and Lakhimpur (3+6).
SURMA VALLEY DISTRICTS ...	...	...	...	...	...	*5*	*877*	*1,047*	*1,056*	*777*	*955*	*836*	
Cachar	...	...	...	...	...	...	171	401	478	297	670	391	
Sylhet	...	...	...	...	...	5	706	646	578	480	285	445	
ASSAM VALLEY DISTRICTS ...	*79*	*26*	*264*	*219*	*85*	*53*	*150*	*137*	*1,155*	*983*	*1,658*	*1,628*	
Goalpara	...	...	...	...	15	14	...	...	6	...	...	...	
Kamrup	41	8	168	158	4	4	...	...	7	6	8	6	
Darrang	33	14	82	50	12	5	73	70	154	172	166	105	
Nowgong	...	...	14	17	4	2	2	3	43	42	45	52	
Sibsagar	...	...	...	...	13	...	57	50	468	356	875	852	
Lakhimpur	5	4	...	...	37	28	18	5	477	407	564	523	

PROVINCIAL TABLE V.—TEA-GARDEN POPULATION BY CASTE. PART A.—HINDUS, ANIMISTS, BUDDHISTS, etc.—*continued.*

Province or District.	BANTIA.		SADGOP.		SANTAL.				SAROGI.				Remarks.
	Hindu.		Hindu.		Hindu.		Animist.		Hindu.		Jain.		
	Males.	Females.	Males.	Females.	Males.	Females.	Males.	Females.	Males.	Females.	Males.	Females.	
1	349	350	351	352	353	354	355	356	357	358	359	360	361
ASSAM	***2,055***	***1,619***	***57***	***22***	***8,657***	***9,165***	***7,335***	***7,292***	***147***	***75***	***16***	...	Bantia includes (12+6) Animists, *viz.*, Darrang (3+2) and Lakhimpur (9+3).
SURMA VALLEY DISTRICTS	***810***	***679***	***8***	***4***	***1,799***	***1,640***	***1,900***	***1,865***	...	...	...	...	
Cachar	453	464	...	...	1,196	1,082	666	676	...	...	...	...	
Sylhet	357	215	8	4	603	558	1,234	1,189	...	...	...	...	
ASSAM VALLEY DISTRICTS	***1,245***	***940***	***49***	***18***	***6,858***	***7,595***	***5,435***	***5,427***	***147***	***75***	***16***	...	
Goalpara	...	...	...	...	...	...	30	39	...	...	...	...	
Kamrup	1	5	...	...	28	30	19	16	...	...	...	...	
Darrang	687	329	4	3	450	433	1,236	1,220	8	9	6	...	
Nowgong	18	29	1	...	...	1	309	370	...	...	...	...	
Sibsagar	420	405	5	4	2,977	2,998	1,831	1,735	29	27	2	...	
Lakhimpur	219	172	39	11	3,403	4,058	2,010	2,047	110	30	8	...	

Province or District.	SARKI.		SAVAR.				SHAHA.		SONAR.		SUDRA.		Remarks.
	Hindu.		Hindu.		Animist.		Hindu.		Hindu.		Hindu.		
	Males.	Females.	Males.	Females.	Males.	Females.	Males.	Females.	Males.	Females.	Males.	Females.	
1	362	363	364	365	366	367	368	369	370	371	372	373	374
ASSAM	***5***	***9***	***1,345***	***1,061***	***493***	***362***	***246***	***191***	***494***	***348***	***728***	***113***	
SURMA VALLEY DISTRICTS	...	...	***214***	***192***	...	...	***205***	***113***	***150***	***126***	***725***	***113***	
Cachar	...	...	30	70	...	...	63	47	150	96	371	92	
Sylhet	...	...	184	122	...	...	142	66	...	30	354	21	
ASSAM VALLEY DISTRICTS	***5***	***9***	***1,131***	***869***	***493***	***362***	***41***	***78***	***344***	***222***	***3***	...	
Goalpara	...	...	...	...	...	...	...	...	...	...	...	...	
Kamrup	...	...	5	4	...	...	2	...	29	19	...	...	
Darrang	1	1	192	140	48	37	1	...	37	15	...	...	
Nowgong	...	...	13	2	...	...	...	...	19	2	...	...	
Sibsagar	2	4	105	189	219	198	9	2	177	93	...	...	
Lakhimpur	2	4	816	534	156	127	29	76	82	93	3	...	

PROVINCIAL TABLE V.—TEA-GARDEN POPULATION BY CASTE. PART A.—HINDUS, ANIMISTS, BUDDHISTS, etc.—*concluded.*

Province or District.	Sunri. Hindu. Males.	Sunri. Hindu. Females.	Sunwar. Hindu. Males.	Sunwar. Hindu. Females.	Surahiya. Hindu. Males.	Surahiya. Hindu. Females.	Sutradhar. Hindu. Males.	Sutradhar. Hindu. Females.	Tanti. Hindu. Males.	Tanti. Hindu. Females.	Teli or Tili. Hindu. Males.	Teli or Tili. Hindu. Females.	Remarks.
1	375	376	377	378	379	380	381	382	383	384	385	386	387
ASSAM	***262***	***216***	***27***	***21***	***15***	***54***	***97***	***73***	***14,736***	***15,853***	***2,984***	***2,765***	Tanti and Tatwa includes (50 + 60) Animists, *viz.*, Darrang (7 + 7), Sibsagar (7 + 7) and Lakhimpur (36 + 46).
SURMA VALLEY DISTRICTS	***56***	***59***	...	...	***5***	***59***	***56***	***47***	***2,204***	***2,712***	***1,561***	***1,398***	
Cachar	12	7	...	...	...	...	39	41	1,026	1,340	688	464	Teli or Tili includes (8 + 6) Animists, *viz.*, Sibsagar (6 + 3) and Lakhimpur (2 + 3).
Sylhet	44	52	...	...	5	52	17	6	1,178	1,372	873	934	
ASSAM VALLEY DISTRICTS	***206***	***157***	***27***	***21***	***10***	***2***	***41***	***26***	***12,532***	***13,141***	***1,423***	***1,367***	
Goalpara	...	...	...	...	...	...	...	...	6	2	2	1	
Kamrup	...	1	...	...	...	...	...	...	46	45	8	9	
Darrang	31	30	7	3	...	...	8	10	2,823	2,974	293	310	
Nowgong	7	7	...	...	...	...	5	1	299	329	63	62	
Sibsagar	42	82	2	3	...	1	7	6	3,529	3,758	494	471	
Lakhimpur	126	87	18	15	10	1	21	9	5,829	6,033	563	514	

Province or District.	Telinga. Hindu. Males.	Telinga. Hindu. Females.	Telinga. Animist. Males.	Telinga. Animist. Females.	Tipara. Hindu. Males.	Tipara. Hindu. Females.	Tipara. Animist. Males.	Tipara. Animist. Females.	Turi. Hindu. Males.	Turi. Hindu. Females.	Turi. Animist. Males.	Turi. Animist. Females.	Vaisya. Hindu. Males.	Vaisya. Hindu. Females.	Remarks.
1	388	389	390	391	392	393	394	395	396	397	398	399	400	401	402
ASSAM	***3,138***	***2,869***	***1,342***	***1,129***	***58***	***59***	***20***	***15***	***6,105***	***5,956***	***254***	***250***	***89***	***27***	
SURMA VALLEY DISTRICTS	***667***	***716***	***20***	***13***	***58***	***59***	***20***	***15***	***2,304***	***2,218***	...	...	***2***	...	
Cachar	92	85	...	...	22	28	20	15	1,217	1,276	...	...	2	...	
Sylhet	575	631	20	13	36	31	...	...	1,087	942	...	...	...	...	
ASSAM VALLEY DISTRICTS	***2,471***	***2,153***	***1,322***	***1,116***	...	...	...	...	***3,801***	***3,738***	***254***	***250***	***87***	***27***	
Goalpara	...	...	...	...	...	...	...	...	4	5	...	...	...	...	
Kamrup	...	3	...	...	...	...	...	...	4	4	...	...	...	...	
Darrang	648	565	641	518	...	...	...	...	460	456	...	2	5	...	
Nowgong	...	1	283	225	...	...	...	...	1	3	81	84	1	4	
Sibsagar	1,203	1,102	230	213	...	...	...	...	2,909	2,872	129	118	24	8	
Lakhimpur	620	482	158	160	...	...	...	...	423	398	44	46	57	15	

PROVINCIAL TABLE V.—TEA-GARDEN POPULATION BY CASTE. PART B.—MUSALMANS.

Province or District.	Population.			Jolaha.		Minor Castes.*		Pathan.		Sayed (Saiad).		Sheikh.		Remarks.
	Persons.	Males.	Females.	Males.	Females.	Males.	Females.	Males.	Females.	Males.	Females.	Males.	Females.	
1	2	3	4	5	6	7	8	9	10	11	12	13	14	15
ASSAM	*18,205*	*10,881*	*7,324*	*1,468*	*1445*	*295*	*173*	*527*	*403*	*130*	*65*	*8,468*	*5,238*	* For details of Minor Castes, see Appendix.
SURMA VALLEY DISTRICTS	*11,238*	*6,963*	*4,275*	*846*	*839*	*270*	*164*	*378*	*310*	*82*	*41*	*5,387*	*2,931*	
Cachar	5,517	3,407	2,110	288	307	151	101	187	152	35	13	2,746	1,537	
Sylhet	5,721	3,556	2,165	558	532	119	63	191	158	47	28	2,641	1,394	
ASSAM VALLEY DISTRICTS	*6,967*	*3,918*	*3,049*	*622*	*616*	*25*	*9*	*149*	*93*	*48*	*24*	*3,081*	*2,307*	
Goalpara	41	25	16	...	...	4	...	...	...	...	...	21	16	
Kamrup	39	28	11	...	...	...	...	...	...	...	...	28	11	
Darrang	778	513	265	49	41	2	1	28	12	15	6	419	205	
Nowgong	225	130	95	...	6	...	...	8	1	1	1	121	87	
Sibsagar	4,461	2,303	2,068	573	557	11	6	84	68	25	12	1,700	1,425	
Lakhimpur...	1,423	829	594	...	13	8	2	[illegible]	[illegible]	7	5	792	563	

APPENDIX TO PROVINCIAL TABLE V.—DETAILS OF CASTES INCLUDED IN THE HEAD "MINOR CASTES." PART A.—HINDUS, ANIMISTS, BUDDHISTS, ETC.

Caste.	Religion.	Males.	Females.	Distribution.
1	2	3	4	5
Abor	Hindu	2	...	Sibsagar.
Ditto	Animist	101	93	Lakhimpur.
Aguri	Ditto	6	...	Sibsagar.
Alton	Buddhist	120	105	Sibsagar.
Amat	Hindu	1	...	Nowgong.
Assamese	Ditto	7	...	Cachar (6+0), Sylhet (1+0).
Atith	Ditto	55	84	Cachar (4+2), Lakhimpur (51+82).
Bahalia	Ditto	18	7	Sylhet (4+0), Sibsagar (14+6), Lakhimpur (0+1).
Baiga	Ditto	23	59	Nowgong (6+0), Lakhimpur (17+59).
Bais Baniya	Ditto	28	9	Cachar (5+0), Sylhet (3+0), Darrang (13+9), Nowgong (2+0), Sibsagar (5+0).
Baite (Chunari)	Ditto	177	151	Cachar (20+0), Sylhet (150+143), Darrang (7+8).
Balija	Ditto	29	...	Cachar.
Banjogi	Ditto	8	8	Lakhimpur.
Baola	Ditto	18	8	Darrang.
Barna Sankar	Ditto	4	...	Sibsagar.
Bhandari	Ditto	76	58	Sylhet (7+5), Nowgong (6+3), Sibsagar (41+49), Lakhimpur (22+1).
Bhaskar	Ditto	5	7	Darrang (0+5), Sibsagar (0+2), Lakhimpur (5+0).
Bhuinmali	Ditto	230	275	Cachar (109+119), Sylhet (164+106), Goalpara (54+50), Kamrup (2+0), Lakhimpur (1+0).
Binjhwar	Ditto	2	...	Lakhimpur.
Brahmo (unspecified)	Brahmo	5	2	Lakhimpur.
Brittial Baniya	Hindu	498	489	Kamrup (20+16), Darrang (142+124), Nowgong (126+97), Sibsagar (117+91), Lakhimpur (93+61).
Buddhist (unspecified)	Buddhist	55	37	Cachar (2+0), Kamrup (1+0), Darrang (0+2), Sibsagar (8+3), Lakhimpur (44+32).
Chain	Hindu	...	10	Kamrup.
Dafla	Animist	220	142	Cachar (4+0), Darrang (117+85), Sibsagar (99+57).
Damai	Hindu	235	145	Cachar (20+12), Sylhet (5+0), Darrang (132+35), Nowgong (1+0), Sibsagar (17+10), Lakhimpur (110+88).
Darzi	Ditto	39	2	Sylhet (2+0), Kamrup (1+0), Lakhimpur (36+2).
Ditto	Buddhist	2	...	Sylhet.
Dehan	Hindu	187	170	Cachar (183+170), Lakhimpur (4+0).
Dhangar	Ditto	19	...	Sylhet.
Dharhi	Animist	44	7	Darrang.
Dharkar	Hindu	...	3	Lakhimpur.
Dhimar	Ditto	27	3	Darrang (26+3), Sibsagar (1+0).
Dholi	Ditto	27	8	Cachar (2+5), Sylhet (19+1), Lakhimpur (6+2).
Doaniya	Ditto	67	60	Sibsagar (67+56), Lakhimpur (0+4).
Ditto	Buddhist	202	185	Sylhet (0+2), Sibsagar (72+68), Lakhimpur (130+116).
Dogara	Hindu	6	...	Lakhimpur.
Eruman	Ditto	3	2	Sibsagar.
Gain	Ditto	1	...	Darrang.
Gandhabanik	Ditto	17	4	Sylhet (1+0), Nowgong (2+1), Sibsagar (14+3).
Gangai Ganesh	Ditto	2	1	Sibsagar.
Ganjhu	Ditto	117	32	Cachar (6+0), Sylhet (111+32).
Gharti	Ditto	1	...	Lakhimpur.
Gola	Ditto	15	8	Sibsagar (13+8), Lakhimpur (2+0).
Gosain	Ditto	5	8	Cachar (4+8), Lakhimpur (1+0).
Gujar	Ditto	6	13	Sibsagar.
Guria	Ditto	7	3	Darrang (5+3), Lakhimpur (2+0).
Gurung	Ditto	21	16	Sylhet (0+6), Darrang (4+2), Nowong (6+2), Sibsagar (5+4), Lakhimpur (6+2).
Ditto	Buddhist	4	3	Darrang (3+2), Lakhimpur (1+1).
Halalkhar	Hindu	2	2	Lakhimpur.
Hindu (unspecified)	Ditto	42	38	Darrang (2+0), Sibsagar (1+2), Lakhimpur (39+36).
Hira	Ditto	7	2	Kamrup (0+2), Darrang (5+0), Sibsagar (2+0).
Ho	Ditto	1	...	Darrang.
Jain (unspecified)	Jain	22	6	Cachar (5+5), Darrang (1+0), Sibsagar (11+0), Lakhimpur (5+1).
Jaladha	Hindu	2	3	Darrang.
Ditto	Animist	11	13	Darrang.
Jat	Hindu	12	2	Sibsagar (1+0), Lakhimpur (11+2).
Jatapu	Ditto	249	197	Sibsagar (14+4), Lakhimpur (235+183).
Ditto	Animist	170	137	Sibsagar (169+137), Lakhimpur (1+0).
Jolaha	Hindu	28	36	Darrang (1+1), Sibsagar (20+12), Lakhimpur (7+23).
Juang	Ditto	5	...	Lakhimpur.
Kachchi	Ditto	...	4	Nowgong.
Kadar	Ditto	43	37	Cachar (12+0), Sylhet (0+3), Kamrup (0+8), Darrang (1+0), Nowgong (1+0), Sibsagar (20+24), Lakhimpur (0+2).
Ditto	Animist	...	1	Lakhimpur.
Kallar	Hindu	2	1	Nowgong (0+1), Sibsagar (1+0), Lakhimpur (1+0).
Kan	Ditto	6	1	Cachar (0+1), Darrang (6+0).
Kanjar	Ditto	30	20	Darrang (3+0), Sibsagar (2+0), Lakhimpur (25+20).
Ditto	Animist	3	...	Lakhimpur.
Kansari	Hindu	51	29	Sylhet (36+13), Darrang (15+16).
Kapali	Ditto	7	...	Lakhimpur.
Kapu	Ditto	20	4	Sibsagar.
Kapuria	Ditto	17	41	Darrang (1+0), Sibsagar (13+41), Lakhimpur (3+0).
Karanga	Ditto	5	7	Darrang (0+1), Sibsagar (0+5), Lakhimpur (5+1).
Karai	Ditto	3	...	Sibsagar.
Kashmiri	Ditto	8	5	Darrang.
Kawali	Ditto	8	...	Sylhet (6+0), Lakhimpur (2+0).
Khandelwal	Ditto	66	54	Darrang.
Khas	Ditto	35	25	Cachar (21+18), Goalpara (1+0), Nowgong (12+4), Sibsagar (1+3).
Khatik	Ditto	45	59	Cachar (31+48), Sylhet (13+10), Darrang (0+1); Nowgong (1+0).
Khawas	Ditto	1	...	Kamrup.
Ditto	Buddhist	1	...	Sibsagar.
Kichak	Hindu	18	30	Darrang (2+0), Sibsagar (16+30).
Konai	Ditto	7	...	Cachar (5+0), Lakhimpur (2+0).
Koshta	Ditto	26	39	Sylhet (22+27), Lakhimpur (4+12).
Kotal	Ditto	10	15	Sylhet (0+8), Darrang (1+0), Nowgong (4+2), Sibsagar (5+5).
Ditto	Animist	1	...	Nowgong.
Kuki (total)	Hindu	83	64	Cachar (70+64), Sylhet (13+0).
Ditto	Animist	83	78	Cachar.
Kunjara	Hindu	1	...	Kamrup.
Kusiari	Ditto	184	47	Sylhet.
Laheri	Ditto	9	14	Cachar (9+11), Sylhet (0+1), Sibsagar (0+2).
Lalbegi	Ditto	16	17	Darrang (12+17), Nowgong (1+0), Lakhimpur (3+0).
Lalung	Animist	100	63	Kamrup (78+57), Nowgong (22+3), Sibsagar (0+3).
Lama	Hindu	1	...	Cachar.
Lushai (total)	Ditto	2	...	Sylhet.
Madrasi	Ditto	45	58	Cachar (28+20), Sylhet (17+38).
Total		4,380	3,375	

APPENDIX TO PROVINCIAL TABLE V.—Details of castes included in the head "Minor Castes." Part A.—Hndus, Animists, Buddhists, etc.—*concld.*

Caste.	Religion.	Males.	Females.	Distribution.
1	2	3	4	5
Brought forward	......	4,380	3,375	
Magh	Hindu	14	...	Sylhet (11+0), Sibsagar (1+0), Lakhimpur (2+0).
Ditto	Buddhist	33	7	Cachar (8+1), Sylhet (2+0), Darrang (5+0), Sibsagar (8+4), Lakhimpur (10+2).
Mahanta	Hindu	2	3	Cachar.
Mahar	Ditto	3	...	Cachar.
Mahara	Ditto	29	9	Cachar (3+0), Sylhet (19+5), Lakhimpur (7+4).
Male (Sauria)	Ditto	75	61	Sibsagar (14+17), Lakhimpur (61+44).
Mar	Ditto	22	17	Kamrup (1+0), Darrang (0+4), Nowgong (12+2), Sibsagar (9+11).
Maram	Ditto	26	14	Sibsagar (5+3), Lakbimpur (21+11).
Maratha	Ditto	5	4	Cachar.
Matak	Ditto	78	5	Lakhimpur.
Miri	Ditto	1	3	Sibsagar (1+0), Lakhimpur (0+3).
Ditto	Animist...	8	10	Sibsagar (4+4), Lakhimpur (4+6).
Mudi	Hindu	62	71	Sylhet.
Mukhi	Ditto	1	3	Sibsagar (0+2), Lakhimpur (1+1).
Naga	Ditto	4	1	Nowgong.
Nagarchi...	Ditto	44	8	Lakhimpur.
Nagesar	Ditto	3	...	Cachar.
Nagpuri	Ditto	13	17	Cachar.
Nahura	Ditto	1	...	Nowgong.
Nat	Ditto	13	5	Sylhet (9+0), Sibsagar (4+5).
Nora	Ditto	5	3	Cachar (3+3), Darrang (2+0).
Ditto	Buddhist...	3	2	Sibsagar.
Ojali	Hindu	17	25	Darrang.
Pahari	Ditto	47	77	Cachar.
Paik	Ditto	...	3	Cachar.
Panjabi	Ditto	2	...	Sibsagar.
Patial (Patikar)	Ditto	64	8	Sylhet (59+0), Darrang (0+5), Nowgong (1+2), Sibsagar (0+1), Lakhimpur (4+0).
Pator	Ditto	567	326	Cachar (54+55), Lakhimpur (513+271).
Patwari	Ditto	2	...	Cachar.
Pawaria	Ditto	12	...	Lakhimpur.
Phakial	Ditto	1	...	Lakhimpur.
Pod	Ditto	6	...	Nowgong (3+0), Lakhimpur (3+0).
Pradhan	Ditto	16	...	Sylhet (12+0), Nowgong (4+0).
Rai	Ditto	35	27	Cachar (7+0), Sylhet (28+27).
Rana	Ditto	10	1	Lakhimpur.
Rauniar	Ditto	10	2	Darrang (2+0), Sibsagar (0+1), Lakhimpur (8+1).
Relli	Ditto	3	...	Darrang.
Ditto	Animist...	2	...	Darrang.
Sahar	Hindu	73	76	Sibsagar (5+0), Lakhimpur (68+76).
Saloi	Ditto	8	...	Darrang (7+0), Sibsagar (1+0).
Sannyasi...	Ditto	13	7	Sylhet (1+0), Darrang (1+1), Nowgong (1+0), Lakhimpur (10+6).
Sarak	Ditto	3	2	Darrang (2+2), Lakhimpur (1+0).
Sikh (unspecified)	Sikh	49	25	Darrang (2+0), Sibsagar (20+8), Lakhimpur (27+17).
Subarnabanik	Hindu	17	2	Cachar (11+0), Sylhet (5+0), Darrang (1+2).
Svarnakar	Ditto	80	18	Sylhet (78+15), Nowgong (2+3).
Tamaria	Ditto	10	25	Sibsagar (8+15), Lakhimpur (2+10).
Tambuli	Ditto	19	21	Cachar (2+3), Kamrup (1+1), Darrang (5+2), Sibsagar (7+9), Lakhimpur (4+6).
Thakuri	Ditto	211	206	Sylhet (115+124), Darrang (77+65), Sibsagar (17+17), Lakhimpur (2+0).
Thami	Ditto	9	...	Lakhimpur.
Thapa	Ditto	50	18	Cachar.
Tharu	Ditto	10	9	Goalpara (9+2), Darrang (1+0), Lakhimpur (0+7).
Thathera	Ditto	17	19	Sibsagar.
Tiyor	Ditto	14	...	Darrang (3+0), Sibsagar (5+0), Lakhimpur (6+0).
Turaha	Ditto	11	3	Darrang (7+3), Sibsagar (2+0), Lakhimpur (2+0).
Uppara	Ditto	13	12	Sibsagar.
Yakha	Ditto	4	3	Darrang (3+3), Lakhimpur (1+0).
Ditto	Buddhist	1	...	Lakhimpur.
	Total	6,231	4,533	

APPENDIX TO TABLE V.—Details of castes included in the head "Minor Castes." Part B.—Musalmans.

Caste.	Males.	Females.	Distribution.
1	2	3	4
Bediya	6	5	Sylhet.
Dhenwar	15	...	Sylhet.
Dhobi	1	...	Cachar.
Dholi	51	47	Sylhet.
Dhunia	8	12	Cachar.
Hajjam	24	22	Cachar (20+20), Sylhet (4+2).
Kalal	8	15	Cachar.
Kunjra	...	3	Cachar.
Mahimal	15	7	Cachar (9+7), Sylhet (6+0).
Mallik	17	19	Cachar.
Moghal	93	35	Cachar (43+23, Sylhet (34+6), Goalpara (4+0), Sibsagar (7+4), Lakhimpur (5+2).
Moria	9	2	Darrang (2+1), Sibsagar (4+1), Lakhimpur (3+0).
Muchi	...	2	Cachar.
Musulman (unspecified)	...	1	Sibsagar.
Nagarchi	2	3	Sylhet.
Sunni	45	...	Cachar.
Total	295	178	

PROVINCIAL TABLE VI.

OCCUPATIONS OF PERSONS LITERATE IN ENGLISH.

This Table follows the headings of Imperial Table XVI and shows each main religion separately.

PROVINCIAL TABLE VI.—Occupations of Persons Literate in English—*contd.*

Religion.	Population dealt with. Actual workers. Males.	Population dealt with. Actual workers. Females.	Population dealt with. Dependants. Males.	Population dealt with. Dependants. Females.	I.—Exploitation of the surface of the soil. Income from rent of land. Males.	Income from rent of land. Females.	Cultivators of all kinds. Males.	Cultivators of all kinds. Females.	Agents and managers of landed estates, planters, forest officers and their clerks, rent collectors, etc. Males.	Agents and managers … Females.	Field labourers and wood cutters, etc. Males.	Field labourers and wood cutters, etc. Females.	Raisers of live-stock, milkmen and herdsmen. Males.	Raisers of live-stock … Females.	Fishing and hunting. Males.	Fishing and hunting. Females.	II.—Extraction of minerals. Owners, managers, clerks, etc. Males.	Owners, managers, clerks, etc. Females.	Labourers. Males.	Labourers. Females.	III.—Industries. Owners, managers, clerks, etc. Males.	Owners, managers, clerks, etc. Females.	Artisans and other workmen. Males.	Artisans and other workmen. Females.
1	2	3	4	5	6	7	8	9	10	11	12	13	14	15	16	17	18	19	20	21	22	23	24	25
All Religions ...	***25,532***	***285***	***8,801***	***1,237***	***2,559***	***1***	***4,363***	***41***	***4,452***	***6***	***233***	***3***	***19***	...	***26***	...	***59***	...	***45***	...	***103***	...	***531***	***25***
Hindu...	19,169	19	6,758	290	2,024	1	3,405	6	3,320	1	190	...	13	...	22	...	40	...	17	...	80	...	253	1
Musalman	3,149	5	1,402	55	527	...	591	4	135	...	13	...	2	...	3	...	2	...	4	...	7	...	86	1
Christian	2,659	249	426	846	6	...	237	29	936	5	27	3	4	...	1	...	10	...	18	...	10	...	102	23
Buddhist	34	—	2	2	...	...	3	...	1	...	...	...	...	...	...	...	...	...	2	...	...	...	18	...
Animist	412	7	184	25	2	...	121	2	13	...	3	...	...	...	...	...	5	...	4	...	5	...	70	...
Parsi	4	...	...	...	...	...	...	...	...	...	...	...	...	...	...	...	...	...	...	...	...	...	...	...
Others	105	5	29	19	...	...	5	...	4	...	...	...	...	...	...	...	2	...	...	...	1	...	2	...

RECORDED PRINCIPAL OCCUPATION OF ACTUAL WORKERS.

Religion.	IV.—Transport. Owners, managers, ships' officers, etc. Males.	Owners, managers, ships' officers, etc. Females.	Labourers, boatmen, carters, palki-bearers, etc. Males.	Labourers, boatmen, carters, palki-bearers, etc. Females.	V.—Trade. Males.	V.—Trade. Females.	VI.—Public force. Commissioned and gazetted officers. Males.	Commissioned and gazetted officers. Females.	Others. Males.	Others. Females.	VII.—Public Administration. Gazetted officers. Males.	Gazetted officers. Females.	Others. Males.	Others. Females.	VIII.—Arts and professions. Religious. Males.	Religious. Females.	Lawyers, doctors and teachers. Males.	Lawyers, doctors and teachers. Females.	Others. Males.	Others. Females.	IX.—Persons living on their income. Males.	IX. Females.	X.—Domestic service. Males.	X. Females.	XI.—Contractors, clerks, cashiers, etc., otherwise unspecified. Males.	XI. Females.	XII.—Labourers unspecified. Males.	XII. Females.	XIII.—Beggars, prostitutes, criminals and inmates of jails and asylums. Males.	XIII. Females.
1	26	27	28	29	30	31	32	33	34	35	36	37	38	39	40	41	42	43	44	45	46	47	48	49	50	51	52	53	54	55
All Religions ...	***2,219***	...	***302***	***1***	***1,558***	***15***	***64***	...	***652***	...	***106***	...	***2,064***	...	***644***	***45***	***3,401***	***75***	***1,104***	***33***	***280***	***8***	***13***	***20***	***454***	***1***	***94***	***7***	***66***	***4***
Hindu...	1,704	...	207	...	1,227	1	...	...	503	...	55	...	1,690	...	450	...	2,543	5	706	...	185	...	64	1	359	...	59	...	53	3
Musalman	288	...	53	...	2 8	...	1	...	111	...	8	...	243	...	39	...	454	...	172	...	41	...	36	...	45	...	8	...	12	...
Christian	209	...	35	1	57	11	63	...	25	...	40	...	81	...	149	45	364	65	179	33	45	8	27	17	25	1	14	7	1	1
Buddhist	1	...	...	...	...	...	...	...	...	...	1	...	2	...	...	...	2	...	1	...	...	...	3	...	...	...	...	...	...	...
Animist	4	...	6	...	34	3	...	...	12	...	...	...	30	...	1	...	20	...	35	...	8	...	4	2	22	...	13	...	...	...
Parsi	3	...	...	...	1	...	...	...	...	...	...	...	...	...	...	...	...	...	...	...	...	...	...	...	...	...	...	...	...	...
Others	10	...	1	...	21	...	...	...	...	...	2	...	18	...	5	...	18	5	11	...	1	...	1	...	3	...	...	...	...	...